Adobe®
Photoshop® 5.0
Certification Guide

Michael Lennox and
Elizabeth Bulger

Adobe

ADOBE® PHOTOSHOP® 5.0 CERTIFICATION GUIDE

Copyright © 1999 by Adobe Press

International Standard Book Number: 0-56830-473-0

Library of Congress Catalog Card Number: 98-86223

Printed in the United States of America

First Printing: January, 1999

01   00   99   4   3   2   1

TRADEMARKS

WARNING AND DISCLAIMER

Figures 10.20 and 10.21 appear courtesy of FoodPix.

EXECUTIVE EDITOR
Chris Nelson

ACQUISITIONS EDITOR
Susan Walton

DEVELOPMENT EDITOR
Karen Whitehouse

TECHNICAL EDITOR
Steve Moniz

MANAGING EDITOR
Sarah Kearns

PROJECT EDITOR
Caroline Wise

COPY EDITOR
Marilyn Stone

INDEXER
Diane Brenner

PROOFREADER
John Etchison

LAYOUT TECHNICIAN
Eric S. Miller

BOOK DESIGNER
Anne Jones

GRAPHIC CONVERSION TECHNICIANS
Tammy Graham
Benjamin Hart

CONTENTS AT A GLANCE

Foreword

Preface

Introduction

Chapter	**Chapter Title**
1	*General Information, 13*
2	*The Photoshop Work Area, 31*
3	*The History Palette, 59*
4	*Scanning & Working with Images, 71*
5	*Image Modes, 91*
6	*Selections, 111*
7	*Paths, 141*
8	*Painting, 171*
9	*Editing & Retouching, 211*
10	*Layers, 239*
11	*Working with Type, 279*
12	*Filters, 303*
13	*Channels & Masks, 339*
14	*Color Correction, 373*
15	*File Formats, 417*
16	*Prepress Production, 439*
17	*Web & Video Production, 455*
18	*Color Management, 471*
19	*Automating Photoshop, 487*
A	*Chapter Review Questions Answer Key, 505*
B	*Glossary, 531*
C	*Bibliography, 543*
	Index, 545

CONTENTS

Foreword

Preface

INTRODUCTION   1

1   GENERAL INFORMATION   13

Common Terms and Concepts 15
    Pixel *15*
    Raster *16*
    Vector *16*
    Path..*17*
    Color Depth *17*
    Color Space *18*
Key Features and Benefits of Adobe Photoshop 18
Photoshop System Requirements 19
    Platform Requirements–Macintosh and Windows *19*
    Hardware Requirements and Recommendations..............................*19*
Installing Adobe Photoshop 20
Optimizing and Customizing Photoshop 21
    General Preferences..*21*
    Saving Files *23*
    Cache Levels *24*
    Memory *24*
    Virtual Memory *24*
    Scratch Disks..*25*
Photoshop Plug-ins 26
Summary 27
Review Questions 28

2   THE PHOTOSHOP WORK AREA   31

The Toolbox 33
    Identifying a Tool *34*
    Activating a Tool..*34*
    Changing the Cursor Appearance for Precision Work *35*
Working with Palettes..36
    Organizing and Customizing Your Palettes *36*
    Setting Palette Preferences *37*
Wizards and Assistants..38
    Resizing and Resampling Images *38*
    Exporting a Transparent Image *38*
Using the Status Bar 40
    Document Sizes *40*
    Scratch Sizes *42*

Efficiency..42

Timing 42

Current Tool 43

Online Help System 43

Adobe Online 43

Keyboard Shortcuts 44

Context-Sensitive Menus 45

Screen Modes 45

Standard Screen Mode 45

Full Screen Mode with Menu Bar 45

Full Screen Mode 46

View Commands...46

View Menu Options 47

Enlarging and Reducing the View of Your Image......................47

The Navigator Palette 48

Changing the View Box Color 49

Changing the View Box Size...49

Multiple Views 49

Arranging Multiple Windows (Windows Only)........................49

Using Rulers 50

Adding Rulers to Your Document...50

Specifying the Ruler Origin 50

Using Guides..51

Placing a Guide 51

Repositioning a Guide 51

Deleting a Guide..51

Locking a Guide 51

Showing and Hiding Guides or Grid 51

Snap to Guides or Grid...51

Setting Guides and Grid Preferences 52

Measure Tool...52

Resizing and Repositioning the Measuring Line 53

Using the Measure Tool as a Protractor 53

Deleting the Measuring Line 53

Setting Preferences 54

Replacing the Preferences File..55

Backing Up Your Preferences File 55

Locking Your Preferences File 55

Summary...56

Review Questions 57

3   THE HISTORY PALETTE   59

Moving Between States..61

Creating Snapshots 63

Deleting States and Clearing the History 65

History Options 66
    Linear Versus Non-linear History 66
    Create Initial Snapshot...67
    History Steps...67
Summary 68
Review Questions 69

4   SCANNING & WORKING WITH IMAGES   71
Key Concepts..73
    Resolution 73
    Interpolation..73
    Resampling 74
Resolution Issues..75
    Intended Use 76
    Prepress..76
    Web and Video 78
    Minimizing File Sizes 79
Common Resolution Problems 80
Image Size Command..81
Canvas Size Command..82
File Info Command 85
Importing and Placing 86
Summary 87
Review Questions 88

5   IMAGE MODES   91
Bitmap 93
Grayscale 95
Duotone..96
    Duotone Curves 97
RGB 99
CMYK 99
Lab 100
Indexed Color 101
Multichannel Mode 105
8-bit and 16-bit Color 106
Summary 106
Review Questions 107

6   SELECTIONS   111
Overview of Selections 113
    Selection Data Versus Pixel Data 113
Using Selection Tools 115
    Marquee Tool 116
    Lasso Tools 119
    Magic Wand Tool 124

Selection Options 128

    Tolerance *128*

    Feather *128*

    Anti-Alias *129*

Using Selection Menu Commands 130

    Color Range *130*

    Grow *133*

    Similar *133*

    Border *133*

    Expand *133*

    Contract *133*

    Smooth *133*

    Deselect *134*

    Reselect *134*

    Inverse *135*

    All *135*

    Feather *135*

Transforming Selections 135

Hiding Edges 136

Summary 136

Review Questions 137

7 PATHS 141

Key Concepts..143

    Paths and Subpaths *143*

    Anchor Points and Direction Lines..............................*143*

    Clipping Path *144*

Creating and Editing Paths..145

    Pen Tool *145*

    Using the Pen Tool *147*

    Magnetic Pen Tool *149*

    Freeform Pen Tool..*152*

    Add Anchor Point Tool *154*

    Subtract Anchor Point Tool *155*

    Direct Selection Tool..*155*

    Convert Point Tool *157*

The Paths Palette...158

Work Paths 160

Paths and Selections 161

Clipping Paths 162

Summary 168

Review Questions 169

8 PAINTING 171

Working with the Foreground and Background Color Swatches 173

Using the Color Picker 173
  Using the Color Field and Color Slider with HSB Values *174*
  Using the Color Picker to Define Lab Values *176*
  Using Numeric Values to Specify a Color...*177*
  The Gamut Warning *177*
  Accessing Custom Colors..*178*
Using the Swatches Palette 180
  Adding Colors to the Swatches Palette *180*
  Replacing and Inserting Colors in the Swatches Palette..........................*180*
  Deleting a Swatch *180*
  Loading Swatches *181*
  Saving Custom Swatch Palettes *181*
  Resetting and Replacing the Swatches Palette *181*
Using the Color Palette...181
  Selecting a Color *182*
  The Eyedropper..*182*
Using the Painting Tools...183
  Cursor Options *183*
  The Options Palette *184*
  The Pencil *190*
  The Eraser...*191*
  The Brushes Palette *192*
  The Line Tool *196*
  The Paint Bucket *198*
  The Gradient Tools *199*
  Fill and Stroke Commands..*204*
  Creating a Pattern *206*
Summary 207
Review Questions 208

9   EDITING & RETOUCHING   211
Using the Transformation Commands 213
  The Scale Command *213*
  The Rotate Command *214*
  The Skew Command *214*
  The Distort Command *215*
  The Perspective Command *215*
  The Transformation Command *215*
  The Free Transform Command *216*
  Cursor Options *218*
  The Options Palette *218*
Using the Rubber Stamp and Pattern Stamp Tools 218
  The Rubber Stamp Tool *219*
  The Pattern Stamp Tool *222*

Using the History Brush 223
  The History Brush 224
Using the Focus Tools 226
  The Blur Tool 227
  The Sharpen Tool 227
  The Smudge Tool 227
Using the Toning Tools 229
  The Dodge Tool 229
  The Burn Tool 229
  The Sponge Tool 230
Using Filters when Editing and Retouching an Image 231
  The Gaussian Blur Filter 231
  The Noise Filters 232
  Using the Sharpen Filters 232
Summary 235
Review Questions 236

10 LAYERS   239
The Layers Palette 241
Viewing a Layered Document 241
Creating a New Layer 242
Reordering Layers 242
Linking Layers 244
Duplicating a Layer 244
Using the Layer Via Copy and Layer Via Cut Commands 245
Repositioning Layer Contents 246
  Aligning and Distributing Layer Contents 246
Editing Layers 249
  Using Preserve Transparency 249
  Changing the Opacity of a Layer 250
  Using the Blend If Option 250
Managing Layered Images 251
Merging Layers 252
  Merging an Adjustment Layer 253
  Using the Clone Merge Command 253
  Using the Copy Merged Command 253
  Flattening an Image 253
Creating a Layer Mask 254
Adding a Layer Mask 254
  Linking and Unlinking a Layer Mask 261
Creating a Clipping Group 261
Creating an Adjustment Layer 263
Using Layer Effects 266
  Adding a Layer Effect 267
  Editing and Removing Layer Effects 269

Converting Layer Effects to Layers *270*
Blending Modes *270*
Summary *275*
Review Questions *276*

11   WORKING WITH TYPE   279
Using the Type Tools *282*
Setting Type..*282*
Working with the Type Tool Dialog Box *283*
Choosing a Font *283*
Choosing a Font Size *283*
Specifying Kerning, Tracking, and Leading *283*
Using Baseline Shift *284*
Specifying Alignment *285*
Rotating Character Direction *285*
Working with Type Layers *287*
Changing the Orientation of a Type Layer *288*
Working with the Type Mask Tools *288*
Rendering a Layer...*289*
Summary *300*
Review Questions *301*

12   FILTERS   303
Filter Overview *305*
3D Transform *306*
Using the Filter *307*
The Cube Tool...*307*
The Sphere Tool *307*
The Cylinder Tool *307*
Selection Tools..*308*
Anchor Point Tools *309*
Camera Controls and the Trackball *309*
Options for Rendering the 3D Transformation *311*
Displace *315*
Noise and Dust & Scratches *318*
Add Noise *318*
Dust & Scratches *319*
Lighting Effects *321*
Adding, Deleting, and Moving Lights *322*
Controlling Lights..*323*
Setting the Properties *324*
Using Preset Styles *325*
Using Texture Channels *328*
Sharpen and Unsharp Mask...*331*
Sharpen and Sharpen More *331*
Unsharp Mask *331*

Blur and Gaussian Blur 333
    Blur and Blur More *333*
    Gaussian Blur *333*
Other Filters 335
Filter Fade 335
Summary 336
Review Questions 337

13   CHANNELS & MASKS   339
Color Channels and Alpha Channels 341
Using the Channels Palette...342
    Setting Channels Palette Options *342*
    Activating Channels *343*
Creating a New Channel...344
Reordering Channels 345
Editing Channels..345
Duplicating a Channel 346
Deleting Channels..348
Multichannel Mode 348
Saving Channels 349
Splitting and Merging Channels 349
Working with Alpha Channels..351
Working in Quick Mask Mode 356
Using Channel Calculations...360
    Using the Duplicate Command *360*
    Using the Apply Image Command *360*
    Calculations *363*
The Channel Mixer...365
Spot Color Channels...366
    Converting an Alpha Channel to a Spot Channel *368*
    Editing a Spot Channel *368*
    Merging Spot Channels *368*
    Printing Composite Images with Spot Colors........................*368*
Summary 369
Review Questions 370

14   COLOR CORRECTION   373
Helpful Hints for Working with RGB and CMYK Images.......................375
Tools and Commands to Consider Before Color Correcting an Image ..375
    Using the Gamut Warning Command....................................*375*
    Using the Info Palette *376*
    Using the Color Sampler Tool..*377*
    Using CMYK Preview..*379*
    Saving and Loading Color Adjustment Settings......................*379*
    Understanding the Histogram *380*
Seven Steps to Better Color and Tonality 383

Using the Levels Command 384
  Using Input Levels *384*
  Using Output Levels *385*
  Setting Target Values for Highlights and Shadows *386*
  Using the Black-Point and White-Point Eyedroppers *387*
  Using the Auto Levels Command *388*
Using the Curves Command 389
Using Variations 394
Using the Color Balance Command 396
Using the Hue/Saturation Command 398
  Changing the Color Range Using the Color Bars....................................*399*
  Using the Colorize Option *400*
Using the Replace Color Command 403
Using the Color Range Command 405
Using the Selective Color Command..408
Using the Brightness/Contrast Command 409
Using the Invert Command 410
Using the Equalize Command 411
Using the Threshold Command 411
Using the Posterize Command...414
Summary 414
Review Questions 415

15   FILE FORMATS   417
Options for Saving Files 419
  Save As *419*
  Save a Copy *419*
Images, Paths, and Other Applications 420
  Adobe Illustrator..*421*
  Page Layout Programs *421*
File Formats...421
  Photoshop Native *422*
  TIFF *424*
  EPS *426*
  EPS and DCS 2.0 ....*429*
  PDF...*430*
  PCX *430*
  PICT *431*
  GIF *432*
  JPEG *433*
  PNG *434*
Choosing Appropriate Formats 436
Summary...436
Review Questions 437

16   PREPRESS PRODUCTION   439

Using the CMYK Setup Command 441

Ink Colors *441*

Dot Gain *442*

Using Black in Separations *443*

Page Setup 445

Screen *446*

Transfer *447*

Background *448*

Border *448*

Bleed *448*

Caption *449*

Calibration Bars *449*

Registration Marks *450*

Corner and Center Crop Marks *450*

Labels *450*

Negative and Emulsion Down *450*

Interpolation *450*

The Print Command 450

Encoding *451*

Print Selected Areas *451*

Space *451*

Trapping 452

Preparing Separations for Page Layout Applications 453

Summary 453

Review Questions 454

17   WEB & VIDEO PRODUCTION   455

Grayscale, Flat-Color, and Full-Color Images 457

Grayscale *457*

Flat Color *457*

Full Color *458*

Optimizing File Sizes 459

Appropriate Image Modes 462

Indexed Color Options and Exporting GIF89a Files 462

Indexed Color Options *462*

Exporting GIF89a Files *464*

Creating Transparency in Other Formats 465

Video and Multimedia 466

Summary 467

Review Questions 468

18   COLOR MANAGEMENT   471

Calibration Procedures 473

Adobe Gamma Utility *473*

ICC Profiles *477*

Color Settings 477
   RGB Setup 478
   CMYK Setup..480
   Grayscale Setup..482
   Profile Setup 482
   Profile to Profile 484
Summary 484
Review Questions 485

19 AUTOMATING PHOTOSHOP 487

Actions..489
   The Actions Palette 489
   Playing Actions 490
   Playback Speed 492
   Button Mode...493
   Creating and Editing Actions 493
   Inserting Commands 494
   Inserting Paths 495
   Inserting Menu Items 495
   Inserting Stops 497
Action Sets and Action Management 498
Automate Command 498
   Batch Processing 499
   Conditional Mode Change 499
   Contact Sheet 500
   Fit Image...501
   Convert Multi-Page PDF to PSD 501
Summary 502
Review Questions 503

A ANSWERS TO REVIEW QUESTIONS 505

B GLOSSARY 531

C BIBLIOGRAPHY 543

INDEX 545

INTRODUCTION

IS THIS BOOK FOR YOU?

This book is specifically designed to present the information required to pass the Photoshop 5 Product Proficiency Exam, which is the primary step toward becoming an Adobe® Certified Expert (ACE). If you plan to take the Photoshop 5 Product Proficiency Exam, this book is for you—whether you are already a Photoshop ACE on a previous version, or you feel that you are ready to prove you know Photoshop at an expert level.

WHAT DOES THIS BOOK COVER?

This book covers all the Domains and Objectives that Adobe expects candidates to understand thoroughly before designating them ACEs. Each chapter contains specific information that will help you pass the Photoshop 5 Product Proficiency Exam. In addition, most of the chapters also contain exercises designed to help you further master the concepts and processes you will need to know. Every chapter also has some sample exam questions to help you assess your skills and become familiar with the way questions will be asked on the actual exam.

One of the goals of this book is to not only help prepare you to take the exam, but to eliminate any surprises you might encounter. Some of the information about Photoshop covered in this book could, in fact, be review for experienced users. Although knowledge of Photoshop is paramount, an understanding of the exam, how it works, and what it covers will help you be as prepared as possible.

OVERVIEW OF ADOBE CERTIFICATION PROGRAMS

Adobe Systems offers certification programs for the following products:

>Adobe Acrobat®
>
>Adobe After Effects®
>
>Adobe FrameMaker®
>
>Adobe FrameMaker+SGML
>
>Adobe Illustrator®
>
>Adobe PageMaker®
>
>Adobe PageMill®
>
>Adobe Photoshop®
>
>Adobe Premiere®

The steps for becoming an ACE are the same for each application, as are the benefits of becoming an ACE. They include the following:

- Professional recognition—ACEs are recognized internationally for their product knowledge.
- A product-specific and customized Adobe wall certificate.
- Use of the ACE signature (logo) on your promotional materials (use the logo on your business cards, advertising, and Web page to announce to the world the quality of your Photoshop skills).

HOW DO YOU BECOME AN ADOBE CERTIFIED EXPERT?

Becoming an ACE is as simple as passing the Product Proficiency Exam. You must agree to Adobe's Terms and Conditions to complete your certification. If you take the exam and pass, the scores will be sent automatically to Adobe. The Terms and Conditions govern the use of the ACE logo and how often recertification is necessary.

You can call Sylvan Prometric between 7:00 A.M., Central Standard Time and 7:00 P.M., Central Standard Time, Monday through Friday, at (800) 356 3926 within the United States and Canada to make an appointment. If you are outside the United States or Canada, check Sylvan Prometric's Web site (www.sylvanprometric.com) for the appropriate phone number. When you call, be sure to have your Social Security Number on hand. When you make the appointment, Sylvan can direct you to the nearest exam site. Sylvan Prometric is one of the largest companies offering computer-based competency exams. They have more than 1,400 testing centers worldwide, so there is probably a testing center near you.

The testing fee is US$150, if you are taking the exam for the first time. Sylvan Prometric handles the billing and the scheduling. The testing centers are where you will sit down at a computer and take the test. You will have an hour and 15 minutes to take the actual exam, but your appointment will be for an hour and a half, giving you some extra time for registration and a brief practice session with the testing software. You must cancel or change your appointment more than one day in advance, or you will forfeit the testing fee. You will need to bring two forms of signature identification, one of which must have a photograph.

WHAT YOU SHOULD EXPECT

The Adobe Photoshop 5.0 Proficiency Exam is a multiple-choice exam, developed by a panel of Photoshop experts at Adobe. It is important to realize that the exam is based on fairly objective topics and it is not necessarily process oriented, although you need to know the steps for performing common Photoshop procedures. You will not be expected to create anything in Photoshop. Rather, you will be asked about tools, commands, dialog boxes, and some techniques. Because of this, it is important that you review all the topic areas, including those about which you feel confident. In fact, the areas where you feel confident are the topics that might require the most review. You might no longer think about what happens when converting from RGB to CMYK or what a certain button or radio box is called. These, however, are the things you need to know for the exam.

PHOTOSHOP PRODUCT PROFICIENCY EXAM TOPICS AND OBJECTIVES

The following are the actual Domains and Objectives taken from the Photoshop 5.0 Exam Bulletin. This list and the entire bulletin are available from Adobe's Web site at `http://www.adobe.com`. You will notice a direct correspondence between the following and the topics covered by this book:

1. **General Information**

    1.1 Define common terms and concepts related to Adobe Photoshop, including but not limited to the following: raster, vector, flatness, path, mask, pixel, color depth, and color space.

    1.2 Identify key features and benefits of Photoshop.

    1.3 Identify installation procedures, memory requirements and plug-ins for Adobe Photoshop, including but not limited to the following: cache levels, virtual memory, Scratch disks, installing third-party plug-ins, and networked and local volumes.

2. **The Work Area**

    2.1 Identify issues regarding the characteristics, function, options, and appropriate use of items in the work area, including using and customizing palettes; using wizards, the History palette, the status bar, and Help/Online Help; setting preferences; and identifying popular keyboard shortcuts.

    2.2 Identify issues regarding the characteristics, function, options, and appropriate use of view menus and commands, including context menus, View commands, screen mode buttons, the Canvas Size command, the Navigation palette, and the Measure tool, rulers, and guides.

3. **Actions/Automation**

    3.1 Determine the appropriate feature, command, or procedure related to the Actions palette, including creating and recording actions, playing actions, editing actions, inserting nonrecordable commands, slowing actions during playback, writing descriptors, creating sets of actions, and batch processing.

3.2   Determine the appropriate feature, command, or procedure related to automating tasks with the Automate command, including Conditional Mode Change, Contact Sheet, Execute JavaScript, Fit Image, and convert Multi-page PDF to PSD.

4. Importing and Adjusting Images

4.1   Define types of resolution and resolution concepts such as interpolation, resampling, fixed image size, and vector versus bitmap graphics.

4.2   Recommend appropriate scanning resolution for typical Photoshop production situations (including minimizing file sizes), and identify and resolve common use problems related to resolution and scanning.

4.3   Identify issues regarding the characteristics, function, options, and appropriate use of the Image Size command, Import command, Place command, and File Info commands.

5. Making Selections

5.1   Identify issues regarding the characteristics, function, and appropriate use of selection tools and commands, including the move tool, lasso, polygon lasso, and magnetic lasso tools, marquee tools, magic wand tool, and the Color Range command.

5.2   Identify issues regarding the characteristics, function, and appropriate use of tools and commands used to make adjustments to a selection in an image, including manually adding, subtracting, and intersecting selections; differentiating between selection data and pixel data; using the Grow, Similar, Expand, Contract, Smooth, Reselect, and Deselect commands, and using the Tolerance, Feather, and Anti-Alias options.

5.3   Identify issues regarding the characteristics, function, and appropriate use of the Paths palette, including using the pen tool, magnetic pen tool, and freeform pen tool; creating and editing paths; the significance of anchor points, their number, and frequency; differentiating between work path, path, and subpath; converting paths to selections; and creating and exporting clipping paths.

5.4   Determine the appropriate feature, command, tool, or procedure to make and modify a selection.

6. Painting and Editing

6.1   Identify issues regarding the characteristics, function, limitations, and appropriate use of the painting tools, functions, and commands, including the paint brush tool, eraser tool, line tool, paint bucket tool, gradient tools, Brushes palette, Options palette, Fill and Stroke commands, Foreground and Background colors, and the relationship between tools and color modes.

6.2   Identify issues regarding the characteristics, function, and appropriate use of the editing and retouching tools, functions, and commands, including the rubber stamp tool; pattern stamp tool; history brush; smudge tool; blur and sharpen tools; burn, dodge, and sponge tools; and transform, matting, and purge commands.

6.3   Identify issues regarding the characteristics, function, and appropriate use of the type tools, functions, and commands, including the type tool, type options, type mask tools, and use of type layers.

6.4   Identify issues regarding the basic characteristics and function of filters, including the 3D Transform Displace, Dust & Scratches, Lighting Effects, Sharpen, and other filters.

6.5   Determine the appropriate feature, command, tool, or procedure to accomplish a stated task related to painting, editing, and creating type.

7. Using Layers

7.1   Identify issues regarding the characteristics, function, and appropriate use of layers and layer options including creation, viewing, moving, editing, reordering, grouping, merging, adjusting opacity, and the Arrange and Align commands.

7.2   Identify features and define steps in the process of creating a layer mask, creating a clipping group, using adjustment layers, and using layer effects.

7.3   Identify issues regarding the characteristics, function and appropriate use of the blending modes, including Dissolve, Behind, Clear, Multiply, Screen, Overlay, Soft light, Hard light, Color Dodge, Color Burn, Darken, Lighten, Difference, Exclusion, Hue, Saturation, Color, and Luminosity.

7.4   Determine the appropriate feature, command, tool, or procedure to accomplish a stated task related to layers.

8. Using Channels and Masks

8.1 Identify issues regarding the characteristics, function, and appropriate use of channels, including creating and editing a selection channel, duplicating and deleting channels, saving and managing channels, channel calculations, the Channel Mixer command, spot color channels, and mode conversion with spot color channels.

8.2 Identify issues regarding the characteristics, function, and appropriate use of masks, including using Quick Mask mode and using alpha channels.

8.3 Determine the appropriate feature, command, tool, or procedure to accomplish a stated task related to channels and masks.

9. Color and Color Correction

9.1 Identify the characteristics, function, and appropriate use of image adjustment commands, including Levels, Curves, Variations, Brightness/Contrast, Hue/Saturation, Color Balance, Equalize, Threshold, histograms, and out-of-gamut colors.

9.2 Identify elements in and differentiate between the applications of the following color models and modes: Bitmap, Grayscale, Duotone, RGB, CMYK, Lab, Indexed color, Multichannel, 8-bit color, and 16-bit color.

9.3 Determine the appropriate feature, command, tool, or procedure to accomplish a stated task related to color correction.

10. File Format/Import/Export

10.1 Identify the characteristics, function, and appropriate use of various file formats, including but not limited to Photoshop native, TIFF, EPS, JPEG, PCX, PDF, PICT, GIF, and relation to production method and file size.

10.2 Determine the appropriate file format and procedure for exporting an Adobe Photoshop file to a specified application to accomplish a particular task.

10.3 Determine the appropriate feature, command, tool, or procedure to import a path into Adobe Photoshop and export a path to Adobe Illustrator.

11. Preparing Files for Production

11.1 Identify issues regarding preparing an image for printing color separations and comps. Issues include but are not limited to adjusting out-of-gamut colors, previewing a printed image, selecting Print options, selecting halftone screen attributes, creating color traps, selecting spot color options, Page Setup options, and Transfer functions.

11.2 Identify the characteristics, function, and appropriate procedure to create a monotone, duotone, tritone, or quadtone and manipulate a duotone curve.

11.3 Identify issues regarding preparing an image for Web publication or other onscreen production. Issues include but are not limited to working with grayscale, flat color, and full-color images; optimizing file sizes; selecting appropriate color modes; selecting Indexed Color options; creating transparency; and selecting file formats.

12. Color Calibration and Setup

12.1 Define the steps in the process of calibration on the Macintosh and Windows platforms, including using the Gamma utility, and the importance of calibration in relation to printing and screen production methods and output.

12.2 Identify issues regarding color management and color settings. Issues include but are not limited to ICC Profile embedding, profile mismatch color space conversion, and selecting Color Settings options including RGB Setup, CMYK Setup, Grayscale, and Profile Setup.

TAKING THE PROFICIENCY EXAM FOR THE SECOND TIME

Whether you are retaking the exam because you didn't pass the first time, or because you are already an ACE for a previous version, you will probably want to review only specific areas of weakness. In both cases, you should have an indication of areas that require additional study.

TIPS FOR PASSING THE SECOND TIME AROUND

If you do not answer the correct number of questions the first time you take the exam, you will need to retake it. If this is the case, when you finish the exam, your score sheet will indicate the topics you need to review. Use that score sheet as a study guide and review the chapters that cover the specific topics. Take extra care to do the lessons in the chapter and experiment with the tools and commands. You should have an accurate confidence level about a certain topic area.

TIPS FOR PHOTOSHOP 4.0 ADOBE CERTIFIED EXPERTS

If you are already an ACE in Photoshop 4.0 and feel comfortable with the topics and objectives from that exam, you might want to review topics that have remained the same at your own discretion and focus mainly on the new features of Photoshop 5.0. The following section lists both the topics new to Photoshop and a chapter-by-chapter strategy for those wanting to focus only on the new material.

NEW FEATURES AND CHANGES

These are the new features, and the chapters in which they are addressed:

FEATURES	CHAPTERS
Scratch Disks	Chapter 1: "General Information"
Measure Tool	Chapter 2: "Photoshop's Work Environment"
History Palette	Chapter 3: "History Palette"
Selection Transformation	Chapter 6: "Selections"
Magnetic Lasso	Chapter 6: "Selections"
Magnetic Pen Tool	Chapter 7: "Paths"
Freeform Pen Tool	Chapter 7: "Paths"
Pen Tool Keyboard Shortcuts	Chapter 7: "Paths"
History Brush	Chapter 9: "Editing & Retouching"
Layer Effects	Chapter 10: "Layers"
Layer Alignment	Chapter 10: "Layers"
Type Layers and options	Chapter 11: "Type"
3-D Transform Filter	Chapter 12: "Filters"
Channel Mixer	Chapter 13: "Channels & Masks"
Spot Color Channels	Chapter 13: "Channels & Masks"
Color Samplers	Chapter 14: "Color Correction"
Support for DCS 2.0	Chapter 15: "File Formats"
Color Management Features	Chapter 18: "Color Management"
Support for Multipage PDF files	Chapter 19: "Automating Photoshop"
Action Sets	Chapter 19: "Automating Photoshop"

CHAPTER-BY-CHAPTER STRATEGY

The following sections indicate ways to implement a chapter-by-chapter strategy.

Chapter 1: "General Information"

Look at the new platform and system requirements. Also be sure to note the changes made to scratch disks.

Chapter 2: "The Photoshop Work Area"

Pay particular attention to the Wizards and the measure tool.

Chapter 3: "The History Palette"

This is a completely new feature; read the entire chapter.

Chapter 4: "Scanning & Working with Images"

Look at the options for importing and placing files, especially the PDF format support.

Chapter 5: "Image Modes"

Review the sections on 16-bit color.

Chapter 6: "Selections"

One selection tool has been added, the magnetic lasso. Make sure that you understand how this new tool operates.

Chapter 7: "Paths"

Another magnetic tool—the magnetic pen tool—will require some attention. There is also now a freeform pen tool. Note also that a keyboard shortcut has been added for the direct selection tool.

Chapter 8: "Painting"

Almost everything in version 5 covered in this chapter is the same as it was in the previous version.

Chapter 9: "Editing and Retouching"

Most of the information in this chapter is also the same. Examine the history brush and how it interacts with the History palette.

Chapter 10: "Layers"

In this chapter, look at aligning layers and applying the new layer effects.

Chapter 11: "Working with Type"

Options for applying type to an image are some of the most significant changes to version 5.0. You should review this entire chapter.

Chapter 12: "Filters"

Most of the filters remain the same. Pay particular attention to the new 3-D Transform filter.

Chapter 13: "Channels and Masks"

Look at the Channel Mixer, and pay particular attention to the new Spot Color channels.

Chapter 14: "Color Correction"

Much of the information is the same as the previous version, but you will want to learn how to use the Color Sampler and its options.

Chapter 15: "File Formats"

The support for DCS 2.0 is new. Although support for the PNG is not, you might want to review its capabilities.

Chapter 16: "Prepress Production"

Pay attention to the areas on the ways that Photoshop now handles spot colors.

Chapter 17: "Web & Video Production"

Almost everything remains the same as in the previous version.

Chapter 18: "Color Management"

You should review this entire chapter. Some of the changes made in the area of color management are the most dramatic in the latest release.

Chapter 19: "Automating Photoshop"

Actions remain essentially the same, but action sets have been added, and several new automation commands have been included.

For many people, a combination of self-paced instruction and instructor-led classes are the most effective way to prepare for an exam. Adobe Certified Training Providers are individual instructors, training businesses, or educational institutions that teach people how to use Adobe products. They have proven training ability and expert product knowledge, and are Adobe's recommended source of highly skilled, expert instruction on Adobe software.

WHAT'S ON THE CD?

The CD provided with this book contains a sample exam that accurately simulates the Proficiency Exam as delivered by Sylvan Prometric. Although the questions are not the same, the material that is covered has been generated directly from Adobe's Domains and Objectives.

The CD also contains all the sample files required to complete the lessons included in this book. The files are organized according to chapter.

CHAPTER 1

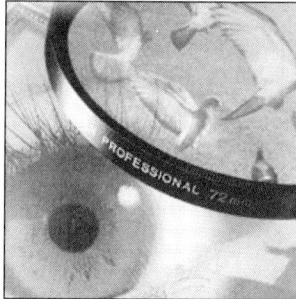

GENERAL INFORMATION

Adobe has determined clear requirements in its Domains and Objectives for the subject matter you need to study for the Photoshop Proficiency Exam. These requirements include defining common terms and concepts important to general Photoshop use, identifying key features and benefits of Photoshop, and installing and configuring Photoshop. This chapter will address each of these, as well as demonstrate their importance in relation to the other Domains and Objectives.

Domains & Objectives

General Information

1.1   Define common terms and concepts related to Adobe Photoshop, including but not limited to the following: raster, vector, flatness, path, mask, pixel, color depth, and color space.

1.2   Identify key features and benefits of Photoshop.

1.3   Identify installation procedures, memory requirements and plug-ins for Adobe Photoshop, including but not limited to: cache levels, virtual memory, scratch disks, installing third-party plug-ins, and networked and local volumes.

COMMON TERMS AND CONCEPTS

As with any subject, there are certain elementary ideas that you must understand before you can master a software application. This is certainly the case for Photoshop users. The following terms and concepts are important to know for the exam, as well as for general Photoshop use. They lay an important foundation upon which you can build a complete knowledge of Photoshop. The most basic and general terms are covered here, and other key terms will be addressed in the appropriate chapters. Most of the terms may seem elementary, but it is important to review them. You will need to understand not only the terms and concepts, but also how they relate specifically to Photoshop and common techniques.

PIXEL

A *pixel* is the fundamental unit of an image in Photoshop. It is a small square block of color. An image often consists of many pixels, arranged in columns and rows. One consequence of this construction is that because the image is made up of square pixels, the image must be rectangular. To understand many of Photoshop's processes, it is valuable to understand what happens at the pixel level. Many fundamental techniques and effects throughout this book will be explained by examining what happens to individual pixels. Figures 1.1 and 1.2 show an example of an image made up of pixels at different magnifications.

Figure 1.1

This image is made up of pixels, magnified at 100%.

Figure 1.2

The same pixel-
based image shown
in Figure 1.1,
at 800%
magnification.

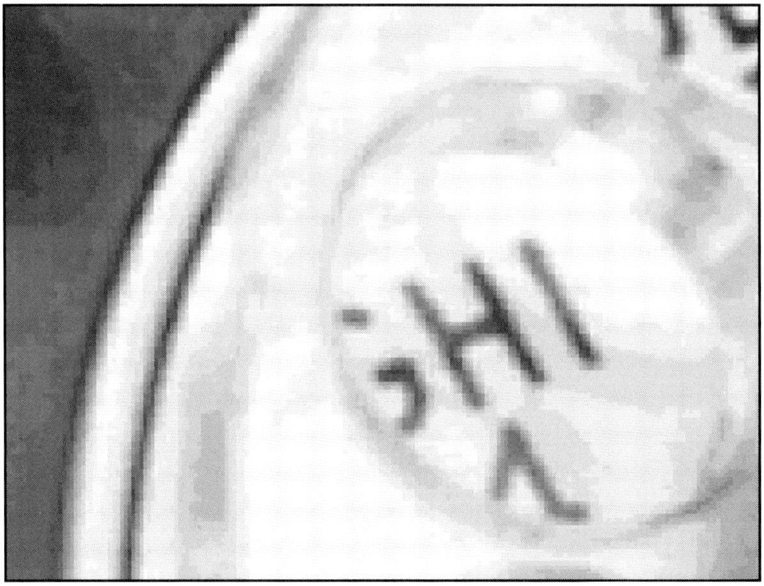

RASTER

A *raster* is the grid into which the pixels are arranged. Consequently, images made up of pixels are often referred to as *raster images*. A raster image cannot be enlarged unlimitedly without the pixels becoming visible. Images enlarged too much often have jagged or "chunky" edges (see Figure 1.3).

VECTOR

A *vector* is a mathematically defined line or curve. While Photoshop utilizes vectors when you create a path, you can only edit raster images with Photoshop. In order to open a vector-based image (from Adobe Illustrator, for example), Photoshop must first rasterize it or convert the vectors to pixels. Because vectors and vector-based images are mathematically defined, they can be enlarged arbitrarily without loss of detail or precision. Figure 1.4 shows a vector-based object. Compare this image with Figure 1.3.

Figure 1.3

A circle made up of pixels, scaled at 800% magnification.

Figure 1.4

A vector-based circle, scaled at 800% magnification.

PATH

A *path* is an entity based on vectors. Paths can be created in Photoshop, but they are more often associated with illustration programs such as Adobe Illustrator. Both the creation of paths and the exchange of information between Photoshop and Illustrator will be covered in detail in later chapters.

COLOR DEPTH

Color depth refers to the possible number of colors in an image. Common color depths are 1-bit, 8-bit, 24-bit, and 32-bit. A bit has two possible values: 0 and 1. These bits are used to define the color of each pixel in an image. By increasing the number of bits used to define the color, the range of colors available for each pixel is also increased.

Because a 1-bit image contains 2^1 colors, a 1-bit image is made up of at most two colors. Each pixel in a 1-bit image can be either black or white. An 8-bit image contains up to 256 (2^8) colors or 256 levels of gray. Every pixel can take on one of the 256 possible colors. A 24-bit image contains 16,777,216 (2^{24}) possible colors. While a 32-bit image does contain 2^{32} possible colors, it is rarely referred to in this way. Rather, a 32-bit image is commonly either a 24-bit image with an added alpha channel, or an image in CMYK mode. In either case, such an image contains four 8-bit channels. While the image mode and color depth are often related (an RGB image and CMYK image can both be 32-bit), this is not always the case. Photoshop also supports 16-bit channels, producing a 16-bit image in Grayscale mode, a 48-bit image in RGB mode, and a 64-bit image in

CMYK mode. Chapter 5, "Image Modes," will cover these and other image modes in depth.

Common color depths		
Color depth	Number of colors	Image mode
1-bit	2 (Black and White)	Bitmap
8-bit	256	Indexed Color
16-bit	65536	Grayscale, 16 Bits / Channel
24-bit	16 Million	RGB
32-bit		CMYK, RGB
48-bit		RGB, 16 Bits / Channel
64-bit		CMYK, 16 Bits / Channel

COLOR SPACE

A *color space* is the range of colors that a device produces. For example, various monitors may have differing color spaces because they combine the red, green, and blue light in slightly different ways. Printers, monitors, and scanners often operate in different color spaces, making calibration among these devices problematic. Photoshop images reside in color spaces that are determined by the device used to display them (a monitor or printer). You can adjust these color spaces by adjusting Photoshop's Color Settings. The Color Settings will be covered in Chapter 16, "Prepress Production," and Chapter 18, "Color Management."

KEY FEATURES AND BENEFITS OF ADOBE PHOTOSHOP

Adobe Photoshop is the industry standard for the manipulation of raster-based images. Photoshop is used to edit photographic images in what is commonly referred to as the "digital darkroom." It provides an array of tools that you can use to enhance and modify images that are comparable to those used by traditional photographic processors. The printing industry uses Photoshop to create color separations and color comps. Web designers and content providers can use Photoshop's powerful features to create an unlimited range of images to suit their needs for electronic publishing. Of course, Photoshop is also renowned for its capability to alter images, from image retouching to dazzling special effects. In addition to these key features, Photoshop serves equally well as a medium for the creation of completely original works of digital art. The powerful features for image creation and manipulation, combined with a universal acceptance by almost every industry that handles images, make Photoshop the clear choice for the creation and manipulation of pixel-based graphics.

Most of Photoshop's other key features are addressed individually through-out this book. For the exam, you should be able to identify the procedures at which Photoshop excels, but you also should be aware of the tasks for which it is inappropriate.

A recognition of Photoshop's limitations is, perhaps, just as important as understanding Photoshop's capabilities. You should know the tasks that you cannot perform in Photoshop. Obviously, this list could grow, depending on what you want to accomplish, but there are some common features found in other graphics programs that Photoshop is not designed to han-dle, such as the manipulation of vector-based objects, the capability to play and save animations, and the capability to create image maps. It is impor-tant to realize that, while Photoshop cannot actually do any of these partic-ular tasks, you may be able to use it as an important starting point. You can create images that you can animate later or that have image maps applied to them, or use images in tandem with vector illustration programs.

PHOTOSHOP SYSTEM REQUIREMENTS

Adobe expects users who pass the Photoshop Proficiency Exam to be aware of the basic system requirements for Photoshop. Pay particular attention to the areas of similarity between the two platforms.

PLATFORM REQUIREMENTS–MACINTOSH AND WINDOWS

Macintosh systems must have Mac OS System 7.5.5 or later; however, Mac OS System 8.1 or later is recommended. Photoshop 5.0 requires an Apple Power Macintosh. Windows systems must be running either Windows 95 or later, or Windows NT 4.0 or later. In either case, an Intel Pentium-class processor is required.

HARDWARE REQUIREMENTS AND RECOMMENDATIONS

For Windows and Macintosh systems, the following requirements and rec-ommendations are the same for both platforms.

Required:
- 32MB RAM
- 80MB free hard drive space

- CD-ROM drive
- 8-bit video card (capable of displaying 256 colors)
- Color monitor

Recommended:

- 64MB RAM or more
- 24-bit video card (capable of displaying millions of colors)

INSTALLING ADOBE PHOTOSHOP

Adobe Photoshop 5.0 is distributed on CD. When you insert the CD into a computer that is running a Windows operating system, the installation program will run automatically if you have your computer set to run CDs. If your computer does not automatically run the setup program, you must locate the Setup program on the CD and start it by double-clicking on the icon or by using the Run command. For Macintosh users, you will need to locate the Installer application and launch it by double-clicking on it.

If you do not already have a version of Photoshop on your computer, the Photoshop setup will guide you through several questions. Photoshop asks you in which folder you would like to place Photoshop, and which installation option you would like. For Windows users, the options are Typical, Compact, or Custom. For Macintosh users, the options are Easy Install or Custom. After you select the installation option, you must enter your registration information: name, business, and serial number. Once this is completed, Photoshop confirms the installation options, and then begins copying the application to your hard drive.

If you already own a copy of Photoshop and have purchased an upgrade, the Photoshop installation program will verify that you own a previous version. You can allow the installation program to search your hard drive for the previous installation, you can point it toward a specific directory that contains the previous version, or you can even use the CD or diskette from a previous version as verification. After the verification is complete and the previous version has been found, the upgrade installation will continue much the same as the new installation process described previously.

Macintosh users who are upgrading from a previous version should delete the Gamma control panel from the System Folder, because Photoshop 5.0 installs a new Gamma utility called "Adobe Gamma."

TIP

One of the greatest improvements you can make to Photoshop's performance is the addition of RAM.

TIP

Keep the serial number for Photoshop in a safe place. You will need it later if you reinstall Photoshop.

TIP

Look in the Goodies folder on the Photoshop CD for free plug-ins and textures.

Once installation is finished, you will be asked to register the program with Adobe. You can do this by filling out and mailing the registration card, or by registering online. In fact, under the File menu, there is an Adobe Online option that links directly to Adobe's Web site where you can go into the registration area.

OPTIMIZING AND CUSTOMIZING PHOTOSHOP

Photoshop enables you to configure how it interacts with the operating system, how it uses RAM and hard drive space, how files are saved, and many other individual preferences. Each of the areas discussed below can be found under File > Preferences. (Only those preferences not specifically addressed in later chapters are covered here.)

GENERAL PREFERENCES

The general Preferences dialog box allows you to set a variety of user preferences. All of the preferences are accessed by choosing File > Preferences (see Figure 1.5). The preferences you can set in the Preferences dialog box range from how to choose colors to whether or not Photoshop beeps when it completes a command.

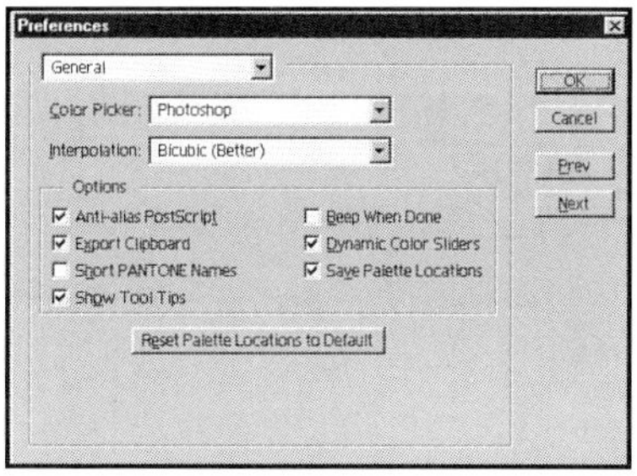

Figure 1.5

The General Preferences dialog box is accessed via the File menu.

Color Picker

The Color Picker option allows you to select between Photoshop's default color picker or the operating system's color picker. Generally, you will want to use the Photoshop color picker. The color pickers for Macintosh and Windows both enable you to select from operating system specific colors. Neither color picker warns you when a color is out-of-gamut.

Interpolation

You can set the default type of interpolation used when resampling an image. *Interpolation* is the mathematical process of determining intermediate values. In the case of images in Photoshop, the values that are determined are those for colors. The options are Bicubic, Bilinear, and Nearest Neighbor. You can override the interpolation type when performing the resampling. More information about resampling and interpolation can be found in Chapter 4, "Scanning & Working with Images."

Anti-Alias Postscript

When placing an EPS file into Photoshop, you can choose whether *anti-aliasing*—the creation of a smooth transition between colors—occurs when the file is rasterized. Turning this option off creates sharp distinctions between colors, but may introduce jagged edges, especially in curves.

Export Clipboard

This option determines whether information is left on the clipboard for use by other applications after exiting Photoshop. Turning this option off saves some time because Photoshop doesn't need to convert the information into a format that can read other applications before exiting.

Short Pantone Names

The Pantone Matching System is a widely used method of designating spot colors. Different programs, such as Adobe Illustrator, Adobe PageMaker, and QuarkXPress, can specify the names for these colors in a variety of ways. To ensure compatibility between the names of spot colors in a Photoshop document and the names in a page layout program, this option should be selected.

Show Tool Tips

Tool tips are the small description boxes that appear when the cursor moves over a command in the toolbox. This option allows tool tips to be turned on or off.

Beep When Done

If a task requires the status bar, you can set this option if you want to hear a beep when Photoshop completes the task.

Dynamic Color Sliders

The sliders in the Color palette display color bars that represent the current color model. By default, the sliders update to show how the colors combine. If this option is turned off, the appearance of the sliders remains fixed.

Save Palette Locations

By default, Photoshop remembers the location of all the palettes when you close and restart it. If you would like the palettes restored to their default locations each time you start Photoshop, turn this option off.

Reset Palette Locations to Default

While working in Photoshop, you can restore all the palettes to their default locations and groupings by clicking this button.

SAVING FILES

The Saving Files preferences give you some control over the ways in which Photoshop saves files. Figure 1.6 shows these options.

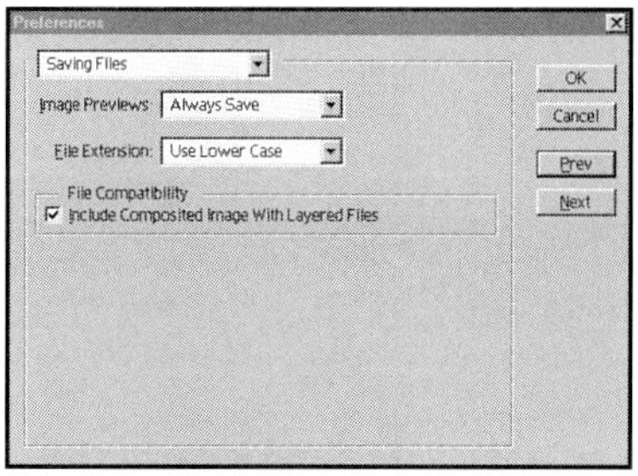

Figure 1.6

Use these Preferences for saving files.

Image Previews

This option controls whether previews of the images are always saved with the document, never saved, or if you are prompted to decide every time you save an image. The previews are visible after selecting an image in the Open dialog box.

File Extension

This option determines whether Photoshop should use uppercase or lower-case file extensions. File extensions are the three character suffixes that follow the file name. For example, the extension for fruit.jpg is jpg. The extension is used by the operating system and by Photoshop to determine the file type. Macintosh users can choose not to use extensions with their files because the Mac OS does not require them. Lowercase extensions are of particular importance to Web developers because Unix servers are case sensitive.

File Compatibility

The Include Composited Image with Layered Files option enables applications that do not support Photoshop's layers, such as Adobe Illustrator, to read the Photoshop image. If this feature is turned on, the size of the file will increase because of the extra information that must be stored.

CACHE LEVELS

Photoshop uses cached images to speed up screen refreshes when certain commands are executed. The cached image is a low resolution copy of the original, which is stored in RAM. The cache levels can be set to values ranging from 1 to 8. A value of 8 uses the maximum caching and provides the fastest redraw times. The default is 4. Because the cached image is stored in RAM, if you are running low on memory, you may want to set the cache level to a lower value.

You can also choose to use the cached image when you calculate a histogram. Photoshop will use the low resolution copy of the image, which provides faster results but a less accurate histogram in the Histogram, Levels, and Threshold dialog boxes

MEMORY

The Memory preference is available only on the Windows platform. Adobe recommends that you have at least 3 to 5 times the size of the image you are working on, plus an additional 5 to 10MB available in RAM. The amount of the RAM that Photoshop can use is either set in the Finder for Macintosh users, or in the Photoshop preferences for Windows users.

For Windows users, the default amount of free RAM that Photoshop uses is 50%. Photoshop will use up to this amount of RAM or an amount of RAM equal to the remaining scratch disk space, whichever is smaller. So even if you have 256MB RAM available, if you have only 16MB of free scratch disk space, Photoshop will use only 16MB of the available RAM, leaving the rest unused. The amount of RAM specified is actually a percentage of the RAM that is left after the operating system loads.

VIRTUAL MEMORY

Virtual memory is the use of hard drive space as additional RAM. The recommended settings for virtual memory vary depending on the operating system. This is because they handle the virtual memory in different ways, and because they interact with Photoshop's own virtual memory scheme differently.

For Windows users, as a general rule, the virtual memory should be set to the amount of actual RAM, plus another 50%. In Windows 95, the settings for virtual memory can be handled automatically by the operating system. In Windows NT, you must set the amount of hard drive space you want to allocate for virtual memory. In either case, if you often run other programs at the same time, you may need to dramatically increase the amount of space allocated, depending in large part on the requirements of these other programs. For Macintosh users, Adobe recommends that you disable Virtual Memory because the space Photoshop could use as scratch disk space may be used by the operating system instead—thus degrading Photoshop's performance. For Macintosh users with plenty of hard disk space available, however, this may not be necessary.

SCRATCH DISKS

Scratch disks are similar to virtual memory. The primary difference between them is that scratch disks are controlled entirely by Photoshop and not by the operating system. It is important that the scratch disk size be at least as large as the amount of available RAM. In some cases, larger values may be necessary. Whenever Photoshop runs out of memory or cannot fit anything else into physical RAM, it uses the scratch disk as virtual memory. When Photoshop is idle, it copies the entire contents of RAM into the scratch disk. (This, incidentally, creates the limitation for the amount of RAM utilization mentioned previously for Windows users.) In addition, Photoshop 5.0 must keep track of more than just the image data. It must store undo and history information, information stored in the pattern buffer, and clipboard data. Because Photoshop uses the scratch disk as additional RAM, proper understanding and control of the scratch disk is one of the more important keys to gaining optimal performance.

By default, Photoshop creates one primary scratch disk on the startup drive. You can set up to four scratch disk areas, and there is no limitation imposed by Photoshop on the amount of scratch disk space you can allocate. The only limit would be one of available disk space. Figure 1.7 shows the Preferences for the scratch disks.

TIP

If you get a warning that Photoshop is unable to complete a task because the primary scratch disk is full, delete unneeded files from your hard drive.

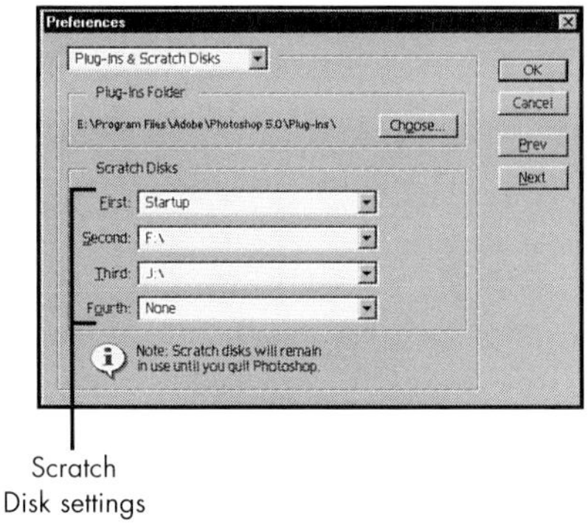

Figure 1.7

Use these options
for Scratch Disks.

Scratch
Disk settings

TIP

If you have multiple hard
disks, use the fastest drive
for your virtual memory
and primary scratch disk
space. Make sure that the
drive is also defragmented
regularly. Ideally, an
entire hard drive would be
dedicated to the
Photoshop scratch disk.

Now you try it...

Checking Your Preferences

1   Go to File > Preferences > General, or type Ctrl+K (Windows)/
Command+K (Macintosh).

2   Click the Next button and scroll through the different preference menus one by one.

3   Notice the settings for some of the preferences. (Some of the
menus will be covered in later chapters.)

PHOTOSHOP PLUG-INS

By default, Photoshop comes with a wide range of plug-ins. The plug-ins
create various special effects from the Filters pulldown menu. They also add
valuable functionality to Photoshop, such as the capability to read and save
different file formats, import and export files, and even to scan.

Plug-ins are typically stored in the Plug-Ins folder inside the Photoshop
folder. There are subfolders within the Plug-Ins folder to help categorize the
filters by purpose and manufacturer. When you start Photoshop, it searches
the Plug-Ins folder and all the subfolders for plug-ins. You can choose to
search a different folder if your plug-ins are at another location by selecting
File > Preferences > Plug-ins and Scratch Disk.

SUMMARY

A thorough understanding of Photoshop's basic terms, advantages and dis-advantages, installation procedures, and especially the preferences and options for optimization are key for not only the exam, but also for using Photoshop successfully in the work environment. Many of the tasks that confront digital artists and graphic designers today can be addressed by Photoshop. In the world of production graphics, however, an understanding of where Photoshop fits into the overall workflow and how it interacts with other graphics tools (such as illustration and page layout programs) is criti-cal if you are to use Photoshop to its fullest potential. In addition, a knowl-edge of the basic terms speaks not only to the fundamentals of Photoshop, but also to the vast array of other graphic programs available, as well as to their relationships. These relationships, in particular with Illustrator, will be examined in greater depth in later chapters.

REVIEW QUESTIONS

1. What is the maximum amount of scratch disk space allowed?

    a.   2GB

    b.   4GB

    c.   8GB

    d.   Unlimited

2. What is the default scratch disk arrangement?

    a.   No scratch disk is created.

    b.   A scratch disk is created on the startup drive.

    c.   A scratch disk is created on any secondary drive.

    d.   Photoshop creates as many scratch disks as it can.

3. What is the maximum number of scratch disk volumes that can be created?

    a.   1

    b.   2

    c.   3

    d.   4

4. You get an error message that Photoshop cannot complete the command because the primary scratch disk is full. What should you do?

    a.   Restart Photoshop.

    b.   Reinstall Photoshop.

    c.   Close any open applications.

    d.   Delete unnecessary files from the disk being used as a scratch disk.

5. What is the minimum amount of RAM that Photoshop 5.0 requires?

    a.   8MB

    b.   16MB

    c.   32MB

    d.   64MB

6. Photoshop cannot do the following (choose the three that apply):

    a.   Play a sound.

    b.   Play an animation.

    c.   Open a raster image file.

    d.   Open a spreadsheet.

7. Which of the following is the fundamental element in a Photoshop image?

    a. Vector

    b. Color Space

    c. Pixel

    d. Path

8. How many colors are supported by an 8-bit image?

    a. 8

    b. 16

    c. 256

    d. 65,000

9. You are working on an image and some of the filters are unavailable. What should you do? (Choose 2)

    a. Turn off virtual memory.

    b. Check the plug-in's search path in the preferences.

    c. Delete the Photoshop preferences file to reset them.

    d. Make sure that the plug-ins are in the correct folder.

10. You are working on a 10MB image. What is the minimum recommended amount of RAM you should have available?

    a. 16–32MB

    b. 30–50MB

    c. 32–64MB

    d. 50–64MB

CHAPTER 2

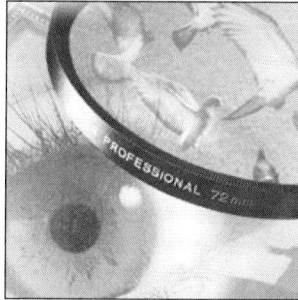

THE PHOTOSHOP WORK AREA

Learning how to navigate the work area is essential to working productively in Photoshop. In this chapter you will be introduced to the Photoshop tools and palettes and how to customize your work area. You will learn keyboard shortcut tips, navigation commands, View commands, and the Navigator palette. You will also learn information about your images; the measure tool, rulers, guides, and the grid for precision work. Finally, you will learn how to use the help resources within the Photoshop application and online.

Domains & Objectives

The Work Area

2.1   Identify issues regarding the characteristics, function, options, and appropriate use of items in the work area, including using and customizing palettes; using wizards, the History palette (which will be covered in Chapter 3), the status bar, and Help/Online Help; setting preferences; and identifying popular keyboard shortcuts.

2.2   Identify issues regarding the characteristics, function, options, and appropriate use of view menus and commands, including context menus, View commands, screen mode buttons, the Canvas Size command, the Navigation palette, and the measure tool, rules, and guides.

The Photoshop work area contains the image window, a series of pulldown menus, and several tools and palettes that enable you to create or edit an image (see Figure 2.1).

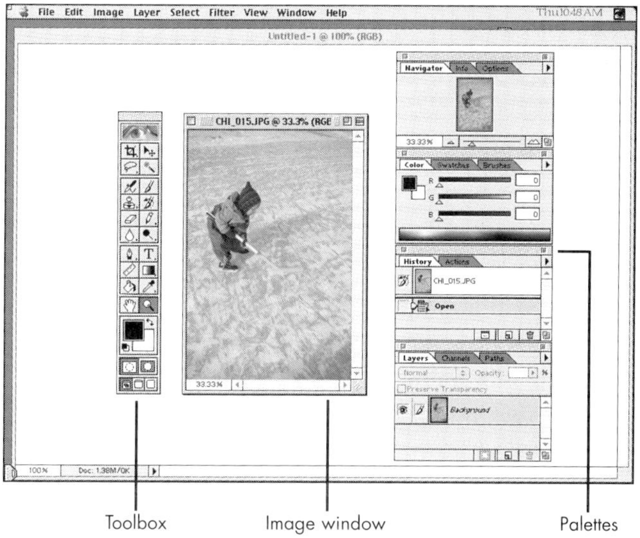
File Edit Image Layer Select Filter View Window Help
Untitled-1 @ 100% (RGB)
CHI_015.JPG @ 33.3% (RGB)
Navigator Info Options
Color Swatches Brushes
History Actions
Open
Layers Channels Paths
Background
Toolbox
Image window
Palettes

Figure 2.1

The Photoshop work area.

THE TOOLBOX

The toolbox offers a variety of tools that you can use to select, paint, retouch, edit, add type, and view images (see Figure 2.2). By default, it is positioned on the left side of your work area, but you can move it to a new location if you prefer.

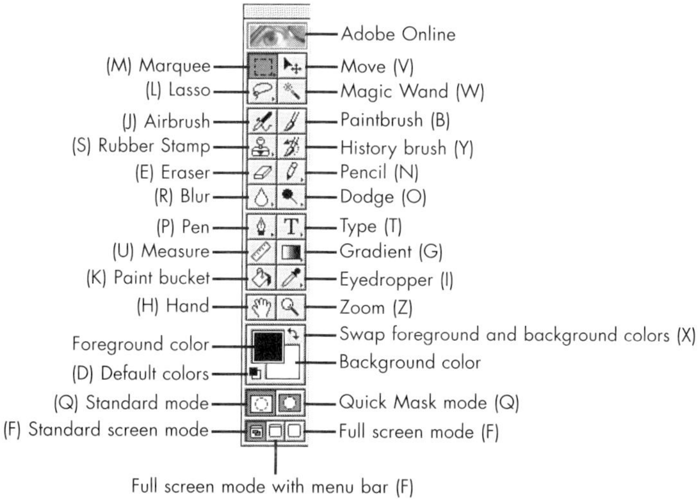
Adobe Online
(M) Marquee
Move (V)
(L) Lasso
Magic Wand (W)
(J) Airbrush
Paintbrush (B)
(S) Rubber Stamp
History brush (Y)
(E) Eraser
Pencil (N)
(R) Blur
Dodge (O)
(P) Pen
Type (T)
(U) Measure
Gradient (G)
(K) Paint bucket
Eyedropper (I)
(H) Hand
Zoom (Z)
Swap foreground and background colors (X)
Foreground color
Background color
(D) Default colors
(Q) Standard mode
Quick Mask mode (Q)
(F) Standard screen mode
Full screen mode (F)
Full screen mode with menu bar (F)

Figure 2.2

The Photoshop toolbox.

Figure 2.3

Hidden tools in
the toolbox.

Elliptical marquee
Single column marquee
Crop
Single row marquee

Polygon lasso
Magnetic lasso

Line

Pattern stamp

Sharpen
Smudge

Burn
Sponge

Magnetic pen
Convert-anchor point
Delete anchor point
Add anchor point
Direct-selection
Freeform pen

Type mask
Vertical Type mask
Vertical Type

Radial Gradient
Reflected Gradient
Diamond Gradient
Angle Gradient

Color sampler

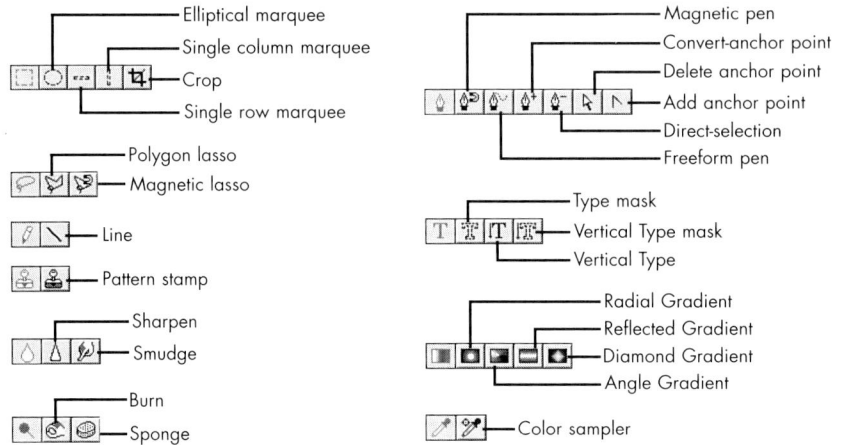

IDENTIFYING A TOOL

To identify a tool, position your mouse pointer over a tool in the toolbox
and pause without clicking on the tool to get the name of the tool as well as
the shortcut key that activates it.

ACTIVATING A TOOL

There are two ways to activate a tool:

- Click the tool icon in the toolbox. The tool button will then appear
  depressed, and its color will be a darker gray.

- Use the shortcut key. For example, when you press the letter E on your
  keyboard, the eraser tool is selected. Unfortunately, not all the tools
  have such obvious letter choices.

A black triangle on a tool button indicates that there are related tools in an
extended menu. To access the hidden tools, click the tool and hold down
your mouse button a little longer than usual. Each tool variation offers different functionality and will be discussed in depth in the tool's relevant
chapter. For example, the paintbrush, airbrush, and pencil are discussed in
Chapter 8, "Painting." You will need to be comfortable with the individual
nature of each variation to be ready for the exam.

To cycle through a set of hidden tools, press Option (Macintosh) or Alt
(Windows), and click the tool in the toolbox. An even faster way is to hold
down your Shift key and press the tool's shortcut key.

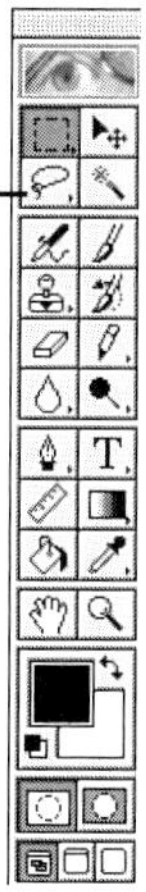

Tool icon with a black triangle

Figure 2.4

Click tools that display a black triangle to access hidden, related tools.

CHANGING THE CURSOR APPEARANCE FOR PRECISION WORK

The Default tool icons are not always helpful when doing precision work on an image. For example, you could have a 300 pixel-wide brush selected and not know it until you begin to paint. You could check the Brushes palette before each use, but you should also know how to change the cursor settings.

Cursor settings for Painting Cursors and Other Cursors are found in the Preferences dialog box (see Figure 2.5). Choose File > Preferences > Display & Cursors. In the lower left area of the dialog box, you have a visual representation of three cursor choices that you can use with the painting tools (the paintbrush, airbrush, pencil, eraser, rubber stamp, pattern stamp, smudge, blur, sharpen, dodge, burn, and sponge). You can choose the default standard tool, the Precise crosshair, or the actual Brush Size.

TIP

You can choose your cursor preference in the Preferences dialog box by first pressing Command/Control+K followed by Command/Control+3 to access the Display & Cursors Preferences.

Figure 2.5

Use the Preferences dialog box to select the type of cursor you want to use.

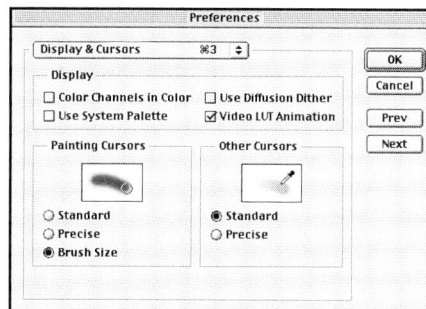

TIP

If you need to switch to a
Precise crosshair, simply
press the Caps Lock key.

TIP

The marquee, line, and
gradient tools appear by
default as crosshairs.

Use the Brush Size cursor so that you have an indication of the size and shape of the selected brush when working with the painting and editing tools.

The Other Cursors option controls the cursor display for the marquee, crop, lasso, polygon lasso, magnetic lasso, magic wand, eyedropper, color sampler, pen, gradient, line, and paint bucket tools.

WORKING WITH PALETTES

Photoshop palettes add functionality to nearly every tool in the toolbox. Some palettes are specific to a tool's use, while others monitor your work and help you stay organized.

You can find all of the palettes listed under the Window menu (see Figure 2.6). Using this menu, you can choose to Show or Hide any palette. When a palette is open, the Window menu option is to hide that palette. When a palette is closed, the menu option is to show it.

Figure 2.6

All of Photoshop's
palettes are listed under
the Window menu.

To display a palette's Options menu, click the black triangle in the upper right corner of the palette (see Figure 2.7).

Figure 2.7

Display the palette's
options by clicking the
black triangle in the
upper-right corner of
the palette.

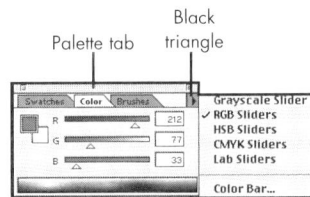

ORGANIZING AND CUSTOMIZING YOUR PALETTES

You can customize the display of your work area to suit the way you like or need to work. All of the palettes and the toolbox can be repositioned or hidden. You can also separate or rearrange palette groups to form new groups. (See Figure 2.8).

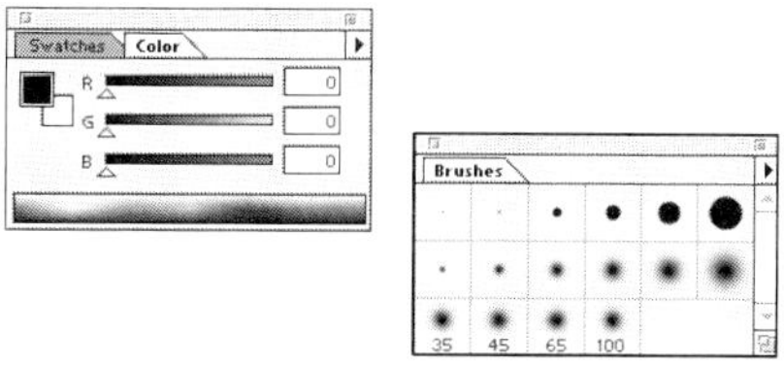

Figure 2.8

Click the tab and drag
to separate a palette
from its group.

- To move a palette group, drag its title bar.
- To separate a palette from its group, click the tab of the chosen palette and drag it away from its group.

  To hide a palette, click the box that appears on the left in its title bar.

- To move a palette to another group, drag the palette tab to the new group. A border appears around the new group indicating that the palette is now part of that group.

- To resize a palette, drag its lower right corner. To bring the palette back to its default size, click the resize box (Macintosh) on the right side of the title bar. Windows users can click the minimum/maximum box.

To collapse a group of palettes to title tabs only, double-click a palette's tab or Option+click the zoom box (Macintosh), or Alt+click the minimize box (Windows). To collapse the palette to its title bar only, double-click the title bar (see Figure 2.9).

TIP

Press Shift+Tab to hide
or show all of the
palettes. Press only the
Tab key to hide or show
all of the palettes including the toolbox.

NOTE

You cannot resize the
Options, Info, or Color
palettes.

Figure 2.9

Double-click the
palette's title bar
to collapse it.

SETTING PALETTE PREFERENCES

Palette groupings and positions are automatically saved from one work session to the next. However, you have the option of choosing whether you'll work with the default palette preferences, in which all of the palettes are stacked on the right side of the screen, or whether you'll customize palette grouping and position. You can save your own custom palette locations or choose the Photoshop default palette locations in the Preferences General dialog box (see Figure 2.10). To make sure Photoshop opens every time with the default positions, deselect Save Palette Locations in the Preferences General dialog box.

TIP

Mac users can click the
zoom box of the palette
to collapse it to include
only the top information.
Windows users can click
the minimize button.

Figure 2.10

To reset your palettes to the default position, choose File > Preferences > General and click the Reset Palette Locations to Default button.

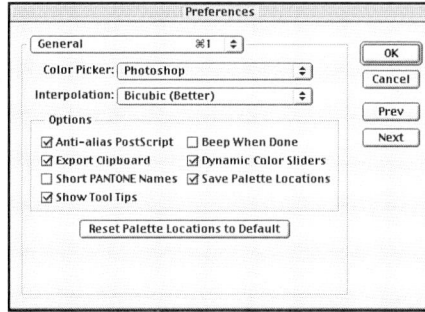

TIP

You can reset the current tool or all the tools back to the default options by clicking on the black triangle in the Options palette.

WIZARDS AND ASSISTANTS

Wizards (Windows) and Assistants (Macintosh) offer step-by-step interactive help in saving an image with transparency as well as resizing and resampling an image for either print or online use. Wizards/Assistants reside in the Plug-ins folder in your Photoshop application folder. To activate them within Photoshop, access the Help menu and choose either Export Transparent Image or Resize Image.

RESIZING AND RESAMPLING IMAGES

For assistance with resizing and resampling images, choose Help > Resize Image. A series of dialog boxes (see Figures 2.11 and 2.12) will take you through the steps and warn you if you will have resolution problems based on the information you have entered.

Figure 2.11

The Resize Image Assistant presents a series of dialog boxes for choosing a desired print size.

EXPORTING A TRANSPARENT IMAGE

You can use the Export Transparent Image command for help when preparing files that contain transparency for the Web, or for preparing a silhouetted image for use in a page layout program. Your image must have either a transparent background or an active selection. To access your Export Transparent Image Assistant, choose Help > Export Transparent Image. Next, choose either Print or Online for Usage (see Figure 2.13).

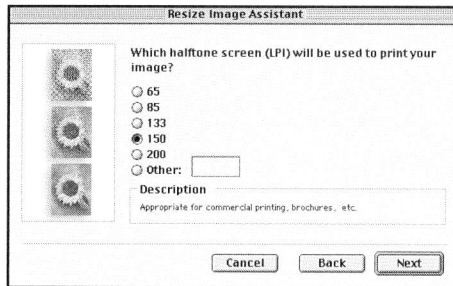

Figure 2.12

Choose an appropriate linescreen.

Figure 2.13

The Export Transparent Image Assistant helps you export your image through a series of dialog boxes.

If you choose the Online option, you will be prompted with a series of dialog boxes (see Figures 2.14 and 2.15) that ask you what file format you want to use, your palette matching preference, dither preference, and color matching quality. Make your choices, click OK, and save the file. For more information on preparing images for the Web, see Chapter 17, "Web & Video Production."

Figure 2.14

Choose an online file format.

If you choose the Print option, make sure that you have an active selection. Photoshop will save a clipping path of the selection and will then prompt you to save the file (see Figure 2.16). For more information on clipping paths, see Chapter 7, "Paths."

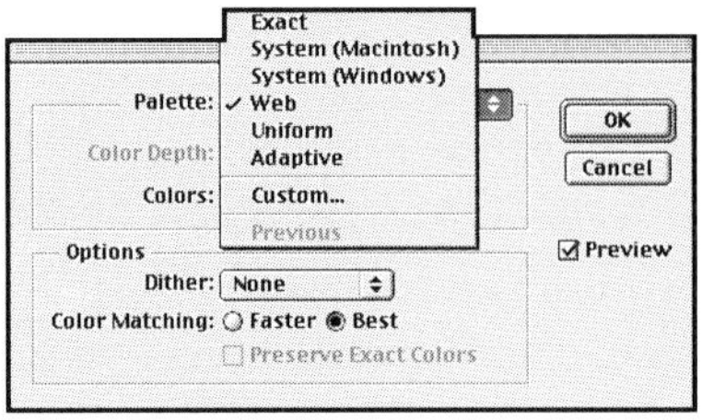

Figure 2.15

Choose a color palette
from the pop-up menu.

Figures 2.16

Photoshop saves a clip-
ping path with the image.

TIP

When saving your file,
note the location on your
hard drive. Photoshop
automatically closes the
file upon saving.

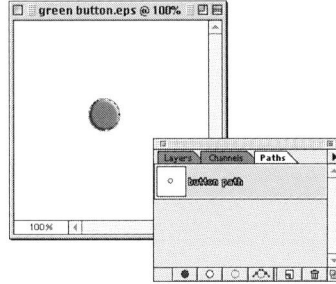

USING THE STATUS BAR

The status bar reveals helpful information regarding your document,
including its current magnification and information related to disk space
and memory. The default setting gives you two sets of numbers that display
information pertaining to the document file size. If you click the triangle in
the status menu, you can get information on Document Sizes, Scratch
Disks, Efficiency, Timing, and the Current Tool (see Figure 2.17).

Figure 2.17

Click the triangle in the
status bar to reveal helpful information regarding
your image.

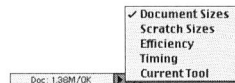

DOCUMENT SIZES

The number on the right tells you the approximate file size of your document with active layers and channels (see Figure 2.18). This number can be
larger than the actual saved file on disk because Photoshop uses compression on data such as alpha channels when saving.

The number on the left gives you what the file size will be after you have
flattened the layers of an image (see Figure 2.18). This number is usually
smaller than the size of the file saved on disk. If the file has been saved in a
compressed format, such as JPEG, the number on the left can be quite a bit
larger than the size of the saved file. Experiment with an image by saving a

copy of the image as a JPEG file, and then comparing the document sizes of both while each document is open.

Figure 2.18

Document sizes of an unflattened image.

TIP

Mac users can check the file size of the document on disk while in the Finder by clicking the document icon once, and then choosing Get Info from the File menu or pressing Command+I.

See Chapter 10, "Layers," for more information on layers and flattening an image. For more information on file formats and compression, see Chapter 15, "File Formats."

Choosing the following Image Previews settings in the Preferences dialog box also creates a larger file (see Figure 2.19).

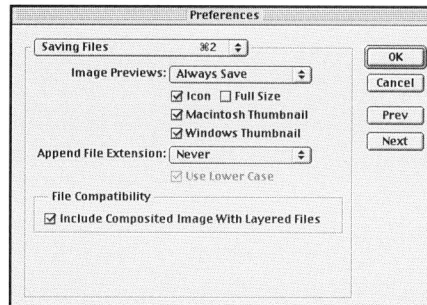

Figure 2.19

Image Previews prefer-ence settings create a larger file.

- **Icon.**   Photoshop will save the file with a Photoshop icon displayed on your hard drive.
- **Thumbnail.**   A picture of the image is displayed in the Photoshop open dialog box when you choose File > Open.
- **Full Size.**   Photoshop creates a full size 72 dpi image to be used by page layout programs and other applications to display the image.
- **Include Composited Image with Layered File.**   A flattened version of a layered file is saved with a layered file which allows you to open the Photoshop file in other applications that don't support Photoshop Layers, such as Adobe Illustrator.

SCRATCH SIZES

The number on the left tells you how much memory is being used to display all open images, including layers, channels, History palette information, the one current undo, pattern or snapshot information, and any information that is on the clipboard (see Figure 2.20). The number on the right tells you how much RAM has been allocated to Photoshop for processing images. This number does not include the amount of memory Photoshop needs to run. For more information about Scratch Disks and memory allocation, see Chapter 1, "General Information."

Figure 2.20

Access Scratch Size information via the black triangle pulldown menu on the Status Bar.

TIP

Be careful when using the Purge command because it will permanently remove the operation stored. You will not be able to get this information back with Edit > Undo (Command/Control+Z). Fortunately, when exercising this command, a warning dialog box appears.

EFFICIENCY

An efficiency percentage below 100% means Photoshop is using the scratch disk for some of its operations instead of using just RAM. To increase efficiency, you can use the Purge command, which frees up memory used by the History palette, the Clipboard, the Undo command, and the pattern buffer. To use the Purge command, choose Edit > Purge and select the memory buffer you want to clear. If the buffer doesn't contain anything to clear, the option is dimmed.

TIMING

Timing tells you how long it took to perform the last operation. This can be helpful for future project planning, especially for large, complex high resolution files as well as for doing benchmark tests to compare hardware speed and performance. Testing an Action before batch-processing several files is an example of how Timing can be used. For more information about using actions, see Chapter 19, "Automating Photoshop."

CURRENT TOOL

This option displays the name of the active tool. The status bar for Windows users also gives brief information about the active tool. In addition, Windows users have the option to Show/Hide the Status Bar from the Window menu.

ONLINE HELP SYSTEM

Within the online help system, you will find complete documentation along with keyboard shortcuts and a description of what's new in Photoshop 5.0. A list of all shortcuts that have changed between version 4.0 and version 5.0 is also included. You can search online help with keywords: Use the Find section by typing in the topic on which you need help (see Figure 2.21). You also can print your results.

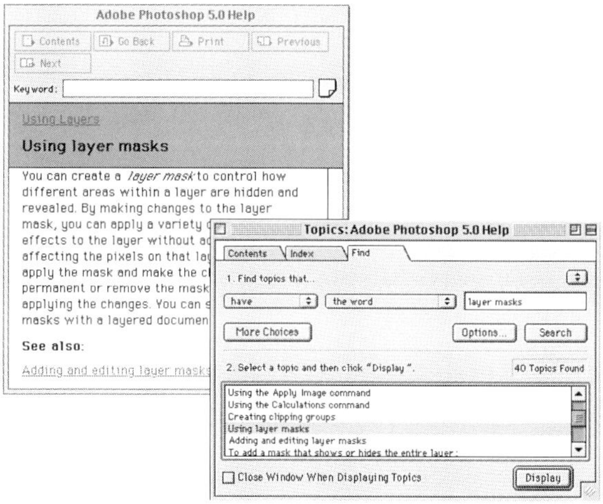

Figure 2.21

Search the online help system by keyword or topic.

For the Macintosh, choose Help > Help Contents. Windows users can press F1 or choose Help > Contents. Windows users can also get context-sensitive help by pressing F1 while a dialog box is open, by pressing Shift+F1 while choosing a command, or when clicking on a palette to display the related help topic.

ADOBE ONLINE

In addition to help offered within the application itself, Adobe provides easy access to the Adobe Web site (http://www.adobe.com) from within

Photoshop. Just choose File > Adobe Online or click the Photoshop icon at the top of the toolbox (see Figure 2.22). You can immediately choose to go to specific areas of the site to find Photoshop tips, plug-ins, user-to-user forums, and access to technical support databases.

The first time you launch Adobe Online, you will need to choose the Configure button to download the opening screen from the Adobe Web site (see Figure 2.23). You can then click on one of the Photoshop topics which will launch your Web browser and connect you to the site.

KEYBOARD SHORTCUTS

Throughout this book, you will find the most common (as well as the most obscure) keyboard shortcuts. Learn them not just for the Product Proficiency Exam but for your own enhanced productivity. But be warned: The Exam will ask you about shortcut keys!

You can learn many of the keyboard commands by simply taking note of them in the pulldown menus. The command is listed to the right of the menu function.

The first letter keyboard commands that activate the tools are the shortcuts that will truly set you free. Once you are familiar with using these commands, you will notice a marked increase in productivity, and you may even start having some fun!

And don't forget to use the shortcut buttons available at the bottom of most palettes (see Figure 2.24). Detailed information about these shortcut buttons can be found in the forthcoming chapters relating to those palettes.

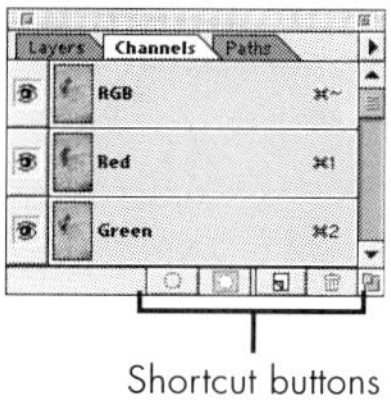

Figure 2.24

Many of the palettes
have shortcut buttons at
the bottom of the
palette.

Shortcut buttons

CONTEXT-SENSITIVE MENUS

In addition to using keyboard shortcuts, you can use context-sensitive
menus for frequently used commands. These menus display options relevant to the active palette, tool or selection, and they change based on what
you're doing (see Figure 2.25).

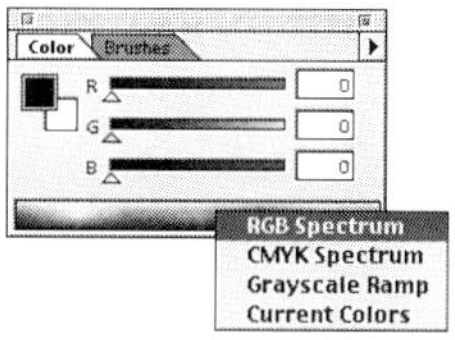

Figure 2.25

Context-sensitive menus
display relevant com-
mand options.

Position the active tool or cursor over an image or palette item and press
Control+click (Macintosh); or, if you are a Windows user, click the right
mouse button.

SCREEN MODES

At the bottom of the toolbox are three different viewing modes (Standard
Screen, Full Screen, and Full Screen with menu bar) that you can toggle
through by pressing F on your keyboard (see Figure 2.26).

STANDARD SCREEN MODE

Standard Screen mode is the default mode, which displays when you press
the left-most button. Standard Screen mode displays the image with a menu
bar at the top and scroll bars on the sides. Mac users may also see the desktop in the background.

FULL SCREEN MODE WITH MENU BAR

Full Screen mode with menu bar is activated when you click the middle button. The title bar and scroll bars are hidden in this mode and the display
background is gray.

NOTE

You must press the
keyboard key before you
click on the image so you
don't inadvertently edit
the image with the
active tool.

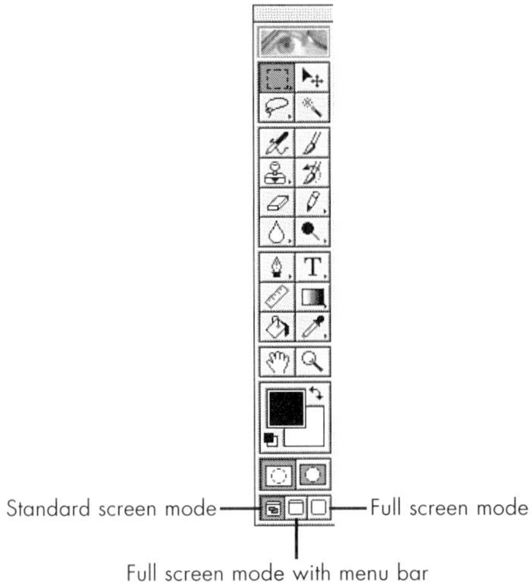

Figure 2.26

Toggle through the dif-
ferent Screen modes
by pressing F.

Standard screen mode ——————— Full screen mode

Full screen mode with menu bar

TIP

To better evaluate your
artwork without the dis-
traction of open palettes,
use Full Screen mode and
temporarily hide your
palettes by pressing the
Tab key.

FULL SCREEN MODE

Full Screen mode is activated when you click the right-most button. The
menu bar, the title bar, and the scroll bars are hidden and the display background is black.

VIEW COMMANDS

Photoshop gives you several ways to view your image at different magnification levels under the View Menu (see Figure 2.27). An image can be viewed
at percentages ranging from 0.03 to 1600 depending on the resolution of
the image.

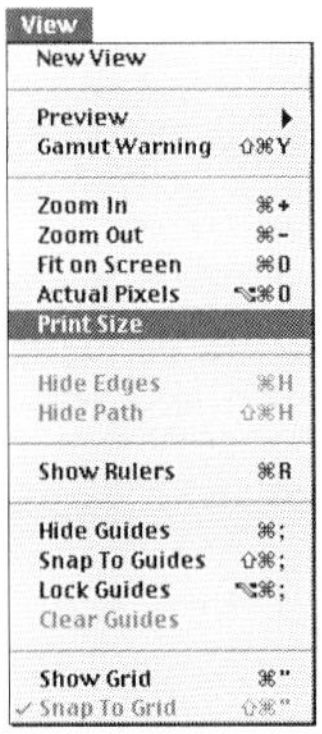

Figure 2.27

The View menu.

VIEW MENU OPTIONS

The View pulldown menu gives you several options including:

- **Zoom In.** Each time you choose Zoom In, your image is magnified by a preset amount.
- **Zoom Out.** Each time you choose Zoom Out, your image is reduced by a preset amount.
- **Fit on Screen.** When all of the palettes and the tool box are hidden, this option scales both the view and the window size to match your monitor size. If the toolbox and palettes are displayed, this option fits the image and window between the toolbox on the left and the palettes on the right.
- **Actual Pixels.** The image is displayed at 100%.
- **Print Size.** The image is displayed as specified in the Print Size fields of the Image Size dialog box.

ENLARGING AND REDUCING THE VIEW OF YOUR IMAGE

ZOOM

ICON	
SHORTCUT	Z
CURSORS	
OPTIONS	Navigator Info Zoom Options ☐ Resize Windows To Fit

You can zoom in to areas of an image up to 1600% for precision detail work.

TIP

You can also highlight the status bar, and then enter a new magnification percentage in the left corner. If you press Shift and Return after entering a view percentage, the Status Bar percentage remains highlighted so you can quickly make further adjustments.

TIP

Press Command/ Control+Spacebar to temporarily access the zoom tool while using another tool.

You can use the zoom tool several different ways:

To magnify:

- Click on the area of the image you want to magnify.
- Click and drag a marquee over the area of the image you want to magnify to isolate that area.

To reduce:

- Press Option (Macintosh) or Alt (Windows) and click on the area of an image that you want to view at a reduced size.

To view at 100%:

- Double-click on the zoom tool in the Tool palette to view your image at 100%.

To change the view to fit the screen:

- Double-click on the hand tool.

THE NAVIGATOR PALETTE

The Navigator palette (see Figure 2.28) not only enables you to view your image at different levels of magnification, it also let's you quickly pan to view specific areas. The thumbnail in the palette represents your image. By default, the View Box surrounds the entire image thumbnail when you first open an image or document.

Figure 2.28

The Navigator palette.

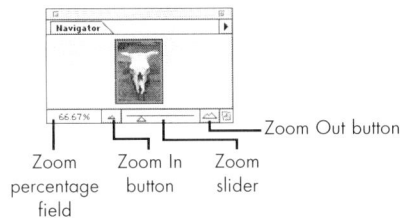

Zoom Out button

Zoom percentage field   Zoom In button   Zoom slider

TIP

To quickly view your image at specific sizes using the Zoom percentage field, hold down the Shift key while pressing the Enter button. This will keep the field highlighted allowing you to continue to enter different percentages.

Experiment changing the view of an image with the Navigator palette:

- Drag the Zoom slider at the bottom of the palette.
- Click the Zoom In and Zoom Out buttons.
- Enter a new magnification percentage and press Enter.

CHANGING THE VIEW BOX COLOR

The View Box is designated by a red border, but the color of the border can be changed, if you prefer, by choosing Options from the Palette triangle pop-up menu (see Figure 2.29).

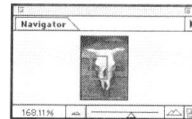

Figure 2.29

Change the View Box color by choosing a pre-set color or click on the swatch button to open the color picker.

CHANGING THE VIEW BOX SIZE

You can change the size of the View Box in the Navigator palette by pressing Command (Macintosh) or Alt (Windows) and dragging a new marquee square around the area of the image you want to view.

The magnifying glass will turn into a hand icon and will then allow you to reposition the View Box anywhere on the thumbnail (see Figure 2.30).

Figure 2.30

Reposition the View Box by clicking and dragging it.

MULTIPLE VIEWS

You can have multiple windows of the same image open with each display-ing a different view. The amount of memory on your machine will deter-mine how many windows you can have open at one time. The Window menu lists all open windows and documents.

To open additional windows, you can either choose View > New View or choose Open again from the File menu, which will warn you that the docu-ment is already open.

NOTE

If you have the same image open in two win-dows and you edit one of them, the other will also be edited. This is because you are working with two windows showing the same image, not two doc-uments.

ARRANGING MULTIPLE WINDOWS (WINDOWS ONLY)

If you're a Windows user, you can display multiple windows by either tiling or cascading them. Both options are listed under the Window menu. Cascade displays the windows stacked and cascading from the top left to the bottom right of the screen. Tile displays the windows from edge to edge.

USING RULERS

You can gain precise control over where you place elements in your image with the use of rulers, guides, and the grid. Photoshop also provides the Snap to Guides and Snap to Grid options for further precision. You also can customize the measurement system as well as the color of your guides and grid.

ADDING RULERS TO YOUR DOCUMENT

The Preferences: Units & Rulers dialog box gives you the option to choose the units of measure with which you like to work. Your choices are inches, pixels, centimeters, points, and picas (see Figure 2.31). Whichever system you choose, it will be reflected in the rulers when you choose View > Show Rulers or press Command/Control+R.

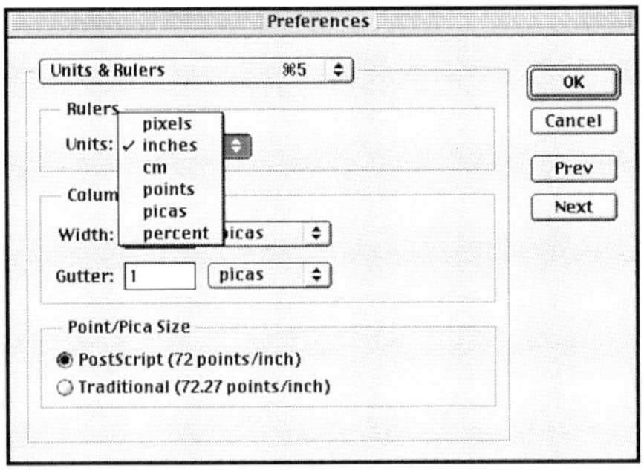

Figure 2.31

The Units measurement pop-up menu.

TIP

You can change the measurement system on-the-fly by double-clicking on either ruler. This will bring up the Preferences: Units & Rulers dialog box. When you change the measurement units in the Info palette, the ruler units change as well.

The rulers appear in the top and left side of the image window. Photoshop also uses the measurement units you specify in Preferences: Units & Rulers for the default units in the Image Size and Canvas Size dialog boxes as well as in the Info palette.

SPECIFYING THE RULER ORIGIN

The ruler origin is where the top ruler and the left ruler intersect in the upper-left corner of your document (see Figure 2.32).

To reposition the ruler origin, click in the square in the upper-left corner of the document and drag the intersection point to the preferred new location.

To reset the ruler origin, simply double-click on the ruler origin box.

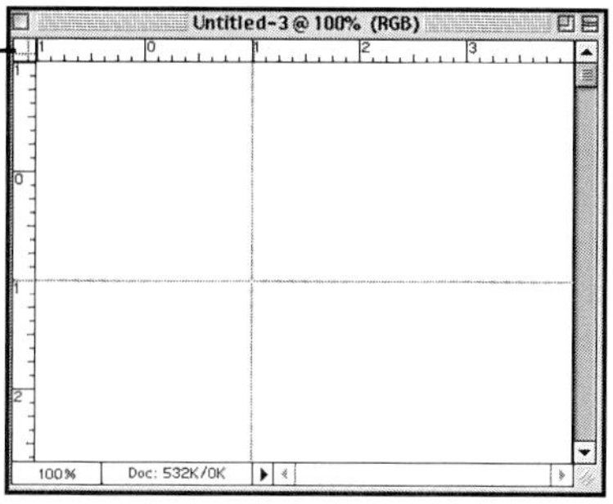

The Ruler Origin box

Figure 2.32

Drag from the ruler intersection to reposition the ruler origin.

USING GUIDES

Non-printing guides can be extremely useful in aligning elements in your image. By default, Show Guides is active in the View menu.

PLACING A GUIDE

In order to place a guide, your rulers must be visible. Click on the horizontal or vertical ruler and drag to place the guide on your image. The pointer will change into a double arrow, indicating that you are moving the guide.

REPOSITIONING A GUIDE

To move a guide, select the move tool, position it over the guide, and drag.

DELETING A GUIDE

With the move tool, click on the guide and drag it outside the image window in either direction. To remove all guides in a document, choose View > Clear Guides.

LOCKING A GUIDE

If you don't want to inadvertently move a guide, you can lock it. Choose View > Lock Guides or press Command+Option+; (Macintosh) or Control+Alt+; (Windows). This option in the View menu acts as a toggle, allowing you to unlock the guide when needed.

SHOWING AND HIDING GUIDES OR GRID

To temporarily Show or Hide guides, choose View > Show/Hide Guides or press Command/Control+;. To temporarily Show or Hide the Grid, choose View > Show/Hide Grid or press Command/Control+".

SNAP TO GUIDES OR GRID

For more precision and control, you can have design elements in your image snap to the guides or to the grid by choosing View > Snap to Guides

TIP

While using another tool, press the Command/Control key to temporarily access the move tool to reposition a guide.

or Grid. Press Command/Control+Shift to snap to guides. Press Command/Control+Shift+; to snap to grid.

SETTING GUIDES AND GRID PREFERENCES

You can change the appearance of the guides and the grid by choosing File > Preferences > Guides & Grid (see Figure 2.32).

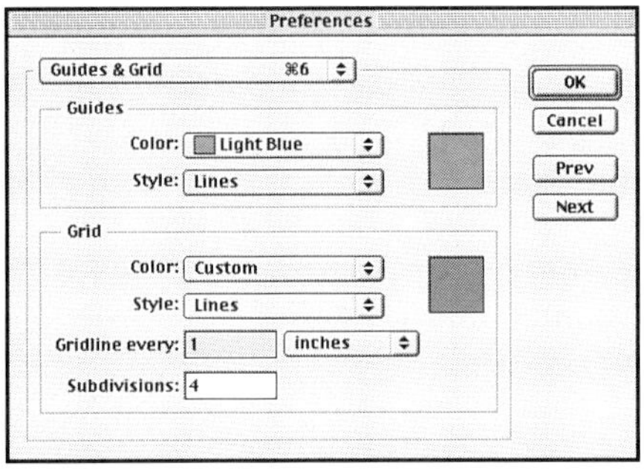

Figure 2.32

The Preferences: Guides & Grid dialog box.

- To change the color of the Guides or Grid, choose the pop-up menu for a list of preset colors or click the Swatch box on the right to choose a color from the color picker.
- To change the Guide Style, click the pop-up menu and choose either solid lines or dashed lines.
- To change the Grid Style, choose solid lines, dashed lines or dotted lines from the pop-up menu. You can also choose the frequency of a grid line and the number of subdivisions needed.

MEASURE TOOL

The measure tool calculates the distance between two points with a non-printing line. The active measurement information is displayed in the Info palette (see Figure 2.33).

Figure 2.33

The measure tool calculates the distance between two points with a non-printing line.

X and Y:	The first click with the measure tool or starting location
W or H:	The width or height from the x and y axis (horizontal or vertical distance)
D:	Total distance
A:	Angle measured relative to the axis

RESIZING AND REPOSITIONING THE MEASURING LINE

With the measure tool active, you can resize the line by dragging either end. To reposition the line, drag it from the middle.

USING THE MEASURE TOOL AS A PROTRACTOR

You can also create a protractor by setting an additional measuring line. Option-drag (Macintosh) or Alt-drag (Windows) at any angle from either end of the measuring line. A protractor icon will appear on the cursor and new distance and angle information about the second line will be displayed in the Info palette (see Figures 2.34 and 2.35).

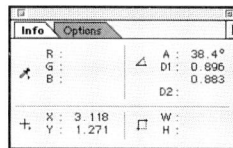

DELETING THE MEASURING LINE

To delete the measuring line, just drag it out of the image with the measure tool.

TIP

To constrain the angle to 45°, press the Shift key while you drag.

TIP

Double-click on either end of the measuring line, then click and drag to create a protractor.

Figure 2.34

Add a second line to create a protractor by Option-dragging (Macintosh) or Alt-dragging (Windows) at any angle from either end of the measuring line.

Figure 2.35

The Info palette displays information regarding the width, height, distance, and angle of the measuring line.

NOTE

You can have only one active measuring line or protractor at a time. When you draw a second line (not a protractor line), it replaces the original.

SETTING PREFERENCES

You can customize Photoshop by choosing preferences that may be required by your work environment, or you can make personal preference changes to suit the way you like to work.

Preference changes such as palette locations, options, ruler units, guides and grid settings, display and cursor options, scratch disk locations, and filesaving settings can be made by choosing File > Preferences (see Figure 2.36). Preference changes to color separation tables and monitor setup can be applied by choosing File > Color Settings.

Figure 2.36

Preference options from
the File menu.

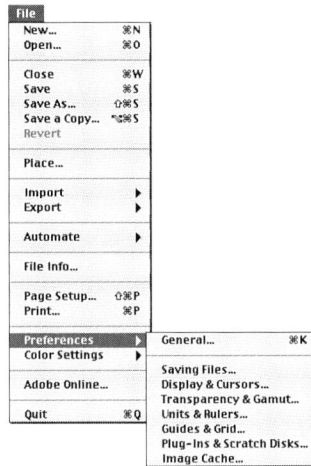

File	
New...	⌘N
Open...	⌘O
Close	⌘W
Save	⌘S
Save As...	⇧⌘S
Save a Copy...	⌥⌘S
Revert	
Place...	
Import	▶
Export	▶
Automate	▶
File Info...	
Page Setup...	⇧⌘P
Print...	⌘P
Preferences	▶
Color Settings	▶
Adobe Online...	
Quit	⌘Q

Preferences submenu	
General...	⌘K
Saving Files...	
Display & Cursors...	
Transparency & Gamut...	
Units & Rulers...	
Guides & Grid...	
Plug-Ins & Scratch Disks...	
Image Cache...	

When you install Photoshop, the default settings are employed until you make changes. The settings are stored in a file in the Adobe Photoshop Settings folder which can be found in the Photoshop application folder. For Macintosh users, this is a new location and is now much easier to access. (Version 4.0 stored the Preferences file in the preferences folder within the System Folder.)

The preference file keeps track of all changes that you make to settings as you work. These changes are stored in RAM as temporary settings and will remain until you make further changes from one work session to the next. The temporary settings are saved to disk when you quit Photoshop. This has both advantages and disadvantages.

For example, let's say in one session you've changed the paintbrush settings to fade from foreground color to background color and kept that option selected when you quit Photoshop. The next time you launch Photoshop and choose to work with the paintbrush, Photoshop remembers the setting. If you are no longer interested in the paintbrush fading to the background color, it may take a moment to figure out what's happening. You'll need to change the option in the Paintbrush Options palette.

REPLACING THE PREFERENCES FILE

The longer you work with the same Preferences file, the bigger it gets and the more likely it will be one day to become corrupted. If it seems Photoshop is suddenly misbehaving, sluggish, or is crashing, it could be that the Preferences file needs to be thrown away and replaced with a fresh default file or a fresh customized file that you have previously backed up.

Don't be afraid to throw away your Preferences file. When you relaunch Photoshop, a fresh file is created based on the default settings. It's a great first step in troubleshooting a Photoshop problem. Often, just doing this can solve speed issues and crashing problems.

BACKING UP YOUR PREFERENCES FILE

You can back up your customized settings so you don't need to change the default settings again when the time comes to throw out your preferences. The best time to make a backup of your Preferences file is when you've had a chance to experiment with the settings you like and Photoshop is functioning smoothly. Just make sure the backup file is saved in a location other than your hard disk. This will provide extra protection in case your hard disk ever crashes.

LOCKING YOUR PREFERENCES FILE

It can be annoying to work with a tool that displays a behavior you aren't expecting, such as the paintbrush fade to background setting example mentioned earlier. Each time you launch Photoshop, it remembers the settings in your palettes and tools from the last session. You can avoid this by locking your Preferences file (see Figure 2.37). This will ensure that your customized settings are reset every time you launch Photoshop.

While in the Finder, Macintosh users can lock the Preferences file by clicking once on the file and choosing Get Info from the File menu. Next, check the Locked checkbox in the lower left area of the window, and then close the Get Info window.

Windows users can click on the "Adobe Photoshop 5 Prefs.psp" file in the Photoshop\Adobe Photoshop Settings folder and choose File > Select

Properties (see Figure 2.37). Next, check the Read-Only box under Attributes and click OK.

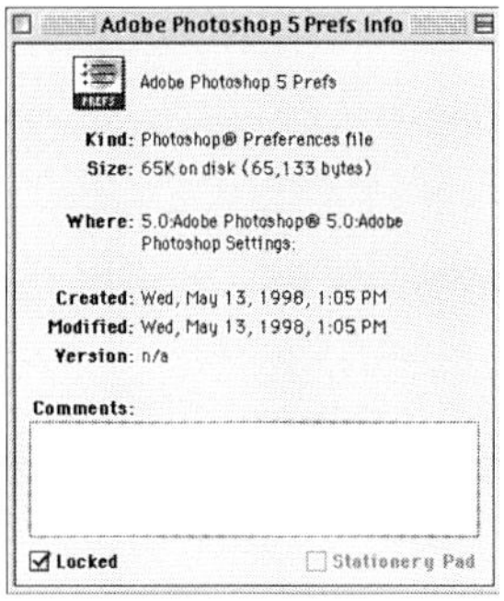

Figure 2.37

Mac users can lock the Preference file by checking the "Locked" box.

SUMMARY

Navigating the Photoshop work area is vital to working efficiently with Photoshop's tools and palettes. In this chapter you were introduced to the Photoshop tools and palettes and how to customize your work area to suit your needs.

REVIEW QUESTIONS

1. When displaying the Document Sizes option in the status bar, what does the number on the left indicate?

    a. Scratch disk size

    b. The size of the document with layers

    c. The size of the document with channels

    d. The size of the document after it is flattened

2. When displaying the Scratch Sizes option in the status bar, what does the number on the left indicate?

    a. How large your document is

    b   How large your scratch disk is

    c. How much RAM has been allocated to Photoshop

    d. How much memory is required for all open images

3. How do you display a Context-Sensitive menu?

    a. Double-click on the image.

    b. Command/Alt+click on the image.

    c. Control+click/right+click on the image.

    d. Position the cursor over the tool in the toolbox.

4. How do you view an image at 100%?

    a. Option-click on the image.

    b. Choose View > Fit in Window.

    c. Double-click the hand tool.

    d. Double-click the zoom tool.

5. What is the function of the measure tool?

    a. To measure a crop before cropping occurs

    b. To measure the distance between two points

    c. To measure the number of pixels in an image

    d. To measure a transform command before the transformation occurs

6. How do you recreate your preferences file after you've thrown it away?

    a. Reinstall Photoshop.

    b. Restart your computer.

    c. Copy the default preferences file to the plug-ins folder and restart.

    d. Launch Photoshop.

7. How do you reposition a guide?

    a. Select the move tool and click and drag.

    b. Option+click and drag while using any tool.

    c. Select any tool in the toolbox and click and drag.

    d. Shift+click and drag key while using any tool.

8. How do you create a protractor when using a measuring line?

    a. Shift+drag at any angle from either end of the measuring line.

    b. You can't create a protractor when using the measuring line.

    c. Click and drag on one of the endpoints of the measuring line.

    d. Option+drag (Macintosh) or Alt+drag (Windows) at any angle from either end of the measuring line.

CHAPTER 3

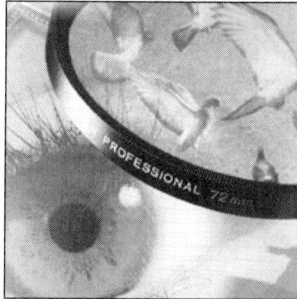

THE HISTORY PALETTE

In versions of Photoshop prior to Photoshop 5.0, you could undo only the last performed operation. While useful, this could be limiting. A new feature in Photoshop 5—the History palette—resolves this.

Domains & Objectives

Actions/Automation

3.1   Identify issues regarding the characteristics, function, options, and appropriate use of items in the work area, including the History palette.

The History palette stores changes made to an image while it is open in Photoshop—that is, it creates a palette of the different states of the image, giving you the freedom to choose the point you want to go back to during your current working session.

For the exam, you should be aware of the basic functions and terminology of the History palette (see Figure 3.1). You should be able to revert the image to a previous state and know how to manage histories and how they use memory.

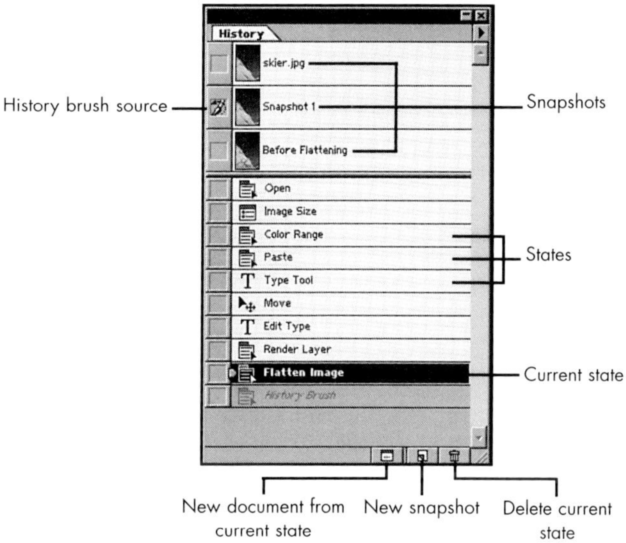

Figure 3.1

The History palette stores the previous states of an image.

MOVING BETWEEN STATES

States are points along an image's history that you can return to. States are placed in the History palette from top to bottom; so those states at the bottom of the palette are the most recent. The states indicate which tool was used to create the state. States are not saved when you save the image; only commands and tools that changed the image are stored as states. Commands and tools—such as setting preferences or view options—that do not change the image are not saved as states.

By default, Photoshop stores the last 20 states of an image. You can return the image to a previous point in its history by selecting any one of these states. By default, states are linear. This means that each state is a necessary causal link; by selecting a previous state and making a change, Photoshop will discard all subsequent states. Photoshop will not immediately discard states created after the selected state, but will instead gray them out. If you then make a change to the image, the grayed-out states will be discarded, and the history from that point forward will begin again (see Figure 3.2).

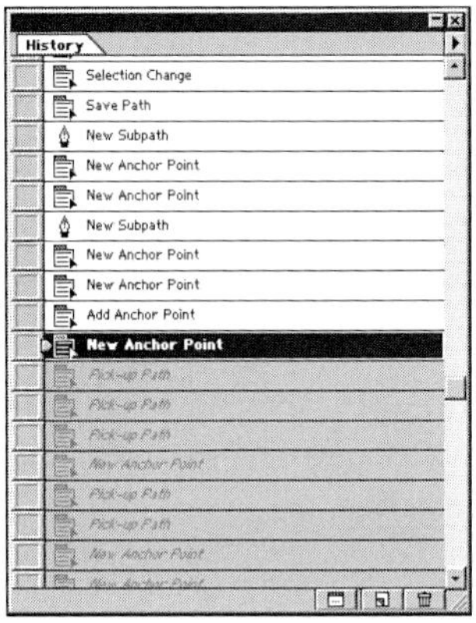

Figure 3.2

By using a tool that will be stored as a history state at this point, all the dimmed states will be discarded.

You can move backward and forward through the states in the History palette by selecting them. You also can navigate among the states by moving the slider up and down. Because the states are related to the capability to Undo, you can also move backward and forward through the history by using Alt+Ctrl+Z (Windows)/Option+Command+Z (Macintosh), or Shift+Ctrl+Z (Windows)/Shift+Command+Z (Macintosh). Using the Alt (Windows)/Option (Macintosh) key with the keyboard shortcut to Undo, Ctrl+Z (Windows)/Command+Z (Macintosh), steps backward through the history states. Stepping backward through the states dims the subsequent states.

If you do restart the history from a selected state, the states that come after it are discarded and can only be recovered by immediately choosing the Undo command. If you would like to store a state that will be discarded, create a snapshot.

CREATING SNAPSHOTS

A *snapshot* is a captured state. A snapshot can be created at any point in the image's stored history. By default, Photoshop creates a snapshot when the image is opened so that you can return to the version of the image that existed when it was first opened. Snapshots, like history states, are not saved with the image, but are reset every time the image is reopened.

To create a new snapshot of an image, use the New Snapshot button or the New Snapshot command in the History palette menu. Photoshop stores a copy of the image in its current state in the History palette. When you create a snapshot, you can rename it by double-clicking the snapshot in the History palette.

You can use a snapshot to try different effects on an image or to create a new set of states. If you save a snapshot, you can return to this image state at any time. You can also save a snapshot or the current state as a new image by using the New Document from Current State button in the History palette or by dragging the state or snapshot onto the button. A new history will be created for the new document.

The History Brush Source icon in the History palette determines which snapshot should be used when painting with the history brush. (The history brush will be covered in more detail in Chapter 9, "Editing & Retouching.")

Now you try it...

Using states and snapshots

1   Open lesson01.psd in the Chapter 3 lessons folder on the CD-ROM (see Figure 3.3).

Figure 3.3

Use this image to practice with states and snapshots.

continues

2 If the History palette is not visible, choose Show History from the Window menu.

3 If Photoshop has been set to the default settings, an initial snapshot will already have been created. Select the airbrush and begin painting anywhere in the image. Note that Photoshop has created a new state.

4 From the Image menu, choose the Adjust submenu, and then the Invert command. Photoshop will create another state (see Figure 3.4).

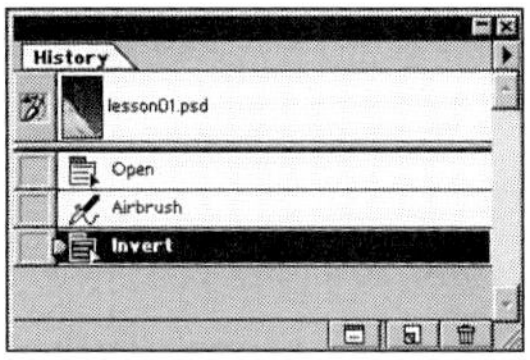

Figure 3.4

The History palette displays each change to the image as a state.

5 In the History palette, select the Airbrush state. The Invert state is grayed-out (see Figure 3.5). If the state is not grayed-out, it may be because the History palette is not using linear history, (Linear and non-linear history are covered later in this chapter.) Check the History Options in the History palette menu to confirm your selection, if necessary.

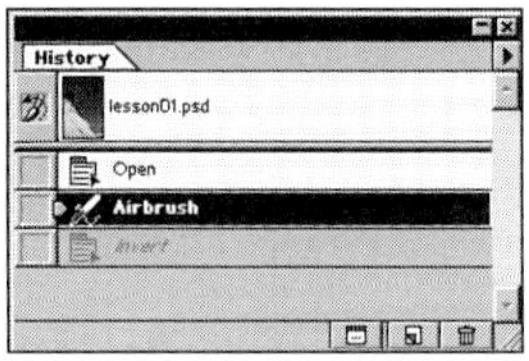

Figure 3.5

The Invert state is grayed-out indicating that if you proceed from this point it will be discarded.

6 Select the Invert state. The image inverts again. Now choose the New Snapshot button in the History palette to capture this current state for later use.

7 Select the Airbrush state again. This time use the airbrush to paint several strokes anywhere in the image. Note that a state is created for each brush stroke and that the previously grayed-out Invert state is discarded.

8 Despite the fact that the Invert state has been discarded, you can return to it at any time by selecting the snapshot you created (see Figure 3.6).

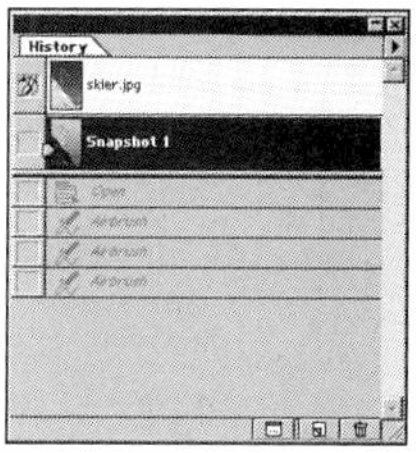

Figure 3.6

You can return to an earlier version of the image if you save a snapshot.

DELETING STATES AND CLEARING THE HISTORY

States can be deleted from the History palette by selecting them, and then dragging them to the Delete State button, clicking the Delete State button, or by choosing Delete from the History palette menu. If you delete a state, all subsequent states will also be discarded.

By using the Clear History command in the History palette menu, you can discard the entire history for the active image. While the history for the image will be discarded, the information is still stored in the Undo buffer. You can immediately use the Undo command to retrieve the history.

Now you try it...

Deleting states and purging

1 Open lesson2a.psd and lesson2b.psd in the Chapter 3 lessons folder on the CD-ROM.

2 Make sure that the History palette is visible. If it isn't, select Show History Palette from the Window menu.

3 With lesson2a active, paint several strokes anywhere in the image with the airbrush tool.

4 Now, select lesson2b to make it active and paint several strokes with the paintbrush anywhere in the image.

TIP

If you hold down the Alt (Windows)/Option (Macintosh) key while selecting Clear History, Photoshop discards the history and the Undo buffer will purge for the active document. This cannot be undone. Choosing Edit > Purge > Histories will discard the histories for all open images. Purging histories can free valuable resources if you are running low on memory.

continues

---

5 Note the History palettes for each image. With lesson2b active, delete the last state you created by selecting the Delete State button.

6 Delete the entire history for this image by choosing Delete History from the History palette menu.

7 Select lesson2a to make it active and note that the history is still intact for this image.

8 Select lesson2b again and choose Undo Clear History from the Edit menu.

9 This time, hold down the Alt (Windows)/Option (Macintosh) key while using the Delete History command in the History palette menu. Note that the Undo command is unavailable from the Edit menu.

10 Select lesson2a and note that the history is intact. Choose Edit > Purge > Histories to purge the histories in both documents.

HISTORY OPTIONS

The History palette has three configurable options: history linearity, the number of history steps, and whether or not Photoshop creates an initial snapshot when you open the image. All are set by choosing History Options from the History palette menu (see Figure 3.7).

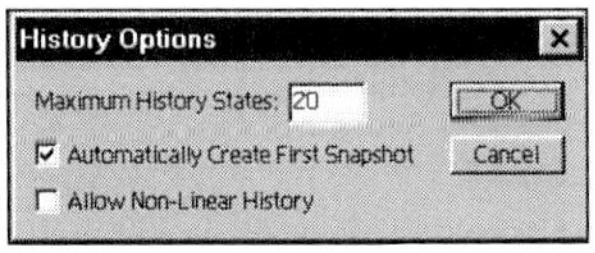

Figure 3.7

There are three configurable options for the History palette.

LINEAR VERSUS NON-LINEAR HISTORY

By default, Photoshop uses linear history. Each step depends on the previous steps. If you select a prior state, all steps that follow are discarded when changes are made starting from that point. Photoshop rewrites the history from the selected state. This is mainly a matter of organizational convenience. If Photoshop uses non-linear history, you can select a prior state and still make changes at that point. The new state that Photoshop creates, however, does not overwrite the states that follow the original; instead, Photoshop places it at the bottom of the list of states. Later states still depend on earlier states, but the order of causality is not readily apparent.

Now you try it...

Using non-linear history

1 Open lesson03.psd in the Chapter 3 lessons folder on the CD-ROM.

2 Make sure that the History palette is visible. If it isn't, select Show History Palette from the Window menu.

3 From the History Palette menu, choose History Options, and then select Allow Non-Linear History.

4 Choose Image > Adjust > Invert.

5 Now choose Image > Adjust > Equalize.

6 Finally, choose Image > Adjust > Desaturate.

7 Select the Invert state by clicking it in the History palette.

8 Paint a few strokes with the airbrush anywhere in the image. Note that instead of replacing the Equalize and Desaturate states from the history, Photoshop has added the Airbrush states.

9 Select the Equalize state. Note that this state does not contain the airbrush strokes because they come later in the history; however, the Equalize state is still based on the Invert state. Because non-linear history is allowed, it is difficult to actually view the history of the image.

10 Select one of the Airbrush states. Note that these are based only on the Invert state and not on the Equalize or Desaturate states.

11 From the History Palette menu, choose History Options and turn off Allow Non-linear History.

CREATE INITIAL SNAPSHOT

By default, Photoshop creates an initial snapshot of the image when you open it. You can use this snapshot to return the image to its original state at any point.

HISTORY STEPS

By default, Photoshop stores 20 history states before it begins to replace the oldest state. You can set this value up to 100 so that Photoshop will store 100 history states. The actual upper limit for the number of stored states may be determined by the amount of memory you have and the size of the image being edited. Therefore, the limit could be considerably fewer than 100. Set this value lower so that Photoshop uses less memory because Photoshop will store less information in the History buffer. You can also set the value as low as 1, in which case Photoshop behaves identically to previous versions, making the last performed operation the only one available.

SUMMARY

The addition of the History palette to Photoshop 5.0 is undoubtedly one of the most anticipated and welcome features. Learning to use the history states and snapshots effectively will not only improve your efficiency in Photoshop, but also will help you answer several questions on the exam correctly.

REVIEW QUESTIONS

1. If Photoshop warns you that you are running low on memory, which of the following is an acceptable solution?

    a.   Delete the Actions.

    b.   Purge the Histogram.

    c.   Purge the History States.

    d.   Purge the preferences file.

2. What is a snapshot?

    a.   A saved pattern

    b.   A saved histogram

    c.   A saved selection

    d.   A saved history state

3. When selecting a previous state, which option retains the subsequent states if turned on?

    a.   Allow Frame Blending

    b.   Allow Linear History

    c.   Allow Non-Linear History

    d.   Allow Bilinear Interpolation

4. What are the default number of states that Photoshop retains?

    a.   5

    b.   10

    c.   20

    d.   100

5. Which of the following are never saved with the file? (Choose 2.)

    a.   Channels

    b.   Snapshots

    c.   ICC Profiles

    d.   History States

6. To delete all the history states in only the current image, which command should you use?

    a.   Clear History

    b.   Hold down the Shift key and choose Clear History

    c.   Hold down the Alt (Windows)/Option (Macintosh) key and choose Clear History

    d.   Hold down the Ctrl (Windows)/Command (Macintosh) key and choose Clear History

7. To delete all the history states in all open images, which command should you use?

   a. Clear History

   b. Edit > Purge > Histories

   c. Hold down the Ctrl (Windows)/Command (Macintosh) key and choose Clear History

   d. Hold down the Alt (Windows)/Option (Macintosh) key and choose Clear History

8. If you select a previous history state and all subsequent states are unavailable or dimmed, what does this indicate?

   a. Continuing to change the image from the current state will discard all the unavailable states.

   b. The unavailable states have been discarded and can be recovered by using Undo.

   c. The Allow Non-Linear history option has been turned on.

   d. You should purge the histories.

9. What will happen if you drag a snapshot to the Create new document from current state button?

   a. A new document will be created from the snapshot and duplicate the history states from the original document.

   b. A new document will be created from the snapshot and the history will start over in the new document.

   c. A new document will be created from the snapshot and the histories will be purged for both the old and new documents.

   d. A new document will not be created from the snapshot, because only history states can be used to create new documents this way.

10. What should you do to delete a state and all states that come after it?

   a. Make sure that Allow Non-Linear History is turned off, select the state, and then select Delete.

   b. Make sure Allow Non-Linear History is turned on, select the state, and then select Delete.

   c. Make sure Allow Non-Linear History is turned off, select all the states you want to delete, and then select Delete.

   d. Make sure Allow Non-Linear History is turned on, select all the states you want to delete, and then select Delete.

CHAPTER 4

SCANNING & WORKING WITH IMAGES

Although this chapter focuses on scanning, it is also about one of the critical issues for those producing digital images: file size. Because file sizes necessary for those publishing electronically differ greatly from those working with paper, one of the key issues to grapple with is knowing the final output of the image. In addition, the tools and commands related to changing image resolution and size are covered.

Domains & Objectives

Importing and Adjusting Images

4.1   Define types of resolution and resolution concepts such as interpolation, resampling, fixed image size, and vector vs. bitmap graphics.

4.2   Recommend appropriate scanning resolution for typical Photoshop production situations, including minimizing file sizes, and identify and resolve common user problems related to resolution and scanning.

4.3   Identify issues regarding the characteristics, function, options, and appropriate use of the Image Size command, Import command, Place command, and File Info command.

You will be expected to know the important concepts underlying the tools and commands used for importing and adjusting images. You should be able to define resolution, interpolation, and resampling. You should also be able to recommend appropriate scanning resolutions as well as identify common problems related to scanning and resolution. Further, you should know how and when to use the Image Size, Canvas Size, File Info, and Place commands.

KEY CONCEPTS

You should be familiar with all the fundamental terms used when scanning and capturing images. Be aware that some terms, such as resolution, are used differently in various industries and contexts.

RESOLUTION

There are three important types of resolution. One is *image resolution*, measured in pixels per inch (ppi). The image resolution is used to determine the actual number of pixels in an image, expressed as width by height. For example, a 4" × 5" image with an image resolution of 300 ppi will have pixel dimensions of 1200 pixels × 1500 pixels. Note that for onscreen images such as those for video or for the World Wide Web, the term *resolution* can also be used to mean the actual pixel dimensions of an image. *Monitor resolution*, which is the number of pixels displayed on a monitor by a video card, is especially important when producing onscreen images. Finally, if you are producing prints on an imagesetter or laser printer, you should know the printer resolution, measured in dots per inch (dpi). The printer resolution is the number of physical dots produced by the device.

INTERPOLATION

Interpolation is the mathematical process of estimating what comes between two things. For example, if you were asked to pick a number that lies somewhere between 2 and 4, you would probably choose 3. That is interpolation. It is important to realize that this process is only an estimate. In the previous example, you also would have been correct to have chosen 2.5 or 3.9; depending on the circumstances, these might have been more appropriate choices.

Photoshop uses interpolation to make estimations about pixels. If it needs to determine an intermediate pixel between black and white, it will choose a 50% gray. It is possible that the color that should have been determined in this situation is not 50% gray, but some other gray. Again, it is important to note that this is a process of mathematical estimation; though you can control the process that Photoshop uses, by definition interpolation introduces inaccuracies. Figures 4.1 and 4.2 show an example of this. The edges in the original image are crisp; however, the edges become blurred after increasing the image resolution. This is caused by the interpolation process and the various gray tones that are added between the black-and-white areas.

Figure 4.1

The original image (100 pixels × 100 pixels) before increasing the pixel dimensions of the image.

Figure 4.2

The image shown in Figure 4.1 after increasing the pixel dimensions to 800 pixels × 800 pixels (zoom at 400%).

RESAMPLING

Resampling is the process of changing the pixel dimensions or number of pixels in an image. The process of resampling uses interpolation to determine the intermediate pixels to use. The process of making the pixel dimensions smaller is commonly referred to as *downsampling* or *resampling down*. Increasing the pixel dimensions of an image is often called *resampling up*.

It is important to note that resampling up does not undo downsampling. Although it might restore the pixel dimensions, it does not restore the details of the image because after pixel information is discarded, it cannot be easily regained. Because Photoshop uses interpolation, it must estimate which colors should be added to an image being resampled up. These colors most likely will not match the original image. Figure 4.3 shows an original image before downsampling. Figure 4.4 shows the image after downsampling, and Figure 4.5 shows the image after returning it to its original pixel dimensions through resampling up. Note that Figure 4.5 appears fuzzy because some image information has been lost, and the process of interpolation can only estimate the pixel colors.

Figure 4.3

The original image before downsampling.

Figure 4.4

The image shown in Figure 4.3 after downsampling.

Figure 4.5

This is the image shown in Figure 4.4, after it has been resampled up.

RESOLUTION ISSUES

When scanning or capturing images by other means—for example, a digital camera—you must take into account many factors throughout the production of the image. What resolution will you need for final output? Will you use only parts of the image? Will you need more pixel information from the

TIP

After performing resampling, you can manually refine the image by running the Unsharp Mask filter. You can use this filter to help sharpen otherwise blurry edges. See Chapter 12, "Filters," for more information about the Unsharp Mask filter.

image at a later time? These are just a few of the questions that you should ask yourself before making an appropriate scan. Some of the decision, however, is subjective. Although there are some common practices and rules that you should know, in the end, it is up to you to decide the best method of capturing an image, the image resolution to use, and the appropriate strategies to produce a final image.

INTENDED USE

The most significant factor in determining the resolution of an image is the eventual use of the image. Rules for scanning an image intended for a Web page differ greatly from those for a magazine cover image.

PREPRESS

For images destined for print using professional printing techniques, you will need to know the line screen of the printed image. This might require that you talk to your printer to find out what he or she recommends and what the printer's equipment is capable of producing. A large part of the decision will be based on the quality you require for the final print.

Professional printing resolution is measured in *lines per inch* (lpi). This is the number of lines of halftone dots in an inch. This differs from the ppi for the image resolution measured in Photoshop. In fact, you can think of there being two dots or pixels for every line. This means that you can determine the scanning resolution in ppi by doubling the intended line screen. For example, if you plan on printing at 150 lpi, you should scan at about 300 ppi. This doubling of the line screen can be adjusted a little. You can scan as low as 1.5 times the line screen in many situations. This is important because files can become very large at these sizes and resolutions. The table below shows some common line screens and suggested scan resolutions.

Scanning for Print	
Line Screen	Scan Resolution
85–150 lpi	150–300 ppi
135–175 lpi	200–350 ppi
150–200 lpi	225–400 ppi

The lower line screens (85–150 lpi) are typical of newspapers. Usually you can see the actual halftone dots used in newsprint. The mid-range values (135–175 lpi) are those generally found in magazines. The halftone dots in the mid-range are much smaller and more difficult to detect. The highest range is typical of high-quality printing, such as that used for photographs in books in which the halftone dots are almost indistinguishable to the naked eye.

After you have determined the line screen of your final output, you might also need to adjust the scan resolution for any scaling of the image that will occur. This can greatly affect the scan resolution. For example, if you have a 4" × 5" image that you would like to print at 8" × 10" at 150 lpi, you will need to scan at 300 ppi × 2 = 600 ppi. The extra value to compensate for the size is commonly referred to as the *size change factor*. To determine the size change factor, divide the desired width by the original width, and the desired height by the original height; then take the larger of the two values. Use this size change factor when determining scan resolution. Note that some scanning software compensates for any scaling of the image, so you might not always need to calculate the size change factor. In general, the scan resolution can be determined by the following formula:

scan resolution (ppi) = line screen (lpi) × size change factor × 2

Now you try it...

Calculate an appropriate scan resolution

You have a 4" × 5" photograph that you would like to reproduce on a flyer in a 6" × 8" space. You find out that you will be printing this on newsprint at 85 lpi. What resolution should you use to scan the photo?

1 Determine the size change factor. Divide the desired width by the original width:

8 / 5 = 1.4

Now divide the desired height by the original height:

6 / 4 = 1.5

The larger of these two values is 1.5, which is the size change factor.

continues

TIP

Not all scanners are capable of scanning at specific resolutions and might only have the most common values available to you. These are usually increments of 75 or 100 ppi and can range from 75 to 800 ppi. For example, you can set most scanners to use a value of 300 ppi, but 350 ppi might not be an option. If this is the case, choose the nearest value to the target resolution. Just keep in mind that it is not recommended that you choose a scan resolution less than 1.5 times the line screen.

> **2**   Now use this formula:
>
> Scan Resolution (ppi) = 85 x 1.5 x 2 = 255
>
> So you should scan the photo at 255 ppi. Some scanners will not have a 255 ppi option, so choose the nearest possible value—which might be 250 or possibly even 200. Because 200 ppi is still greater than 1.5 times the line screen (in this case, it would be about 191 ppi), this resolution would probably be fine.

Black-and-white line art should be scanned at the same resolution of the final output device. For example, for a 1200 dpi imagesetter, generally the artwork should be scanned at 1200 ppi. In reality, you cannot discern a significant increase in quality after a scan resolution of 800 ppi, and you certainly don't need to scan line art at a resolution greater than 1200 ppi before compensating for the size change factor, regardless of the output device. As a general rule, however, scan resolution should equal the printer resolution.

WEB AND VIDEO

For electronic publishing on the World Wide Web and for images that will be used in video presentations, the scanning situation is very different than for paper printing. When scanning an image for use on a Web page or for a video application, the image should be scanned at actual size, and the image resolution should be set to 72 ppi. This is the standard image resolution for onscreen images. The image will be viewed on most Web pages at between 640×480 pixels and 1024×768 pixels. For images displayed on a television screen, 640×480 pixels is also typical.

On the other hand, for even a relatively small printed image, say 3" × 3" at 300 ppi (or 150 lpi), the image will contain 900×900 pixels. Compare the 900×900 pixels for the 3" × 3" printed image with a 640×480 pixels image that fills the screen on a 14-inch monitor, and you can see the vast differences in scale. For larger printed images, the number of pixels required is much greater. Because of this significant difference between paper publishing and electronic publishing, the resolution requirements are also very different. Whereas printed images often require very large files, images destined to display on Web pages are optimized to be as small as possible.

MINIMIZING FILE SIZES

One of the fundamental problems with scanning is managing—which usually means minimizing—file size. For printing, as file sizes can escalate to 50MB and beyond, anything you can do to decrease the file sizes not only makes working on the image easier, but also allows for easier transmission of the file to the final location. Similarly, for electronic publishing, when users are downloading images over modems, some still only 14.4 baud, size is a critical issue as well. The problems are similar, but the scales vary greatly.

The most important thing to realize when managing file size is that the size of the file is related directly to the number of pixels in the image. Because of this, minimizing file sizes is a matter of minimizing the number of pixels. If an image that will be printed is growing too large to work on effectively, you might need to cut corners to reduce pixels whenever possible. You might need to aim closer to the 1.5 times line screen value instead of using a scan resolution twice the line screen. Further, you might be able to strip a number of pixels out of the image by allowing a little less bleed around the edges. On very large images, small conservation techniques quickly add up to megabytes of saved space.

For Web graphics, the issue of file size is perhaps even more critical because of bandwidth considerations. Because file size is directly related to the number of pixels, small changes made to the dimensions of the image can dramatically alter the file size. One of the primary reasons for this is that because the image is two-dimensional—that is, it contains both width and height—global changes made to the dimensions will change the number of pixels not linearly, but geometrically. For example, if an image is made twice as large in both width and height, the number of pixels does not double; rather, it quadruples. Similarly, if the number of pixels on each axis is halved, the size of the image will be reduced by a factor of four. Figures 4.6 and 4.7 show examples of this.

Figure 4.6

This is a 2 × 2 pixel image (4 pixels total).

Figure 4.7

This is the same image doubled (16 pixels total).

Because of this relationship, decreasing an image to about 75% in both directions (70.7% to be absolutely accurate) cuts the size of the file to about half of the original.

TIP

To quickly zoom to 100%, double-click the zoom tool in the toolbox.

When making images to be published on Web pages, make the images the actual size at which they will display on the page. To check this, set the zoom to 100%. This displays the image at one image pixel to one monitor pixel, which is the eventual goal when producing images for Web pages. For more information about producing files for Web pages and minimizing file size, see Chapter 15, "File Formats," and Chapter 17, "Web & Video Production."

COMMON RESOLUTION PROBLEMS

The most common resolution problems for printed images are images originally scanned too small. Resampling up often will not produce the quality needed for a large print. This is a common mistake made when using digital cameras. Many lower-end digital cameras are incapable of producing resolutions required for professional quality printing. Resampling up does not add pixel and color detail because of the estimation performed by interpolation. To combat these issues, make sure that you can capture the image at a sufficient resolution for the final output. If you are unsure of the final output, you might want to scan the image at a higher resolution than you need just in case you need more detail in the final output. You can then downsample if necessary to remove unnecessary image information before the final production begins.

For Web graphics, the most common problem is the exact opposite: The images are scanned too large. Although it is common to scan images at a higher resolution than necessary so you can work on them easily, you must resize the image before placing it on a Web page to minimize download time. Whereas images for print often range in the tens of megabytes, images for the Web should rarely exceed 100KB and will often be much smaller. Some graphics can even be made smaller than they will appear on the Web page, and then scaled up when viewed by the browser (see Chapter 17 for more detail).

IMAGE SIZE COMMAND

The most common command for resampling is the Image Size command found under the Image pulldown menu. This command works for both downsampling and resampling up. Figure 4.8 shows the options for this command.

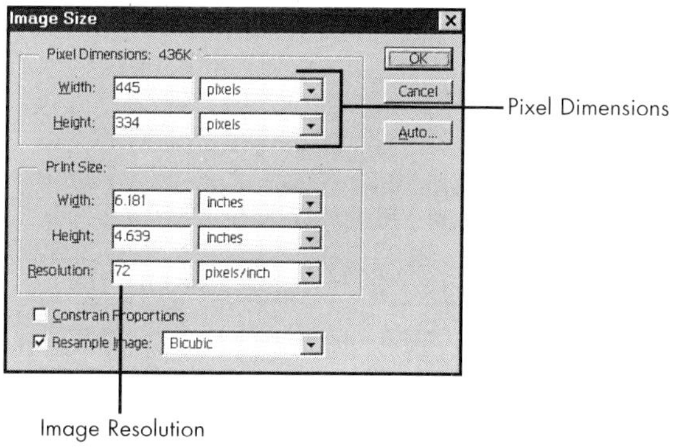

Figure 4.8

The Image Size dialog box is used to change both image resolution and pixel dimensions.

You can change the image size by either specifying the actual pixel dimensions of the image or using percentages. If you would like the ratio of width to height to remain fixed, use the Constrain Proportions checkbox. The Resample Image checkbox enables Photoshop to change the pixel dimensions of the image if the print size is changed. The print size can be specified in inches, centimeters, points, picas, or columns, or, similar to the pixel dimensions, as a percentage of the current value. The resolution can be specified either in pixels per inch or pixels per centimeter. It is important to note that different combinations of print size values can produce identical pixel dimensions. For example, a 2" × 2" image at 100 ppi has the same pixel dimensions as a 1" × 1" image at 200 ppi.

If the Resample Image checkbox is selected, Photoshop will use one of three methods of interpolation: Bicubic, Bilinear, and Nearest Neighbor. Bicubic provides the most accurate interpolation but takes the longest to perform. Nearest Neighbor gives the least accurate results but is the fastest of the three. Nearest Neighbor is often preferred for images with sharply delineated areas of color such as line art because it adds the fewest intermediate colors. Bilinear is a middle method, both in accuracy and speed.

TIP

When changing the image size, carefully watch the projected file size at the top of the dialog box.

Now you try it...

Resampling an image

1   Open the Lesson01.psd file in the Chapter 4 folder on the CD.

2   Select Image > Image Size.

3   Note the current file size. Make sure that the Resample Image checkbox is selected. Increase the image size by **200%** in width by selecting percent from the units list in the Pixel Dimensions area. Note that the file size has doubled. Now enter **200%** for the height as well, and note the file size is approximately four times larger than the original.

4   Hold down the Alt/Option key and click the Reset button.

5   Change the Resolution to **144 ppi**. Note the new pixel dimensions and file size.

6   Hold down the Alt/Option key and click the Reset button again.

7   Now make sure that the Resample Image checkbox is not selected, and enter **144 ppi** for the resolution again. Note that the file size stays the same because the pixels dimensions are now fixed.

8   Click the Cancel button and close the file.

CANVAS SIZE COMMAND

Similar to the Image Size command, the Canvas Size command also alters the file size of an image; however, instead of performing resampling, the Canvas Size command either crops the image into a specified area if the desired canvas size is smaller than the current image size, or it adds pixels around the image in the background color. Figure 4.9 shows the Canvas Size dialog box.

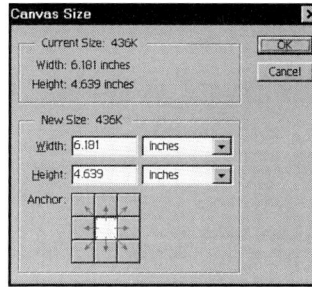

Figure 4.9

The Canvas Size dialog box is used to change the overall size of an image.

The size of the new image can be specified in all the units fields that are used for print size: pixels, inches, centimeters, points, or picas, or as a percentage of the current size. In addition to the new canvas size, you can direct Photoshop where to place the current image by using the Anchor grid. By default, Photoshop places the current image into the center of the new canvas, but you can place it in any of the other eight locations by clicking on the approprivate box in the grid.

The Crop Tool trims an image to a selected boundary.

There are two methods of cropping an image. One is to use the crop tool located with the marquee selection tools. With the crop tool selected, you can specify a rectangular area that will be cropped. This area will be enclosed in a bounding border. The area that you select can be resized by dragging any of the control handles; moved by clicking within the bounding border and dragging; and rotated by selecting the bounding border along the outside edge until the rotate icon is visible. The control point in the center is the pivot point for the rotation. Figure 4.10 shows just such a crop selection.

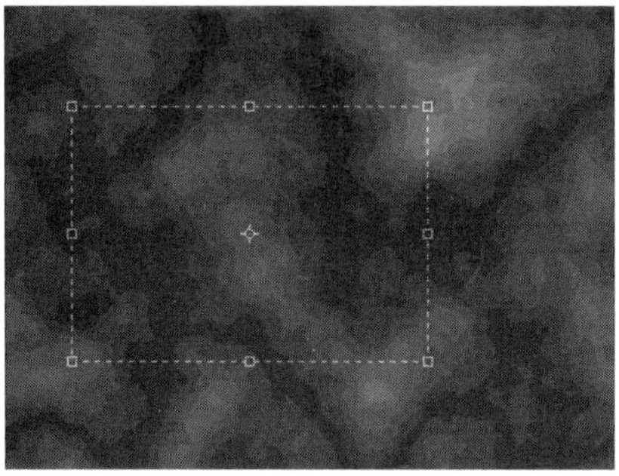

Figure 4.10

The crop bounding border defines the area that will remain after the image is cropped.

When the bounding border is positioned, sized, and rotated correctly, either double-click or press the Enter key for the crop to take effect.

The size of area that will remain after cropping takes place can be precisely controlled by turning on the Fixed Target Size checkbox in the Crop Options palette. This area can be specified in any of the units that Photoshop supports.

The other option for cropping an image is to select a rectangular area with the rectangle marquee, and then choose Image > Crop. The selection must be perfectly rectangular, so make sure that feathering is off, or the crop command will not be available.

TIP

Press the Escape key if you don't want to apply the crop to your image.

Now you try it...

Cropping an image

1 Open the Lesson02.psd file in the Chapter 4 folder on the CD.

2 Select the crop tool from the toolbox and select a rectangular area.

3 Move the pointer over the dashed border of the rectangular area until it turns into the rotate icon.

4 Rotate the rectangle to match the angle of the red diamond in the image.

5 Resize the rectangle as necessary to match the red diamond.

6 When you have finished, press the Enter key or double-click to complete the crop.

FILE INFO COMMAND

The File > File Info command enables you to add extra information to your image, such as caption information, keywords and categories for searches and cataloging, copyright and origin information, and credits. Caption information entered through the File Info command can be printed under an image by checking the Caption checkbox in the Page Setup dialog box. This file information added to images is based on the standards created by the Newspaper Association of America and the International Press Telecommunications Council. On Windows systems, only JPEG, TIFF, and Photoshop Native File formats support the extra information; on the Macintosh, any image can contain the information. Figure 4.11 shows the File Info dialog box used for the addition of caption information to an image.

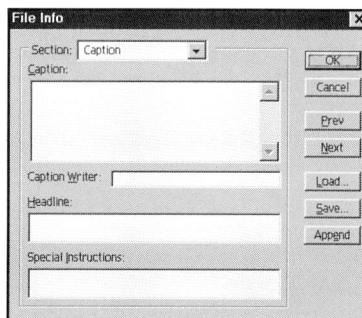

Figure 4.11

The File Info dialog box enables you to enter specific file information about your image.

Now you try it...

Using file info

1 Open the Lesson3 file in the Chapter 4 folder on the CD.

2 Use File > File Info to access the file information.

3 Examine the file information attached to this file. Use the Next button to move to each new information area.

IMPORTING AND PLACING

Importing images into Photoshop is primarily accomplished through the use of a scanner. Photoshop either communicates with the scanner through the TWAIN interface, which is supported by most scanners, or through an Adobe Photoshop-compatible plug-in module. TWAIN interfaces enable software applications to communicate with image acquisition devices such as scanners and digital cameras. To scan using Photoshop, select the TWAIN source or plug-in module, and then acquire the image using the software provided with your scanner. Note that because Photoshop now runs on only 32-bit Windows platform—that is, Windows 95, 98, and NT— you will need a 32-bit TWAIN source module. The TWAIN source module should be provided with your scanner.

Placing images is the process of importing Encapsulated Postscript (EPS), Adobe Illustrator (AI), and Acrobat Portable Document Format (PDF) files into Photoshop. Because such files often contain vector information or text, the file must be rasterized before Photoshop can use it. In other words, the information in the file must be converted to pixels.

To place an EPS or Illustrator file into Photoshop, select File > Place, choose the file to be placed, and then make changes to the image by resizing, mov-ing, or rotating the placed image. When you have finished resizing, moving, or rotating the placed image, either double-click on the image or press the Enter key. The result will be a raster image that can be edited in Photoshop.

PDF files are placed in an identical manner. Note, however, that because PDF files commonly contain more than one page and Photoshop only reads the first page when using the Place command, there is an automation tool for converting multipage PDF files to Photoshop documents. You can use the Multi-Page PDF to PSD command by selecting it from the Automate submenu of the File menu. For more information about the automation tools, see Chapter 19, "Automating Photoshop."

Now you try it...

Placing an EPS file

1 Open the Lesson4 file in the Chapter 4 folder on the CD.

2 Choose File > Place. From the Chapter 4 folder, choose the `Lesson04.eps` file and click the Place button.

3 Move the text so that it fits around the circle and either press the Enter key or double-click.

SUMMARY

One of the most important topics to understand in Photoshop is the balance between resolution and file size based on the intended use of the image. As an ACE, you should know how the major concepts covered in this chapter interrelate, the appropriate resolutions and sizes of files, and how to use the Photoshop commands related to these concepts. Further, you will need to understand the process of placing and importing images into Photoshop and when these techniques should be used.

REVIEW QUESTIONS

1. What is the appropriate image resolution for graphics that will appear on Web pages?

    a. 72 ppi

    b. 144 ppi

    c. 150 ppi

    d. 300 ppi

2. What is the appropriate scan resolution for an image that will be printed at 75 lpi?

    a. 75 ppi

    b. 150 ppi

    c. 175 ppi

    d. 300 ppi

3. Which types of files can be placed into Photoshop? (Choose 2.)

    a. TIFF

    b. JPEG

    c. PDF

    d. EPS

4. For a 3" x 5" image to be printed at 6" x 10" at 150 lpi, what is an appropriate scan resolution?

    a. 150 ppi

    b. 300 ppi

    c. 600 ppi

    d. 1200 ppi

5. Which interpolation method gives the most accurate results?

    a. Nearest Neighbor

    b. Bilinear

    c. Bicubic

    d. Downsampling

6. If a 100 x 100-pixel image is resampled up to a 200 x 200-pixel image, what will happen to the file size?

    a. It will approximately double.

    b. It will approximately triple.

    c. It will approximately quadruple.

    d. It will remain the same.

7. Which command should you use to include copyright information with an image?

    a. File Info

    b. Export

    c. Preferences

    d. History

8. You are planning to print a black-and-white technical illustration (line art) on a 1200 dpi imagesetter. What scan resolution should you use?

    a. 300 ppi

    b. 600 ppi

    c. 1200 ppi

    d. 2400 ppi

9. You make an elliptical selection in a CMYK image and try to use Image > Crop, but the tool is unavailable (dimmed-out). What might be wrong?

    a. You cannot use cropping in CMYK mode.

    b. You cannot crop an elliptical selection.

    c. You cannot crop a selection in CMYK mode.

    d. You cannot crop a selection with anti-aliasing on.

10. The crop tool is located with what other tool in the toolbox?

    a. The pen tool

    b. The dodge tool

    c. The polygon lasso

    d. The elliptical marquee

CHAPTER 5

IMAGE MODES

For the Photoshop 5 Product Proficiency Exam, you will be expected to know the different types of image modes available in Photoshop. It is important to understand not only the definitions and common uses of each mode, but also to know about the availability of various tools and filters, as well as the steps to convert an image from one mode to another. As a certified expert, you will be expected to identify elements in, and differentiate between, the applications of the following color models and modes: Bitmap, Grayscale, Duotone, RGB, CMYK, Lab, Indexed color, Multichannel, 8-bit color, and 16-bit color.

Domains & Objectives

Color and Color Correction

9.2   Identify elements in and differentiate between the applications of the following color models and modes: Bitmap, Grayscale, Duotone, RGB, CMYK, Lab, Indexed color, Multichannel, 8-bit color and 16-bit color.

You change the image mode by selecting Image > Mode, and then choosing the appropriate option (see Figure 5.1). Some image modes are not always available, and an intermediate mode must be used. In general, changing image modes alters the layer composition, so layers often need to be flattened. You will be prompted if this is the case. Figure 5.1 shows the submenu used to change image modes.

Figure 5.1

From the Image > Mode menu, choose the image mode you want.

BITMAP

An image in Bitmap mode is made up of only black-and-white pixels. Because the image has only two colors, it is a 1-bit image. Bitmaps are most often produced by scanning or importing line art.

Only Grayscale or Duotone images can be converted to Bitmap mode. Further, to convert an image from Bitmap mode to any other mode, it must first be converted to Grayscale.

During the conversion process, Photoshop will prompt you to determine the resolution of an image and to choose which method of selecting black or white pixels to use. The possibilities are 50% Threshold, Pattern Dither, Diffusion Dither, Halftone Screen, and Custom Pattern. The 50% Threshold chooses white for any luminance greater than a gray level of 128, and black for any darker gray (see Figure 5.2).

Figure 5.2

The 50% Threshold method uses the luminance of each pixel to determine whether or not to convert it.

Pattern Dither uses geometric patterns of black-and-white dots to approximate the gray tones in an image (see Figure 5.3).

Figure 5.3

The regular pattern caused by the Pattern Dither is clearly discernible.

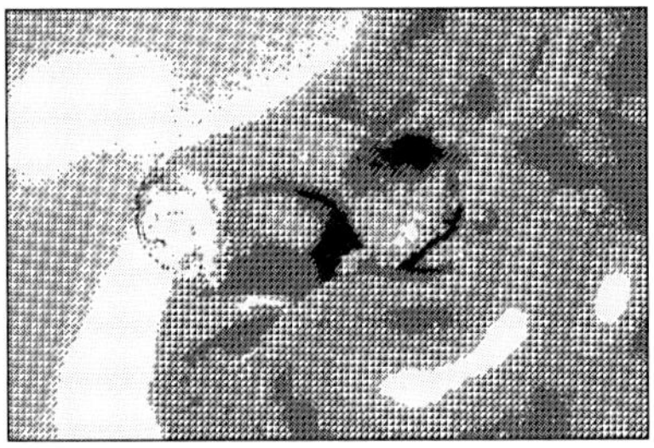

Diffusion Dither uses surrounding pixels to determine whether a pixel should be black or white (see Figure 5.4).

Figure 5.4

The Diffusion Dither method is best used when displaying images on a monochrome monitor.

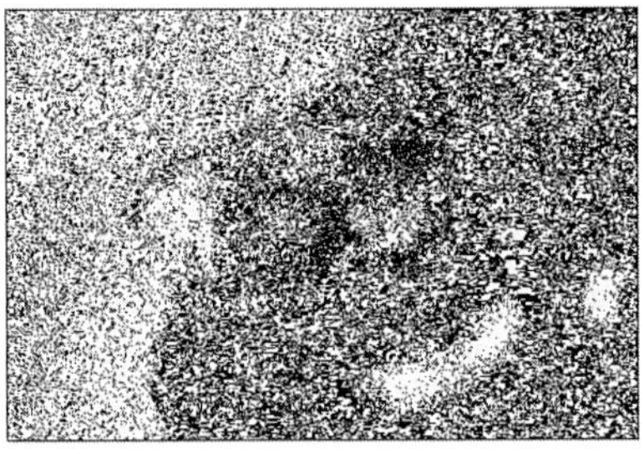

Halftone Screen converts the Grayscale image to Bitmap mode by using simulated halftone dots (see Figure 5.5). Photoshop will prompt you to choose the halftone options such as the line screen (lpi), the angle of the screen, and the shape of the dot. Note that the simulated halftone screen may produce moiré patterns if the printer is also producing a halftone.

Figure 5.5

You can increase the size of the dots used in the simulated halftone screen by decreasing the line frequency.

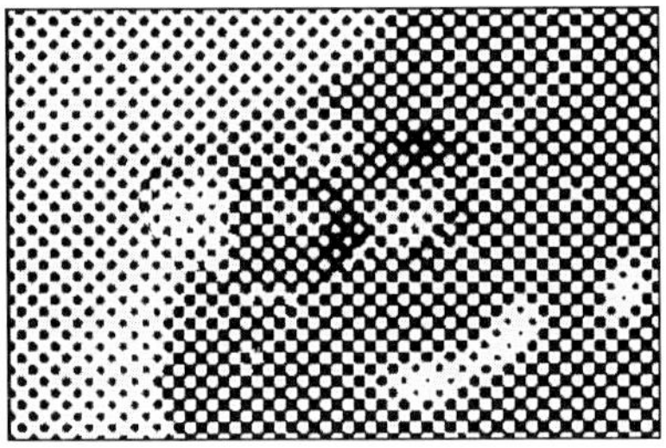

Finally, the Custom Pattern option allows the image to be dithered using a pattern that has been defined using Edit > Define Pattern (see Figure 5.6).

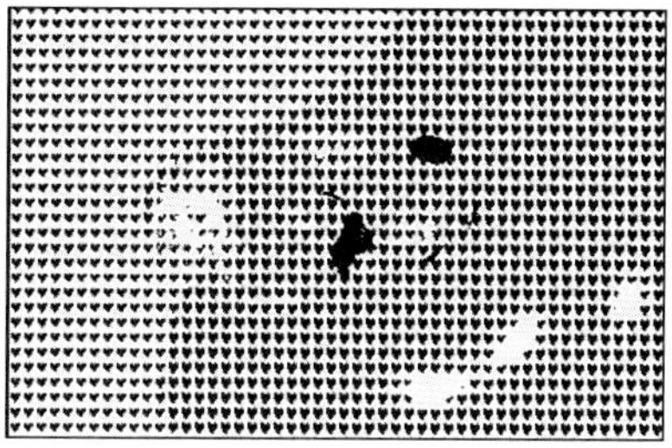

Figure 5.6

The Custom Pattern method of converting to Bitmap mode uses whatever is currently stored in the pattern buffer.

Only some tools are available in Bitmap mode. All of the toning tools are unavailable because they do not have enough information to work with if the image is in Bitmap mode. None of the filters are available. In addition, only one layer, the Background layer, and one channel named Alpha are permitted.

Now you try it...

Converting to bitmap mode

1   Open lesson01.psd in the Chapter 5 folder on the CD-ROM.
2   Convert the image to Bitmap mode using the 50% Threshold.
3   Undo.
4   Convert the image to Bitmap mode using the Pattern Dither.
5   Undo.
6   Convert the image to Bitmap mode using a Halftone Screen. Set the Frequency to **15**, the Angle to **45** degrees, and the Shape to Round.
7   Close the image when you have finished.

GRAYSCALE

Grayscale images are usually 8-bit and therefore contain 256 levels of gray. Grayscale images in 16-bit/channel mode contain 65,536 levels of gray. They are similar to black-and-white photographs. Figure 5.7 shows an image in Grayscale mode.

An image in any mode can be converted to Grayscale. If the image originally contained color information, this will be discarded. All of the tools and almost all of the filters are available. Images in Grayscale mode can have multiple layers and channels, and they contain one primary channel, Black.

Figure 5.7

Grayscale mode contains
256 levels of gray.

Figure 5.7

Grayscale mode contains
256 levels of gray.

DUOTONE

Duotone is not a single type of image mode, but an entire category. While you do have the option to create Duotones, options for Monotones, Tritones and Quadtones are also available. The rules for each type of image are similar except for the number of colors used.

In general, a Duotone is a method to increase the dynamic range of a printed grayscale image by adding another color. Often Duotones consist of Black, which is used in the shadow areas, and another spot color, used for the mid-tones and highlights (see Figure 5.8). This gives the image an added tint.

Figure 5.8

A Duotone is usually
made of Black and
another spot color.

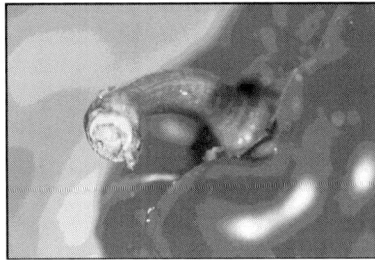

Monotones are essentially grayscale images in which you have the ability to substitute any other color for the black ink (see Figure 5.9).

Figure 5.9

A Monotone replaces the
black ink in a Grayscale
image with another color.

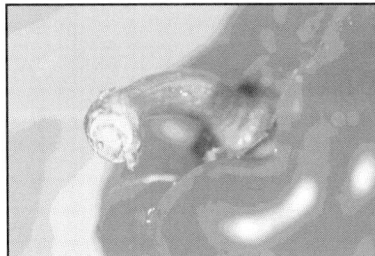

Tritones and Quadtones use three and four inks, and similar to Duotones, continue to increase the dynamic range of the image.

Only images in Grayscale mode can be converted to Duotones. As with Grayscale images, all of the painting tools and most of the filters are available. There are no limitations on the creation of layers or alpha channels while in Grayscale mode.

To convert an image to a Duotone, select Image > Mode > Duotone, and then set the options in the Duotone dialog box (see Figure 5.10).

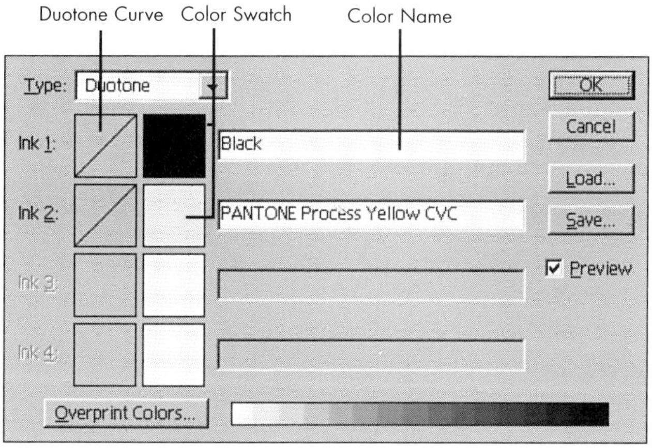

Duotone Curve   Color Swatch   Color Name

Figure 5.10

Set the options for the Duotone in the Duotone Options dialog box.

From the Duotone dialog box, you should select whether you want a Monotone, Duotone, Tritone, or Quadtone. By clicking in the color swatch, you can select the color from the Color Picker. By default, Photoshop assumes that you will want to choose a spot color from the Custom Color dialog for the Duotone, Tritone, and Quadtone. Photoshop will fill in the name of the color, but you can change it if you need to specify another name to match a page layout or illustration program.

TIP

In the General Preferences dialog, turn on the Short PANTONE names so that Photoshop will use names for spot colors recognized by many page layout programs.

DUOTONE CURVES

While Duotones, Tritones, and Quadtones consist of more than one color, they each have only one channel, named for the specific type. Monotones also have only one channel, named Monotone. The densities of each of the colors are not determined by separate channels, but by Duotone curves.

Duotone curves are set in the Duotone Options dialog box by clicking on the curve associated with each used ink. By setting Duotone curves, you are controlling the amount of ink that will be placed at various points along a grayscale continuum, from black to white. By default, each ink is spread evenly over this grayscale continuum. The ratio of each ink can be altered by directly manipulating the curve, or by entering percentages of ink coverage next to the corresponding gray value (see Figure 5.11). Duotone curves can be saved to reproduce results on other images.

Figure 5.11

Set the ink coverage through the Duotone by adjusting the Duotone curves.

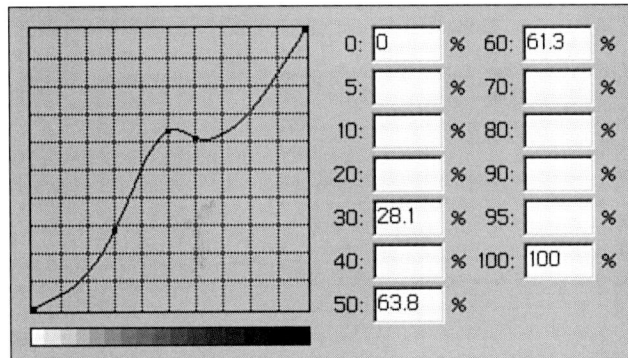

Now you try it...

Converting to duotone mode

1   Open lesson02.psd in the Chapter 5 folder on the CD-ROM.

2   Select Image > Mode > Duotone.

3   In the Duotone dialog box, select Duotone from the Type menu.

4   Click in the second color swatch, select PANTONE Process Yellow CVC from the Custom Color menu, and then click OK. Photoshop creates a preview image so that you can see the results before accepting them.

5   Click in the Duotone curve next to the black swatch. Enter **60** in the box next to the number 50. This will increase the amount of black ink in the midtones, thus darkening the image. Click OK.

6   When you have finished with the Duotone, click OK.

7   Experiment with other colors and Duotone curve settings. Try creating a Tritone and Quadtone.

8   When you have finished, close the image.

RGB

RGB mode, by far the most common mode to work in, combines red, green, and blue in an additive fashion to produce a large spectrum of colors. Images displayed on the World Wide Web or on a monitor are commonly RGB. In addition, scanners and digital cameras capture RGB image information, but some can also convert the data to other image modes.

Most images in RGB mode contain three 8-bit channels, making them 24-bit. This means that they can contain up to 16.7 million colors. The three channels are named Red, Green, and Blue (see Figure 5.12).

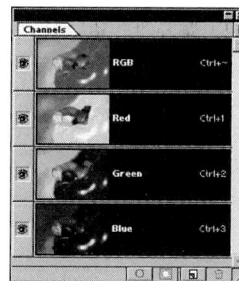

Figure 5.12

An image in RGB mode contains three channels.

Most image modes can be converted into RGB. All painting tools and filters are available in the RGB image, and there are no layer restrictions.

CMYK

An image in CMYK mode is often created immediately before printing, when using a four color process. The four colors are Cyan, Magenta, Yellow, and Black. Some care must be taken when converting from RGB to CMYK because the gamuts, or colors available in each color mode, are different. The RGB color gamut is larger than the CMYK color gamut. This means that some colors displayed on your monitor in RGB mode may not look the same when printed in CMYK. When a color in RGB does not have an equivalent color in CMYK, the color is said to be out-of-gamut. Photoshop chooses the nearest color in the CMYK gamut for an out-of-gamut color.

Images in CMYK mode contain four channels: Cyan, Magenta, Yellow, and Black (see Figure 5.13). Because the image contains four 8-bit channels, an image in CMYK mode is 32-bit. About half the default filters are available in a CMYK image, and there are no layer restrictions.

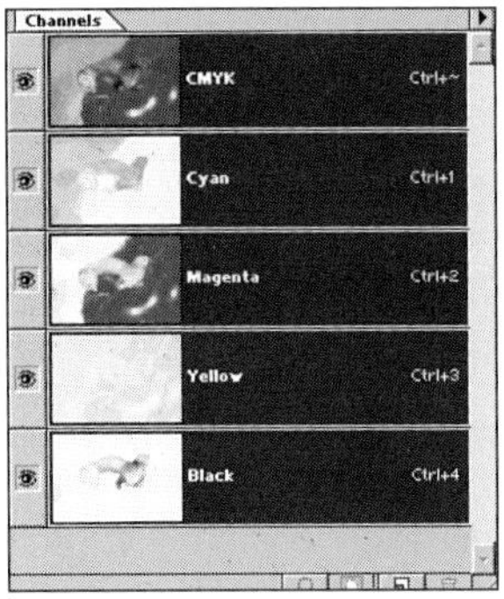

Figure 5.13

An image in CMYK
mode contains four
channels that correspond
directly to color separa-
tions used for process
printing.

When working with printed images, the most common mode conversion is
from RGB to CMYK. To make this conversion, Photoshop uses Lab mode as
an intermediate because Lab mode contains all the colors from the other
modes. There are multiple steps involved in the process, though the steps
are transparent to the user. The RGB image is converted to Lab mode using
the RGB settings found under File > Color Settings > RGB setup. The
image is then converted from Lab to CMYK using the CMYK settings from
File > Color Settings > CMYK setup. The RGB setup and CMYK setup will
be examined in depth in Chapter 18, "Color Management."

Monitors are capable of displaying only RGB images, so Photoshop must
make a final conversion from CMYK through Lab to RGB. While the image
is made up of cyan, magenta, yellow, and black, you are actually viewing an
RGB version of the CMYK image on your monitor.

The settings in the CMYK setup are used only during the actual conversion
from RGB to CMYK. While Photoshop may display an image in CMYK
mode differently after modifying the CMYK setup, it is important to realize
that Photoshop has not actually made any changes to the CMYK values.
Instead, Photoshop has only changed the RGB monitor version.

LAB

The Lab image mode is used by Photoshop as an intermediate mode
between RGB and CMYK because the color space defined by Lab mode
contains both the RGB and CMYK color gamuts. The three components of
Lab mode are Lightness (L), and two chromatic components, a and b (see
Figure 5.14).

Each of these components is depicted in an 8-bit grayscale channel. About
half the default filters are available while in Lab mode, and all of the painting tools are available. Any image type, with the exception of Bitmap
images, can be converted to Lab mode.

Figure 5.14

Images in Lab mode
contain three channels.

Images in Lab mode are designed to be device independent. Colors remain consistent between different printers, monitors, and operating system platforms.

INDEXED COLOR

Indexed Color images are commonly found on the Web and in animations. Images converted to Indexed Color can contain at most 256 colors and are often referred to as 8-bit images, though Photoshop creates images of different bit depths. An Indexed Color image contains a Color Table, or CLUT (Color Lookup Table), which defines every color in the image. The Color Table can be defined during the conversion or modified after the Indexed Color image has been created. Figure 5.15 shows a Color Table.

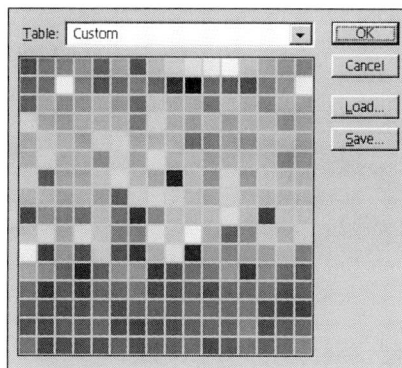

Figure 5.15

You can modify the col-
ors in the Color Table
after converting to
Indexed Color mode.

Only Grayscale and RGB images can be converted to Indexed Color. When converting from RGB to Indexed Color, the Indexed Color dialog box enables you to remove all but 256 colors. It also allows you to use dithering and choose which 256 colors or Color Table to use. Figure 5.16 shows the dialog box used during the conversion process.

Figure 5.16

The Indexed Color dialog box is used to set your preferences during the conversion.

To create the Indexed Color image, you can allow Photoshop to use dithering, which is the replacement of missing colors with combinations of colors available from the Color Table. Options for dithering are None, Diffusion, or Pattern. If None is selected, no dithering occurs, and each original color is replaced with the closest color available from the Color Table (Figure 5.17).

Figure 5.17

This image was converted to Indexed Color using the Uniform palette and Dithering set to none.

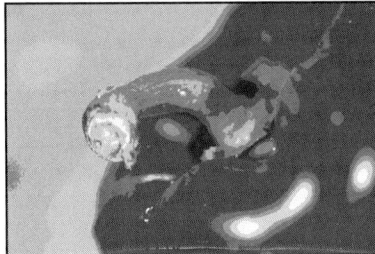

If Diffusion is chosen, pixels of available colors from the Color Table are added to the image using an error-diffusion process to simulate colors not available from the Color Table (see Figure 5.18).

Figure 5.18

This image was converted to Indexed Color using the Uniform Palette and the Diffusion Dither.

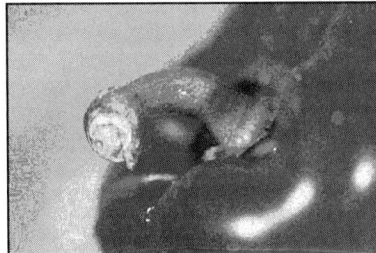

If the Pattern Dither option is chosen, patterns of squares, similar to halftone dots, are used to dither the image (see Figure 5.19). Only the Web, Macintosh Systems, and Uniform palettes can be used if using a Pattern Dither.

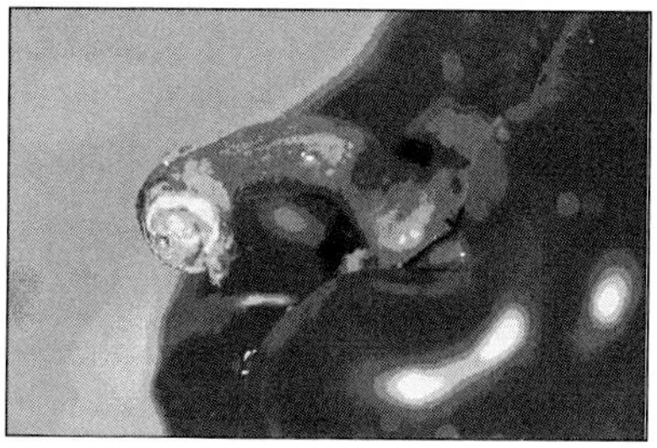

Figure 5.19

This image was converted to Indexed Color using the Uniform Palette and the Pattern Dither.

While using either a setting of Diffusion or None for the dither, you can choose between a faster conversion or a more accurate one by selecting either Faster or Best from the Indexed Color dialog box. The Preserve Exact Colors option prevents Photoshop from dithering colors that are in the palette you select, and it is available only if you are using the Diffusion Dither. This is of particular importance when producing graphics with small details for the World Wide Web.

In addition to the dithering options, at the time of conversion, a specific Color Table, or palette, and the actual number of colors to be used can be selected. Photoshop has several palettes already defined, including system palettes for the Macintosh and Windows operating systems, a Web palette for producing images for Web publication, Uniform palettes that consist of samples taken from the RGB spectrum at regular intervals, and an Adaptive palette that samples the original image for the most commonly used colors. If the RGB image already contains 256 colors or fewer, an Exact option is available, since the resulting Indexed Color image will exactly match the original image. If a conversion to Indexed Color mode has already occurred, the Previous palette can also be used. Finally, there is an option to use a Custom palette that can be loaded from a saved Color Table or set of swatches.

Images in Indexed Color mode have many of the same restrictions as images in Bitmap mode. None of the filters are available, and some of the painting tools cannot be used. In addition, images in Indexed Color mode can contain only one layer and have one channel called Index.

Now you try it...

Converting to indexed color

1   Open lesson03.psd in the Chapter 5 folder on the CD-ROM.

2   Select Image > Mode > Indexed Color.

3   Move the Indexed Color dialog box out of the way so that you can see part of the image.

4   Make sure the Preview option is turned on and the Dither is set to None in the Indexed Color dialog box. From the Palette menu, select System (Macintosh) and wait for Photoshop to show a preview. Select each of the other Palette options in order and wait for Photoshop to make a preview. Note how Photoshop changes the image based on the Color Table.

5   Select the Uniform palette option. Select each of the Dithering options in succession and wait for Photoshop to make a preview. Note how the Dithering options affect the image.

6   With the Dither set to Diffusion and the Color Matching set to Best, pick the Adaptive palette option and click OK.

7   The image has now been converted to Indexed Color using a Diffusion Dither and the 256 most commonly used colors in the image. Note the result.

8   Now select Image > Mode > Color Table. This Color Table shows the 256 colors used throughout the image. Only these 256 colors are being used.

9   Select the color in the upper-left corner of the Color Table. The Color Picker will appear so that you can choose a replacement color. Change this color to Red: 0, Green: 255, Blue: 0. Click the OK button in the Color Picker and the OK button in the Color Table dialog box.

10   Note that green dots have appeared throughout the image because you have replaced the color assigned to those pixels in the Color Table.

11   Try modifying some of the other colors in the Color Table and note the results.

12   Close the image.

MULTICHANNEL MODE

This mode splits any image containing multiple channels into individual spot color channels. The channels created are 8-bit grayscale and reflect the Grayscale values of the original channels (see Figure 5.20). Multichannel mode is used primarily in specialized printing applications and for some advanced channel manipulations.

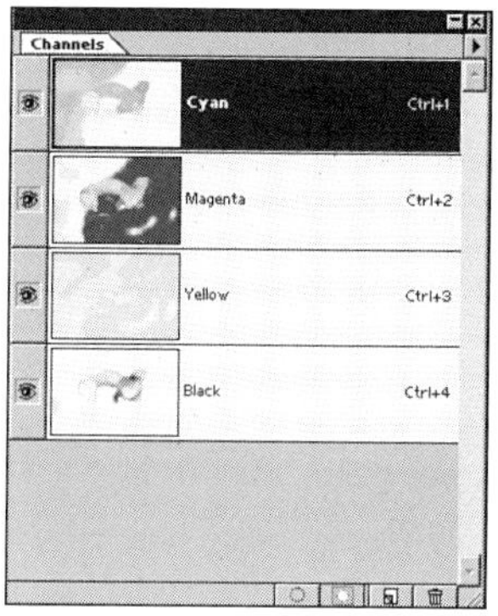

Figure 5.20

This image was convert-ed from CMYK to Multichannel mode.

If an individual channel is deleted from an image in a mode that contains multiple channels, it is converted to Multichannel automatically.

- When a CMYK image is converted to Multichannel mode, the channels produced are Cyan, Magenta, Yellow, and Black.
- When an RGB image is converted to Multichannel mode, the channels produced are Cyan, Magenta, and Yellow.
- When an image in Lab mode is converted to Multichannel mode, three alpha channels are created, each called Alpha.

Grayscale images and Duotones can also be converted to Multichannel mode, even though they each contain only one channel. In the case of Grayscale images, the channel is still called Black. In the case of a Duotone, each spot color used is placed on a separate channel.

When working in Multichannel mode, you are manipulating the separate color channels individually. There is no composite channel to work in. Almost all of the filters are available and all of the tools can be used, but they affect only one channel at a time.

TIP

To see the separations created for an image in Duotone mode, you can convert to Multichannel mode. You may want to do this to a copy of the image because you cannot convert from Multichannel mode back to Duotone mode.

8-BIT AND 16-BIT COLOR

One of the options you have if you are in Grayscale, RGB, or CMYK modes, is to work with 16-bit color instead of the default 8-bit. By default, the channels that make up the images in these modes contain 256 levels of gray. By increasing the color depth of the channels to 16-bit, 65,536 levels of gray can be achieved, allowing for much finer color detail. Photoshop has the ability to read and import images with this higher bit depth.

In the default mode, 8-bit, all the limitations outlined previously exist. In a 16-bit/channel mode, there are severe restrictions on the changes that can be made to the image. None of the filters are available, and only one layer is allowed. Of the painting tools, only the rubber stamp tool can be used, and some of the image adjustment commands, such as Levels and Curves, are available. Furthermore, an image in a 16-bit/channel mode cannot be printed.

SUMMARY

The following chart summarizes some of the most important features of each image mode in Photoshop.

Summary of Image Modes					
Mode	Layers	Channel Names	Painting Tools	Filters	Converts From
Bitmap	Background Only	Alpha	Some	None	Grayscale
Grayscale	Unrestricted	Black	All	Most	Any Other Mode
Duotone	Unrestricted	Duotone	All	Most	Grayscale
RGB	Unrestricted	Red, Green, Blue	All	All	All but Bitmap
CMYK	Unrestricted	Cyan, Magenta, Yellow, Black	All	Most	All but Bitmap
Lab	Unrestricted	Lightness, a, b	All	Most	All but Bitmap
Indexed Color	Background Only	Index	Most	None	Grayscale or RGB
Multi-channel	Background Only	Varies	All	Most	All but Bitmap

REVIEW QUESTIONS

1. In which mode does your image need to be in order to convert it to Bitmap mode?

    a.   RGB

    b.   Grayscale

    c.   Multichannel

    d.   Indexed Color

2. When converting from CMYK to Multichannel mode, what are the names of the channels produced?

    a.   Cyan, Magenta, and Yellow

    b.   Four channels named Alpha

    c.   Four channels named Black

    d.   Cyan, Magenta, Yellow, and Black

3. None of the filters are available. Which image mode is your image in (assume 8-Bit/Channel color where applicable)?

    a.   CMYK

    b.   Grayscale

    c.   Multichannel

    d.   Indexed Color

4. You try to add a layer, but the New Layer button in the Layers palette is dimmed. What is a possible reason (assume 8-Bit/Channel color where applicable)?

    a.   The image is in CMYK mode.

    b.   The image is in Duotone mode.

    c.   The image is in Grayscale mode.

    d.   The image is in Indexed Color mode.

5. What does the Halftone Screen option do when converting from Grayscale to Bitmap mode?

    a.   It simulates halftone dots.

    b.   It creates a custom Dot Gain.

    c.   It uses the printer's halftone screen settings.

    d.   It sets the halftone screen for the image, but does not display the halftone information.

6. How many channels does a Quadtone image have?

   a.   One

   b.   Two

   c.   Three

   d.   Four

7. Which color mode is used as an inter-mediate when converting from RGB to CMYK?

   a.   Lab

   b.   Grayscale

   c.   Multichannel

   d.   Indexed Color

8. What does adjusting the Duotone curves accomplish?

   a.   It determines where the spot color should be applied throughout the image.

   b.   It determines where trapping should be applied throughout the image.

   c.   It determines where the CMYK profile should be applied through-out the image.

   d.   It determines where out-of-gamut colors should be corrected throughout the image.

9. While converting from RGB to Indexed Color, the Pattern dither is unavailable. What is a possible reason?

   a.   You are trying to use the Web palette.

   b.   You are trying to use the Uniform palette.

   c.   You are trying to use the Adaptive palette.

   d.   You are trying to use the Macintosh System palette.

10. How many colors can an image in Indexed Color mode contain?

   a.   2

   b.   256

   c.   65,000

   d.   16 million

11. When converting an image to Bitmap Mode from Grayscale, the Custom Pattern dither option is unavailable. What is a possible reason?

    a. You have not defined a pattern.

    b. You are trying to use the Uniform palette.

    c. You are trying to use the Adaptive palette.

    d. You cannot convert a Grayscale image to Bitmap Mode.

12. Which color model is device independent?

    a. RGB

    b. CMYK

    c. Lab

    d. Indexed Color

CHAPTER 6

SELECTIONS

For Photoshop professionals, quite possibly the most important technique to master is the selection process. Selecting in Photoshop is unlike the selection process in other object-based applications in which an object is either selected or not. In Photoshop, pixels can be selected at any one of 256 levels. While you can select individual pixels in Photoshop, it is perhaps more appropriate to think in terms of selecting areas of an image. This chapter will examine the primary tools and commands used to create and modify selections.

Domains & Objectives

Making Selections

5.1   Identify issues regarding the characteristics, function, and appropriate use of selection tools and commands including the move tool, lasso, polygon lasso, and magnetic lasso tools, marquee tools, magic wand tool, and the Color Range command.

5.2   Identify issues regarding the characteristics, function, and appropriate use of tools and commands used to make adjustments to a selection in an image including manually adding, subtracting and intersecting selections, differentiating between selection data and pixel data, using the Grow, Similar, Expand, Contract, Smooth, Reselect, and Deselect commands and using the Tolerance, Feather, and Anti-Alias options.

5.4   Determine the appropriate feature, command, tool, or procedure to make and modify a selection.

OVERVIEW OF SELECTIONS

Photoshop shows which pixels in an image are selected by using a selection boundary. This selection boundary or edge is sometimes referred to as the "marching ants." Figure 6.1 shows a selection boundary. Selections can be discontinuous and can contain holes. A selection can be of an entire image or a single pixel.

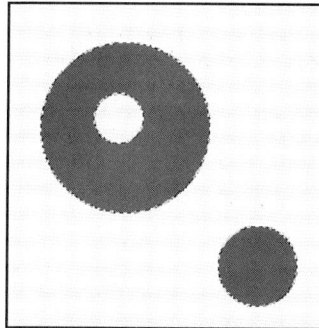

Figure 6.1

The pixels in the "marching ants" are selected.

Selections are used as masks so that only selected areas can be changed, either through painting or through the use of other commands. You can also use selections to move and copy pixels within an image and between images. Often the first step to cutting or copying and pasting involves a selection.

SELECTION DATA VERSUS PIXEL DATA

When making selections, two fundamental concepts must be clearly understood, and both require an understanding of how pixels make up an image. The first thing to recognize is that only whole pixels can be selected. Because pixels are the most elementary building block of a raster image, a selection must contain at least one whole pixel. Figures 6.2 and 6.3 show an attempt to select half a pixel and the result.

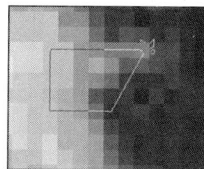

Figure 6.2

The lasso appears to be selecting only parts of a pixel.

Figure 6.3

The resulting selection,
however, contains only
complete pixels.

The other significant concept to remember when making selections is that while only whole pixels can be selected, they can be selected at any of 256 levels. Often selections contain pixels that are either completely selected or completely deselected. A pixel can, however, be variably selected. The selection boundary, or "marching ants" shows only those pixels that are more than 50% selected. Figures 6.4 and 6.5 show two selection boundaries that look identical. The pixels in Figure 6.4 are either completely selected or completely deselected. The pixels in Figure 6.5 are all partially selected. While the two figures look identical, they contain very different selections.

Figures 6.6 and 6.7 show the results from filling the selections from the previous figures with black. While two selection boundaries may appear the same, the selection information may be very different.

Figure 6.4

The pixels in this image
are either completely
selected or completely
deselected.

Figure 6.5

The pixels in this image
are all partially selected.
Note the similarity to
Figure 6.4.

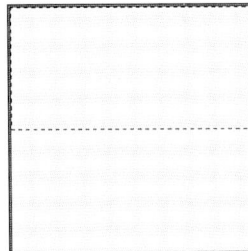

Figure 6.6

The selection from Figure 6.4 is filled with black.

Figure 6.7

The selection from Figure 6.5 is filled with black.

Pixels in Photoshop can be partially selected at 256 levels. These 256 levels of selection correspond precisely to the 256 levels of gray available in an alpha channel. In fact, when you save a selection, it is saved as an 8-bit (256 levels of gray) channel. See Chapter 13, "Channels & Masks," for more information on channels and their relationship to selections. If you make a selection and none of the pixels are over 50% selected, Photoshop will warn you that a selection boundary will not display (see Figure 6.8).

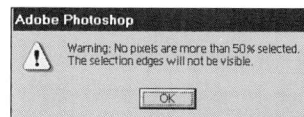

Figure 6.8

Photoshop warns you if it cannot display the selection boundary.

USING SELECTION TOOLS

The primary selection tools are all located in the upper part of the toolbox. Figure 6.9 shows the default toolbox and the selection tools that are available. Note that many of the toolbox's buttons have related tools hidden underneath the buttons.

TIP

Because selection borders can be ambiguous, carefully keep track of your selections. If you become unsure of what you have selected, try switching to Quickmask mode, and then switching back.

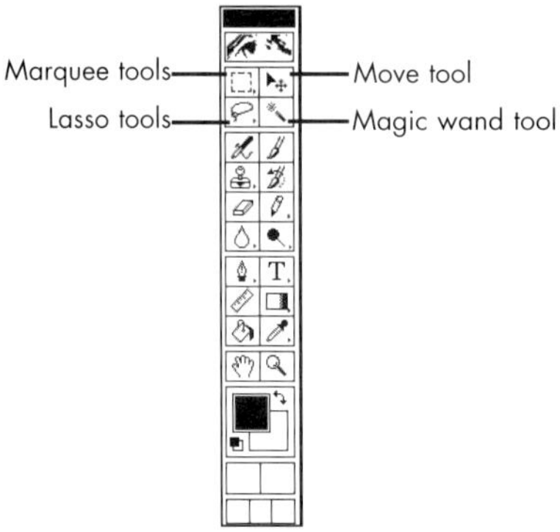

Figure 6.9

The upper part of the
toolbox contains the
main selection tools.

Marquee tools ——————— Move tool
Lasso tools ——————— Magic wand tool

All of the selection tools use common keys to modify the selection as it is being made. If you already have made a selection, holding down the Shift key will add to the existing selection, and holding down the Alt (Windows)/ Option (Macintosh) key will subtract from the selection. Holding down both the Shift and Alt (Windows)/Option (Macintosh) keys will intersect the selection. An intersection is the area common to the original and new selections. Hold these keys only until you start the selection. After that, the keys can be used again to constrain the selection area or to draw the selection from the center, if the tools support it.

MARQUEE TOOL

The Marquee tools are actually a collection of tools that include the rectangular marquee, the elliptical marquee, and tools for selecting a single row or column of pixels. The crop tool is also included in this tool group.

Rectangular Marquee

Use the rectangular marquee tool to select rectangular areas of an image. Holding down the Shift key constrains the selection to a square. Holding down the Alt (Windows)/Option (Macintosh) key draws the rectangle from the center. Be careful about the order of the key strokes. If you already have a selection and you hold down the Shift key before dragging, you will be adding to the selection. If you hold the Shift key down after you start dragging, you will constrain the selection. If you would like to do both, hold down the Shift key, begin dragging, release, and then hold down the Shift key again. (The Alt (Windows)/Option (Macintosh) keys work identically.)

Both the rectangular marquee and the elliptical marquee (see below) have three styles available in the Marquee Options palette: Normal, Constrained Aspect Ratio, and Fixed Size. The Normal style draws a rectangle or ellipse, according to the points you select. The Constrained Aspect Ratio draws the rectangle or ellipse with a specified relationship between the width and height. If you want to create a selection that is proportional to an 8.5 × 11-inch sheet of paper, for example, you could enter these values (8.5 and 11) for the width and height. The Fixed Size style enables you to specify the exact size of the marquee in pixels.

The rectangular marquee tool selects rectangular areas of an image.

Elliptical Marquee

With the elliptical marquee, you can select an elliptical area of an image. Similar to the rectangular marquee tool, you can constrain the selection to a circle by holding down the Shift key, and you can draw the selection from the center by holding down the Alt (Windows)/Option (Macintosh) key.

Note that because only whole pixels can be selected, the resulting selection when using this tool is only an approximation to an ellipse or circle that is made up of squares. Figures 6.10 and 6.11 show a selection made with the elliptical marquee tool and the results.

ELLIPTICAL MARQUEE

ICON	
SHORTCUT	M
CURSORS	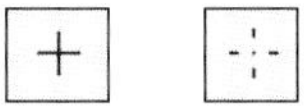 + ⊹
OPTIONS	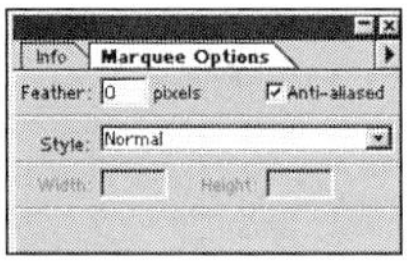

The elliptical marquee tool selects elliptical areas of an image.

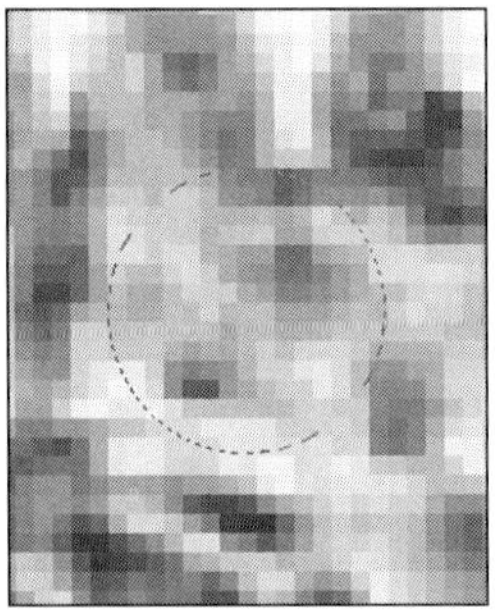

Figure 6.10

This is a circular selection made with the elliptical marquee tool and by holding down the Shift key.

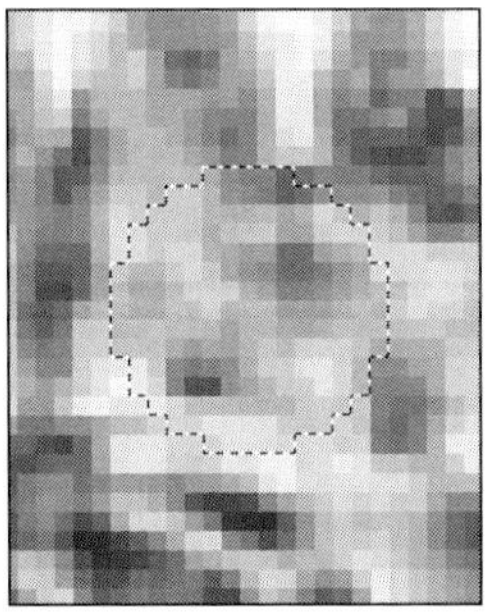

Figure 6.11

This is the result of the selection made in Figure 6.10.

Single Column and Single Row Tools

The single column and single row tools select either an entire column of pixels in an image or an entire row of pixels. These are used most often for specialized effects.

LASSO TOOLS

Photoshop has three lasso tools: the standard lasso, the polygon lasso, and the magnetic lasso. The magnetic lasso is new to Photoshop 5.0.

Lasso

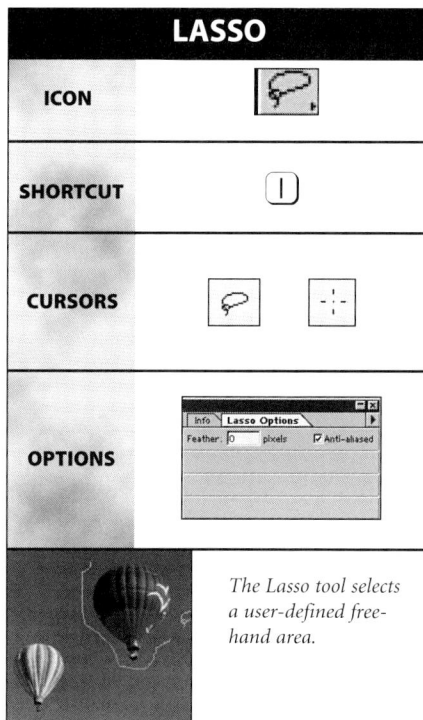

LASSO	
ICON	
SHORTCUT	
CURSORS	
OPTIONS	

The Lasso tool selects a user-defined free-hand area.

The lasso tool is a freehand drawing tool that defines a selection area. It is often used to refine selections, but it also can be used as a good starting point in making sophisticated selections. When using the lasso tool, it is helpful to define an enclosed area. If you don't, Photoshop will close the boundary by connecting the start and end points with a straight line (see Figures 6.12 and 6.13).

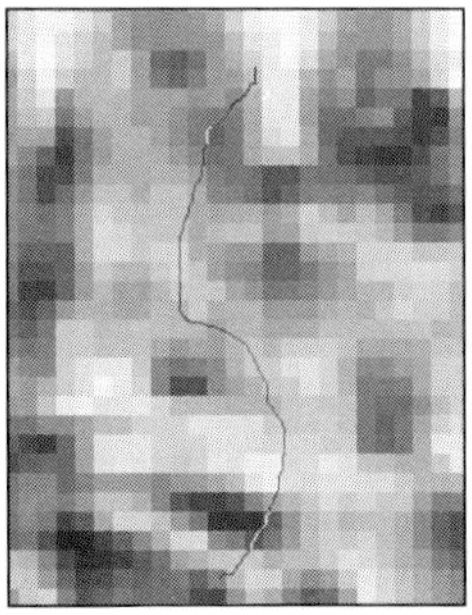

Figure 6.12

This is a selection made
with the Lasso tool.

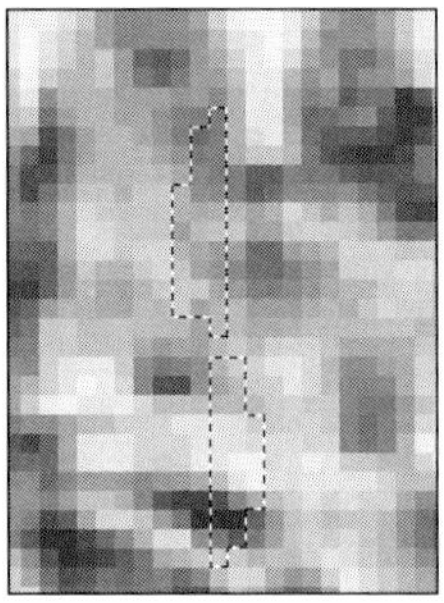

Figure 6.13

Photoshop draws a line
between the start
and end points to
close the shape.

Polygon Lasso

The polygon lasso tool is similar to the lasso tool. It makes freehand selections but, in this case, the selection is bounded by straight lines to form a polygon. You can create a selection with the polygon lasso tool either by selecting the tool from the toolbox, or by holding down the Alt (Windows)/ Option (Macintosh) key while using the standard lasso tool. The polygon lasso is very useful for selecting geometric objects such as buildings and architectural elements. When you move the cursor over the start point once the polygon is started, a circle displays under the cursor (see Figure 6.14), denoting that the polygon will close and the selection will be complete. If you want to finish the selection without placing the cursor on top of the start point, you can either double-click or press the Enter or Return key, and Photoshop will finish the selection by drawing a straight line between the start point and the last point drawn. If you want to start over without completing the selection, you can press the Esc key. If you hold down the Alt (Windows)/Option (Macintosh) key while dragging with the polygon lasso tool, it will temporarily become the standard lasso tool.

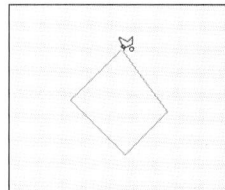

POLYGON LASSO

ICON	
SHORTCUT	⬆Shift + I
CURSORS	
OPTIONS	Info / Polygonal Lasso Options Feather: 0 pixels ☑ Anti-aliased

The polygon lasso tool selects a user-defined polygonal area.

Figure 6.14

Photoshop will close the polygon and complete the selection if you click while this cursor displays.

Magnetic Lasso

The magnetic lasso tool is a new tool to Photoshop 5.0. It is used to select areas of an image, but selection is made easier because it automatically snaps to the edges of contrasting color areas. The magnetic lasso is very useful for tracing objects in an image or for selecting complicated areas. Like the polygon lasso, when you move the cursor over the start point, the cursor changes to indicate that the selection path will close. You can also double-click or press the Enter or Return key to complete the path. If you want to start over without completing the selection, you can press the Esc key. If you hold down the Alt (Windows)/Option (Macintosh) key while dragging with the magnetic lasso tool, it will temporarily become the standard lasso tool.

MAGNETIC LASSO

ICON

CURSORS

OPTIONS

The magnetic lasso selects a freehand area by finding the edges formed by contrasting colors.

The magnetic lasso creates fastening points as it detects edges in the image. Figure 6.15 shows the magnetic lasso tool, the path that it creates, and the fastening points. You can manually insert a fastening point at any time while using the magnetic lasso tool by clicking as you move the pointer.

Figure 6.15

The magnetic lasso tool creates a selection path and fastening points as it detects the edges in an image.

Selection path

Cursor

Fastening point

When you use the magnetic lasso tool, it utilizes several settings in the magnetic lasso Options palette to determine the edges of the image. The Lasso Width is the area around the cursor's position in which Photoshop will look for edges. The values can range from 1 to 40 pixels. The Frequency determines how quickly fastening points are placed along edges or how quickly the selection path is finalized. Values for frequency can range from 0 to 100. The higher values indicate faster placement of fastening points. You can also set the Edge Contrast for the magnetic lasso tool. This determines how sensitive the tool is at detecting edges. The higher the value, the more contrast the tool will require between the edges to make an accurate detection. Values for Edge Contrast can range from 1% to 100%.

Now you try it...

Using the magnetic lasso tool

1. Open the lesson01.psd image (see Figure 6.16) in the Chapter 6 lessons folder on the CD.

Figure 6.16

Start with this image and isolate the black areas from the contrasting orange color.

2. Select the magnetic lasso tool. Make sure that the options are visible by double-clicking on the tool.

3. Set the Lasso Width to **10** pixels, the Frequency to **90**, and the Edge Contrast to **60%**.

4. Start in the lower right corner and move the pointer to the left toward the other corner. Move the pointer slowly so that Photoshop can find the edges accurately and you can adjust the path as you move the pointer.

5. When you reach the lower left corner, Photoshop tends to round the corner, so click once in the corner to make a sharp point.

continues

6 Now move the cursor up to the top of the black area of the image. When you reach the peak, click the mouse button again to insert a fastening point at the peak and continue down the mountain and over the figure.

7 When you reach the right edge, click to add another fastening point at this sharp corner, and then continue down the edge until the pointer indicates that Photoshop will close the path. Click once to close the path.

8 Subtract the area between the figure's legs by holding down the Alt (Windows)/Option (Macintosh) key when you start to make the path. You may want to zoom in on this area to get a better view of what you are doing. When finished, the selection should look like the one shown in Figure 6.17.

Figure 6.17

When you have completed the selection, it should look like this.

Before you close the file, try using other settings for the Lasso Width, Frequency, and Edge Contrast to practice further.

MAGIC WAND TOOL

The magic wand tool is one of the most versatile of all the selection tools. Selections are often started with this tool, and then refined using the other selection tools. The magic wand tool selects contiguous areas of similar color. When you select a pixel with the magic wand tool, Photoshop will examine the adjacent pixels and add them to the selection if they are within the color tolerance. Photoshop will continue to add to the selection with adjacent pixels until no more pixels within the tolerance are detected. The Tolerance can be set in the magic wand Options palette. Values for

Tolerance range from 0 to 255. If set to 0, the magic wand will select only an area of a single color. Higher values will select broader areas of color. Figures 6.18 and 6.19 show a similar area selected using two different Tolerance values. The magic wand tool can also be set to examine pixels under the cursor. Doing this disregards the current layer of pixels if you have selected the Use All Layers option. In addition, as with all the selection tools, holding down the Shift key while selecting will add to an existing selection and holding down the Alt (Windows)/Option (Macintosh) key will subtract.

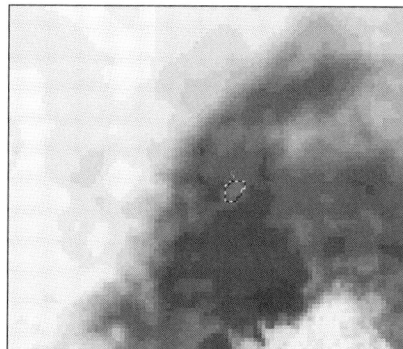

MAGIC WAND

ICON	
SHORTCUT	W
CURSORS	
OPTIONS	

The Magic Wand tool selects contiguous areas of similar color.

Figure 6.18

This selection was made with the Tolerance set to 10.

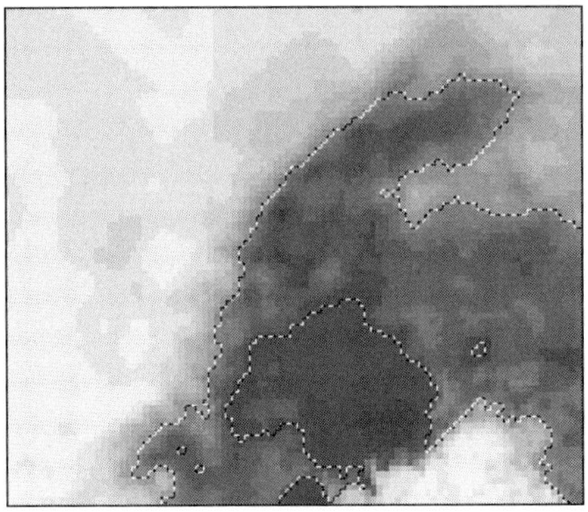

Figure 6.19

This selection was
made with the Tolerance
set to 32.

Figure 6.19

This selection was made with the Tolerance set to 32.

Now you try it...

Using the magic wand tool

1   Open the lesson02.psd image in the Chapter 6 lessons folder on the CD.

2   Set the Tolerance in the magic wand Options palette to **0**.

3   Using the magic wand tool, click in the upper area of the image, anywhere in the orange. Notice that only one or two pixels are selected.

4   Now click in the lower left corner or in the black area. Notice that much of the black area is selected. This is because many of the pixels are the identical color black.

5   Set the tolerance to **32** and click in the body of the figure. Note that much of the darker area in the image is selected. This selection resembles that made previously with the magnetic lasso tool.

6   Now set the tolerance to **255** and click in the unselected area. The entire image should be selected because the range of colors is wide enough to choose every pixel in the this particular image.

Before you close the file, experiment on your own with different Tolerance values.

MOVE TOOL	
ICON	
SHORTCUT	Ctrl / ⌘ + V
CURSORS	
OPTIONS	
	The move tool moves the selected pixels.

Once you have made a selection, the selected pixels can be moved with the move tool by clicking in the selection and dragging it to a new location. You can also move a selection by holding down the Ctrl (Windows)/Command (Macintosh) key and dragging while any tool other than the pen tool is active. The move tool cuts out the pixels from the background by default. The pixels are replaced by either the background color (if the selection is on the Background layer), or by transparent pixels on any other layer. As you move a selection, it can be constrained to horizontal, vertical, or a 45-degree angle if you hold down the Shift key while moving. Holding down the Alt (Windows)/Option (Macintosh) key makes a copy of the pixels and moves the copy rather than the original pixels.

The arrow keys can also be used to move a selection. With the move tool selected, the arrow keys move the selected pixels one pixel at a time. If the Shift key is held down while using the arrow keys, the selected pixels will move 10 pixels at a time. The Alt (Windows)/Option (Macintosh) key can be used with the arrow keys to make a copy of the selected pixels.

TIP

If you want to move pixels, make sure that the move tool is selected. If a selection tool is currently active, the selection boundary will move instead.

If you use the move tool without first making a selection, the entire layer will move. If the layer that is moved is the Background layer, it will be renamed "Layer 0." If you turn on the Auto Select Layer option in the move Options palette, Photoshop will select the pixels in the uppermost layer at the point you click with the cursor instead of in the current layer.

The Pixel Doubling option creates a lower-resolution (half, to be precise) preview of the pixels being moved. This can improve system performance while dragging.

You can move selections within an image or between images using the move tool. Select the pixels in one image and use the move tool to drag and drop them into another. If you hold down the Shift key while dragging and dropping between Photoshop images, the pixels will be placed in the center of the new image. The advantage of using the drag-and-drop method over cutting and pasting is that the clipboard is not used and some system resources are saved.

SELECTION OPTIONS

Many of the selection tools and commands share similar options and settings.

TOLERANCE

The Tolerance option, described above in the section "Magic Wand Tool" and specified in the magic wand Options palette, is used not only for the move tool, but also for the Grow and Similar commands. Further, the Fuzziness specified in the Color Range command is similar in its use to the Tolerance option for the magic wand tool.

FEATHER

There are two types of feathering that can be used on a selection. The first is the feathering that is applied as you use a selection tool to select an area of an image. This is set in the Options palette for the specific tool. All of the selection tools—except for the Magic Wand—have a feathering option. When a selection is feathered, the edges are softened by an amount that you specify. Photoshop softens the edges of the selection by providing a smooth transition between selected pixels and unselected pixels. The maximum feather value is 250 pixels. A feather value of 0 produces a normal selection. When used with a rectangular marquee, the corners of the rectangle will become rounded as the selection softens. The selection is softened on either side of the selection boundary the amount of the feather radius by creating a blend between the colors inside the selection and the colors outside the selection. Figure 6.20 shows a rectangular selection with a feather applied to it and the effects after filling the selection with black.

Figure 6.20

This is a feathered rectangular selection filled with black. The feather was set to 10 pixels.

The second type of feathering is identical to that used while creating selections, but it is performed after the selection has been made using the Feather command from the Select menu.

ANTI-ALIAS

Anti-aliasing is the introduction of an intermediate color along the edges of a selection to smooth the selection. This intermediate color is actually produced by providing a thin border of partially selected pixels. This option is most commonly used to enhance the appearance of curves in Photoshop, because the curves must be approximated using square pixels. All the lasso tools and the elliptical marquee have anti-aliasing options because the shapes you draw with these tools must be approximated. The rectangular marquee does not need an anti-aliasing option because the rectangle can be exactly constructed from square pixels. Figures 6.21 and 6.22 show circles with and without anti-aliasing. Both were created using the elliptical marquee tool.

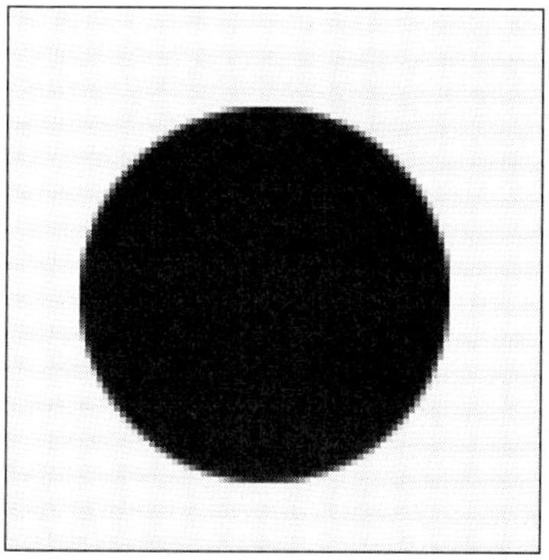

Figure 6.21

A circle created with anti-aliasing turned on. Note the smoothing along the edges of the circle.

Figure 6.22

A circle created with
anti-aliasing turned off.

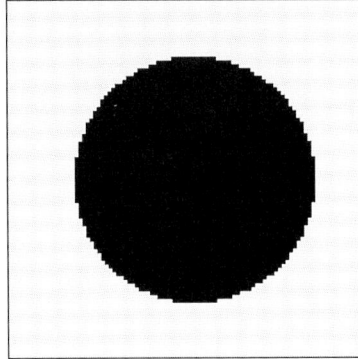

Anti-aliasing can be turned on and off by selecting the Anti-aliased button
in the tool's respective Options palette. Rectangular selections do not
require anti-aliasing because a rectangle can be built from square pixels
without requiring any approximations.

USING SELECTION MENU COMMANDS

Photoshop comes with a wide range of options for modifying and creating
new selections. All of these commands are located in the Select menu. See
Figure 6.23.

Figure 6.23

The Select menu has
many commands used to
modify existing selections
and to create new ones.

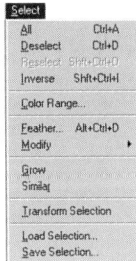

COLOR RANGE

The Color Range command can be used to modify an existing selection or
to create a new selection. The Color Range command is used to select a
range of colors, either throughout the image or within an existing selection.
Figure 6.24 shows the Color Range dialog box.

The Color Range command can be used to select a range of colors based on
a specified Fuzziness value and a pixel selected with the eyedropper. The
Fuzziness is similar to the Tolerance used by the magic wand tool. Fuzziness
values range from 0 to 200. At 0, only the pixels that exactly match the
selected color within the image or selection are selected. If the value is set

larger, the number of selected pixels grows because there are more pixels that fall within the range of the original selection. Colors can be added to the base color by using the plus eyedropper or subtracted by using the minus eyedropper. When any eyedropper is selected, hold down the Shift key to temporarily toggle to the plus eyedropper in order to add colors and the Alt (Windows)/Option (Macintosh) key to toggle to the minus eyedropper in order to subtract colors. You can pick with the eyedroppers either in the preview area of the dialog box or in the image. The eyedroppers and fuzziness slider are available only if the Color Range command is selecting from Sampled Colors.

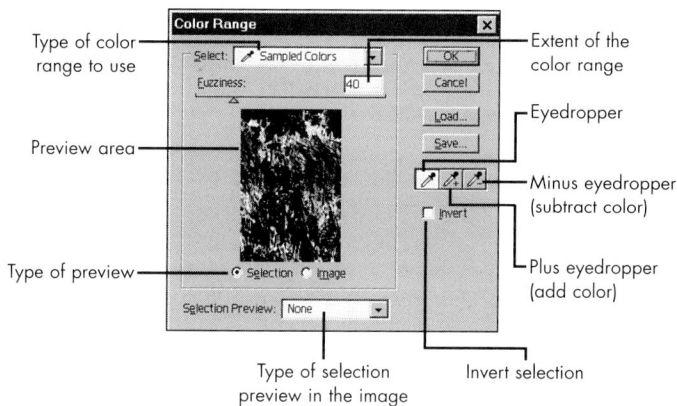

Type of color range to use

Preview area

Type of preview

Type of selection preview in the image

Color Range

Select: Sampled Colors

Fuzziness: 40

OK

Cancel

Load...

Save...

Invert

Selection   Image

Selection Preview: None

Extent of the color range

Eyedropper

Minus eyedropper (subtract color)

Plus eyedropper (add color)

Invert selection

Figure 6.24

Use the Color Range command to select a range of colors.

If you choose not to use Sampled Colors, you can select color ranges based on the reds, greens, blues, cyans, magentas, or yellows in an image. You can also select the highlights, midtones, or shadows of an image. Further, in an RGB or Lab image (see Chapter 5, "Image Modes"), you can choose to select all the colors that are out-of-gamut or that will not reproduce correctly in CMYK mode.

The preview area can be set to display either a preview of the selection or the actual image. If you use a preview of the selection, white represents areas completely selected; black represents areas completely unselected; and any gray tones represent partially selected areas. Keep in mind that a pixel may be partially selected, and if it is less than 50% selected, the selection boundary will not highlight that pixel.

The Selection Preview option determines how the selection is shown in the actual image. It can be shown in grayscale, in which case the preview of the selection in the image will match the preview window in the dialog box. It can also be shown as a black-or-white matte, where black or white is used to show the unselected areas. If Quick Mask is selected, the unselected areas are shown with a color cast determined in the Quick Mask options. By default the color cast is red and 50% transparent to simulate a rubylith mask. You can set the Quick Mask options by double-clicking on the Quick Mask icon in the toolbox.

Color range settings can be saved and loaded. In addition, you can reset the values in the dialog box at any time by holding down the Alt (Windows)/ Option (Macintosh) key. The Cancel button will become a Reset button.

The Color Range command can be used to refine an existing selection, even one originally created using the Color Range command. For example, you can select an area with a marquee, run the Color Range command to select only those colors within the original selection that are out-of-gamut, and then run the Color Range command again to select the reds within this selection. A selection constructed with the Color Range command can also be inverted by using the Invert option in the dialog box.

Now you try it...

Using the Color Range Command

1   Open the lesson03.psd image in the Chapter 6 lessons folder on the CD.

2   From the Select menu, choose Color Range.

3   From the Select menu within the Color Range dialog box, choose out-of-gamut. Note the preview in the dialog box.

4   From the Selection Preview menu, choose Black Matte. All the colors that are safe to print are now shown in black, while those out-of-gamut are clearly visible.

5   Now click the Invert checkbox to show only the out-of-gamut colors in black.

6   Hold down the Alt (Windows)/Option (Macintosh) key and click the Reset button. Turn off the Invert option and set the Selection Preview back to None.

   Before you close the file, make sure that you are using the Sampled Colors selection and experiment with the eyedroppers and the fuzziness slider.

GROW

The Grow command increases a current selection based on the Tolerance set in the Magic Wand Options palette. The Grow command only detects similar-colored pixels in areas adjacent to the existing selection.

SIMILAR

The Similar command selects colors similar to those in an existing selection throughout an image based on the Tolerance setting. Note that unlike the magic wand tool and Grow command, the pixels added to the selection with the Similar command do not need to be adjacent. They can be anywhere in the image.

BORDER

This command, located in the Modify submenu of the Select menu, creates a border around an existing selection by a specified amount. Values from 1 to 64 pixels are acceptable. Whatever the value, the border is created by offsetting the selection boundary one-half the value inward and outward.

EXPAND

This command is in the Modify submenu of the Select menu. The Expand command offsets the selection boundary outward by a specified amount. This amount can range from 1 to 16 pixels. If used with a rectangular selection, the corners will become rounded.

CONTRACT

Like the Expand command, this command is located in the Modify submenu of the Select menu. The Contract command offsets a selection boundary inward by a specified amount. This amount can range from 1 to 16 pixels. If you specify an offset amount that is greater than the number of pixels available in the existing selection, nothing will be selected, and Photoshop will warn you that no pixels are selected. When used on a rectangular selection, the corners stay sharp.

SMOOTH

The Smooth command is also located in the Modify submenu of the Select menu. The Smooth command examines the pixels within a specified radius to determine if they are within the color range of the rest of the selection. Pixels that are within the color range are added to the selection, while those outside are subtracted. The detection radius can be set from 1 to 16 pixels. Smoothing is particularly useful when making color-based selections, and isolated pixels are inadvertently selected or deselected. Figures 6.25 and

6.26 show a color-based selection and the same selection cleaned up through smoothing.

Figure 6.25

A color-based selection may contain some stray pixels.

Figure 6.26

After running the Smooth command on the selection shown in Figure 6.25, note that the two pixels inside the area are now part of the selection.

TIP

If a painting tool is not working correctly or a command is not working the way you expect, try deselecting. Because of the ambiguity of the selection boundary and because sometimes it is impossible to determine if anything is selected (especially when zoomed in), there may be a selection that is interfering with your tools or commands.

DESELECT

The Deselect command is used to deselect any active selection. Often you may need to deselect before running other selection commands. The keyboard shortcut for this command is Ctrl+D (Windows) or Command+D (Macintosh). You can also deselect by using one of the selection tools and clicking outside the canvas but within the gray area of the active window. This area is often not visible if the image is zoomed to any magnification.

RESELECT

If at any time you have nothing selected and want to reload the last selection, you can use the Reselect command. This command is particularly useful if you accidentally deselect.

INVERSE

The Inverse command inverts the current selection. Any pixels which were selected become deselected. Any pixels that weren't selected become selected. In addition, Photoshop truly inverts the selection. So if a pixel was 75% selected, it would become only 25% selected after you run the Inverse command. The Inverse command is useful in many selection instances because many times it is simpler to select the pixels you don't want. In this case, the selection can be inverted to produce the desired result.

ALL

This command selects all the pixels in an image or in a layer. Note that if no pixels are selected on a layer, then the layer behaves as though they were all selected for the purpose of moving, painting, and applying effects.

FEATHER

The Feather command behaves identically to the Feather option for the selection tools and must be applied to an existing selection. Feathering provides a smooth transition between the areas selected and those areas not selected based on a specified value.

TRANSFORMING SELECTIONS

Selection boundaries can be moved, and now in Photoshop 5.0, they can also be scaled and rotated. A selection can be moved by placing the cursor in the selected area while one of the selection tools is active. The cursor will look like the move tool, but it will have a selection box under it (see Figure 6.27).

Figure 6.27

Note the cursor in this selection that is being moved.

If you choose Transform Selection from the Select menu, the current selection will get handles (at each corner, the sides, and top and bottom) for scaling, and a pivot point for rotating. To scale the selection boundary, choose any one of the handles and drag. To rotate the selection boundary, move the cursor to the edge of the boundary until the cursor changes to a rotate tool, and then apply the rotation. You can move the pivot point for the rotation if necessary. Holding down the Shift key while scaling from one of the corner handles keeps the width and height of the selection boundary proportional. Holding down the Shift key while rotating rotates the selection in 15-degree increments. Once the transformation is complete, either double-click or press the Enter key. Figure 6.28 shows a selection being transformed.

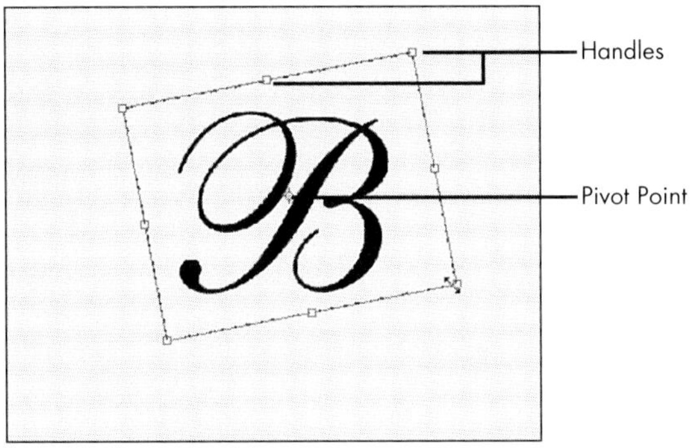

Figure 6.28

A selection boundary can be transformed just as selected areas can.

HIDING EDGES

In many instances, the selection boundary becomes distracting. This is especially true when making color-based selections, such as selecting the out-of-gamut colors in an image with the Color Range command. In this case, it can be advantageous to turn off the selection boundary, or hide the edges. From the View menu, choose Hide Edges. The selection boundary is no longer visible, but the selection remains.

SUMMARY

Photoshop provides numerous methods for producing selections in an image. Selecting can be one of the most sophisticated and complicated processes in Photoshop. Mastery of the selection process is necessary for mastery of Photoshop. While most of the selection options have been covered in this chapter, some still remain. In Chapter 7, "Paths," the relationship between selections and paths will be examined, and the relationship between selections and channels, which is an extremely important one, will be looked at closely in Chapter 13.

REVIEW QUESTIONS

1. Which tool selects contiguous areas of similar color?

    a. Grow

    b. Similar

    c. Magic wand

    d. Magnetic lasso

2. Which command is used to select areas of similar color throughout an image?

    a. Expand

    b. Similar

    c. Magic wand

    d. Magnetic lasso

3. Which commands or tools, other than the magic wand, rely on the Tolerance setting? (Choose 2.)

    a. Similar

    b. Grow

    c. Expand

    d. Contract

4. To adjust the range of colors in the Color Range dialog box, you should adjust which value?

    a. Tolerance

    b. Anti-aliasing

    c. Fuzziness

    d. Feather

5. Which tool does not have an anti-aliasing option?

    a. Magnetic lasso

    b. Elliptical marquee

    c. Rectangular marquee

    d. Polygon lasso

6. Which command creates a smooth transition between selected and unselected pixels?

    a. Grow

    b. Expand

    c. Feather

    d. Transform Selection

7. Which key should you use to copy a selection to the center of another image while dragging and dropping?

    a. Shift

    b. Alt (Windows)/Option (Macintosh)

    c. Ctrl (Windows)/Command (Macintosh)

    d. Alt (Windows)/Command (Macintosh)

8. Which key should you hold down to add to a selection?

    a. Shift

    b. Alt (Windows)/Option (Macintosh)

    c. Ctrl (Windows)/Command (Macintosh)

    d. Alt (Windows)/Command (Macintosh)

9. Which key should you hold down to constrain the elliptical marquee to a circle?

    a. Shift

    b. Alt (Windows)/Option (Macintosh)

    c. Ctrl (Windows)/Command (Macintosh)

    d. Alt (Windows)/Command (Macintosh)

10. To specify the magnetic lasso's sensitivity to edges in the image, which value should be adjusted?

    a. Tolerance

    b. Edge Contrast

    c. Fuzziness

    d. Lasso Width

11. You want to copy a selected area in an image, but when you drag the cursor, only the selection boundary moves. What might you need to do to fix the problem?

    a.   Set the tolerance.

    b.   Feather the selection.

    c.   Select the move tool.

    d.   Select the magnetic lasso tool.

12. You click a point with the magic wand tool and only one pixel is selected. What is probably the value of the tolerance?

    a.   0

    b.   100

    c.   255

    d.   256

13. How can you soften the hard edges of a selection? (Choose 2.)

    a.   Grow

    b.   Feather

    c.   Smooth

    d.   Anti-alias

14. What is the minimum part of an image that can be selected?

    a.   1/2 pixel

    b.   1 pixel

    c.   1/10 pixel

    d.   1/256 pixel

15. The crop tool is located with what other tool in the toolbox?

    a.   The pen tool

    b.   The dodge tool

    c.   The polygon lasso

    d.   The elliptical marquee

CHAPTER 7

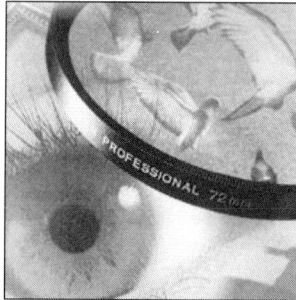

PATHS

Although vector-based objects such as paths are more frequently associated with illustration programs such as Adobe Illustrator, Photoshop uses paths for a variety of purposes. They can be used for special painting and fill effects, to create and modify selections, and to isolate which parts of an image are visible in page layout programs.

Paths are a topic that you will need to know to become an Adobe Certified Expert (ACE), but for many Photoshop users, they are a bit foreign. As an ACE, you will be expected to identify the characteristics, function, and appropriate use of the Paths palette and tools.

Domains & Objectives

Making Selections

5.3   Identify issues regarding the characteristics, function, and appropriate use of the Paths palette, including using the pen, magnetic pen, and freeform pen tools; creating and editing paths; knowing the significance of anchor points, their number, and frequency; differentiating among work path, path, and subpath; converting paths to selections; and creating and exporting clipping paths.

File Format/Import/Export

10.3   Determine the appropriate feature, command, tool, or procedure to import a path into Adobe Photoshop and export a path to Adobe Illustrator.

KEY CONCEPTS

The following key concepts are related specifically to Photoshop and its use of paths. Although many of the terms might seem familiar if you have used other programs that rely on paths, take care to know how the term or concept applies to Photoshop.

PATHS AND SUBPATHS

A *path* is an object defined mathematically with vectors. In Photoshop, a path is a collection of *subpaths*. A subpath can be open or closed. In Photoshop, a path can be saved and used for a variety of purposes, and a subpath is a component part of a path. Figure 7.1 shows a path with some different subpaths.

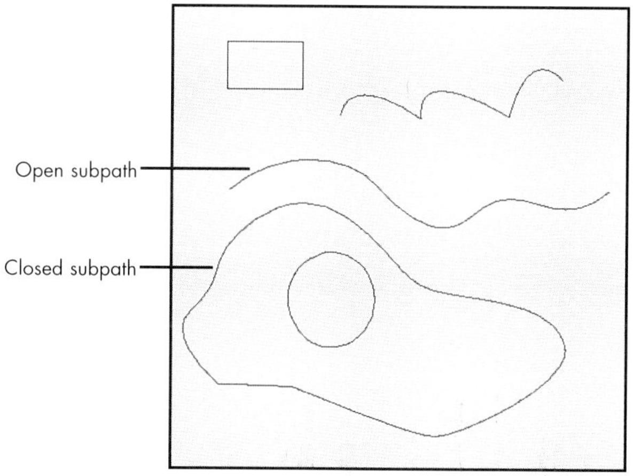

Open subpath

Closed subpath

Figure 7.1

A path is a collection of subpaths.

ANCHOR POINTS AND DIRECTION LINES

A subpath in Photoshop is a *Bézier curve*. Such curves are made up of path segments, anchor points, direction points, and direction lines. Figure 7.2 shows the anatomy of a Bézier curve.

Each path segment must pass through its corresponding anchor point. As the path segment passes through the anchor point, the amount of curvature in the path segment is determined by the direction lines. The direction lines are defined at each end by direction points and control not only the curvature, but also the direction of tangency of the path segment. If a direction line's length is increased, the curve will flatten out. As the length of the direction line decreases, the curve becomes sharper at that point until, at the extreme, the curve at that point becomes so sharp that the point becomes a corner point. Figures 7.3 and 7.4 show what happens to a path as the direction lines are changed.

Figure 7.2

A Bézier curve has several structural components.

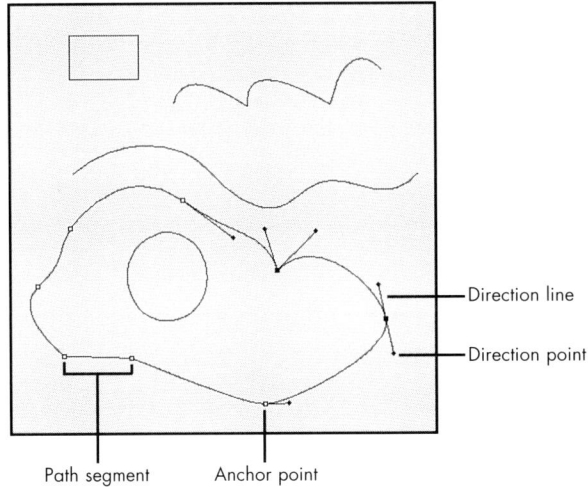

Direction line

Direction point

Path segment   Anchor point

Figure 7.3

These two subpaths have identical anchor points and direction lines.

Figure 7.4

These two subpaths still have identical anchor points, but the direction lines are very different.

CLIPPING PATH

A *clipping path* is a path that is saved with the image and is used by a page layout program such as QuarkXPress or Adobe PageMaker to determine which parts of an image show and which are hidden. Figures 7.5 and 7.6 show a raster image being clipped in a page layout program and the same raster image without a clipping path applied.

Figure 7.5

A raster image being clipped in a page layout program.

Figure 7.6

The same image in a page layout program without a clipping path.

CREATING AND EDITING PATHS

Photoshop provides several methods to create and edit paths and subpaths. If you are familiar with editing paths in illustration programs, these tools will probably be familiar.

PEN TOOL

The pen tool is the basic path creation tool. With it you can draw Bézier curves. The operation of the pen tool is unlike most of the painting tools in Photoshop. It does not directly create subpaths to match the motion of your cursor; rather, it requires some additional information about where to place the direction lines.

To start a subpath with the pen tool, you click once inside the image area to place the first anchor point, and then—before releasing the mouse button or selecting the next anchor point—you determine the length of the direction line. This is accomplished by dragging until the direction line is correct, and then releasing the mouse button. This determines curvature of the subpath at the start point. When you have finished, you can continue to place anchor points by clicking and dragging to create their corresponding direction lines. Figure 7.7 shows the creation of a subpath's direction line.

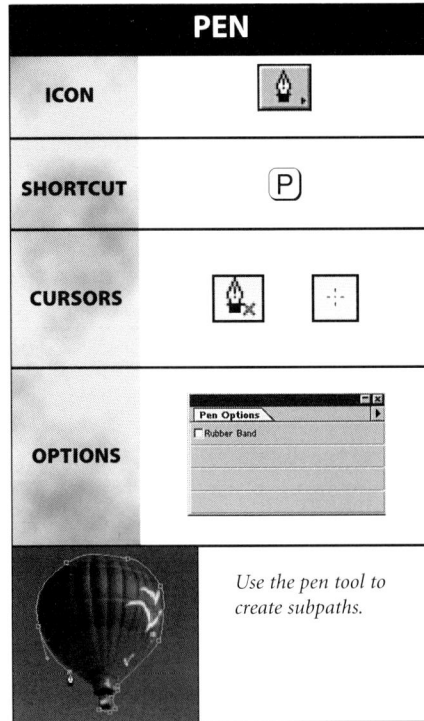

PEN	
ICON	
SHORTCUT	P
CURSORS	
OPTIONS	Pen Options ☐ Rubber Band
	Use the pen tool to create subpaths.

Figure 7.7

This is a path being created.

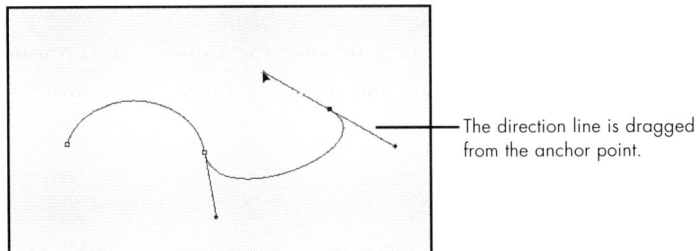

The direction line is dragged from the anchor point.

If Rubber Band mode is selected from the Pen Options palette, Photoshop shows a preview of the next path segment until the next anchor point is placed.

USING THE PEN TOOL

If a subpath remains open, any new point selected with the pen tool will add a segment to the subpath until the subpath is closed or until the pen tool is reselected from the toolbox. If, on the other hand, you want to continue adding segments to an open subpath, moving the cursor over either the start point or end point and clicking will begin to append path segments to the subpath.

If you click without dragging a direction line, no direction line will be made, and a corner point will be made at that anchor point. If both ends of a segment of the path have corner points, the segment will be a straight line. Therefore, the process to create straight line segments is to click without dragging a direction line. To constrain the pen tool to horizontal, vertical, and 45° angles when creating straight line segments, hold down the Shift key while clicking points. Figure 7.8 shows the creation of a path or straight line segments.

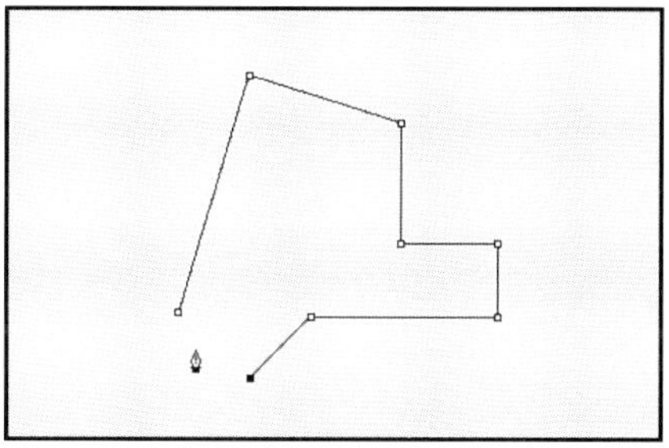

Figure 7.8

Straight line segments are created by clicking points without dragging direction lines.

By default, Photoshop creates parallel direction lines extending from each anchor point in opposite directions. Figure 7.9 shows such a direction line.

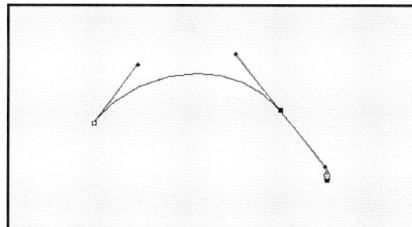

Figure 7.9

By default, direction lines extend from anchor points opposite but parallel.

If you would like to create direction lines that are not parallel, you can change the last direction point you created by holding down the Alt (Windows)/Option (Macintosh) key while creating a direction line. This is useful for creating points or curves that cross over themselves. Figure 7.10 shows a path with these types of direction lines and an existing direction point being moved during the creation process.

Figure 7.10

Hold down the Alt (Windows)/Option (Macintosh) key to change individual direction lines.

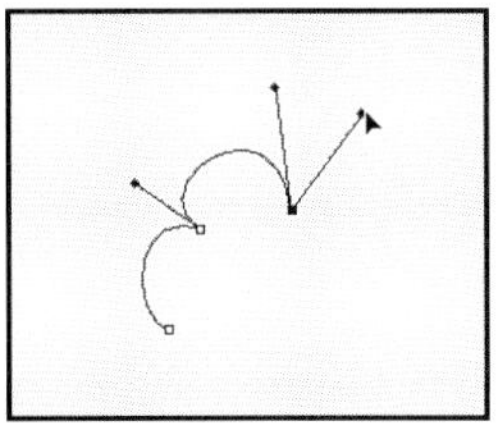

You can edit a subpath as you are creating it with the pen tool. If you move the cursor over an existing anchor point, the tool will change to the subtract anchor point tool. If you move the cursor over an existing path segment, the tool will change to the add anchor point tool. Holding down the Alt (Windows)/Option (Macintosh) key and moving the cursor over an existing anchor point will change the tool to the convert point tool. Consistent with all the path tools, holding down the Control (Windows)/Command (Macintosh) key will change the tool to the direct selection tool.

Now you try it...

Using the pen tool

1   Open "lesson01.psd" in the Chapter 7 lessons folder on the CD.
2   Using the pen tool, trace over the shapes to make paths that match them (see Figure 7.11). Be sure that you choose the tool again between each subpath segment to restart the pen tool.

Figure 7.11

Trace over these shapes to practice using the pen tool.

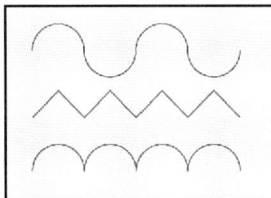

3 For the top subpath, starting at the leftmost point, click to place the anchor point, and then, before releasing the mouse button, drag the direction line straight up. Continue to trace the path by placing an anchor point at each change of direction.

4 For the middle subpath, click at each point without dragging a direction line.

5 For the bottom subpath, starting at the leftmost point, pick to place the anchor point, and then drag the direction line straight up. Place the cursor at the next change of direction, pick the point, and then hold down the Alt (Windows)/Option (Macintosh) key to drag the next direction line straight up as well. Repeat the process for each path segment.

MAGNETIC PEN TOOL

MAGNETIC PEN

ICON	
SHORTCUT	(⬆Shift) + (P)
CURSORS	
OPTIONS	Magnetic Pen Options Curve Fit: 0.5 pixels Pen Width: 40 pixels Frequency: 10 Edge Contrast: 50 % Stylus: ☐ Pressure

Use the magnetic pen tool to create subpaths by tracing over the edges between contrasting colors.

The magnetic pen tool, which is a new addition to Photoshop 5.0, works much as the magnetic lasso. It detects edges between contrasting areas of color in an image, which makes it a very effective tool for tracing raster images. To use the magnetic pen tool, click to place the first anchor point, and then move the mouse along the edge you want to trace. The subpath snaps to this edge as you move the cursor. Holding down the Alt (Windows)/ Option (Macintosh) key while dragging with the mouse button creates a freeform path. If you continue to hold down the Alt (Windows)/Option (Macintosh) key and then pick instead of dragging with the mouse, you can create straight line segments as well. Figure 7.12 shows the creation of a sub-path with the magnetic pen tool.

Figure 7.12

The center subpath was created with the magnetic pen tool. The outside subpath is being created with the magnetic pen tool.

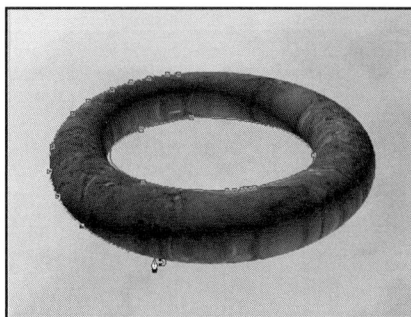

If you want to place an anchor point manually, you can click at any time. When the subpath is complete, if you have placed the cursor for the final point over the start point, the cursor will change showing a circle in the lower-right corner; this indicates that the subpath will be closed. You also can double-click at any time, and Photoshop will join the start point and end point with a magnetic path segment to create a closed subpath. Holding down the Alt (Windows)/Option (Macintosh) key while double-clicking joins the start and end points with a straight line segment. If you use the Enter key, Photoshop will end the subpath, leaving it open. Whatever the method used to end the subpath, Photoshop converts the subpath to a Bézier curve. Figure 7.13 shows a subpath about to be closed.

The magnetic pen tool has options similar to the magnetic lasso tool. The magnetic pen tool uses several settings in the Magnetic Pen Options palette to determine the edges of the image and where to place the path segments. The Curve Fit option controls how sensitive the placed path segments are to the movement of the cursor. The values can range from 0.5 to 10.0. If the value is set higher, fewer anchor points are used, creating a simpler, more efficient, but possibly less accurate path.

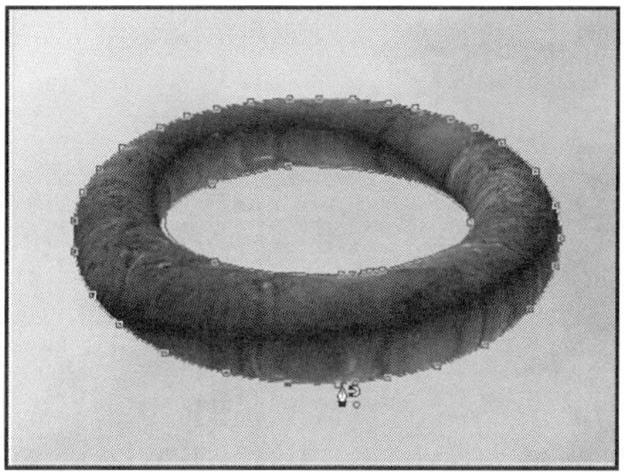

Figure 7.13

The outer subpath will be closed by ending at the start point.

The Pen Width is the area around the cursor's position in which Photoshop will look for edges. The values can range from 1 to 40 pixels. The Frequency determines how quickly fastening points are placed along edges or how quickly the subpath is finalized. Values for Frequency can range from 0 to 100. The higher values indicate faster placement of fastening points. You also can set the Edge Contrast for the magnetic pen tool. This determines how sensitive the tool is with respect to detecting edges. The higher the value, the more contrast the tool will require between the edges to make an accurate detection. Values for Edge Contrast can range from 1% to 100%.

Now you try it...

Using the magnetic pen tool

1   Open the "lesson02.psd" image in the Chapter 7 lessons folder on the CD (see Figure 7.14).

Figure 7.14

Begin with this file by using the magnetic pen tool to create a path around the text.

continues

2   In the Magnetic Pen Options palette, set the Curve Fit to **0.5** pixels and the Frequency to **10**. This will create a subpath with many segments but helps to maintain some of the sharpness in the corners. Set the Edge Contrast to **50%**, which makes it easier for the magnetic pen tool to find the contrasting edges between the light color of the letters and the background. Set the Pen Width to **40** pixels.

3   Starting with the letter A, use the magnetic pen tool to trace around the letter (see Figure 7.15). You might want to zoom in to see the letter better. Don't move the cursor too quickly, or you could create subpath segments that you don't want. When you have finished tracing the outside of the letter A, trace the inside.

Figure 7.15

Create a subpath around the letter A using the magnetic pen tool.

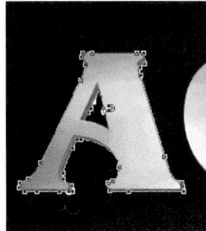

4   Continue tracing the rest of the letters.

FREEFORM PEN TOOL

Like the magnetic pen tool, the freeform pen tool is a new addition to Photoshop 5.0. With the freeform pen tool, you can draw freeform subpaths directly. Where the cursor moves, a subpath is created. As with the other pen tools, to create a subpath you must first click to place the starting anchor point. Then, as long as you hold down the mouse button, the subpath will continue to be created. When you release the mouse button, the subpath is completed and will be transformed into a Bézier curve.

If you position the cursor for the last point over the start point, the cursor will change to show that the subpath will be closed. If you release the mouse button at this point, a closed subpath is created. Holding down the Control (Windows)/Command (Macintosh) key while releasing the mouse button also closes the subpath. Figures 7.16 and 7.17 show the freeform pen tool being used to create a subpath and the resulting subpath.

FREEFORM PEN

ICON	
SHORTCUT	⬆Shift + P
CURSORS	
OPTIONS	Freeform Pen Options Curve Fit: 2 pixels
	Use the freeform pen tool to create sub-paths by drawing with the mouse.

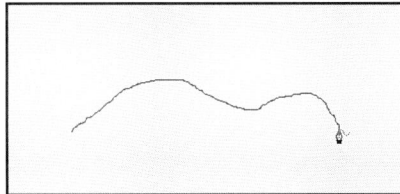

Figure 7.16

This is a subpath being created with the freeform pen tool.

Figure 7.17

This is the resulting sub-path created with the freeform pen tool in Figure 7.16.

The freeform pen tool has only one option: Curve Fit, which is similar to this same option for the magnetic pen tool. It controls how closely the path follows the movement of the cursor as you draw. Larger values create longer path segments and fewer anchor points.

Now you try it...

Using the freeform pen tool

1   Open the "lesson03.psd" image in the Chapter 7 lessons folder on the CD.

2   Use the freeform pen tool to draw a path around the canoe by starting where it meets the water on the left. Follow its silhouette and the fisherman until you reach the point where the canoe meets the water on the right side. Hold down the Control (Windows)/Command (Macintosh) key before releasing the mouse button to close the subpath.

ADD ANCHOR POINT TOOL

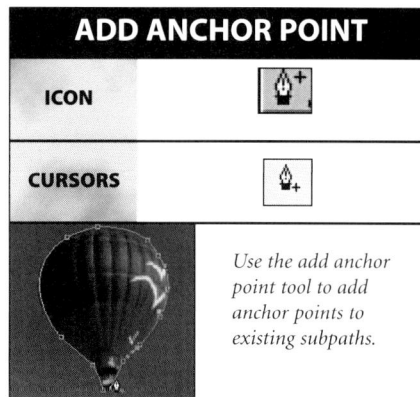

ADD ANCHOR POINT

ICON	
CURSORS	

Use the add anchor point tool to add anchor points to existing subpaths.

After you have created a subpath, you can add anchor points by using the add anchor point tool. If the cursor is moved to a point on a path segment, you can click to add an anchor point. Direction lines also accompany the anchor point and are determined by the curvature of the path segment at the point where the new anchor point is added. If you click and drag, you can adjust the newly created direction lines, changing the curvature of the path segment at the new anchor point. Holding down the Shift key while creating the direction lines constrains them to horizontal, vertical, and 45-degree angles.

If you place the cursor over an existing anchor point or direction point, the add anchor point tool will become the direct selection tool (see the "Direct Selection Tool" section). If you hold down the Alt (Windows)/Option (Macintosh) key, the subpath will be copied as you drag.

SUBTRACT ANCHOR POINT TOOL

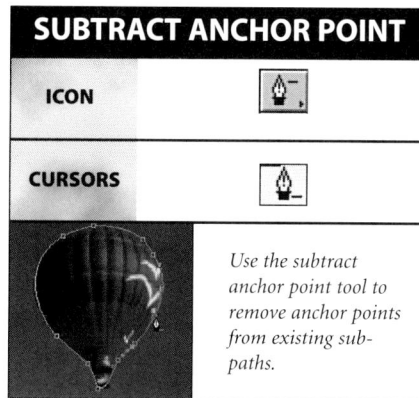

SUBTRACT ANCHOR POINT

ICON	
CURSORS	

Use the subtract anchor point tool to remove anchor points from existing sub-paths.

The subtract anchor point tool is similar to the add anchor point tool—except, of course, that it removes anchor points. If the cursor is placed on an anchor point, it will be removed when you click. If the cursor is placed on a path segment instead of an anchor point, the tool will become the direct selection tool.

DIRECT SELECTION TOOL

The direct selection tool is used to select and modify the subpath. If you place the tool on an anchor point, you can adjust the point's position by clicking and dragging. In addition, clicking on an anchor point displays the direction lines for the anchor point. The direction lines can then be adjusted by clicking and dragging the direction points. If placed on a path segment, the segment can be adjusted. The anchor points remain fixed, and the direction lines change. In either case, holding down the Shift key while dragging constrains the movement to horizontal, vertical, and 45° angles.

The keyboard shortcuts for the path tools in Photoshop 5.0 more closely match those of Adobe Illustrator: You can press the A key to access the direct selection tool. While any other path tool is selected, hold down the Control (Windows)/Command (Macintosh) key to toggle to the direct selection tool while the key is held down.

DIRECT SELECTION	
ICON	
SHORTCUT	Ⓐ
CURSORS	
	Use the direct selection tool to select and modify subpaths

In addition to adjusting the subpath, the direct selection tool can be used to select parts of the path or subpath. Hold down the Shift key while clicking to select multiple anchor points. When selected, these points can be moved together. If you click off a subpath, a selection marquee will be started. With the marquee, multiple anchor points can be selected. To select an entire subpath, either drag a marquee over all the anchor points in the subpath, or hold down the Alt (Windows)/Option (Macintosh) key and pick the subpath. If you drag while holding down the Alt (Windows)/Option (Macintosh) key, the entire subpath will be copied. As always, the Shift key constrains the movement.

A path segment can be deleted by selecting it and then pressing the Delete or Backspace key. When you have deleted one segment, the rest of the sub-path is selected. Because of this, you can delete an entire subpath by selecting any part of the subpath and pressing Delete or Backspace twice. Note that if the subpath is closed, deleting a segment will open it. To delete a single anchor point, use the subtract anchor point tool.

Path segments and selected points can also be transformed using the transformation tools from the Edit menu. The Free Transform command can be used as well as the other transformation commands such as Rotate, Scale, and Skew. The tools behave identically to the transformation commands used to transform selections. Figure 7.18 shows points being transformed.

TIP

With parts of a path selected, you can also use the context-sensitive menu to start the Free Transform command.

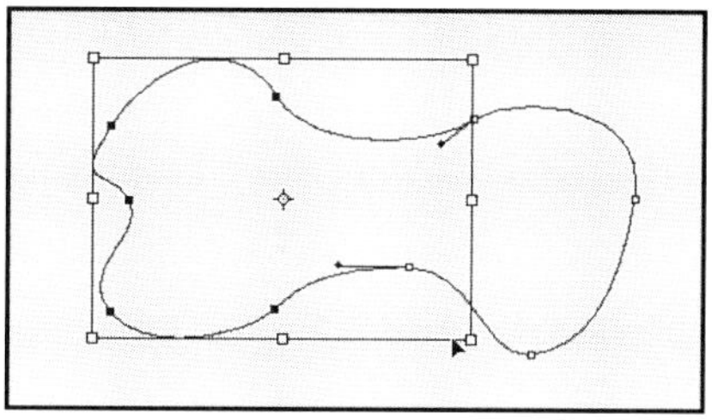

Figure 7.18

Only the selected anchor
points and path seg-
ments are being trans-
formed in this subpath.

CONVERT POINT TOOL

CONVERT POINT	
ICON	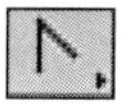
CURSORS	
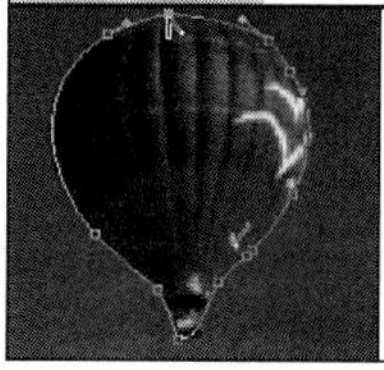	*Use the convert point tool to convert anchor points on a curve to corner points, or vice versa.*

The convert point tool is used to toggle anchor points between corner
points and points that define a smooth curve. With this tool, you can either
remove the direction lines, making the curvature of the path segment at that
point very sharp, or add direction lines if the anchor point is at a corner. To
create a corner point, position the cursor on an anchor point and click. To
create direction lines for an anchor point that lacks them, click and drag.
Holding down the Alt (Windows)/Option (Macintosh) key while dragging
enables you to adjust the direction lines individually from that anchor point
so that the direction lines are not necessarily parallel and opposite.

You also can change the direction lines independently by clicking and dragging a direction point. If the direction points are not visible, you can use the
direct selection tool to select the anchor point associated with the direction
lines. If the cursor is placed over a path segment instead of an anchor point,
it becomes the direct selection tool.

THE PATHS PALETTE

Photoshop provides the Paths palette as a convenient way to manage paths (see Figure 7.19). Each path in the palette is a named object. These paths can be any collection of subpaths.

Figure 7.19

The Paths palette provides a convenient place to manage paths.

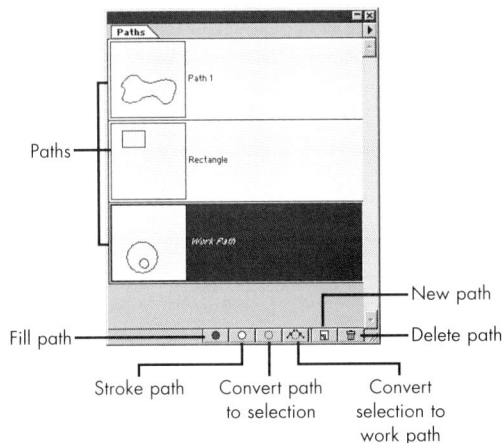

Figure 7.20

The commands in the Paths palette pop-up menu give you more advanced options for using paths.

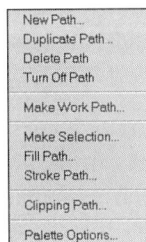

Paths can be deleted from the palette by dragging them to the delete current path button in the Paths palette or by selecting a path in the palette and clicking the delete current path button (the Trash Can). New paths can be created by selecting the new path button. Existing paths can be copied by dragging them onto the new path button. A path can be saved or renamed by double-clicking the path's name in the Paths palette.

The Paths palette menu contains many commands that duplicate the buttons in the palette, with some more advanced options (see Figure 7.20).

A path in the palette or a subpath also can be stroked or filled. If the stroke path button is clicked, the path or selected subpath will be stroked using the current painting tool, brush size, and foreground color (see Figure 7.21). Any painting tool or toning tool can be used to stroke a path.

Figure 7.21

These subpaths were stroked using the airbrush.

To change your painting tool to use for stroking, either hold down the Alt (Windows)/Option (Macintosh) key and click the stroke path button or choose the Stroke Path/Stroke Subpath command from the Paths palette menu, which prompts you to select a tool (see Figure 7.22).

Figure 7.22

The Paths palette menu prompts you to select which tool you will use to stroke the path.

A path also can be filled with the foreground color by using the Fill Path button in the Paths palette. If the path to be filled is open, Photoshop will connect the start and end points with a straight line and fill the closed areas. Figure 7.23 shows a filled path.

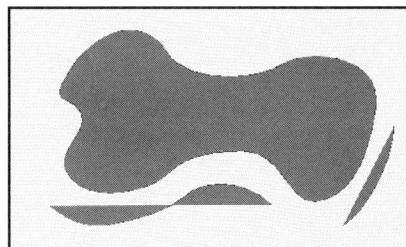

Figure 7.23

The subpaths in this image have been filled.

You can control the color, opacity, painting mode, and feathering of the fill by holding down the Alt (Windows)/Option (Macintosh) key while clicking the fill path button or by using the Fill Path/Fill Subpath command from the Paths palette menu (see Figure 7.24).

Figure 7.24

Use the Fill Path sub-
menu to set the fill
options when filling a
path or subpath.

Figure 7.24

Use the Fill Path sub-
menu to set the fill
options when filling a
path or subpath.

If a subpath has been selected, stroking or filling will take place only on the
subpath. To stroke or fill the entire path, deselect by clicking with the direct
selection tool in an area where there are no path segments before applying
the stroke or fill.

Paths can be turned off by using the Turn Off Path option in the Paths
palette menu or deselecting the path by clicking in the area of the Paths
palette where there are no paths (see Figure 7.25).

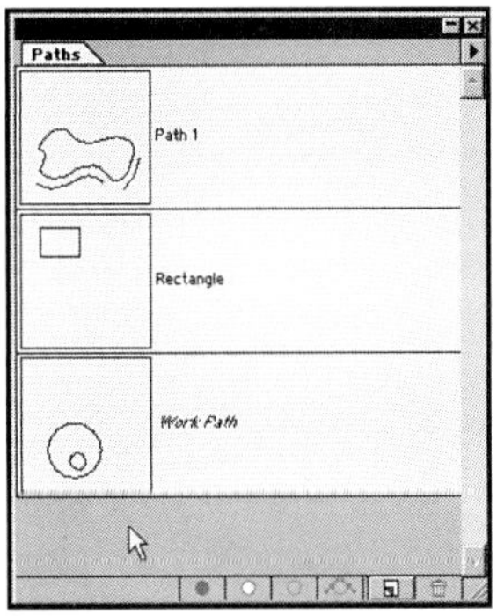

Figure 7.25

Click in the area under
the path thumbnails to
turn off any paths.

WORK PATHS

If you create a path using one the of the pen tools instead of using the new
path button in the Paths palette, the path created becomes the *work path*.
The work path is also the path created when a selection is transformed into
a path. Photoshop saves the work path with the file, but it cannot be used as
a clipping path because it is not yet saved as such. In addition, any action or
command that creates a new work path overwrites an existing work path,
unless it is saved with another name. To save the work path so that it can
be used as a clipping path, double-click on the Work Path thumbnail and
name it.

PATHS AND SELECTIONS

One of the most useful aspects of paths is that they can be converted into selections, and selections can be converted to paths. To convert a path into a selection, use the make selection button in the Paths palette or use the Make Selection command from the Paths palette menu. Using the command from the menu enables you to set the feathering and anti-aliasing, and also control how the new selection should be combined with any existing selections. These options also can be set by holding down the Alt (Windows)/Option (Macintosh) key while clicking the make selection button. Figure 7.26 shows the options available while converting paths into selections.

TIP

You can quickly convert a path into a selection by holding down the Control (Windows)/ Command (Macintosh) key and clicking on the path in the Paths palette.

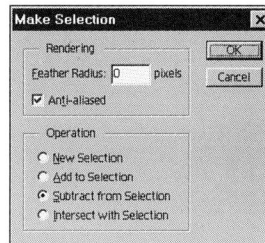

Figure 7.26

You can set how a selection converted from a path will behave after it is converted.

Selections also can be converted into paths, specifically, into a work path. This can be accomplished by either clicking the make work path from selection button in the Paths palette or selecting the Make Work Path command in the Paths palette menu. If you use the menu command, or if you hold down the Alt (Windows)/Option (Macintosh) key while the button is clicked, Photoshop will prompt you to set the Tolerance for the new path (see Figure 7.27). The Tolerance value can range from 0.5 to 10.0 and is similar to the Curve Fit options for the magnetic and freeform pen tools. It controls how closely the created path conforms to the selection boundary. Higher values create longer segments with fewer anchor points. Complex selection boundaries might require smaller values.

Figure 7.27

When converting a selection into a work path, set the Tolerance to control how closely the work path conforms to the selection boundary.

CLIPPING PATHS

A *clipping path* is used by page layout programs to determine which parts of the image to display and which to hide. To create a clipping path, choose the Clipping Path option from the Paths palette menu. Because only saved paths can be used, the work path cannot be a clipping path. Photoshop prompts you to select which path to use as the clipping path and to set the flatness (see Figure 7.28). The Flatness value ranges from 0.2 to 100. The clipping path is made up of straight line segments. The higher the flatness value, the longer the segments used to approximate the curve, creating a less accurate clipping path. If the value is lower, the segments used are shorter and the resulting path is more accurate. For the best results, leave the value blank to use the printer's default settings.

Figure 7.28

For the best results, leave the Flatness value blank.

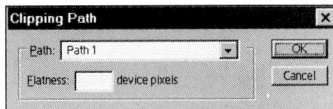

Paths can be exported in Illustrator format for use in Adobe Illustrator. Select the Export command from the File menu and then choose Paths to Illustrator. You can choose which path to export or you can export all of them.

Now you try it...

Practicing with paths

1   Open the "exer1a.psd" and "exer1b.psd" images in the Chapter 7 lessons folder on the CD (see Figures 7.29 and 7.30).

2   Make sure that the exer1a image is active. Double-click on the magnetic pen tool to set the options in the Options palette, and set the Curve Fit to **2**, the Pen Width to **40**, the Frequency to **20**, and the Edge Contrast to **10**.

3   Select the magnetic pen tool and trace around the moon.

Figure 7.29
This is a picture of
the moon from the
Adobe Image Library
(`exer1a.psd`).

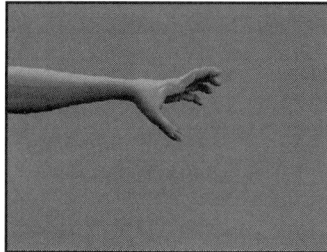

Figure 7.30
This is the
`exer1b.psd` image.

4   With these settings, the path that has been created around the moon contains more anchor points than are necessary (see Figure 7.31). Select the subtract anchor point tool and begin deleting points. Reduce the total number of points around the circle to only four or five. You might want to experiment with how few anchor points are required to make a circle.

Figure 7.31
Note the path around
the moon and the
number of anchor
points that it
contains.

continues

5 When the anchor points are removed, some parts of the path might begin to deviate from the circle. Use the direct selection tool to adjust the path so that it fits closely around the moon (see Figure 7.32). Remember that you can adjust anchor points, direction points, and path segments.

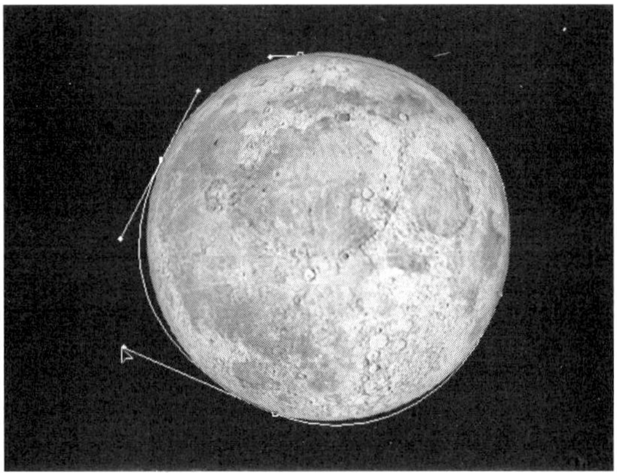

Figure 7.32

Adjust the path around the moon so that it matches the shape of the moon.

6 When the path is complete, double-click on the work path in the Paths palette and rename the path **moon**.

7 Now convert the path to a selection by choosing the Make Selection from the Paths palette menu. Make sure that anti-aliasing is turned on and that the selection is not feathered (see Figure 7.33).

Figure 7.33

Make sure that Anti-Aliased is selected and that there is no feather applied to the finished selection.

8 Now that the moon is selected, select the move tool and drag the moon from the current image to the "exer1b" image. Position the moon just inside the hand (see Figure 7.34).

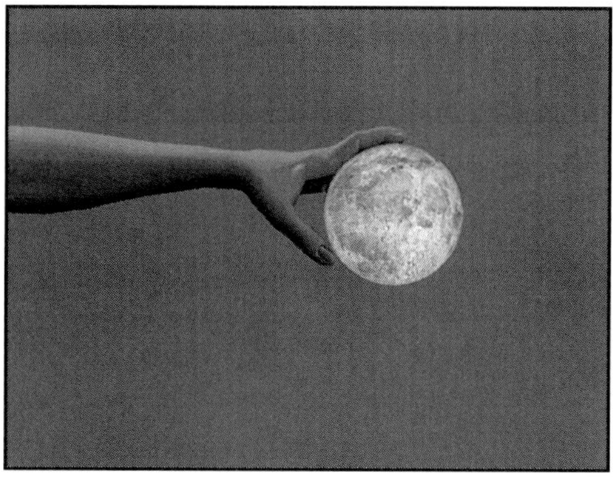

Figure 7.34

Position the moon just inside the out-stretched hand.

9 A new layer was created, so from the Layer menu, choose Flatten Image to make one layer: Background (see Figure 7.35).

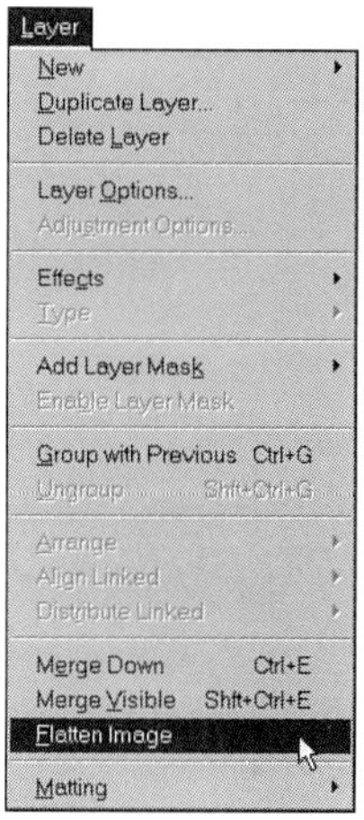

Figure 7.35

Choose Flatten Image from the Layer menu.

continues

10 Select the gray background around the hand and moon by using the magic wand tool. Double-click the magic wand tool and set the Tolerance in the Magic Wand Options palette to **0**, so that only gray pixels are selected (see Figure 7.36). Click anywhere in the gray, but not in the area between the moon and hand.

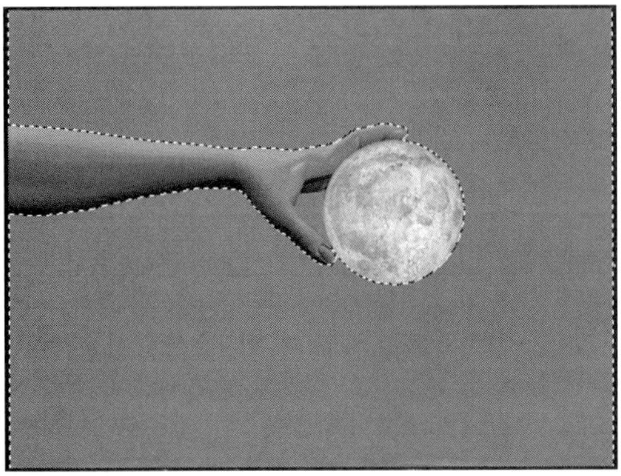

Figure 7.36

Use the magic wand tool to select the gray pixels in the image.

11 This selection now contains all the gray pixels in the image except those between the moon and the hand. Hold down the Shift key and, with the magic wand tool still selected, and click in the area between the moon and hand to select these gray pixels (see Figure 7.37).

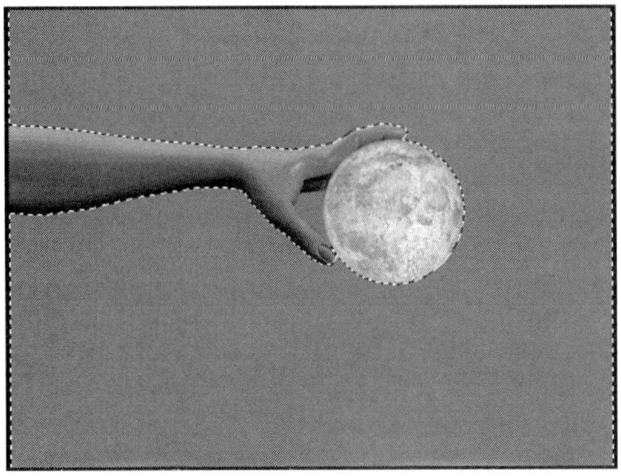

Figure 7.37

Use the magic wand tool to select the gray pixels between the hand and the moon.

12 Now all the gray pixels are selected, but the selection should be just the hand and moon; so from the Select menu, choose Inverse (Shift+Control/Command+I).

13 Now from the Paths palette, convert this selection into the work path by choosing Make Work Path from the Paths palette menu. Set the Tolerance to **0.5** to make the path more closely match the selection boundary and click the OK button (see Figures 7.38 and 7.39).

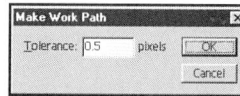

Figure 7.38

Set the Tolerance to 0.5 in the Make Work Path dialog box.

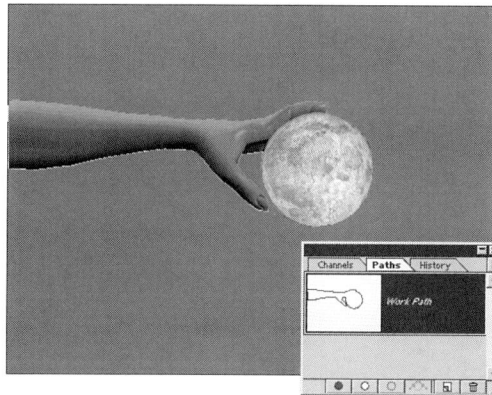

Figure 7.39

The work path has been created.

14 Now, to make a clipping path from the work path, the path must be saved. Either double-click on the work path or choose Save Path from the menu and call this path **moon in hand**.

15 Create a clipping path from this new path by choosing Clipping Path from the Paths palette menu. Specify the path you just created and leave the Flatness value blank to use the printer's default value (see Figure 7.40).

Figure 7.40

Choose the moon in hand path and leave the Flatness value blank.

continues

16 If you have a page layout program, try saving this file as an Encapsulated Postscript (EPS) file and importing it into a document in a page layout program (see Figure 7.41).

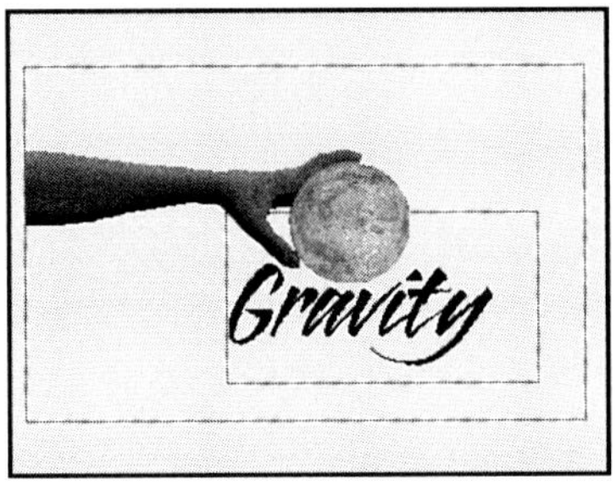

Figure 7.41

The image is clipped when imported into a page layout program.

SUMMARY

Paths are used in Photoshop for a variety of purposes. Although used most often by those incorporating raster images into page layout programs, paths can also be used to create and enhance selections and to create painting effects. An understanding of how Photoshop handles paths provides a basis for the use of paths in other illustration programs as well.

REVIEW QUESTIONS

1. To create a clipping path, you must use which type of object?

    a. A work path

    b. A saved path

    c. A selection

    d. A clipping group

2. When using the magnetic pen tool, which option should you set to change the length of the segments produced?

    a. Tolerance

    b. Curve Fit

    c. Pen Width

    d. Edge Contrast

3. If you increase the length of the segments produced by the magnetic pen tool, what happens to the number of anchor points?

    a. They will increase.

    b. They will decrease.

    c. They will stay the same.

    d. You cannot change the length of the segments produced by the magnetic pen tool.

4. Which of the following cannot be selected with the direct selection tool?

    a. Anchor points

    b. Direction points

    c. Direction lines

    d. Path segments

5. When stroking a path, which key should you use when clicking the Stroke Path button in the Paths palette to select the type of painting tool to use?

    a. Shift

    b. Alt (Windows)/Option (Macintosh)

    c. Ctrl (Windows)/Command (Macintosh)

    d. Shift+Ctrl (Windows)/Command (Macintosh)

6. When converting a selection to a path, what type of path will be created?

    a. Work Path

    b. Open Subpath

    c. Clipping Path

    d. Filled Subpath

7. When creating a corner point while using the pen tool, which key should you hold down while dragging the direction line?

    a. Shift

    b. Alt (Windows)/Option (Macintosh)

    c. Ctrl (Windows)/Command (Macintosh)

    d. Alt (Windows)/Command (Macintosh)

CHAPTER 8

PAINTING

Adobe Photoshop provides a great selection of painting tools. Each tool has a myriad of settings and color mode options to help you create your Photoshop images. In this chapter, you will learn how to select colors with the Swatches palette, the Color Picker, and the Color palette. You will also learn how to use the following tools: paintbrush, airbrush, pencil, line tool, eraser, gradient tool, paint bucket, and eyedropper.

Domains & Objectives

Painting and Editing

6.1   Identify issues regarding the characteristics, function, limitations, and appropriate use of the painting tools, functions, and commands, including the paintbrush tool, eraser tool, line tool, paint bucket tool, gradient tools, Brushes palette, Options palette, Fill and Stroke commands, Foreground and Background colors, and the relationship between tools and color modes.

6.2   Determine the appropriate feature, command, tool, or procedure to accomplish a stated task related to painting…

WORKING WITH THE FOREGROUND AND BACKGROUND COLOR SWATCHES

The Foreground and Background color swatches in the toolbox enable you to add color to your canvas or image by painting, or by filling or stroking a selection or layer element with the foreground color (see Figure 8.1). You can also blend between the foreground and background colors to create a gradation or erase part of an image with the background color.

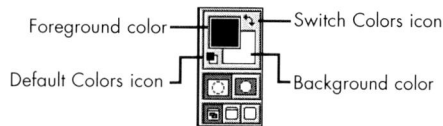

Foreground color — Switch Colors icon
Default Colors icon — Background color

Figure 8.1

The Foreground and Background color swatches enable you to select colors as well as fill and stroke elements.

When using the Foreground and Background color swatches, you are essentially working with any two colors at one time. The default foreground color is black, which is the active color if you start painting with the paintbrush, airbrush, or pencil. The default background color is white.

To change the foreground color, click the top swatch in the toolbox and the Color Picker appears. You can click anywhere in the Color Field in the left window of the Color Picker to choose a color, and then click OK. (You'll find more on how to use the Color Picker in the following paragraphs.)

To change the background color, click the swatch underneath the foreground swatch to gain access to the Color Picker.

To reverse the foreground and background colors, click the Switch Colors icon. You can now paint with the color you selected for the background.

To set the colors back to the default black-and-white settings, click the Default Colors icon or press D on your keyboard.

TIP

You can press X on your keyboard to switch between foreground and background colors.

USING THE COLOR PICKER

You can use the Photoshop Color Picker to select the foreground and background colors using the following color models: HSB, RGB, Lab, and CMYK. An advantage to using the Color Picker over the Color palette or Swatches palette is that you can see the values of all the color models simultaneously. In addition, you can choose colors from several different color matching libraries such as PANTONE or Trumatch.

The Adobe Photoshop Color Picker is the default color picker when you launch the program. However, you can choose to work with either the Apple or Windows Color Picker in the General Preferences dialog box.

The Photoshop Color Picker offers many more options than either the Windows or Apple Color Pickers, including several color modes to choose from such as RGB, CMYK, Lab, and HSB. It also has a much more extensive selection of custom color matching libraries, and it offers an out-of-gamut warning to let you know when you've selected a color that may not print accurately with standard CMYK printing inks. (You'll find information on all of these features in this chapter.)

See your operating system user guide for more information on the Apple or Windows Color Picker.

To display the Color Picker, click either the foreground or background swatches in the toolbox (see Figure 8.2).

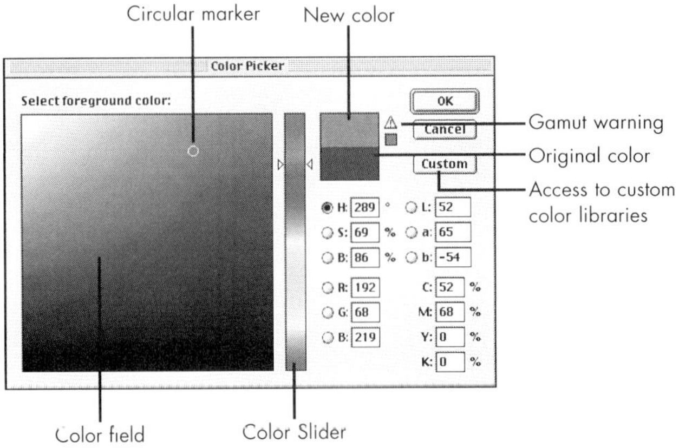

Figure 8.2

Click the Foreground or Background swatches in the toolbox to display Photoshop's Color Picker.

USING THE COLOR FIELD AND COLOR SLIDER WITH HSB VALUES

By default, the Hue component of the Hue, Saturation, and Brightness model is selected when you open the Color Picker. However, you can select other individual color components, such as Saturation and Brightness, or you can choose to work with the RGB, Lab, or CMYK modes.

The Color Slider represents the range of colors available to the selected component.

The Color field displays the range of available colors to the other two related components based on the position of the white triangle sliders.

Now you try it...

Using the Color Picker to define HSB values

1 Open the Color Picker by clicking the Foreground swatch in the toolbox. With the Hue component selected, drag the triangles up and down the Color Slider to display the range of saturation and brightness values in the Color field that are related to that hue.

2 Drag the circular marker from left to right in the Color field to affect the saturation. (Saturation is represented on the horizontal axis.)

3 Drag the circular marker from top to bottom in the Color field to affect the brightness. (Brightness is represented on the vertical axis.)

4 Click on the Saturation component and drag the triangles up to display colors that are more saturated. Drag the triangles down to display colors that are less saturated.

5 Click the Brightness component to display the available brightness values.

In the RGB Color Model, each of the red, green, and blue components has a range in color value from 0 to 255. If all three values are set to 0, the resulting color is black. If all three are set to 255, the resulting color is white. If you combine the 255 values possible, the total number of possible colors is 16.7 million ($256 \times 256 \times 256$).

The RGB Color Model works much the same way as the HSB Model when selecting colors in the Color Picker. When you select one component, its color range is represented in the Color Slider, and the other two components are represented in the Color field along either the horizontal or vertical axis.

Now you try it...

Using the Color Picker to define RGB values

1 Open the Color Picker by clicking on the Foreground swatch in the toolbox.

2 Choose the red component so that it is displayed in the Color Slider and drag the triangles while watching the corresponding values. The higher you drag up the slider, the higher the value (255). Drag the triangles all the way down to the bottom and the value changes to 0. Notice that the green and blue components do not change.

3 Blue is represented on the horizontal axis, so dragging the circular marker left to right increases the blue values. With a steady hand, click in the Color field and drag horizontally. If you're dragging in a perfectly straight line, only the blue values will change in the numeric field. Study the changes in the Color Slider as well as the numeric fields.

4 Now try dragging the circular marker vertically to adjust the green values.

5 Experiment with choosing the green component and you'll note the blue values change as you drag horizontally and the red values change as you drag vertically.

6 Now experiment with choosing the blue component and you'll note the red values change as you drag horizontally and the green values change as you drag vertically.

USING THE COLOR PICKER TO DEFINE LAB VALUES

In Photoshop's Lab mode, the "L" component represents Lightness, which ranges in value from 0 to 100. The "a" component represents the green-red axis, and the "b" component represents the blue-yellow axis where values range from +120 to –120.

For more detailed information about the Lab mode, see Chapter 5, "Image Modes."

Using the Color Picker to define Lab values

1 Open the Color Picker by clicking on the Foreground swatch in the toolbox.

2 Choose the "L" (Lightness) component so that it is displayed in the Color Slider and drag the triangles while watching the corresponding values. The higher you drag up the slider, the higher the brightness value, up to 100. Now drag the triangle all the way down to the bottom of the slider and the value changes to 0.

3 Select the "a" component and note that the Color field represents blue to yellow values.

4 Select the "b" component and note that the Color field now displays green to red values.

USING NUMERIC VALUES TO SPECIFY A COLOR

In addition to selecting colors in the Color field, you can also enter numeric values in the corresponding fields of the color mode you are using.

- **CMYK.** Specify a percentage up to 100% for each color.
- **RGB.** Specify component values from 0 to 255.
- **HSB.** Specify Hue as an angle from 0°–360° based on the color's location on the color wheel. Specify saturation and brightness as percentages.
- **Lab.** Specify Lightness from 0 to 100, as well as the a axis (green to magenta) and the b axis (blue to yellow) values from −128 to +127.

THE GAMUT WARNING

Some colors in the HSB and RGB Color Models cannot be reproduced by commercial printers' CMYK inks. The gamut warning, a triangle with an exclamation point inside it, will appear in the Color Picker and Color palette to alert you if you've selected a color that is not reproducible. The closest CMYK color match is displayed in a small color swatch beneath the triangle alert in the Color Picker and to the right of the triangle alert in the Color palette.

TIP

Press the Tab key to cycle through the numeric fields.

TIP

Even if you've selected an out-of-gamut color while working in CMYK mode, Photoshop won't let you use it. Try picking a hot pink color and close the Color Picker without clicking the gamut alert. Note the hot pink color is your foreground color. Select the paintbrush and begin painting. It isn't hot pink because Photoshop converts the out-of-gamut color to the closest CMYK equivalent.

To find the closest CMYK equivalent, click on the alert triangle. The circular marker jumps to the reproducible color. Note that the CMYK percentages don't change, just the circular marker's position changes.

ACCESSING CUSTOM COLORS

You can access custom color libraries by clicking the Custom button in the Color Picker, which displays a pop-up menu of color matching books. (An explanation of each book can be found at the end of this section.)

Now you try it...

Choosing custom colors

1   Choose PANTONE Coated in the pop-up menu for this exercise. The swatches open and you now can select a color (see Figure 8.3).

Figure 8.3

The PANTONE
Coated Swatch
library.

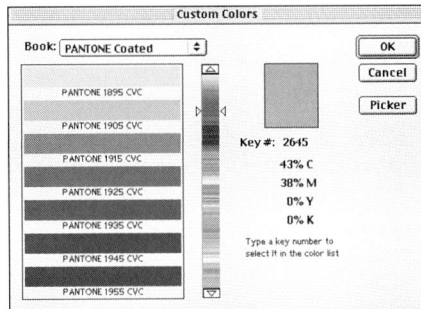

2   You can either click on the vertical slider or use the up and down arrow keys to scroll through the colors, and then click on the swatch you want. If you know the swatch number of the PMS (PANTONE Matching System) color you want to use, enter it, and click OK.

3   Notice your foreground color is now your new PMS color. To add custom colors to your Swatches palette, see page 180.

It's important to note that Photoshop prints custom colors as CMYK equivalent colors in every mode but Duotone, Tritone, and Quadtone unless you use Spot Channels. For more information on Spot Channels, see Chapter 13, "Channels & Masks." For more information on Duotones, Tritones, and Quadtones, see Chapter 5.

- **ANPA Color.** These colors are intended to be printed on newsprint. Contact the Newspaper Association of America to obtain The ANPA-COLOR ROP Newspaper Color Ink Book. 11600 Sunrise Valley Drive, Reston, VA 22091. (703) 648-1367. www.naa.org

- **DIC Color Guide.** A commonly used guide in Japan. To obtain this guide, contact Dainippon Ink and Chemicals, Inc. 3-7-20 Nihonbashi, Chuo-ku, Tokyo 103, Japan. (011) 81-3-3272-4511. www.dic.co.jp

- **Focaltone.** 763 process colors represented that help avoid trapping and registration issues. The guide depicts sample overprint colors. For more information, contact Focaltone International, Ltd., Churchview House, Penkridge, Acton Trussell, Stafford, ST170RJ, United Kingdom. (44) 0785-712667.

- **PANTONE.** Probably the most popular spot color matching system in the U.S. Available options include:

  - **PANTONE Coated.** 1,012 inks intended to print on coated stock.

  - **PANTONE Uncoated.** 1,012 inks intended to print on uncoated stock.

  - **PANTONE Process.** 3,000 CMYK choices.

  - **PANTONE ProSim.** 942 colors represented as the CMYK equivalent. The Prosim book places the solid PANTONE color next to its CMYK equivalent in the color matching guide.

    Acquire PANTONE color matching books by contacting PANTONE, Inc. 590 Commerce Blvd., Carlstadt, NJ 07072. 201-935-5500. www.pantone.com

- **Toyo Color Finder.** The Toyo Color Finder contains 1,050 spot colors and is used widely in Japan. To obtain a swatch book contact Toyo Ink Manufacturing Co., Ltd., 3-13-2-chome Kyobashi, Chuo-ku, Tokyo 104. (011) 81-3-3272-0781

- **Trumatch.** Gaining popularity in the United States, the Trumatch system contains over 2,000 achievable, computer-generated colors. For more information, contact Trumatch, Inc., 25 West 43rd St., 8th floor, New York, NY 10036. (212) 302-9100. www.trumatch.com

TIP

To identify the swatch number without going back into the Color Picker, hold your cursor over the Foreground swatch in the Color palette; the number of the swatch appears in the tab.

NOTE

Choose Short PANTONE names in the General Preferences dialog box before you select your PANTONE colors if you plan to export your Photoshop file to a program that uses only short PANTONE names, such as Adobe Illustrator, Adobe PageMaker, or QuarkXPress.

USING THE SWATCHES PALETTE

The Swatches palette displays a set of easily accessible default colors that you can add to or delete. You can also create and save custom swatch palettes or load a custom palette from the Photoshop Goodies folder. To use the Swatches palette, choose Window > Show Swatches (see Figure 8.4).

Figure 8.4

Create, reset, load, and save custom Swatches in the Palette Options menu.

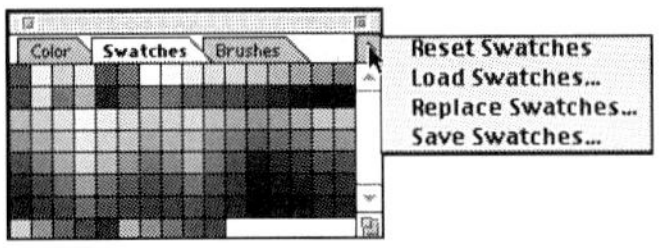

- Place your cursor over a color in the Swatches palette. The cursor turns into an eyedropper.
- Click on a swatch color to activate it as your new foreground color. To activate a swatch as a background color, press Option (Macintosh)/Alt (Windows) while you click.

ADDING COLORS TO THE SWATCHES PALETTE

Choose a color that you want to add to your Swatches palette by either selecting a color with the Color Picker or using the eyedropper tool to sample a color from an image. See page 182 to learn how to use the Eyedropper tool.

Once your new color is selected as your foreground color, you can add it to the palette by clicking an empty area in the Swatches palette. If an empty area isn't visible, scroll down in the palette or click and drag the lower right corner of the palette to reveal the empty area. Your cursor will turn into a Paint Bucket icon enabling you to add the new swatch.

REPLACING AND INSERTING COLORS IN THE SWATCHES PALETTE

To replace an existing color in the Swatches palette with the foreground color, press the Shift key while clicking the swatch.

To insert a new color swatch in a specific location, position your cursor over the swatch where you want the new color to appear and press Option+Shift (Macintosh)/Alt+Shift (Windows), and then click the swatch.

DELETING A SWATCH

You can delete individual swatches by pressing Command (Macintosh)/ Control (Windows) and clicking the swatch. The cursor turns into the scissors icon to warn you that you will delete the swatch when you click.

LOADING SWATCHES

The Goodies folder contains several Swatches palettes that you can load including PANTONE, Toyo, Focaltone, Trumatch, ANPA, System, and Web safe colors. To load a custom swatch palette, click on the black triangle in the upper-right corner of the swatches palette and choose Load Swatches.

SAVING CUSTOM SWATCH PALETTES

If you've spent some time customizing a palette and know that you'll be using it again, it makes sense to save the palette. Click on the black triangle in the upper-right corner of the Swatches palette and choose Save Swatches. Save the file to the Photoshop Goodies folder along with the other custom palettes. You may also want to make a backup file and store it in a location other than your hard drive.

RESETTING AND REPLACING THE SWATCHES PALETTE

You can reset your current Swatches with the Photoshop default palette by clicking the black triangle in the upper-right corner of the Swatches palette and choosing Reset Swatches. If you choose Append in the dialog box, Photoshop will add another set of default color swatches to the existing set of swatches.

Choosing Replace Swatches enables you to replace your current swatches with one of the custom color matching palettes found in the Photoshop Goodies folder or a custom set that you have previously saved.

USING THE COLOR PALETTE

Another way to choose a color is with the Color palette. It displays the color values for the active foreground and background colors from the mode in which you're working. To select a different color mode, click the black triangle in the upper-right corner of the Color palette and choose: RGB, CMYK, Lab, HSB, or Grayscale (see Figure 8.5). The sliders reflect the individual components of each color mode.

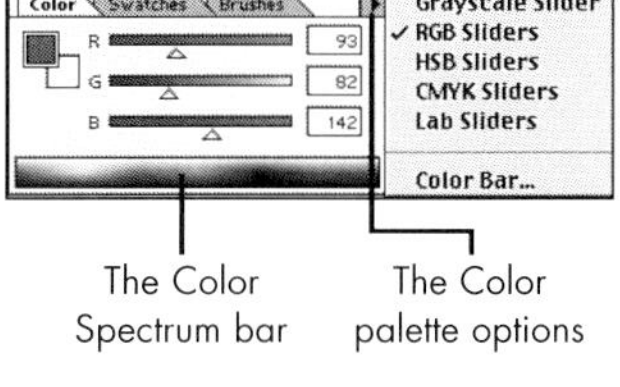

The Color Spectrum bar / The Color palette options

Figure 8.5

The Color palette options include RGB, CMYK, Lab, HSB, and Grayscale.

You can change either the foreground or background color in this palette by clicking either swatch. You'll know when it's the active swatch because it will be surrounded by a white border. Double-clicking on these mini swatches opens the Color Picker.

SELECTING A COLOR

When selecting a color with the sliders, drag toward the color that you want or enter the values in the corresponding fields. You can also click on the color bar at the bottom of the Color palette to select a color.

The color bar at the bottom of the Color palette also reveals the spectrum of the active color mode. However, you can choose a different mode for the color bar by either choosing Color Bar from the Color palette menu or you can Control and click (Macintosh) or right-click (Windows) on the bar to show the options in a context-sensitive menu (see Figure 8.6).

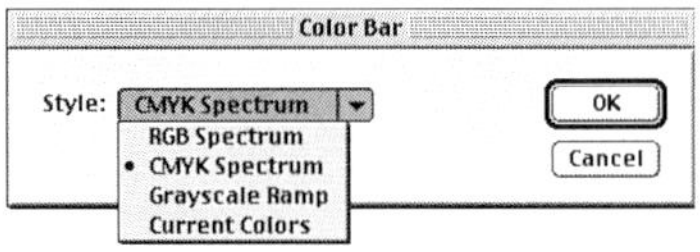

Figure 8.6

The Color Bar spectrum options.

```
                     Color Bar
Style:  [ CMYK Spectrum  ▼ ]           [   OK   ]
          RGB Spectrum
        • CMYK Spectrum                [ Cancel ]
          Grayscale Ramp
          Current Colors
```

THE EYEDROPPER

The eyedropper enables you to sample different colors of an image to create a new foreground or background color based on which pixel on the image you've clicked. Using the eyedropper is a great way to pick up an existing color in an image that you'd like to match for text or other elements.

By default, the eyedropper selects a new foreground color. If you want to change the background color using the eyedropper, hold down Option (Macintosh)/Alt (Windows) and click on the image.

You can sample colors from any open image. Sampling a color in a non-active window won't activate the window when using the eyedropper. The The Info palette also displays the CMYK or RGB color information that makes up the sample color. To access the Info palette, choose Window > Show Info. See Chapter 14, "Color Correction," for more information on using the eyedropper, its related color sampler tool, and the Info palette for use in color correction.

By default, the area you sample with the eyedropper is a single pixel. This option is called the point sample. If you want to sample a larger area, you can choose a 3 × 3 pixel or 5 × 5 pixel area by clicking on the Point Sample pop-up menu in the eyedropper Options palette (see Figure 8.7). If you choose a larger sample size, Photoshop will average the value of the specified number of pixels within the area you click.

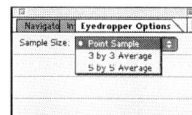

EYEDROPPER	
ICON	
SHORTCUT	
CURSORS	
OPTIONS	

The eyedropper enables you to sample different colors that appear in an image.

TIP

Control+click (Macintosh)/right+click (Windows) on your image to display the sample size choices in a context-sensitive menu.

Figure 8.7

The pop-up menu displays the eyedropper sample size choices in the Eyedropper Options palette.

USING THE PAINTING TOOLS

Now that you know how to select foreground and background colors using the Color Picker, Color palette and Swatches palette, it's time to learn how to put those colors to work using the Photoshop painting tools. In this section, you'll learn how to use and customize brushes to take advantage of the wide variety of options that each painting tool offers.

CURSOR OPTIONS

The paintbrush, airbrush, pencil, and eraser have cursor options that you can specify in Preferences. Choose File > Preferences > Display & Cursors (see Figure 8.8). Of the three choices, Standard, Precise, and Brush Size, the Brush Size option is your best bet for use with the painting tools. The cursor turns into a circle, square, or custom brush shape, which visually represents the pixel diameter of the selected brush in the Brushes palette.

Figure 8.8

The Display & Cursors Preferences dialog box displays options for set- ting your brush cursor.

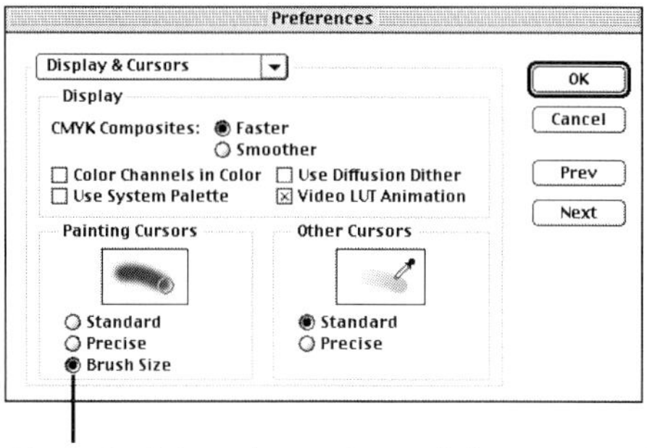

Choose Brush Size when working with the painting tools

TIP

Double-click on a tool to display the tool's Options palette.

THE OPTIONS PALETTE

To take full advantage of all of the options available to the painting tools, it's best to keep the Options palette, the Brushes palette, and either the Swatches palette or Color palette open for easy access.

The paintbrush, airbrush, pencil, and eraser share a few common options; using any of these options with each tool will bring a different result. These options are Color mode (except the eraser), Opacity level (except airbrush, in which case it uses Pressure level), Fade-out rate, and Stylus pressure. Each option is explained in the following paragraphs.

Blending Modes

You have access to a wide variety of blending modes in the Options palette for each of the painting tools (see Figure 8.9). The results achieved with each mode depend on how the colors on the underlying image and the fore- ground color interact. Blending mode options are also available in the Layers palette.

As you read about each blending mode, it might be helpful to experiment with each mode to compare the results. You can create a new document with a white background and select and paint with different colors from the Swatches palette. Double-click on one of the painting tools, such as the paintbrush to access the blending modes. You can also open the file "Color Grid.psd" located in the Chapter 8 lessons folder and follow the lesson at the end of this section.

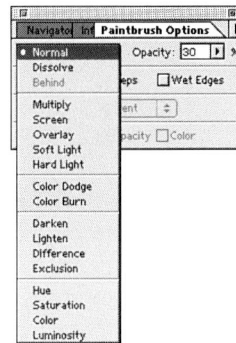

Figure 8.9

The Paintbrush Options palette displaying the blending modes.

- **Normal.**   As the default blending mode, Normal mode replaces the values of the pixels with the foreground color with which you're painting. When working with a bitmap or indexed-color image, the Normal mode is called "Threshold."

- **Dissolve.**   The Dissolve mode paints pixels randomly with the foreground color if used with the airbrush or paintbrush. You can also apply the Dissolve mode to a layer. Results will depend on the opacity setting of the brush in the brush Options palette or the opacity setting in the Layers palette and the underlying Layer.

- **Behind.**   The Behind mode paints only on the transparent areas of a layer. Preserve Transparency must be off for the selected layer for this mode to work.

- **Clear.**   The Clear mode is only available for the line tool, the paint bucket tool, and the Fill and Stroke commands. This mode paints with transparent pixels.

- **Multiply.**   The Multiply mode multiplies the color values of the image or element with the foreground color and creates a darker complimentary color. Multiplying any color with black will produce black. Multiplying any color with white yields no result. Painting over the same area repeatedly will continue to produce a darker color.

- **Screen.**   The Screen mode is the opposite of the Multiply mode. It blends the foreground color with the underlying image or element and will produce a lighter color. Screening with white will produce white. Screening with black yields no result.

- **Overlay.**   Related to the Multiply and Screen modes, the Overlay mode will use either mode depending on what the base color of the image is. It combines the foreground color with the underlying image pixels but preserves the highlight and shadow detail of the image.

- **Soft Light.**   The Soft Light mode darkens or lightens the underlying image based on the how dark or light the foreground color is.

- **Hard Light.**   The Hard Light mode will multiply or screen the underlying image or element based on how dark or light the foreground color is. If the foreground color is lighter than 50% gray, the image is lightened. If the foreground color is darker than 50% gray, the image is darkened.

- **Color Dodge.**   The Color Dodge mode lightens the color of the image pixels to reflect the lightness value based on the color with which you're painting.

- **Color Burn.**   The opposite of Color Dodge is the Color Burn mode; the base colors are darkened depending on the color with which you're painting.

- **Darken.**   The Darken mode darkens the underlying pixels that are lighter than the color with which you're painting. Pixels darker than the color you're painting with remain unchanged.

- **Lighten.**   The opposite of Darken mode, the Lighten mode lightens underlying pixels that are darker than the color with which you're painting. Pixels lighter than the color you're painting with remain unchanged.

- **Difference.**   The result of using the Difference mode depends on whether the underlying pixels or the color you're painting with has a lighter value. Either the color you're painting with is subtracted from the underlying color, or the underlying color is subtracted from the color with which you're painting.

- **Exclusion.**   The Exclusion mode is similar to the Difference mode but creates an effect lower in contrast, thus producing a softer effect. Experiment painting with light and dark colors on top of other colors.

- **Hue.**   The Hue mode replaces only the hue value of the image with the Saturation values of the foreground color. The saturation and luminance values remain unaffected.

- **Saturation.**   The Saturation mode replaces only the saturation value of the image with the color with which you're painting. The hue and luminance values remain unaffected.

- **Color.**   The Color mode preserves the gray levels of the image while replacing the hue and saturation of the underlying image with the hue and saturation values of the color with which you're painting.

- **Luminosity.**   Luminosity represents the brightness of a color. The Luminosity mode changes the luminosity of the underlying image but maintains the hue and saturation.

Now you try it...

Using the Blending Modes

In this lesson, you can experiment with the different blending modes available to the painting tools. You will access the blending modes in the Layers palette. Before you begin, open the file named "Color Grid.psd" in the Chapter 8 lessons folder on the CD.

1   Make sure the Layer palette and Swatches palette are open by choosing Window > Show Layers, and then Window > Show Swatches.

2   Select the Blending Mode Result Layer and select the Move tool in the toolbox.

3   Because the Layer palette displays the default Normal Blending mode, the circle appears opaque on top of the Color Grid image. Experiment changing the Blending mode and moving the circle over different portions of the underlying image to see how that color and Blending mode interacts with the underlying image.

4   Next, choose a new color from the Swatches palette and fill the circle with the new color by choosing Option+delete (Macintosh)/Alt+delete (Windows).

5   Continue experimenting with each Blending mode and filling the circle with lighter and darker colors to compare the results.

TIP

Press Shift+ the plus symbol (+) on your keyboard to select the next Blending mode in the list. Press Shift+ the minus symbol on your keyboard (–) to select the previous Blending mode.

Opacity

Opacity settings range from 1 to 100%. The lower the number, the more transparent the color; the higher the number, the more opaque the color. If you want to paint with an opacity less than 100%, you must specify the opacity setting before you begin painting (see Figure 8.10).

There are several ways to change the opacity setting:

- Enter a number in the percentage box of the Options palette.
- Click on the Opacity triangle to display the drop-down slider.

• Type in a percentage on your keyboard. To enter an opacity value in multiples of ten, enter a number from 0 through 9. For example, type 7 for 70% or 0 for 100%. You can also type in a double-digit number, such as 89, to change the opacity to 89%.

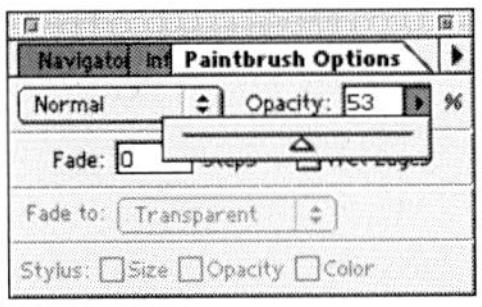

Figure 8.10

Specify an opacity setting by clicking the triangle to access the opacity slider or change the percentage in the Opacity field.

Changing the Paint Fade-Out Rate

To simulate actual painted brush strokes, you can set a paint fade-out rate that starts with the foreground color, and then fades to either transparency or the background color (see Figure 8.11).

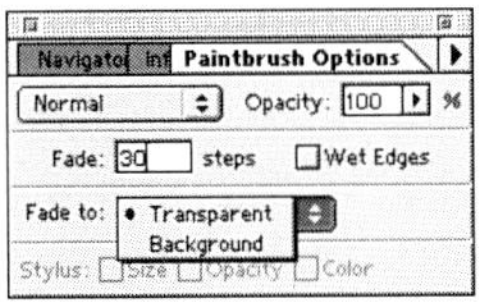

Figure 8.11

Access the fade-out rate for your blend in the paintbrush Options palette.

The number of steps you can enter in the Options palette ranges from 1 to 9999 (see Figure 8.12). (Your canvas would have to be pretty big to see the results of 9,999 steps!) Each step is equal to one click of the mouse, or one mark of the brush tip, but the actual length of the stroke depends on the spacing.

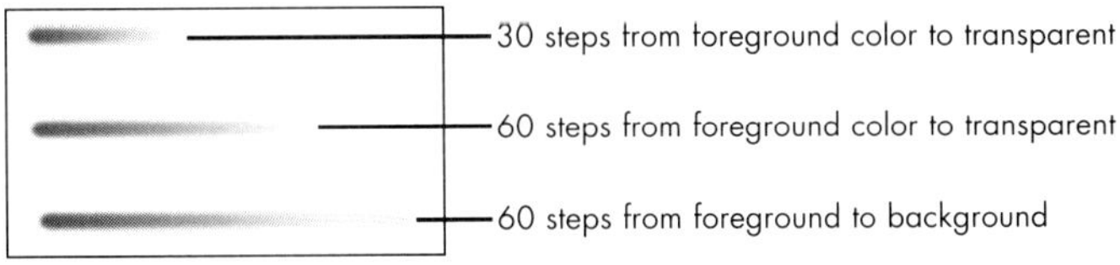

Figure 8.12

The paint fade-out rate can be set from 1 to 9,999 steps.

30 steps from foreground color to transparent

60 steps from foreground color to transparent

60 steps from foreground to background

Using a Pressure-Sensitive Tablet

All of the painting tools can be controlled with the use of a pressure-sensitive stylus in conjunction with the popular Wacom or Calcomp tablets. The Options palette for each painting tool enables you to adjust the pressure by size and opacity of the stylus.

You must have the tablet software installed before you can change any of the related options in the tool's Options palette. See the user manual that accompanies your tablet for the proper installation procedure. Click the corresponding checkboxes if you want to activate the following options:

- **Size.** The brush size increases as the pressure increases.
- **Opacity.** Stylus pressure will affect the opacity of the color that you are painting with. Painting with light pressure on the stylus results in a lower opacity of the color. Painting with heavier pressure on the stylus results in a more opaque color.
- **Color.** Applying light pressure on the stylus results in painting with the background color; applying heavy pressure results in painting with the foreground color. Painting with medium pressure will give you a color somewhere in between the foreground and background colors.
- **Pressure.** To affect the pressure of the stylus, drag the slider to where you want your lowest pressure setting. This becomes your starting point to increase pressure up to 100%. The higher the pressure setting, the stronger the effect.

TIP

To quickly change the settings of opacity, pressure, or exposure for any of the painting or editing tools, type the desired value on your keyboard. Type 1 through 9 to set values in multiples of 10%. You can also type a double-digit number such as 89 to change the opacity to 89%.

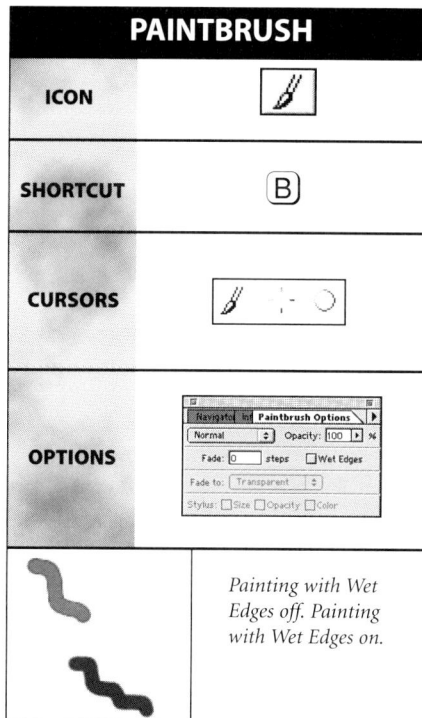

PAINTBRUSH	
ICON	
SHORTCUT	B
CURSORS	
OPTIONS	
	Painting with Wet Edges off. Painting with Wet Edges on.

NOTE

You cannot turn off
anti-aliasing for the
paintbrush tool.

You can create soft strokes with the paintbrush that are more dense than an airbrush stroke. You'll also get varying effects depending on whether you use a soft-edged brush or a hard-edged brush. For example, the Wet Edges option gives your stroke a watercolor effect with edges lighter in color.

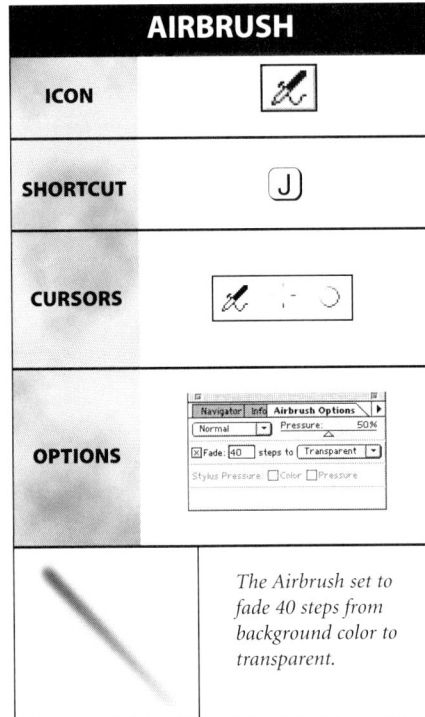

AIRBRUSH

ICON	
SHORTCUT	J
CURSORS	
OPTIONS	

The Airbrush set to fade 40 steps from background color to transparent.

TIP

To paint a straight line
with even pressure,
don't click and drag. Hold
down the Shift key
and click once at your
starting point and once
at your ending point.

The airbrush works a lot like the paintbrush but the edges of the stroke are softer. Because you set the amount of pressure, you can control how light or heavy the color will be. You can build up color on one area of your canvas or image by holding down your mouse button without dragging.

If you're not using a pressure-sensitive tablet, as explained earlier, you can still adjust the pressure settings for the airbrush in the airbrush Options palette.

THE PENCIL

The pencil works like the paintbrush but paints with a hard, non-anti-aliased edge. Even if you choose a soft-edged brush in the Brushes palette, you will still paint with a hard-edged brush. The pencil is a perfect tool for single-pixel editing.

PENCIL	
ICON	✏
SHORTCUT	Ⓝ
CURSORS	✏ · ○
OPTIONS	Navigator | Info | **Pencil Options** | ▶ Normal ▾ Opacity: 100% ☐ Fade: ___ steps to [Transparent ▾] Stylus Pressure: ☐ Size ☐ Color ☐ Opaci... ☐ Auto Erase
	The pencil draws hard-edged bitmapped lines.

You can use the Auto Erase option in the pencil Options palette to paint the background color over areas that are painted with the foreground color. If you paint over areas that don't include the foreground color, you paint with the foreground color in the normal fashion.

THE ERASER

If you are working on the background layer or a layer with the Preserve Transparency option turned on, the eraser enables you to remove pixels in an image and replace them with the current background color. For more information on Layers and the Preserve Transparency option, see Chapter 10, "Layers."

If you select Return to History in the eraser Options palette, you can return the affected area to a saved state or Snapshot in the History palette. For more information on using the History palette, see Chapter 3.

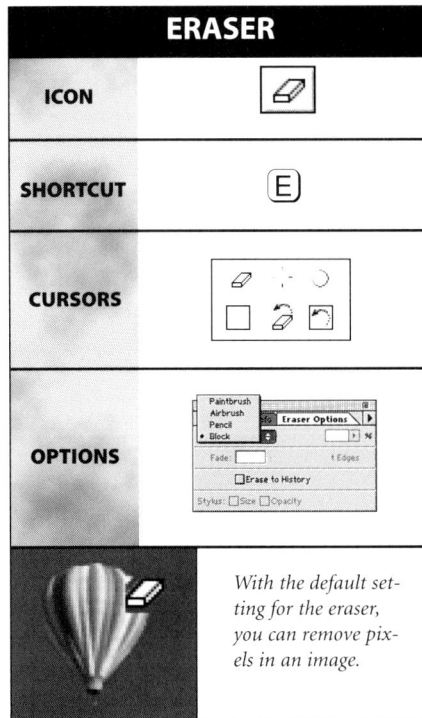

ERASER	
ICON	
SHORTCUT	E
CURSORS	
OPTIONS	

With the default setting for the eraser, you can remove pixels in an image.

There are several way to access the eraser:

- Double-click on the eraser in the toolbox to open the eraser Options palette. You'll notice that you have the same options as many of the other painting tools discussed in this chapter, such as adjusting opacity, fade-out rate, and stylus options.

- The Options palette also lets you choose which type of brush stroke will be applied, including Block, Pencil, Paintbrush, or Airbrush. Experiment painting on a blank canvas with these different options and try adding additional layers to paint and erase.

- The Erase to History option activates the magic eraser letting you restore parts of the image to a previous state. You can temporarily activate this option by pressing Option (Macintosh)/Alt (Windows) as you brush across the image.

THE BRUSHES PALETTE

The default Brushes palette contains a number of round brushes with both hard and soft edges in a variety of sizes (see Figure 8.13). You can modify any brush by double-clicking it, or you can easily create a new brush by choosing New Brush from the palette menu. Photoshop also includes a variety of custom brushes that you can import into the palette from the Goodies folder. You can also create your own custom brushes.

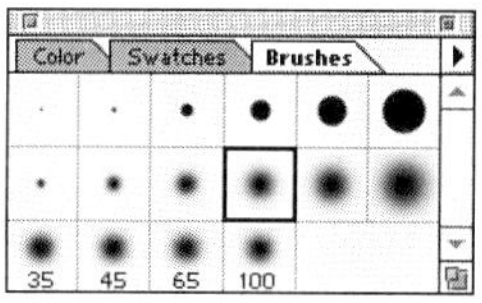

Figure 8.13

Access a variety of brushes via the default Brushes palette.

Specify a Brush in the Brushes Palette

To display the Brushes palette choose Window > Show Brushes. The brushes are displayed as actual size unless a brush is too large to fit on the palette, in which case it appears with a number underneath it indicating the pixel diameter. Select a brush by clicking it.

Creating a New Brush

To create a new brush, choose New Brush from the Brushes palette menu or click on an empty area in the Brushes palette. If the empty area of the palette isn't visible, make the palette bigger by clicking and dragging the lower-right corner of the palette.

The last brush you chose in the Brushes palette displays in the preview box and can be modified to create the new brush.

Setting the Brush Diameter, Hardness, and Spacing

You can set the diameter, hardness, and spacing by dragging the sliders or entering values in the corresponding fields (see Figures 8.14, 8.15, and 8.16).

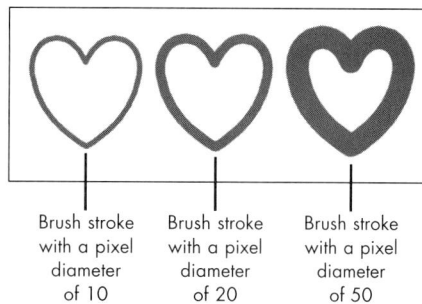

Brush stroke with a pixel diameter of 10

Brush stroke with a pixel diameter of 20

Brush stroke with a pixel diameter of 50

Figure 8.14

The brush diameter defines the thickness of the brush.

Figure 8.15

The brush hardness defines the edge of the brush.

Brush stroke Hardness set at 100%

Brush stroke Hardness set at 50%

Brush stroke Hardness set at 0%

Figure 8.16

The brush spacing controls the distance between the brush marks based on the percentage of the brush size.

Brush Spacing set at 135%

Brush Spacing set at 25%

Brush Spacing set at 100%

- **Roundness and Angle.** You can set the roundness and angle of the brush by entering a value in the corresponding fields. You can also click and drag the arrow on the brush in the preview box on the left to change the angle, or click on the small black circles to change the shape or roundness of the brush (see Figure 8.17).

Figure 8.17

The Brush Options dialog box.

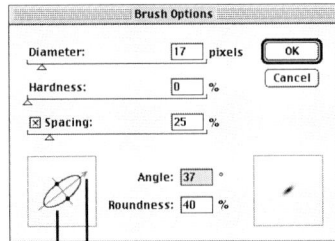

Drag the circle to change the shape of the brush

Drag the arrow line to change the angle of the brush

TIP

In any highlighted field in the Brush Options dialog box, you can use the up and down arrow keys on your keyboard to change the values in one unit increments. Add the Shift key to change the increments by 10 units.

Brushes Palette Options

The following options are available from the Brushes palette menu (see Figure 8.18).

- **Delete Brush.** Make sure the brush you want to delete is the one selected in the Brushes palette and choose Delete from the palette's options menu. You can also press the Command key (Macintosh)/ Control key (Windows) and click on the brush you want to delete. The scissors cursor icon warns you that if you click, you will delete your selection.

- **Reset Brushes.** Choose Reset Brushes if you want to restore the default brushes.
- **Load Brushes.** Add brushes stored in the Goodies folder by choosing Load Brushes. You can also load brushes that you have saved using the Save Brushes option described below.
- **Replace Brushes.** Choose Replace Brushes to replace the current brush set with one stored in the Goodies folder.
- **Save Brushes.** To save a brush set, choose Save Brushes. Windows users need to append an .abr extension to the filename.

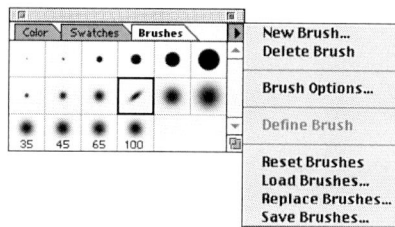

Figure 8.18

The Brushes palette options menu.

Loading and Saving Custom Brushes

Photoshop provides a few sets of custom brushes that you can load into the brushes palette by clicking on the palette triangle and choosing Load Brushes. The Brush sets are located in the Goodies folder, which is located in the Photoshop application folder. You can choose Assorted Brushes, Drop Shadow brushes, or Square brushes.

The custom brushes are added to the brushes palette underneath the default brushes. The palette can hold as many brushes as you like (see Figure 8.19).

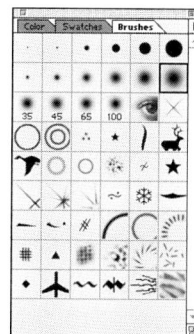

Figure 8.19

Drag the lower right corner of the palette to reveal the added brushes.

You can also create your own custom brushes and save them as a set that you can load when you need them. It's recommended that you make a backup file and store it in a location other than your hard drive in case you need to replace your Preferences file. To learn more about replacing the Preferences file, see Chapter 2, "The Photoshop Work Area."

Creating a Custom Brush

You can create a custom brush by first selecting an area of an image with any of the selection tools, or by copying and pasting an object you've created in Adobe Illustrator or other drawing application. The object must be an active selection before you can define it as a brush (see Figure 8.20).

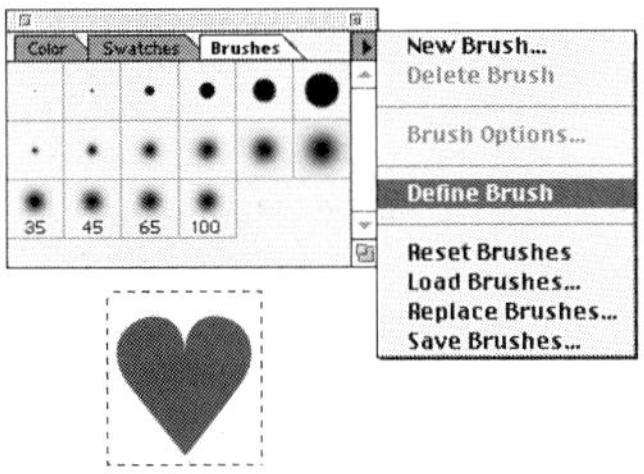

Figure 8.20

Select the area you want to define as a brush and choose Define Brush from the Brushes palette menu.

To create a custom brush:

- Select part of an image. If you select with a rectangular or circular marquee, the selection edges will be the edges of your brush. You can also make a selection with the Magic Wand or any of the Lasso or Pen tools. See Chapter 6, "Selections" for information on the selection tools.
- Click on the black triangle in the upper-right corner of the Brushes palette and choose Define Brush. Your new brush now appears in the Brushes palette. Double-click on the new brush to set the spacing. The Anti-alias option is only available to smaller-sized brushes. However, when creating a brush with one of the painting tools or selecting an area with a marquee, you can check the Anti-aliasing option in the tools' options palette before creating the brush.

NOTE

If you define a brush from a selection of a color image, the brush won't reproduce the color. Instead, it will reproduce as a grayscale image and will paint with the active foreground color.

THE LINE TOOL

The line tool draws straight lines horizontally, vertically, or at any angle. Holding down the Shift key while you draw a line constrains it to a 45° angle. Specify the line weight in the line tool Options palette.

Adding Arrowheads

You can add Arrowheads to one end or both ends of a line as well as specify the length, width, and concavity of the Arrowhead in the Options palette (see Figure 8.21).

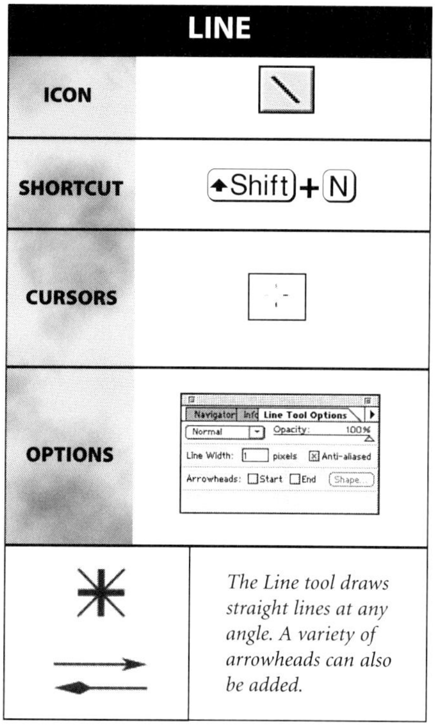

LINE	
ICON	◻
SHORTCUT	⬆Shift + N
CURSORS	⊹
OPTIONS	Navigator Info **Line Tool Options** ▶ / Normal ▾ Opacity: 100% / Line Width: 1 pixels ☒ Anti-aliased / Arrowheads: ☐Start ☐End (Shape...)

✳ ⟶ ⬧⟶	*The Line tool draws straight lines at any angle. A variety of arrowheads can also be added.*

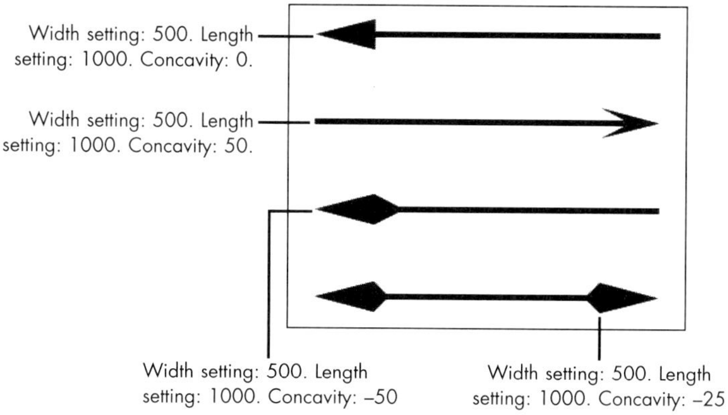

Width setting: 500. Length setting: 1000. Concavity: 0.

Width setting: 500. Length setting: 1000. Concavity: 50.

Width setting: 500. Length setting: 1000. Concavity: –50

Width setting: 500. Length setting: 1000. Concavity: –25

Figure 8.21

By adjusting the width, length, and concavity of an Arrowhead, your Arrowhead choices are many.

Now you try it...

Creating Arrowheads

1 Specify a line weight in the Options palette.

2 Click the Shape button and choose Start, End, or both.

3 Set the width of the Arrowhead by entering a value from **10%** to **1000%**.

4 Set the length of the Arrowhead by entering a value from **10%** to **5000%**.

5 Set the concavity of the Arrowhead by entering a value from **–50%** to **+50%**. The concavity setting defines the amount of curvature on the widest part of the Arrowhead, where the Arrowhead and the line meet.

6 Finally, draw a line. Take a few minutes to experiment with different settings.

THE PAINT BUCKET

PAINT BUCKET	
ICON	
SHORTCUT	K
CURSORS	
OPTIONS	Navigati Paint Bucket Options ▶ / Normal ▾ Opacity: 100% / Tolerance: 32 ☒ Anti-aliased / Contents: Foreground ▾ / ☐ Sample Merged
	Quickly fill image areas with the paint bucket tool.

You can use the paint bucket to quickly fill areas of an image with either the foreground color or a defined pattern without making a selection first and without choosing Fill from the Edit menu. The paint bucket works a lot like the magic wand because you can set a tolerance level to designate which pixels will be filled.

Paint Bucket Options

The Options palette for the paint bucket includes options for setting the opacity and using a blending mode similar to the other painting tools discussed earlier in this chapter. The palette also includes an area where you can set a tolerance level for filling a designated area of an image with a new color or pattern. For more information on defining a pattern, see page 206.

Setting the Tolerance

The Tolerance setting defines how similar in color a pixel must be to be filled with the foreground color or pattern. Tolerance values range from 0 to 255. The lower the tolerance, the smaller the filled area. The higher the tolerance, the larger the filled area.

After you've set the tolerance level, click on the part of the image you want to fill. If you're working in a layered document and don't want to fill transparent areas, click Preserve Transparency in the Layers palette. See Chapter 10 for more information about preserving transparency and layers.

Using the Anti-Alias Option

Click on the Anti-alias option to smooth the edges of the filled area. Choosing this option adds gradated pixels to the edge of the selection.

Choosing the Use All Layers Option

If you're working in a layered document and you want to fill pixels on the visible underlying layers in addition to the active layer with the same foreground color, click the Use All Layers option.

THE GRADIENT TOOLS

The gradient tools enable you to create gradual blends between multiple colors. The gradient tool Options palette offers 15 preset gradients that you can choose from, or you can create your own. In addition to the linear and radial gradients, Photoshop 5.0 sports three new gradient tools: angular, reflected, and diamond.

GRADIENT

ICON	
SHORTCUT	G / ⬆Shift + G
CURSORS	
OPTIONS	

The gradient tool fills a selected area or layer with transitional colors.

- **Linear Gradient.** Creates a blend between two or more colors that runs horizontally, vertically, or at any angle.
- **Radial Gradient.** Creates a blend between two or more colors in a circular pattern radiating from a center point.
- **Angular Gradient.** Creates a blend between two or more colors in a counter-clockwise sweep around a starting point.
- **Reflected Gradient.** Creates a blend between two or more colors using symmetric linear gradients on either side of a starting point.
- **Diamond Gradient.** Creates a blend between two or more colors from the starting point outward in a diamond pattern.

Applying Gradients

You can fill an entire layer with a gradient or apply the gradient to an active selection.

Now you try it...

Applying a gradient

   1   Create a new document, 5" by 5" at 72 dpi, for experimentation.

   2   Double-click on the Gradient tool in the toolbox to open the Options palette. The palette displays 15 preset gradients in a pop-up menu (see Figure 8.22).

Figure 8.22

Photoshop's preset gradient choices.

   3   Select a gradient and click and drag across the document. Experiment dragging the different gradient tools at different angles and lengths.

Similar to the other painting tools discussed in this chapter, the Gradient Options palette lets you adjust the opacity and apply a Blending mode to your gradient. The palette also provides options for the following:

 • Adding a transparency mask (See "Editing the Gradient Transparency" on page 203).

 • Apply dithering for a smoother gradation with less banding.

 • Reversing the order of the colors in the gradation.

Using the Gradient Editor

You can edit the existing gradient styles or create your own using the Gradient Editor. Click the Edit button in the Gradient Options palette. The Gradient Editor dialog box opens and displays choices for creating a new gradient or editing an existing one (see Figure 8.23).

TIP

Add the Shift key while you drag with the gradient tool to constrain the gradient either horizontally, vertically, or at a 45° angle.

TIP

Press Shift+G to toggle through the gradient tools.

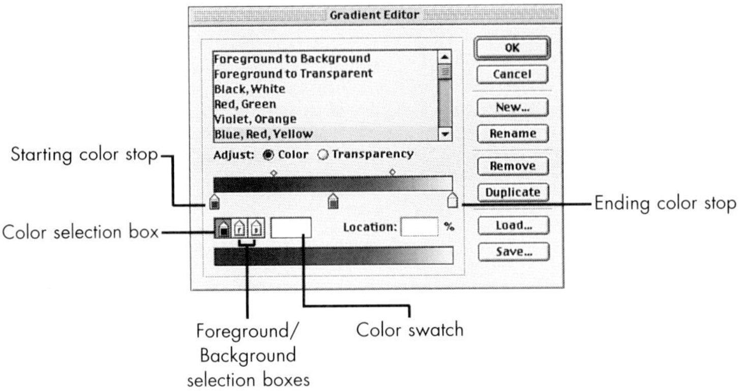

Figure 8.23

Create and edit
gradients in the Gradient
Editor dialog box.

Starting color stop

Color selection box

Foreground/
Background
selection boxes

Color swatch

Ending color stop

Now you try it...

Creating a new gradient

1   Click the New button and give the gradient a name. Make sure the Color button is checked. You can modify an existing gradient by choosing the duplicate button and renaming it.

2   When you click New, only the foreground color displays in the Gradient Bar as both your starting and ending color. Click on the left color stop under the Gradient Bar (it looks like a little house).

3   To select a new color, either double-click the color stop or click the color box below the Gradient Bar. The Color Picker opens, enabling you to specify a new color.

4   You can also click the Foreground and Background buttons to apply the current foreground or background colors in the toolbox.

5   To add other colors to the gradient, choose a location where you want to add a color stop, and click underneath the Gradient Bar. Double-click the new color stop and specify the color.

6   When you click on the Gradient Bar, the eyedropper tool appears, enabling you to set the active color in that location of the gradient.

7   To adjust the length of each of the colors in the gradient, drag the color stop in the direction you want or enter a number in the Location percentage field.

TIP

Press the Tab key to
cycle through the color
stops and Diamond
midpoint buttons.

8 To adjust the location of the midpoint, drag the diamond above the Gradient Bar or enter a value in the locations settings box.

9 To remove a color, drag the color stop down and off the Gradient Bar or press the Delete key (Macintosh), Backspace key (Windows).

10 Click OK to add your new gradient to the list.

Editing the Gradient Transparency

Editing the transparency mask of the gradient enables you to adjust the opacity of the colors that make up the gradient (see Figure 8.24). By default, the transparency mask is off which means it's set at 100% opacity.

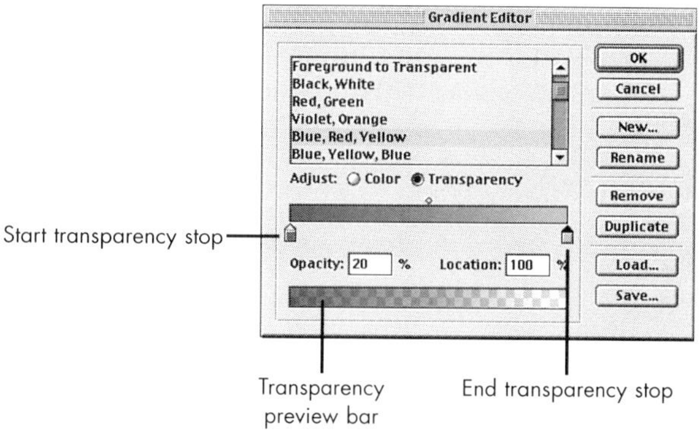

Figure 8.24

Adjust the transparency of a gradient by clicking on the Transparency button.

Start transparency stop

Transparency preview bar

End transparency stop

Now you try it...

Editing the gradient transparency mask

1 Select a gradient and click the Duplicate button. Give the gradient a new name.

2 Next, click the Transparency button and the actual mask is displayed. Black represents an opacity of 100%. White represents an opacity 0%; and gray represents opacity anywhere between 0 and 100%.

continues

> **3** Change the opacity of the left color stop to 50%. The Gradient Bar at the bottom displays the new opacity setting. Experiment with different opacities on the right color stop.
>
> **4** To adjust the midpoint of the opacity, drag the diamond above the bar to the left or right or enter a value in the locations settings box.
>
> **5** To add an intermediate opacity to the mask, click under the bar to define a new transparency stop.
>
> **6** To delete a transparency stop, click and drag it down and off the Transparency Gradient Bar or press the Delete key (Macintosh)/Backspace key (Windows).

Loading, Saving, and Deleting Gradients

You can save and load sets of custom gradients as well as delete existing gradients from the list by clicking the Edit button in the Gradient Options palette to access the Gradient Editor dialog box. The following options appear:

- **Remove.**   Select the gradient in the list that you want to delete and click the Remove button.

- **Load.**   Click the Load button to add gradients that you have previously saved.

- **Save.**   To save your custom gradients, Shift+click (if you want to save more than one) of the gradients in the list and click the Save button.

To reset the gradient list back to the default list, click the black triangle in the upper-right corner of the gradient Options palette and choose Reset.

FILL AND STROKE COMMANDS

There are several quick and easy ways to fill a selection or layer with either the foreground or background color. The key commands listed below are some of the most valuable in helping you save time.

Filling a Selection or Layer

With an active selection or layer, choose Edit > Fill. Several options appear in the Fill dialog box including Foreground, Background, White, Black, or 50% Gray (see Figure 8.25).

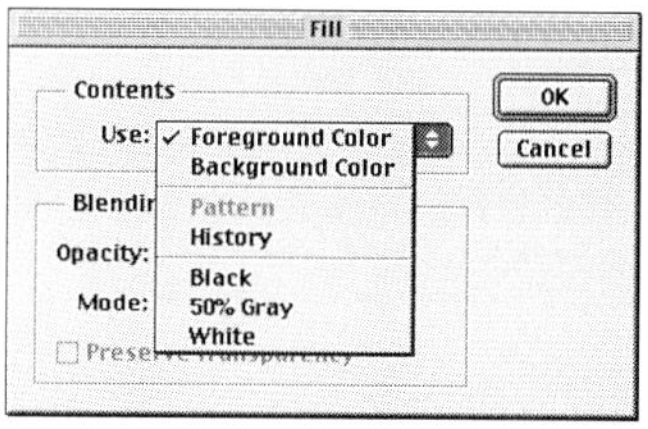

Figure 8.25

The Fill dialog box displays content options in a pop-up menu.

You can also choose Pattern, which fills the selection or layer with the most recently defined pattern. The pattern option isn't available unless you have previously defined a pattern. You'll learn how to define patterns later in this chapter.

You can choose History as an option, which restores the selection or layer to a previous state or snapshot. For more information on History, see Chapter 3.

If you want to fill just an element on a layer, make sure Preserve Transparency is checked in the either the Layers palette or the Fill dialog box. This option doesn't require an active selection around the element on the layer.

Now you try it...

Using key commands to fill and stroke

1   To fill an active selection or layer with the foreground color, press Option+Delete (Macintosh)/Alt+Backspace (Windows).

2   To fill an active selection or layer with the background color press Command+Delete (Macintosh)/Ctrl+Backspace (Windows).

3   To fill an object on a layer with the foreground color while preserving the transparency of the layer, press Option+Shift +Delete (Macintosh)/Alt+Shift+Backspace (Windows).

4   To fill an object on a layer with the background color while preserving the transparency of the layer, press Command+ Shift+Delete (Macintosh)/Ctrl+Shift+Backspace (Windows).

5   To display the Fill menu options, press Shift+Delete (Macintosh)/Shift+Backspace (Windows). This is handy when you want to fill an object with a pattern, white or black, 50% gray or history, or if you want to change the opacity or blending mode.

Stroking a Selection, Object, or Layer

To stroke an active selection, choose Stroke from the Edit menu and in the resulting Stroke dialog box, choose a width for the stroke from 1 to 16 pixels (see Figures 8.26, 8.27, and 8.28). You can also specify the location of the stroke by choosing inside, outside, or directly over the object. Opacity and Blending mode options are also available in the Stroke dialog box. To stroke an element on a layer without a selection, make sure Preserve Transparency is not checked in the Stroke dialog box.

Figure 8.26

The Stroke dialog box.

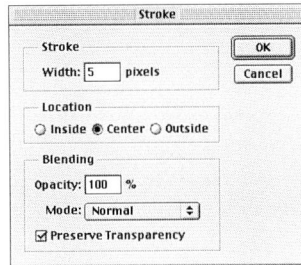

Figure 8.27

The star with no stroke applied.

Figure 8.28

The star with a stroke applied.

CREATING A PATTERN

In Photoshop, you can define a pattern from any part of an image. Only one pattern can be used to fill an area at a time, because each time you define a new pattern, it replaces the previous one. The defined pattern will fill a selection in tiles when you choose Edit > Fill > Pattern.

TIP

To select the area to be defined as a pattern from the center, press the Option key and click and drag.

1. Make a selection with the rectangular marquee tool around part of an image that you want to define as a pattern and choose Define Pattern from the Edit menu (see Figure 8.29).

2. Next, make a new selection somewhere else on the canvas or open a new image and choose Edit > Fill > Pattern. Click OK to view the results (see Figure 8.30).

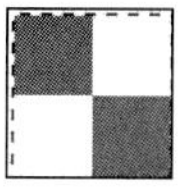

Figure 8.29

Define a pattern by using the rectangular marquee tool.

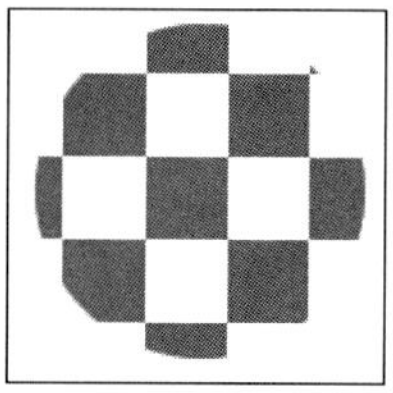

Figure 8.30

An elliptical selection filled with a pattern.

SUMMARY

Photoshop provides a variety of painting tools, each with its own settings and color mode options to help you create your image. In this chapter, you learned how to select colors with the Swatches palette, the Color Picker, and Color palette, work with brushes, use the paintbrush, airbrush, pencil, line tool, eraser, gradient tool, paint bucket, and eyedropper.

TIP

One way around using only one pattern at a time is to create a document that contains the pattern art as individual swatches on the canvas. When you want to use one of the patterns, simply make a selection around that pattern and choose Define Pattern from the Edit menu.

REVIEW QUESTIONS

1. What are the steps to paint a straight line?

    a. Press the Shift key while dragging.

    b. Press the Option key while dragging.

    c. Press the Control key while dragging.

    d. You can't draw a straight line with the painting tools.

2. How do you access custom colors?

    a. Choose Import from the File menu.

    b. Choose Open Colors from the File menu.

    c. Click the Custom button in the Color Picker.

    d. Double-click on a swatch in the Swatches palette.

3. What is displayed in the Color Field when the Hue button is selected in the Color Picker?

    a. Saturation on both axes

    b. Brightness on both axes

    c. Saturation on the vertical axis

    d. Saturation on the horizontal axis

4. How do you define a pattern?

    a. Choose Define Pattern from the File menu.

    b. Choose Define Pattern from the Edit menu.

    c. Add the pattern to the pattern list by clicking on the Add button in the Patterns palette.

    d. Control+click/right+click on the pattern, and choose Define Pattern from the context-sensitive menu.

5. How do you apply a stroke to a layer element?

    a. Choose Stroke from the Select menu and enter an amount in the Stroke field.

    b. Choose Stroke from the Layer menu and enter an amount in the Stroke field.

    c. Control+click/right+click on the selection, and choose Stroke from the context-sensitive menu.

    d. Press Command+Shift+Delete (Macintosh) or Control+Shift+Delete (Windows) to stroke with the background color.

6. How do you activate the eyedropper tool while using the painting
    tools?

    a. Press the Shift key.

    b. Press the Alt/Option key.

    c. Press Command (Macintosh) or Control (Windows).

    d. Press Command+Option (Macintosh) or Control+Alt (Windows).

7. How do you add a color to the Swatches palette?

    a. Choose New Color in the Swatches Options palette.

    b. Drag the foreground color swatch into the Swatches palette.

    c. Choose Add foreground color in the Swatches Options palette.

    d. Click an empty area in the Swatches palette to add the foreground
        color.

8. What is the function of the Clear?

    a. To delete a layer in an image

    b. To delete any active selection

    c. To remove pixels in an image using the Paintbrush or Airbrush

    d. To make pixels transparent using the paint bucket, line tool, and Fill
        and Stroke commands

9. What is the function of the Screen mode?

    a. Set the linescreen for the image.

    b. Change the opacity of an image or selection.

    c. Blend the foreground color with the underlying image to produce a
        darker color.

    d. Blend the foreground color with the underlying image to produce a
        lighter color.

10. How do you delete a swatch from the Swatches palette?

    a. Alt/Option+click on the swatch.

    b. Press the Delete key.

    c. Command+click (Macintosh) or Control+click (Windows) on the
        swatch.

    d. Choose Reload Swatches from the Swatches palette menu, and then
        delete the color.

CHAPTER 9

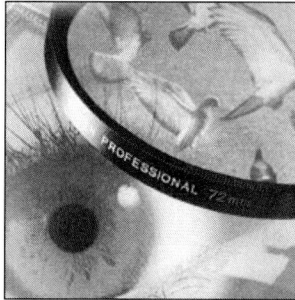

EDITING & RETOUCHING

The most notable strengths of Photoshop have always been its image editing and retouching capabilities. With Photoshop 5.0, there is even greater flexibility when editing and experimenting with images because of Photoshop's new history brush and History palette (see Chapter 3, "The History Palette," for more information). In this chapter, you will learn how to use the numerous tools that are available to edit an image. These tools include the transformation commands, rubber stamp and pattern stamp, history brush, toning tools (dodge burn and sponge), focus tools (blur and sharpen), smudge tool, plus a few filters that can really make a difference when editing an image.

Domains & Objectives

Painting and Editing

6.2   Identify issues regarding the characteristics, function, limitations, and appropriate use of the editing and retouching tools, functions and commands, including the transformation commands, rubber stamp tool, pattern stamp tool, history brush, smudge tool, blur and sharpen tools, burn, dodge and sponge tools, and purge command.

USING THE TRANSFORMATION COMMANDS

The Photoshop transformation commands enable you to resize, rotate, skew, distort, flip, and add perspective to an image, layer, path, or selection. You can also transform alpha channels and layer masks.

When executing a transformation command, it's important to note that pixels are added and deleted using a mathematical calculation called interpolation. It's best to keep transformations to a minimum or apply multiple transformations simultaneously to maintain image quality. Every time you apply a transformation, the image quality is degraded because of interpolation. The default interpolation method is bicubic, which is slower than the other interpolation options but provides far better results (see Chapter 1, "General Information," for more information on interpolation settings).

The transformation commands described in the following sections are now available in the Edit menu, not in the Layer menu as in previous versions of Photoshop.

THE SCALE COMMAND

By choosing Edit > Transform > Scale and dragging either a corner or side handle, an object can be scaled in the direction you wish (see Figure 9.1). If you press the Shift key while you drag, the object scales proportionately. You can also press the Alt (Windows)/Option (Macintosh) key to scale from the center.

A transformation can be applied to your image or selection by either pressing the Enter/Return key or double-clicking on the image. If you decide you don't want to apply the command, press the Escape key or Control (Windows)/Command (Macintosh)+. [period], or select a different tool in the toolbox.

NOTE

When transforming the background layer of an image, turn it into a regular layer by double-clicking and then naming it. However, an element on the background layer can be transformed first by selecting the element. Also, the transformation commands are not available to 16-bit images.

TIP

To see the numeric transformation information as you use the scale, rotate, or skew commands, display the Info palette by choosing Window > Show Info or press the F8 key if you have an extended keyboard.

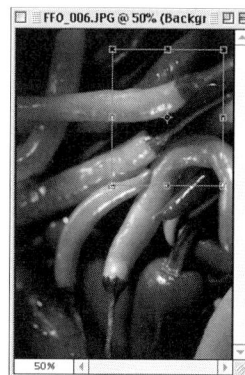

Figure 9.1

Scale an element proportionately by dragging a corner handle while pressing the Shift key.

THE ROTATE COMMAND

Rotating an active selection or layer can be achieved by choosing Edit > Transform > Rotate and clicking on either a corner or side handle (see Figure 9.2). The cursor displays curved arrows. Click and drag in the direction you wish. If you press the Shift key while dragging, the object can be rotated in 15-degree increments. The center axis point also can be repositioned by clicking and dragging it.

To apply the rotation to your image, either press the Enter/Return key or double-click on the image. If you decide you don't want to apply the command, press the Escape key or Control (Windows)/Command (Macintosh)+. [period], or select a different tool in the toolbox.

You can also rotate a layer or selection by choosing Edit > Transform > Rotate 180°, 90° CW (clockwise), or 90° CCW (counter clockwise), or choose Flip Horizontal or Flip Vertical in the same menu.

Figure 9.2

The rotate command enables you to rotate an element 360 degrees.

THE SKEW COMMAND

To use the Skew command, choose Edit > Transform > Skew. The corner handle of the bounding box can be moved up, down, left, or right. When dragging a side handle, the closest two corner points also move. Dragging the middle handle located at the top or bottom of the bounding box skews the element left and right. If you press Alt (Windows)/Option (Macintosh) while dragging a corner handle, the handle on the opposite corner moves in the opposite direction. For example, if you Alt (Windows)/Option (Macintosh)+drag down on the lower-right corner handle, the upper-left corner handle moves up (see Figure 9.3).

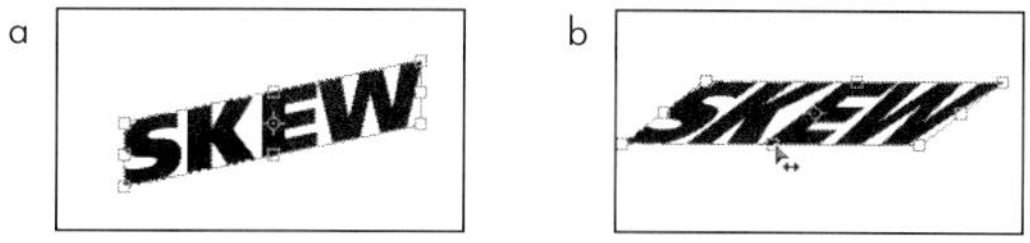

a b

Figure 9.3

a. Skew an element by dragging a corner handle.

b. Skew an element by pressing the Alt (Windows)/Option (Macintosh) key while dragging a middle handle.

THE DISTORT COMMAND

The Distort command is similar to both skew and perspective, but you have more control over the direction of the handles when dragging and can achieve both the skew and perspective effect depending on which handle you drag. Also, by pressing Alt (Windows)/Option (Macintosh) as you drag on a side point, you can rotate an element around its axis point. To distort a layer or selection, choose Edit > Transform > Distort (see Figure 9.4).

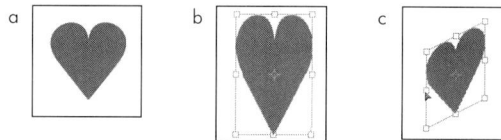

a b c

Figure 9.4

a. An element with no distortion applied.

b. An element vertically scaled with the Distort command.

c. An element distorted by dragging a side handle.

THE PERSPECTIVE COMMAND

Use the Perspective command to make one side of the element shorter or longer without affecting the opposite side by dragging a corner handle (see Figure 9.5). Dragging a side handle gives you the same result as dragging a side handle using the Skew command. To use the Perspective command, choose Edit > Transform > Perspective.

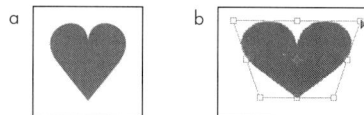

a b

Figure 9.5

a. An element with no perspective applied.

b. Perspective added by dragging a corner handle.

THE TRANSFORMATION COMMAND

The Numeric Transform command gives you precise control over the position, size, rotation, and degree of skew of an active selection or layer. You can perform any combination of these transformations while in the Numeric Transform dialog box; however, it might be difficult to anticipate the results because this command does not offer a preview. One benefit of using Numeric Transform is that you can perform all the transformations to an image or element at once rather than after each transformation, lessening the degradation that interpolation causes. To use the Numeric Transform

command, choose Edit > Transform > Numeric. The Numeric Transform
dialog box displays four transformation options (see Figure 9.6):

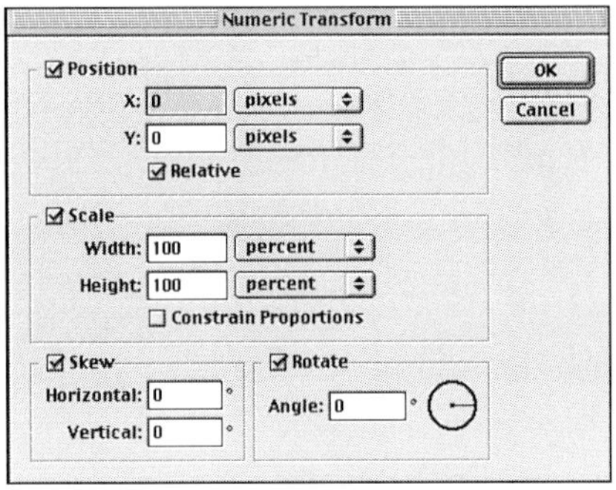

Figure 9.6

Use the Numeric
Transform command to
simultaneously position,
scale, skew, or rotate a
layer or selection.

- **Position.**   In the Position fields, X (horizontal distance) and Y (vertical
  distance), enter a number in either pixels, inches, centimeters, points, or
  picas to reposition an element. To move an element horizontally or vertically, relative to its current position, check the Relative box; otherwise,
  the movement is relative to the top-left corner of the image (The x and
  y coordinates are from the zero point on the rulers).

- **Scale.**   Enter the percentage that you'd like to use to scale the selection
  or layer. If you check the Constrain Proportions box, you can scale an
  element proportionately, and you need only enter an amount in either
  the Height X or Width Y field.

- **Skew.**   You can skew a selection or layer element at a horizontal or vertical slant from –89.9 degrees to 89.9 degrees. Entering a negative number skews the element outward and increases its size. Entering a positive
  number skews the element inward and decreases its size.

- **Rotate.**   To rotate a selection, you can either enter a value between
  –360 degrees and 360 degrees for the angle in the Rotate field or click
  and drag on the line in the circle and drag.

TIP

You can transform just
the selection border and
not the contents of the
selection by choosing
Select > Transform
Selection and then choos-
ing Edit > Transform
Numeric or by clicking
and dragging on
the handles.

THE FREE TRANSFORM COMMAND

Using the Free Transform command enables you to actively scale, rotate,
and skew an element all at the same time. If used in conjunction with the
Info palette, you can apply these transformations by the numbers as you can
with Numeric Transform.

Press Control (Windows)/Command (Macintosh)+T or choose Edit > Free
Transform to display the Free Transform bounding box around an active
selection or layer.

To scale an element, drag either a side or corner handle. Press Shift while you drag a corner handle to scale an element proportionately. Press Control (Windows)/Command (Macintosh) while dragging on a handle to scale an element from its center.

To rotate an element, you must position the cursor between the side and corner points or outside the selection box. The cursor will display curved arrows. Click and drag in the direction you wish. To rotate in 15-degree increments, press the Shift key while you drag.

To distort an element, press Alt (Windows)/Option (Macintosh) while dragging a handle.

Apply the transformation to your image, by either pressing the Enter/Return key or double-clicking on the image. If you decide you don't want to apply the command, press the Escape key, press Control (Windows)/Command (Macintosh) +. (period), or select a different tool in the toolbox. When using the Free Transform command, use the shortcuts in the table below for scaling, rotating, and distorting.

Best Free Transform Command Shortcuts

Command	Mac OS
Free Transform	Command+T
Scale proportionately	Shift+drag handle
Rotate 15-degree increments	Shift+drag outside bounding box
Scale or reflect from center	Option+drag handle
Distort	Command+drag handle
Create perspective	Command+Option+Shift+drag handle
Transform again	Command+Shift+T
Transform with duplicate	Command+Option+T
Transform Again with duplicate	Command+Option+Shift+T
Apply transformation	Return or Enter or double-click on element
Cancel transformation	Escape or Command+. [period]

Command	Windows
Free Transform	Control+T
Scale proportionately	Shift+drag handle
Rotate 15-degree increments	Shift+drag outside bounding box
Scale or reflect from center	Alt+drag handle
Distort	Control+drag handle
Create perspective	Control+Option+Shift+drag handle
Transform again	Control+Shift+T
Transform with duplicate	Control+Alt+T
Transform Again with duplicate	Control+Alt+Shift+T
Apply transformation	Return or Enter or double-click on element
Cancel transformation	Escape or Control+. [period]

TIP

All the transform commands are available in the Edit menu even when you're actively transforming an element. You can also Control/right+click to display all the transformation options in a context-sensitive menu.

CURSOR OPTIONS

The rubber stamp, pattern stamp, history brush, smudge tool, and focus and toning tools have cursor options that you can specify in Preferences. Choose File > Preferences > Display and Cursors. Of the three choices in the Preferences dialog box (see Figure 9.7), Standard, Precise, and Brush Size, the Brush Size or Precise option works best when using the retouching and editing tools.

Figure 9.7

The Display & Cursors dialog box displays options for setting your brush cursor.

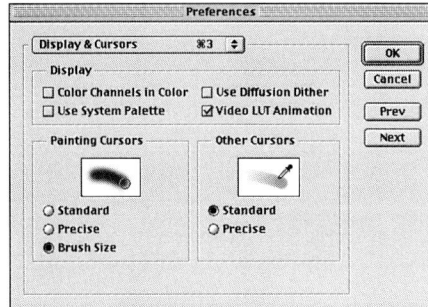

THE OPTIONS PALETTE

To take full advantage of all of the options available to the editing and retouching tools, it's best to keep open the Options palette and the Brushes palette.

Many of the editing and retouching tools share the same options as the painting tools, such as opacity setting, stylus settings, and blending modes. For more detailed information on these options, see Chapter 8, "Painting."

USING THE RUBBER STAMP AND PATTERN STAMP TOOLS

The rubber stamp and the pattern stamp tools are both used to duplicate pixel information. In addition to the blending modes, opacity, and stylus choices in the Options palette, the rubber stamp and pattern stamp tools also have options such as Aligned and Use All Layers.

When you select the Aligned option in the Options palette, the crosshair where you sample travels at the same distance and in alignment with your brush regardless of how often you click and lift up the mouse button or stylus.

If you deselect the Aligned option, the tool remembers your initial sample and crosshair position; it will paint with the same area every time you click and lift up the mouse button or stylus regardless of how near or far away your brush is from the sampled area.

When the Use All Layers box option is checked in the Options palette, you can sample data from all visible layers. If the box is left unchecked, the tool samples only from the active layer.

THE RUBBER STAMP TOOL

RUBBER STAMP	
ICON	
SHORTCUT	S
CURSORS	
OPTIONS	
	The rubber stamp enables you to clone portions of an image on to other areas of the same image.

The rubber stamp tool is used for duplicating or cloning one area of an image over another area of an image or different image. Achieving professional results, however, takes practice and technique development. Cloning is a two-step process:

1. Sample the area you want to clone by pressing Alt (Windows)/Option (Macintosh) and clicking on the area with the rubber stamp tool.

2. Release the mouse button and then the Alt (Windows)/Option (Macintosh) key, and reposition the rubber stamp in the area where you want to clone the sample. As you click and drag, a crosshair is displayed over the sampled area, showing you precisely which pixels you're cloning.

TIP

To avoid obvious patterns when retouching, sample different areas often and use single clicks when painting rather than clicking and dragging.

Now you try it...

Retouching an old photograph

1   Before you begin, delete the Adobe Photoshop Preferences file to restore the program's default settings. Open the files `FamFinal.psd` and `Family.psd` located in the Chapter 9 lessons folder on the CD (see Figure 9.8). You will use the `FamFinal.psd` file as a reference as you learn to use the rubber stamp tool and the Dust & Scratches filter.

Figure 9.8

a. The image before cloning with the rubber stamp tool.

b. The image after cloning.

a

b

Resize the reference image to **50%** and click the Zoom box in the upper-right corner of the image window to reduce the size of the window for that image.

2   To retouch the tape at the top of the image, select the rubber stamp tool and zoom in to **200%**. Select the brush that is third from the right in the middle row of the Brushes palette.

3   Next, take a sample of an area nearby the tape by pressing the Alt (Windows)/Option (Macintosh) key and click. (The rubber stamp displays a white triangle when sampling.) Release the mouse button and then the Alt (Windows)/Option (Macintosh) key and move your cursor over the tape area and click. Note there is a crosshair where you are picking up pixels from the sampled area.

4   Continue to resample new areas nearby the tape to achieve realistic results.

5   You can use the Dust & Scratches filter to easily remove the small black dots that are in the foreground of the image. Make a tight selection around one of the black dots using the lasso tool and choose Filter > Noise > Dust & Scratches (see Figure 9.9). The filter blurs and blends the pixels together inside the selection.

TIP

Rather than clicking and dragging over the tape area to be cloned, you will receive better results if you repeatedly click in different areas. This method enables you to avoid a pattern.

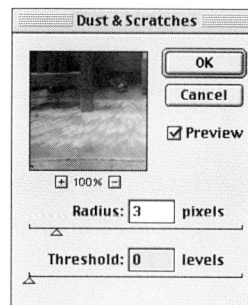

Figure 9.9

Remove defects in a scanned image using the Dust & Scratches filter.

To more clearly see the effect of this filter and to make sure that not too much blur is added, hide the edges of the selection by pressing Control (Windows)/Command (Macintosh)+H. Just don't forget to either turn the edges of the selection back on by again pressing Control (Windows)/Command (Macintosh) +H or deselecting after clicking OK in the filter dialog box. To deselect, press Control (Windows)/Command (Macintosh)+D.

6   To practice further, clone the tape at the bottom of the image as well as other areas in the image that are flawed.

THE PATTERN STAMP TOOL

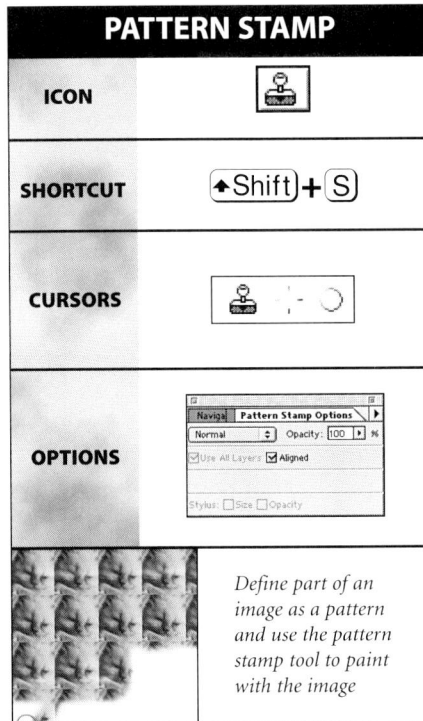

PATTERN STAMP	
ICON	[stamp icon]
SHORTCUT	⬆Shift + S
CURSORS	[cursor icons]
OPTIONS	[Pattern Stamp Options palette]
[pattern of kittens]	*Define part of an image as a pattern and use the pattern stamp tool to paint with the image*

Use the pattern stamp tool to paint or fill a selection with a tiled pattern. To paint a tiled pattern with the pattern stamp tool, first define part of an image as a pattern. By default, the Aligned box is checked in the pattern stamp tool Options palette, which enables you to paint the pattern in an aligned fashion. If you uncheck the Aligned box, the pattern starts over each time you lift up the mouse button and start painting again.

Now you try it...

Creating a tiled pattern with the pattern stamp tool

1   Open the file Iris.psd, located in the Chapter 9 lessons folder on the CD.

2   Select the rectangular marquee tool and make a selection around the kitten's face (see Figure 9.10). To originate the

selection from the center, press Alt (Windows)/Option (Macintosh) as you drag; to constrain the selection to a perfect square, also press the Shift key while dragging.

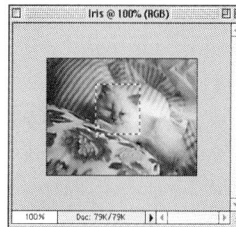

Figure 9.10

To define a pattern, select an area of an image with the rectangular marquee tool and choose Define Pattern from the Edit menu.

3 Choose Edit > Define Pattern.

4 Next, create a new document by choosing File > New. Enter **5** inches for both the height and width, select RGB for the image mode, set background to white, and enter **72** ppi for the resolution; click OK.

5 Select the pattern stamp tool and paint on the new document background (see Figure 9.11). Experiment with different brush sizes, opacity, and mode settings in the pattern stamp Options palette. Experiment painting with the Aligned option unchecked. You can also experiment painting inside a selection with the pattern stamp tool.

Figure 9.11

Painting an area with the pattern stamp tool.

USING THE HISTORY BRUSH

A new tool introduced in Photoshop 5.0, the history brush enables you to selectively paint a copy of one state or snapshot of an image in the active image window. It's a great tool to use if you've cloned areas of an image that you didn't intend to clone with the rubber stamp tool, because you can use the history brush to paint those areas back into your image.

THE HISTORY BRUSH

HISTORY BRUSH

ICON	
SHORTCUT	Y
CURSORS	
OPTIONS	

Use the history brush to selectively paint the contents of a previous state or snapshot.

The action of the history brush is the same as using the eraser with the Erase to History option checked in the eraser Options palette. When using the eraser with this option checked, the state of the eraser in the history palette is named "magic eraser" to denote the difference between it and the regular eraser in the toolbox.

In the history brush Options palette, you can also adjust the opacity and blending mode as well as select the impressionist effect, which will paint with an impressionistic copy of the source state or snapshot.

For more information about using the history palette and snapshots, see Chapter 3.

Now you try it...

Using the history brush

1   Before you begin, delete the Adobe Photoshop Preferences file to restore the program's default settings. Open the files `Orange Flower.psd` and `Orange Flower Final.psd`, located in the Chapter 9 lessons folder on the CD. You will use the `Orange Flower Final.psd` file as a reference as you learn how to clone the flower with the rubber stamp tool, resize it, and flip it horizontally for a more realistic effect. You'll also clean up the edges of the duplicate flower using the history brush and applying a Gaussian Blur to make the flower appear to be in the background of the image (see Figure 9.12).

Figure 9.12

a. The image before adding the flower to the upper-right corner.

b. The image after adding the flower.

2   Choose the second brush from the right in the top row of the Brushes palette. Select the rubber stamp tool and make sure the Aligned option is checked in the rubber stamp Options palette. Sample the center of the flower by pressing Alt (Windows)/Option (Macintosh)+click. (Click the mouse button before releasing the Alt (Windows)/Option (Macintosh) key.)

3   Next, create a new layer in the Layers palette and begin cloning the flower onto the new layer. Watch the crosshair as you paint. It's often easier to first outline the object you are cloning and then clone the inside area with a larger brush (see Figure 9.13).

continues

Figure 9.13

With the rubber stamp tool, outline the edges of the object you're cloning first.

4   Select the move tool and reposition the duplicate flower in the upper-right corner of the image.

5   For a more realistic effect, choose Edit > Free Transform or Control (Windows)/Command (Macintosh)+T and scale the flower down in size by pressing the Shift key and dragging. Next, choose Edit > Transform > Flip Horizontal.

6   If you cloned background areas around the flower by mistake, zoom in on the duplicate flower and select the history brush. Paint around the edges of the flower to bring back those areas of the background layer.

7   To make the flower appear as if it's in the background, choose Filter > Gaussian Blur. Set the Radius to approximately **1.9** and click OK.

USING THE FOCUS TOOLS

The focus tools include the blur and sharpen tools and enable you to either blur or sharpen particular areas of an image by painting with a brush. Both tools have pressure settings and blending mode options in their Options palettes.

THE BLUR TOOL

You can use the blur tool to make subtle corrections in areas where an image might have too much contrast or when an area of an image appears oversharpened. The blur tool is also useful when blending images together for a smoother transition.

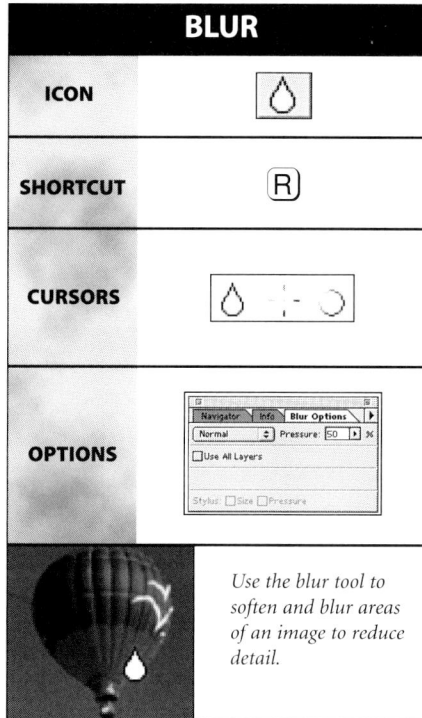

BLUR	
ICON	△
SHORTCUT	R
CURSORS	△ ⋅ ◡
OPTIONS	*Navigator* *Info* *Blur Options* ▶ Normal ▾ Pressure: 50 ▸ % ☐ Use All Layers Stylus: ☐ Size ☐ Pressure

Use the blur tool to soften and blur areas of an image to reduce detail.

THE SHARPEN TOOL

The opposite of the blur tool, the sharpen tool increases contrast in the area where you paint and can help bring slightly blurry areas of an image into focus.

THE SMUDGE TOOL

The smudge tool works as if you're smearing paint with your finger. By default, if you click and drag with your mouse over an area of an image, the color you first clicked on will be used. If you check the Finger Painting box in the Smudge tool Options palette, the tool will smudge with the foreground color.

TIP

To toggle the Finger Painting option on and off while using the smudge tool, press Alt (Windows)/Option (Macintosh) as you click and drag.

SHARPEN

ICON	
SHORTCUT	⇧Shift + R
CURSORS	
OPTIONS	

Use the sharpen tool to increase focus and clarity of an area in an image.

SMUDGE

ICON	
SHORTCUT	⇧Shift + R
CURSORS	
OPTIONS	

Click and drag the smudge tool to simulate dragging your finger through wet paint.

USING THE TONING TOOLS

The toning tools include the dodge and burn tools and enable you to lighten or darken areas of an image. Simulating traditional darkroom techniques that photographers use, both tools aid in enhancing detail in an image by affecting exposure in the highlights, midtones, and shadows.

THE DODGE TOOL

Traditionally, when dodging, a photographer withholds or blocks out light with either his or her hand or a piece of cardboard to lighten a specific area on a print. The dodge tool in Photoshop can be effective in lightening shadow areas in an image that lacks detail or can even be used to whiten a person's teeth.

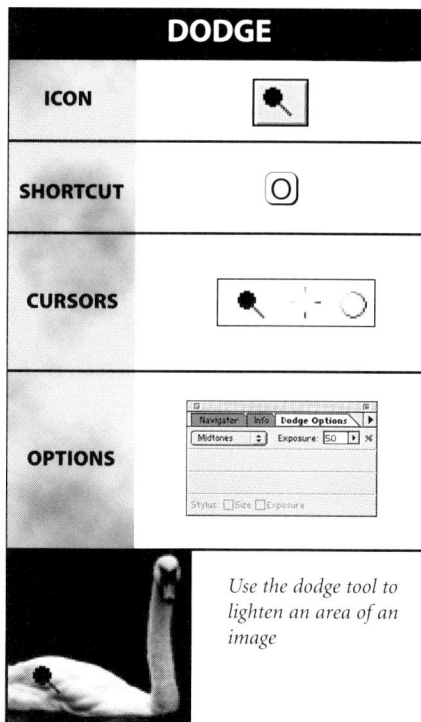

Use the dodge tool to lighten an area of an image

THE BURN TOOL

Traditionally, when burning, a photographer increases exposure with either his or her hand formed as a circle or a piece of cardboard that has a hole punched through it to darken areas on a print. In Photoshop, burning can be effective in adding detail to blown out highlights and darkening shadow tones.

With either the dodge or burn tool, it's important to use the Options palette to set the tool to work with highlights, midtones, or shadows as well as adjust the exposure setting depending on the area of the image you want to affect. The size and edge of the brush you choose in the Brushes palette is also an important factor in achieving the effect you want.

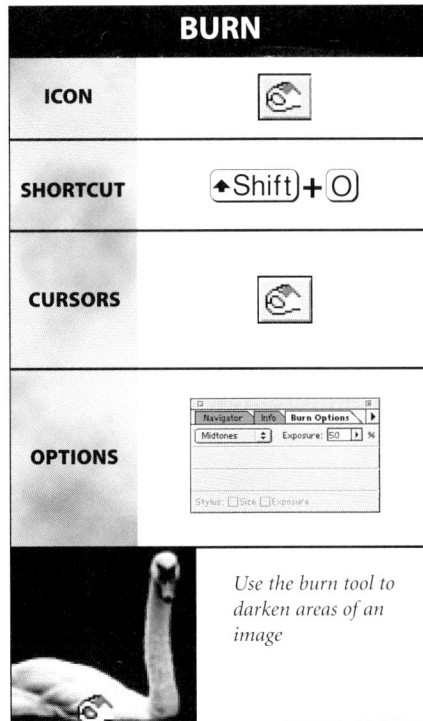

BURN

ICON	[burn tool icon]
SHORTCUT	⬆Shift + O
CURSORS	[burn cursor icon]
OPTIONS	Navigator / Info / **Burn Options** ▸ Midtones ⬍ Exposure: 50 ▸ % Stylus: ☐Size ☐Exposure

Use the burn tool to darken areas of an image

THE SPONGE TOOL

You can use the sponge tool to saturate or desaturate areas of an image. When saturating a portion of an image, the sponge tool should be used in conjunction with the Gamut Warning command to make sure that the image isn't oversaturated, which results in colors that cannot be printed. For more information on the Gamut Warning command, see Chapter 14, "Color Correction."

You can also use the sponge tool to desaturate areas of a color image to create a combination of both color and grayscale within the same image for an interesting effect. If you use the sponge tool on a grayscale image, you increase or decrease contrast by adjusting gray levels away from or toward the middle gray tones in an image.

SPONGE	
ICON	🔲
SHORTCUT	⬆Shift + O
CURSORS	🔲
OPTIONS	*(Sponge Options panel: Navigator / Info / Sponge Options; Desaturate, Pressure: 50%; Stylus: Size Pressure)*
	Use the sponge tool to saturate or desaturate areas of an image

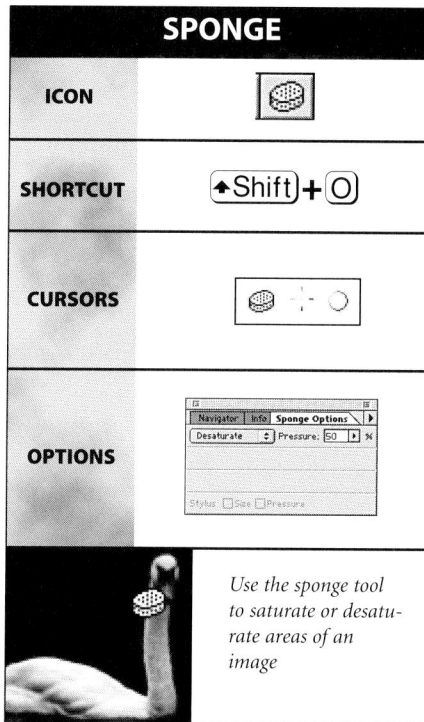

USING FILTERS WHEN EDITING AND RETOUCHING AN IMAGE

Although there are a variety of blur, sharpen, and noise filters that you can use when working with images in Photoshop, only a few give you the necessary control over settings to help restore or improve an image when editing and retouching. The most useful include the Gaussian Blur, Unsharp Mask, and the various Noise filters. Following is an overview of how you can use these filters effectively when editing and retouching an image. For more information on other Photoshop filters, see Chapter 12, "Filters."

THE GAUSSIAN BLUR FILTER

When editing an image, the Gaussian Blur filter is effective on areas that need to be put slightly out of focus. The benefit of using the Gaussian Blur filter over the Blur and Blur More filters is that not only do you have a preview of the effect, but you can also adjust the amount of blur that you apply. See the lesson on page 334 in this chapter to learn how to use the Gaussian Blur filter to alter the focus of an image.

THE NOISE FILTERS

Photoshop's Noise filters include Add Noise, Despeckle, Dust & Scratches, and Median. All can be used to correct poorly scanned images or defective originals.

Noise

You can use the Add Noise filter to add grain to an image, thus creating a mezzotint effect. Noise can also be used on individual channels to reduce banding in gradient blends. For more information on the Add Noise settings, see Chapter 12.

Despeckle

The Despeckle filter removes noise in an image by blurring everything but the edges of a selection or the edges of high-contrast areas. You can use the Despeckle filter on an individual channel such as the Blue channel, which has a reputation of picking up the most noise when an image is scanned, or to help eliminate a moiré pattern in a previously printed grayscale image. Follow the Despeckle filter with the Unsharp Mask filter to sharpen the image if the Despeckle filter applied too much blur.

Dust & Scratches Filter

The Dust & Scratches filter can be helpful in eliminating spots, hairs, and blemishes on an image that might have been caused by either dirty glass on the scanner bed or on an original that might have defects caused by age or mishandling.

To use this filter effectively, make a tight selection around the spot or scratch and choose Filter > Noise > Dust & Scratches. Depending on the contrast between the offending mark and the background, results will vary with how you set both the Radius and Threshold settings. If you don't get the results you expect, you can always use the rubber stamp tool.

Median

Like the Despeckle filter, the Median filter removes noise and can help eliminate a moiré pattern if you've scanned a previously printed color image. It also can be useful in cleaning up a bitmap image destined for line art. A setting between one and three pixels is usually sufficient.

USING THE SHARPEN FILTERS

Nearly every image that is scanned—whether on an expensive high-end drum scanner or on a low-end flatbed—will need some amount of

TIP

Use Control (Windows)/Command (Macintosh)+H to hide the edges of your selection as you adjust the radius and threshold settings to better see the filter work. Just don't forget to deselect after applying the filter. To deselect, press Control (Windows)/Command (Macintosh)+D.

sharpening due to either an out-of-focus original or blurring that occurs during the scanning process. In addition, you will receive far better quality if you sharpen an image after any color correction work or resampling.

Although there are four sharpening filters listed under Sharpen in the Filter menu, your best bet is to use the Unsharp Mask filter, because not only do you have a preview in the Unsharp Mask dialog box, but you also have control over the amount, radius, and threshold settings.

Unsharp Mask

Unsharp masking, also known as USM, is the preferred method by professionals for sharpening a scanned image. You might think the name is a bit contradictory, but it makes sense when you understand that USM applies a slightly blurry version of the image with the original image. The blurred image is then subtracted from the original and is essentially used as a mask to determine the edge pixels of contrasting areas on the original image. When the two versions are combined, the result is a higher contrast image with more detail.

In the Unsharp Mask Preview dialog box, you can control the amount, radius, and threshold:

- **Amount.**   The Amount setting, from 1% to 500%, determines how much contrast is added to the image. Because Photoshop is comparing edge pixels for contrasting areas, the farther you drag the slider to the right, the more pronounced the edges of tonal contrast will be. For high-resolution images, an amount between 150% and 200% is recommended, but the setting will depend on the contrast and tonality of your image.

- **Radius.**   The Radius setting, from 0.1 to 250 pixels, determines the number of pixels surrounding the edge pixels that will be affected. A setting between 1 and 2 is recommended on high-resolution images. Again, the setting will depend on the contrast and tonality of your image.

- **Threshold.**   The Threshold can be set from 0 to 255. The default threshold setting of 0 sharpens all pixels in the image with no regard to tonality and contrast. As you move the slider to the right, you exclude more gray values in the shadows. The higher the setting, the more pixels are excluded from sharpening. That's why when you start dragging the threshold slider to the right, the image appears to blur; but this just reflects a lack of sharpening, which in effect is taking you back to the original version of the image.

TIP

By first converting to Lab mode, you can sharpen an image without affecting the color by applying the Unsharp Mask filter to only the Lightness channel.

It's important to get the threshold setting right so you can retain smooth gradations in low-contrast areas while avoiding noise or artifacting due to oversharpening. A Threshold setting from 2 to 10 is recommended but will depend on the tonality and contrast of the image.

Now you try it…

Using the Unsharp Mask filter

1   Open the image Andy.psd in the Chapter 9 lessons folder on the CD.

2   Convert the image to Lab mode by choosing Image > Mode > Lab. Select the Lightness channel in the Channels palette.

3   Choose Filter > Sharpen > Unsharp Mask to open the Unsharp Mask dialog box. Make sure the Preview button is checked (see Figure 9.15).

Figure 9.15

Use the Unsharp Mask filter to sharpen and add detail to a soft image.

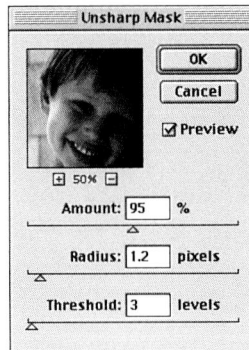

4   Experiment with the settings to understand how each affects the image. Click on and off the Preview button to compare the before and after versions of the image. Next, adjust the Radius setting to **1.2**, the amount to **95**, and the Threshold to **3**; click OK.

5   Notice that part of Andy's hair has been oversharpened. This can be fixed by using the blur tool. In the blur tool Options palette, set the pressure to approximately **30**. Select the blur tool and choose the brush on the far right in the middle row in the Brushes palette. Brush over the portion of his hair that is slightly oversharpened.

SUMMARY

Mastering the editing and retouching tools takes practice, patience, and time devoted to experimentation. Learning how to combine the use of these tools to achieve convincing and professional results will help prepare you to become an Adobe Certified Expert and ultimately set you apart as one.

NOTE

Applying the correct amount of sharpening on a high-resolution image can be tricky, because the image onscreen appears sharper than it will actually be when printed. Experimentation with your service provider is recommended.

REVIEW QUESTIONS

1. How do you sample an area of an image using the rubber stamp tool?

    a. Click on the area you want to sample and drag.

    b. Shift+click to select multiple sample pixels.

    c. Option (Macintosh) or Alt (Windows)+click on the area.

    d. Command (Macintosh) or Control (Windows)+click on the area.

2. You use the dodge tool when editing an image to achieve what result?

    a. Darken areas of an image

    b. Delete pixels in an image

    c. Lighten areas of an image

    d. Saturate areas of an image

3. Which filter is commonly applied to channels to reduce banding in a gradient blend?

    a. Noise

    b. Diffuse

    c. Displace

    d. Unsharp Mask

4. How do you rotate a layer or selection?

    a. Choose Rotate from the Select menu.

    b. Click and drag with the rotate tool.

    c. Choose Edit > Transform > Free Transform.

    d. Press Control/Command and drag with the move tool.

5. How do you add perspective to an element using the Free Transform command?

    a. Click on a side handle.

    b. Press Option/Alt+Shift and drag on a side handle.

    c. Shift+click and drag from the center of the bounding box.

    d. Press Command+Option+Shift (Macintosh) or Control+Alt+Shift (Windows) and drag on a side or corner handle.

6. Which is one way you cannot cancel a transformation?

    a. Press the Escape key.

    b. Select a different tool.

    c. Press Control/Command+D.

    d. Press Control/Command+. (period).

7. What happens when you drag the Threshold slider to the right in the Unsharp Mask dialog box?

    a. The amount of sharpening increases.

    b. The amount of sharpening decreases.

    c. The number of pixels surrounding the edge pixels increases.

    d. The number of pixels surrounding the edge pixels decreases.

8. The action of the history brush is the same as using what other tool?

    a. The eraser.

    b. No other tool works like the history brush.

    c. The eraser with the Magic Eraser option checked in the eraser Options palette.

    d. The eraser with the Erase to History option checked in the eraser Options palette.

9. Which tool desaturates areas of an image?

    a. The burn tool

    b. The dodge tool

    c. The sponge tool

    d. Any painting tool that has a Saturation slider in its Options palette

10. How do you change the size of a layer or selection?

    a. Choose Edit > Transform > Scale.

    b. Choose Scale from the Select menu.

    c. Select the scale tool and click and drag the corner points.

    d. Enter the new percentage in the scale tool Options palette.

CHAPTER 10

LAYERS

Every file or image opened in Photoshop contains one or more layers. When you scan an image into Photoshop, it is automatically placed on a layer named *Background* and is displayed in the Layers palette. When you create a new document, it contains a default blank background layer; or you can choose to create it with a transparent background, in which case it would be named *Layer 1*, rather than *Background*. A Photoshop image can have a maximum of 100 layers, including the background layer and adjustment layers.

Domains & Objectives

Using Layers

7.1   Identify issues regarding the characteristics, function, limitations, and appropriate use of layers and layer options including creating, viewing, moving, editing, re-ordering, grouping, merging, adjusting opacity, and the Arrange and Align commands.

7.2   Identify features and define steps in the process of creating a layer mask, creating a clipping group, using adjustment layers, and using layer effects.

7.3   Identify issues regarding the characteristics, function and appropriate use of the blending modes, including Dissolve, Behind, Clear, Multiply, Screen, Overlay, Soft Light, Hard Light, Color Dodge, Color Burn, Darken, Lighten, Difference, Exclusion, Hue, Saturation, Color and Luminosity.

7.4   Determine the appropriate feature, command, tool, or procedure to accomplish a stated task related to layers.

THE LAYERS PALETTE

Each new layer you create is placed above the active layer in the Layers palette and displays a thumbnail icon that depicts the contents of the layer (see Figure 10.1).

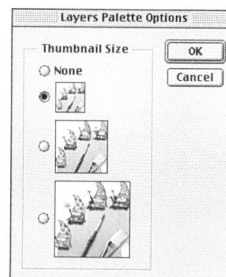

Figure 10.1

The Layers palette displays each layer in an image as a thumbnail.

To display the Layers palette, choose Window > Show Layers. The Layers palette enables you to manage the layers in your document. You can create new layers, delete or merge layers, show or hide layers, and apply special effects to individual layers.

To activate a layer, click on the layer name in the Layers palette. The paintbrush icon is displayed, which indicates that you can edit the layer. The name of the layer is also displayed to the right of the filename in the image window's title bar.

VIEWING A LAYERED DOCUMENT

You can choose to show or hide a layer by clicking the eye icon in the Layers palette (refer to Figure 10.1).

To change the display of the layer thumbnails, choose Palette Options from the Layers palette menu. In the Layers Palette Options dialog box, click a preferred size or click None to turn off the layer thumbnail, and then click OK (see Figure 10.2).

TIP

Right/Control+click in the image window to display a context-sensitive menu to choose a different layer.

Figure 10.2

The size of the thumbnail that displays in the Layers palette can be changed using these options.

By default, layer transparency is displayed as a gray-and-white checker-board. If the checkerboard interferes with the display of your image, you can display transparency as white by choosing None, or you can change the color and size of the checkerboard. To change the way layer transparency is displayed, choose File > Preferences > Transparency & Gamut (see Figure 10.3).

Figure 10.3

You can change how Layer transparency is displayed in the Transparency & Gamut Preferences dialog box.

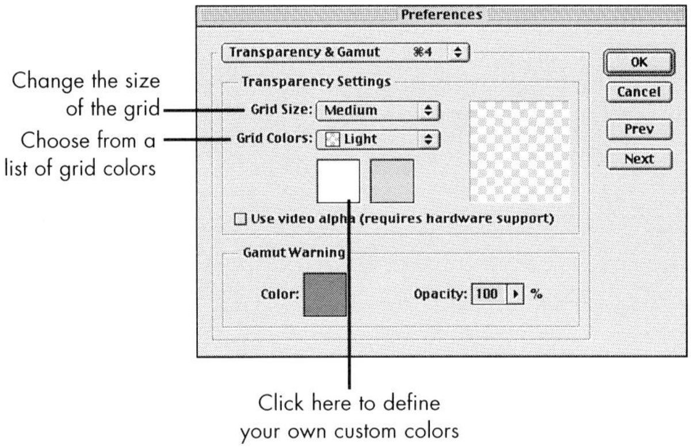

Change the size of the grid

Choose from a list of grid colors

Click here to define your own custom colors

TIP

Alt/Option+click the New Layer icon at the bottom of the Layers palette to display the New Layer dialog box, and then name the layer.

CREATING A NEW LAYER

To create a new layer, you can choose New Layer from either the Layers palette menu (see Figure 10.4) or the Layer pulldown menu. You can also click the New Layer button at the bottom of the Layers palette (see Figure 10.4). If you choose the latter option, double-click the layer to name it.

Figure 10.4

The Layers palette menu accessed by clicking the black triangle.

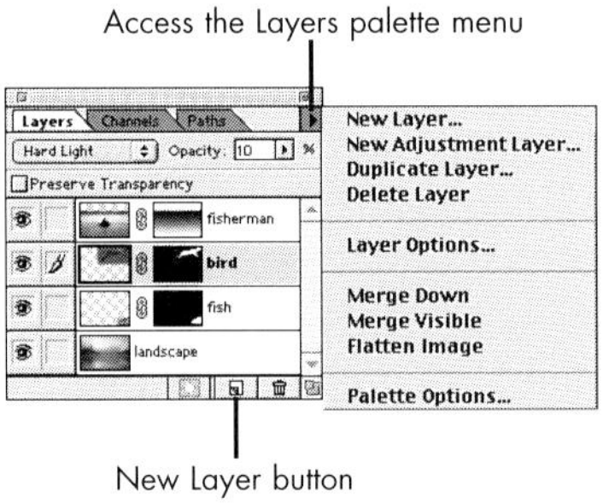

Access the Layers palette menu

New Layer button

REORDERING LAYERS

There are several ways to change the stacking order of layers in an image. The stacking order determines the placement of a layer either behind or in front of the other layers in the image. To reorder a layer, do one of the following:

- Select the layer you want to move in the Layers palette, and then drag the layer either above or below another layer. When the black line is displayed above or below the layer you're moving, release the mouse button (see Figure 10.5).

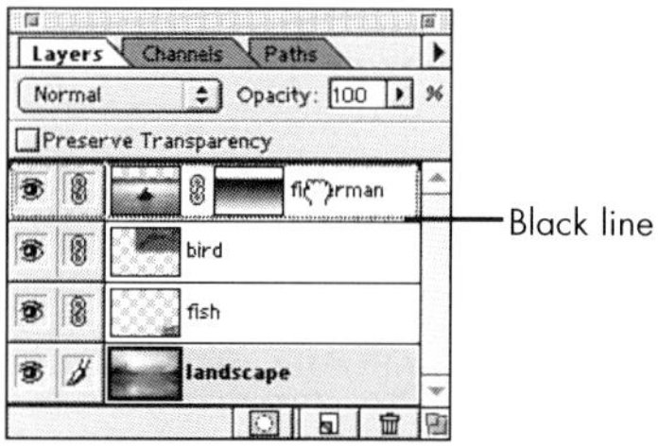

Black line

Figure 10.5

Click and drag a layer to reposition it above or below another layer. When the black line is displayed, release the mouse button.

- Select the layer you want to move in the Layers palette, and choose Layer > Arrange (see Figure 10.6). Your options in the Arrange menu include the following:

  - **Bring to Front**, which places the layer as the topmost layer in the image
  - **Bring Forward**, which moves the selected layer one level up in the stacking order
  - **Send Backward**, which moves the selected layer one level down in the stacking order
  - **Send to Back**, which makes the selected layer the bottommost layer

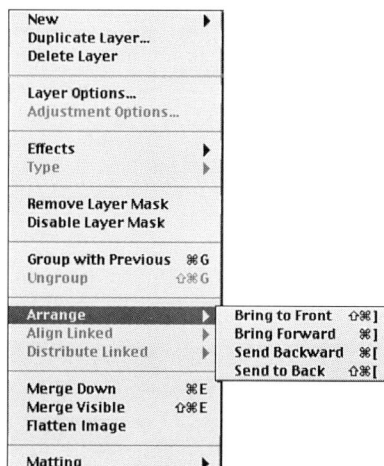

Figure 10.6

Use the Arrange submenu to reorder layers in your image.

- To move a selected layer one level up in the stacking order, press Control (Windows)/Command (Macintosh)+]; to move one level down, press Control (Windows)/Command (Macintosh)+[. Adding the Shift key moves the layer to the topmost or bottommost level (but above the background layer) in the Layers palette.

LINKING LAYERS

You can move and transform elements on multiple layers simultaneously by linking. Linking one or more layers to another can be accomplished by clicking the column to the left of the layer thumbnail that you want to link to the selected layer. The link icon appears in the column identifying that layer as a linked layer (see Figure 10.7).

To unlink a layer, click the link icon in the Layers palette.

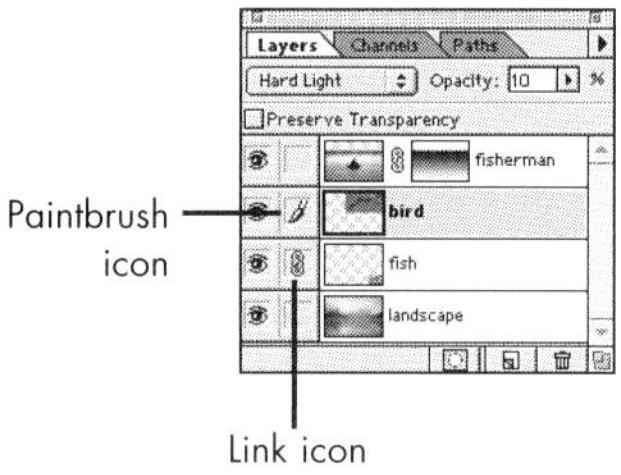

Figure 10.7

Two layers that are linked. One layer is active as designated by the paintbrush icon; the other layer displays the link icon.

Paintbrush icon

Link icon

DUPLICATING A LAYER

You can duplicate any layer—including the background layer—within the same image, as well as duplicate a layer to another image. When duplicating layers between two images, the size of the image or element on the duplicate layer will depend on the resolution of the destination image. For example, if the source image has a lower resolution than that of the destination image, the source image will appear smaller in the destination image and also when printed. It's best to first make sure both the source and destination image have the same resolution by choosing Image Size from the Image menu. For more information on resolution and image size, see page 77, Chapter 4, "Scanning & Working with Images."

To duplicate a layer within the same image, do one of the following:

1. Select the layer you want to duplicate and choose Duplicate Layer in the Layers palette menu. Name the layer, and then click OK.

2. Drag the layer you want to duplicate on top of the New Layer button at the bottom of the Layers palette. Double-click the duplicate layer to rename it, and then click OK.

To duplicate a layer between different images, do one of the following:

- Open both the source image and destination image and select the layer you want to duplicate in the Layers palette. Drag the Layer on top of the destination image.
- Select the layer you want to duplicate. Select the move tool; then click and drag the source image into the destination image window. The layer is displayed on top of the active layer in the destination image.
- Select the layer you want to duplicate, choose Duplicate layer from the Layers palette menu, and specify the destination document from the destination pop-up menu (see Figure 10.8). The destination document must be open for it to show up in the menu. You can also choose New from the same pop-up menu, and Photoshop creates a new image window with the same dimensions, resolution, and color mode as the source image.

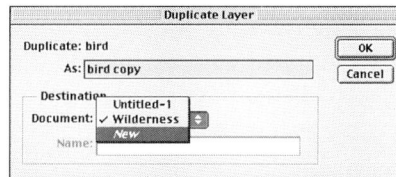

Figure 10.8

Select the destination document in the Duplicate Layer dialog box.

- Select the layer you want to duplicate and choose Select > All or Control/Command+A. Copy the source image to the clipboard by choosing Edit > Copy (Control/Command+C) and paste the duplicate layer into a new file or destination image that is open by choosing Edit > Paste (Control/Command +V).

USING THE LAYER VIA COPY AND LAYER VIA CUT COMMANDS

You can turn an active selection and copy it to a new layer by using the Layer Via Copy command, or you can cut the selection from one layer and paste it into a new layer by using the Layer Via Copy command.

To turn a selection into a new layer, follow these steps:

- Make a selection and choose New from the Layer pulldown menu.
- Choose Layer Via Copy to duplicate the selection and its contents into a new layer. The duplicate selection will be displayed in the exact same location on the new layer as the original layer.

TIP

Press the Shift key as you drag the layer to the destination image to place it in the same position it had in the source image. This works only if both images have the same pixel dimensions. If not, it will be centered in the destination image.

TIP

Press Control (Windows)/ Command (Macintosh)+J to quickly use the Layer Via Copy command.

TIP

Press Control (Windows)/
Command (Macintosh)+
Shift+J to quickly use the
Layer Via Cut command.

TIP

To temporarily activate
the move tool while using
a another tool, press
Control/Command.

TIP

To nudge an element in
1-pixel increments, use the
arrow keys on the your
keyboard. Add the Shift
key to nudge in 10-pixel
increments. The move tool
must be activated by
either selecting it in the
toolbox or by pressing
Control (Windows)/
Command (Macintosh) for
the arrow keys to work.

To cut and paste a selection into a new layer, follow these steps:

- Make a selection and choose New from the Layer pulldown menu.
- Choose Layer Via Cut. The selection is displayed on the new layer in the exact same location it had in the original layer. The original layer is now empty.

REPOSITIONING LAYER CONTENTS

You can reposition the contents of individual layers and linked layers using the move tool or the Align and Distribute commands.

To move a layer element with the move tool, select the layer you want to move. Select the move tool, and click and drag the element into the desired position. To constrain the movement to a multiple of 45°, press the Shift key as you drag the element.

ALIGNING AND DISTRIBUTING LAYER CONTENTS

You can reposition elements of both single and linked layers by using the Align and Distribute commands. You can also use an active selection to align multiple elements that are on different layers.

With the Align Linked commands, you can align the elements on linked layers to the element on the active layer or to a selection border. The Distribute Linked commands enable you to position the contents of linked layers at evenly spaced intervals. To align or distribute multiple linked layers, link the layer and choose Layer > Align Linked or Layer > Distribute Linked, and then choose one of the following alignment options (see Figure 10.9):

- **Top.**   Choose Top to align the topmost pixel on the active layer to the topmost edge of the selection border or active layer.

Figure 10.9

Options for aligning
linked layer elements.

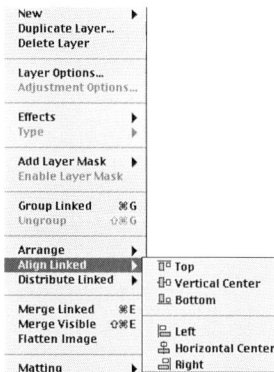

- **Vertical Center.**   Choose Vertical Center to align the vertical center-most pixel on the selection border or active layer.

- **Bottom.**   Choose Bottom to align the bottommost pixel on the selection border or active layer.

- **Left.**   Choose Left to align the leftmost pixel on the selection border or active layer.

- **Horizontal Center.**   Choose Horizontal Center to align the horizontal centermost pixel on the selection border or active layer.

- **Right.**   Choose Right to align the leftmost pixel on the selection border or active layer.

Now you try it...

Aligning and distributing linked layers

1   Open the `Card art.psd` file located in the Chapter 10 Lessons folder on the CD (see Figure 10.10).

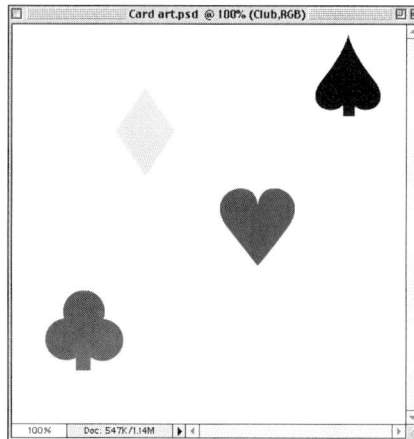

Figure 10.10

Artwork before using the Align and Distribute commands.

2   Notice that each layer in the Layers palette contains a separate piece of art and that the layers are linked.

3   With the Spade layer selected, choose Layer > Aligned Linked > Bottom. The other layer elements align with the bottom pixels of the Spade. Choose Edit > Undo or Control (Windows)/ Command (Macintosh)+Z to undo the move.

continues

4   Next, make the Heart layer the active layer by clicking on it and choose Layer > Align Linked > Top. This time the other layer elements align with the top pixels of the Heart layer (see Figure 10.11).

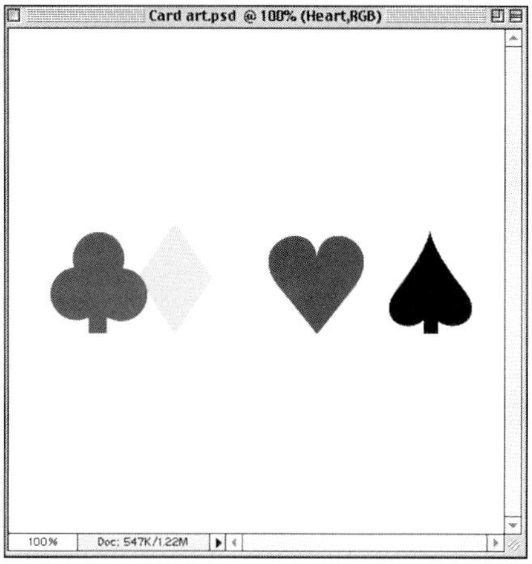

Figure 10.11

Artwork after using
the Align Linked >
Top command.

5   Now choose Layer > Distribute Linked > Horizontal Center. This distributes the elements evenly (see Figure 10.12).

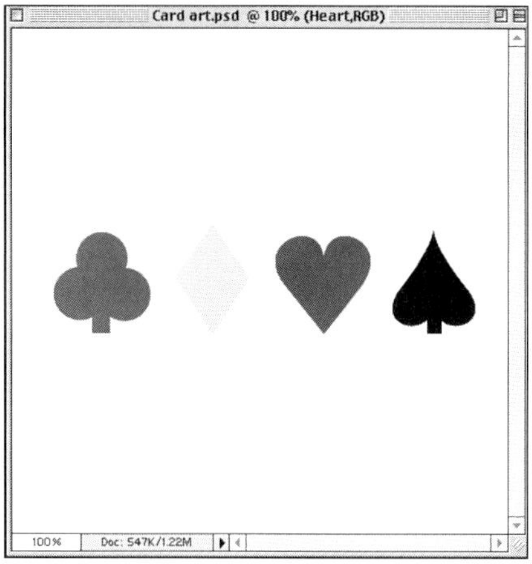

Figure 10.12

Artwork after using
the Distribute Linked
Horizontal command.

6   Continue to experiment by selecting different layers and alignment and distribution options.

EDITING LAYERS

When you create a new layer, it is by default a transparent layer. You can paint on the layer, add filter effects, adjust the opacity of the entire layer, and add blending mode effects.

USING PRESERVE TRANSPARENCY

When the Preserve Transparency box is checked in the Layers palette, the transparent areas of the layer are protected, and you can paint or use the Fill command to edit an element on the active layer without having an active selection. However, when the Preserve Transparency box is not checked, painting is not confined to the shape of the element and using the Fill command results in filling the entire layer.

In addition, you cannot change the transparency of the background until you convert it into a layer. To do so, double-click Background in the Layers palette, give it a name, and click OK. You can, however, create a new document and choose transparent for the contents instead of the default color, white, or a background color.

Now you try it...

Using Preserve Transparency

1   Choose File > New and create a document that measures 5 inches in both height and width. Select **72 dpi** for the resolution and RGB as the color mode. Select Transparency for Content color and click OK.

2   Note that in the Layers palette, Preserve Transparency is not checked and that the image window displays the default gray-and-white checkerboard pattern to indicate transparency.

3   Make a square selection with the rectangular marquee tool and fill the selection with a color.

4   Choose a new color in the Swatches palette and click the Preserve Transparency checkbox in the Layers palette. Select the paintbrush and paint over both the colored square and the transparent areas. Note how the color is confined to just the square and is not affecting the transparent pixels surrounding the square.

5   Click off the Preserve Transparency checkbox in Layers palette, and once again paint over the square and transparent areas. Both the square and transparent areas around it are now affected.

CHANGING THE OPACITY OF A LAYER

You can change the opacity of a layer by either changing the Opacity percentage in the upper-right corner of the Layers palette (see Figure 10.13) or double-clicking the layer and entering a new percentage in the Opacity field. The lower the percentage, the more transparent the pixels are on that layer.

Figure 10.13

The Opacity field in Photoshop 5.0 now has a pop-up slider.

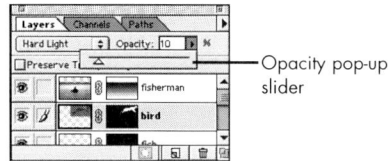

Opacity pop-up slider

USING THE BLEND IF OPTION

The Blend If option in the Layer Options dialog box enables you to blend two layers together by either including or excluding grayscale values of one or both layers. Blending is based on the position of the sliders with brightness values ranging from 0 (black) to 255 (white). You can blend the composite channels of the image by choosing gray in the Blend If pop-up menu or blend individual channels, such as red, green, or blue in an RGB image.

TIP

To quickly change the opacity of a layer, use the number keys on your keyboard. Press 0 for 100%, Press 1 for 10%, press 83 for 83%, and so forth. With the Opacity field highlighted, you can also press the up and down arrow keys to adjust the opacity in 1% increments and 10% increments when you also press Shift.

Now you try it...

Using the Blend If option

1   Open the "Big Sky" image, which is located in the Samples folder within the Goodies folder in the Photoshop application folder.

2   Double-click and name the background layer to give the layer transparency capability and name the layer **Clouds**.

3   Create a new layer by clicking the New Layer button at the bottom of the Layers palette. Name the layer **Yellow Highlight**.

4   Select the Yellow Highlight layer and drag it beneath the Clouds layer. Select a pale yellow in the Swatches palette and fill the layer by pressing Alt (Windows)/Option (Macintosh) +Delete.

5   Next, double-click on the Clouds layer to open the Layer Options Dialog box (see Figure 10.14). To blend the yellow layer beneath the Clouds layer into the highlights of the clouds, choose gray in the Blend If pop-up menu and click on the highlight slider labeled This Layer. Drag the slider to the left to approximately **198**.

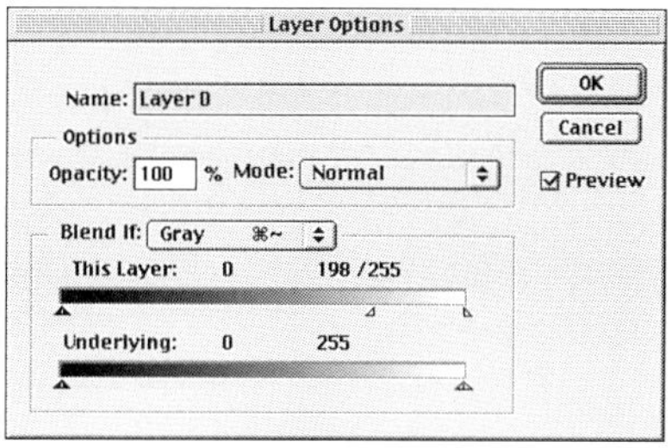

Figure 10.14

Double-click on a layer to display the Layer Options dialog box.

6 To partially blend the pixels, split the triangle sliders by pressing Alt (Windows)/Option (Macintosh) and then drag the right triangle back to **255** to create a more subtle effect. Click OK to exit the dialog box.

MANAGING LAYERED IMAGES

The more layers you have in an image, the larger the file size. If you need to conserve disk space, you have the option of merging or deleting layers or ultimately flattening all the layers into one base image.

You can track the file size of an image by displaying Document Sizes in the Status Bar in the lower-left corner of the screen/image window (see Figure 10.15). The number displayed on the left indicates the size the file will be when it's flattened. The number on the right shows the estimated file size with channels and layers intact and unflattened.

Figure 10.15

Document sizes are displayed in the Status Bar.

Flattened file size   Unflattened file size

MERGING LAYERS

When you are satisfied with your work on some layers, you can merge them into one layer to help manage the file size of your image (see Figure 10.16).

Figure 10.16

Manage the file size of
an image by choosing
Merge Down or Merge
Visible from the
Layers menu.

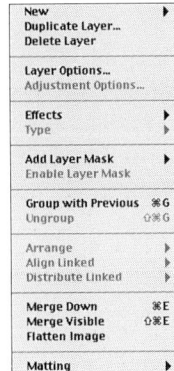

NOTE

If you are merging layers
containing blending
modes that affect under-
lying layers which aren't
being merged, the blend-
ing effect won't be
applied to those layers.

There are several ways to merge layers:

- **Merge Down.** To merge a layer with the layer below it, make sure both layers are visible and the layer you want to merge is selected in the Layers palette. You can either choose Layer > Merge Down, choose Merge Down from the Layer palette menu, or press Control/ Command+E.

- **Merge Visible.** Merge Visible enables you to merge all visible layers in the Layers palette. The eye icon must be on for each layer you want to merge. Hidden layers will not be merged. You can choose either Merge Visible from the Layer pulldown menu or Merge Visible from the Layers palette menu.

- **Merge Linked.** Merge Linked enables you to merge Layers that are linked. You can choose either Merge Linked from the Layer pulldown menu or Merge Linked from the Layers palette menu. The image must have linked layers for this option to be available in both the Layer pull-down menu and Layers palette menu. Keep in mind only one of the linked layers needs to be visible. The other linked layers need not be visible to be merged.

- **Merge Grouped.** Merge Grouped enables you to merge Layers that are part of a clipping group. The layers must be visible. Any hidden layers that are part of the group are discarded. Select the base layer of the clipping group and choose Merge Grouped from either the Layer pulldown menu or the Layer palette menu. The image must have layers that are part of an active clipping group for this option to be available in the Layers pulldown menu and Layers palette menu. For more information on clipping groups, see page 261 in this chapter.

MERGING AN ADJUSTMENT LAYER

When you merge an adjustment layer, you will permanently apply the adjustments to the layers below it—depending on whether you choose Merge Down, Merge Visible, Merge Linked, or Merge Grouped. The adjustment will only apply to those layers you choose to merge. Any remaining underlying layers not included in the merge will return to their previous state. For more information on adjustment layers, see page 263 in this chapter.

USING THE CLONE MERGE COMMAND

The Clone Merge command enables you to combine selected layers into one layer while retaining the layers separately. You can do this by pressing Alt/Option when you choose Merge Visible, Merge Linked, or Merge Group. The visible or linked layers merge into the active layer.

To avoid the layers merging into the active layer, create a new blank layer and select it before pressing Alt (Windows)/Option (Macintosh) and the Merge command. This way, all layers are merged into the blank layer, keeping the individual layers intact.

USING THE COPY MERGED COMMAND

The Copy Merged command copies any selected area on all visible layers to the clipboard. You can either make a selection or press Control (Windows)/ Command (Macintosh)+A to select the entire area of each layer. Press Control (Windows)/Command (Macintosh)+Shift+C to copy the layers to the clipboard. Press Control (Windows)/Command (Macintosh)+V to paste the selection or layers into a new merged layer.

FLATTENING AN IMAGE

When an image is flattened, all visible layers are merged into one layer named Background and any layers that are hidden are discarded. Flattening an image is necessary if the image needs to be saved in a file format other than the native Photoshop file format. If you plan to use the image in a page layout or illustration program, the image must be flattened and saved in the appropriate format. For more information on file formats, see Chapter 15, "File Formats."

To flatten an image, make sure that all the layers to be included are visible. Choose Flatten Image from either the Layer pulldown menu or the Layers palette menu (see Figure 10.17).

Figure 10.17

a) Before flattening
the image.

b) After flattening
the image.

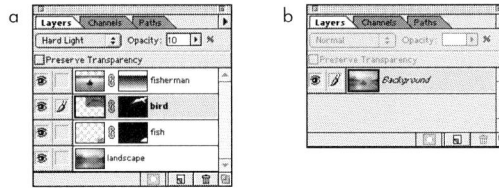

![NOTE icon]

NOTE

It is highly recommended
that you keep a copy of
the Photoshop file with
layers intact in case you
need to edit the image
at a later date. Choose
File > Save a Copy, select
a file format, and give the
new flattened image file
a name.

The table below lists the best key commands for merging layers.

Best Key Commands for Merging Layers	
Action	Command
Merge Down:	Control (Windows)/Command (Macintosh)+E
Merge Visible:	Control (Windows)/Command (Macintosh)+Shift+E
Merge Down and keep active layer intact:	Alt (Windows)/Option (Macintosh)+Merge Down
Merge a copy of all visible layers into a target layer:	Alt (Windows)/Option (Macintosh)+Merge Visible
Merge a copy of linked layers into a layer below:	Alt (Windows)/Option (Macintosh)+Merge Linked

CREATING A LAYER MASK

Layer masks can be used to hide or reveal areas of an image or to blend images together that are on separate layers for interesting collage effects. A layer mask is an 8-bit grayscale channel that you can edit just like any alpha channel. You can experiment with a wide variety of effects without affecting the pixels on that layer until you're ready to apply the mask to the image.

Each layer can contain only one layer mask and is automatically saved within layered documents. When working with a layer mask, you can use it in one of three ways:

- To hide portions of an image layer where areas on the mask are black
- To reveal portions of an image layer where areas on the mask are white
- To create semitransparency on an image where areas on the mask are gray

ADDING A LAYER MASK

When you add a layer mask, it automatically creates an alpha channel in the Channels palette. The alpha channel remains active until you either apply the layer mask to the layer or discard it. You have four options when adding a layer mask from the Layer pulldown menu (see Figure 10.18):

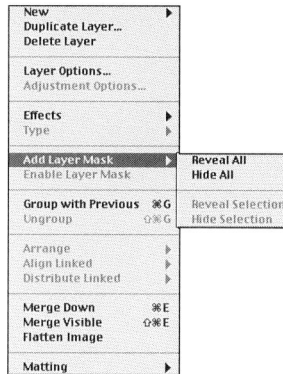

Figure 10.18

Add a layer mask to an image by accessing the Layers menu.

- **Reveal All.** A layer mask added to an active layer will be displayed as white. It allows you to see the entire image on that layer until you paint the image with black to hide pixels, paint with gray to create semitransparency, or add a gradation to the layer mask.

- **Hide All.** A layer mask added to an active layer will be displayed as black and will hide the image on that layer until you paint with white or gray or add a gradation to the layer mask.

- **Reveal Selection.** This option is only available when you have an active selection on an image layer. The selected area of the image is revealed and shows up as white in the layer mask thumbnail. The area outside the selection is black, thus hiding that portion of the image.

- **Hide Selection.** This option is only available when you have an active selection on an image layer. The selected area of the image is hidden and shows up as black in the layer mask thumbnail. The area outside the selection is white, thus revealing that portion of the image.

In the following lessons, you will learn how to blend images together using the linear gradient tool and a layer mask, paint on a layer mask to edit the transparency of the mask, paint on a layer mask channel to edit the transparency of the mask, view and hide a layer mask, apply and remove a layer mask, and link and unlink a layer mask.

Before you begin, delete the Adobe Photoshop Preferences file to restore the program's default settings. See page 55 in Chapter 2, "The Photoshop Work Area," for information on how to delete the preferences file.

Now you try it…

Using a layer mask to blend images with the linear gradient tool and paint brush

1 Open the files "Peprs.psd" and "PeprsFnl.psd", located in the Chapter 10 folder on the CD. You will use the "PeprsFnl.psd" file as a reference as you learn to create this image from the beginning using the Peprs.psd image.

2 If the layer palette isn't open, choose Window > Show Layers. Make sure that the Tabasco layer is active and choose Layer > Add Layer Mask > Reveal All. (You can also click the New Layer Mask button at the bottom of the Layers Palette.) The layer mask thumbnail will be displayed next to the image thumbnail on that layer.

3 To blend the two images together, choose the linear gradient tool in the toolbox and click and drag diagonally across the image. Experiment with different gradient lengths and directions. The layer mask thumbnail will reflect a grayscale gradation, and the two images will appear to fade into each other (see Figure 10.19).

Figure 10.19

A layer mask applied to the image using the linear gradient tool.

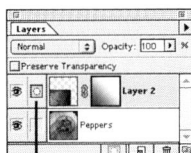

Layer mask icon

When you examine the image, you'll see that areas of the mask that are black completely hide that portion of the Tabasco while revealing the Peppers image on the layer underneath. The areas of the layer mask that are white completely reveal that part of the Tabasco image while hiding that same area of the Peppers layer underneath. The gray shades of the layer mask indicate different levels of transparency in the image, depending upon how light or dark the gray is.

4 Choose the paint brush and a small soft-edged brush from the Brushes palette. Make sure the layer mask thumbnail is active. You can tell it's active if the layer mask icon is displayed (see Figure 10.19). The layer mask thumbnail will also have a black border around it.

5 Experiment painting with black to hide portions of the background of the Tabasco label (see Figure 10.20) and then with white to reveal portions. Next, choose a few different grays in the swatches palette to make areas of the image semitransparent.

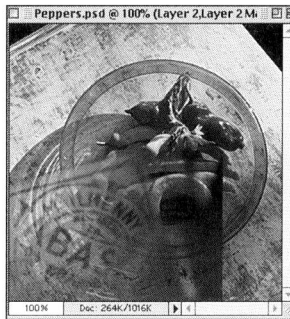

Figure 10.20

Hide areas of the image by painting with black.

6 Choose File > Save a Copy and save the file in Photoshop format for use in the next lesson.

Now you try it...

Viewing and editing a layer mask

1 Open your saved file from the previous lesson.

2 You can view and edit the layer mask on top of your image by pressing Option+Shift and clicking on the layer mask thumbnail (see Figure 10.21). It might be necessary to change the default overlay (50% red) to a different color to better see and work with the underlying image.

continues

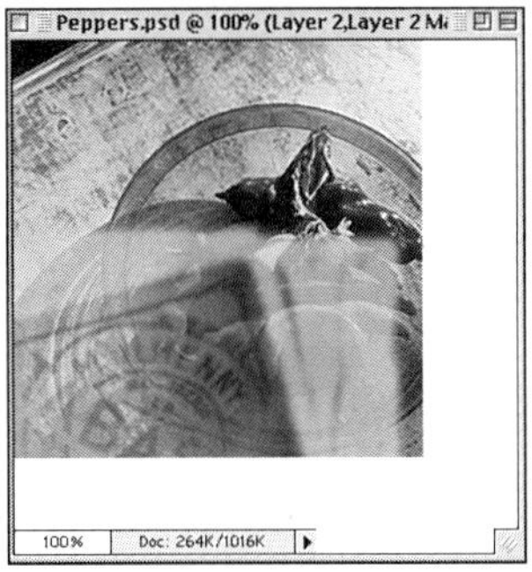

Figure 10.21

Display the layer mask on top of your image by pressing Option+Shift and clicking on the layer mask thumbnail.

Right/Control+click the layer mask thumbnail to display a context-sensitive menu and choose Layer Mask Options, or choose it in the Channels palette menu (see Figure 10.21). Double-click on the color swatch to change the color in the Color Picker and click OK. You can also change the opacity of the mask in the same dialog box.

In addition to painting directly on the image or overlay mask, you can also paint on the layer mask channel in the Channels palette. This can be helpful if precision is important, and often it's easier than painting on the ruby overlay mask if you need to fix small holes that otherwise wouldn't be visible in the other views.

3 To view or hide the layer mask channel, Alt (Windows)/ Option (Macintosh)+click on the layer mask thumbnail (see Figure 10.22). You can also click off the eye icons of all the channels except the layer mask channel at the bottom of the Channels palette.

Figure 10.22

Paint directly on the layer mask channel by Option+clicking on the layer mask thumbnail.

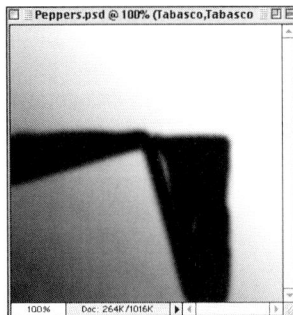

4 With black as your foreground color, choose an appropriate brush and clean up the areas where you had painted directly on the image. You might see areas where you'll want the image to be completely opaque.

When finished painting on the channel, Option+click on the layer mask thumbnail again or turn the eye icon off in the layer mask channel and turn all other channel eye icons back on. Activate the Layer palette and view the results.

5 If you want to see before and after versions of your image, you can temporarily hide the layer mask by holding down the Shift key and clicking on the layer mask thumbnail. A red X will display on the thumbnail, indicating the mask is disabled (see Figure 10.23). To view the layer mask effect again, click on the layer mask thumbnail. You can also choose Disable/Enable Layer Mask from the Layers pulldown menu.

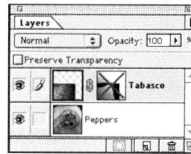

Figure 10.23

To temporarily hide a layer mask, press the Shift key and click on the layer mask thumbnail.

When your layer mask is complete, you can choose to apply or discard the mask, either of which reduces the file size of your document. There are three ways to apply or discard a layer mask:

- Choose Layer > Remove Layer Mask.
- Drag the layer mask thumbnail to the trash in the Layers palette. Make sure you're discarding the layer mask thumbnail and not the image thumbnail, so you don't inadvertently delete the image layer.
- Use the Context-sensitive menu by right/Control+clicking on the layer mask thumbnail.

6 Choose Layer > Remove Layer Mask. A dialog box will be displayed giving you a choice to apply, discard, or cancel. Choose Apply and click OK. Merge the layers by choosing Merge Down from the Layer Menu or Control (Windows)/Command (Macintosh)+E. Choose Save As from the File menu and name your new document for use in the next lesson.

You can use any of the selection tools to first define an area of an image that you would like to mask with a layer mask. Adding a feather to a selection before adding a layer mask will give the mask a soft, subtle edge.

Using a layer mask to blend images with a selection

2   Open the file you saved from the previous lesson, or open "Lmask.psd" located in the Lesson 10 folder on the CD.

2   Select the elliptical marquee tool in the toolbox. Select part of the image by clicking and dragging and choose Feather from the Select menu (Control+Alt/Command+Option+D) and enter an amount of 10 pixels. This will create a soft edge when the layer mask is added.

3   Next, add the layer mask by choosing Layer > Add Layer Mask > Reveal Selection or click on the New Layer Mask Button at the bottom of the Layers palette. The layer mask thumbnail represents the new mask with a soft vignette edge (see Figure 10.24).

Figure 10.24

A layer mask applied to an image with a feathered selection

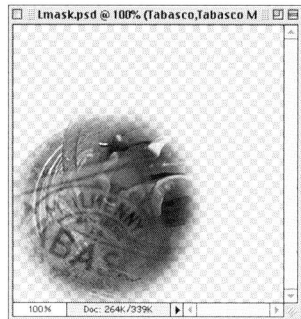

LINKING AND UNLINKING A LAYER MASK

By default, the layer mask is linked to the image, but you can reposition the mask or image by unlinking the two thumbnails in the Layers palette. Click off the Link icon and use the move tool to reposition the mask.

The table below lists the best layer mask shortcuts.

Best layer mask shortcuts	
Create layer mask with Reveal All/Reveal Selection:	Click on the Layer Mask button
Create layer mask with Hide All/Hide Selection:	Alt/Alt/Option+Click on Mask button
Toggle layer mask on/off:	Shift+Click layer mask thumbnail
Toggle viewing/hiding layer mask/composite:	Alt/Option+Click layer mask thumbnail
Toggle rubylith mode mask on/off:	Alt+Shift/Option+Click layer for layer mask thumbnail
Toggle rubylith modemask on/off:	Alt+Shift/Option+Click layer for layer mask thumbnail

CREATING A CLIPPING GROUP

A *clipping group* is composed of at least two elements on separate layers. The element on the bottommost layer acts as a mask for the elements on the layers above it. For example, if you want to place an image inside a shape, such as a circle, the circle is on the bottom layer, and the image is on the top layer. When the elements are defined as a clipping group, the image appears inside the circle, and the remaining portion of the image is masked.

Now you try it...

Using a clipping group to mask an image inside text

Before you begin, replace the Adobe Photoshop Preferences file to restore the program's default settings. See page 55 in Chapter 2 for information on how to replace the preferences file.

1   Open the files "Snow.psd" and "snowfnl.psd" located in the Chapter 10 folder on the CD. You will use the "SnowFnl.psd" file as a reference as you learn to create this image from the beginning using the Snow.psd image (see Figure 10.25).

continues

Figure 10.25

A clipping group
applied to an image
using type as a mask.

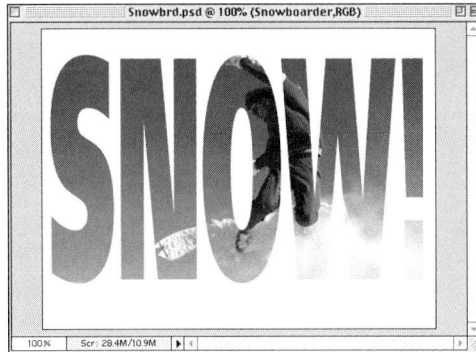

2   Select the horizontal Type tool and click on the image to open the Type dialog box.

3   Click in the text field at the bottom of the dialog box and type the word **SNOW!** in all caps. Highlight the text and change the size of the type. (We used **110** point Frutiger Ultra Black.) Click OK.

4   Position the type over the image with the move tool.

5   Because the type will be used as a mask, it must be positioned underneath the image layer in the Layers palette (see Figure 10.26). Click on the type layer and drag it underneath the image layer.

Figure 10.26

Position the type layer
underneath the image
before creating the
clipping group.

6   To create the clipping group, make sure the Snowboarder layer is active and choose Layer > Group with Previous or Control (Windows)/Command (Macintosh)+G.

7   Next, select the SNOW! layer. In order to have more of the image show through the type, vertically scale it by selecting Edit > Transform > Scale or press Control (Windows)/Command (Macintosh)+T. Drag the handle on the top of the box to the top of the image. To apply the transformation, either double-click on the image or press Enter on the keyboard.

🖐 **TIP**

Adjustment layers can be
stacked to combine more
than one color adjustment
to individual or
multiple layers.

Now you try it...

Using an adjustment layer to color correct an image

1 Open the file "Rose.psd" in the Chapter 10 folder on the CD. This image needs a basic tonal correction to adjust the high-lights, midtones, and shadows. If the Layers palette isn't open, choose Window > Show Layers or press F7 on your keyboard.

2 Choose New Adjustment Layer in the Layers palette menu, click on the pop-up menu, and choose Levels. Keep Opacity at 100% and the mode set to Normal; leave the Group with Previous box unchecked. Click OK.

3 The Levels dialog box displays a histogram of the image and enables you to adjust the tonal range of the image by using the Input or Output sliders, Auto Levels adjustment, or eye-droppers. In this lesson, you will adjust the image using the highlight and shadow eyedroppers. (For more detailed infor-mation on correcting the tonal range of an image using Levels, see Chapter 14, "Color Correction.")

4 Make sure the Preview box is checked. To set the black point in the image, select the black eyedropper tool, position the eye-dropper over the darkest area of the image, and click (see Figure 10.29).

5 To set the white point in the image, select on the white eye-dropper tool and position the eyedropper over the lightest area of the image and click (see Figure 10.29).

6 Click on the midtone (gamma) slider and experiment adjusting the midtones by dragging in either direction. When satisfied with the results, click OK.

Notice the Layers palette now includes a layer named Levels, the layer is identified as an adjustment layer by the adjust-ment layer icon placed to the right of the name (see Figure 10.30).

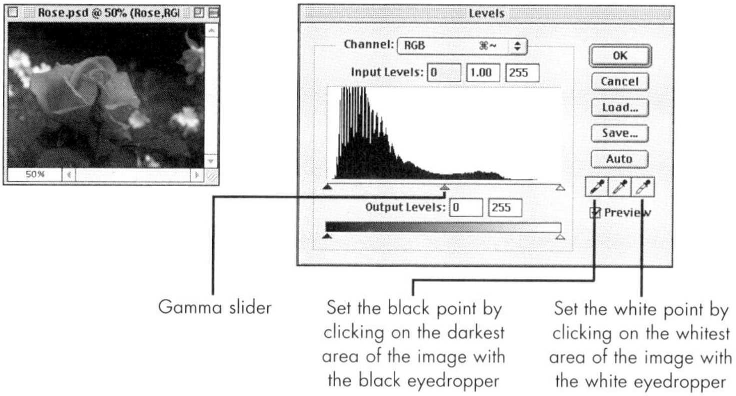

Figure 10.29

Adjust the tonal range of an image using levels.

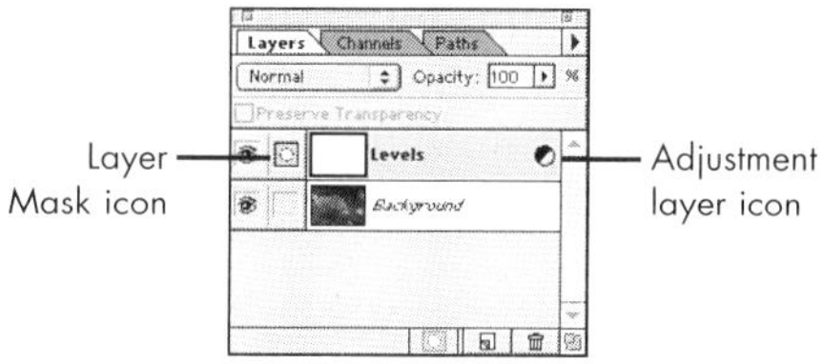

Gamma slider

Set the black point by clicking on the darkest area of the image with the black eyedropper

Set the white point by clicking on the whitest area of the image with the white eyedropper

Figure 10.30

The Levels adjustment layer in the Layers palette.

Layer
Mask icon

Adjustment
layer icon

Adjustment layers are also layer masks, indicated by the mask icon to the left of the layer thumbnail (see Figure 10.30). Because it's a layer mask, you can create or load a selection or paint on the mask to hide or reveal the adjustments on the layer.

7 Add another adjustment layer to change the color of the rose. A selection of the rose has been previously saved with the Rose.psd file. Choose Select > Load Selection > Rose.psd (see Figure 10.31).

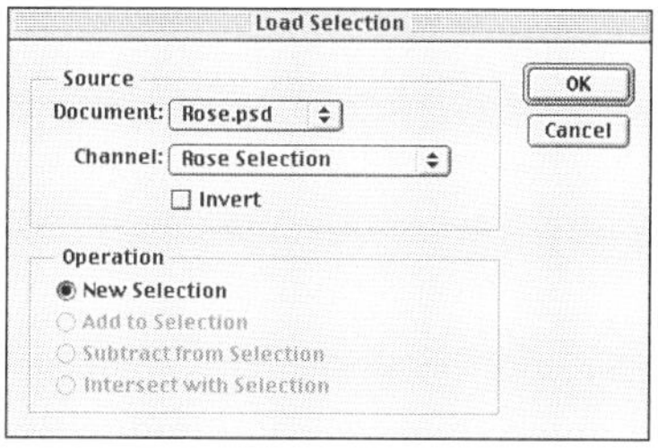

Figure 10.31

When you choose Load Selection from the Select menu, you can activate a previously saved selection.

continues

8   In the Layers palette menu, choose New Adjustment layer to display the New Adjustment Layer dialog box and then choose Color Balance from the pop-up menu. Make sure the Preview box is checked and experiment with the sliders (see Figure 10.32).

Figure 10.32

In the Color Balance dialog box you can adjust the color of a selection or image using the sliders.

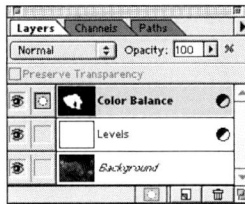

Move the top slider toward Red and the bottom slider toward Blue to create a pink rose. Click OK. Note that the Color Balance thumbnail displays the mask (see Figure 10.33).

Figure 10.33

The color balance thumbnail displays the mask because a selection was used to isolate the color correction.

9   Experiment showing and hiding each adjustment layer to compare your results with the original image. If you want to further correct the image with either the Levels or the Color Balance command, double-click on either adjustment layer to open the corresponding dialog box.

TIP

Change the name of the adjustment layer by double-clicking on the layer thumbnail.

USING LAYER EFFECTS

New to Photoshop 5.0, layer effects enable you to quickly apply drop shadows, glows, beveling, and embossing to layer elements. You can also apply more than one effect to a layer. An "f" icon is displayed to the right of the layer name in the Layers palette when you've applied one of these effects. The Layer Effects are linked to the layer contents, so when you move or edit the contents, the effect is updated accordingly (see Figure 10.34).

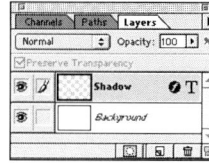

Figure 10.34

The "f" icon indicates a layer effect applied to the Layer.

ADDING A LAYER EFFECT

To add a Layer Effect, select a layer in the Layers palette and choose Layer > Effects. The following effects can be applied to a layer in any combination:

- **Drop Shadow.**   The drop shadow effect adds a shadow behind the contents of the layer. You can adjust the blending mode, opacity, angle, distance, blur, and intensity, as well as the color of the shadow (see Figure 10.35).

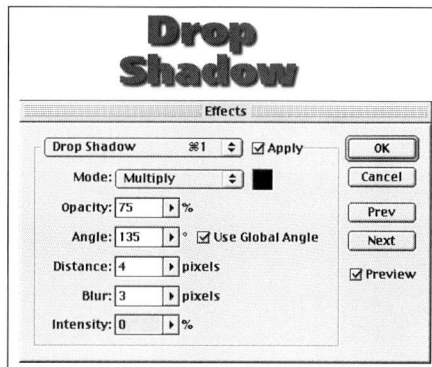

Figure 10.35

Drop Shadow options in the Layer Effects dialog box.

- **Inner Shadow.**   The inner shadow effect adds a shadow that is placed inside the edges of the layer contents. You can adjust the blending mode, opacity, angle, distance, blur, and intensity, as well as the color of the shadow (see Figure 10.36).

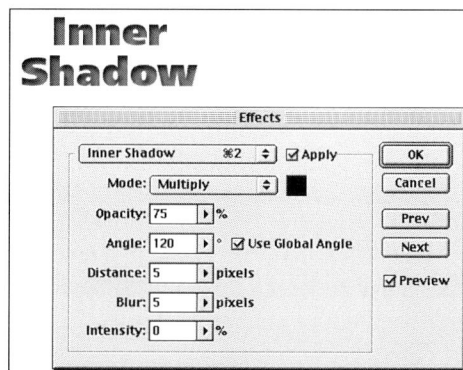

Figure 10.36

Inner Shadow options in the Layer Effects dialog box.

• **Outer Glow.** The outer glow effect adds a glow that emanates from the outside of the layer contents. You can adjust the blending mode, opacity, blur, intensity, and color of the shadow (see Figure 10.37).

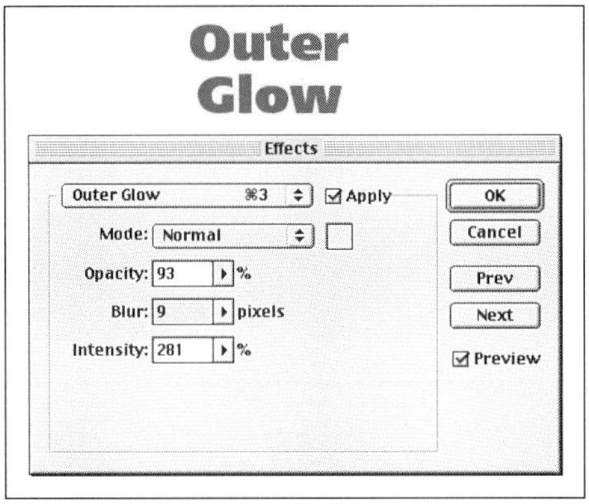

Figure 10.37

Outer Glow options in the Layer Effects dialog box.

Figure 10.37

Outer Glow options in the Layer Effects dialog box.

• **Inner Glow.** The inner glow effect adds a glow that emanates from the inside of the layer contents. You can adjust the blending mode, opacity, blur, and intensity, as well as the color of the shadow (see Figure 10.38).

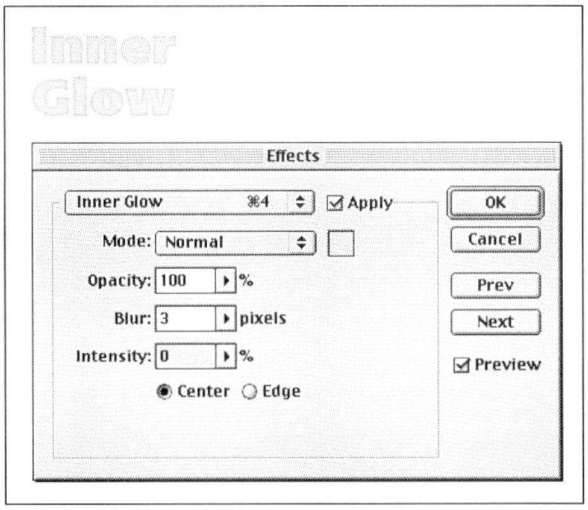

Figure 10.38

Inner Glow options in the Layer Effects dialog box.

• **Bevel.** The bevel effect adds either an inner or outer bevel to the layer contents. You can adjust the blending mode and opacity for both the highlight and shadow as well as the angle, depth, and blur (see Figure 10.39).

• **Emboss.** The emboss effect adds either a regular emboss or pillow emboss to the layer contents. You can adjust the blending mode and opacity for both the highlight and shadow as well as the angle, depth, and blur (see Figure 10.40).

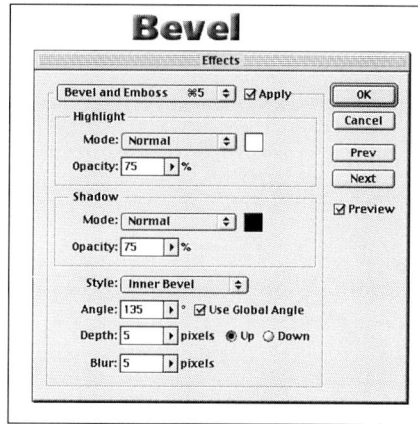

Figure 10.39

Bevel options in the Layer Effects dialog box.

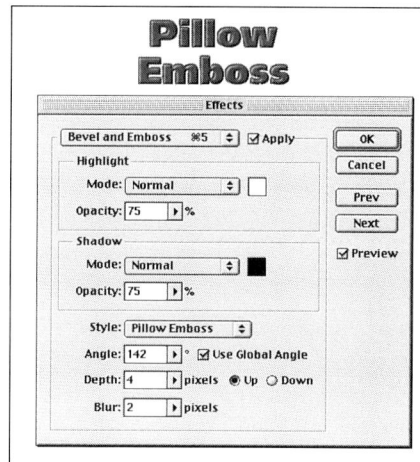

Figure 10.40

Emboss options in the Layer Effects dialog box.

EDITING AND REMOVING LAYER EFFECTS

Layer effects are fully editable until you convert an effect to an image layer, merge layers, or flatten the image. You can also copy effects between layers and remove an effect that you've applied to a layer element.

To edit a layer effect, double-click on the layer effect icon in the Layers palette to open the Effects dialog box, and then choose the desired effect in the pop-up menu. You can also click the Prev or Next buttons to cycle through the options.

You can copy effects among layers by first selecting the source layer that you want to copy and choosing Layer > Effects > Copy Effects. You can then choose to paste the effect into an existing layer or a new layer by selecting

Layer > Effects > Paste Effects. It's also possible to paste into multiple layers if the destination layer is linked to others. To do this, select Layer > Effects > Paste to Linked.

To remove a layer effect, select the layer that has the effect you want to remove and press Alt (Windows)/Option (Macintosh) and select Layer > Effects and the Effect you want to remove. An applied effect has a check mark next to its name. Removing the effect removes the check mark. You can also remove an effect in the Effects dialog box by deselecting the Apply button.

To remove all effects applied to a layer, choose Layer > Effects > Clear effects.

CONVERTING LAYER EFFECTS TO LAYERS

After you convert a layer effect into a regular layer, the effect will no longer be editable. You can, however, apply additional special effects with filters or painting tools, both of which are not available until you convert the layer.

To convert a layer that has an effect, select the layer in the Layers palette and choose Layer > Effects > Create Layers. The Drop Shadow, Inner Shadow, and Outer Glow effects create one additional layer, and the Bevel and Emboss effects create two layers: one for the shadows and one for the high-lights. The Inner Glow effect creates a clipping group.

Right/Control+click the Effects icon in the Layers palette to quickly display related commands (see Figure 10.41).

Figure 10.41

The context-sensitive menu for Layer effects gives you quick access to related commands.

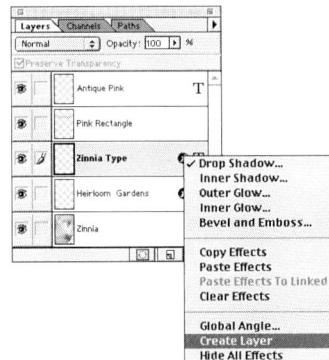

BLENDING MODES

You have access to a wide variety of blending modes in the Layers palette. The results achieved with each mode depend on how the colors on the underlying layer interact with the layer on which you're applying an effect. Blending mode options are also available for all the painting tools in the tools' Options palette.

As you read about each blending mode, experiment with the file `Color Grid.psd` located in the Chapter 10 folder on the CD. You can also follow the lesson at the end of this section.

Normal

As the default blending mode, Normal mode replaces the values of the pixels with the foreground color with which you're painting. When working with a bitmap or indexed-color image, the Normal mode is called Threshold and is only available as a mode choice in the Fill dialog box, not in the Layers palette.

Dissolve

The Dissolve mode paints pixels randomly with the foreground color if used with the airbrush or paintbrush. You can also apply the Dissolve mode to a layer. Results will depend on the opacity setting in the Layers palette.

Behind

The Behind mode paints only on the transparent areas of a layer. Preserve Transparency must be off for the selected layer for this mode to work.

Clear

The Clear mode is only available for the Line tool, the paint bucket tool, and the Fill and Stroke commands; and Preserve Transparency must be off in the Layers palette for it to work. This mode makes pixels transparent.

Multiply

The Multiply mode multiplies the color values of the image or element with the foreground color and creates a darker complementary color. Multiplying any color with black will produce black. Multiplying any color with white yields no result. Painting over the same area repeatedly will continue to produce a darker color.

Screen

The Screen mode is the opposite of the Multiply mode. It blends the foreground color with the underlying image or element and will produce a lighter color. Screening with white will produce white. Screening with black yields no result.

Overlay

Related to the Multiply and Screen mode, the Overlay mode will use either mode depending on what the base color of the image is. It combines the foreground color with the underlying image pixels but preserves the highlight and shadow detail of the image.

Soft Light

The Soft Light mode darkens or lightens the underlying image based on the how dark or light the foreground color is.

Hard Light

The Hard Light mode will multiply or screen the underlying image or element based on how dark or light the foreground color is. If the foreground color is lighter than 50% gray, the image is lightened. If the foreground color is darker than 50% gray, the image is darkened.

Color Dodge

The Color Dodge mode lightens the color of the image pixels to reflect the lightness value based on the color with which you're painting.

Color Burn

The opposite of Color Dodge is the Color Burn mode wherein the base colors are darkened based on the color with which you're painting.

Darken

The Darken mode darkens the underlying pixels that are lighter than the color with which you're painting. Pixels darker than the color with which you're painting remain unchanged.

Lighten

The opposite of Darken mode, the Lighten Mode lightens underlying pixels that are darker than the color with which you're painting. Pixels lighter than the color with which you're painting remain unchanged.

Difference

The result of using the Difference mode depends on whether the underlying pixels or the color with which you're painting has a lighter value. Either the color with which you're painting is subtracted from the underlying color, or the underlying color is subtracted from the color with which you're painting.

Exclusion

The Exclusion mode is similar to the Difference mode but creates an effect lower in contrast, producing a softer effect. You might want to experiment painting with light and dark colors on top of other colors.

Hue

The Hue mode replaces only the hue value of the image with the Hue values of the foreground color when painting or the Hue values on the layer. The saturation and luminance values remain unaffected.

Saturation

The Saturation mode replaces only the saturation value of the image with the saturation of the color with which you're painting or the saturation of the colors on the layer. The hue and luminance values remain unaffected.

Color

The Color mode preserves the gray levels of the image while replacing the hue and saturation of the underlying image with the hue and saturation values of the color with which you're painting or the hue and saturation values of the layer.

Luminosity

Luminosity represents the brightness of a color. The Luminosity mode changes the luminosity of the underlying image but maintains the hue and saturation.

In the following lesson, you can experiment with the different blending modes available in the Layers palette.

Now you try it...

Using the blending modes

1   Open the file named "Color Grid.psd" in the Chapter 10 folder on the CD. Make sure the Layer palette and Swatches palette are open by choosing Window > Show Layers, Window > Show Swatches.

2   Select the layer named "Blending Mode Result" and select the move tool in the toolbox.

continues

TIP

To quickly toggle through the blending modes, press Shift++ (the plus sign) to select the next blending mode in the list. Press Shift+ – (the minus sign) to select the previous mode.

3 Because the Layer palette displays the default Normal blending mode, the circle appears opaque on top of the Color Grid image. Experiment with changing the blending mode and moving the circle over different portions of the underlying image to see how that color and the blending modes interact.

4 Next, choose a new color from the Swatches palette and fill the circle with the new color by choosing Alt (Windows)/Option (Macintosh)+delete.

5 Continue experimenting with each blending mode and filling the circle with lighter and darker colors to compare the results.

The following table lists the best Layer shortcuts.

Best layer shortcuts	
Toggle show all layers/ show active layer only:	Alt/Option+Click on Eye icon
Create new empty layer with Layer Options dialog box:	Alt/Option+Click New Layer button
Delete layer while bypassing Warning Alert:	Alt/Option+Click Delete Layer button
Create new adjustment layer with Adjustment Layer dialog box:	Control+Alt/Command+Opt+Click New Layer icon
Toggle preserve transparency for target layer:	/ (Forward Slash)
Load layer transparency as selection:	Control+Click Layer thumbnail
Add layer transparency to selection:	Control (Windows)/Command (Macintosh)+Shift+Click Layer thumbnail
Subtract layer transparency to selection:	Control+Alt/Command+Option+ Click Layer thumbnail
Intersect layer transparency with selection:	Control+Alt/Command+Option+ Shift+Click thumbnail
Select top layer:	Alt/Option+Shift+]
Select next layer up:	Alt/Option+]
Select previous layer down:	Alt/Option+[
Select bottom layer:	Alt/Option+Shift+[
Move target layer up:	Control+Alt/Command+Option+] (Windows)
Move target layer down:	Control+Alt/Command+Option+[
Create Layer Mask with Hide All/Hide Selection:	Alt+Click Option+Click on Layer Mask button

Open Layer Mask Options dialog box:	Double-click Layer Mask thumbnail
Toggle Layer Mask on/off:	Shift+Click Layer Mask thumbnail
Toggle viewing Layer Mask/composite:	Alt/Option+Click Layer Mask thumbnail
Toggle rubylith mode for Layer Mask on/off:	\ (backslash)
Toggle rubylith mode for Layer Mask on/off:	Alt/Option+Shift+Click Layer Mask thumbnail
Merge down a copy of current layer into layer below:	Alt/Option+Merge Down
Merge a copy of all visible layers into target layer:	Alt/Option+Merge Visible
Merge a copy of linked layers into layer below:	Alt/Option+Merge Linked
Toggle Group with Previous/Ungroup:	Alt/Option+Click line between layers
Clear each Effect on a layer one at a time:	Alt/Option+Double-click effect icon

SUMMARY

As you've learned in this chapter, layers are fundamental to image compositing. However, an understanding beyond the basics is essential in creating professional artwork and preparing for the exam. A Photoshop ACE is well versed in the use of adjustment layers, layer masks, and clipping groups, as well as how to work with layered images in the most productive manner.

REVIEW QUESTIONS

1. How do you duplicate a layer?

   a. Choose Edit > Duplicate.

   b. Choose Image > Duplicate.

   c. Choose File > Duplicate Layer.

   d. Drag the layer on top of the New Layer button.

2. How do you change the background into a layer?

   a. Choose Layer > New Layer.

   b. Choose Layer > Transform.

   c. Option-click on the layer thumbnail.

   d. Double-click on the background layer.

3. Which is not a method of changing the stacking order of layers?

   a. Choose Layer > Align Up (or Align Down).

   b. Drag the layer above or below another layer.

   c. Press Control (Windows)/Command (Macintosh)+] (or [).

   d. Choose Layer > Arrange > Bring to Front, Bring Forward, Send to Back, Send Backward.

4. Which blending mode is not available to layers?

   a. Color

   b. Clear

   c. Dissolve

   d. Exclusion

5. When is it appropriate to use a clipping group?

   a. To group layers

   b. To move linked elements

   c. To mask an image inside type or a shape

   d. To create a silhouette for use in a page layout program

6. How do you turn off a layer mask?

   a. Shift+click the layer mask thumbnail.

   b. Option+click the layer mask thumbnail.

   c. Choose Hide Layer Mask from the Layers menu.

   d. Choose Hide Layer Mask from the Layers palette.

7. How do you show a layer mask in the image window?

    a. Shift+click the layer mask thumbnail.

    b. Alt/Option+click the layer mask thumbnail.

    c. Choose Load Layer Mask from the Select menu.

    d. Choose Load Layer Mask from the Layers palette.

8. When an adjustment layer is applied to a clipping group, what happens?

    a. You can't apply an adjustment layer to a clipping group.

    b. Only the layers in the clipping group are affected by the adjustment layer.

    c. An adjustment layer only affects a clipping group when the clipping group is merged.

    d. All layers in an image are affected by the adjustment layer, regardless of the clipping group.

9. Which is not a choice when the Adjustment Layer command options are displayed?

    a. Invert

    b. Threshold

    c. Replace color

    d. Channel Mixer

10. How do you create an adjustment layer?

    a. Choose New Adjustment Layer from the Layer pulldown menu.

    b. Choose New Adjustment Layer from the Layers palette menu.

    c. Shift+click on the Layer thumbnail.

    d. Command+click (Macintosh) or Control+click (Windows) on the Layer thumbnail.

CHAPTER 11

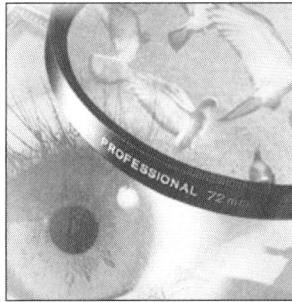

WORKING WITH TYPE

Photoshop 5.0 now includes more control in setting and editing type. In addition to setting horizontal type, you can now set type vertically. You can also adjust kerning, tracking, leading, and the baseline. Because Photoshop now supports character-based formatting, you can apply multiple fonts, styles, and attributes to type on an individual type layer, and the layer remains fully editable until you render it. You can also specify color while previewing your type in the image window.

Domains & Objectives

Painting and Editing

6.3   Identify issues regarding the characteristics, function, limitations, and appropriate use of the type tools, functions, and commands, which include the type tool, type options, type mask tools, and use of type layers.

Type in Photoshop is typically created for special effects such as drop shadows, ghosting, and embossing; or it is used as an artistic element in painting and montage art in both print and Web graphics. If it's important for
the type to retain crisp, clean edges, it's best to place your Photoshop image
into a page layout or illustration program, and then set the type using that
program.

Because Photoshop is a raster-based program, the type you set is composed
of pixels. When anti-aliasing is turned on in the Type Tool dialog box, the
edges of the type are blurred to give a smoother appearance. If anti-aliasing
is turned off, the edges will appear jagged and bitmapped (see Figure 11.1).
Unless you want the type to appear jagged as a special effect, always keep
anti-aliasing turned on (see Figure 11.2).

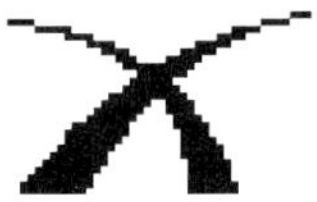

Figure 11.1

The effect created by
turning off anti-
aliasing in the Type
Tool dialog box.

Figure 11.2

The effect created by
turning on anti-
aliasing in the Type
Tool dialog box.

Page layout and illustration programs support outline type. Outline type is
composed of straight lines and Bézier curves, which are mathematically
defined shapes that can be scaled, rotated, or distorted without losing
smooth, crisp edges (see Figure 11.3).

Figure 11.3

Outline type created
in Adobe Illustrator.

There is no need to scale type in Photoshop because of its new, editable type
layers. If you do scale type up in size with the Transform > Scale command,
your type will appear jagged. Instead, simply double-click the type layer and
enter a new amount in the Size field of the Type Tool dialog box.

USING THE TYPE TOOLS

The type tools are located in the toolbox (see Figure 11.4). The horizontal and vertical type tools enable you to set colored type that is stored in an editable type layer. The horizontal type mask and vertical type mask tools enable you to set type as an active selection that you can fill or stroke just like any other selection.

Figure 11.4

To access the hidden type tools, click on the type tool and hold down your mouse button a little longer than usual to display an extended menu.

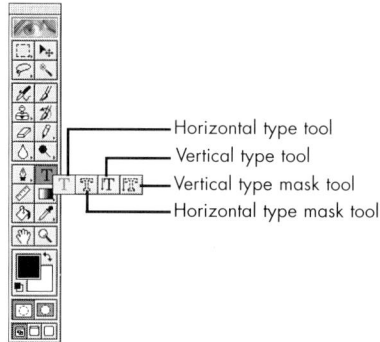

— Horizontal type tool
— Vertical type tool
— Vertical type mask tool
— Horizontal type mask tool

SETTING TYPE

To create type in Photoshop, select one of the type tools and click anywhere in the image window to open the Type Tool dialog box (see Figure 11.5), which displays formatting choices that include setting your font, size, style, alignment, kerning, tracking, leading, baseline, rotation, and color.

Figure 11.5

Set your formatting choices in the Type Tool dialog box.

To open the Type Tool dialog box:

- Select the horizontal text tool. Notice how the cursor changes into an I-beam when in the image window. The small line through the I-beam indicates the type baseline. For vertical type, the small line indicates the center axis of the type characters.

- Click anywhere in the image area to open the Type Tool dialog box.

WORKING WITH THE TYPE TOOL DIALOG BOX

You can resize the text area by dragging the lower-right corner of the Type Tool dialog box. In addition, you can change the view magnification up to 800% in increments of 100 by clicking the left Zoom button (with the plus) in the lower-left corner of the Type Tool dialog box (see Figure 11.5 above). The Zoom Minus button reduces the magnification in increments of 100.

Click the Fit in Window checkbox so the magnification scales with the text to fit in the window as you type. Note the Zoom button percentage changes dynamically as you type.

With Photoshop 5.0 you no longer need to close the Type Tool dialog box to reposition your type. However, you must have the box checked in order for the cursor to change to the move tool to reposition the type in the image window.

CHOOSING A FONT

Photoshop supports Type 1, TrueType, and CID fonts. CID fonts are double-byte fonts that support Chinese, Japanese, and Korean text. All fonts installed in your system are available in the Font pop-up menu in the Type Tool dialog box.

If you have a font family installed, the style pop-up menu (next to the Font pop-up menu in the Type Tool dialog box) will reflect the styles available to that font, for example regular, bold, and italic. Type styles can vary within font families.

CHOOSING A FONT SIZE

In Photoshop, the default type measurement setting is given in points (72 PostScript points equals 1 inch). If you prefer to use the traditional measurement system (72.27 points equals 1 inch), choose File > Preferences > Units & Rulers.

SPECIFYING KERNING, TRACKING, AND LEADING

Photoshop 5.0 features character-level formatting that enables you to adjust kerning, tracking, leading, and baseline shift within the Type Tool dialog box.

TIP

Press T on your keyboard to activate the type tool. Shift+T toggles through all the type tools.

- **Kerning.**   You can manually adjust the spacing between characters by inserting the cursor between two characters in the text area at the bottom of the Type Tool dialog box (see Figure 11.6). Enter a negative value to tighten up the space or a positive value to add space. Checking the Auto Kern option automatically kerns the type based on the kerning table built into the font.

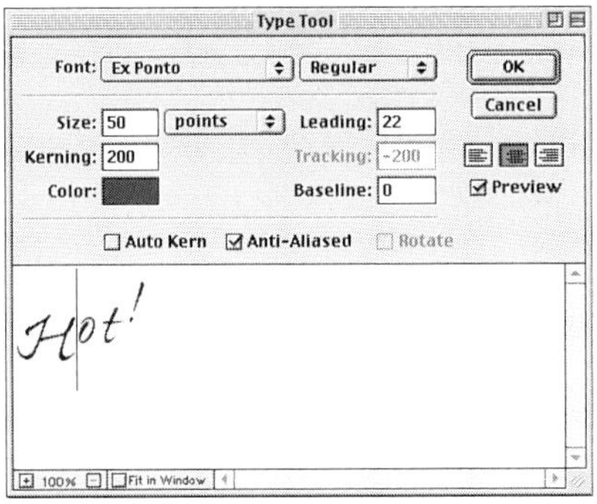

Figure 11.6

Place the cursor between two characters to tighten or loosen the kerning.

- **Tracking.**   In the Type Tool dialog box, you can uniformly adjust the space between more than two characters by selecting the text and entering an amount in the tracking field. A negative tracking value tightens the space between characters, and a positive value loosens the space (see Figure 11.7).

  Kerning and tracking values are measured in units that are 1/1000 of an em space. The em space width is relative to the current type size. For example, if your text is set at 12 points, the em space width is also 12 points.

Figure 11.7

You can use tracking to uniformly adjust the spacing between characters in a word or multiple lines of text.

G a r d e n

Tracking set at 500

Garden

Tracking set at –500

- **Leading.**   Leading is the spacing between multiple lines of text and is measured from baseline to baseline (see Figure 11.8). The default setting for leading is 120% of the font size. To specify a leading value, enter it in the Leading field of the Type Tool dialog box.

USING BASELINE SHIFT

You can raise or lower individual letters or lines of text using baseline shift. A negative value in the Baseline field of the Type Tool dialog box lowers the text below its baseline; a positive value raises the text above its baseline (see Figure 11.9).

HEIRLOOM

GARDENS

Leading set at 50 points

HEIRLOOM
GARDENS

Leading set at 30 points

Figure 11.8

You can use leading to adjust the spacing between multiple lines of text.

Heirloom
Gardens

No baseline shift
applied

Heirloom
Gardens

Baseline shift applied at 14.5

Figure 11.9

You can use baseline shift to raise or lower words or individual characters.

SPECIFYING ALIGNMENT

Alignment controls the position of the type based on where you first clicked the insertion point on the image. You can set single or multiple lines of type to align to the left, right, or center of the insertion point in the Type Tool dialog box by clicking on the Alignment buttons (see Figure 11.10).

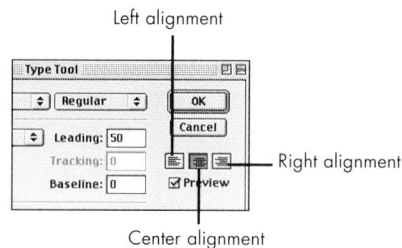

Left alignment

```
Type Tool
  [ Regular  ]      [  OK  ]
                    [ Cancel ]
  [ Leading: 50 ]
    Tracking: 0   ≣ ≣ ≣  — Right alignment
    Baseline: 0   ☑ Preview
```

Center alignment

Figure 11.10

You can set type to align left, right, or to the center of the insertion point.

ROTATING CHARACTER DIRECTION

Checking the Rotate box turns vertical text 90° (see Figure 11.11). This option is not available for horizontal type or double-byte characters.

Type layers as well as regular layers are not supported by Bitmap, Indexed-color, or Multichannel modes. If you are working in one of these modes, the type will be set on the background layer and cannot be edited. The Preview option in the Type Tool dialog box is also not available.

You can copy and paste text into the type area of the Type Tool dialog box from other applications, although any local formatting that you might have applied, such as bold or italics, will be lost.

Figure 11.11

You can rotate
vertical text 90° by
checking the Rotate
box in the Type Tool
dialog box.

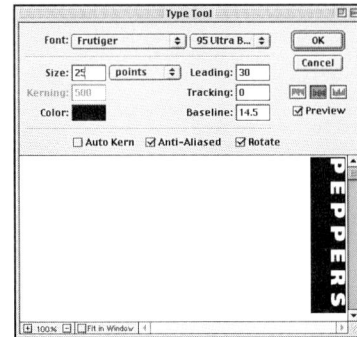

Default vertical text

Text rotated 90°

TIP

Instead of clicking OK or
pressing the Return key
(Macintosh) to exit a dialog box, get into the habit
of pressing the Enter key
on the numeric keypad. If
you press Return while in
the text field, you'll move
the insertion point to the
next line rather than exit
the dialog box.

When in the Type Tool dialog box, use the following shortcuts for font siz-
ing, kerning, tracking, leading, and baseline shift.

Best Type Tool dialog box shortcuts

Macintosh Commands

Select all characters:	Command+A
Align type left, center, or right:	Command+L, C, R
Increase/decrease 1 point/pixel increments	Up or down arrow keys
Increase/decrease 10 point/pixel increments	Shift+up or down arrow keys
Increase/decrease type size in 2 point/pixel increments	Command+Shift+<>
Increase/decrease type size in 10 point/pixel increments	Command+OptionShift+<>
Increase/decrease leading in 2 point/pixel increments	Option+up/down arrow keys
Increase/decrease leading in 10 point/pixel increments	Command+Option+up/down arrow keys
Increase/decrease baseline shift in 2 point/pixel increments	Option+Shift+up/down arrow keys
Increase/decrease baseline shift in 10 point/pixel increments	Command+Option+Shift+ up/down arrow keys
Increase/decrease kerning/tracking in 20/1000 em increments	Option+left/right arrow keys

Windows Commands

Select all characters	Control+A
Align type left, center, or right	Control+L, C, R
Increase/decrease 1 point/pixel increments	Up or down arrow keys
Increase/decrease 10 point/pixel increments	Shift+up or down arrow keys

Increase/decrease type size in 2 point/pixel increments	Control+Shift+<>
Increase/decrease type size in 10 point/pixel increments	Control+Alt+Shift+<>
Increase/decrease leading in 2 point/pixel increments	Alt+up/down arrow keys
Increase/decrease leading in 10 point/pixel increments	Control/Alt+up/down arrow keys
Increase/decrease baseline shift in 2 point/pixel increments	Alt+Shift+up/down arrow keys
Increase/decrease baseline shift in 10 point/pixel increments	Control+Alt+Shift+ up/down arrow keys
Increase/decrease kerning/tracking in 20/1000 em increments	Alt+left/right arrow keys
Increase/decrease kerning/tracking in 100/1000 em increments	Control+Option/Alt+ left/right arrow keys

WORKING WITH TYPE LAYERS

When setting horizontal or vertical type, Photoshop creates a type layer in the Layers palette (see Figure 11.12). Preserve Transparency is automatically enabled and cannot be disabled. For more information on Preserving Transparency, see page 249 in Chapter 10, "Layers." The text is fully editable at any time before rendering or merging the layers or flattening the image.

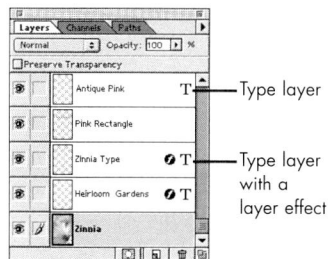

Figure 11.12

The Layers palette with type layers and effects.

In addition to editing the content and attributes of a text layer, you can continue to edit the text even after applying a Layer Effects command or a Transform command such as Rotate and Scale (but not Perspective or Distort). However, you will need to render the type layer as a regular layer if you want to apply a filter effect or transform just part of the layer.

Editing type layers

1   Double-click on the name of the type layer in the Layers palette to open the Type Tool dialog box.

2   To select all of the text, press Command/Control+A. To select a portion of the text, click and drag your cursor over the characters you want to select.

3   Change the font, size, and style of the text and click OK.

CHANGING THE ORIENTATION OF A TYPE LAYER

To change the horizontal or vertical orientation of text on a type layer, select the layer in the Layers palette, and then choose Layer > Type > Horizontal or Vertical (see Figure 11.13).

Figure 11.13

Change the orientation of the text to horizontal or vertical.

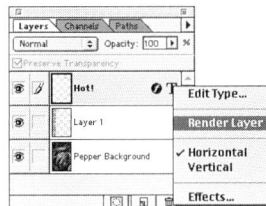

WORKING WITH THE TYPE MASK TOOLS

When you use the type mask tools, an active selection is created that you can stroke, or fill with a color, an image, or a pattern (see Figure 11.14). The type selection can also be used to select parts of an image on which to apply a filter effect or Adjustment command.

Figure 11.14

An active selection is created with the type mask tool.

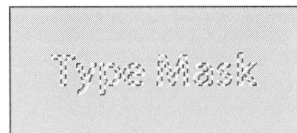

Now you try it...

Creating a type mask

1 Select the horizontal type mask tool in the toolbox.

2 Click in the image area to open the Type Tool dialog box.

3 Set a line of text in the text area at the bottom of the Type Tool dialog box and choose a font size and style. Click OK.

4 The type appears as an active selection in the image window. After the type is filled and deselected, it is placed on the active layer.

5 To fill the type selection, you must make sure Preserve Transparency is not checked in the Layers palette. Choose Edit > Fill > Foreground Color or Option+Delete (Macintosh) or Alt+Delete (Windows).

NOTE

When working with the horizontal or vertical type mask tools, it's important to create a new layer in the Layers palette. If you don't, you cannot alter or move the type after it's deselected because it merges with the active layer in the Layers palette.

RENDERING A LAYER

To render a type layer into a regular layer, select the type layer in the Layers palette and choose Layer > Type > Render Layer. Keep in mind, you can no longer edit the text on the layer, after it is rendered.

You can quickly render a layer by using the context-sensitive menu (see Figure 11.15). Press Control+click (Macintosh) or click the right mouse button (Windows) on the "T" icon to the right of the name of the type layer to display the shortcut menu.

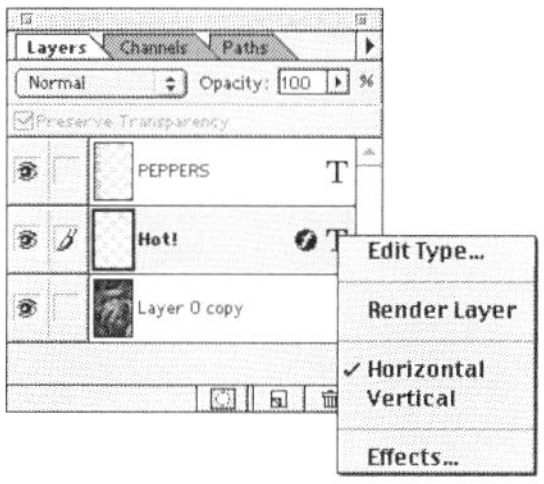

Figure 11.15

Render a layer using a context-sensitive menu.

In the following lesson, you will learn how to set horizontal type, adjust tracking and leading, and fill type with a color using the Color Picker and eyedropper.

Now you try it...

Setting horizontal type

Before you begin, delete the Adobe Photoshop Preferences file to restore the program's default settings. (See page 55 in Chapter 2, "The Photoshop Work Area," for information on how to delete the Preferences file.)

1   Open the files, "Heirloom Gardens Seed Pack.psd" and "Zinnia.psd" located in the Chapter 11 folder on the CD (see Figure 11.16). You will use the Heirloom Gardens Seed Pack.psd file as a reference as you learn to create this image from the beginning using the Zinnia.psd image.

Figure 11.16

The finished seed packet art.

2   Select the horizontal text tool and click anywhere on the Zinnia image to open the Type Tool dialog box.

3   Make sure the Preview box is checked so you can see the type on top of the image in the image window.

4   In the text field at the bottom of the palette, type **Heirloom** and press the return key on your keyboard. Next, type **Gardens** (see Figure 11.17).

5   Highlight the text by clicking and dragging your cursor over the text or pressing Command/Control+A.

6   Choose a font (Trajan was used for this example at **33** points) from the Font menu and enter a size. Adjust the space between the two lines of text by entering an amount for leading (this example used **22**).

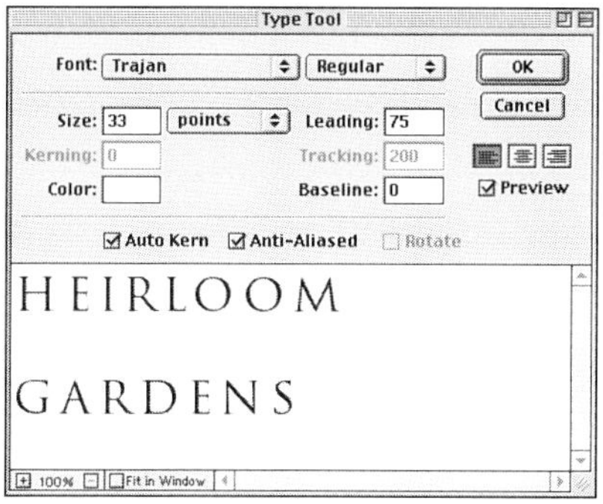

Figure 11.17

Enter the text in the area at the bottom of the Type Tool dialog box.

7 Change the tracking amount (**200** was used here). Center the text by clicking the Centered text box button (see Figure 11.18).

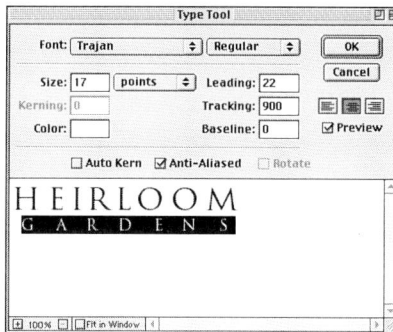

Figure 11.18

Adjust the leading, tracking, and alignment in the Type Tool dialog box.

8 Next, highlight just the **Gardens** text and make the font size smaller (17 points was used for this example). Adjust the spacing between the letters by entering an amount for tracking.

9 Click OK to exit the Type Tool dialog box. Select the move tool to position your text at the top of the image. Notice you now have a type layer in the Layers palette named Heirloom Gardens.

10 Fill the type with white by pressing Command+Delete (Macintosh), Control+Backspace (Windows), or choosing Edit > Fill > White.

11 Create a new layer by clicking the New Layer button at the bottom of the Layers palette. Double-click the thumbnail and name the layer **Pink Rectangle**. Click OK.

continues

12 Double-click the rectangular marquee tool to open the Options palette for that tool. Select Fixed Size from the style pop-up menu and enter the values **197** for width and **22** for height.

13 Click on the image with the marquee tool and position the selection (see Figure 11.19).

Figure 11.19

Position the marquee selection.

14 Select the eyedropper tool and click on a pink area of the image to fill the selection with a shade of pink. Fill the selection by pressing Option+Delete (Mac OS), Alt+Return (Windows), or choose Edit > Fill > Foreground Color.

15 Press Command/Control+D to deselect the rectangle. Change the opacity of the pink rectangle to **50%** in the Layers palette. This will allow the underlying image to partially show through.

16 Select the horizontal type tool once more and position the insertion point over the rectangle. Click to open the Type Tool dialog box. Change the font (Snell Roundhand Black Script at **20** points for the font size was used here).

17 Click inside the text area at the bottom of the Type Tool dialog box and type **Antique Pink**. Highlight the text and change the tracking amount to **495**.

18 Change the color of the type by clicking on the color swatch in the Type Tool dialog box to open the Color Picker and choose a dark gray. Click OK. With the move tool, center the type on top of the pink rectangle.

19 Choose File > Save As and give the image a name for use in the following lesson.

In this next lesson, you will learn how to create a drop shadow with the Layer effects command and how to duplicate and edit a type layer.

Now you try it...

Creating drop shadows for type using the Layer Effects command

Before you begin, delete the Adobe Photoshop Preferences file to restore the program's default settings. (See page 55 in Chapter 2 for information on how to delete the Preferences file.)

1 Open the file "Heirloom Gardens Seed Pack.psd" located in the Chapter 11 folder on the CD and also the file you saved from the previous lesson. You will use the Heirloom Gardens file as a reference as you learn to create drop shadows with the Layer Effects command.

2 To add a drop shadow to the Heirloom Gardens type, make sure the type layer is selected and choose Layer > Effect > Drop Shadow from the Layer Effects menu (see Figure 11.20).

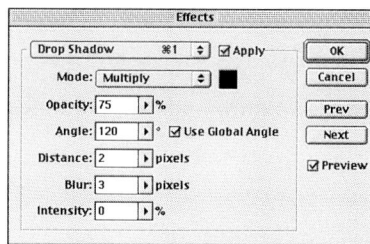

Figure 11.20

The Effects dialog box enables you to select an effect and instantly add it to images, graphic elements, and type.

3 In the Effects menu, check the Preview box as well as the Apply checkbox. The Apply checkbox acts as a toggle, and the effect is applied only when the box is checked.

4 Experiment with the different settings, and then choose the settings in Figure 11.21.

continues

Figure 11.21

The Drop Shadow Effects dialog box enables you to adjust the attributes of a shadow instantly.

5   Because the Zinnia type will have the same drop shadow attributes as the Heirloom Gardens type, you can save a step by making a duplicate layer of the Heirloom Gardens layer and edit that type.

6   Click on the Heirloom Gardens layer and choose Duplicate Layer from the Layers palette menu, or drag the layer on top of the New Layer button at the bottom of the Layers palette (see Figure 11.22).

7   Double-click the thumbnail of the layer copy and rename the layer **Zinnia Type**. Click OK.

8   Next, double-click on the new layer name to open the Type Tool dialog box and edit the text. Highlight the text and change it to read **Zinnia**. Change the font to another style (Book Antiqua was used here).

Figure 11.22

Drag the type layer to the New Layer button to create a duplicate layer.

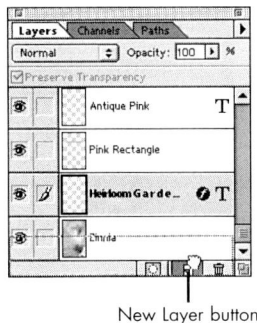

New Layer button

9   With the Type Tool dialog box still open, reposition the type in the correct position in the image window.

10 Change the font size to **40** points. With the font Size field still highlighted, experiment with the type size by pressing the up- and down-arrow keys on your keyboard. This changes the size of the text in one point increments. Add the Shift key and the font size changes in 10 point increments.

11 Press the tab key until the tracking field is highlighted and change the tracking amount. Click OK to exit the dialog box.

12 Choose File > Save.

NOTE

Because you're working with a type mask tool, you won't see a preview of the text in the image window. The type mask tool makes an active unfilled selection.

In the next step-by-step tutorial, you learn how to set vertical type, use a type mask, and fill and stroke type with a color using the Color Picker and the eyedropper.

Now you try it...

Setting vertical type with the type mask tool

Before you begin, delete the Adobe Photoshop Preferences file to restore the program's default settings. See page 55 in Chapter 2 for information on how to delete the Preferences file.

1   Open the files "Hot Peppers Final.psd" and "Hot Peppers.psd" located in the Chapter 11 folder on the CD. You will use the "Hot Peppers Final.psd" file as a reference (see Figure 11.23) as you learn to create this image from the beginning using the Hot Peppers.psd image.

2   Create a new layer, select the vertical type mask tool, and click anywhere on the Pepper image to open the Type Tool dialog box. Make sure the Preview box is checked so you can see the type on top of the image in the image window.

3   In the text field at the bottom of the palette, type **PEPPERS** in all caps (see Figure 11.24).

NOTE

It's important to create a new layer when using the type mask tool. If you don't create a new layer, you won't be able to alter or move the type once it's deselected, because it merges with the active layer in the Layers palette.

continues

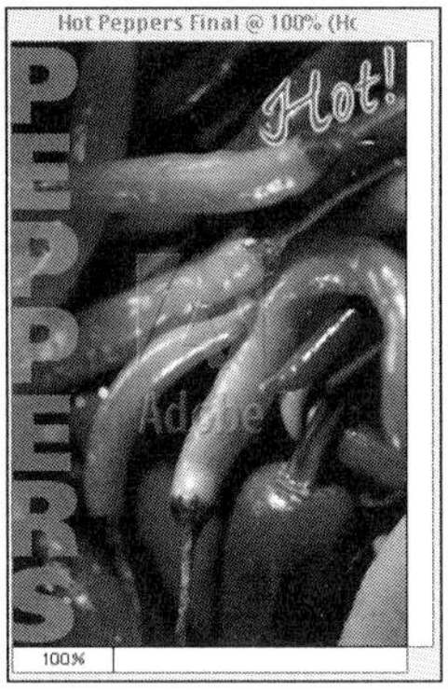

Figure 11.23

The finished Hot
Peppers image.

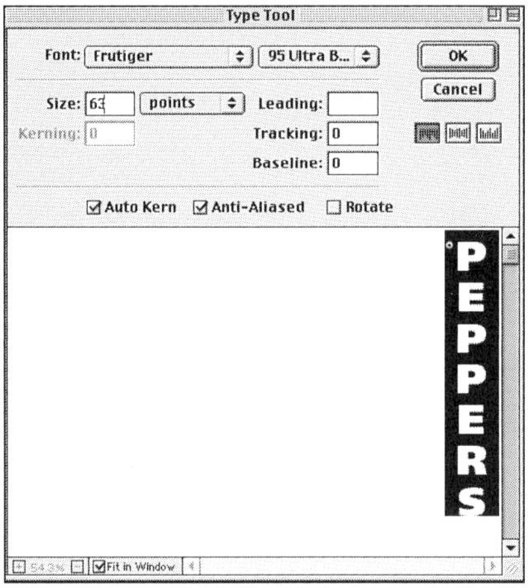

Figure 11.24

The Type Tool
dialog box using the
vertical type mask
tool.

4 Highlight the text by clicking and dragging your cursor over it or
by pressing Command/Control+A. Choose a font from the Font
menu. (This example used Frutiger Ultra Black at **63** points.)
Tighten the tracking amount (–**200** was used here). Click OK.

5 The text is now an active selection. With the type mask tool
still selected, reposition the text to the left side of the image.

6 To fill the type with yellow, select the eyedropper and click
bright yellow in the image. Choose Edit > Fill > Foreground
color.

7 To stroke the type with red, again use the eyedropper and click
on a red area of the image. Choose Edit > Stroke and enter an
amount of **2** pixels in the Stroke dialog box (see Figure 11.25).

Choose Center and click OK. By choosing Center with an amount of **2** pixels, one pixel will be on the inside of the selection and the other pixel will be outside the selection.

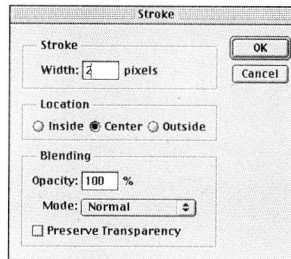

Figure 11.25

Specify a width, location, opacity, and blending mode of a stroke in the Stroke dialog box.

8   Press Command/Alt+D or choose Select > Deselect to deselect the type.

9   To adjust the opacity of the type, click on the opacity slider in the Layers palette or type the opacity percentage on your keyboard.

In this final lesson, you'll learn how to work with kerning, tracking, and baseline shift; and how to create an outer glow on type using the Layer Effects command.

Now you try it...

Adjusting Kerning, Tracking, and Baseline Shift

Before you begin, delete the Adobe Photoshop Preferences file to restore the program's default settings. See page 55 in Chapter 2 for information on how to delete the Preferences file.

1   Open the files "Hot Peppers Final.psd" located in the Chapter 11 folder on the CD and the file you saved from the previous lesson. You will use the "Hot Peppers Final.psd" file as a reference (see Figure 11.23) as you learn to work with kerning, tracking, and leading and create an outer glow effect with the Layer Effects command.

continues

2   Select the horizontal type tool and click anywhere on the image to open the Type Tool dialog box. Change the font and size. (This example used ExPonto Regular at **50** points with tracking set to **0**.)

3   In the text field at the bottom of the Type Tool dialog box, type **Hot!** and click OK.

4   To add the outer glow effect to the type, make sure the type layer is selected. From the Layer pull-down menu choose Effects > Outer Glow.

5   In the Effects dialog box, make sure the Preview box and the Apply button are checked (see Figure 11.26). Reposition the dialog box so you can preview the effect.

Figure 11.26

The layer Effects dialog box for the outer glow effect.

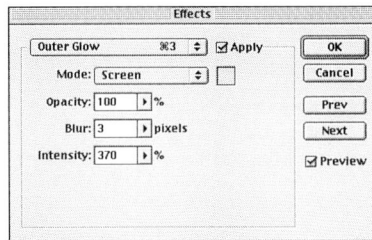

6   Click on the color swatch and choose a bright yellow in the Color Picker. Change the opacity to **100%**, enter **3** for the blur amount, and change the intensity to **255**. Click OK to apply the effect. You can quickly edit the layer effect by using the context-sensitive menu (see Figure 11.27). Control+click (Mac OS) or click the right mouse button (Windows) on the Layer Effect icon to the right of the type layer name to display the shortcut menu.

Figure 11.27

A context-sensitive menu enables you to edit or apply additional effects to the active type layer.

7 To adjust the baseline of each individual letter, first double-click on the Hot! type layer to open the Type Tool dialog box (see Figure 11.28). Highlight the letters "O" and "T" and change the baseline amount to **12**. This moves the two letters up 12 points. Next highlight just the exclamation point and change the baseline amount to **27**. Note your adjustment amounts may need to be different based on the font you've chosen.

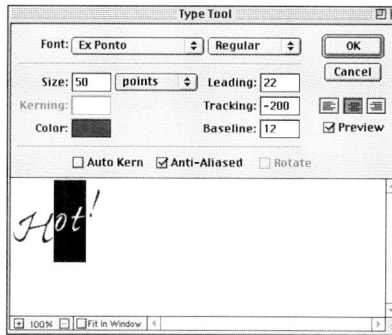

Figure 11.28

Adjust the baseline by highlighting the characters and entering the amount in the Baseline field.

8 To adjust the kerning between the letters, click the Auto Kern button off, position the cursor between the "H" and the "O," and enter an amount of **20** in the kerning field (see Figure 11.29). Next position the cursor between the "0" and the "T" and enter a kerning value of **75**. It may be necessary to continue to click the Auto Kern button off. Last, position the cursor between the "T" and the exclamation point and enter a kerning value of **300**. Click OK to apply the modification to the type.

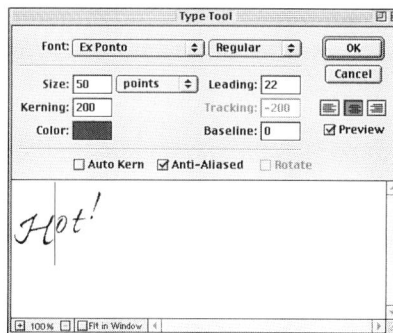

Figure 11.29

Adjust the space between characters by placing the insertion point between two characters and changing the kerning value.

continues

> **9** Select the move tool and position the text in the upper right corner of the image. Choose File > Save As and give your new image a name.

SUMMARY

Editable type layers, Layer Effects, and increased formatting control give new strength to Photoshop 5.0 and provide more flexibility than ever when adding type to images or preparing type for usage in both print and Web page design. Because there are several new capabilities to the type features in Photoshop, you can expect to see questions about creating type on the exam. By studying this chapter, practicing the lessons, and experimenting on your own, you should be well prepared.

REVIEW QUESTIONS

1. What happens when the anti-aliasing option is turned on in the Type Tool dialog box?

    a. The text is bitmapped.

    b. The text retains the font outline.

    c. The edges of the text are blurred for a smoother appearance.

    d. It has no affect on the text if set in Adobe Illustrator and imported into Photoshop.

2. What does kerning do to text?

    a. It raises or lowers the selected text.

    b. It adjusts the amount of space between two characters.

    c. It equally adjusts spacing between more than two characters.

    d. It adjusts the spacing between two lines of text depending on where the cursor is inserted.

3. What happens when you check the Rotate box in the Type Tool dialog box?

    a. Vertical text is rotated 90°.

    b. Horizontal text is rotated 90°.

    c. Text is rotated in 45° increments.

    d. The Edit > Transform command is enabled.

4. What do you do to increase/decrease type size in 10 point/pixel increments?

    a. Press up and down arrow keys.

    b. Press Shift+up/down arrow keys.

    c. Press Option+Shift+up/down arrow keys.

    d. Press Command+Option+Shift+up/down arrow keys (Macintosh) or Control+Alt+Shift+up/down arrow keys.

5. When applying a filter to a text layer, what must you do first?

    a. Render the layer.

    b. Choose a filter from the Filter menu.

    c. Make sure the layer isn't linked to another layer.

    d. Make the text an active selection and choose a filter from the Filter menu.

6. How do you reposition text in the image window while still in the Type dialog box?

    a. You must close the Type dialog box in order to move the type in the image window.

    b. Click and drag on the type in the image window.

    c. Select the move tool, and then click and drag the type in the image window.

    d. Move the type with the move tool while in the Type dialog box.

7. What does tracking do to text?

    a. It raises or lowers the selected text.

    b. It adjusts spacing between two characters.

    c. It adjusts the amount of space between characters and words.

    d. It adjusts the spacing between two lines of text depending on where the cursor is inserted.

8. How do you edit a layer effect applied to text?

    a. Choose Text effects from the Edit menu.

    b. Choose Edit > text effects from the Layers palette.

    c. Double-click on the Type icon in the Layers palette.

    d. Double-click on the text effect "f" icon in the Layers palette.

CHAPTER 12

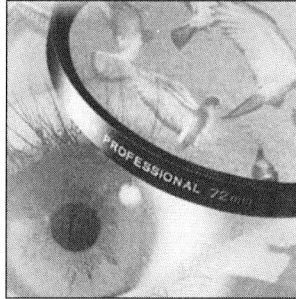

FILTERS

You can use Photoshop's filters to create a wide range of image effects. More than 100 filters are installed when you install Photoshop. These range from special effects such as lens flares, to artistic effects such as watercolors, to texture effects such as mosaic tiles. Filters are a specific type of plug-in. Because others can write plug-ins for Photoshop, filters can be purchased from several sources to provide an even greater variety of effects. Further, some filters are freely available on the World Wide Web. Photoshop 5.0 even comes with a Filter Factory plug-in that enables you to create your own filter effects.

Domains & Objectives

Painting and Editing

6.4 Identify issues regarding the basic characteristics and function of filters, including the 3D Transform, Displace, Dust & Scratches, Lighting Effects, Sharpen, and other filters.

FILTER OVERVIEW

Only some of the filters that come with Photoshop are described in this chapter. They were chosen in part because they are explicitly required for the exam, and also in part for their importance and wide use. You are encouraged to experiment with all the filters. Whereas some of the filters have purposes easily apparent from their names, some are a little ambiguous, and still others are commonly used to produce effects for which they might not have been originally intended.

Filters are plug-ins and are usually located in Photoshop's Plug-Ins folder. For more information about choosing the folder for Photoshop to search for plug-ins, see Chapter 1, "General Information."

In general, the filters can be selected from the Filter menu in Photoshop. The Filter menu has further submenus, which categorize all the filters (see Figure 12.1).

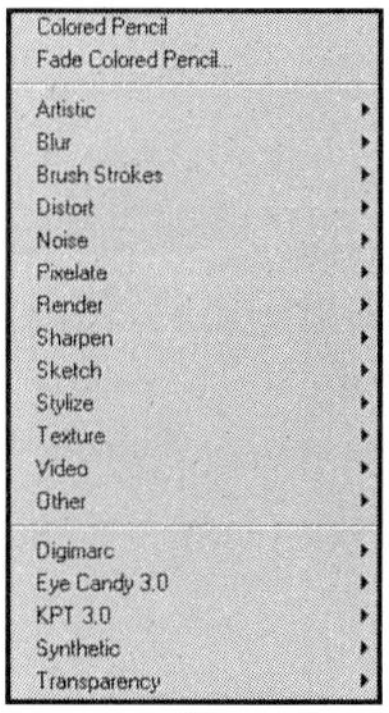

Figure 12.1

You choose the filter you want to run from the appropriate category within the Filter menu.

All filters will work on an image in RGB mode. Bitmap and Indexed Color modes and any mode in 16 Bits/Channel do not support the use of any filters. Grayscale mode supports all the filters except those especially intended for RGB images: Lens Flare, Lighting Effects, and NTSC Colors. In CMYK and Lab mode, about half the filters are available. If you need to run a specific filter and it is unavailable or dimmed, the image could be in the wrong image mode.

Filters change the information contained on a single layer at a time, even if layers are linked. If the layer is empty, Photoshop warns you if it cannot run the filter (see Figure 12.2). You cannot apply any of the filters to a layer that is turned off.

NOTE

If you want to apply a filter to more than one layer, merge the layers. You can make copies of the layers and merge the copies if you need the separated layer information. For more information about layers, see Chapter 10, "Layers."

Figure 12.2

Make sure that the layer is not empty before running the filter.

TIP

To compare the results of applying a filter with a copy of the image before the filter was run, make a snapshot of the image.

If a selection is present, Photoshop applies the filter's effect to the selected pixels. You can run filters on individual channels, but because they are 8-bit grayscale, you have the same limitations as an image in Grayscale mode.

Using filters can be time-consuming, especially on larger images. Photoshop shows you the progress of applying the filter in the status bar. If you want to test the effect of a filter on a very large image, either apply the filter to a small selected area or make a low-resolution copy of the image and apply the filter.

3D TRANSFORM

The 3D Transform filter is new to Photoshop 5.0. You can use it to make adjustments in size, shape, position, and rotation of 3D objects. Whereas images in Photoshop are only 2D, the 3D Transform filter enables you to make changes to pixels in the image as though they were 3D objects.

The 3D Transform filter enables you to select one or more 3D objects. The objects can be any collection of spheres, cylinders, or boxes. To use the 3D Transform filter, select 3D Transform from the Render submenu in the Filter menu. You then can use the 3D Transform dialog box to create wireframe objects and change them (see Figure 12.3).

Figure 12.3

Use the 3D Transform dialog box to select and transform objects in an image.

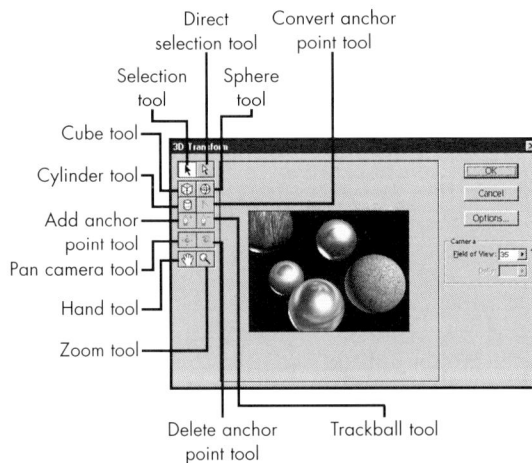

USING THE FILTER

When Photoshop displays the 3D Transform dialog box, you can use the wireframe creation tools to create a cube, sphere, or cylinder around the objects in an image. When created, the 3D wireframes can be modified using the selection and anchor point tools and moved and rotated using the pan camera and trackball tools. The selection and anchor point tools work like the tools used to modify paths. A preview of the change displays in a window in the dialog box. You can pan and zoom in the preview window using the hand and zoom tools, which work identically to the hand and zoom tools in the Photoshop toolbox. When you have finished, click the OK button to accept the transformation.

THE CUBE TOOL

Use the cube tool to draw a cube to match a boxlike object in an image (see Figure 12.4). Start by clicking in one corner and drag to the opposite corner. You might need to adjust the cube using the direct selection tool and the camera's field of view after you have created the cube.

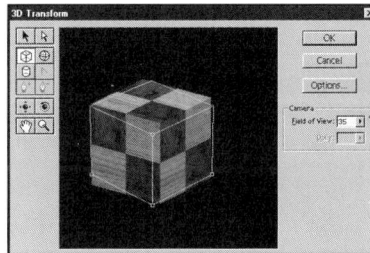

Figure 12.4

Click and drag a cube over a boxlike object in the image. You can adjust it after it is created.

THE SPHERE TOOL

The sphere tool is used to create spheres to match spherical objects in the Photoshop image. To use the sphere tool, select it, click on a point along the edge of the sphere, and drag to choose the second point (see Figure 12.5). It is best to pick a point along the horizontal diameter because Photoshop creates the sphere based on the horizontal distance between the two points you pick while clicking and dragging. If the sphere is not perfectly placed or sized from the outset, you can change it afterward using the direct selection tool.

THE CYLINDER TOOL

The cylinder tool can be used to create cylindrical wireframes to match similar shapes in an image. As with the cube and sphere, click and drag to create a cylinder. When created, it can be modified using some of the other tools similar to those in the Photoshop toolbox (direct selection, convert anchor point, add anchor, and delete anchor point tools). The cylinder's sides can be modified to match a variety of other shapes such as cones, bottles, and hourglass-shaped objects (see Figure 12.6).

Figure 12.5

Use the sphere tool to create spheres over spherical objects in the image.

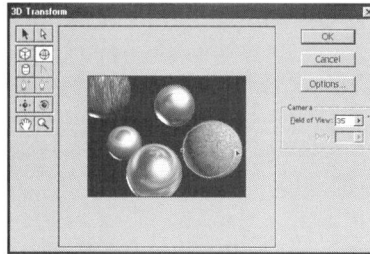

Figure 12.6

The cylinder that you create with the cylinder tool can be modified to match a variety of other shapes.

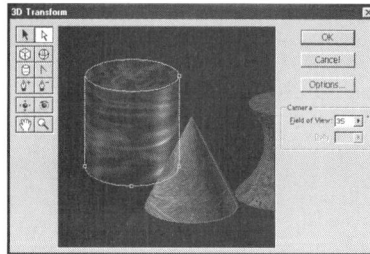

SELECTION TOOLS

Use the selection tool to select and move the wireframes you create in the 3D Transform window. To select a wireframe, click on it. When the wireframe is selected, Photoshop outlines the wireframe with a brighter shade of green. You can select only one wireframe at a time. To move a wireframe, click on it and drag.

The direct selection tool is used to select the anchor points of a wireframe. By clicking on and dragging the anchor points, the wireframe can be modified to fit more closely over the appropriate area of the image. The wireframes can be resized and rotated by clicking and dragging with the direct selection tool. A cylinder's anchor points can be moved to make the cylinder into a cone, or if anchor points have been added to the cylinder, they can be moved to create concavity or bulging areas.

To delete a wireframe, select it with either the selection or the direct selection tool and use the Delete or Backspace key. Like any action taken in the 3D Transform window, this cannot be undone.

ANCHOR POINT TOOLS

The convert anchor point, add anchor point, and delete anchor point tools are only available if a cylinder is selected. These tools can be used to transform the shape of the cylinder (see Figure 12.7). These tools work much like the tools you use to edit paths. Click on the right side of the cylinder to add an anchor point. Photoshop mirrors this added anchor point on the left side. With the delete anchor point tool, click on an added anchor point to remove it. The convert anchor point tool changes an added anchor point to a corner point. If you attempt to change the wireframe into a shape that cannot actually be constructed, Photoshop will warn you by changing the wires to red.

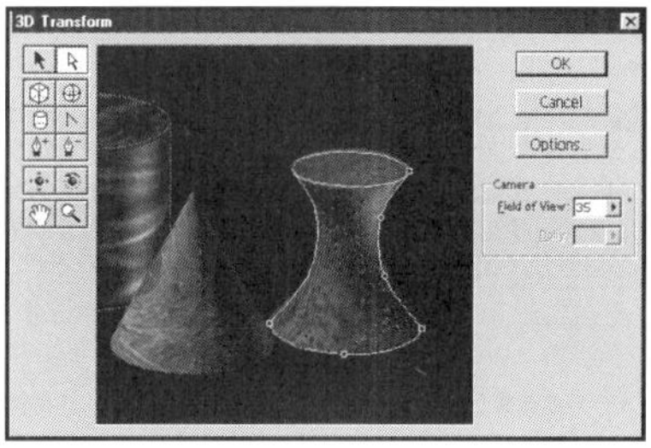

Figure 12.7

Anchor points can only be added to the right side of a cylinder.

CAMERA CONTROLS AND THE TRACKBALL

There are two values used to control the camera in the 3D Transform window: the Field of View and Dolly values. Change the Field of View value with any of the selection, wireframe creation, or anchor point tools to make the wireframes better match those in the image (see Figure 12.8).

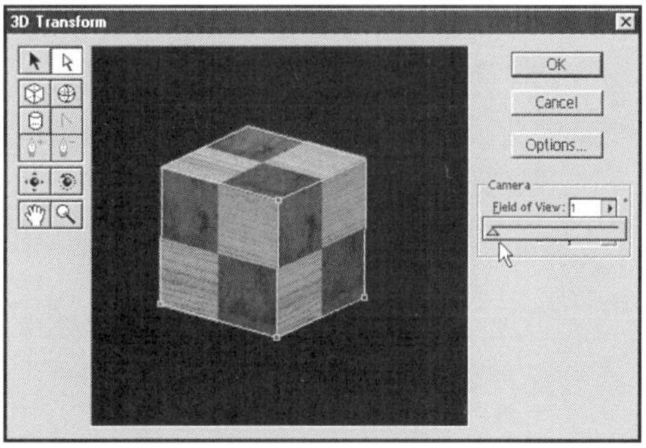

Figure 12.8

Change the value for the Field of View to make the wireframe more closely match the object in the image.

You can match the field of view used to create the original image if it is known. Values for the Field of View range from 1 degree to 130 degrees. If you change the Field of View value while the pan camera tool is selected, the objects are scaled as the camera's field of view increases or decreases.

The Dolly value can be set only while the pan camera tool or trackball tool is active. The Dolly value controls the relative scale of the wireframes and preview objects in the window as the camera moves closer or farther from the wireframes and objects (see Figure 12.9).

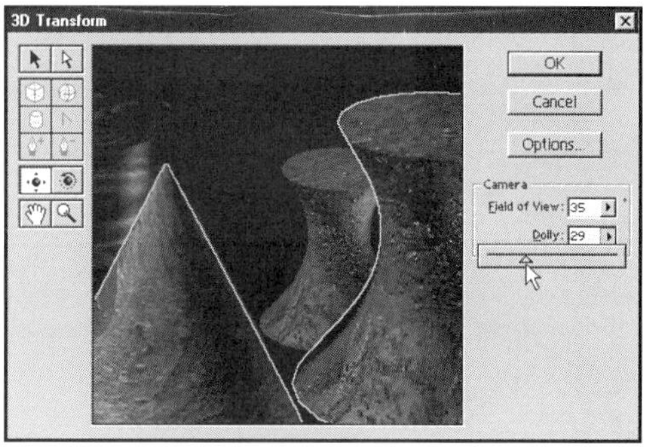

Figure 12.9

The Dolly value is used to scale the wireframes and objects in the 3D Transform window.

The pan camera tool and trackball tool move and rotate the wireframes and objects they define. To move the wireframes and objects, select the pan camera tool, and then click and drag (see Figure 12.10).

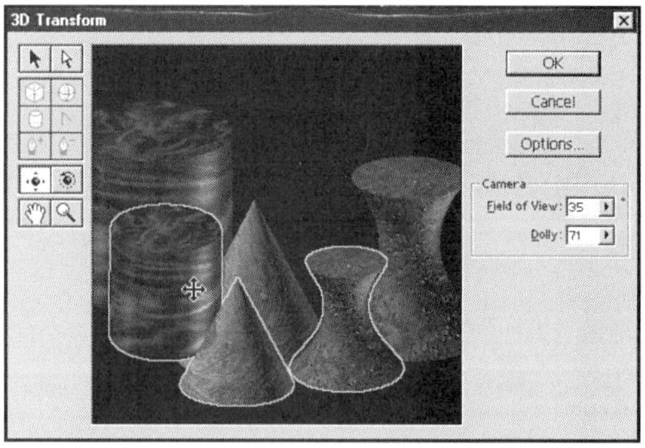

Figure 12.10

The pan camera tool is used to move all the wireframes and objects in the image.

To rotate the wireframes and objects in 3D space, click and drag with the trackball tool selected. If the wireframes and objects are rotated so far that Photoshop cannot use any pixels to continue a pattern on the surface, the faces of the 3D object without any pattern on the surfaces will be shown (see Figure 12.11).

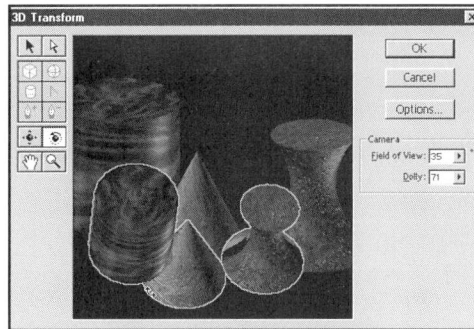

Figure 12.11

If Photoshop can't find enough pixels to continue the pattern, it will show the faces of the 3D object defined by the wireframe.

OPTIONS FOR RENDERING THE 3D TRANSFORMATION

Clicking on the Options button in the 3D Transform dialog box enables you to determine how the transformed objects render. You can set the Resolution to Low, Medium, or High. This controls the quality of the rendering of the objects defined by the wireframes, particularly spheres and cylinders. You can also control the amount of anti-aliasing that Photoshop applies to the rendered objects or turn off anti-aliasing by choosing the None option. You can also control whether the background is displayed in the 3D Transform window and in the resulting image after the filter is applied.

Now you try it...

Using the 3D Transform filter

1　Open the "lesson01.psd" image in the Chapter 12 lessons folder on the CD (see Figure 12.12).

Figure 12.12

Begin with this image to apply the 3D Transform filter.

continues

2 Start the 3D Transform filter by selecting Filter > Render > 3D Transform. Use the sphere tool to create a wireframe around the ball in the image by clicking and dragging. Use the selection tool to move the wireframe and the direct selection tool to resize the wireframe to match the underlying image. Zoom in using the zoom tool if necessary (see Figure 12.13).

Figure 12.13

Use the sphere tool to create a wireframe sphere to match the underlying ball.

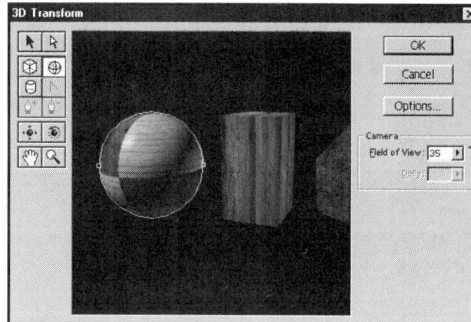

3 Use the box tool to create a wireframe box over the underlying box in the image by clicking in one corner and dragging to the other. Use the selection, direct selection, and zoom tools as necessary. Change the Field of View value to **110** degrees (see Figure 12.14). This was the field of view used to create the original image and will help the object you have created more closely match the block in the image.

Figure 12.14

Change the Field of View to match that used to create the image.

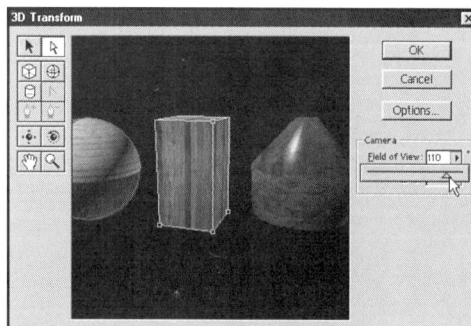

4 Because the Field of View value applies to all wireframes, you might need to slightly adjust the sphere wireframe.

5   Use the cylinder tool to create a rough cylinder wireframe over the final object in the image. Change its position using the selection tool. Use the direct selection tool to move the anchor points to match the top and bottom of the underlying object. The result is a cone (see Figure 12.15).

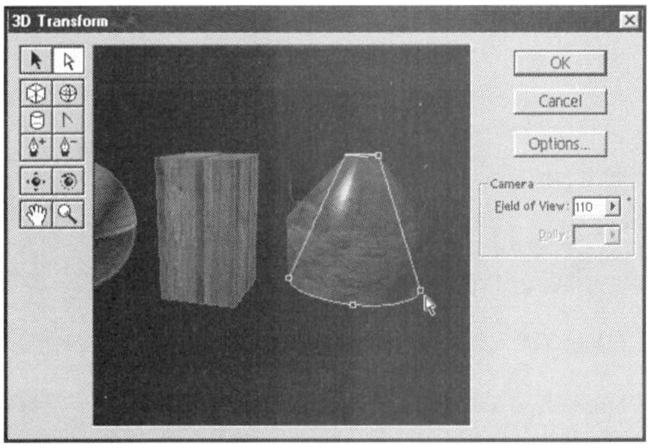

Figure 12.15

Use the cylinder tool to create a cylinder and make it match the underlying object using the direct selection tool.

6   Use the add anchor point tool to add an anchor point on the right side of the cone. Click on this newly created anchor point with the convert anchor point tool and use the direct selection tool to change the shape of the wireframe (see Figure 12.16).

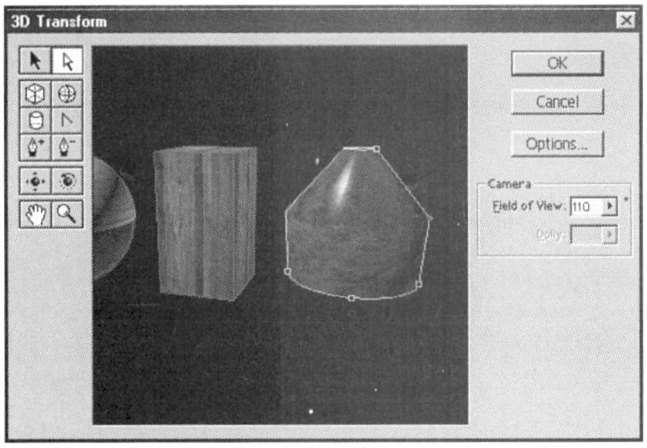

Figure 12.16

Add an anchor point, convert it, and then drag it to match the underlying object.

7   Click the Options button and turn off the Display Background option. Select the pan camera tool. Adjust the Field of View to **65** degrees and the Dolly value to **99**. With the pan camera tool, click in the 3D Transform window and drag the objects toward the top of the windows (see Figure 12.17).

continues

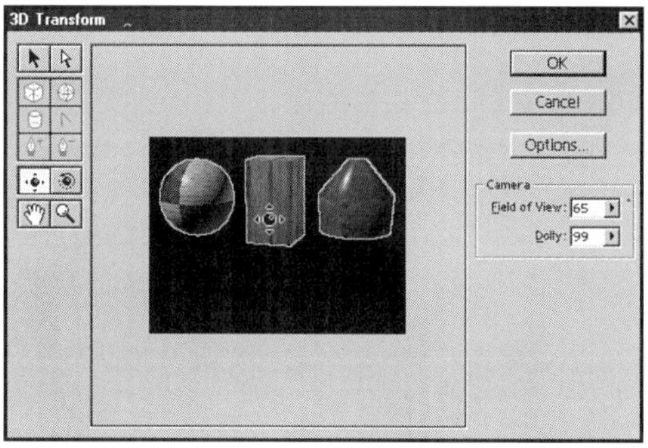

Figure 12.17

Use the pan camera tool to move the wire-frames and objects they define.

8 Click and drag with the trackball tool to rotate the objects in 3D space. Try dragging with the trackball tool into different positions. Note what happens when Photoshop does not have enough information to apply a map over the complete wireframe. Rotate the objects until you are viewing them from above (see Figure 12.18).

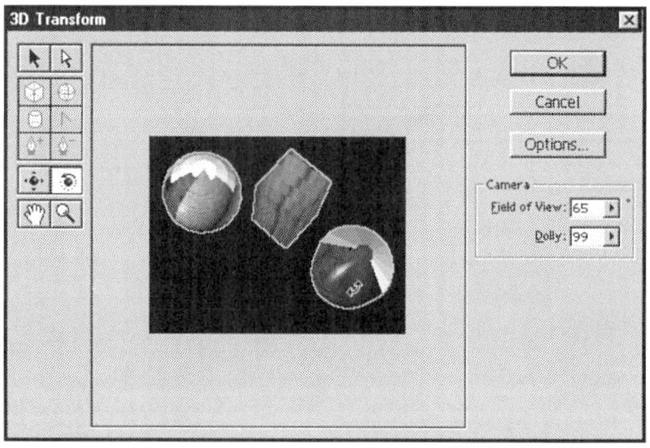

Figure 12.18

Rotate the objects in 3D space with the trackball tool.

9 Click OK. Note what happened in the areas of missing texture on the sphere and cylinder, and that the map on the cube was repeated to fill in the missing area (see Figure 12.19). Close the file.

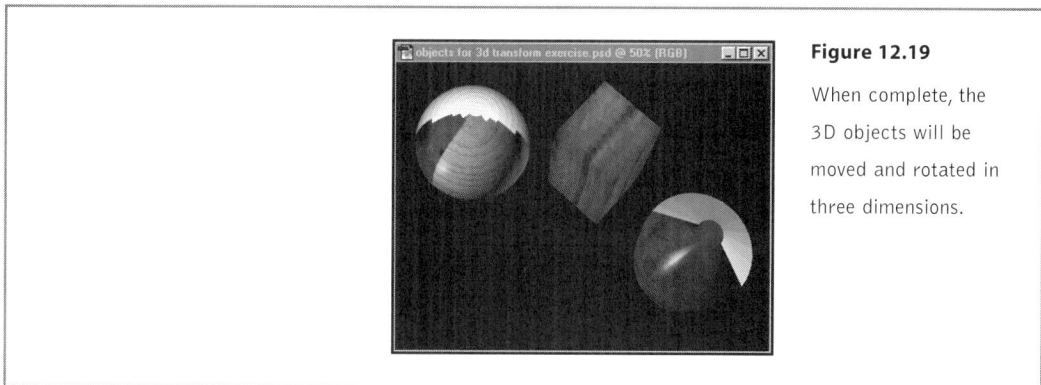

Figure 12.19

When complete, the
3D objects will be
moved and rotated in
three dimensions.

DISPLACE

The Displace filter uses a displacement map to apply a horizontal and vertical
scale to an image. The Displace filter is commonly used to make an image
appear that it is on a surface that is irregular, either in shape or texture. Found
in the Distort submenu of the Filters menu, the Displace filter prompts you to
provide horizontal and vertical scales as well as how to use the displacement
map and what to do about undefined areas (see Figure 12.20).

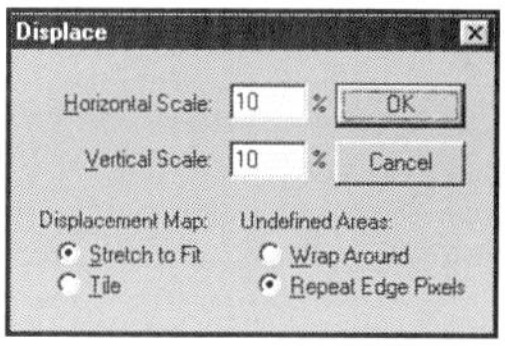

Figure 12.20

Use the Displace filter
settings to control how
the displacement map is
applied to the image.

After you choose the scales and options and you click OK, Photoshop will
prompt you to choose a file to use as a displacement map. The displacement
map should be an image in any mode but Bitmap, and it should be flattened
or include a composite image with layer information. The Displace filter
examines the displacement map image, and where it finds color values of 0
(black) or 255 (white), it performs the maximum negative and positive
shifts. A middle gray value of 128 performs no shift. Figures 12.21, 12.22,
and 12.23 show the original image, the displacement map, and the displacement map applied to the original image.

Figure 12.21

This is the original image before the Displace filter is applied.

Figure 12.22

The areas of the displacement map that are 50% gray have no effect on the final image.

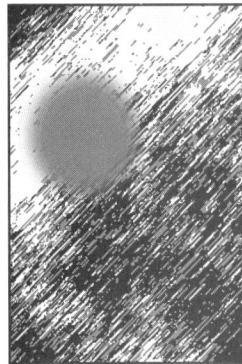

Figure 12.23

The effects of the Displace filter are most apparent in high contrast areas of the image.

Now you try it...

Using the Displace filter

1   Open the "lesson02.psd" image in the Chapter 12 lessons folder on the CD (see Figure 12.24).

Figure 12.24

Apply a displacement map using the Displace filter.

2   Start the Displace filter by choosing Filter > Distort > Displace.

3   In the Displace dialog box, enter a horizontal and vertical scale of **25%**. Click the Stretch to Fit radio button and the Repeat Edge Pixels radio button. Click OK.

4   When prompted to select a file for the displacement map, choose "lesson02d.psd" in the Chapter 12 lessons folder on the CD.

5   The Displace filter will be applied using the selected displacement map. See Figure 12.25 for the resulting image.

Try using the Displace filter with different settings or with your own displacement map. When finished, close the file.

Figure 12.25

The original image is displaced using the displacement map image.

NOISE AND DUST & SCRATCHES

The noise filters in Photoshop are used to add to or remove noise from an image. There are four noise filters: Add Noise, Despeckle, Dust & Scratches, and Median. The Add Noise filter randomly adds noise to an image. The Despeckle filter searches the image for edges and then blurs all but the detected edge areas, removing noise while attempting to maintain detail. The Dust & Scratches filter can be used to remove dust and scratches from an image. Finally, the Median filter reduces noise in an image typically caused by motion.

ADD NOISE

The Add Noise filter changes the color of pixels randomly throughout an image in a specified amount. When you choose the Add Noise filter, Photoshop prompts you to choose the amount of noise to add and how it should be added (see Figure 12.26). Values for the Amount of noise to add can range from 1, which is a minimal amount, to 999. At the maximum setting, only the highest contrast areas are faintly distinguishable.

Figure 12.26

Specify the amount and type of noise to be added in the Add Noise dialog box.

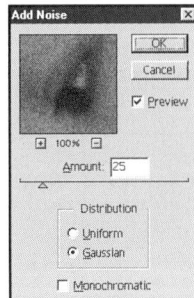

TIP

To save time on a very large image, turn off the preview in the Filter dialog box.

The Add Noise dialog box displays a small preview of the effect in a window. You can use the plus and minus buttons in the dialog box to zoom in and out in the preview window. If you click inside the window, a hand tool enables you to pan to different areas of the image. If you click on the number found between the plus and minus buttons, the image in the preview window zooms to 100%. You can also choose whether to display a preview of the effect in the actual image. Many filters with similar dialog boxes behave identically.

There are two types of noise you can add: Uniform and Gaussian. If Uniform is selected, the color values for the changed pixels are determined by selecting randomly from a range of colors determined by the Amount value.

If Gaussian is selected, the same range is used, but the pixels are selected along a bell-curve distribution. The Uniform option produces smoother noise (see Figure 12.27), and the Gaussian option produces a more apparent speckled effect (see Figure 12.28). You can also choose to add noise mono-chromatically, so that the underlying color is preserved.

Figure 12.27

Noise added uniformly produces a smoother effect than if Gaussian is used.

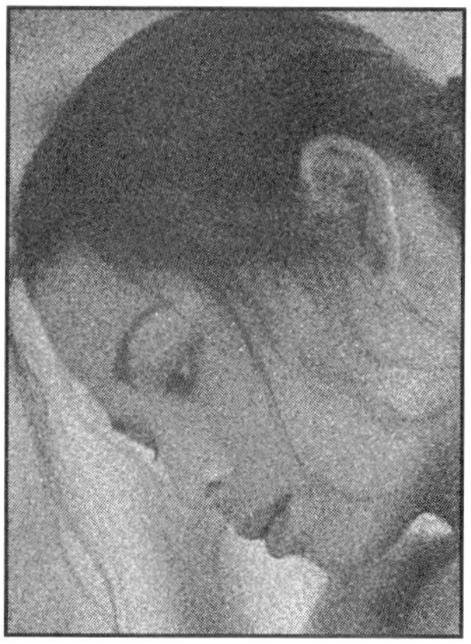

Figure 12.28

Using the Gaussian option produces speckled noise.

TIP

Use the Add Noise filter to add randomness to an area that has been re-touched if it looks too smooth.

DUST & SCRATCHES

The Dust & Scratches filter enables you to eliminate small blemishes on a photograph. Small blemishes can be introduced to the digital image at many stages, such as when the picture is originally taken and developed or when it is scanned. This filter helps eliminate some of these imperfections by mak-ing areas of color match, specifically by removing pixels whose colors do not match their surrounding areas. When the Dust & Scratches filter is selected from the Noise submenu of the Filter menu, a dialog box is displayed (see Figure 12.29).

Figure 12.29

You can control exactly how Photoshop corrects the blemishes in the image by changing the Radius and Threshold values.

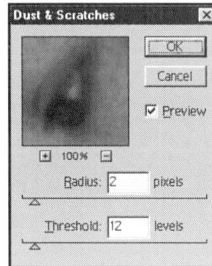

When the Dust & Scratches filter is started, the Radius is set to 1 and the Threshold to 0. The Radius determines the area to be searched for pixels of dissimilar color. Values for the Radius range from 1 to 16. The higher the value, the blurrier the image becomes, so the goal is most often to choose the smallest value that still produces the desired effect. The Threshold value determines the range of acceptable colors for pixels within the area determined by the Radius. The higher the value, the greater the range of acceptable colors. For the Threshold value, the goal is most often to choose the highest value that still produces the desired effect. Figures 12.30, 12.31, and 12.32 show an application of the Dust & Scratches filter.

Figure 12.30

Small blemishes, black marks, and gray scratches were intentionally added to the wall of this building.

Figure 12.31

These are the results with a Radius of 1 and a Threshold of 26. Only the larger blemishes remain.

Figure 12.32

With the Radius set to 2 and the Threshold set to 16, the blemishes are no longer apparent, although the image is slightly blurred.

LIGHTING EFFECTS

The Lighting Effects filter, available in the Render submenu of the Filter menu and applicable only to images in RGB mode, is one of the most versatile of the filters. It can be used to make subtle changes to the lighting of an object or area; or you can use it to make dramatic changes to an image and the way it appears to be lit. Like the Displace filter, it can even make use of a map—in this case, to apply texture to an area. The Lighting Effects concept is relatively simple. You define the types of lights and properties of the lights to control how the image appears to be lit in the Lighting Effects dialog box (see Figure 12.33). The lights can be used to either lighten or darken an image. There are infinite possibilities available when using this filter. The same suggestion about experimentation for discovering the use of filters in general is applicable to this filter in particular: The best way to learn exactly how the Lighting Effects filter changes an image is to play with it. The basic use and options for the filter are outlined in the following sections.

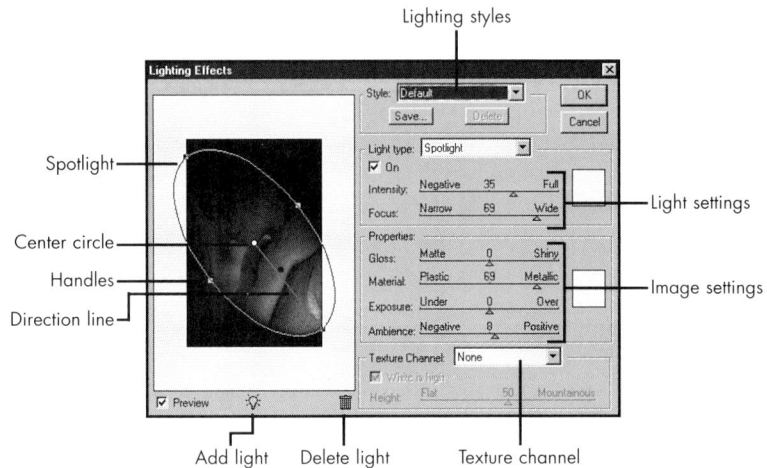

The Lighting Effects filter contains three kinds of lights, with controls for each, and four controls to determine the surface quality of the image. The filter also has 17 preset light combinations. There are several tools that are used to move, resize, add, and delete lights.

ADDING, DELETING, AND MOVING LIGHTS

Click the add light icon in the Lighting Effects dialog box and drag into the preview windows to create a new light. After a light is created, it has a center circle to determine position, handles to determine the area of effect, and a direction line to determine the direction of the light. You can move the light by clicking the center circle and dragging. You can change the area of effect for omni lights and spotlights by clicking and dragging the handles. You can change the direction for spotlights and directional lights by clicking and dragging on the endpoint of the direction line (see Figure 12.34).

You can delete any light by clicking on the center circle and dragging it to the delete light (Trashcan) icon. You can also select the light and press the Backspace or Delete key to remove the light. You must have at least one light defined, so if you only have one light in the preview window, you cannot delete it.

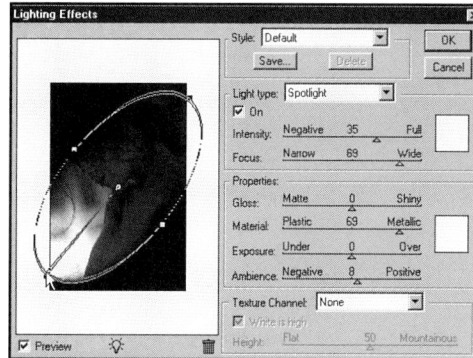

Figure 12.34

Drag the handles of a
spotlight to control the
area of effect and the
endpoint of the direction
line to control the direction of effect.

CONTROLLING LIGHTS

After a light has been created, you can change its type by selecting from the
Light type pop-up menu. You can choose spotlight, omni light, or directional light. A *spotlight* has a direction, an area of effect, and a position. It behaves like a spotlight that can be directed onto an image. Figure 12.33 shows
an example of a spotlight. The spotlight has an elliptical area of effect, controlled by the handles. An *omni light* has an area of effect and position but
no direction. An omni light is similar to a spotlight that shines perpendicu-
lar to the surface of the image (see Figure 12.35). The area of effect is circular and can be increased or decreased by dragging any of the handles.

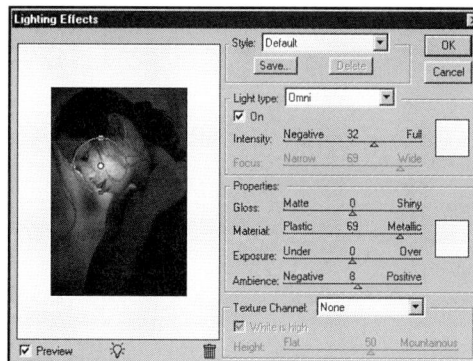

Figure 12.35

An omni light is a point
light source without any
direction.

A *direction light* has a direction and position, but affects the entire image
equally, like the rays of the sun (see Figure 12.36). The length of the direction line controls the height of the light and therefore the amount of added
light as the light is moved closer to or farther from the image.

Figure 12.36

A directional light either
lightens or darkens the
entire image equally.

All the light types can be turned on and off by selecting the light and then
using the on/off toggle. All the lights also have an Intensity value. The values for Intensity range from –100 to 100. At –100, the light darkens the
image at the maximum, and at 100, the light applies a maximum amount of
light. All lights also have a color control. Clicking in the color swatch causes
the Color Picker to display; you can choose any color for the light color (see
Figure 12.37).

Figure 12.37

Adjust the color of the
lights to produce
different effects.

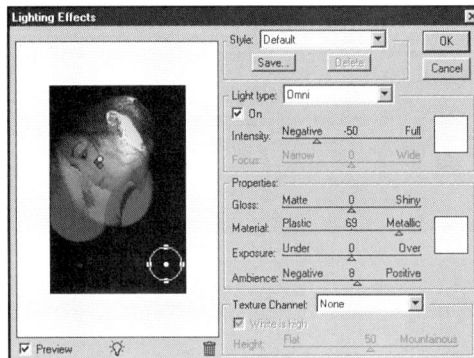

Spotlights have an additional control for the Focus. The Focus can range
from –100 to 100, like the Intensity. At –100 (narrow), the spotlight is
focused on a very small area. At 100 (wide), the spotlight fills the ellipse,
which defines the area of effect more evenly (see Figure 12.38).

SETTING THE PROPERTIES

The Properties in the Lighting Effects dialog box determine how the light
should interact with the surface of the image. The Properties are set globally
and apply to every light. All values range from –100 to 100. The Gloss

property determines whether the surface should be treated as a matte or glossy surface. Setting a high value increases the specular highlight for a spotlight or omni light, and setting a low value creates a more diffused effect.

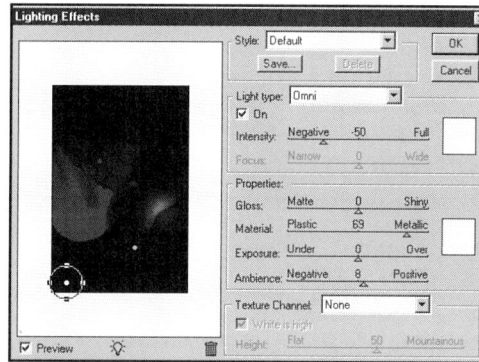

Figure 12.38

The spotlight on the right has a very narrow focus (−100), and the spotlight on the left has a very wide (100) focus.

The Material property determines the intensity of the specular highlight. As the value increases, the surface is treated more like a metal, which is typically very shiny and has a small, intense highlight so that more of the surface color is reflected. As the value decreases, the surface is treated like a plastic, with a more diffused highlight, so that more of the light's color is reflected.

If the Gloss property is very low (matte), the Material property will have no effect. The Exposure property controls the degree to which the lights are added or subtracted. If a negative value is chosen, the image will be very dark (underexposed). If a positive value is chosen, the image will be very bright (overexposed). A value of 0 will have no effect on the added lights.

The Ambience property controls the ambient light in the image. A high setting will wash out the image and use only the ambient light, whereas a low setting will darken the entire image. You can control the color of the ambient light by clicking on the color swatch in the Properties area of the Lighting Effects dialog box.

USING PRESET STYLES

The Lighting Effects filter comes with numerous predefined styles (see Figure 12.39). You can use these or define your own by setting the lights and clicking the Save button. You can redefine the default style using this same procedure.

Figure 12.39

You can use any of the
17 predefined styles that
come with the Lighting
Effects filter or define
your own.

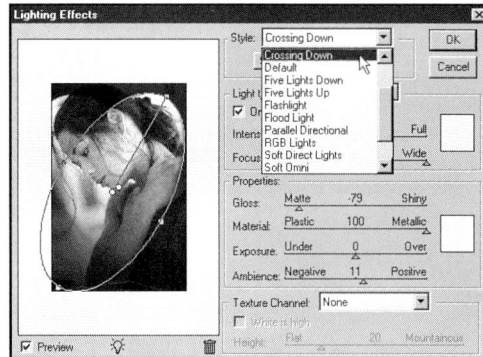

Now you try it...

Using Lighting Effects

1 Open the "lesson03.psd" image in the Chapter 12 lessons folder on the CD (see Figure 12.40).

Figure 12.40

Begin with this image
and apply the
Lighting Effects filter.

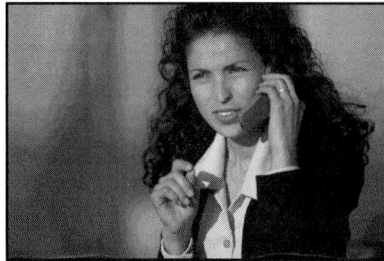

2 Select Filter > Render > Lighting Effects.

3 From the Style pop-up menu, choose Crossing Down.

4 Click and drag the endpoint of the selected light's direction line until the elliptical area of effect is almost circular (see Figure 12.41).

5 Click and drag on the center circle of the selected light and move the center to the woman's face.

6 Adjust the intensity of the selected spotlight until the image is not washed out by the light (about 7 or 8).

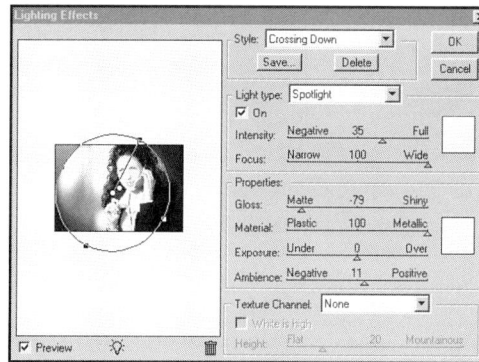

Figure 12.41

Drag on the handles
of a spotlight to
change the area of
effect.

7   Select the other spotlight by clicking on the other center circle and change its shape to match the other spotlight. Move
this light to the woman's face, but make sure that the center
doesn't match the other light's exactly (see Figure 12.42).
Adjust the intensity of the spotlight to match the other spotlight's intensity.

Figure 12.42

Move the light by
clicking and dragging
on the center circle.

8   Set the Gloss property for the surface to **–100** (matte). Click OK
when you have finished (see Figure 12.43).

9   Experiment with other lighting styles and options by undoing
the last filter. When you have finished, close the file.

continues

Figure 12.43

The final image has two rings of layered light.

USING TEXTURE CHANNELS

When using the Lighting Effects filter, you can use an alpha channel in the image as a bump map to create areas of impression and relief (see Figure 12.44). The alpha channel can be created using any of the methods outlined in Chapter 13, "Channels & Masks." An alpha channel contains 256 levels of gray. By default, areas in the alpha channel that are white create areas of relative depression, whereas darker areas will make areas of relative relief, but you can select the White is high option to invert the light and dark relationship. When an alpha channel has been selected to be used as a bump map, you can determine the apparent emboss or deboss by adjusting the height slider. Values for the height range from 0 to 100. The smaller the value, the less apparent the emboss or deboss, until at 0, the texture is completely removed.

Figure 12.44

Use an alpha channel as a texture map to create embossing and debossing effects.

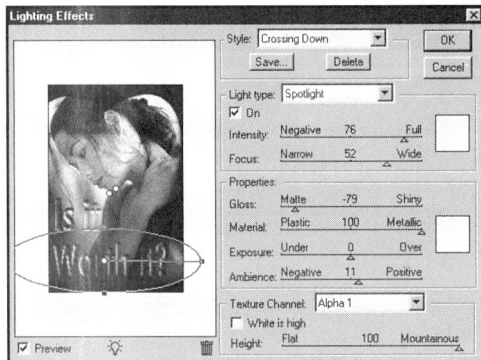

Now you try it...

Using Lighting Effects

1 Open the "lesson4.psd" image in the Chapter 12 lessons folder on the CD (see Figure 12.45).

Figure 12.45

Practice using the Lighting Effects filter with a texture channel.

2 From the Render submenu of the Filter menu, select Lighting Effects.

3 In the Lighting Effects style, select Default. If you have changed the default lighting style, create a single spotlight.

4 Adjust the spotlight intensity value to **33** and the focus value to **100**.

5 Move the handles of the spotlight area until most of the upper-right part of the image is illuminated. Move the center circle to the side of the man's head (see Figure 12.46).

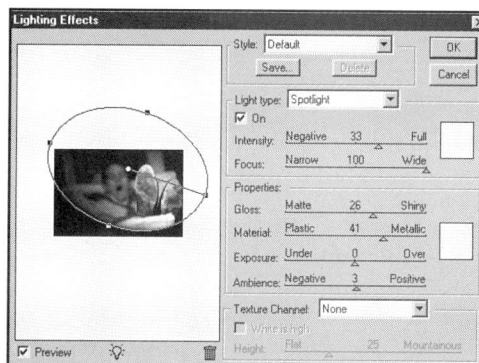

Figure 12.46

Move the light by clicking and dragging the center circle.

continues

6   For the surface properties, set the Gloss to **26**, the Material to **41**, the Exposure to **0**, and the Ambience to **3**.

7   For a Texture Channel, select Hardly Working Copy from the pop-up menu (see Figure 12.47).

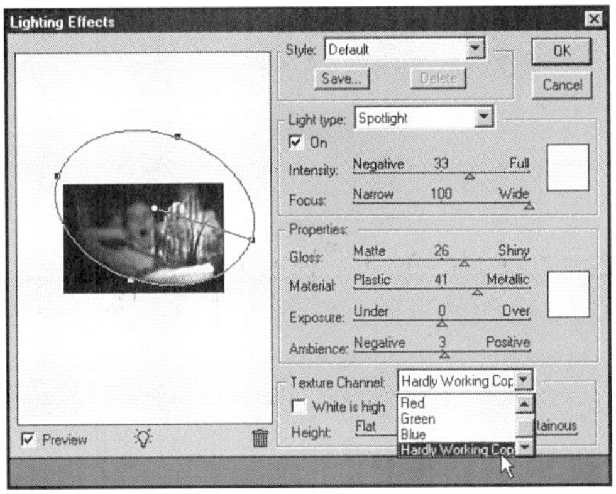

Figure 12.47

Any alpha channel can be used as a texture map.

8   Make sure that White is high is not selected. Set the height to **34** using the slider. Press the OK button when finished (see Figure 12.48).

Figure 12.48

When finished, the text should appear to be part of the texture of the image.

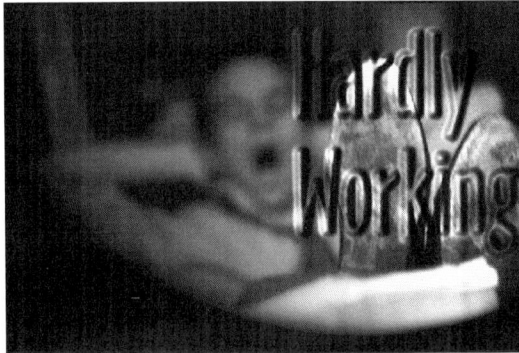

9   For more practice, undo the Lighting Effects filter and try some different light combinations. When you have finished, close the file.

SHARPEN AND UNSHARP MASK

Like the noise filters, there are actually several filters that perform sharpening. When sharpening, Photoshop increases the contrast between pixels of dissimilar colors, giving the illusion of adding more detail.

While this can often help correct some blurriness, like that caused by interpolation, the sharpening techniques use a mathematical process, so some detail may be irretrievable. All the filters used for sharpening are in the Sharpen submenu of the Filter menu.

SHARPEN AND SHARPEN MORE

The Sharpen filter works much like the sharpen tool in the toolbox. The Sharpen filter does not have any configurable options but simply improves the focus in the area of effect. The Sharpen More filter performs a stronger sharpening. Because these filters are not configurable and they do not provide a preview, many users prefer the Unsharp Mask filter over these filters.

UNSHARP MASK

The Unsharp Mask filter is commonly used after resampling to counteract some of the blurriness naturally introduced by interpolation. The Unsharp Mask filter has three configurable options and a preview window (see Figure 12.49). The Unsharp Mask filter also displays a preview of the effect in the image window.

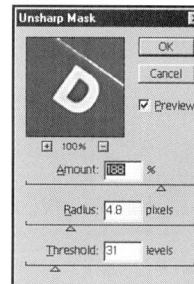

Figure 12.49

Use the Unsharp Mask filter to sharpen a blurry image.

There are three configurable options in the Unsharp Mask filter: Amount, Radius, and Threshold. The Amount determines the overall amount of sharpening. The Amount value can range from 1% to 500%. The Radius determines how far from any one pixel Photoshop should increase contrast to sharpen the area. Radius values range from 0.1 to 250.0 pixels. The Threshold value determines the number of levels allowed before sharpening occurs. Values can range from 0 to 255. At a Threshold value of 0, all pixels can be sharpened. At a Threshold value of 100, only pixels that vary by more than 100 levels are changed. At higher values, edges must have more contrast for sharpening to occur. Figures 12.50, 12.51, and 12.52 show the effect of some different Unsharp Mask settings.

Figure 12.50

This is the original image with no sharpening.

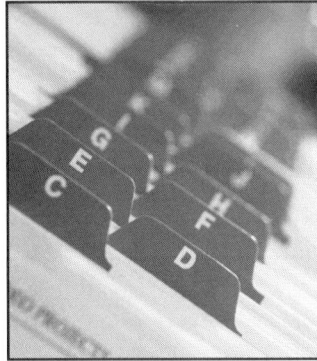

Figure 12.51

This is the same image, using 100% for the Amount, 5.0 for the Radius, and 0 for the Threshold. Notice especially the edges of the tabs and the letters.

Figure 12.52

For this image, the Amount was set to 200%, the Radius to 50.0, and the Threshold to 5.

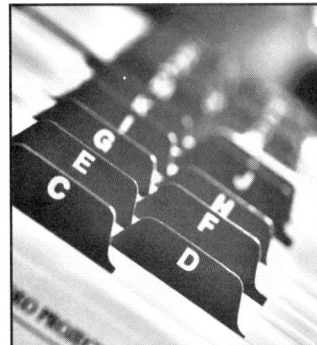

BLUR AND GAUSSIAN BLUR

The blur filters, the opposite of the sharpen filters, soften selected areas by smoothing transitions. The blur filters can be used to create depth of field, glow and shadow effects, and the illusion of motion. There are six blur filters, each of which perform different functions ranging from the straightforward Blur and Blur More filters, which are analogous to the Sharpen and Sharpen More filters, to the Motion Blur and Radial Blur. All the blur filters are found in the Blur submenu of the Filter menu. Only the most elementary blur filters are covered here.

BLUR AND BLUR MORE

The Blur filter softens a selected area, whereas the Blur More filter intensifies the blurring effect. The Blur filter is similar to the blur tool found in the toolbox. These filters do not have any configurable options and do not provide a preview.

GAUSSIAN BLUR

The Gaussian Blur is probably the most widely used blur filter. It provides a preview and can be configured by adjusting the Radius of effect (see Figure 12.53).

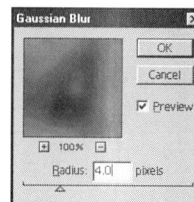

TIP

Because the Blur filters create pixel information on all sides of any given pixel, if the Preserve Transparency option is checked for a layer being blurred, the blur will not enter the transparent areas. Be sure to turn off Preserve Transparency if you want to completely blur a group of pixels on a layer that contains transparency.

Figure 12.53

You can adjust the Gaussian Blur by increasing or decreasing the Radius value.

The Radius ranges from 0.1 to 250.0 pixels. Like the Gaussian Noise option, the Gaussian Blur uses a bell-shaped curve to determine the distribution of the blur. The higher the Radius value, the more the image is blurred (see Figure 12.54). Note that because the radius of the blur area is measured in pixels, images at different resolutions will blur differently.

Figure 12.54

This image was blurred with a radius of 20.

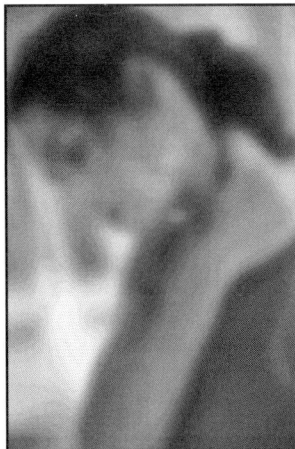

Now you try it...

Using the Gaussian Blur filter

1 Open the "lesson05.psd" image in the Chapter 12 lessons folder on the CD (see Figure 12.55).

Figure 12.55

Use this image to practice with the Gaussian Blur.

2 Copy the Background layer by dragging it to the Create new layer button in the Layers palette. Make this layer active by clicking on it.

3 Start the Gaussian Blur by selecting Filter > Blur > Gaussian Blur.

4   Enter a value of **9.0** for the Radius and click OK.

5   Change the opacity of the uppermost layer (the one you creat-
    ed) to **50%**. The image will now be slightly diffused (see Figure
    12.56). To see the difference between the new image and the
    original, turn the Background Copy layer on and off to com-
    pare.

Figure 12.56

The final image
should look
slightly diffused.

6   Experiment with different opacities, and if you like, undo the
    blur and try different Radius values. When you have finished,
    close the file.

OTHER FILTERS

For more practice with the filters, you might want to experiment on your
own. If you are interested in applying texture effects, there is a series of
Texture filters. In particular, the Texturizer filter enables you to load a file as
a bump map. The Glass filter, found with the Distort filters, also enables you
to load a file as a displacement map like the Displace filter. The Blur filters
not covered in this chapter, especially the Motion Blur and Radial Blur, are
useful in a variety of applications. Finally, you should experiment with combinations of filters. If you find a combination that works particularly well,
you can save that series of filters as an Action so that it can be repeated (see
Chapter 19, "Automating Photoshop").

FILTER FADE

Any filter or tool can have a fade applied to it after it has been applied to an
image. Select Filter > Fade to change the opacity and blending mode of the

filter as though it were on a separate layer (see Figure 12.57). The Fade command will affect only the last command or tool used to alter the information in the image.

Figure 12.57

Use the Filter Fade command to change the opacity and blending mode of the filter.

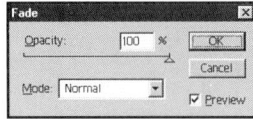

The Fade command can be used to further add to the functionality of the filters. Figure 12.58 uses the Glowing Edges filter, found in the Stylize submenu.

Figure 12.58

The glowing edges filter was faced to 35% opacity and the blending mode was left set to Normal.

SUMMARY

Photoshop has filters for many special effects, and more are available through other sources, such as third-party vendors and the World Wide Web. As an ACE, you should have a general idea of how the filters work and know the major filters covered in this chapter. You should practice with these and with some of the others on your own.

REVIEW QUESTIONS

1. You can add anchor points to which type of wireframe in the 3D Transform dialog box?

    a. Cube

    b. Toroid

    c. Sphere

    d. Cylinder

2. Which filter should be used to remove small dark spots caused by a dirty scanner bed?

    a. Find Edges

    b. Gaussian Blur

    c. Lighting Effects

    d. Dust & Scratches

3. In the 3D Transform filter, what is the Trackball tool used for?

    a. Moving Wireframes and Objects

    b. Rotating Wireframes and Objects

    c. Resizing Wireframes and Objects

    d. Deleting Wireframes and Objects

4. Which of the following filters has configurable options?

    a. Blur

    b. Sharpen

    c. Sharpen More

    d. Unsharp Mask

5. Which of the following is not a wireframe that you can create using the 3D Transform filter?

    a. Cone

    b. Cube

    c. Sphere

    d. Toroid

6.   Which file could not be used as a displacement map by the Displace filter?

    a.   An image in RGB mode

    b.   An image in Lab mode

    c.   An image in CMYK mode

    d.   An image in bitmap mode

7.   You are attempting to apply the Lighting Effects filter, but it is not available (dimmed). What is a possible reason?

    a.   The image is in CMYK mode.

    b.   The image contains a selection.

    c.   The image does not have a background layer.

    d.   The image does not contain an alpha channel.

8.   You are attempting to apply the Gaussian Blur filter, but it is not available (dimmed). What is a possible reason?

    a.   The image is in CMYK mode.

    b.   The image contains a selection.

    c.   The current layer is not visible.

    d.   The image does not contain a background layer.

9.   Which filter can load a channel as a texture map?

    a.   Sharpen

    b.   Displace

    c.   3D Transform

    d.   Lighting Effects

10.   Which filter should you use to soften the edges of an image?

    a.   Blur

    b.   Add Noise

    c.   Dust & Scratches

    d.   Lighting Effects

CHAPTER 13

CHANNELS & MASKS

Understanding and mastering the use of channels
and masks enables you to take full advantage of
Photoshop's power and strength in several areas,
including silhouetting, compositing, and color correction. In this chapter, you will learn about color channels and alpha channels, how to use Quick Mask mode
and Calculations, as well as how to use two new features in Photoshop 5.0: spot color channels and the
Channel Mixer.

Domains & Objectives

Using Channels and Masks

8.1 Identify issues regarding the characteristics, function, and appropriate use of channels, including creating and editing a selection channel, duplicating and deleting channels, saving and managing channels, channel calculations, the Channel Mixer command, spot color channels, and mode conversion with spot color channels.

8.2 Identify issues regarding the characteristics, function, and appropriate use of masks, including using Quick Mask mode and using alpha channels.

8.3 Determine the appropriate feature, command, tool, or procedure to accomplish a stated task related to channels and masks.

COLOR CHANNELS AND ALPHA CHANNELS

Channels are fundamental to every image you open in Photoshop. When you open an image in Photoshop, what you are looking at onscreen is a composite image—that is, an image made up of individual color channels that, when combined, result in a simulated full-color image.

For example, if you're working with a CMYK image and display the Channels palette, you'll see each of the individual process color plates displayed: cyan, magenta, yellow, and black. At the top of the palette is the composite channel, which is the result of the four process colors when combined. If you're working with an RGB image, the Channels palette will reflect each of the red, green, and blue channels as well as the composite channel.

Painting, color correcting, or manipulating an image in any way affects each of the channels. You can also edit each channel individually.

In addition to color channels, there is a second type of a channel called an *alpha channel*. An alpha channel is where a selection is stored. When you make a selection and you choose Save Selection from the Select menu, you are saving a mask as an alpha channel. The alpha channel is displayed under the color channels in the Channels palette. The best analogy to illustrate how a mask works is that of a stencil. The holes of a stencil fill with paint or ink when applied to a surface. The solid part of the stencil protects or masks the areas where you don't want the paint or ink applied (see Figure 13.1).

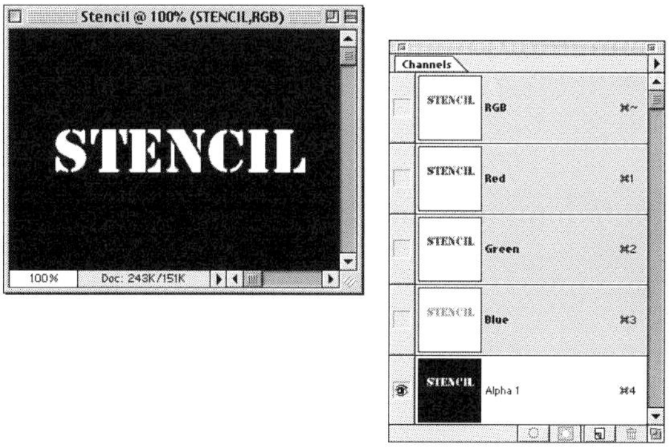

Figure 13.1

An alpha channel works like a stencil.

In Photoshop, an active selection represents the holes in a stencil. The part of the image that is surrounded by the "marching ants" can be manipulated, and all other areas outside the selection are masked or protected.

When a selection is saved, it becomes an alpha channel, resulting in a mask that you can edit. When looking at the alpha channel, the selection appears as white (the hole of the stencil) and the masked portions appear as black (the part of the image that is protected). See page 351 to learn how to create an alpha channel.

USING THE CHANNELS PALETTE

Choose Window > Show Channels to display the Channels palette. The Composite channel is always displayed first, followed by each of the individual channels. The eye icon in the left column indicates visible channels (see Figure 13.2). If you click the eye icon for any of the individual channels, you can temporarily hide it. Experiment with hiding different combinations of channels to understand how each channel affects the composite image. You cannot turn all the eye icons off at the same time; at least one channel must be visible.

Figure 13.2

The Channels palette displays the composite channel at the top and the component channels that make up the composite channel below.

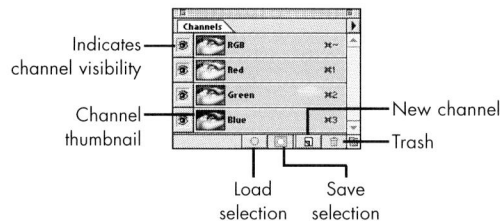

Indicates channel visibility

Channel thumbnail

New channel

Trash

Load selection

Save selection

✋ **TIP**

Click and drag down the eye icons to quickly hide or show the channels.

The bottom of the palette displays four shortcut buttons for performing routine tasks including: load selection, save selection, create a new channel, and discard a channel (see Figure 13.2).

Click on the black triangle in the Channels palette to display the palette menu choices; with these, you can create, duplicate, delete, split, or merge channels (see Figure 13.3).

SETTING CHANNELS PALETTE OPTIONS

The thumbnail icons are a visual display of each channel, and you can easily enlarge or reduce their display size. Click on the black triangle in the palette and choose Palette Options. Select the largest thumbnail and click OK (see Figure 13.4). Use this option only if you need a detailed reference of each channel. Next, go back to Channels Palette Options and select None. Click OK to view the channels without thumbnail icons. Use this option if the channel thumbnail information is irrelevant to the task at hand. Working with a small or medium thumbnail icon is usually sufficient.

Figure 13.3

The Channels Palette menu.

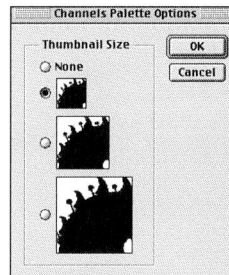

Figure 13.4

Choose a thumbnail size from the Channels Palette Options dialog box.

TIP

Control (Windows)/ Command (Macintosh)+1 is a tricky shortcut in Photoshop for those who use this command in Adobe Illustrator®, Adobe PageMaker®, or Quark-XPress®. In these programs, it resizes the view of your document to 100%. If your Photoshop document displays in grayscale when you are expecting it to resize, remember that you've activated the first channel, not resized the view of your image.

ACTIVATING CHANNELS

A channel is active only if the name bar is highlighted. It's important to note that a channel can be visible but not active. Having more than one channel visible is helpful when you want to use one channel as a reference while editing another.

You can choose to view your thumbnails and channels in color rather than grayscale by choosing File > Preferences > Display & Cursors > Color Channels in Color. This is helpful for a more literal indication of how the individual colors combine to make up the composite image, but it's not a great way to evaluate the tonal range of an individual channel. It is recommended that you view the channels with the Color Channels in Color option turned off for a more accurate representation of the pixel information contained in each channel.

You can activate individual channels with the following keyboard shortcuts:

- Control (Windows)/Command (Macintosh)+~ activates the composite channel
- Control (Windows)/Command (Macintosh)+1 activates the first color channel

- Control (Windows)/Command (Macintosh)+2 activates the second color channel

- Control (Windows)/Command (Macintosh)+3 activates the third color channel

Additional channels follow in numeric order.

CREATING A NEW CHANNEL

TIP

Press Alt/Option while clicking on the New Channel button to open the Channel Options dialog box.

When adding a new channel to an image, it will always be an alpha channel, and by default Photoshop names it "Alpha," unless you decide to give it a different name. You also can also change the color and opacity that represents the mask in the alpha channel to aid in editing the mask. When you create a new channel without a selection, it will appear as black until you edit it with either the painting or selection tools.

Now you try it...

Adding a new channel to an image

1 Click on the black triangle in the Channels palette and choose New Channel. The New Channel dialog box is displayed. You can also click on the New Channel button at the bottom of the palette (refer back to Figure 13.2) and then double-click on the channel to open the Channel Options dialog box if you want to rename it or change the color and opacity of the mask.

2 Give the channel a name.

3 By default, the color of the mask is red, which can make it difficult to see your image if the image is also red. To change the color of the mask, click on the color swatch (see Figure 13.5); the Color Picker dialog box is displayed. Select a color and click OK. You also can change the opacity of the mask by entering a new percentage.

Figure 13.5

The New Channel dialog box enables you to give the channel a name and change the color and opacity of the mask.

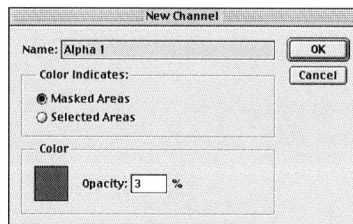

> **4** To see the mask displayed over the image, click on all of the eye icons, including the new alpha channel eye icon in the Channels palette. The mask is fully editable with any of the painting or selection tools. See page 351 for more information on editing alpha channels. To turn off the mask, click on the eye icon of the new channel once more.

REORDERING CHANNELS

You cannot change the order of color channels, but you can change the order of alpha channels. You must also have more than one alpha channel to change the order. (This capability is primarily for organizational purposes, because reordering the alpha channels does not affect the image.) You cannot place an alpha channel above any of the color channels. To reposition an alpha channel in the channels palette, follow these steps:

- Click on the name or thumbnail of the alpha channel you want to move and drag it above or below another alpha channel (see Figure 13.6).

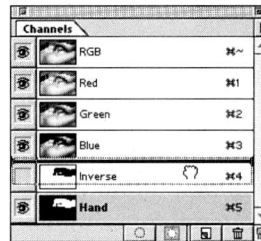

Figure 13.6

Reposition an alpha channel by clicking and dragging it above or below another alpha channel.

- When the black line is displayed, release the mouse button, and the channel will appear in its new position.

EDITING CHANNELS

You can manipulate individual channels of an image using Levels, Curves, or Brightness/Contrast from the Image > Adjust menu. This approach is often used when an image has a visible color cast. When you make changes to individual channels, you are affecting the grayscale values of the channel. You can select and edit more than one channel by pressing the Shift key while clicking on the channels. It's helpful to have the Composite channel visible in addition to the individual channel so you have an onscreen representation of the changes you make.

Now you try it...

Editing channels using Curves

1   Open the Temple image in the Samples folder, which is in the Goodies folder located in the Photoshop applications folder. This image has an overall green cast.

2   Select the red channel in the Channels palette. Click on the eye icon of the Composite channel for a preview in the image window.

3   Choose Image > Adjust > Curves. The Curves dialog box tells you which channel you are manipulating. Experiment adjusting the curve and click OK.

4   Next, select the red and blue channels in the Channels palette by Shift-clicking on the channel. Make sure the eye icon is still on for the Composite channel.

5   Open the Curves dialog box once more by pressing Control (Windows)/Command (Macintosh)+M.

6   Notice that the dialog box now displays a pop-up window with three channel choices: a combination channel (red and blue) as well as the individual channels.

7   Experiment manipulating the curve with the combination channel selected and click OK.

To learn more about using Levels, Curves, and the Brightness/Contrast adjustment commands, see Chapter 14, "Color Correction."

DUPLICATING A CHANNEL

You can duplicate a channel for use in the same image or for use in another document. If you're experimenting with a particular channel, you can make a backup of the channel, compare your results, and then later discard the one you don't want to use. You can also use a duplicate channel to apply filter effects for use with the original channels. You cannot duplicate the Composite channel.

Duplicating alpha channels into a separate document can be useful because you can treat the separate document as a library that stores the individual channels. This will keep the original document file size down, because you can load individual alpha channels from the library document whenever you need to.

NOTE

The Duplicate Channel command can be used with any image mode except Indexed Color and Bitmap.

Now you try it...

Duplicating a channel by using menu commands

1   Open an image, select the channel you want to duplicate in the Channels palette, and choose Duplicate from the Palette menu (see Figure 13.7).

Figure 13.7

You can name the duplicate channel, specify a destination document, and choose to invert the channel information in the Duplicate Channel dialog box.

2   Type in a name for the duplicate channel and choose a destination. You can choose to duplicate it within the existing document, to another open document, or to a new document.

3   If you want to make a duplicate of the opposite area of your selection or mask, check the Invert box. This saves you from going back to the image, loading the selection, choosing Inverse from the Select menu, and then saving the inverted selection.

Now you try it...

Duplicating a channel by dragging

1   Select the channel you want to duplicate in the Channels palette.

2   To duplicate the channel within the same document, drag the channel onto the new channel button at the bottom of the palette (refer to Figure 13.2).

    To duplicate the channel to a different document, make sure the destination document is open and drag the channel into the image window.

NOTE

When duplicating a channel to a different document, both documents must be the same size and resolution, and the destination document must also be open.

✍ **TIP**

Right/Control+click on a component channel to display a context-sensitive menu that gives you the option of either duplicating or deleting the channel. If you choose Duplicate, the Duplicate Channel dialog box opens, enabling you to name the channel and specify a destination document. If you choose Delete, the channel is discarded with no warning, but you can choose Edit > Undo or Control (Windows)/ Command (Macintosh)+Z to immediately restore the channel.

DELETING CHANNELS

Because channels can substantially add to the file size of your image, it's a good habit to delete the channels you are no longer using before saving a document. You cannot delete the Composite channel because it's linked to the other component channels that make up the composite. However, it is possible to delete one of the component color channels. If you do this, the composite channel is removed, because it no longer has the support of all of the component channels. The document mode then becomes Multichannel. Keep in mind that you can no longer print a composite image. However, the information on the remaining channels remains the same.

There are several ways to delete a channel:

- Select a channel and choose Delete from the Palette menu.
- Drag the channel to the Trash at the bottom of the Channels palette.
- Select the channel and click on the Trash button. A confirmation message is displayed. Click Yes. To bypass the confirmation message, press Alt (Windows)/Option (Macintosh) when you click on the Trash.

MULTICHANNEL MODE

If you convert an image to multichannel mode and the image contains more than one channel, the channels become spot color channels. Each channel is represented in grayscale and contains 256 levels of brightness based on the color values of the pixels in the image. When you convert an image to multichannel mode, you can no longer print a composite image.

When converting a CMYK image to multichannel mode, Photoshop converts the channels to four spot color channels: cyan, magenta, yellow, and black. When converting an RGB image to multichannel mode, Photoshop creates three spot color channels: cyan, magenta, and yellow.

Double-clicking on one of the spot channels will open the Color Picker, enabling you to choose a spot color by clicking on the Custom Button. See page 366 for more information on working with spot channels. The channels are also editable with the image adjustment commands including Levels, Curves, and Brightness/Contrast (see Chapter 14).

A Multichannel mode document can also be used to store channels that contain selections or layer masks that belong to another document, thus keeping the original document's file size down. Before Photoshop supported spot channels, Multichannel mode was also used to view the individual channel results of duotone, tritone, or quadtone images.

When you initially create a duotone, for example, the color information is combined into one channel. Each color of the duotone can only be edited when you choose Image > Mode > Duotone. If you change the Duotone mode to Multichannel, you will create two channels in the Channels palette, which reflect the two colors you chose when you created the duotone. This can be helpful if you'd like to examine the tonality of each of the duotone plates.

Although it is possible to edit each of these channels individually, it is not recommended, because the onscreen preview might not be accurate. If you need to edit a duotone, it's best to do so in the Duotone dialog box and not convert to multichannel. See Chapter 5, "Image Modes," for more information on duotones, tritones, and quadtones.

SAVING CHANNELS

Be careful which file formats you choose when saving a document with alpha channels. If you know you will need to further edit an alpha channel, save the document in Photoshop, Photoshop 2.0 (Macintosh only), DCS 2.0, Pict, Pict Resource, Pixar, PNG, Raw, or TIFF formats. In any other format, the mask will be applied, and you can no longer edit the alpha channel.

SPLITTING AND MERGING CHANNELS

You might need to split the channels of a file if the file is too large to be saved or transported. The channels can be saved individually and merged at a later date. You can also split channels if you need to retain the channel information when you are saving the image in a file format that doesn't preserve channel information such as Photoshop EPS or JPEG.

Before you can split the channels of an image, you must flatten the image. See Chapter 10, "Layers," for information on layers and flattening an image.

Now you try it...

Splitting and merging channels

1   Open the Rockies image in the Samples folder, which is in the Goodies folder located in the Photoshop application folder. Choose Split Channels from the Channels palette menu (see Figure 13.8).

NOTE

You will not be able to revert back to duotone mode if you make any changes in Multichannel mode.

TIP

When saving Photoshop 5.0 files with the Save a Copy command in the File menu, you have the option of including or excluding alpha channels for use with formats that support channels. For those formats that don't support channels, this option is grayed out. You can also choose to exclude nonimage data such as paths.

continues

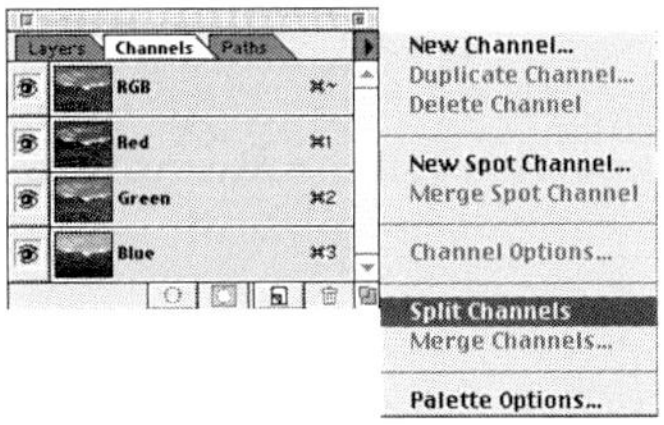

Figure 13.8

The Split channels command is located in the Channels palette menu.

2 The original file is closed, and each individual channel is displayed as a separate 8-bit grayscale file. The document name includes the original name plus the channel abbreviation (Windows) or full name (Macintosh). For example, the RGB file named Rockies splits into three files named "Rockies.Red," "Rockies.Green," and "Rockies.Blue" (see Figure 13.9).

Figure 13.9

An RGB file split into three files.

3 To merge channels back into a single document, each separate document you want to merge must be open. Select one of the documents you want to merge and choose Merge Channels from the Channels palette menu. The Merge Channels dialog box is displayed (see Figure 13.10).

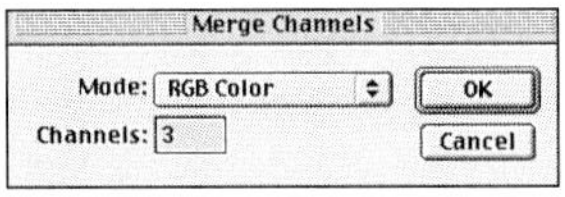

Figure 13.10

The Merge Channels dialog box enables you to choose a mode and specify the number of channels to merge.

4 In the Merge Channels dialog box, choose a mode for the merged image by clicking on the pop-up menu (refer back to Figure 13.10). You must have the correct number of documents for the mode you select. For example, to choose RGB, three documents must be open. To choose CMYK, four documents must be open. The documents must also be exactly the same size. If you choose Multichannel, Photoshop does not recomposite the image and will save each document as an alpha channel in an untitled document.

After you have selected a mode, you can specify which channels to merge. For example, you can keep them the same (merge Red with Red) or merge different channels (merge Red with Green) by using the pop-up menu (see Figure 13.11).

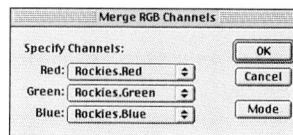

Figure 13.11

After you've chosen a mode, you can specify which channels to merge from the pop-up menu.

5 Click OK to apply the command. The separate channel documents are now merged, and the original documents are closed with no changes.

6 Save the new untitled document.

WORKING WITH ALPHA CHANNELS

When you select an area of an image, you are actually creating a temporary mask. The area inside the selection is the only part of the image that can be affected. The rest of the image outside of the selection is masked and protected and cannot be affected. When you choose to save a selection, you are creating an alpha channel. The alpha channel holds your selection or mask. The terms *mask* and *alpha channel* are used interchangeably.

When you save an alpha channel, it is displayed in the channels palette below the color channels. The black areas of the channel represent what is masked in the image. The white areas of the channel represent that area of the image that is selected. Because an alpha channel is an 8-bit channel, it supports 254 different levels of gray in addition to black and white. This means that alpha channels can support varying levels of transparency.

A selection with a feathered edge illustrates this well, as you will see in the following lesson.

Now you try it...

Creating a vignette by using an alpha channel from a feathered selection

1   Open the Rockies image in the Samples folder, which is in the Goodies folder located in the Photoshop application folder.

2   If the Channels palette isn't open, choose Window > Show Channels.

3   Make a selection of part of an image with the elliptical marquee tool. Press the Option key to draw the selection from the center, and then add the Shift key to constrain the selection to a perfect circle.

Figure 13.12

An elliptical marquee selection of the image is constrained to a circle by using the Shift key.

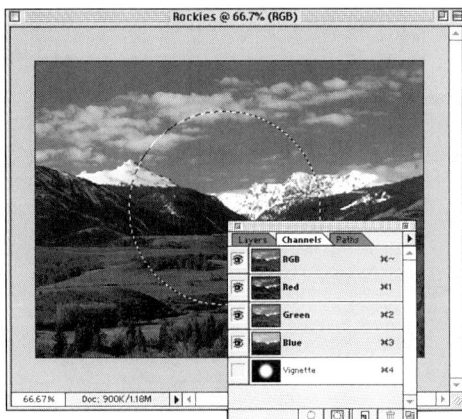

4   Choose Feather from the Select menu and enter the amount **30**. Click OK.

5   Choose Save Selection from the Select menu and give it a name. The new alpha channel is placed beneath the component channels at the bottom of the Channels palette.

6   Click the eye icon off for all the channels but the alpha channel and make sure the alpha channel is selected in the Channels palette. The alpha channel will display in the image window (see Figure 13.13). Here the channel is fully editable by using any of the painting tools, adjustment commands, or filters.

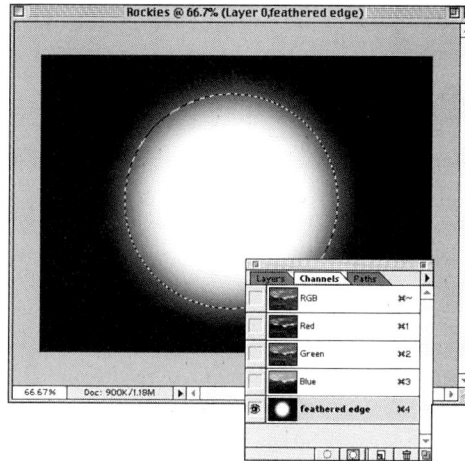

Figure 13.13

The alpha channel selection with a feathered edge.

7 Click on the composite eye icon and click off the eye icon of the alpha channel.

If you turn on the eye icon for at least one of the channels in addition to the alpha channel, you will activate the ruby mask overlay. See page 356 for more information on using the ruby mask mode.

8 Choose Inverse from the Select menu. This selects the opposite areas of your selection.

9 To create the vignette effect, fill the selection with white by choosing Edit > Fill > White, and then click OK (see Figure 13.14). Deselect by pressing Control (Windows)/Command (Macintosh)+D.

Figure 13.14

The vignette is created by filling the inverse selection with white.

You can create interesting effects using filters on alpha channels. In the following lesson, you will learn how to create a colorful textured background
using an alpha channel with a gradient, the Difference Clouds filter, and the
Brightness/Contrast command.

Now you try it...

Using filter effects on an alpha channel

1   Create a new document by choosing New from the File menu.
Enter **5** inches for both the height and width, enter a resolution of **72**, and then choose RGB mode. Click OK.

2   Double-click the linear gradient tool in the toolbox to open the
tools' Options palette and choose the Violet, Orange gradient
from the Gradient pop-up menu (see Figure 13.15).

Figure 13.15

The Gradient Options
palette offers several
gradient style choices,
blending mode options,
and opacity settings.

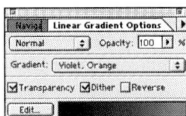

3   Press the Shift key to constrain the gradient 90 degrees. Click
and drag the gradient tool from the top of the canvas to the
bottom.

4   Create an alpha channel by clicking the New Channel button
at the bottom of the Channels palette (see Figure 13.16).
Double-click the channel and name it **Clouds**.

Figure 13.16

To quickly create a
new channel, click the
New Channel button.

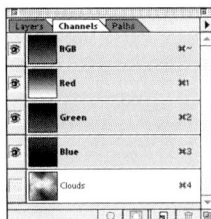

New Channel button

5   With the new channel selected, choose Filter > Render >
Difference Clouds. By pressing Control (Windows)/Command
(Macintosh)+F, you can cycle through various renditions of the
filter effect. The end result will depend on the contrast of the
Render Difference Clouds filter.

6 Click the eye icon for the composite channel so all the channels are visible.

7 Load the alpha channel as a selection by choosing Select >
Load Selection. This displays the Load Selection dialog box
(see Figures 13.17 and 13.18). Choose the Clouds channel and
click OK. You can also click on the Load Selection button at the
bottom of the Channels palette when the alpha channel is
selected.

Figure 13.17

The Load Selection
dialog box enables
you to load a selec-
tion from the same
document or a differ-
ent one, as well as
load an inverted
selection.

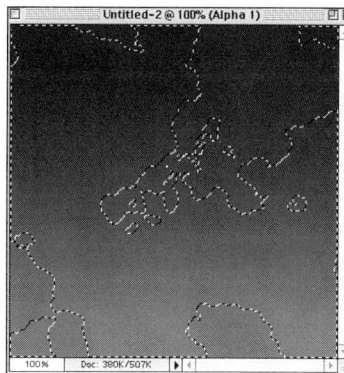

Figure 13.18

The Clouds alpha
channel loaded on
the image.

8 To create a mottled effect, choose Image > Adjust >
Brightness/Contrast. Experiment with the sliders and click OK.

TIP

You can press Control (Windows)/Command (Macintosh)+H to temporarily hide the edges of the selection while you're still in the Brightness/ Contrast dialog box (or any other image adjustment dialog box). Just don't forget to deselect (Control (Windows)/ Command (Macintosh)+D) when you have finished.

NOTE

The ruby overlay metaphor comes from a traditional prepress masking technique in which a sheet of acetate with a thin coating of red plastic was used in the creation of masks. An X-Acto™ knife or similar cutting tool was used to cut away areas of the ruby to allow that part of the image or page to be exposed when shooting film for printing plates. The area of the image masked by the opaque part of the overlay was protected.

WORKING IN QUICK MASK MODE

Create Quick Mask Mode is a great tool for improving an existing selection that you've made with one of the selection tools. Many use Quick Mask for improving difficult selections, such as silhouetting hair or other intricate areas of an image. Although you need not have an active selection to use Quick Mask, it does make it an easier place to start.

When you turn on Quick Mask, a ruby overlay is displayed over areas of the image that are not part of the selection.

Now you try it...

Using Quick Mask mode

1   Open the image "Mushrooms.psd" in the Chapter 13 lessons folder on the CD (see Figure 13.19). Select the mushrooms Quick Mask by using one of the selection tools.

Activate the Quick Mask by clicking on the right button (see Figure 13.20). The button on the left is the Standard mode; by clicking it, you will turn the Quick Mask off. Pressing Q on your keyboard enables you to quickly toggle Quick Mask Mode on and off.

2   It might be difficult to work with the default Quick Mask color (red) if the image you're editing is also red, as with this mushroom image. Change the color of the Quick Mask ruby overlay by double-clicking on either the Standard Mode button or Quick Mask button. This opens the Quick Mask Options dialog box (see Figure 13.21). Click on the color box, select green in the Color Picker, and click OK. You can also change the opacity of the Quick Mask overlay.

3   With Quick Mask Mode activated (see Figure 13.22), you can use any of the painting tools to edit the mask. Select the paintbrush and begin to paint on an exposed area of the image. Similar to layer masks and alpha channels, your foreground and background color options are either black or white or a shade of gray. The Swatches palette also now displays grayscale swatches.

Figure 13.19

Make a selection by using the selection tools before applying Quick Mask Mode.

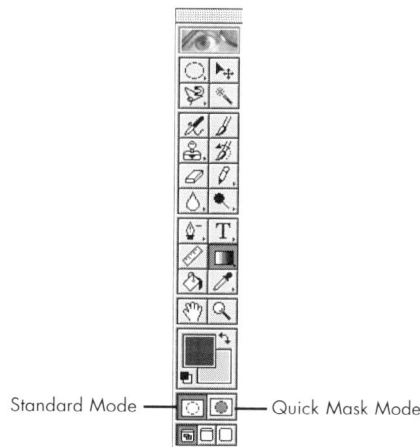

Figure 13.20

Click the Quick Mask Mode button to display the mask overlay. Click the Standard Mode button to hide the mask overlay.

Standard Mode ——— ⬜⬜ ——— Quick Mask Mode

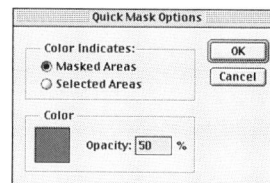

Figure 13.21

Use the Quick Mask Options dialog box to change the color and opacity of the mask.

continues

Figure 13.22

The Quick Mask
overlay on top of
the selection.

Figure 13.22

The Quick Mask overlay on top of the selection.

4   Quick Mask is very forgiving if you make a mistake while you're painting on it. For example, you might mistakenly paint over an area of the mushrooms while painting with black. To correct this, switch the foreground color to white by clicking on the arrows next to the swatches in the toolbox or press X on your keyboard. You can now fix the mistake by painting back over it.

To add to the mask, paint with black as your foreground color. This will subtract from the selection.

Paint with white as your foreground color to remove from the mask. This will add to the selection.

Paint with a shade of gray from the Swatches palette, and you'll affect the transparency of that portion of your selection.

5   Press Q on your keyboard to hide the Quick Mask and evaluate the changes you made to your selection.

6   It can be helpful to toggle back and forth between viewing the Quick Mask as Masked Areas and as Selected Areas. So far, you've been working in the default Masked Areas mode. To view the mask over your selection, double-click either the standard Mode or Quick Mask mode button in the toolbox to display the Quick Mask Options dialog box. Choose Selected areas and click OK. This is a great way to double-check your work in the complementary mode.

7 When you're satisfied with the silhouette, click on the standard mode button, choose Select > Save selection, and give the channel a name. Your selection is now stored as an alpha channel in the channels palette.

Keep in mind, creating and editing a Quick Mask is a temporary step. The selection (mask) isn't saved until you choose Save Selection from the Select menu or click on the Save Selection as Channel button at the bottom of the Channels palette (see Figure 13.23).

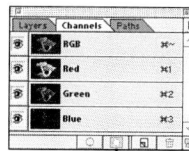

Save Selection as Channel button

Figure 13.23

Instead of choosing Save Selection from the Select menu, click on the Save Selection as Channel button.

If you know that you will need to edit and save the selection for later use, you can create an alpha channel from an active selection, completely bypass Quick Mask, and edit the alpha channel with the ruby overlay capability turned on in the Channels palette. Using this approach allows you to avoid having to save the selection every time you make a change. To use Quick Mask on an active alpha channel, all channel eye icons including the alpha channel must be on.

You will save a tremendous amount of time if you get into the habit of using the shortcut keys listed in the table below while in Quick Mask Mode.

TIP

In addition to using the painting tools in Quick Mask mode, you can use the selection tools, which can be extremely useful in masking and unmasking large areas of an image.

TIP

Be careful using the brackets to change the size of your brush if you're using the default brushes, because you will be switching to brushes that have different edges.

Best Shortcut Keys to Use When Editing in Quick Mask Mode.	
Q	Toggle Quick Mask on and off
X	Switch between foreground and background (black and white) for painting and erasing on the mask
B	Paintbrush
Z	Zoom in
Control/Command + – (minus)	Reduce magnification
Control/Command++ (plus)	Increase magnification
Spacebar	Pan around different areas of the image
Control/Command+Z	Undo
[	Choose a smaller brush
]	Choose a larger brush

USING CHANNEL CALCULATIONS

You can blend two channels together from two different images or within the same image, and then apply the results to a new channel or new document using channel calculations. If you want to blend channels from two different images, they must be exactly the same size and resolution. This is because Photoshop needs to compare the corresponding pixels appearing in the same location that will be affected and ultimately replaced in the channel.

Because channels are grayscale images, each pixel can possess a value from 0 to 256 based on brightness. Depending on the value for the corresponding pixel, you can create a variety of different effects by using the Apply Image and Calculation commands. Although the Duplicate command is not a channel calculation command, it is listed with the Apply image and Calculations commands in the Image menu.

USING THE DUPLICATE COMMAND

A quick way to make a copy of your active document is to use the Duplicate command. You can choose to duplicate a document with all its layers and channels intact, or you can duplicate a merged copy. A merged duplicate document will flatten all the layers into one composite image.

For experimentation, the duplicate command is ideal. You can experiment with the duplicate image while keeping the original intact, comparing both on screen while you work. In addition, when you use the Duplicate command, a temporary version of your image is stored in RAM rather than saved to disk. To duplicate an image, choose Duplicate from the Image pull-down menu. The Duplicate Image dialog box is displayed (see Figure 13.24).

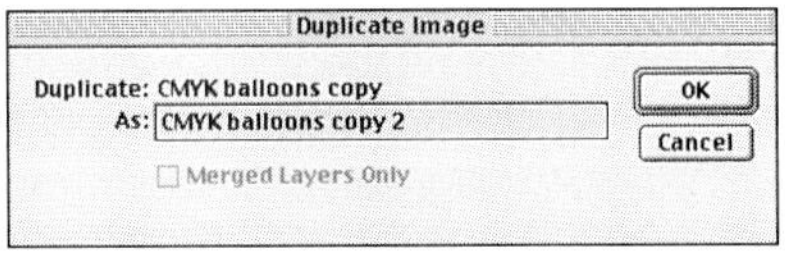

Press Alt/Option while selecting the Duplicate command to duplicate the document without the Duplicate dialog box displaying. If you want to duplicate a merged version of the document, you must choose Duplicate from the Image pull-down menu and check the Merged Layers Only checkbox in the dialog box.

Figure 13.24

The Duplicate Image dialog box enables you to give the duplicate document a name as well as the option to duplicate a merged version of a multilayer document.

USING THE APPLY IMAGE COMMAND

You can use the Apply Image command to blend one document's layer and channel with another document's layer and channel. Many of the functions of the Apply Image command can be easily achieved with layers—but at a price. When blending images using layers and layer masks, Photoshop must store files for display, undo, and revert purposes and recomposite every layer every time you make a change to your image. All of this slows Photoshop down and uses a lot of RAM. If you're working on large files at high resolution, you might want to consider using the Apply Image function for some of your compositing work. The only drawback is that you lose the flexibility layers provide for positioning and deleting elements.

When you use the Apply Image command, Photoshop compares the pixels of the two documents, layers, or channels and, based on the options you've chosen in the Apply Image dialog box, throws away the pixels it no longer needs and creates new ones.

When you choose Apply Image from the Image menu, the following options are available:

- **Source.** This is the active document when you choose the Apply Image command. This can be a different document than the target, but the file size and resolution must be the same—otherwise, it won't be the listed.

- **Layer.** The Layer pop-up menu reveals the available layers in the source document that can be used. Choosing the Merged option will include all visible layers in the source document.

- **Channel.** You can choose the composite channel or an individual color channel. You can also choose transparency mask if you have chosen a particular layer.

- **Target.** The target is the document that has the elements you want to apply to the source.

- **Blending.** Choose a blending mode from the pop-up menu. With the preview button checked, it's easy to experiment to get the effect you're looking for. For a description of the different blending mode options, see Chapter 8, "Painting."

- **Opacity.** Choose an opacity setting from 1% to 100%. Again, make sure the preview button is checked to see the results before you commit.

- **Preserve Transparency.** If you want to preserve the transparency of the target layer, click this button.

- **Mask.** If you want the calculation to be applied through a mask, you can choose document, layer, or channel for the mask.

- **Invert.** This option is available for both the source and the mask. If you want to use the opposite area of the selection, you can click the Invert button instead of having to create and save an inverted selection beforehand.

- **Preview.** The results of your settings are displayed in the active document.

NOTE

Keep in mind, when using the Apply Image command, both the source document and the destination document must be the exact same size and pixel resolution. Both documents must also be open.

Now you try it...

Blending images with the Apply Image command

1   Open the images "Lake.ps" and "Birds.ps" located in the Chapter 13 lesson folder on the CD. Position the images on your screen so both are visible (see Figure 13.25). You might need to reduce the view size of each image.

Figure 13.25

Two images with the same dimensions and resolution are neces- sary to use the Apply Image command.

2   With the Lake image active, choose Image > Apply Image to display the Apply Image dialog box (see Figure 13.26).

Figure 13.26

The Apply Image dialog box.

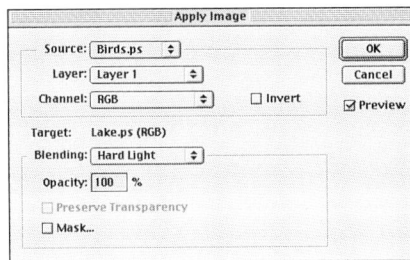

3   Click on the Preview button.

4   For the Source image, choose "Birds.ps."

5   Choose Layer 1.

6   Choose RGB for Channel.

7   The target should be "Lake.ps" (see Figure 13.27).

8   Experiment with the different blending options and opacity settings. For more information on blending options, see Chapter 8. Click OK.

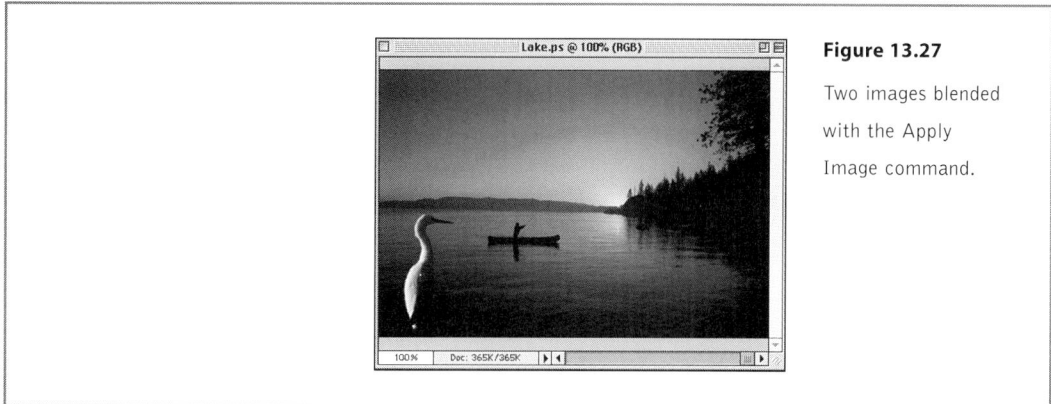

Figure 13.27

Two images blended with the Apply Image command.

CALCULATIONS

At first glance, it might seem that the Apply Image and Calculations commands are the same. However, upon a closer look, you will recognize there are substantial differences. With Apply Image, composite images can be used for both the source and target. With Calculations, only individual channels can be specified for both source and target.

With Apply Image, the actual channel information changes when you invoke the command. With Calculations, the changes you make are reflected in a new channel, selection, or document, leaving the original channels intact.

Calculations also offer a gray channel option that will result in a grayscale image of the combined channels. If saved to a new document, the image will be in Multichannel mode.

Now you try it...

Creating a multichannel image by using Calculations

1 Open the images "Lake.psd" and "Birds.psd" located in the Chapter 13 Lesson folder on the book CD. Position the images on your screen so both are visible. You might need to reduce the view size.

2 With the Lake image active, choose Image > Calculations to display the Calculations dialog box (see Figure 13.28).

continues

Figure 13.28

The Calculations dialog box enables you to mix channel information into a new channel, selection, or document.

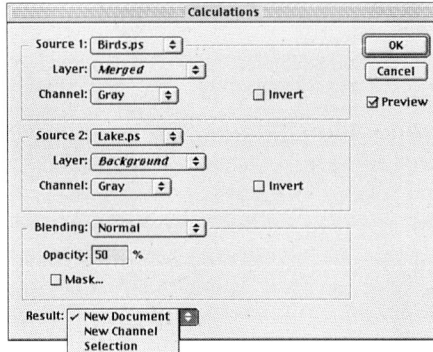

3   Click on the Preview button.

4   For the Source 1 Image, choose `Birds.psd`.

5   Choose Layer Merged.

6   Choose Gray for Channel.

7   For the Source 2 Image, choose `Lake.psd`.

8   Choose Background for Layer.

9   Choose Gray for Channel.

10   Choose Normal for Blending and an opacity of **50%**.

11   For Result, choose New Document. Click OK.

12   The result will be a new multichannel document displaying one grayscale channel (see Figure 13.29).

Figure 13.29

Two images merged together into a new document by using the Calculations command.

THE CHANNEL MIXER

Photoshop 5.0 now gives you the capability to dynamically mix pixel information on multiple channels. This new feature can be used to adjust the color balance of an image because you can adjust the tonality contribution of each channel simultaneously. You can also convert color images into rich grayscale or sepia tone images or easily create a hand-tinted effect.

When working with a CMYK image with the Channel Mixer (see Figure 13.30), decreasing the values on a specific channel will decrease the amount of that color in the image. However, if you're working with an RGB image, decreasing the values on a specific channel will shift the color toward the complementary color of that channel. For example, decreasing red shifts the color toward cyan; decreasing green shifts the color to magenta; and decreasing blue shifts the color to yellow. Yet when you increase color values of a particular channel in an RGB image, you increase that color in the image.

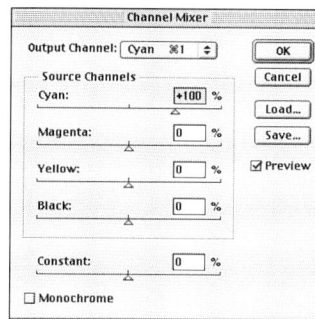

Figure 13.30

The Channel Mixer dialog box enables you to adjust the tonality contribution of each channel in an image.

In the following lesson, you will learn how to adjust the tonality of an image by using the Channel Mixer as well as convert an image to grayscale and create a hand-tinted effect.

Now you try it...

Using the Channel Mixer

1   Open the CMYK balloons image located in the Samples folder, which is in the Goodies folder in the Photoshop application folder.

continues

TIP

You can also use the Channel Mixer on an adjustment layer for experimentation. An adjustment layer allows you to work on an image without permanently changing the pixel values. You can edit the adjustment layer at any time, temporarily hide the adjustment layer to compare before and after adjustments, or delete the adjustment layer to return to the original image. For more information on using adjustment layers, see Chapter 10.

TIP

Keep your swatch books protected and away from light to avoid faded colors.

NOTE

If your image has spot color channels, you cannot split or merge the channels. The spot color channels will be merged as alpha channels.

2   Choose Image > Adjust > Channel Mixer to display the Channel Mixer dialog box. Make sure the Preview button is checked to display a Preview. If the Preview button isn't checked, click it to display a preview.

3   The Output channel is the channel that you want to affect with information from the other channels. Drag a slider for one of the individual channels to either increase or decrease its contribution to the output channel. Experiment with different output channels from the pop-up menu.

4   The Constant slider affects the opacity of the Output Channel. Negative values act as a black channel and will decrease the opacity of the Output channel. Positive values act as a white channel and increase the opacity of the Output Channel. Experiment with the Constant slider with different Output Channel colors selected. Note the opacity changes to the channel you are affecting by viewing the Channels palette thumbnail as you experiment.

5   To create a rich four-color, black-and-white image, choose the Monochrome option. You'll notice that now you only have one output channel, which is named black. Each channel is now grayscale.

6   If you click the Monochrome option again, you will have color output channels once more, and you can add colors to the grayscale image. This is also a great method to create a hand-tinted effect.

SPOT COLOR CHANNELS

Photoshop 5.0 now supports spot colors as dedicated channels. You can use spot colors, which are premixed inks from PANTONE or Toyo instead of, or in addition to, the process CMYK colors for a print job. Spot colors are often used when a color cannot be reproduced with the process colors, such as metallic and neon colors. Adding a spot color to a four-color job gives you a fifth channel and will ultimately give you a fifth printing plate. You can add more than one spot color to a job, but the more you add, the more expensive the print run will be.

Many times, a spot color is added to a four-color piece as a varnish plate or bump plate. The varnish can be applied over the entire piece or just selected areas. A bump plate is typically used to give an added punch of color on a selected area of an image. For example, if you want to make that little red sports car really red, you can mask just the parts of the car you want to include and create a spot channel to represent that area of the bump plate.

Spot colors are also used when creating monotone, duotone, tritone, and quadtone images. When creating a duotone, for example, the spot color is typically added as an additional plate to the black plate of a grayscale image. The highlights, midtones, and shadows take on different tints of the spot color. However, it isn't necessary to use Spot Color channels when creating monotones, duotones, tritones, and quadtones. To learn more about these modes, see Chapter 5.

TIP

When creating a varnish channel, choose a warm gray PMS spot color and set the solidity to a low value, such as 5%, so you can have a visual indication of where the varnish is applied.

Now you try it...

Creating a spot color channel

1   Load or make a selection of part of an image and choose New Spot Channel from the Channels palette menu to display the New Spot Channel dialog box (see Figure 13.31).

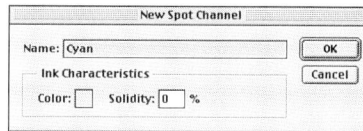

Figure 13.31

The New Spot Channel dialog box enables you to select a spot color from the Color Picker, name the color, and adjust the onscreen solidity.

2   In the New Spot Channel dialog box, click on the color box to choose a color. In the Color Picker dialog box, click on the Custom button.

3   Choose PANTONE Coated, PANTONE Uncoated, or Toyo from the book pop-up menu and select a color. Click OK to exit the dialog box. For more information on the color matching systems, see Chapter 8.

4   Choose a Solidity value between **0%** and **100%**. The solidity value gives you an onscreen representation of the printed spot color. 100% represents total opacity. Any percentage lower than 100% will have transparency. 0% is total transparency. Note: The Solidity value does not affect the printed output.

continues

TIP

If you want to use a tint
percentage of a spot
color, fill the selection
first using the paint bucket with the color slider in
the color palette set to
the tint percentage you
desire, and then choose
New Spot Channel in the
Channels palette.

TIP

Control (Windows)/
Command (Macintosh)+
click the New Channel
button to open the New
Spot Channel dialog box.

5   Click OK. If you're planning on exporting the image to Adobe
Illustrator, Adobe PageMaker, or QuarkXPress, make sure that
you have chosen the option of short PANTONE names (if
you're using PANTONE colors) in the General Preferences dialog box. The file might not print correctly if these applications
can't recognize the filenames.

CONVERTING AN ALPHA CHANNEL TO A SPOT CHANNEL

You can designate areas of an image that will contain a spot color by first
creating a selection and saving it as an alpha channel. You can then convert
the alpha channel to a spot color channel by double-clicking on the Alpha
channel and selecting spot color.

EDITING A SPOT CHANNEL

You can edit spot channels just like any other channel with any of the painting or editing tools. The swatch selected on the Swatches palette or color set
in the Color palette will directly affect the actual ink density on your printed output. For example, if you want to paint with a tint percentage of 20%
of the spot color, the color slider in the Color palette should be set to 20%.

MERGING SPOT CHANNELS

You can merge spot channels into the other color channels, but be aware
that by doing so, you will flatten the image if you have a layered document.
Fortunately, a warning dialog box is displayed asking if you want to flatten
the layers before you actually merge the spot channel. For more information on layers and flattening an image, see Chapter 10.

To merge a spot channel, select the spot channel in the Channels palette
and choose Merge Spot Channel from the palette menu.

When you merge spot channels into the other color channels, Photoshop
converts the spot color to the closest color equivalent. Don't expect the
color to exactly match, especially if you're working in CMYK, because
CMYK inks cannot adequately match all the available spot color inks.

PRINTING COMPOSITE IMAGES WITH SPOT COLORS

When printing images with spot colors to a composite printer, the spot colors print out as separate pages. To print a composite image that contains
spot colors, make a copy of the document and merge the spot channels into
the other color channels by choosing Merge Spot Colors from the Channels

palette menu. The names of the spot channels will display on each plate when the image is separated. Each spot channel is overprinted on top of the image in the order in which they appear in the Channels palette. Save the Photoshop document in DCS 2.0 format. For more information on the DCS 2.0 file format, see Chapter 15, "File Formats."

SUMMARY

You can understand and master the use of channels and masks by applying what you've learned in this chapter, augmented by your own experimentation. This will not only help prepare you to become an Adobe Certified Expert but also enable you to achieve sophisticated and professional results in your color correcting, silhouetting, and compositing work.

REVIEW QUESTIONS

1. Which answer is true when using the Apply Image command?

    a.   The new image will be in Multichannel mode.

    b.   The original channel information in the image is affected.

    c.   The individual channels can be specified for both the source and the target.

    d.   The original channel information in the image is not affected because you can create a new channel, selection, or document.

2. How do you change the order of color channels?

    a.   Color channels cannot be reordered.

    b.   Click on the channel name and drag it above or below another channel.

    c.   Click on the channel thumbnail and drag it above or below another channel.

    d.   Click on the black triangle in the Channels palette and choose Reorder Channels.

3. What does the Solidity value of a spot color represent?

    a.   The ink density of the spot color

    b.   The opacity of the spot color when printed

    c.   An onscreen display of the printed spot color

    d.   The tint percentage of the spot color when printed

4. Which answer is true when using the Channel Mixer?

    a.   Increasing the values of a specific channel of a RGB image will shift the color toward its complimentary color.

    b.   Decreasing the values of a specific channel of a CMYK image will shift the color toward its complimentary color.

    c.   Increasing the values of a specific channel of a CMYK image will shift the color toward its complimentary color.

    d.   Decreasing the values of a specific channel of an RGB image will shift the color toward its complimentary color.

5. Which answer is incorrect on how to load an alpha channel as a selection?

    a.   Choose Select > Load Selection.

    b.   Alt/Option+click on the channel thumbnail.

    c.   Control/Command+click on the channel name.

    d.   Click the load selection button in the Channels palette.

6. What do you need to do first when using Quick Mask mode?

    a. Create a selection.

    b. Select the alpha channel.

    c. Click on the Quick Mask button.

    d. Choose Quick Mask from the Edit menu.

7. Where is a saved selection stored?

    a. In the Select menu

    b. To your hard drive

    c. In the Layers palette

    d. In the Channels palette

8. How do you edit the mask of a saved alpha channel?

    a. Paint on the Layer.

    b. Paint on the layer mask.

    c. Paint on the Quick Mask overlay.

    d. Paint on the alpha channel with black, white, or a shade of gray.

CHAPTER 14

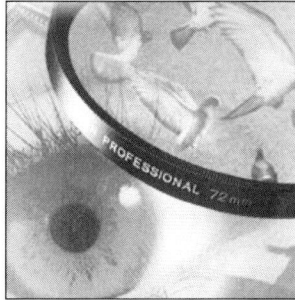

COLOR CORRECTION

This chapter focuses on the appropriate use of the image adjustment commands; the lessons will help you understand and distinguish between their similarities and differences. Before using the individual image adjustment commands, it's important to first learn about the tools that can make color and tonal adjustments more accurate and easier to perform, such as the Gamut Warning command, CMYK Preview, the Histogram, the Info palette, the color sampler tool, and the Auto Levels command. The remainder of the chapter explains the use of the image adjustment commands, including Levels, Curves, Color Balance, and more.

Domains & Objectives

Color and Color Calibration

9.1   Identify the characteristics, function, and appropriate use of image adjustment commands, including Levels, Curves, Variations, Brightness/Contrast, Hue/Saturation, Color Balance, Equalize, Threshold, Histogram, and out-of-gamut colors.

9.3   Determine the appropriate feature, command, tool, or procedure to accomplish a stated task related to color correction.

HELPFUL HINTS FOR WORKING WITH RGB AND CMYK IMAGES

Following are a few general guidelines to keep in mind when working with color images destined for film output:

- If an image has been scanned in RGB mode, keep it in RGB while making tonal and color adjustments as long as possible. Convert the image to CMYK as your last step, and fine-tune the image if needed before film output.

- Save an unflattened copy of the RGB file before converting to CMYK so that if any major corrections need to be made, you have the option of correcting the original file.

- If an image is scanned in CMYK mode, stay in CMYK. There's no use compromising the pixel information twice by converting to RGB to make corrections, and then converting the file back to CMYK for film output.

- You'll work faster in RGB mode because the file size is approximately 25% smaller than a CMYK file. In RGB, each channel is equal to 1/3 the size of the total image, whereas in CMYK, each channel is equal to 1/4 the size of the total file.

- Take advantage of the CMYK dot percentage display in the Info palette while working with an RGB image. For more information on using the Info palette, see page 376 in this chapter.

- Don't forget that you can make tonal and color corrections without affecting the actual pixels by using adjustment layers. See page 263 for more information on using adjustment layers.

TOOLS AND COMMANDS TO CONSIDER BEFORE COLOR CORRECTING AN IMAGE

Photoshop includes several tools and commands that can help you achieve more accurate color. Understanding how these tools and commands work in conjunction with the image adjustment commands will lead to not only more professional results but increased efficiency as you work with images. These tools include the Gamut Warning command, CMYK Preview, the Histogram, the Info palette, the color sampler tool, and the Auto Levels command.

USING THE GAMUT WARNING COMMAND

Gamut warning can be used to identify colors in an image that cannot be matched and printed correctly when converted to CMYK. Even though

Photoshop automatically converts out-of-gamut colors to reproducible colors when the CMYK conversion takes place, you can view and manually correct the out-of-gamut colors before the conversion if you wish.

To display the Gamut Warning, choose View > Gamut Warning. To turn off the Gamut Warning display, reselect Gamut Warning in the View menu. By default, the Gamut Warning color is gray, but you can change the color by choosing File > Preferences > Transparency & Gamut (see Figure 14.1). Click the color box located at the bottom of the dialog box to display the Color Picker and then choose a new warning color. You also can change the opacity of the warning color here.

To bring colors back into a printable gamut range, you can use the sponge tool (see page 230), the Saturation blending mode (see page 186), or the Saturation slider in the Hue/Saturation dialog box (see page 398-399).

Figure 14.1

If it's difficult to see the Gamut Warning when it is displayed over the image, change its color in the Transparency & Gamut preferences.

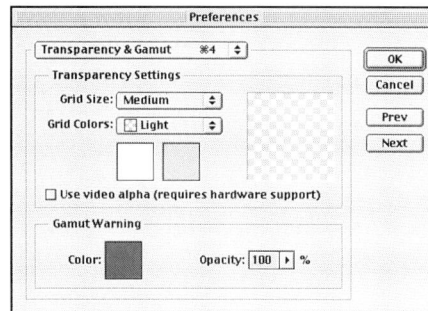

USING THE INFO PALETTE

When color correcting RGB images that are destined for CMYK output, use the Info palette to display the approximate CMYK values. You can select the eyedropper tool in the toolbox to monitor corrections in specific areas of an image before making adjustments by dragging over different areas of the image. In addition, while in an image adjustment dialog box such as Levels or Curves, the active tool turns into the eyedropper tool, enabling you to take samples of different areas. Both methods display the values in the Info palette.

When working with one of the image adjustment commands such as Levels and Curves, the Info palette displays two sets of values. The numbers to the left of the slash reflect the pixel values before a color correction, and the numbers to the right of the slash reflect the pixel values after the correction. If you select colors that are out-of-gamut, an exclamation point will display next to the colors in the Info palette (see Figure 14.2). The CMYK values that display are based on the settings in the RGB Setup and CMYK Setup preferences. (See Chapter 16, "Prepress Production," for more information on these topics.)

Figure 14.2

An exclamation point displays next to colors that are out-of-gamut in the Info palette.

The information displayed in the Info palette can be changed to reflect what's appropriate for the image on which you're working. For example, the image mode can be changed for the before and after readouts using the pulldown menus; the measurement units also can be changed from inches to pixels or another measurement type (see Figure 14.3). To access these options, click the black triangle in the Info palette and select Palette Options.

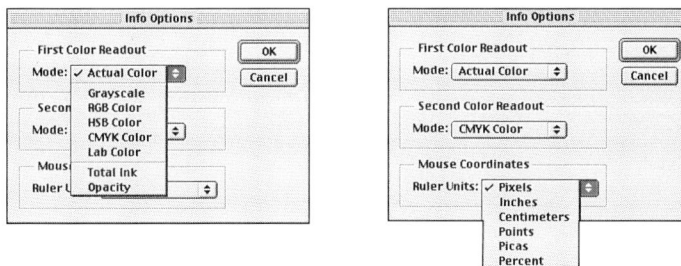

Figure 14.3

Customize the Info palette by changing modes for more accurate feedback when editing an image.

USING THE COLOR SAMPLER TOOL

The color sampler tool, new to Photoshop 5.0, enables you to record up to four color samples in an image. Using the color sampler tool is a great way to keep track of certain colors so that you can make accurate before-and-after comparisons when adjusting an image. Photoshop stores the color sample values in the Info palette, and the sampled area is marked on the image. The sampled color information is also saved with the image. The following options are available to the color sampler tool:

- **Display or hide the color sampler information in the Info palette.** Choose Show or Hide Color Samplers from the Info palette menu.

- **Place a color sampler on an image.** Select the color sampler tool in the toolbox (located as a hidden tool with the eyedropper) and click on the image. The Info palette records the sample (see Figure 14.4).

Figure 14.4

The Info palette displays
information for up to
four color samplers.

- **Change the color mode for the color sampler display in the Info palette.** Click the color sampler icon to display the color mode menu in the Info palette (see Figure 14.5).

Figure 14.5

After setting a color
sampler on an image, you
can change the color
sampler mode display
by clicking the Color
Sampler icon in the
Info palette.

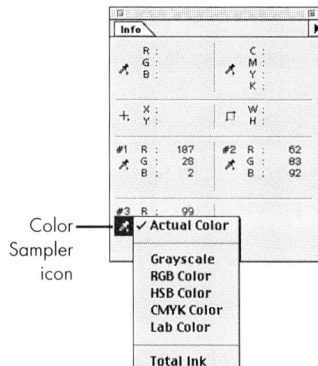

- **Move a color sampler.** Select the color sampler tool in the toolbox. Click and drag the sampler to a new location. (The new value will not display until the mouse button is released.)

- **Delete a color sampler.** Select the color sampler tool and drag the sampler out of the image window; or press Alt/Option, position your cursor over the sampler, and click on it when the cursor becomes the scissors icon.

- **Change the sample size measured by the color sampler tool.** Click on the black triangle in the color sampler Options palette and choose Point Sample to read the value of a single pixel, 3 by 3 Average to read the average value of a 3-by-3-pixel area, or 5 by 5 Average to read the average value of a 5-by-5-pixel area (see Figure 14.6).

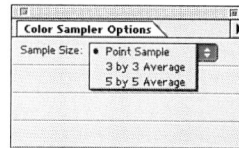

Figure 14.6

Change the sample size
measured by the sampler
tool in the Color
Sampler Options palette.

USING CMYK PREVIEW

The CMYK Preview option is extremely helpful when color correcting or
adjusting out-of-gamut colors in an RGB image. By choosing View >
Preview > CMYK, Cyan, Magenta, Yellow, Black, or CMY, you can display a
CMYK preview of an image (see Figure 14.7). To turn off the preview, reselect CMYK Preview in the View menu.

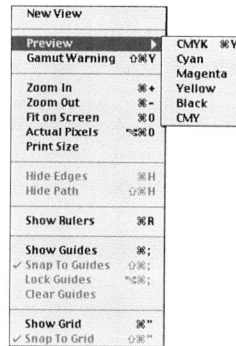

Figure 14.7

Preview the composite
CMYK image, individual
plates, or CMY combi-
nation plates by choos-
ing CMYK Preview from
the View menu.

Keep in mind that Photoshop displays the CMYK equivalents using the current separation and calibration values in the CMYK Setup dialog boxes. The
actual CMYK color conversion doesn't take place until you choose the
CMYK mode in the Image menu.

SAVING AND LOADING COLOR ADJUSTMENT SETTINGS

The Save and Load buttons in the Levels, Curves, Hue/Saturation, Replace
color, Selective color, Variations, and Duotone dialog boxes enable you to
save color adjustments you've performed on one image, and then apply the
adjustment to other images.

As an example, let's say a line of products is photographed on a white background with the same roll of film. After scanning all the images, you discov-
er each exhibits the same color cast. Using the Save and Load buttons, you
can adjust one image, save the adjustment, and then apply it to the others.

TIP

While correcting an RGB
image, you can monitor
the changes you make in
a second image window
by turning on the CMYK
Preview. Choose View >
New View to open a sec-
ond image window, and
then turn on the CMYK
Preview for that window.

Now you try it...

Using the Save and Load buttons

1   Open your first image and make your correction with one of
     the color adjustment commands.

2   Click the Save button and give the file a name.

3   Open the file that you want to apply the correction to and
     reopen the same Color Adjustment dialog box used earlier.

4   Click the Load button and locate the saved color correction
     file. Click OK.

UNDERSTANDING THE HISTOGRAM

The Histogram is your roadmap to where all the pixels in an image reside.
Depicted visually and numerically as a graph, the Histogram tells you how
many pixels are in the image and where they are located in terms of brightness, from 0 (black) to 255 (white). The x-axis represents the color values
(0–255), and the y-axis represents the total number of pixels at a particular
level of brightness (see Figure 14.8).

Figure 14.8

The Histogram reveals
information about the
tonality of an image.

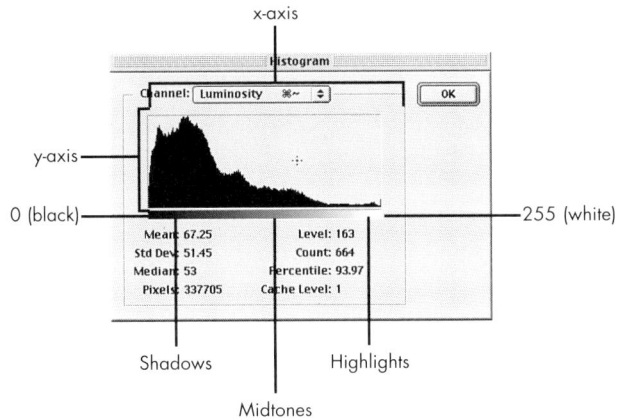

The Histogram helps you determine the image key type or tonal range,
which can help you decide how to best correct the image. Access the
Histogram by choosing Image > Histogram. There are three key types: low-
key, average-key, and high-key. The Histogram for a low-key image displays
most of the pixels on the left side, which means the image is heavy in the
dark tones or shadow areas (see Figure 14.9).

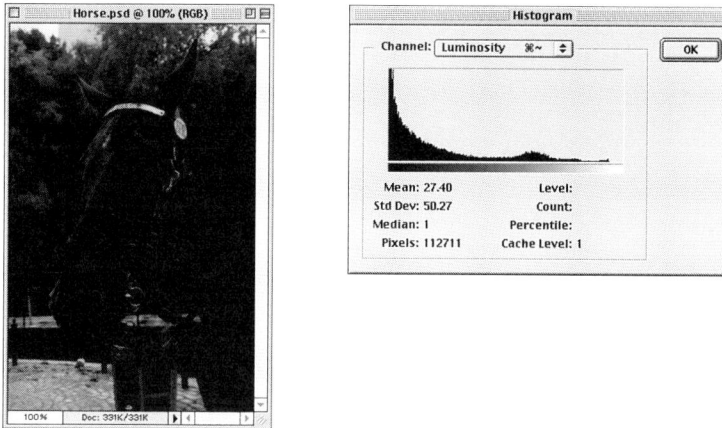

Figure 14.9

A low-key image
Histogram in which
most of the pixels are
in the shadow areas
of the image.

With a high-key image, the Histogram displays most of the pixels on the
right side. This means the image is light in color (see Figure 14.10).

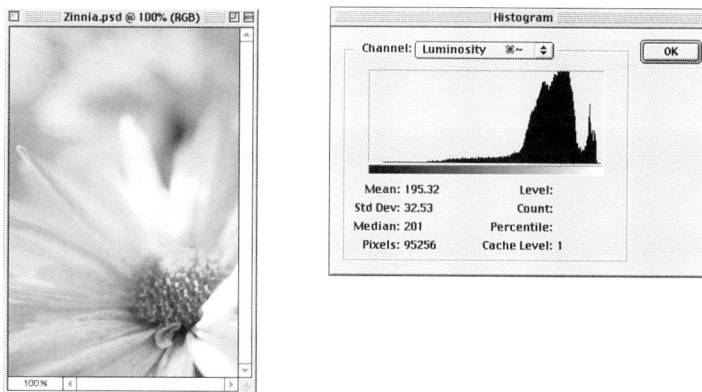

Figure 14.10

A high-key image
Histogram in which
most of the pixels are
in the highlight areas
of the image.

An average-key image with balanced tonality is displayed with a somewhat
equal distribution of pixels (see Figure 14.11).

TIP

A low-key or high-key
image isn't necessarily a
bad thing, because the
subject of the image
could be inherently dark
or light. More than likely,
however, it's a poorly
scanned image or a bad
original.

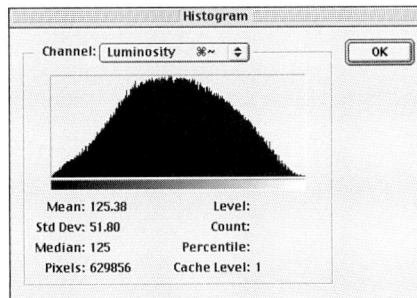

The following statistical information is also available in the Histogram dialog box:

- **Mean.**   Represents the average brightness value in the image or selection.
- **Std Dev.**   Standard Deviation indicates how widely the values vary.
- **Median.**   Represents the middle value in the image or selection.
- **Pixels.**   Indicates the total number of pixels used to calculate the Histogram in the image or selection.
- **Level.**   You can find out the brightness level of a specific area or range of pixels by placing the cursor over areas of the graph or clicking and dragging for range-level information.
- **Count.**   You can display a count of the total number of pixels of a specific area or range by placing the cursor over an area of the graph or clicking and dragging for a range count.
- **Percentile.**   You can display a percentage of the total number of pixels at or below a specific area or range by placing the cursor over an area of the graph or clicking and dragging for the range percentage.
- **Cache Level.**   The number displayed for Cache Level is set in the Image Cache Preferences dialog box. The higher the number, the faster

the Histogram is displayed, but the lower the accuracy of the information for high resolution images. When the Use Cache for Histograms box is checked, Photoshop takes a representative sampling of the image based on the screen display, not the actual pixel data. Therefore, if your image is at a magnification other than 100%, the Histogram won't display true information.

Uncheck the Cache Level box when color quality is more important than speed. To do this, choose File Preferences > Image Cache, uncheck the Use Cache for Histograms box, and click OK. The change doesn't take effect until you relaunch Photoshop (see Figure 14.12).

NOTE

If you're using adjustment layers in an image, the information displayed in a Histogram depends on which layers are visible beneath the Adjustment Layer.

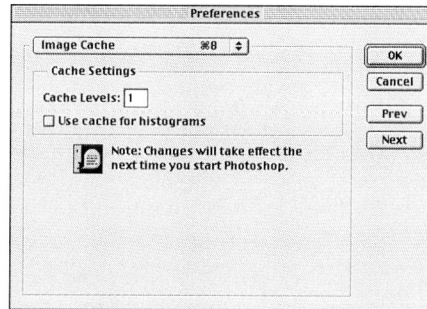

Figure 14.12

For greater accuracy in the Histogram display, it's a good idea to leave the Use cache for histograms box unchecked.

SEVEN STEPS TO BETTER COLOR AND TONALITY

The following steps can help ensure better color and tonality when correcting images. Keep these steps in mind as you read through this chapter and experiment with your own images after you have learned about each command:

TIP

When working in RGB, CMYK, Lab, and Indexed color mode, you can also view individual channel information in the Histogram dialog box, in addition to the Luminosity (composite) channel, by clicking on the Channel pop-up menu.

- **Calibrate your system.** This first step is a crucial one in the process of producing accurate color.

- **Evaluate the tonality of the image.** Read the Histogram to understand the dynamic range of the image before you use the color adjustment commands. See page 380 in this chapter for information on reading a Histogram.

- **Determine if the image contains a color cast.** If so, choose to fix the cast before adjusting the tonality of the image. This chapter explains several ways to adjust a color cast, including using the Color Balance, Variations, and Curves commands.

- **Adjust the highlights and shadows.**   Set the black point and white point of an image using Levels or Curves. See pages 386-390 in this chapter for information on using Levels and Curves.

- **Adjust the midtones.**   Use Levels or Curves to adjust the midtones. See page 389 in this chapter for more information.

- **Fine-tune the color.**   Use Color Balance, Selective Color, or another color-specific adjustment command explained in this chapter.

- **Apply the Unsharp Mask filter.**   Sharpen and improve the contrast of the image. See page 233 in Chapter 9, "Editing and Retouching."

USING THE LEVELS COMMAND

If you haven't noticed, the Levels dialog box displays the same information as the Histogram. Whereas the Histogram is just a visual display of the information, the Levels command enables you to adjust the tonal balance of an entire image, selection, or channel. Specifically, you can adjust the highlights, midtones, and shadows by using either the Input or Output sliders or the black-point and white-point eyedroppers (see Figure 14.13).

Figure 14.13

Use the Levels command to adjust highlights, midtones, and shadows.

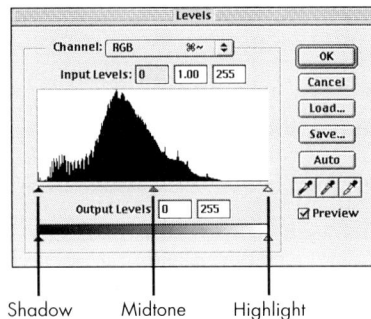

USING INPUT LEVELS

The Input Levels sliders in the Levels dialog box enable you to adjust the black-point (shadow), white point (highlight), and gamma (midtone) in an image on a scale from 0 (black) to 255 (white), as explained by the following:

- **Adjusting the shadows.**   The black triangle represents the shadows, or darker tones in an image, and the default setting is set to 0. By dragging the slider to the right you can increase the shadow tones in the image. Dragging the slider to a higher level sets all pixels at that level and below to 0.

- **Adjusting the highlights.**   The white triangle represents the highlights, or lighter tones in an image, and the default setting is set to 255. By dragging this slider to the left, you can increase the highlights in the image. Dragging this slider to a lower level causes all pixels at that level and above it to become 255.

- **Adjusting the midtones.**   The gray slider adjusts the midtones or (gamma) of an image without affecting the highlight and shadow points.

USING OUTPUT LEVELS

Using the Output sliders at the bottom of the Levels dialog box compresses the tonal range of an image into fewer than the available 256 levels of gray; they also are effective for setting the maximum shadow points and minimum highlight points. There are two sliders:

- **Black Output.**   By sliding the black Output triangle to the right you decrease the shadows in the image. For example, if you slide the black Output triangle to 10, all pixels at level 0 change to level 10, pixels at level 1 change to level 11, pixels at level 2 change to level 12, and so on.

- **White Output.**   By sliding the white Output triangle to the left, you decrease the highlights in the image. For example, if you slide the white Output triangle to 245, all pixels at level 255 change to level 245, pixels at level 254 change to level 244 and so on.

The following lesson reviews how to use the Levels command sliders to adjust the shadows, midtones, and highlights of an image.

Now you try it...

Using the Levels sliders to adjust the tonality of an image

1   Open the "Andy.psd" image in the Chapter 14 lessons folder located on the CD.

2   Choose Image > Adjust > Levels to open the Levels dialog box. Notice there are no pixels to the immediate left of the white triangle and few pixels to the right of the black triangle (see Figure 14.14). This indicates a dull, flat image.

3   Click and drag the white triangle to the left to the position where the pixels in the graph end to add highlight pixels.

4   Click and drag the black triangle to the position where the pixels start to adjust the shadows and further increase contrast (see Figure 14.15).

continues

Figure 14.14

Levels before adjust-
ing the highlight and
shadow points.

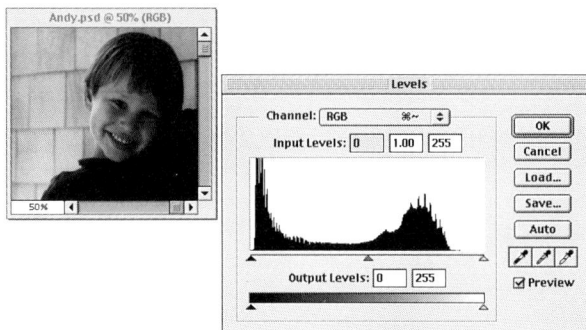

Figure 14.15

Levels after
adjusting the
highlight and
shadow points.

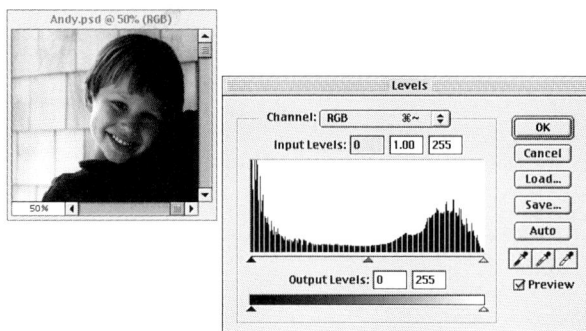

5   Experiment adjusting the midtones by dragging the gray slider
to the left to lighten the midtones, and then dragging the slider to the right to darken the midtones.

6   Click the Cancel button to leave the image uncorrected for use
in the next lesson.

SETTING TARGET VALUES FOR HIGHLIGHTS AND SHADOWS

You can change the target values for both the highlight and shadow areas in
an image to increase detail or to avoid too much contrast. There are two good
reasons why you might want to do this. First, you want to avoid *specular highlights* (often called blown-out highlights) in your image. These areas contain
no dot; hence, they contain no detail, and no ink will be applied to that area
of the paper. When working with shadow areas, it's important that you maintain detail so the shadow areas don't plug up on press and print as solid ink.

When the target values are set for both the highlights and shadows, you can
use the black-point and white-point eyedroppers in the Levels (or Curves)
dialog box to set the highlight and shadow values in the image.

When assigning a recommended target value for shadows, open either the Levels or Curves dialog box and double-click the black eyedropper to open the Color Picker. In the CMYK fields, enter the values **65**, **53**, **51**, and **95** (or **10**, **10**, and **10** in the RGB fields) (see Figure 14.16). These are recommended target values for shadows when printing an average key image on white paper. However, if you're working with a high-key image, you might need a higher target value for the shadows to avoid too much contrast.

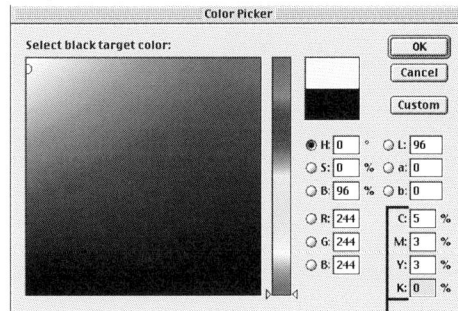

Setting the highlight target values

Figure 14.16

Change the target values for highlights and shadows by double-clicking the black-point and white-point eyedroppers in the Levels or Curves dialog box.

To assign target values for highlights, double-click the white eyedropper and in the CMYK fields, and enter the values **5**, **3**, **3**, and **0** (or **244**, **244**, and **244** in the RGB fields). These are the recommended target values for highlights when printing an average key image on white paper. However, if you're working with a low-key image (more pixels in the shadow areas), you might need a lower target value for the highlights to avoid too much contrast.

USING THE BLACK-POINT AND WHITE-POINT EYEDROPPERS

Similar in function to the Levels sliders, the black-point and white-point eyedroppers are used with either the Levels or Curves command to adjust the darkest and lightest values in an image.

Now you try it...

Using the Levels eyedroppers to adjust the tonality of an image

1   Open the "Andy.psd" image in the Chapter 14 lessons folder located on the CD.

continues

NOTE

When one of the eye-dropper buttons is selected in the Levels or Curves dialog box, the button turns gray. To deselect it, just click it.

NOTE

If you changed the black-point and white-point values by double-clicking the white-and-black eyedroppers, the Auto Levels command will use those values as well as the black and white clipping specified when you click the Options button in the Levels dialog box.

2   Choose Image > Adjust > Levels to open the Levels dialog box. Notice there are no pixels to the right of the white triangle or to the left of the black triangle. This indicates a dull, flat image.

3   Visually determine the darkest area of the image. Select the black eyedropper and click in that area (try the lower-right corner of Andy's shirt). This sets the black point and is similar to dragging the black Input triangle to the right.

4   Select the white eyedropper and click in the brightest area of the image (try the highlight on Andy's cheek). This sets the white point and is similar to dragging the white Input triangle to the left.

5   Experiment adjusting the midtones by dragging the gray slider to the left to lighten the midtones and to the right to darken them.

USING THE AUTO LEVELS COMMAND

The easiest (but not the most precise) way to adjust the tonality of an image is to use the Auto Levels command or the Auto buttons in the Levels or Curves dialog box. The Auto Levels command adjusts the tonality of an image by defining the lightest and darkest pixels in the image, and then proportionately redistributing the pixels in between. It is most effective on an image that is dull and flat or of an average key type.

The Auto Levels command clips or discards the white-and-black pixels by a default amount of 0.5%. However, the clipping amount can be changed when in the Levels or Curves dialog box by pressing Alt/Option and clicking the Options button. The Auto Range Options dialog box displays, enabling you to enter a new clipping percentage (see Figure 14.17).

Figure 14.17

The Auto Range Options dialog box can be accessed by pressing the Alt/Option key and clicking the Options button in the Levels or Curves dialog box.

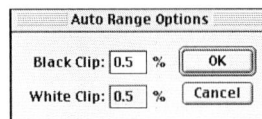

For example, if you enter **2%** in both the Black Clip and White Clip fields, Photoshop will ignore the darkest 2% and lightest 2% when you use the Auto Levels command or when you click on the Auto button in either the Levels or Curves dialog box. A clipping amount between 0.5% and 1% is recommended.

Use the following keyboard shortcuts when in the Levels dialog box:

Best Levels dialog box shortcuts	
Mac OS Commands	
Open Levels dialog box	Command+L
Increase/decrease in increments of 1	Up/down arrow keys
Increase/decrease in increments of 10	Shift+Up/down arrow keys
Toggle channels	Command+~, 1, 2, 3, 4
Move to next field	Tab
Move to previous field	Shift+Tab
Reset Levels	Option+Click on Cancel button
Auto Levels	Command+Shift+L
Zoom in/out while in dialog box	Command++ (plus) or – (minus)
Zoom in while in dialog box	Command+Spacebar
Pan around image while in dialog box	Spacebar
Windows Commands	
Open Levels dialog box	Control+L
Increase/decrease in increments of 1	Up/down arrow keys
Increase/decrease in increments of 10	Shift+Up/down arrow keys
Toggle channels	Control+~, 1, 2, 3, 4
Move to next field	Tab
Move to previous field	Shift+Tab
Reset Levels	Alt+Click on Cancel button
Auto Levels	Control+Shift+L
Zoom in/out while in dialog box	Control++ (plus) or – (minus)
Zoom in while in dialog box	Control+Spacebar
Pan around image while in dialog box	Spacebar

TIP

Press Control/
Command+Shift+L
to quickly apply Auto
Levels to an image.

USING THE CURVES COMMAND

Similar to the Levels command, the Curves command enables you to control the highlight, midtone, and shadow areas of a composite image, selection, or channel(s). However, the Curves command gives you precise control in adjusting the tones between the shadows and midtone (three-quartertones) and between the midtones and highlights (quartertones).

The Curves dialog box displays a graph that represents the relationship between the original pixels and the adjusted pixels of an image. The horizontal axis represents the original pixel values, which are called the *input values.* The vertical axis represents the adjusted pixel values, which are called *output values.*

When you first open the Curves dialog box, the graph displays a line at a 45 degree angle. Because you haven't made any changes to the curve, the input and output values are the same. The bottom-left corner designates

NOTE

When identifying the lightest and darkest points in the image, you should use your cursor. (It turns into the eyedropper when you open the Curves dialog box.) When you are ready to actually set the black point and white point, you need to switch to the eyedroppers in the Curves dialog box.

NOTE

When the eyedropper is selected in the Levels or Curves dialog box, the eyedropper button turns gray. To de-select it, just click it.

the shadows and a 0 value at the corner point. The top-right corner designates the highlights and a value of 255 at the corner point. The middle of the graph represents the midtones (see Figure 14.18).

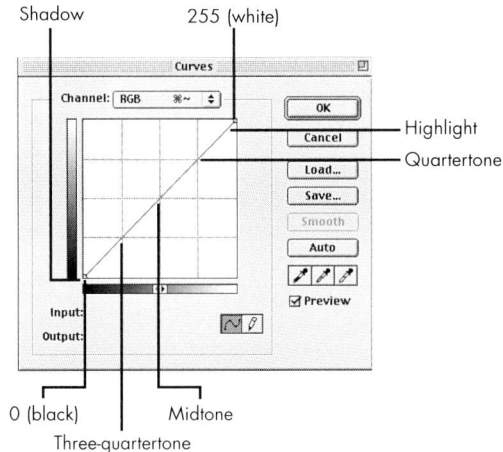

Below the graph is a grayscale that displays the pixel values from black (0) on the left to white (255) on the right. You can reverse the display and work with percentages (0%–100%) instead of levels by clicking on the double arrow. Manipulate the curve by clicking and dragging on the diagonal line.

You can sample areas in the image to plot the pixel values on the grid in the Curves dialog box. For example, if you click and drag over the darkest areas of an image, those values will be designated by a small circle indicating its position on the grid. The input and output numbers are also displayed (see Figure 14.19).

In the following lesson, you will learn how to use the Curves command with the black-point and white-point eyedroppers to adjust the shadows and highlights. In addition, you'll learn how to adjust the midtones, including the quartertone and three-quartertone areas of an image.

Figure 14.19

The grid displays
the sampled value,
designated by a circle.

Now you try it...

Setting the Black-and-White points of an image using Curves

1   Open the "Dark.kit.psd" image in the Chapter 14 lessons folder located on the CD. This image is very dark, with little range in the midtones. Choose Image > Histogram to evaluate the image, and then Click OK (see Figure 14.20).

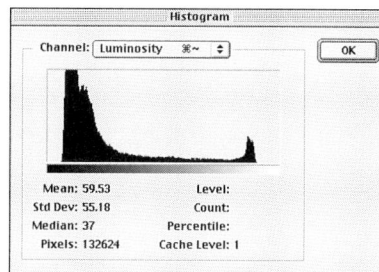

Figure 14.20

The Histogram indi-
cates a dark image
with flat midtones
and few highlights.

2   Choose Image > Adjust > Curves or press Control/Command+M to open the Curves dialog box. Notice that your cursor has switched to an eyedropper when it's placed over the image.

Click and drag on the image to determine the darkest and lightest points in the image. The grid displays the sampled value designated by a circle with numeric values.

continues

3   When you've found the darkest and lightest points in the image, first select the black eyedropper in the Curves dialog box and click on the area that you determined was the darkest (try the tip of the kitty's nose). Then select the white eyedropper and click on the lightest area of the image (try the upper-right corner of the image).

4   Set the three-quartertone point by clicking on the grid and dragging the point up (see Figure 14.21). This will lighten the area between the darkest shadows and the midtone.

5   Set the quartertone point by clicking on the grid and dragging the point up (refer to Figure 14.21). This will lighten the area between the midtone and the highlight.

6   Continue experimenting by moving the points individually. Then try moving the points at the same time by Shift+clicking on each point and dragging. If you want to delete a point, Control/Command+click on it or drag the point off the grid.

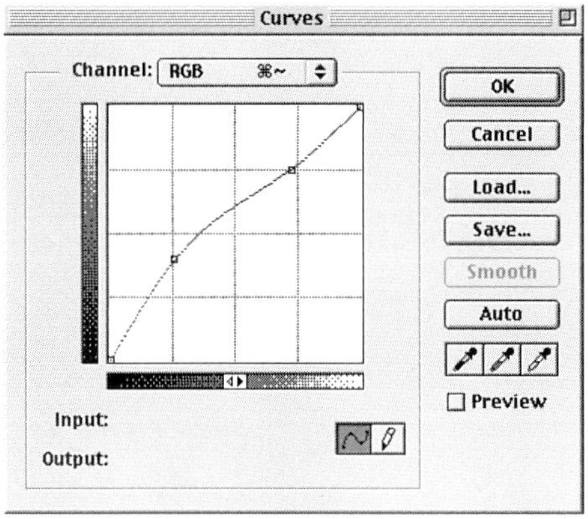

Figure 14.21

Adjust the three-quartertone and quartertone areas of the image.

Use the following keyboard shortcuts when in the Curves dialog box:

TIP

You can add points to the curve by Control/Command+clicking on the image.

Best Curves dialog box shortcuts	
Mac OS Commands	
Open Curves dialog box	Command+M
Add point	Click in grid
Delete point	Command+Click on point
Select multiple control points	Shift+Click
Deselect all points	Command+D
Add color as new point on curve	Command+Click in image
Add color as individual points for each channel curve	Command+Shift+Click
Move points	Up/down arrow keys
Move points in multiples of 10	Shift+up/down arrow keys
Select next control point	Command+Tab
Select previous control point	Command+Shift+Tab
Toggle grid between fine/coarse	Option+Click in grid
Reset Curve	Option+Click on Cancel button
Toggle channels	Command+~, 1, 2, 3, 4
Zoom in/out of image when in dialog box	Command++ (plus) or – (minus)
Zoom in while in dialog box	Command+Spacebar
Pan around image while in dialog box	Spacebar
Windows Commands	
Open Curves dialog box	Control+M
Add point	Click in grid
Delete point	Control+Click on point
Select multiple control points	Shift+Click
Deselect all points	Control+D
Add color as new point on curve	Control+Click in image
Add color as individual points for each channel curve	Control+Shift+Click
Move points	Up/down arrow keys
Move points in multiples of 10	Shift+up/down arrow keys
Select next control point	Control+Tab
Select previous control point	Control+Shift+Tab
Toggle grid between fine/coarse	Alt+Click in grid
Reset Curve	Alt+Click on Cancel button
Toggle channels	Control+~, 1, 2, 3, 4
Zoom in/out of image when in dialog box	Control++ (plus) or – (minus)
Zoom in while in dialog box	Control+Spacebar
Pan around image while in dialog box	Spacebar

USING VARIATIONS

If working with color is new to you, the Variations command can be a good place to begin to understand how colors interact with each other. The Variations command is a quick and easy way to visually adjust an image or selection and is effective in correcting an image that has a color cast. In addition to adjusting the color balance, it also adjusts the contrast and saturation and works best on average-key type images. The Variations command is not available to indexed-color or Lab images.

In the top-left area of the Variations dialog box, two thumbnails display that represent the Original image and the Current Pick. These thumbnails should be identical, unless you have made previous corrections with the Variations command (see Figure 14.22).

Figure 14.22

Use the Variations command to simultaneously adjust the color balance, contrast, and saturation of an image.

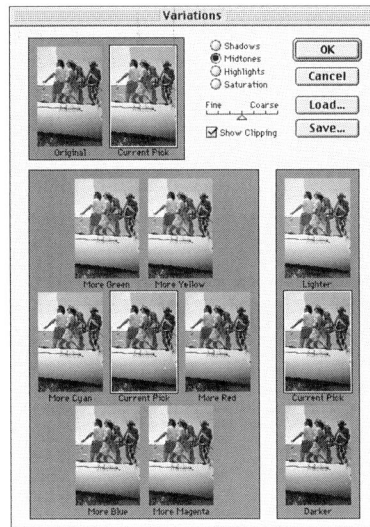

In the top-right area of the Variations dialog box, you have the following adjustment options:

- **Shadows, Midtones, and Highlights.**   Check the corresponding button to affect the color and brightness of these areas of an image.
- **Saturation.**   Check the Saturation button to saturate or desaturate the image. Make sure the Clipping option is checked to ensure that you have not oversaturated the image. A neon preview displays over areas in the image that will be clipped by the adjustment. Clipping does not occur when you adjust the midtones.

- **Fine/Coarse.**   The Fine/Coarse slider enables you to specify the amount of each adjustment when you click a thumbnail. By default, the triangle slider is centered on the scale. For each move of the triangle slider above or below the middle, the adjustment is doubled.

The thumbnails displayed in the bottom-left area of the dialog box enable you to adjust the color balance of the image. These thumbnails are arranged according to their position on the color wheel. For example, green and magenta are complementary colors and appear diagonally across from each other; same with blue and yellow, because they are also complementary. So, for example, if an image has too much blue in the midtones, you can reduce the blue by clicking the yellow thumbnail.

The thumbnails displayed in the right column of the dialog box enable you to adjust the brightness in the image.

The following lesson covers how to use the Variations command to correct an image that has a color cast.

Now you try it...

Using the Variations command to adjust an image with a color cast

1   Open the "Family Sail.psd" image located in the Chapter 14 lessons folder on the CD. This image has a heavy blue cast most noticeable in the midtones and shadows.

2   Before using the Variations command, it can be helpful to first identify the highlights, midtones, and shadows in the image by using the Color Range command. (This is also useful with the other color adjustment commands.) Choose Select > Color Range. First identify the midtones in the image by choosing Midtones from the pop-up menu (see Figure 14.23). The midtones are displayed as white in the Color Range dialog box. Compare these areas with the actual image.

Next, identify both the highlights and shadows using the pop-up menu while analyzing the image. Click cancel to exit the dialog box. (To learn more about the Color Range command, see page 405 in this chapter.)

Now that you know where the highlights, midtones, and shadows are, you can use the Variations command with a little more knowledge of the image.

Figure 14.23

The Color Range com-
mand can be helpful in
visually determining
where the highlights,
midtones, and shadows
are in an image.

3   Choose Image > Adjust > Variations. Make sure the Fine/
Coarse triangle slider is positioned in the middle of the slider
and that the Midtones button is selected. To decrease the blue
cast in the midtones, click once on the More Yellow thumbnail.
If the image still appears too blue, experiment with lowering
the Fine/Coarse triangle slider so the next change to the
image isn't as exaggerated.

4   Adjust the blueness in the shadows by clicking the Shadow
button and lowering the Fine/Coarse triangle slider all the way
to the left and click once again on the More Yellow thumbnail.

5   Continue experimenting by adding and subtracting color with
different settings and colors to understand the relationship
between adding and subtracting colors in an image.

USING THE COLOR BALANCE COMMAND

Similar to the Variations command, the Color Balance command enables
you to increase or decrease particular colors in an image or selection in the
highlight, midtone, and shadow areas; however, only the composite channel
can be corrected. Therefore, if you need to make a more precise color correction in an image that has a cast, for example, your best bet is to use the
Curves command. The Curves command gives you control in these three
tonal areas—highlight, midtone, and shadows—and also the quartertone
and three-quartertone areas of an image. Using Curves also enables you to
correct individual channels or combinations of two or more channels
simultaneously. (See page 389 in this chapter to learn more about the
Curves command.)

When in the Color Balance dialog box, you have the following options available to you for adjusting the color balance of an image:

- **Color adjustment sliders.**   The color sliders display the complementary CMYK and RGB colors. For example, to decrease a particular color in an image or selection, drag the slider away from the color you want to reduce and toward its complement. So, if you want to decrease blue in an image, drag the slider toward yellow (see Figure 14.24).

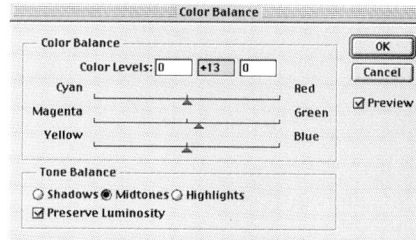

Figure 14.24

To reduce a particular color, drag the slider away from that color and toward its complementary color.

You can also increase or decrease a color by adjusting the two adjacent colors on the color wheel, or the two adjacent colors to the opposite color. For example, to decrease green, add blue and red. To increase blue, subtract green and red.

- **Shadows, Midtones, Highlights.**   Check the corresponding button and use the adjustment sliders to affect the color values in these areas of the image.

- **Preserve Luminosity.**   When the Preserve Luminosity box is checked, the tonality of the image is maintained. Only the color values change, and the brightness values of the pixels are unaffected.

Now you try it...

Using the Color Balance command to color correct a selected area of an image

1   Open the "Canoe.psd" image located in the Chapter 14 lessons folder on the CD. The trees in the background of this image are a bit dull in color. By adjusting the color balance on only a selection of the trees, you can make a big improvement to this image.

2   With the rectangular marquee tool, make a selection around the trees (see Figure 14.25).

continues

Figure 14.25

Apply the Color
Balance command to
a selected area of
an image.

Figure 14.25

Apply the Color Balance command to a selected area of an image.

3   Choose Image > Adjust > Color Balance or press
Control/Command+B to open the Color Balance dialog box
(see Figure 14.26).

Figure 14.26

The Color Balance
dialog box enables you
to adjust the color in
highlights, midtones,
and shadows in
an image.

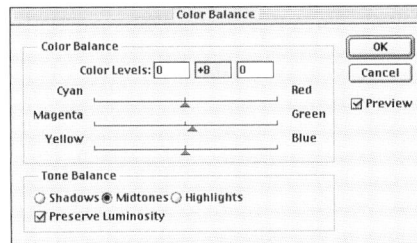

4   To add more green to the trees, click and drag the slider
toward green with the midtone button selected. Then experiment adding green to the shadows and highlights.

5   Press the Alt/Option key to set the Cancel button to the Reset
button and experiment decreasing the blue and red values.
Click OK.

USING THE HUE/SATURATION COMMAND

The Hue/Saturation command enables you to adjust the hue and saturation
as well as the lightness of an image or selection.

You can choose Master from the pop-up menu in the dialog box to adjust
all the colors in the image simultaneously, or choose just one color component to adjust it individually, and then drag the Hue adjustment slider (see
Figure 14.27).

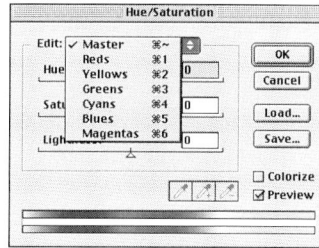

Figure 14.27

Use the Hue/Saturation command to adjust one color component at a time or all components simultaneously.

The Saturation adjustment slider enables you to increase saturation by dragging it to the right and decrease saturation by dragging it to the left. As you drag, the color shifts away from or toward the center of the color wheel relative to the original values of the selected pixels.

With the Lightness adjustment slider you can increase the lightness of the pixels by dragging it to the right or decrease the lightness by dragging it to the left.

The Hue/Saturation dialog box in Photoshop 5.0 now includes an option for modifying a range of colors for the hue, saturation, and lightness of an image (see Figure 14.28).

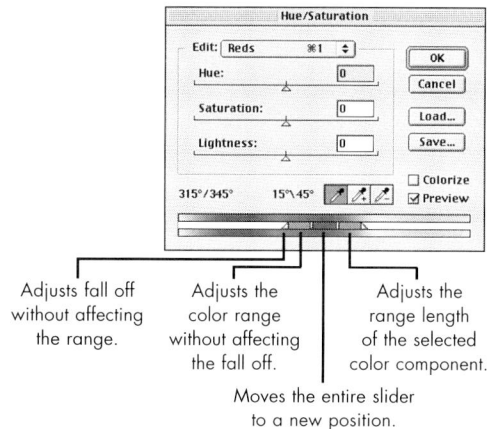

Figure 14.28

The new color bar in the Hue/Saturation dialog box.

Adjusts fall off without affecting the range.

Adjusts the color range without affecting the fall off.

Adjusts the range length of the selected color component.

Moves the entire slider to a new position.

CHANGING THE COLOR RANGE USING THE COLOR BARS

The two color bars at the bottom of the Hue/Saturation dialog box are based on the color wheel. The upper color bar shows the active color range, based on the color selected from the Edit menu. Clicking and dragging the dark gray field of the slider is the same as selecting a color in the Edit menu.

🖐 **TIP**

Press Control/Command
and drag the color bar to
reposition the display of
the color wheel.

If you make an adjustment with the Hue adjustment slider and drag the
color bar slider to a new range, the bottom color bar moves around the
color wheel. The numeric values displayed represent the number of degrees
of rotation around the color wheel from the pixel's original color.

Not only can you increase and decrease the range of colors included in the
adjustment, you can adjust the fall off of the colors, which can help blend
the new hue with existing colors in the image.

When you modify the range selected in the color bar so that it falls into a
different color range, the name is reflected in the Edit menu. This means
you can create customized color ranges for your image. For example, if you
choose Red and alter the range so that it includes Yellow, the name changes
to Yellow 2 (see Figure 14.29). You can create up to six ranges of each of the
preexisting color ranges (for example, Yellow through Yellow 6).

Figure 14.29

You can create up to six
customized ranges with
the Hue/Saturation com-
mand, shown here in
the Edit menu.

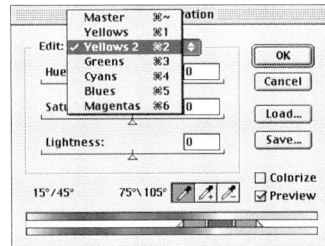

You can edit the color range by sampling colors in your image with the eyedropper tools located in the Hue/Saturation dialog box. Use the + (plus)
eyedropper to add to the range; use the – (minus) eyedropper to subtract
from the range. You can also press Shift to add to the range when the regular eyedropper is selected or Alt/Option to subtract.

USING THE COLORIZE OPTION

The Colorize option reduces the hue to one color, which can be used to create a duotone effect. The lower color bar displays the hue as you drag the
Hue adjustment slider. Keep in mind this is not a true duotone. Because
you're working with more than two colors, you have the opportunity to add
elements to the image that possess other colors, such as type, graphics, or
even another image. You can also use the Colorize option to achieve a hand-
tinted effect by adding color to a selection in a grayscale image that's been
converted to RGB.

The following lesson takes you through the process of adjusting colors in an image using the Hue, Saturation, and Lightness sliders, as well as how to adjust the range of colors in the color bar.

Now you try it...

Using the Hue/Saturation command to adjust colors in an image

1   Open the "Rose.psd" image in the Chapter 14 lessons folder located on the CD.

2   Adjust the color of the rose by selecting Reds from the Edit pop-up menu. Notice that the slider now is displayed in the color bar at the bottom of the Hue/Saturation dialog box and is positioned in the Red range (see Figure 14.30).

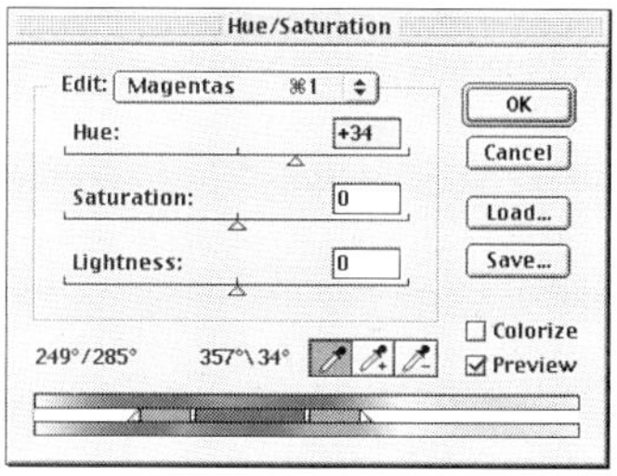

Figure 14.30

The color bar displays the color component selected in the Edit pop-up menu.

3   Drag the Hue adjustment slider to the left to approximately **–23** to add Magenta to the image. If you continue to slide the Hue slider to the left, you successively change the reds in the image to the colors that appear to the left of the red range in the color bar. This is just like moving clockwise through the color wheel (see Figure 14.31).

4   Drag the white triangles to adjust the amount of fall off of the colors selected without affecting the range.

5   Drag one of the lighter gray bars to adjust the range without affecting the amount of fall off.

6   Add colors to the current selected range by selecting the + (plus) eyedropper and clicking on the colors in the image you want to add. Note the range change in the color bar.

continues

Figure 14.31

Drag the Hue adjustment slider and notice how it changes the color based on the color wheel.

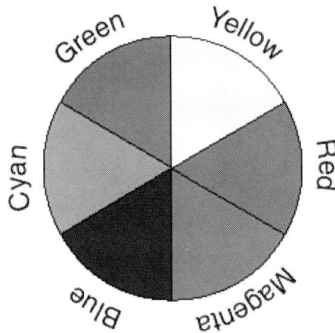

7   Subtract colors from the current selected range by selecting the – (minus) eyedropper and clicking on the colors in the image you want to subtract. Note the range change in the color bar.

8   Reset the image back to the original by pressing the Alt/Option key and clicking the Reset button if you want to experiment further.

Use the following keyboard shortcuts when in the Hue/Saturation dialog box (Image/Adjust menu):

Best Hue/Saturation dialog box shortcuts	
Macintosh Commands	
Open Hue/Saturation dialog box	Command+U
Increase/decrease in increments of 1	Up/down arrow keys
Increase/decrease in increments of 10	Shift+Up/down arrow keys
Move to next field	Tab
Move to previous field	Shift+Tab
Move range to new location	Click in image
Add to range	Shift+Drag in image
Subtract from range	Option+Drag in Image
Edit master	Command+tilde (~)
Edit individual colors	Command+1–6
Slide color spectrum	Command+Drag on ramp
Reset Hue/Saturation	Option+Click on Cancel button
Zoom in/out while in dialog box	Command++ (plus) or – (minus)
Zoom in while in dialog box	Command+Spacebar
Pan around image whle in dialog box	Spacebar

Windows Commands	
Open Hue/Saturation dialog box	Control+U
Increase/decrease in increments of 1	Up/down arrow keys
Increase/decrease in increments of 10	Shift+Up/down arrow keys
Move to next field	Tab
Move to previous field	Shift+Tab
Move range to new location	Click in image
Add to range	Shift+Drag in image
Subtract from range	Alt+Click/Drag in image
Edit master	Control+tilde (~)
Edit individual colors	Control+1–6
Slide color spectrum	Control+Drag on ramp
Reset Hue/Saturation	Alt+Click on Cancel button
Zoom in/out while in dialog box	Control++ (plus) or – (minus)
Zoom in while in dialog box	Control+Spacebar
Pan around image whle in dialog box	Spacebar

USING THE REPLACE COLOR COMMAND

Using the Replace Color command enables you to change the hue, saturation, and lightness of selected pixels in an image by first creating a mask.
The mask you create is temporary and is visible only in the Replace Color
dialog box. It does not result in an active selection. The mask is displayed in
the Replace Color dialog box after you click on the first pixel value in the
image. The masked areas appear as black, the selected areas appear as white,
and the gray areas represent partially selected areas (see Figure 14.32).

TIP

Right-click/press the
Control key to toggle
between previewing the
image and the mask in
the Replace Color
dialog box.

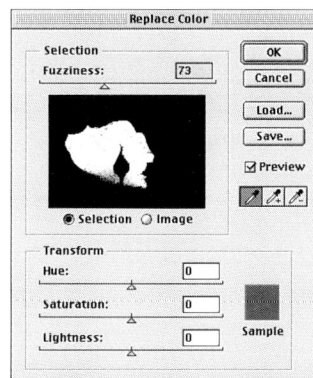

Figure 14.32

The Replace Color pre-
view box displays the
sampled colors in white.
The black areas repre-
sent the masked areas
that are protected from
change.

You can select multiple colors by using the + (plus) eyedropper or pressing
Shift while clicking with the regular eyedropper. To subtract areas, use the –
(minus) eyedropper and click on the image. You can also Alt/Option+click.

In addition to adding and subtracting pixels by clicking in the image window, you can also add or subtract areas of a selection by clicking on the mask in the Preview box displayed in the Replace Color dialog box.

The Fuzziness slider enables you to partially select pixels and interactively add or delete pixel ranges in the selection. Using the Fuzziness slider to increase or decrease the number of pixels selected is similar to setting the tolerance for the magic wand or paint bucket tools.

When you are satisfied with the mask, you can adjust the hue, saturation, and lightness of the selected pixels. It's important that the last color you sample in the image has the same color properties you want in the new color. For example, if the last pixel you click is a muddy color, the new color will also be muddy.

The following lesson reviews how to use the Replace Color command to create a temporary mask of a rose and to change its color by adjusting the hue, saturation, and lightness of the sample pixels.

Now you try it...

Using the Replace Color command

1   Open the "Rose.psd" image in the Chapter 14 lessons folder located on the CD and choose Image > Adjust > Replace Color.

2   Select the + (plus) eyedropper and make sure the Preview displays Masked areas by clicking on the Selection button.

3   Click on a few of the rose pixels and notice that the preview box now displays areas of white. This indicates the area of sampled pixels (refer to Figure 14.33).

Figure 14.33

Sampled areas appear as white in the Preview box.

The black areas indicate the mask, or areas that are protected from change. Any gray areas or stray pixels can be picked up by clicking on those pixels in the Mask Preview box with the + (plus) eyedropper. Experiment clicking and dragging to select large tonal areas.

4   Use the Fuzziness slider to adjust the tolerance. If you've picked up too many pixels in the image, drag the slider to the left and continue sampling a few more pixels with the + (plus) eyedropper.

5   When you have a clean mask (see Figure 14.34), you can change the hue, saturation, and lightness of the rose by using the sliders at the bottom of the palette. The last color you sample will be displayed in the color box, and its properties will be the same in the new color. (Remember, a muddy sample color leads to a muddy new color.) Click OK.

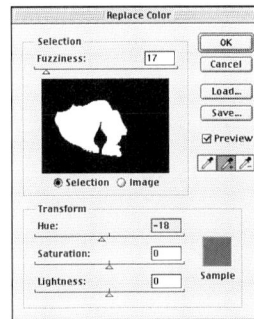

Figure 14.34

Work with the Fuzziness slider and the plus and minus eyedroppers to obtain a clean mask.

USING THE COLOR RANGE COMMAND

The Color Range command operates the same way as the Replace Color command, only it results in an active selection by selecting sampled colors, default preset colors, or highlight, midtone, and shadow areas. Keep in mind that you will likely need to use other selection tools such as the lasso tool, Quick Mask, or the Smooth command after using Color Range to refine the selection.

When using Color Range, you are sampling pixel information from all visible layers, so if you don't want certain layers included, you need to hide those layers before using the command.

Use the Color Range command to make a selection by choosing Select > Color Range. The Select pop-up menu enables you to view and select particular colors or tonal ranges in the image (see Figure 14.35).

TIP

Press Control/Command++ (plus) or − (minus) to change the view of the image while working in any of the Image adjustment dialog boxes.

Figure 14.35

You can select specific colors and tonal ranges using the Color Range command.

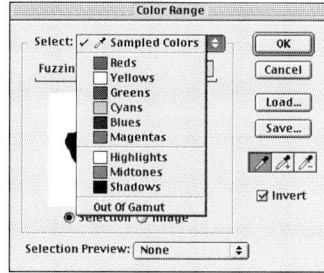

TIP

Press Control/ Command+Spacebar to zoom in on the image while in any of the Image adjustment dialog boxes. Pressing just the Spacebar enables you to pan around the image.

TIP

For realistic results, the Replace Color command is best used on areas where you don't desire a huge color shift from the original image.

When you select Sampled Colors from the Select pop-up menu, you have access to the eyedroppers, which enable you to add or subtract colors in the same manner as the Replace Color command.

Use the + (plus) eyedropper or press Shift while clicking to include multiple colors in the selection; use the – (minus) eyedropper and click on the image to subtract areas. You also can Alt/Option+click using the regular eyedropper in the dialog box.

Using the Fuzziness slider to increase or decrease the number of pixels selected is similar to setting the tolerance for the magic wand or paint bucket tools. The Fuzziness slider enables you to partially select pixels and interactively add or delete pixel ranges in the selection and is useful for creating selections that have a slightly feathered edge.

At the bottom of the dialog box you have several selection preview options, including Grayscale, Black Matte, White Matte, and Quick Mask (see Figure 14.36). All are useful in making selections when the Sampled Colors option is selected from the Select pop-up menu. An explanation of each follows:

Figure 14.36

Check the accuracy of your selection while creating it by toggling between the Preview options.

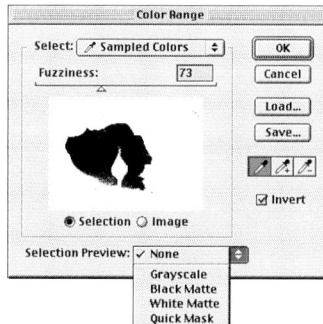

TIP

When working in the None mode, Press Control for a quick grayscale preview in the color range dialog box.

- **None.**   This default setting doesn't display the mask in the image window as the other preview options do; however, it is definitely the fastest option because you don't need to wait for the information to update in the image window. If time isn't on your side, work in the None mode and periodically switch to one of the preview options described next to check your work.

- **Grayscale.**   This preview option displays the selection mask as it would look if saved as an alpha channel. This preview is effective when adding and deleting sampled pixels using the eyedroppers.

- **Black Matte and White Matte.**   The Black Matte and White Matte previews show what the selection would look like if copied and pasted on a black or white background. Both of these options are also effective when adding and subtracting sample pixels and are especially useful in checking the edges of the selection.

- **Quick Mask.**   Using the Quick Mask preview displays the Quick Mask overlay over your selection. If you want to change the Quick Mask options—such as the mask color or the display of selected areas or masked areas—press the Alt/Option key while selecting Quick Mask from the pop-up menu; the Quick Mask options dialog box is displayed.

The following lesson covers how to use the Color Range command to create a selection of a rose.

Now you try it...

Using the Color Range command to create a selection

1   Open the "Rose.psd" image in the Chapter 14 lessons folder located on the CD and choose Select > Color Range.

2   Take a moment to go through each of the options in the Select pop-up menu to display a preview of each option. Then choose the Sampled Colors option.

3   Select the + (plus) eyedropper. Click and drag over areas of the rose to begin selecting multiple pixel values. You can select pixels in either the image window or in the Preview display in the dialog box (see Figure 14.37).

continues

TIP

If you press the Shift key while using the plus eyedropper, you can add a color sampler to the image. (See page 377 for more information on color samplers.)

TIP

You can add or subtract areas of a selection by clicking on the image or on the mask in the Preview box.

TIP

If it's easier to select the opposite area (such as a white background), you can check the Invert check box in the Color Range dialog box rather than choose Invert from the Select menu after using Color Range.

Figure 14.37

Use the eyedroppers
to either select or
deselect areas of the
image in both the
image window and
the Preview display.

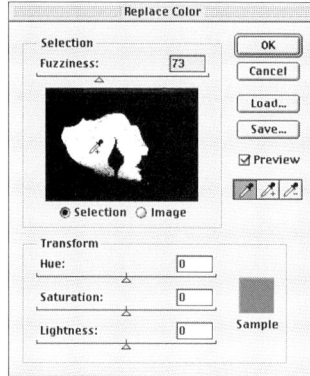

4   Adjust the Fuzziness to a lower setting if you have mistakenly picked up pixels in the background area of the image or use the – (minus) eyedropper to deselect areas.

5   Continue refining the selection by experimenting with each Preview setting from the pop-up menu at the bottom of the dialog box. Click OK.

6   To add areas of the rose that weren't included in the selection, use the lasso tool with the Shift key held down and click and drag a circle around those pixels. To subtract background areas included in the selection, hold down the Alt/Option key and click and drag around those pixels to exclude them. (For more information on using the lasso tool, see Chapter 6, "Selections.")

USING THE SELECTIVE COLOR COMMAND

Selective color correction is a technique used by high-end drum scanners and separation programs. Within Photoshop, it's a command that's especially useful in making final color corrections to CMYK proofs. The Selective Color command enables you to increase or decrease the amount of a process color in an additive or subtractive color. For example, you can decrease the cyan in the red areas of an image while keeping the cyan in the blue areas intact. The Colors pop-up menu in the Selective Color dialog box lists the primary additive and subtractive colors plus whites, neutrals, and blacks (see Figure 14.38).

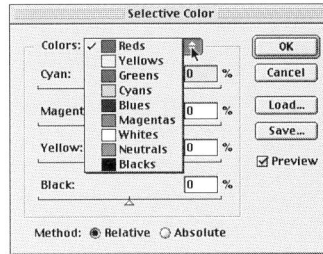

Figure 14.38

The Selective Color
command is useful
when fine-tuning
CMYK images.

NOTE

The composite channel
must be active to use the
Selective Color command.

NOTE

You cannot use the
Relative option on specu-
lar highlights (areas that
contain no color) in an
image.

It's important to understand the difference between using the Relative and
Absolute mode methods, because they work quite differently in the way
each adjusts color. An explanation of each follows:

- **Relative**.   Relative adjusts all four CMYK values to match the desired
  increased or decreased percentage you choose for a particular color. For
  example, if you add 10% to a 50% cyan pixel, the result is 55% cyan
  (10% of 50% = 5%).

- **Absolute**.   Absolute adjusts only the desired percentage increase or
  decrease for that particular color. For example, if you reduce an 85%
  cyan pixel by 10%, the new value is 75% cyan.

Now you try it...

Using the Selective Color command

1   Open an image that contains colors you would like to selec-
     tively adjust and choose Image > Adjust > Selective Color.

2   Choose the color you would like to adjust from the Colors pop-
     up menu at the top of the Selective Color dialog box. Make
     sure the Preview box is checked.

3   Select either Relative or Absolute and drag the sliders to
     increase or decrease the components of a selected color.

TIP

When using the Selective
Color command, display
the Info palette to see
the before and after
color values.

USING THE BRIGHTNESS/CONTRAST COMMAND

The Brightness/Contrast command makes a global adjustment to your
image without regard to the highlights, midtones, shadows. It adjusts the
pixels in each of these areas equally. For example, if you increase the
brightness value to 10, all the pixels in the image increase in brightness
by a value of 10.

The Brightness/Contrast command is the least effective in adjusting the tonal range of an image and should never be used as the only means of correction. If you need to use it at all, it's best to use it after you have adjusted the image using either Levels (see the section "Using the Levels Command") or Curves (see the section "Using the Curves Command"). The Brightness/Contrast command is not recommended for high-resolution output. To access the Brightness/Contrast command, choose Image > Adjust > Brightness/Contrast.

USING THE INVERT COMMAND

The Invert command can be used to turn a scanned black-and-white negative into a positive image, or it can be used to turn a positive black-and-white image into a negative (see Figure 14.39). When you use the Invert command, the brightness value of each pixel is inverted. For example, a pixel that has a value of 0 (black) is changed to 255 (white), and a pixel that has a value of 15 is changed to 240. To access the Invert command, choose Image > Adjust > Invert or press Control/Command+I.

Figure 14.39

The Invert command inverts the brightness values of the pixels.

A scanned negative before using the Invert command

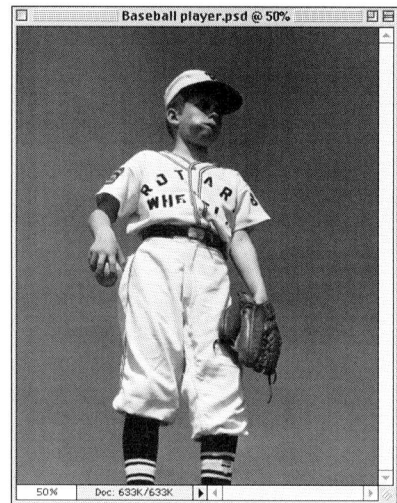

The positive image after using the Invert command

NOTE

You cannot use the Invert command to make a positive from scanned color film; however, you can use the command on color images as a special effect.

TIP

You can also use the Invert command on alpha channels and layer masks to reverse the alpha mask.

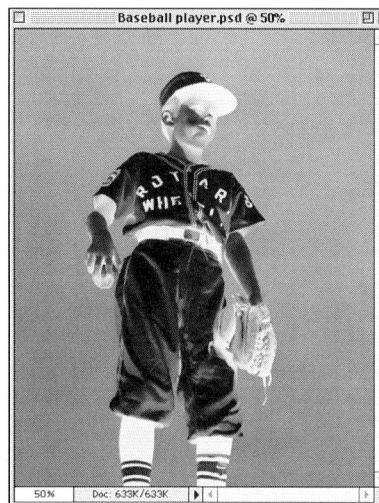

USING THE EQUALIZE COMMAND

The Equalize command redistributes dark and light values over the full tonal range of an image (0–255). It locates the darkest and lightest values and makes them absolute black and white. All the pixels in between are then averaged and distributed evenly.

You can apply the Equalize command on an entire image or on a selection. When applying the command to a selection, the Equalize dialog box opens and displays two choices (see Figure 14.41):

- **Equalize selected area only.**   Choose this option to equalize only the pixels within the selection.

- **Equalize entire image based on selected areas.**   Choose this option to equalize the pixels in the entire image based on the pixels within the selection.

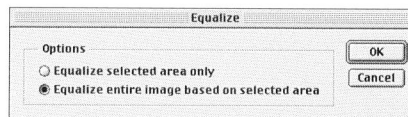

Figure 14.41

When you have an active selection and choose the Equalize command, you can apply the command to either the selection or to the entire image based on the pixels in the selection.

Now you try it...

Using the Equalize command

1   Open the "Bottles" image in the Samples folder, which is in the Goodies folder located in the Photoshop application folder.

2   Select the magic wand and set the tolerance for the magic wand to **32** in the Options palette. Display the Options palette by either double-clicking on the magic wand in the toolbox or choosing Window > Show Options.

3   Select only the white background area with the magic wand. You might need to Shift+click on areas that weren't included with your first click.

4   Choose Image > Adjust > Equalize to change the color of the background. In the Equalize dialog box, choose Selected Area Only. Click OK.

USING THE THRESHOLD COMMAND

You can use the Threshold command to convert color or grayscale images to high-contrast black-and-white images. The Threshold dialog box enables you to specify a threshold level by using a slider. Dragging the slider to the right turns the pixels above the 128 midpoint value to black, whereas dragging the slider to the left increases the number of white pixels.

The Threshold command can also be used to make selections in conjunction with an alpha channel by first duplicating the channel that has the most contrast, and then applying the Threshold command. Results vary depending on the image. You will usually need to add or subtract areas to refine the selection. You can make these additional edits by painting on the alpha channel or using either the lasso tool or Quick Mask.

The following lesson reviews how to use the Threshold command in combination with the alpha channel to create a selection.

Now you try it...

Using the Threshold command to create a selection

1   Open the "Red bird.psd" image in the Chapter 14 lessons folder located on the CD.

2   Display the Channels palette by choosing Window > Show Channels. Examine each component channel individually to determine which channel has the most contrast. In this case, the Blue channel contains the most contrast between the bird and the background.

3   Make a duplicate of the Blue channel by dragging it on top of the New Channel icon at the bottom of the palette or by clicking the black triangle in the Channels palette and choosing Duplicate channel. Make sure that the new alpha channel is the active channel.

4   Choose Image > Adjust > Threshold and drag the slider to the left. It's important to watch the detail around the bird and to settle on a Threshold level (59 works well) that gives you the most distinction between the bird and the background (see Figure 14.42). Click OK.

Figure 14.42

Concentrate on the detail of the silhouette as you drag the Threshold slider.

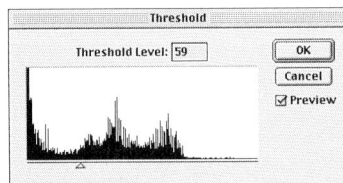

5 Select the paint brush and, with black as your foreground color, paint over the areas in the background that are white to add those areas to the selection. Switch the foreground color to white and paint the black areas within the bird silhouette to deselect those areas. Press X on your keyboard to switch between black and white as you edit the mask (see Figure 14.43).

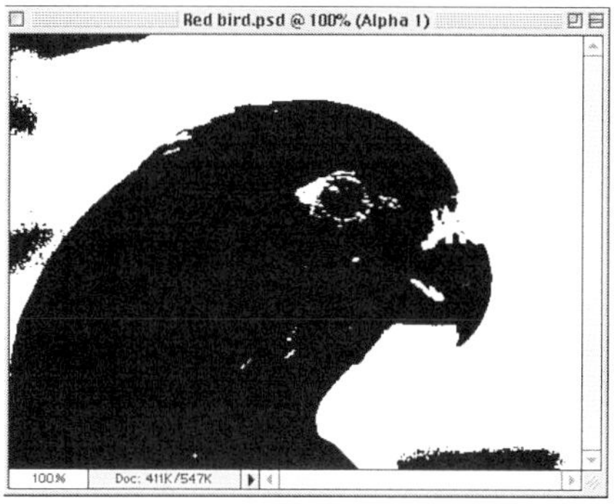

Figure 14.43

Paint on the mask to add or delete areas of the selection after using the Threshold command.

6 To check the selection, activate the RGB composite channel by clicking it. Load the alpha channel as a selection by Control/Command+clicking on the channel. Choose Select > Inverse to select the bird rather than the background (see Figure 14.44). If you want to save the selection for later use, Choose Save Selection from the Select menu. (For more information on saving and loading alpha channels, see Chapter 13, "Channels & Masks.")

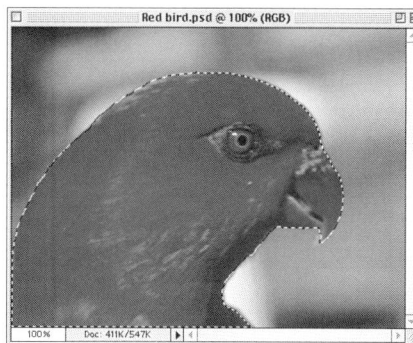

Figure 14.44

The finished selection after using the Threshold command on an alpha channel and inverting the selection.

USING THE POSTERIZE COMMAND

The Posterize command can be used to reduce the number of tonal levels in a color or grayscale image. The number of colors that result are based on the number you enter in the Posterize dialog box and the number of pixels at a certain tonal level. For example, if you posterize a color image at six levels, Photoshop finds the six most popular colors in the image and forces the other colors to match those six (refer to Figure 14.45).

Figure 14.45

Use the Posterize command to reduce the number of tonal colors in an image.

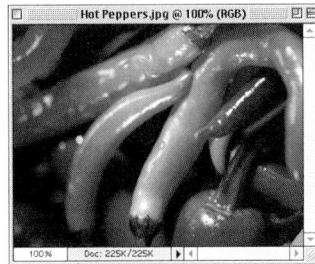

Before applying the
Posterize command

After applying the
Posterize command

TIP

When in the Posterize dialog box, use the up and down arrows on your keyboard to quickly experiment with different posterization levels.

SUMMARY

Spending time up front evaluating your images and reading the Histogram are necessary steps in choosing the most appropriate command when color correcting images. The more you work with the various adjustment commands, the better you'll be able to make an educated decision. Having a conceptual understanding of the similarities and differences between the image adjustment commands not only prepares you to become an Adobe Certified Expert, but also helps you achieve excellent results in your professional work.

REVIEW QUESTIONS

1. What color should you add to an image that has a blue cast?

    a.   Blue

    b.   Green

    c.   Yellow

    d.   Magenta

2. How does the Relative option affect an image when using the Selective Color command?

    a.   The Relative option enables selective color correction only on selected channels.

    b.   The Relative option enables selective color correction only within an active selection.

    c.   The Relative option adjusts only the desired percentage increase or decrease for a particular color.

    d.   The Relative option adjusts all four CMYK values to match the desired percentage increase or decrease chosen for a particular color.

3. When using the Color Range command, how do you add colors to the selected range?

    a.   Press the Alt/Option key and click on the image.

    b.   Press the Shift key and click on the image.

    c.   Press Alt/Option+Shift and click on the image.

    d.   Select the eyedropper from the toolbox and click on the image.

4. Which color adjustment command is ap-propriate for an image that has a color cast?

    a.   Equalize

    b.   Tolerance

    c.   Color Balance

    d.   Brightness/Contrast

5. How does a high Image Cache Level setting affect the Histogram display?

    a.   Accurate pixel information

    b.   Inaccurate pixel information

    c.   It has no affect on the Histogram information.

    d.   It increases the amount of pixel information displayed.

6.   Where do you turn off the Image Cache?

    a.   Uncheck the Image Cache box in the Histogram dialog box.

    b.   Uncheck the Image Cache box in the Levels dialog box.

    c.   Toggle the option off by selecting View > Image Cache.

    d.   Select File > Preferences > Image Cache.

7.   How do you set the white point in an image?

    a.   Select the eyedropper tool in the toolbox and click on a highlight in the image.

    b.   Select the color sampler tool in the toolbox and click on a highlight in the image.

    c.   Select the white eyedropper in the Levels dialog box and click on a highlight in the image.

    d.   Select the white eyedropper in the Color Range dialog box and click on a highlight in the image.

8.   How do you set the target values for shadows and highlights?

    a.   Adjust the settings in the Separations setup dialog box.

    b.   Use the eyedropper to select sample pixels in the shadow and highlight areas in an image.

    c.   Double-click the eyedroppers in the Curves or Levels dialog box and enter the values in the Color Picker.

    d.   Double-click the eyedroppers in the Curves or Levels dialog box to open the Target Value dialog box and enter the values.

CHAPTER **15**

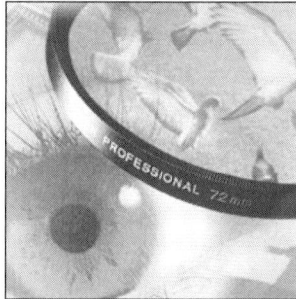

FILE FORMATS

When you save an image file, it is saved in a specific file format. The format of a file determines how the file can be viewed and edited, how the data the file contains is compressed, and how well the file is suited for a particular purpose. It is important to understand how Photoshop uses the various formats for a thorough understanding of how Photoshop interacts with other graphics applications. In addition, many of the file formats available have been developed for use by particular industries. Knowledge of the file formats aids in an understanding of industry requirements and limitations.

Domains & Objectives

File Format/Import/Export

10.1   Identify the characteristics, function, and appropriate use of various file formats, including but not limited to Photoshop native, TIFF, EPS, JPEG, PCX, PDF, PICT, GIF, and relation to production method and file size.

10.2   Determine the appropriate file format and procedure for exporting an Adobe Photoshop file to a specified application to accomplish a particular task.

10.3   Determine the appropriate feature, command, tool, or procedure to import a path into Adobe Photoshop and export a path to Adobe Illustrator.

OPTIONS FOR SAVING FILES

Although Photoshop has a standard save option, there are two other methods of saving files that also enable you to create new images.

SAVE AS

The Save As command, similar to other programs, saves the current document as a new file with a new filename. If you have not yet saved the current document, the Save As dialog box will prompt you to provide a filename (see Figure 15.1). Further, if you are working on a document and have made changes that are not supported by the current file format, the Save As dialog box will prompt you to save the image file in another format. For example, if you are working on a file in a format that does not support layers and you create a new layer, you will need to save the file in the Photoshop native format to preserve the layer information. If you want to save the file in the original format, use the Save a Copy command described in the following section.

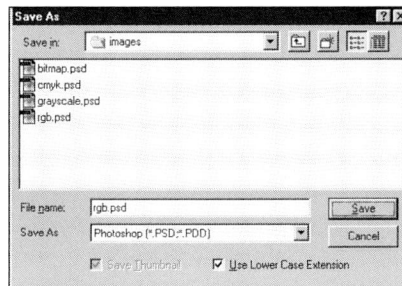

Figure 15.1

The Save As dialog box enables you to save the current file with a new filename.

SAVE A COPY

The Save a Copy command saves another copy of the current file with a new filename, while leaving the current file open for editing with its original name. The Save a Copy command also provides options to flatten the layers, discard alpha channels, and discard nonimage data based on the requirements of a specific file format (see Figure 15.2). For example, only the Photoshop native format supports layers, so using the Save a Copy command and choosing any other file format automatically flattens the layers in the image. When using the Save a Copy command, Photoshop adds the word *copy* to the end of the filename.

Figure 15.2

The Save a Copy com-
mand flattens layers or
discards alpha channels
if necessary.

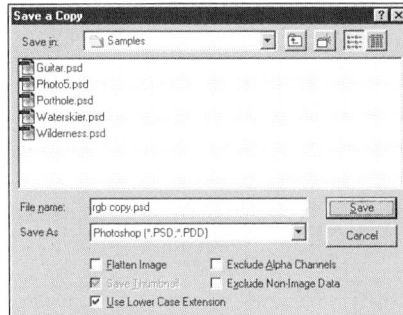

The Save a Copy command can be used to save an image at different stages
of its development while preserving the original file. Using the Save As
command would necessitate closing the copy of the file that is created by
the Save As command and reopening the original file. By using the Save a
Copy, you can avoid these extra steps.

The Save a Copy command can be very useful for creating images that will
actually be used for printing and display onscreen, while preserving the
original Photoshop file complete with layers and alpha channels. Many
times, two or even three copies of a file can be stored together. In electronic
publishing, there is often an original source file in Photoshop native format
that still has all the layers and alpha channels intact and a JPEG or GIF file
that can be used in the electronic document. When changes need to be
made, they are changed in the source file, and then the JPEG or GIF is
recreated. Similarly, in print publishing, there are often three files: an RGB
master file in Photoshop native format, a CMYK file in Photoshop native
format, and then the EPS or TIFF, which is given to the printer for publication. In both of these cases, you can make excellent use of the Save a Copy
command.

IMAGES, PATHS, AND OTHER APPLICATIONS

Images created in Photoshop are often viewed or edited in other applications before the final publication is created. In the case of images intended
for print, the images often are imported into page layout or illustration programs so that they can be combined with text or vector graphics.

ADOBE ILLUSTRATOR

Images created in Photoshop can be imported into an Adobe Illustrator document using Illustrator's Place command. Illustrator can import many of the formats that Photoshop 5.0 can create, including the Photoshop native format. If you want to mask certain areas of the image, create a clipping path and save the file as a Photoshop EPS. When imported into Illustrator, the areas inside the clipping path are visible; the other areas are transparent. (See Chapter 7, "Paths," for more information about creating clipping paths.)

In addition to saving clipping paths with EPS files, you can use the Export command in the File menu in Photoshop to export paths in the Photoshop document to an Adobe Illustrator file. You can export the Document Bounds, selected paths, or all the paths in the document. These paths can be used in Illustrator or any application that can open or import Adobe Illustrator files. The document bounds can be used as a placeholder for the raster image in Illustrator. Exporting paths from Photoshop can be helpful to precisely control where you place effects or objects in documents created using different applications. For example, to control where text placed on a path in Illustrator will occur in a Photoshop image, the path should first be created in Photoshop, and then exported to Illustrator to apply the text. Finally, the text placed along the path can be placed into the Photoshop image.

PAGE LAYOUT PROGRAMS

Most page layout programs, such as Adobe PageMaker and QuarkXPress, can also import many of the file formats that Photoshop can create. They also use a clipping path saved with an EPS file to mask parts of the image. In addition, some page layout programs can use alpha channels to determine areas of transparency. In this case, a file format that supports alpha channels must be used.

FILE FORMATS

Each file format stores image data in a slightly different fashion. It is not terribly important that you understand exactly how image information is stored in every particular format. Rather, a broad understanding of each file type is needed to become an ACE. You might need to know very specific information about a file format for a particular industry application.

By default, Photoshop can open more than 20 different types of files and can save almost as many. You might never use some of these file formats, depending on how you use Photoshop. What seems like a relatively unknown format could actually be a common standard within a specialized industry. The following sections present the most common file formats found in a Photoshop work environment.

PHOTOSHOP NATIVE

Photoshop's native file type (PSD) supports all of Photoshop's features: alpha channels, spot color channels, multiple layers, and clipping paths and it also supports any color depth or image mode used by Photoshop.

This format is used most frequently as a working format—that is, versions of the image are stored with all layer and channel information intact before saving the image in a format that flattens layers or discards extra channels.

If an image contains more than one layer or the Background layer has been renamed, the image must be saved in the Photoshop native format if you want to preserve the layer information.

If you want to open the file in an application that doesn't understand Photoshop files, you must save the file in a format that is supported using the Save As or Save a Copy commands.

The Photoshop native format is compressed and optimized for use by Photoshop with Run Length Encoding (RLE). *Run Length Encoding* is lossless, so no pixel data is removed. Run Length Encoding groups rows of identical color pixels or patterns of pixels together, defining them only once to save file space. The following table shows relative file sizes for some common image modes. The pixel dimensions for the image used are 1000 pixels high by 1000 pixels wide.

Photoshop Native Format File Sizes

	Image	File Size
	Bitmap	133KB
	Grayscale	982KB
	RGB	2938KB
	CMYK	3748KB

TIFF

The Tagged Image File Format (TIFF) is one of the most versatile image file formats. Supported by a wide range of applications on several platforms, the TIFF is capable of efficiently handling multiple color depths, alpha channels, and most of Photoshop's image modes.

TIFF files support Bitmap, Grayscale, Indexed Color, RBG, CMYK, and Lab Image Modes. Alpha channels are supported in RGB, CMYK, and Grayscale images. TIFF files can also contain captions created using the File Info command.

By default, the TIFF supports RLE. The TIFF also supports optional Lempel-Ziv-Welch (LZW) compression, one of the most commonly used compression schemes for raster images. Because LZW compression is lossless, no image data is removed. It searches for repetition in the strings of data in a file. Such repetition is usually prevalent in raster image files. Using LZW compression dramatically decreases the size of some files, particularly those containing large areas of uniform color; however, LZW compressed files take longer to open and save because the file must be decompressed and compressed. The following table shows a comparison to compressed and uncompressed sizes as well as a comparison to the Photoshop native file format.

TIFF and Photoshop Native Format File Sizes

Image	File Size for TIFF Uncompressed	File Size for TIFF Compressed	File Size for Photoshop Native
Bitmap	133KB	137KB	133KB

TIFF and Photoshop Native Format File Sizes

Image	File Size for TIFF Uncompressed	File Size for TIFF Compressed	File Size for Photoshop Native
Grayscale	982KB	817KB	982KB
RGB	2938KB	2592KB	2938KB
CMYK	3923KB	3594KB	3748KB

You are prompted to choose whether you want to compress the file and whether to use a byte order appropriate for use on IBM PC or Macintosh systems when saving (see Figure 15.4).

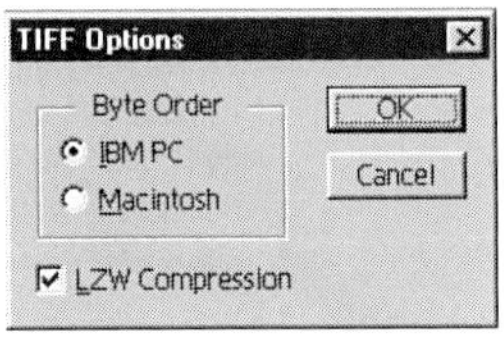

Figure 15.4

When saving a TIFF file, choose the appropriate method and compression.

Because of its wide acceptance by page layout programs and its versatility, TIFF is frequently used in the prepress and print industries. Further, most scanners also support the TIFF format, making it a good choice throughout the digital imaging process.

EPS

When Adobe created the PostScript™ language, it revolutionized digital printing. The PostScript language has become the standard throughout the printing industry and is supported by a wide array of applications, operating systems, and output devices. PostScript can store both mathematically defined vector objects and raster image data. Placing the PostScript defined objects and raster images within a bounding box, or page boundary, creates an Encapsulated PostScript (EPS) file. The EPS file is unique among the other non-native image formats that Photoshop can save because it is designed to contain both raster and vector information. When saved from Photoshop, however, the file that is created is commonly called a Photoshop EPS and contains only raster information (unless the Photoshop image included paths).

An EPS file saved from Photoshop can support any image mode except Multichannel. Although alpha channels are not supported, a derivation of the EPS format, the Desktop Color Separations (DCS) format, does support alpha and spot color channels. (The DCS 2.0 variation of the EPS is dealt with in the section "EPS and DCS 2.0.") The EPS format does support the inclusion of clipping paths to mask areas of an image in page layout or illustration programs. For more information about clipping paths, including how to create them, see Chapter 7.

Encapsulated PostScript files are most commonly used for printing and exchanging image data between Photoshop and page layout applications.

When you save an EPS, Photoshop shows the EPS Options dialog box (see Figure 15.5).

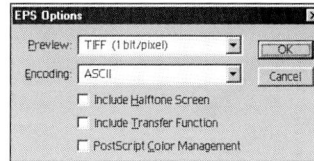

Figure 15.5

When saving a Photoshop EPS file, you need to determine what information the EPS file will contain.

You will need to specify what kind of preview, if any, is included with the EPS, how the EPS is encoded, and whether to include certain common printing elements such as a Halftone Screen, Transfer Function, and PostScript Color Management. For more information about the printing elements that you can include in an EPS file, see Chapter 16, "Prepress Production."

The kind of preview you specified when saving your file as an EPS determines what a page layout program displays when the EPS file is imported. You can choose from including no preview, in which case the page layout program shows only a gray box; a 1-bit preview; or an 8-bit preview. Note that the preview is a low-resolution version of the file for display purposes only. The encoding options are ASCII, Binary, and four JPEG resolutions.

The ASCII is the most common format, particularly in the Windows environment, but it also produces the largest files. The Binary encoding produces a smaller file than the ASCII encoding but is not supported by every application and printing device. It is, however, more commonly used on the Macintosh platform.

The JPEG encoding uses JPEG compression, a lossy compression method. Some data is discarded to make the file smaller. You can choose how much information is discarded by selecting the appropriate JPEG option. If you set the quality setting higher, less information will be lost. The JPEG encoding option is not supported by all applications and printing devices. See the following table for a comparison of the relative sizes of files created using the different encoding methods. Note the dramatic differences in file size caused by different EPS encoding options.

EPS Encoding and File Sizes

Image	File Size for EPS Using ASCII Encoding	File Size for EPS Using Binary Encoding	File Size for EPS Using JPEG Encoding (High)
Bitmap	294KB	165KB	n/a
Grayscale	2087KB	1049KB	243KB
RGB	8139KB	3989KB	307KB

EPS Encoding and File Sizes			
Image	File Size for EPS Using ASCII Encoding	File Size for EPS Using Binary Encoding	File Size for EPS Using JPEG Encoding (High)
 CMYK	10,173KB	4985KB	473KB

EPS AND DCS 2.0

Photoshop 5.0 now supports the DCS 2.0 derivation of the EPS format. Originally created by Quark, the purpose of the DCS file is evident from its name: Desktop Color Separations. This format is actually used to produce a collection of EPS files, one for each separated color. Typically, for a four-color separation, five files are produced: one each for the cyan, magenta, yellow, and black plates and an additional composite file—although this is not necessary.

The DCS format supports only Photoshop images in CMYK and Multi-channel modes. Similar to the standard Photoshop EPS, clipping paths are supported. Unlike the standard EPS, DCS 2.0 files support alpha channels and spot color channels, making them the best choice for images that include spot colors. (DCS 1.0 does not support additional channels.) Most page layout programs that support EPS files also support the DCS form.

When saving DCS files from Photoshop, you are actually creating one or more EPS files. Photoshop prompts you for information about a preview and encoding, just like the standard EPS. In addition, however, you will need to choose whether a single file or multiple files should be created, and whether a composite file should be created. If you choose to create a composite file, you must also select whether it will be grayscale or color (see Figure 15.6). Making only a single file, or a file with no composite image, creates a smaller file.

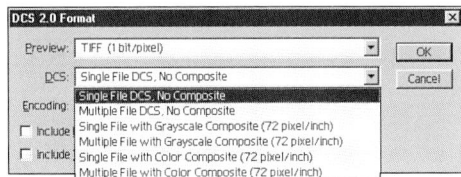

PDF

The Portable Document Format, or PDF, is the format used by Adobe Acrobat, which is a format intended to be viewed within most of the major operating systems. Although the PDF format is usually thought of as a format for layout of both graphics and text, it can contain raster information. This image data is usually compressed using a JPEG compression scheme, but a ZIP compression is also supported; CCITT Group 4 compression, commonly used for fax data, is used for images in Bitmap mode. Images saved in PDF format can be transmitted over the World Wide Web or imported into other PDF files for use as either complete pages or as buttons for navigational structures.

Files saved in the Photoshop PDF format can be in Bitmap, Grayscale, Indexed Color, RGB, CMYK, and Lab color modes. Alpha channels are not supported. When saving a PDF file, you must choose the type of compression to use and, if it is JPEG, the amount of compression.

PCX

One of the very first graphic file formats to gain wide acceptance, the PCX file is still commonly used for scanning, facsimiles and by some older raster image applications, especially in the Windows environment. The PCX file format supports some of the most common color depths, including 1-bit (Bitmap), 8-bit (Grayscale and Indexed Color), and 24-bit (RGB). Additional channels and CMYK mode are not supported. The PCX format uses RLE. Although both the Photoshop native format and PCX format use RLE, Photoshop files are typically smaller. The following table shows files sizes relative to the Photoshop native format.

PCX and Photoshop Native Format File Sizes

Image	File Size for PCX	File Size for Photoshop Native
Bitmap	167KB	133KB
Grayscale	1336KB	982KB
RGB	4305KB	2938KB

PICT

The PICT format is the default raster image file format for Macintosh systems. The PICT format is a versatile and widely used method for storing raster images and for exchanging raster data between graphic programs on the Macintosh.

The PICT file format supports Bitmap, Grayscale, Indexed Color, and RGB image modes. In RGB mode, one extra alpha channel can also be saved in the image. In addition, the PICT file format supports Photoshop's use of

16 bits per channel color, creating 16-bit Grayscale and 48-bit RGB images. When saving an RGB image in PICT format, Photoshop will prompt you to choose between 16 bits/pixel or 32 bits/pixel.

The PICT file format compresses image data using RLE. If QuickTime is installed, the PICT format can also use JPEG compression.

GIF

The Graphic Interchange Format, or GIF, is one of the most widely used image file formats found on the World Wide Web. Literally millions of images in GIF format are viewed daily as Web pages are loaded. Used for banner ads, buttons, and backgrounds, the GIF is well suited to the specific graphic needs of the World Wide Web. Photoshop supports two variations of the GIF format: the CompuServe GIF and the more recent GIF89a format.

Only Indexed Color and Grayscale images can be saved as GIFs. If a Grayscale image is saved as a GIF, the 256 different gray values become the 256 indexed colors. This limitation becomes an advantage in a medium in which transmission speeds are important, because the resulting files are typically small.

Further, the GIF89a file supports several features that are indispensable for use on the World Wide Web. The GIF89a supports transparency in any of the indexed colors. On a Web page, the transparent pixels show through to the page color below the image. The GIF89a also supports limited animation and small flip-book style animations that populate the Web in the form of banner ads and cartoon graphics. Although Photoshop does not offer direct support for animated GIFs, successive GIFs can be saved and combined using a number of other utilities designed specifically for this purpose.

Both the CompuServe GIF and GIF89a also support interlacing. If a GIF image is *interlaced*, every other row of pixels in the image is transmitted and displayed first; then the rest of the lines are filled in. The result is that half of the image, constructed by every other line, is visible, giving the viewer something to look at while the rest of the image loads.

The GIF format uses the lossless LZW compression scheme and is very good for storing images with large areas of identical color.

Instead of saving CompuServe GIFs from Photoshop, images are most often exported as GIF89a files. Only images in Indexed Color mode and RGB mode can be exported. The advantage of using the GIF89a export from the File menu is that a transparent color can be specified during export (see Figure 15.7). If an alpha channel is defined, it can be used to determine the transparency as well. In addition, if the image is in RGB mode, the image can be converted to Indexed Color mode during the export process. For more information about converting to Indexed Color mode, see Chapter 5, "Image Modes."

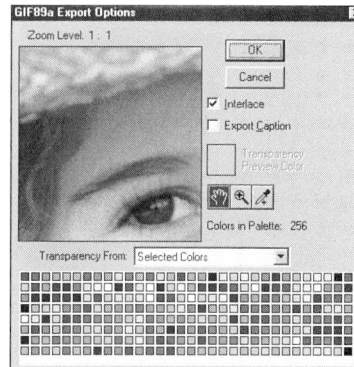

Figure 15.7

Using the Export option instead of saving enables you to choose a transparent color.

JPEG

Devised by the Joint Photographic Experts Group, the JPEG is not actually a format but is more accurately described as a compression algorithm. Some other file formats, such as the PICT and EPS, can use the JPEG compression algorithm to store image data. What is commonly thought of as the JPEG format is actually the JPEG File Interchange Format, or JFIF, but it is commonly referred to simply as a JPEG. JPEG compression works best on continuous tone or photographic images.

The JPEG shares the bulk of the image responsibilities for the World Wide Web with the GIF format. The JPEG is not limited to Indexed Color images as the GIF is, but rather it is capable of storing images in both RGB and CMYK modes. Further, although JPEG files cannot store any extra alpha channels and do not support transparency, they can contain embedded paths. The capability to contain path information, coupled with the support for CMYK, makes the JPEG format an excellent tool for not only electronic publishing, but both prepress applications such as proofing and the distribution of images for use in page layout programs.

The JPEG compression algorithm is a lossy compression scheme. Image data is removed from the file every time it is saved in JPEG format. Repeated saves in JPEG format degrades the image and produce artifacts, and eventually, the image noticeably breaks apart into blocks.

When saving the JPEG format, Photoshop prompts you to choose a number of options from the JPEG Options dialog box (see Figure 15.8). You will need to select an image quality and a format option. The image quality can range from 1 to 10.

Figure 15.8

When saving a JPEG, select the Maximum setting to discard the least amount of image data.

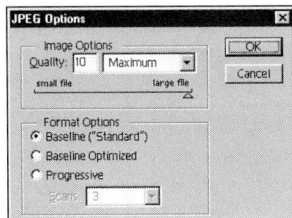

The higher the image quality you select, the larger the resulting file will be, but the better the quality. The quality is better because less information is discarded when saving. The options for format of the JPEG are Baseline or Standard, Baseline Optimized, and Progressive. The Baseline or Standard option produces JPEG files that are recognized by most Web browsers and image viewers. The Baseline Optimized option creates a file that optimizes the color quality but that is not supported by all browsers and viewers. The Progressive option enables you to choose a number of scans so that the image is displayed gradually as it is downloaded. The Progressive option produces a slightly larger file and is not supported by all browsers and viewers.

PNG

The Portable Network Graphics (PNG) format was designed to combine the best features of the GIF and JPEG formats. The PNG format is free of the patent difficulties associated with the GIF and can support both Indexed Color and RGB modes. In addition, the PNG format uses a lossless compression, unlike the JPEG, and can support levels of transparency defined by an alpha channel. See the table below for a comparison of file sizes for the JPEG, PNG, and Photoshop native format. The JPEG file is usually smaller than the PNG or Photoshop native format but discards image data. The primary drawback of the PNG format is that older browsers might not support this format.

The PNG format supports images in Indexed Color, Grayscale, and RGB modes. In Grayscale and RGB, an alpha channel is supported to define areas of transparency.

When saving an image in PNG format, you determine whether the image should be displayed gradually by selecting the Adam7 option from the PNG

TIFF and Photoshop Native Format File Sizes

Image	File Size for JPEG (Maximum)	File Size for PNG (no filter)	File Size for Photoshop Native
Grayscale	608KB	857KB	982KB
RGB	1401KB	2721KB	2938KB
CMYK	2019KB	n/a	3748KB

Options dialog box. When Adam7 is enabled, a process similar to interlacing but occurring bidirectionally, displays the image in increasing detail. You can also select one of four compression filters. Choosing None applies no compression, and any of the other options—Sub, Up, Average, and Paeth—compress the image based on the image's contents. Using the Adaptive option uses the most appropriate compression filter for the image. In any case, the compression is lossless, so no image data is discarded.

CHOOSING APPROPRIATE FORMATS

Although the categories and uses of the various formats are broad and often defy categorization, there are some general rules to follow. Specific industries make use of some of the other file formats (not mentioned earlier) for various applications; but in general, there are some reasonable expectations about when file formats might be encountered and used.

Using Appropriate File Formats	
General Use	**Comments**
Photoshop Native	Suppports all Photoshop features
PCX	Used especially on Windows platforms and with older software.
PICT	Exclusively Macintosh
Print	**Comments**
TIFF	Used to exchange raster data between Photoshop and other applications and for exchanging raster data between platforms.
EPS	Used for printing and for importing into page layout programs especially if you need a clipping path.
DCS 2.0	Used for similar purposes as the EPS, but especially if you need spot color channels.
Electronic Publishing	**Comments**
PDF	Used with other Acrobat documents.
GIF	Used for the World Wide Web.
JPEG	Used for the World Wide Web, especially for photographic images.
PNG	Used for the World Wide Web. Make sure it is supported by your target browsers.

SUMMARY

This chapter provides some basic information about the most commonly used file formats when using Photoshop. Although you are probably familiar with the file formats used by your industry, review the formats that are new to you. Make sure you feel comfortable with the capabilities and limitations of the various formats and when you are most likely to encounter them.

REVIEW QUESTIONS

1. Which format does not support lossless compression?
    a. PNG
    b. JPEG
    c. TIFF
    d. Photoshop Native

2. Which format supports spot color channels?
    a. TGA
    b. BMP
    c. DCS 1.0
    d. DCS 2.0

3. Which format only supports 256 colors?
    a. GIF
    b. JPEG
    c. TIFF
    d. PCX

4. Which format is commonly used for the World Wide Web?
    a. EPS
    b. DCS 2.0
    c. TIFF
    d. JPEG

5. Which format supports layers?
    a. Photoshop Native
    b. TIFF
    c. EPS
    d. DCS 2.0

6. Which of the following is a lossy compression?
    a. Run Length Encoding (RLE)
    b. Tagged Image File Format (TIFF)
    c. Lempel-Ziv-Welch (LZW)
    d. Joint Photographic Experts Group (JPEG)

7.   Which file format supports images in CMYK mode?

    a.   GIF

    b.   PCX

    c.   PNG

    d.   TIFF

8.   Which file format can be exported instead of saved?

    a.   JPEG

    b.   GIF

    c.   PNG

    d.   TIFF

9.   Which format cannot contain an alpha channel?

    a.   TIFF

    b.   DCS 2.0

    c.   JPEG

    d.   Photoshop Native

10. Which format is most commonly found on Macintosh systems?

    a.   PCX

    b.   PICT

    c.   PDF

    d.   PNG

11. Which format should be used with other Acrobat files?

    a.   PDF

    b.   PNG

    c.   PICT

    d.   Photoshop Native

12. Which file format does not support clipping paths?

    a.   EPS

    b.   GIF

    c.   DCS 1.0

    d.   DCS 2.0

CHAPTER **16**

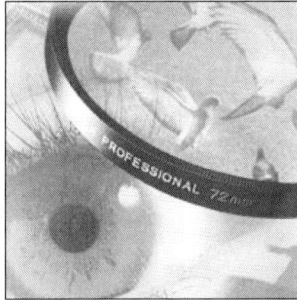

PREPRESS PRODUCTION

This chapter focuses on the Page Setup and Printing options for separating and printing images directly from Photoshop. As an Adobe Certified Expert (ACE), you should know the CMYK Setup options. You also should know how to create halftones specifically for your print environment and prepare your image for output, including how to add crop marks, labels, and registration marks.

Domains & Objectives

Preparing Files for Production

11.1   Identify issues regarding preparing an image for printing color separations and comps. Issues include but are not limited to selecting Print options, selecting halftone screen attributes, creating color traps, Page setup options, and Transfer Functions.

USING THE CMYK SETUP COMMAND

The CMYK Setup dialog box enables you to specify the separation settings for printing by using the built-in color space parameters, ICC profiles, or a custom color separation table. The CMYK Setup dialog box is accessed by choosing File > Color Settings > CMYK Setup (see Figure 16.1). Separation settings are selected from the CMYK Setup dialog box and include the following:

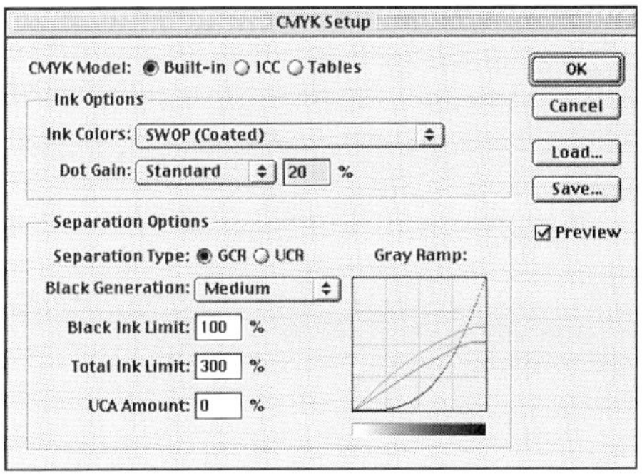

Figure 16.1

The CMYK Setup dialog box gives you several options for preparing separations.

- **ICC Profiles.**   You can define the CMYK color space using the ICC profile for your printer. See page 481 in Chapter 18, "Color Management," for information on the ICC Profile options.

- **Tables.**   You can load a previously defined separation table created in an earlier version of Photoshop or created by a third-party compatible program by first clicking the Table option and then the Load button. This option can be used to save the CMYK setup created using the Built-in option and then used as an ICC profile.

- **Built-in.**   The Built-in option enables you to specifically adjust the separation settings that your printing environment might require. Customized settings can be saved and loaded as an ICC profile. The options available in the Built-in color settings dialog box are explained in the following sections.

INK COLORS

The Ink Colors pop-up menu displays a list of predefined color sets for printing on coated and uncoated paper stock, including SWOP (Specifications for Web Offset Publication), Toyo, and Eurostandard, among others (see Figure 16.2). You also have the option of customizing the color sets used by Photoshop if you need to use colors that are not included in one of the Photoshop profiles.

DOT GAIN

Dot gain is the most important variable when printing CMYK images. Dot gain most often occurs in the midtones of an image, making these areas appear dark and muddy because ink spreads when applied to paper. The dot gain can be anywhere from 5% to 35%, depending on the absorbency of the paper (see Figure 16.3). Factors to consider when specifying a dot gain percentage include the paper, ink, and press. Dot gain can also result when a miscalibrated imagesetter has been used.

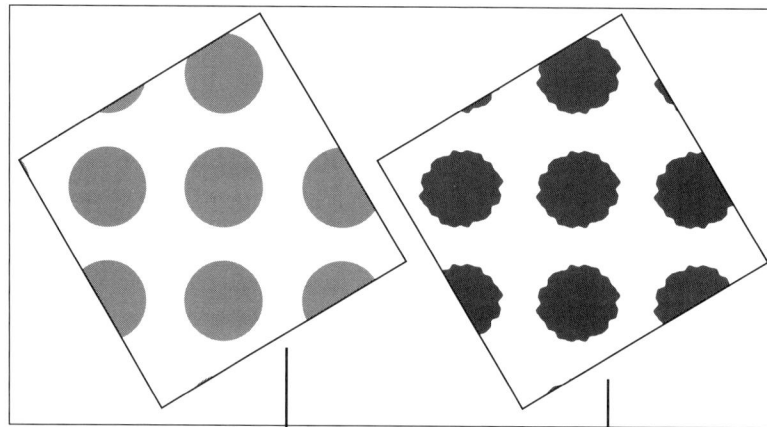

A 50% dot on film   A dot gain of 26% when printed

Following are guidelines you can use when specifying the dot gain amount; it's important to note these are typical dot gain amounts. It is recommended that you double-check these percentages with your printer:

- Newsprint, 85 lpi: 25%–35% dot gain
- Sheetfed, coated stock, 133/150 lpi: 10%–15% dot gain
- Sheetfed, uncoated stock, 133/150 lpi: 18%–22% dot gain
- Web, coated stock, 133/150 lpi: 15%–22% dot gain

You can also compensate for dot gain in the midtones by adjusting the dot gain curve. The Dot Gain Curve dialog box can be accessed by clicking on the Dot Gain pop-up menu and choosing Curves. Following are recommended percentages for the midtone dot gain for each of the process plates. Enter the desired value for the 50% dot in the appropriate field. Again, because press conditions vary, you must confirm these settings with your printer:

- Newsprint, 85 lpi: C=50%, M=50%, Y=28%, K=32%
- Sheetfed, coated stock, 150 lpi: C=20%, M=20%, Y=18%, K=22%
- Sheetfed, uncoated stock, 150 lpi: C=22%, M=22%, Y=20%, K=24%
- Web, coated stock, 133 lpi: C=22%, M=22%, Y=20%, K=26%
- Web uncoated stock, 110 lpi: C=26%, M=26%, Y=24%, K=28%

USING BLACK IN SEPARATIONS

In theory, if you mix equal amounts of cyan, magenta, and yellow, the resulting color is black. However, this is not the case in the printing world: Mixing equal amounts of these three inks results in brown because printing inks contain impurities. Each color contains traces of its complementary color—that is, yellow contains blue, magenta contains green, and cyan contains red. To compensate for this, a black plate is added when creating process color images and can be manipulated in different ways using gray component replacement (GCR) undercolor removal (UCR) and undercolor addition (UCA). (Each black generation method is explained in the following sections.)

GCR

When GCR is used, cyan, magenta, and yellow inks are reduced in the neutral areas as well as some colored areas of an image. These reduced neutral values are placed on the black plate and result in a broader coverage of black. (Undercolor addition is often used to add back some of the color that is depleted by using GCR. See the section "UCA.") Gray component

NOTE

Dot gain is based on the size of the 50% dot; therefore, a 10% dot gain, for example, doesn't mean every value gains by 10%. Because dot gain works on a bell curve, shadows and highlights will experience less dot gain that midtones. Also, in CMYK printing, each color can have a different dot gain value.

replacement is typically used when printing on coated stock and produces dark saturated colors based on your choice in the Black Generation pop-up menu (see the following paragraphs on Black Generation).

The Black Generation pop-up menu is available only to GCR separations. The following options are available:

- **None.**   When the None option is selected, the separation is generated without the black plate.
- **Light.**   The Light option decreases the effect of the Medium setting.
- **Medium.**   Medium is the default setting and usually produces the best results on an average key image.
- **Heavy.**   Heavy increases the effect of the Medium setting.
- **Maximum.**   The Maximum setting is useful for images that have a large amount of solid black against a light background.
- **Custom.**   The custom setting enables you to manually adjust the black generation curve. To use the Custom option, first choose one of the Black Generation options that best matches the type you need and then choose Custom. A dialog box opens and displays the curve. The cyan, magenta, and yellow curves adjust automatically, relative to the black curve.

UCA
Undercolor addition is used in conjunction with GCR to compensate for loss of ink density in the shadow areas. It produces richer shadow areas in an image in which these areas appear flat by increasing the amount of cyan, magenta, and yellow.

UCR
When undercolor removal is used, the cyan, magenta, and yellow are removed in the shadow tones and midtone, and highlight values are left intact. The resulting black plate is a skeleton black with black ink in the contrast and shadow areas only. With UCR, colors often appear more vibrant; however, the overall tonality of the image could suffer. Also, UCR can significantly reduce the amount of ink used and is often the method of choice when printing on uncoated stock.

Black Ink Limit and Total Ink Limit
The Black Ink Limit is the total amount of black ink used in the darkest shadows of an image. The Total Ink Limit, or maximum density, is the total

amount of ink the press can support. A setting between 270 and 300 is appropriate for uncoated stock, and a setting between 300 and 340 is appropriate for coated stock. For newsprint, a setting between 220 and 280 is recommended. Again, it's important to discuss these settings with your printer.

Gray Ramp

The Gray Ramp grid in the CMYK Setup dialog box displays how neutral colors will separate. The horizontal axis represents the neutral color value from 0% (white) to 100% (black). The vertical axis represents the amount of each of the CMYK inks that will be generated for any given value.

PAGE SETUP

The Page Setup dialog box is accessed by choosing File > Page Setup or Control/Command+Shift+P (see Figure 16.4). It is important that you discuss the appropriate settings in the Page Setup dialog box with your service provider.

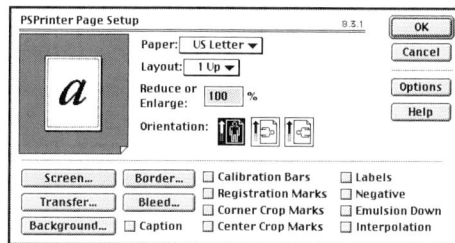

The Macintosh Page Setup dialog box

Figure 16.4

The appearance of the Page Setup dialog box varies with different operating systems, printer drivers, and printers.

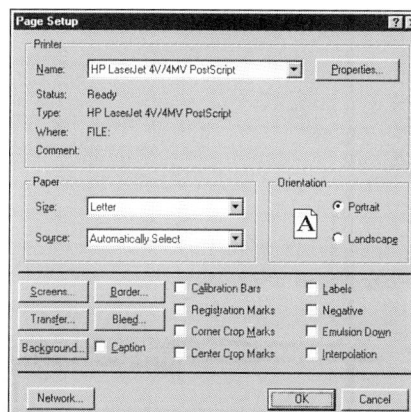

The Windows Page Setup dialog box

At the top of the Page Setup dialog box, general printing options such paper size, orientation, and reduction or enlargement percentages are displayed. The halftone options discussed in the following sections are available at the bottom of the dialog box.

SCREEN

Click the Screen button to access the Halftone Screens attributes dialog box (see Figure 16.5). If you uncheck the Use Printer's Default Screens option, you can specify the screen frequency, angle, and dot shape.

Figure 16.5

The Halftone Screens dialog box enables you to specify screen frequency, screen angle, and dot shape.

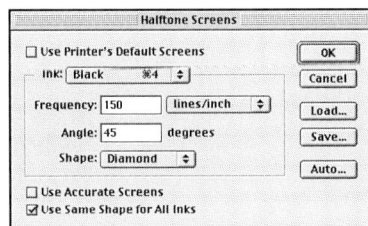

Frequency

Screen frequency, also known as screen ruling or line screen, refers to the number of printer dots per inch used to print grayscale images or color separations. Screen frequency is measured in lines per inch (lpi).

Paper, ink, and the press that will be used to print your image are all factors that need to be considered when selecting a screen frequency. Typical screen frequencies include 150 for sheetfed coated stock and web offset coated stock; 133 for web offset coated (SWOP); and 85 or 100 for web offset newsprint.

Remember, the quality of the printed halftone also depends on the resolution of an image. As a general guideline, scan an image at 1.5 to 2 times the screen frequency. For more information on determining the best resolution for an image, see Chapter 4, "Scanning & Working with Images."

Angle

The correct screen angle settings are extremely important to avoid moiré patterns in your printed image. The standard combination of the halftone angles are cyan 15°, magenta 75°, yellow 0°, and black 45°. Talk with your service provider regarding the appropriate screen angles for your job.

Shape

You can specify the shape of the dot used in your separations by accessing the Shape pop-up menu after deselecting the Use Printer's Default Screens check box. If you want all four screens to have the same dot shape, check the Use Same Shape For All Inks option check box.

A description of the most often used dot shapes follows:

- **Round dots.** Round dots do not connect. This option can be used to minimize midtone and highlight gain. This is a good option for high-speed web offset printing.

- **Diamond dots.** Diamond dots are fast becoming the dot of choice; they are effective on images in which detail in the midtone and three-quartertone areas are important.

- **Square dots.** Square dots connect in all four directions and can help control density variation while on press. This option is often used for sheetfed, web offset, and letterpress printing.

- **Elliptical dots.** Elliptical dots are elongated and connect in only one direction. This option can provide smoother gradations in the midtones.

Use Accurate Screens

Check the Use Accurate Screens option if you're using a PostScript Level 2 output device (or higher) or one equipped with an Emerald controller (a raster image processor [RIP] controller that uses a RISC processor). If not, checking this option has no effect on the output.

TRANSFER

The Transfer Functions option is most often used when an imagesetter is miscalibrated. The values you enter in the Transfer Functions dialog box are based on a transmissive densitometer reading to bring halftone values into range on the film output. (A *densitometer* is an instrument used to measure the density of printed halftones.) The settings are employed when the image is rasterized by a PostScript imagesetter or printer based on the curve that is set in the Transfer Functions dialog box.

When using Transfer Functions, choose Page Setup from the File menu and click the Transfer button to open the Transfer Functions dialog box (see Figure 16.6). Enter the desired value for the 50% dot in the appropriate field. You can set the dot for all plates by clicking the All Same box. To set the dot for individual plates, click off the All Same box, and then click OK.

Figure 16.6

The Transfer Functions
dialog box enables you
to adjust the midtone
curve to compensate for
a miscalibrated
imagesetter.

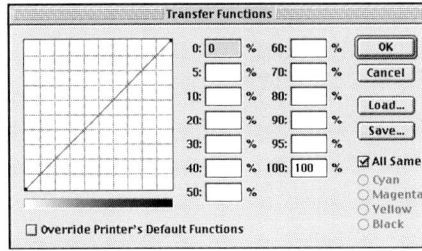

BACKGROUND

Under normal circumstances, when you print an image directly to a printer from Photoshop, the area surrounding the image is white. If you're printing to an imagesetter, the surrounding area is clear on the film. The Background option enables you to select a color from the Photoshop Color Picker to fill this blank area and prints the chosen color to the edges of the page. This can be useful when outputting slides on a film recorder. Because it's a printing option, it does not affect the actual image.

BORDER

The Border option enables you to print a black border around an image (see Figure 16.7). The border is centered on the edge of the image; half of the border overlaps the image and the other half overlaps the background. You can specify a width amount up to 10 points, .15 inches, or 3.5 millimeters.

Figure 16.7

Enter a width value to
create a black border
around an image
when printing.

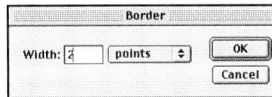

BLEED

You can reposition and print the corner crop marks to crop inside of the image with the Bleed option (see Figure 16.8). This option is useful if the image will be manually stripped into a page. The maximum amount of bleed you can specify is 9.01 points, .125 inches, or 3.18 millimeters.

Figure 16.8

Enter a bleed amount to
reposition the corner
crop marks inside
the image.

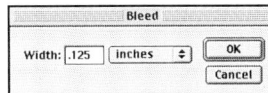

CAPTION

If you check the Caption box, Photoshop prints the caption you created in the File Info dialog box, and it will be displayed beneath the image. This can be an extremely useful option for photo identification and copyright information. The caption prints in 9 point Helvetica Plain, and the font cannot be changed (see Figure 16.9). For more information on using the File Info command, see Chapter 4.

Figure 16.9

A printed plate displaying printer's marks.

CALIBRATION BARS

The Calibration Bars option adds a 10-step grayscale bar under the image and also adds color bars to the right of the image (refer to Figure 16.9). An additional grayscale bar is also placed on each individual color plate to the left of the image. The grayscale bar is divided into 10 separate swatches that display the density range from 0% to 100%. The color bars enable you to measure the individual swatches with a densitometer and then make a comparison of the onscreen values.

REGISTRATION MARKS

Use the Registration Marks option so when the image is separated, the printer can align the films accurately. This option will add eight bull's-eyes and two star target marks (refer to Figure 16.9).

CORNER AND CENTER CROP MARKS

Use Corner and Center crop marks to indicate where the image is to be trimmed (refer to Figure 16.9).

LABELS

When separating an image, it's very important to use the Labels option to print the filename and the color plate name (cyan, magenta, yellow, and black, as well as spot channels or other channels) on each piece of film (refer to Figure 16.9).

NEGATIVE AND EMULSION DOWN

Both the Negative and Emulsion Down checkboxes act as toggles. When not checked, you print a positive, which is appropriate for printing comps and preliminary proofs on paper. When Negative is checked, you print a negative of the image, which is appropriate for separations in most cases. However, ask your service provider and printer, because some jobs require film positives and, depending on the job specifications for stock, quantity, and press used, film emulsion right reading up or down. Also, your service provider might want to have the imagesetter rather than Photoshop handle these options, so it's best to check.

INTERPOLATION

The interpolation option is specifically for low-resolution images to be printed on a PostScript Level 2 device. This option provides on-the-fly resampling as it processes the image data.

THE PRINT COMMAND

Choose File > Print or Control/Command+P to open the Print dialog box (see Figure 16.10). The Print dialog box provides options to print selected areas of an image and print composite or separated images, as well as image data transfer options. (Each is explained in the following sections.)

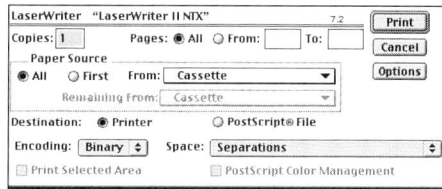

Figure 16.10

The appearance of the
Print dialog box varies
with different operating
systems, printer drivers,
and printers.

Macintosh Print dialog box

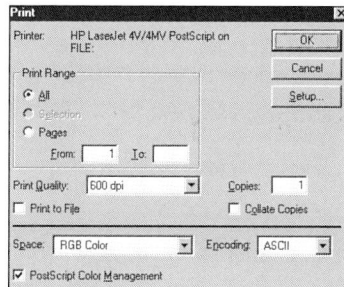

Windows Print dialog box

ENCODING

You can choose either ASCII or Binary as the format to use when image
data is transferred to the output device. Binary is the default format and
transfers data faster than ASCII. However, ASCII is universally understood
by PostScript devices, so if you're using DOS or Unix servers, ASCII might
be more appropriate for your print environment.

PRINT SELECTED AREAS

To print only a specific area of an image, make a selection of the area with
the rectangular marquee tool and choose File > Print. In the Print dialog
box, check the Print Selected Areas option and click OK. This option is only
available to a nonfeathered rectangular selection. If any other type of selection is made, the option is not available.

SPACE

By default, a single page is printed as a CMYK or duotone composite unless
you choose Separations from the Space pop-up menu (refer to Figure 16.10)
in the Print dialog box. When you choose separations for a CMYK image,
each plate is printed on a separate piece of paper or film.

When printing only selected plates, such as the black plate and the yellow plate, you need to make sure that they are the only visible channels in the Channels palette (see Chapter 13, "Channels & Masks"). You can also specify which plates to print by setting the Page Range in the Print dialog box. The Page Range acts as though Photoshop is a multi-page document because of the channels. For example, if you only wanted to print the black plate, you would enter a page range of 4 to 4.

TRAPPING

Like most page layout and illustration programs, Photoshop has trapping capabilities, although they are limited. *Trapping* is used as a solution for misregistration problems that can occur on press. As the paper is fed through the press, it can shift anywhere from .25 to 4.5 points, depending on the press and the paper used. This shift causes white gaps (where no ink is printed) or colored halos between adjacent solid colors (see Figure 16.11).

Figure 16.11

Trapping can compensate for misregistration on press.

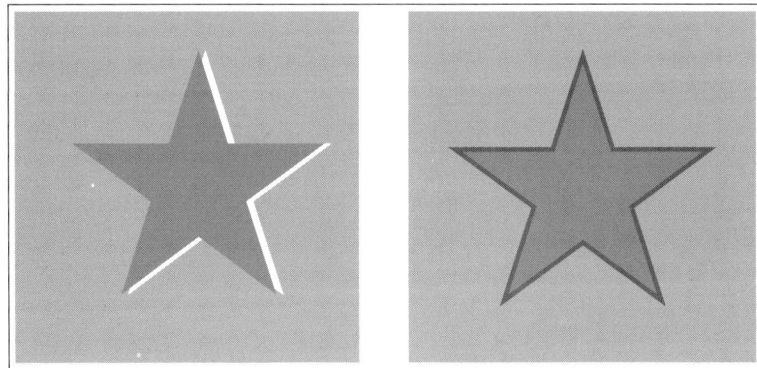

Misregistration with no trap applied   Object with trap applied

Photoshop uses the spreading method of trapping by slightly overlapping the colored areas based on the amount you enter in the Trap dialog box. Photoshop spreads lighter colors under darker ones. However, pure cyan and pure magenta spread equally under each other. The choking method of trapping is not available in Photoshop. To access the Trap dialog box, choose Image > Trap. Your image must be in CMYK to use the trapping command.

PREPARING SEPARATIONS FOR PAGE LAYOUT APPLICATIONS

If your Photoshop file will be placed in a page layout program, you can either use the screening information from that program or save the Photoshop file as an EPS file and include the Photoshop screening information along with it. The Photoshop screening information overrides the page layout program screening information only for that image on the page. The Save as EPS dialog box gives you options to include the halftone screen and transfer function information (see Figure 16.12).

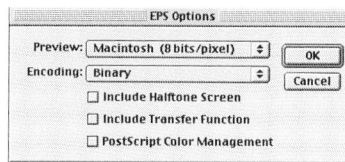

Figure 16.12

You can save customized Photoshop screening information in an EPS file for placement in a page layout program.

SUMMARY

It is important to understand the general concepts of prepress and printing presented in this chapter as you prepare to become an ACE. It is highly recommended that when preparing your own images for separation and printing, you discuss all the options in the CMYK Setup and Page Setup dialog boxes with your service provider and printer. They have an intimate knowledge of the equipment they use and can make appropriate recommendations for achieving the best quality output and printing for your job.

REVIEW QUESTIONS

1. What happens to an image when GCR is applied?

    a. Cyan, magenta, and yellow are reduced.

    b. Black is added to cyan, magenta, and yellow.

    c. Cyan, magenta, yellow, and black are reduced.

    d. Cyan, magenta, and yellow are replaced with black.

2. Which term is NOT used to describe screen frequency?

    a. Screen angle

    b. Linescreen

    c. Screen ruling

    d. LPI

3. Why would you adjust dot gain?

    a. To create separations

    b. To adjust the color settings

    c. To apply more ink to the paper

    d. To prevent the midtones from printing dark and muddy on press

4. How do you print only one color separation plate?

    a. Convert the plate to a matching spot color.

    b. You can't because the Separation option in the Print dialog box will only print all four plates.

    c. Click on the corresponding cyan, magenta, yellow, or black button in the Print dialog box.

    d. Click off the eye icons of the channels you don't want to print and choose Print.

5. Which is the fastest method for transferring image data to an output device?

    a. PDF

    b. ASCII

    c. Binary

    d. Encoded

CHAPTER 17

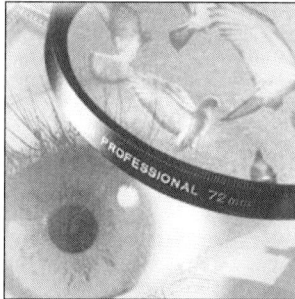

WEB & VIDEO PRODUCTION

With the explosion of online content on the World Wide Web, Photoshop, which has been a long-time favorite among professionals in the traditional print field, has rapidly become an essential tool for Web and multimedia professionals. Publishing for the World Wide Web and producing images destined for video—whether broadcast or part of a multimedia application—all have similar rules and requirements. The most important aspects of producing images for Web and video are understanding file formats, file sizes, compression, and how Photoshop elements relate to these key concepts.

Domains & Objectives

Preparing Files for Production

11.3   Identify issues regarding preparing an image for Web publication
or other onscreen production. Issues include but are not limited to
working with grayscale, flat-color, and full-color images; optimizing file sizes; selecting appropriate color modes; selecting Indexed
Color options; creating transparency; and selecting file formats.

If you have not already done so, it would be helpful to read Chapter 4, "Scanning & Working with Images," Chapter 5, "Image Modes," and Chapter 15, "File Formats." Some of the information is also covered in this chapter, but the other chapters examine the concepts and issues in greater detail.

To become an Adobe Certified Expert (ACE), you will be expected to know the basic concepts and ideas about preparing images to be published electronically, even if your primary interest and expertise in Photoshop is in the print arena. Specifically, you should be able to identify issues regarding preparing an image for Web publication or other onscreen production. Issues include but are not limited to working with grayscale, flat-color, and full-color images; optimizing file sizes; selecting appropriate color modes; selecting Indexed Color options; creating transparency; and selecting file formats.

GRAYSCALE, FLAT-COLOR, AND FULL-COLOR IMAGES

The most important aspect for determining how to deal with different types of images is to understand both the image mode requirements and the file format requirements for a specific type of image.

GRAYSCALE

In general, images in Grayscale mode should be saved or exported as GIF files. The GIF format is specifically intended to contain only 256 colors, and an image in Grayscale mode contains 256 levels of gray. Although you can save an image in Grayscale mode as a GIF, in order to use the GIF89a Export plug-in from the File menu, you must first convert the image to Indexed Color or RGB mode. When you convert from Grayscale to Indexed Color mode, you don't need to choose any dithering or color table options because the image already contains only 256 colors. Using the GIF89a Export plug-in enables you to specify colors for transparency.

FLAT COLOR

For images that contain large areas of flat-color, GIF is the best format to use because the Lempel-Ziv-Welch (LZW) compression scheme works particularly well with areas of identical color. Because line art typically meets this criterion, the GIF should be used when exporting line art for use on the Web. Another good example of GIF files that commonly contain large areas of flat-color are Web banner ads, which populate most commercial Web pages. Almost all of these banner ads have been standardized and use GIF.

FULL COLOR

Currently, the best format for saving full-color images for the World Wide Web is the JPEG file interchange format. The JPEG format uses the Joint Photographic Experts Group (JPEG) compression method. This is a lossy compression scheme that discards graphic information to decrease the file size. It supports 24-bit color and is the most commonly used format for displaying photographic images on the World Wide Web.

In the near future, the Portable Network Graphics (PNG) format could become the preferred file format for full-color images on the Web. Right now, however, the PNG format does not have the support of all browsers; it cannot be considered a viable replacement for either JPEG or GIF until it has the wide support that they have. The PNG format does support 24-bit color, transparency, and lossless compression. Although it will never completely replace JPEG or GIF, it does have some useful properties that could make it an excellent third choice for creating onscreen images.

The table below shows the relative file sizes for grayscale, flat-color, and full-color images in the GIF, JPEG, and PNG file formats. Note especially the size of the flat-color image in GIF format, especially compared with the JPEG. The GIF format is designed to compress areas of similar color very well, whereas JPEG is designed to compress photographic information. Also be aware that though the full-color image is smaller in the GIF format, it contains only 8-bit color; the JPEG and PNG formats both contain 24-bit color.

File Size and Format				
	Image	GIF	JPEG	PNG
	Grayscale	265KB	173KB	250KB
	Flat Color	10KB	116KB	22KB
	Full Color	186KB	337KB	854KB

These are general rules for using file formats for specific types of images; there could be other requirements of the publication that force you to use a nonpreferred format. For example, because the JPEG format does not support the use of transparency, you might need to choose between the 24-bit color of the JPEG and the transparency capabilities of GIF. You might want to use the GIF format with an adaptive color palette so that you can use transparency but still maintain the 256 dominant colors in the image.

When you create an image for use in an onscreen presentation in any form, you will need to keep in mind the tool that you will use to create the final composition. For example, although you generally want to use the GIF format for all grayscale images, if you are using a page layout program to create a PDF file that does not support the GIF format, you might need to choose a format that is supported by the specific application. Another example is file formats used for multimedia and video production. Many nonlinear video editing applications do not support the GIF or JPEG formats and could in fact have their own specific file format requirements. Many video applications can import and export sequences of TGA files but do not understand many of the other major file formats that Photoshop supports.

OPTIMIZING FILE SIZES

One of the fundamental issues for those creating graphics for both Web pages and multimedia presentations is speed. Loading graphics over modems is limited by the speed of the modem. Loading a graphic or playing an animation from a CD is limited by the speed of the CD player. Therefore, the goal of those who create images for onscreen publishing is to make them small enough to load quickly while maintaining the quality of the image. Sometimes trade-offs are necessary, and some quality is sacrificed in the name of speed. The JPEG compression method is an excellent example of this: some image data is discarded to make the file size as small as possible.

Before optimizing an image's file size, you must determine how big the image should be on screen. To do so, use the magnification in the Photoshop status bar and set it to 100% or double-click on the zoom tool in the toolbox, which displays the image at the size it will display on screen. If the image fills the screen but is only supposed to occupy a small part of a Web page, the image is too large and needs to be downsampled by choosing Image > Image Size.

Most Web page designers work toward the lowest common denominator of monitor resolution: 640 × 480 pixels. An image that completely fills the screen should be no larger than this. All other graphics should be proportionally smaller. If you are designing a Web page for an intranet or multimedia application, you might be able to design the graphics with a larger base monitor resolution. Keep in mind that the size at which a graphic displays on a monitor is a function of both the monitor size and the monitor resolution set at the computer.

When attempting to make files as small as possible, the fundamental issue to be addressed is image resolution. The image resolution, or actual number of pixels in the image, should be made as small as possible. Any extra pixels must be transmitted and processed, so remove any pixels that are not absolutely necessary. Figure 17.1 shows a GIF image from a Web page that can be cropped to remove some of the pixels.

Figure 17.1

This image is 80.2KB; the size of the file is too large.

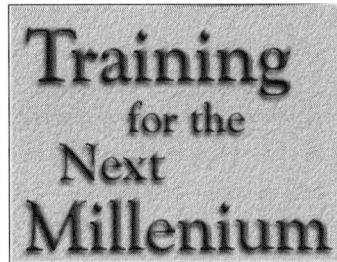

Cropping the image and removing the pixels that are not necessary decreases the file size. Figure 17.2 shows the cropped image. By removing the pixels along the edges of the image, the total number of pixels in the image was reduced from 92,750 to 81,740.

Figure 17.2

After cropping extraneous pixels, this image was reduced to 60.8KB.

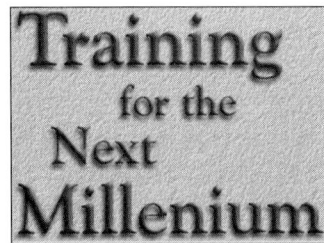

This process applies to any file format; if you are saving the file in the GIF format, you might be able to reduce the final file size even more. In the case of Figure 17.1, the background of the image was deliberately chosen to match the Web page background. This was necessary because although GIF supports transparency, it supports only one level; therefore, each pixel must be either transparent or opaque. The levels of transparency that are required for the drop shadow areas and for anti-aliasing the text against the background are not attainable using the GIF format. Areas that do not need to contain the background texture, however, can be changed to a single color, which in turn can be made transparent when exporting the file in GIF. Because the LZW compression scheme works especially well with areas of identical color, adding blocks of a color that can be made transparent takes advantage of the LZW compression. Figure 17.3 uses the smaller image from Figure 17.2 but adds rectangular areas of transparency.

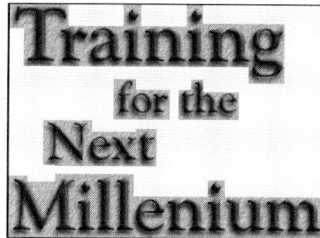

Figure 17.3

This image is only 41.9KB when exported. Removing unneeded pixels and employing the LZW compression and transparency cut the file size almost in half.

If the file were in JPEG format, a higher JPEG compression could be used while saving the file. Although more image information would be discarded, the file would be smaller.

Another solution for reducing the size of a file is to decrease the pixel dimensions of the image. Although often not an acceptable alternative for multimedia presentations, in some cases Web-page image sizes can be decreased slightly to decrease the file size. For example, in the case of Figure 17.3, if the image were scaled down by 10% in both the horizontal and vertical directions, the new file size would be only 31.1KB.

When placing the image into a Web page, you can explicitly specify the pixel dimensions of an image; so although the image is 10% smaller, it can be made full size on the Web page. Not all images, especially smaller ones, can withstand this scaling process. Experiment with the image to determine if it can be decreased in resolution without losing too much quality. In Photoshop, you can decrease the image's pixel dimensions and set the zoom percentage in the status bar to the inverse of the amount scaled. For example, if you want a preview of how an image looks on a Web page after scaling the resolution to 50%, view it at 200% magnification.

TIP

It is generally accepted that onscreen images should have a print resolution of 72 pixels per inch.

To decrease the image resolution, choose Image > Image Size. You can use a percentage for the value if you select percent from the units menu. Leave the Constrain Proportions option checked if you want to keep the ratio between the horizontal and vertical dimensions fixed.

APPROPRIATE IMAGE MODES

There are only four image modes typically encountered on the World Wide Web and in any electronic publishing: Bitmap, Grayscale, Indexed Color, and RGB. Bitmap and Grayscale can be treated as subsets of the Indexed Color mode because they each contain 256 or fewer colors. In addition, images in Grayscale mode and Bitmap mode should be either exported or saved as GIF files. The only image modes that are commonly used for publishing on the World Wide Web are Indexed Color in the form of GIF files, and RGB in the form of JPEG and PNG files.

The applications of the GIF file point directly to the use of the Indexed Color mode. Indexed Color mode should be used for grayscale images and images that contain key line art. Similarly, RGB mode should be used for continuous tone or photographic images.

Even when working in an Indexed Color image, the values of each color in the color table are typically defined by their red, green, and blue components. Because monitors and television sets both display combinations of red, green, and blue light, RGB is the dominant image mode. When displaying images on computer monitors, you do not need to be concerned with CMYK mode or out-of-gamut colors.

INDEXED COLOR OPTIONS AND EXPORTING GIF89A FILES

For many images that are displayed on Web pages, ranging from banners and backgrounds to buttons and navigational aids, GIF files are desirable. For images that do not contain transparency, you can save an image in Indexed Color mode as a CompuServe GIF. For images that require transparency values or images for some specialized applications such as animation programs, the GIF89a format is required. Although images in RGB mode can be exported using the GIF89a Export plug-in, converting the image to Indexed Color mode first enables you to control the conversion to a greater degree.

For a complete description of the process for converting to Indexed Color mode, see Chapter 5, "Image Modes."

INDEXED COLOR OPTIONS

When you convert an image from an image mode that can contain more than 256 colors to Indexed Color in Photoshop, you can choose the color table and dithering options that will be used during conversion (see Figure 17.4). Images in Bitmap and Grayscale mode do not require that you choose a color table or dithering option because they already contain 256 colors or fewer. If you are preparing images for use on the World Wide Web, you can choose the Web palette for images that contain flat-color or key line art, and the Adaptive palette for photographic images. If you are preparing graphics that will be displayed entirely on a Windows or Macintosh system, you can choose their respective system palettes to limit the colors to the 256 used by that platform. This option should be used when a limited palette is either necessary or desired and works best for flat-color images and screen captures.

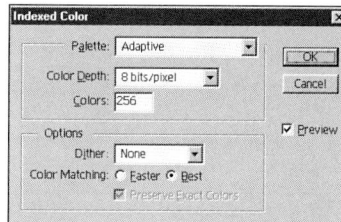

Figure 17.4

Set the color table and dithering options for images to be viewed on screen in the Indexed Color dialog box.

You can also choose from the different dithering options—None, Diffusion, and Pattern—to control how Photoshop converts images that contain more than 256 colors to 256 colors or fewer. If None is selected, no dithering occurs, and Photoshop replaces each original color with the closest color available from the Color Table. If Diffusion is selected, pixels of available colors from the Color Table are added to the image using an error-diffusion process to simulate colors not available from the Color Table. If the Pattern dither option is chosen, patterns of squares, similar to halftone dots, are used to dither the image. A Pattern dither can only be used with the Web, Macintosh System, and Uniform palettes.

While using either Diffusion or None for the dither, you can choose between a faster conversion and a more accurate one by selecting either Faster or Best from the Indexed Color dialog box. The Preserve Exact Colors option prevents Photoshop from dithering colors that are in the palette you select, and it is available only if using the Diffusion dither.

If you are converting a flat-color image that was constructed using colors from the Web Safe color swatches, you should set the dithering to None with color matching set to Best to preserve the colors selected from the Web Safe color swatches. If you are converting a flat-color image that does not necessarily use colors from the Web palette but is using the Web color table, you should use the Diffusion dither, with the Best and Preserve Exact Colors boxes checked to maintain the Web-safe colors whenever possible. If you are using an adaptive palette to convert a photographic image, you should use a Diffusion dither with the Best and Preserve Exact Colors boxes checked because the colors that Photoshop chooses for the adaptive palette most likely will not match those in the Web palette.

EXPORTING GIF89A FILES

To create a GIF file, you should use the File > Export > GIF89a Export command. By using this command rather than Save As, you can export an RGB image without first converting it to Indexed Color mode, you can turn interlacing on or off, and—most importantly—you can specify a transparency color or area. The GIF89a Export command is available only if the image is in either Indexed Color or RGB mode.

If the image is already in Indexed Color mode, the GIF89a Export dialog box will prompt you to specify whether the file should be interlaced, and you can also select a transparency color (see Figure 17.5). You can select colors to be transparent by either clicking on them in the preview window with the eyedropper or clicking on the colors from the color table displayed at the bottom of the dialog box. If you want to reset the transparency color and start over, holding down the Alt/Option key will change the Cancel button to a Reset button. You can use the zoom tool and hand tool to change the area viewed in the preview window.

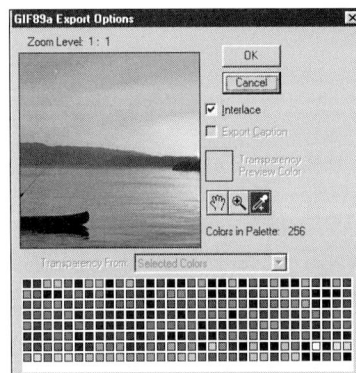

You can also use an alpha channel to define areas of transparency when exporting an image in Indexed Color mode. Define an alpha channel by creating a selection and saving it or by creating a new channel in the Channels palette. When you use the GIF89a Export command, you can specify whether to use selected colors for the transparency or an alpha channel in the Transparency From menu.

TIP

Although Photoshop 5.0 for Windows users can be set to use only lowercase extensions, the GIF89a Export plug-in still uses an uppercase extension by default. For consistency, you might want to change the extension to lowercase when exporting.

Figure 17.5

If the image is already in Indexed Color mode, choose a transparency color from the color table or from the image.

If the image is in RGB mode when the GIF89a Export command is used, the GIF89a Export Options dialog box will prompt you to specify the color table to be used to convert the image to Indexed Color, whether the file should be interlaced, and the number of colors (see Figure 17.6). By using the Load button, you can load any saved color table or palette to convert the image. If you are exporting an image in RGB mode using this command, the transparency is determined by the transparent pixels in the layers that are visible when the command is executed. Make sure any layers that you do not want in the final GIF file are turned off. You can change the preview color for the transparency to something other than the default gray by clicking in the color swatch in the transparency area of the GIF89a Export Options dialog box. This color only changes the color that Photoshop uses to represent the transparent pixels when the Preview button is clicked.

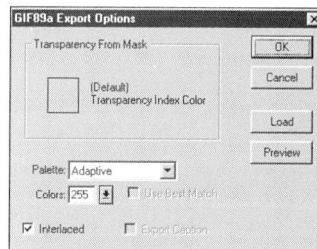

Figure 17.6

Specify a color table and number of colors when exporting from an image in RGB mode.

If you want to create transparency in an image with only one layer, you should first rename the Background layer by double-clicking on it. If the Background layer has been renamed, when pixels are deleted from the layer they become transparent instead of changing to the background color.

You can export a series of Indexed Color or RGB images to GIF89a by using an action in a batch process. The Override Action Save In Commands option will not affect the creation of the GIF89a files because the export plug-in is used rather than the Save command. For more information about creating actions and their options, see Chapter 19, "Automating Photoshop."

CREATING TRANSPARENCY IN OTHER FORMATS

The PNG format also supports transparency and derives the areas of transparency from an alpha channel. Only one alpha channel can be used, but the PNG format does support varying levels of transparency and opacity. To create transparency in a PNG file, create a single alpha channel to define the transparent and opaque areas. When the file is saved, the alpha channel information is saved with it.

The TGA format, commonly used for video applications, also supports a single alpha channel that can be used to define areas of transparency.

Although the JPEG format does not support transparency, illusions of transparency are often created by copying the background area into the undefined areas. A similar technique must be used if gradual transparency effects are needed when using a GIF file (refer to Figure 17.1).

VIDEO AND MULTIMEDIA

When preparing images for use in broadcast video or for a video editing application such as Adobe Premiere or Adobe After Effects, some care must be taken to ensure that the colors produced will display correctly on a television screen. Computer monitors are generally capable of displaying a greater range of the RGB gamut than television sets.

To convert colors in an image to video-safe colors that display correctly on a television set, run the NTSC Colors filter by selecting Filter > Video > NTSC Colors. The NTSC Colors filter desaturates highly saturated colors so that they do not bleed when displayed on a television. You can apply the NTSC Colors filter only to images in RGB mode. To accurately view the colors for television applications, change the RGB setup to NTSC or one of the SMPTE color spaces. The National Television Standards Committee (NTSC) format was the predominant video format throughout the United States but has been largely superseded by the Society of Motion Picture and Television Engineers (SMPTE-C) standard. You should also be aware that any true white values should be dropped down to gray tones so they display correctly on a television screen.

In addition to compensating for the colors displayed on television screens, you might also need to compensate for D-1 NTSC pixels, which, unlike the pixels displayed on a computer monitor, are not square. Your video editing software might compensate for this; but, just as with print applications, you must be aware of the intended use of the image and the applications being used to composite the final video.

Similarly, for images that will be part of a multimedia presentation created in programs such as Macromedia Director or Adobe Premiere, attention must be paid to the system palette of the computer. For Windows applications, the native BMP format is widely implemented. For Macintosh applications, the native PICT format is commonly used. Both formats support images in Indexed Color mode, and an appropriate system palette can be selected when converting from RGB mode to Indexed Color. Such images are useful when developing video presentations that will be viewed on a computer monitor, and for interface design.

SUMMARY

There are several issues specific to the creation of onscreen images. Although the most important issues center around file size and image resolution, as an ACE you should also be aware of the different file formats, how they are created, and when they are used. In addition, you should know how to determine an appropriate image size and image mode for an image that will be displayed on the Web or in a multimedia presentation.

REVIEW QUESTIONS

1. Which format should be used to display a photographic image on the World Wide Web?

    a. GIF

    b. EPS

    c. JPEG

    d. TIFF

2. Which format should be used to display a line drawing on the World Wide Web?

    a. GIF

    b. EPS

    c. JPEG

    d. TIFF

3. What is an appropriate print resolution for an image that will be displayed on a monitor?

    a. 72 pixels/inch

    b. 72 lines/inch

    c. 600 pixels/inch

    d. 133 lines/inch

4. Which format should be used to display a photographic image on the World Wide Web without discarding any image information?

    a. EPS

    b. PNG

    c. TIFF

    d. JPEG

5. Which color table should you use to make the colors match as closely as possible to the original image when exporting a GIF file?

    a. Uniform

    b. System

    c. Adaptive

    d. Black Body

6. Which of the following formats uses lossy compression?

    a. GIF

    b. PNG

    c. TIFF

    d. JPEG

7. Which of the following formats does not support transparency?

    a. GIF

    b. PNG

    c. TGA

    d. JPEG

8. In which image mode must an image be in order to run the NTSC Colors filter?

    a. RGB

    b. CMYK

    c. Grayscale

    d. Indexed Color

9. How many colors does the GIF file format support?

    a. 256

    b. 32,000

    c. 65,000

    d. 24 million

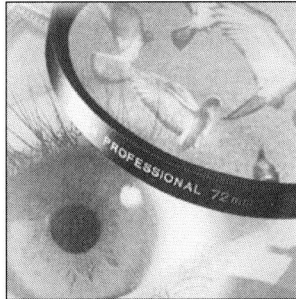

CHAPTER 18

COLOR MANAGEMENT

The process of calibration is used to maintain consistent color between different monitors and between the monitor and printer. Photoshop 5.0 has added several features to aid in the calibration process, including a Gamma utility for Windows users—similar to those available to Macintosh users—and ICC profile embedding. Managing color and ICC profiles will help guarantee predictable results throughout the life of an image.

Domains & Objectives

Color Calibration and Setup

12.1   Define the steps in the process of calibration on the Macintosh and Windows platforms, including using the Gamma utility, and the importance of calibration in relation to printing and screen production methods and output.

12.2   Identify issues regarding color management and color settings. Issues include but are not limited to ICC profile embedding, profile mismatch color space conversion, and selecting Color Settings options including RGB Setup, CMYK Setup, Grayscale, and Profile Setup.

CALIBRATION PROCEDURES

Calibration can be divided into two major categories depending on the output of the final images: onscreen or print. If you are producing images that will be displayed either onscreen or in print, the first step is to calibrate the monitor using the Adobe Gamma utility or another monitor calibration tool. If you are only producing images for the Web, you might be able to stop after monitor calibration because the Photoshop defaults will probably work in most cases. Options do exist for further adjustment in the RGB setup. If you are producing images that will appear in print, you will also need to make changes in the CMYK setup in addition to running the Adobe Gamma utility.

ADOBE GAMMA UTILITY

Calibration procedures for the Macintosh and those for Windows systems are now very similar because the Adobe Gamma utility is now included for Windows users: Adobe Gamma will be installed in the control panel for those using Windows 95, Windows 98, and Macintosh systems. On Windows NT systems, the Adobe Gamma utility should be manually copied to the Control Panel by copying the Adobe Gamma.cpl file from the \Program Files\Common Files\Adobe\Calibration folder to the \Winnt\System32 folder. To do this, you will need administrative rights. On the Macintosh platform, the Adobe Gamma utility will automatically be installed, but any previous versions of the Adobe Gamma utility should first be deleted.

If you have another calibration utility and an ICC profile generator that is ICM 2.0 (Windows 98 and NT 5.0) or ColorSync (Macintosh) compatible, you can use these instead of the Adobe Gamma utility. Further, if you have already calibrated your monitor with an ICC-aware calibration utility, you will not need to recalibrate your monitor. Note, however, that if you make any changes to the ambient light in the room or to the brightness and contrast controls on the monitor, the system must be recalibrated.

When installed, the Adobe Gamma utility can be executed by double-clicking on its icon in the Control Panel. The Adobe Gamma utility will prompt you to choose between going through a step-by-step calibration or jumping directly to the calibration control panel (see Figure 18.1)

TIP

Avoid changing the brightness and contrast controls on the monitor. You can tape them in place if necessary. In addition, maintain consistent lighting conditions in your workspace.

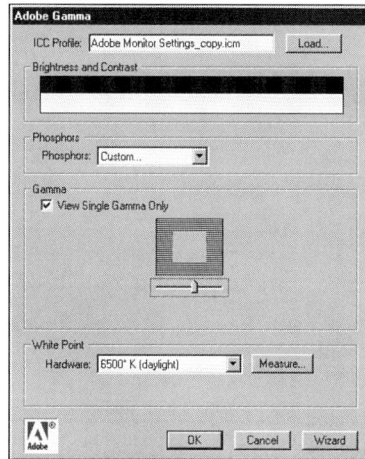

The step-by-step wizard guides you through the same settings that are in
the control panel one option at a time. The first step is to load a monitor
ICC profile by clicking on the Load button in either the wizard or Adobe
Gamma control panel. If your monitor is listed, you can use this as a starting point for the rest of the calibration process.

Using the control panel, adjust the brightness and contrast controls on the
monitor to make the gray squares as dark as possible (though not black)
while maintaining a bright white in the bar immediately below the black
and gray boxes (see Figure 18.2).

In the Phosphors section of the control panel, enter an appropriate description of the phosphor in your monitor (see Figure 18.3). Inside the tube of
your monitor, there is a thin layer of *phosphor*, a material that emits light
when bombarded with electrons. Your monitor also contains an electron
gun that "paints" the phosphor with a stream of electrons to produce an
image on the monitor. It repeatedly paints the image and updates it with
information sent by the computer based on the setting of the refresh rate.
If you know what type of phosphors your monitor uses, use that value here.
If your monitor's phosphor type is not listed but you were provided with
chromaticity coordinates with your monitor, you can enter them by selecting the Custom option.

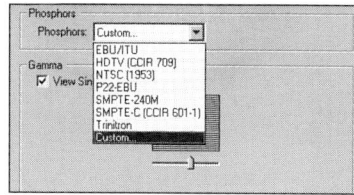

Figure 18.3

Choose the type of
phosphors used by your
monitor.

To adjust the Gamma setting, drag the slider until the center box matches
the patterned frame as closely as possible. You can choose to adjust the
gamma as a single value (see Figure 18.4) or as three separate red, green,
and blue components (see Figure 18.5). The gamma setting adjusts how
bright the midtones in an image will be displayed on your monitor. You
should back away from the monitor far enough so that the dithering pattern
is no longer discernable.

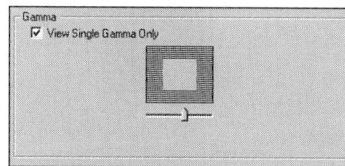

Figure 18.4

Drag the slider until the
center box matches the
patterned frame.

Figure 18.5

Drag the sliders until all
three boxes match the
corresponding patterned
frames.

On the Macintosh and on Windows systems whose monitors are being controlled by the operating system, you can specify a target gamma setting. For
Windows systems, the default gamma is between 2.2 and 2.5; for Macintosh
systems, it is 1.8.

The last adjustment to be made in the Adobe Gamma utility is to the white
point. The *white point* is the whitest white that a monitor is capable of displaying and is a measurement of color temperature in degrees Kelvin. Many
monitors have adjustable white points. If you know the white point of your
monitor, select it from the list (see Figure 18.6).

If you don't know the white point for your monitor but were provided with
the values, you can select Custom. If you do not know the white point for
your monitor and were not provided with the appropriate values, you can

use the Measure button in the Adobe Gamma utility control panel to determine the white point. After you click on the Measure button, three squares will be displayed on screen (see Figure 18.7). The goal here is to make the center square as neutral a gray as possible.

Figure 18.6

Select your monitor's
white point from the list.

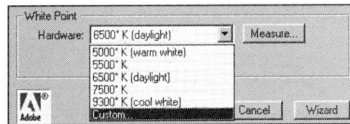

Figure 18.7

Use the three gray
squares to help the utility
determine the white point
of your monitor.

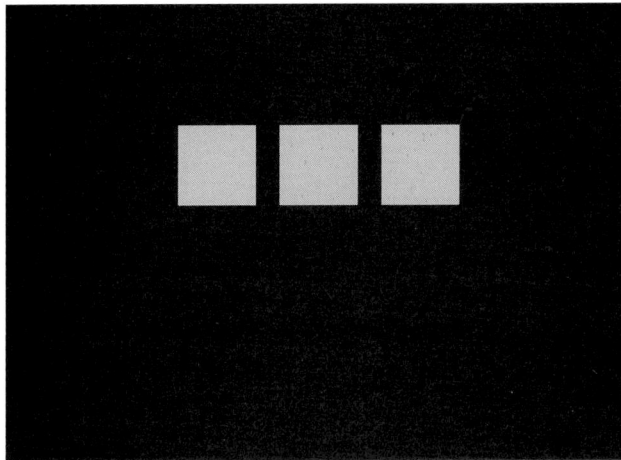

Clicking on the right square will reset all the squares a shade warmer. Clicking on the left square will reset all the squares a shade cooler. Click on the left or right squares until the center square is a neutral gray. When complete, commit the changes by clicking on the center square or by pressing Enter.

On the Macintosh and on Windows systems whose monitors are being controlled by the operating system, you can specify an adjusted white point value. This value should be changed only if you know the color temperature that will be used to view the image and it is different than the white point of the monitor being calibrated. If you don't know the final viewing color temperature, choose Same As Hardware.

When complete, the Adobe Gamma utility will save a monitor profile to be used by Photoshop to display images. You can save multiple profiles for different monitors. The display characteristics for the monitor, including the gamut it can represent, or color space, are saved in an ICC profile.

ICC PROFILES

When the monitor has been properly calibrated, the rest of the calibration process is completed within Photoshop. Photoshop calibrates the display of images to other displays and to printed output by comparing the ICC profile created to define your monitor and other known profiles and then making any necessary adjustments. For this to work properly, you must accurately describe your own display capabilities through the Adobe Gamma utility, and you must also define the characteristics of the final output, whether it be an onscreen or printed image.

ICC profiles, defined by the International Color Consortium, are a cross-platform standard and describe the color spaces of output devices such as monitors and printers. They ensure that images will display correctly in any ICC-compliant applications and on output devices. This is accomplished by embedding the profile information in the file.

The ICC profiles are interpreted through the use of a Color Management Module (CMM). By default, Photoshop uses its own built-in CMM, but you can choose to use other CMMs such as the Kodak Digital Science Color Management System, installed with the Kodak Photo CD Acquire plug-in; Apple ColorSync 2.1.2 (or later); or Microsoft ICM 2.0. The CMM acts as a coordinator, managing the color issues when an image is converted between image modes and correctly displaying the image on the monitor and in the final print.

For the CMM to correctly compensate for color differences among your monitor, the monitor used to create or view the image, and the printer, you must either specify the ICC profile or create a new one for each of these different devices. You must also specify how Photoshop should handle profiles when saving files, and when opening files with profiles not matching the current settings.

COLOR SETTINGS

When adjusting Photoshop's color settings, you are defining the working color spaces for each image mode. These spaces are used when viewing and editing images. Photoshop has a variety of existing ICC profiles to use, or you can define your own for your particular input and output requirements. All the settings for color management in Photoshop are found in the Color Management submenu of the File menu (see Figure 18.8). The three setup dialog boxes—RGB, CMYK, and Grayscale—have Preview check boxes to display the results of any changes you make. A small flashing bar under the checkbox indicates that a preview is being generated.

Figure 18.8

All the settings for
color management in
Photoshop are found in
the Color Management
submenu.

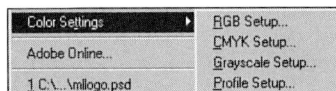

RGB SETUP

The color space described by the RGB Setup is independent of your monitor's color space. This has two important benefits: First, you are not subject to the limitations of your monitor to display RGB information; and second, you can be assured that colors will display correctly on different monitors, so that multiple people on multiple monitors can edit and view images while maintaining accurate color information.

In many cases, Photoshop's default choice for an RGB color space will provide acceptable results. By default, when an RGB file is opened, if there is a profile embedded in the image that differs from the one that describes the working space or if the file is untagged (no profile is embedded), the profile is converted to the current working space. This automatic conversion can be controlled in File > Color Management > Profile Setup; it is described in detail in the following paragraphs.

To control the working RGB space, choose File > Color Management > RGB Setup. The settings in the RGB Setup dialog box describe the working space for images in RGB mode (see Figure 18.9).

Figure 18.9

The RGB Setup dialog
box controls the working
space for RGB images.

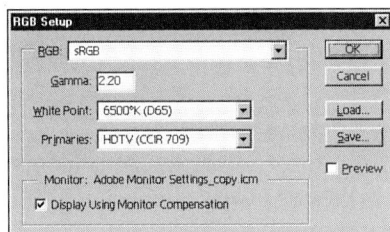

You can specify an appropriate RGB color space (see Figure 18.10); however, the setting is largely dependent on the final use of the image. Changing the RGB profile to use will also change the values for Gamma, White Point, and Primaries in the RGB Setup dialog box. A description of the options follows:

- **sRGB.** The sRGB space is the default and is probably the best option, especially for those creating image that will be displayed online.

The sRGB standard is widely accepted and is supported by many scanners, low-end printers, and other graphics applications.

- **Apple RGB.** Apple RGB reproduces the color space used by previous versions of Photoshop and other desktop publishing applications such as Adobe Illustrator and can be a good choice for online images that will be displayed only on Macintosh computers.

- **CIE RGB.** The CIE RGB color space is defined by the Commission Internationale d'Eclairage and has largely been superseded.

- **ColorMatch RGB.** This color space is defined by Radius for the PressView monitor, a monitor common to prepress applications.

- **NTSC (1953), PAL/SECAM, SMPTE-240M, and SMPTE-C.** These color spaces are all used for specific video applications, though the SMPTE-240M is often used for prepress work because it has a wide gamut.

- **Wide Gamut RGB.** This color space uses the widest possible RGB gamut and includes most of the visible spectrum, though many of the colors cannot be accurately represented on a monitor.

Note that the working space for editing RGB images does not need to be faithfully reproduced on your monitor. Photoshop will use the CMM to translate the colors in the profile that describes the working color space to the monitor's profile.

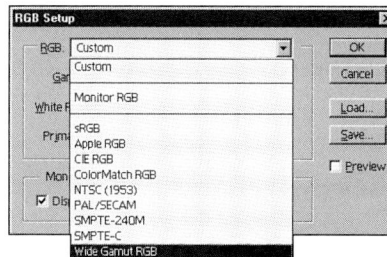

Figure 18.10

Select an appropriate RGB profile for the working space.

You can define a custom RGB profile by selecting Custom from the RGB menu and entering Gamma, White Point, and Primaries information. This color space is only used to edit the images. The monitor profile you defined using the Adobe Gamma utility is used to display the RGB color information. The Custom profile option can be used to define an ICC profile for a scanner or other image acquisition device so images can be edited in the same color space as the device. You can save this custom ICC profile or load other ICC profiles by using the Save and Load buttons in the dialog box.

You can also set the working space to match the monitor color space you defined using the Adobe Gamma utility. This will make Photoshop behave similarly to earlier versions, and you can edit in your own personal monitor's color space. This can be useful if you are using many older application versions that do not read embedded profile information and you want consistently displayed color between these applications.

The Display Using Monitor Compensation check box determines whether Photoshop should use the ICC profile defined from the Adobe Gamma utility and does not change the image information; only the display of RGB values is altered. If this option is selected, the display will be more accurate, though slightly slower, because some conversion of color between the profiles must be performed to display properly.

CMYK SETUP

Possibly the most important reason for the calibration process is to attempt to match what is displayed onscreen to what is printed. This is accomplished by choosing proper settings in the CMYK Setup dialog box (see Figure 18.11).

Figure 18.11

Enter the specific printer information in the CMYK Setup dialog box.

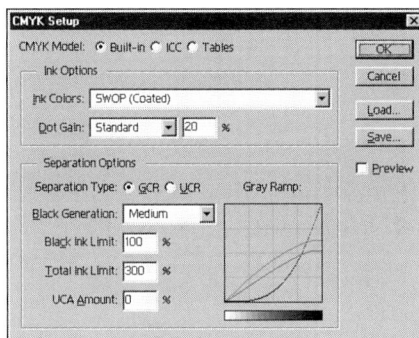

Photoshop provides three options for defining a CMYK color space: You can specify the properties of the inks and paper that will be used by selecting the Built-in CMYK Model, an ICC profile, or an externally defined separation table.

The Built-in CMYK Model

The settings in the Built-in CMYK Model must be obtained from your printer and are described in detail in Chapter 16, "Prepress Production." Figure 18.11 shows the options for the Built-in CMYK Model.

ICC Profiles

If the ICC Profiles option is selected for defining the CMYK color space, you can select the ICC profile of a specific printer. Select the appropriate printer option, the Engine or CMM to use in the conversion process, and the Intent (see Figure 18.12).

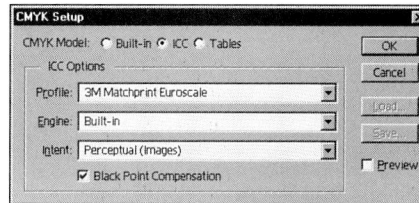

Figure 18.12

Select the Printer, Engine, and Intent when using a CMYK color space determined by an ICC profile.

There are 26 printer options built into Photoshop. You can define others or load ICC profiles provided with your printer. For the Engine, you can chose the built-in Photoshop CMM, the Kodak Digital Science ICC CMS, or another CMM available on your system.

For Intent, you can specify how Photoshop converts out-of-gamut colors. A description of the settings follows:

- The **Perceptual** (Images) setting maintains the relationship between the colors in the image. Most of the colors in the image will change as out-of-gamut colors are mapped to the CMYK gamut. Colors that are not out of gamut will also change as Photoshop attempts to maintain the relationship between these colors and the out-of-gamut colors.

- The **Saturation** (Graphics) setting maintains the relative saturation values of the colors. Colors that are out of gamut are converted to colors inside the CMYK gamut while maintaining their saturation values.

- The **Relative Colorimetric** setting typically converts out-of-gamut colors to colors inside the CMYK gamut while maintaining lightness values. This setting does not change the values of colors inside the CMYK gamut.

- The **Absolute Colorimetric** setting disables white point matching during the conversion process and might not produce acceptable results.

By selecting the Black Point Compensation checkbox, Photoshop will map the darkest neutral color in the unconverted image to the darkest neutral color in the target color space. If the checkbox is not selected, Photoshop will map the darkest neutral color in the unconverted image to black.

Color Separation Tables

This option should be used to load a separation table defined in Photoshop 4.0 or another application that produces separation tables compatible with Photoshop. This option can also be used to save the CMYK setup created by using the Built-in option as an ICC profile.

GRAYSCALE SETUP

The Grayscale setup only has two options (see Figure 18.13) You can either define Grayscale Behavior to act as equal amounts of red, green, and blue or as black ink. The RGB option should be used for images that will be displayed onscreen, whereas the Black Ink option should be used for Grayscale images that will be printed.

Figure 18.13

There are only two settings for the Grayscale setup.

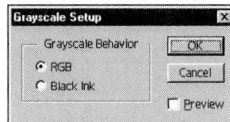

PROFILE SETUP

One of the most important aspects of managing ICC profiles is handling images whose embedded profiles do not match the defined RGB, CMYK, or Grayscale working color spaces. Files that do not have an ICC profile embedded also need to be handled. The Profile Setup dialog box also controls which types of images should have profiles embedded in them (see Figure 18.14).

Figure 18.14

The Profile Setup dialog box controls how ICC profiles are handled when opening and saving files.

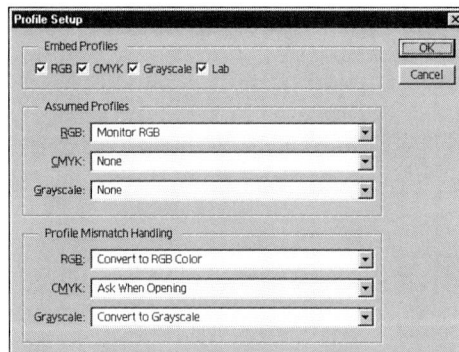

You can choose to embed ICC profiles in Grayscale, RGB, CMYK, and Lab mode images. Only Encapsulated PostScript (EPS), JPEG, PICT, TIFF, and the Photoshop native format support ICC profile embedding in the modes that they support. Files in PDF format can also have embedded ICC profiles in RGB and Grayscale images. If you turn off the embedding for an image mode, Photoshop will still tag the file, noting that there is no embedded profile.

The Assumed Profiles section specifies which profile Photoshop should use when an untagged file is opened. By default, when opening an untagged RGB image, Photoshop will convert the colors to the working color space based on an assumed Monitor RGB profile. If you know that the image was originally in a different RGB space, you can choose the appropriate ICC profile. You can also instruct Photoshop to ask about the assumed profile when opening an untagged image.

The default when opening CMYK and Grayscale images is to not make any assumption about the original color space used to create the file.

When a profile in the opened image either does not exist because the image is untagged or does not match the profile of the working space, there is a profile mismatch. You can control how Photoshop handles profile mismatches for RGB, CMYK, and Grayscale images. By default, Photoshop converts RGB images automatically and prompts you to make decisions about CMYK and Grayscale images.

Automatic conversion of RGB images is safe in many instances. When the original image uses specific RGB values—for example, a Web-safe palette or client-specified colors—you should be cautious when converting between RGB color spaces because some color values could change.

When opening a CMYK image, automatic conversion can be dangerous and can produce unwanted color changes because of the wide variety in CMYK ICC profile gamuts, and the ways that black generation is handled. You should leave the setting for CMYK to Ask When Opening. Another option would be to automatically convert the image mode of the file being opened to RGB or Lab color. This will force the values in the CMYK setup to have an effect when the image is converted to CMYK mode.

The options for images in Grayscale mode are similar to those for CMYK. You can automatically convert grayscale images if they will be used for onscreen applications. For print purposes, however, you should leave the option set to Ask When Opening.

PROFILE TO PROFILE

By selecting Image > Mode > Profile to Profile, you can translate an image from its current profile to any other defined profile, including the working spaces defined for Grayscale, RGB, CMYK, and Lab modes (see Figure 18.15). Doing so will shift the colors in the image from one color space to another. It does not alter the working space that will be embedded in the image when it is saved. This command can be used when you have changed the working space and also need to convert open images. It can also be used if you ignored the ICC profile when opening an image but subsequently need to convert the file to a working space.

Figure 18.15

Use the Profile to Profile command to change the data in an open file from one color space to another.

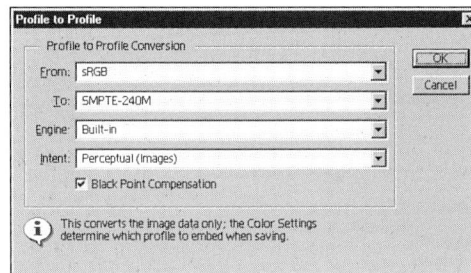

SUMMARY

Photoshop 5.0 has largely improved its capability to maintain consistent color throughout the life of an image. Through the Adobe Gamma utility and ICC profile embedding, you can be assured of accurate color reproduction on virtually any well-behaved output device. As an Adobe Certified Expert, you should be able to identify the steps and importance of calibration. You should also understand how ICC profiles are managed and be able to work with them.

REVIEW QUESTIONS

1. What is the default RGB ICC profile used by Photoshop to define the working RGB space?

    a. sRGB

    b. CIE RGB

    c. SMPTE 240M

    d. Colormatch RGB

2. For which device does the Adobe Gamma utility create an ICC profile?

    a. Scanner

    b. Printer

    c. Monitor

    d. Entire system

3. Which of the following RGB color profiles is NOT a standard video format?

    a. NTSC

    b. SMPTE-240M

    c. PAL/SECAM

    d. Colormatch RGB

4. Which file type supports ICC profile embedding?

    a. TIFF

    b. TGA

    c. BMP

    d. PCX

5. Which file type supports ICC profile embedding in Lab mode?

    a. JPEG

    b. PICT

    c. PCX

    d. Photoshop Native

6. Which image mode should never be set for automatic conversion when a profile mismatch is encountered?

    a. Lab

    b. RGB

    c. CMYK

    d. Indexed Color

7. What command should you use to convert the profile of an open image to match the current working profile?

   a.   Space to Space

   b.   Channel Mixer

   c.   Colormatch RGB

   d.   Profile to Profile

8. Which of the following is NOT an option to use as a CMYK color space definition?

   a.   ICC

   b.   CMM

   c.   Tables

   d.   Built-in

9. What should you do to force Photoshop to display an RGB image directly, with no compensation for the monitor profile?

   a.   Select Monitor RGB as the working RGB color space.

   b.   Set the primaries to Standard Illuminant A in the RGB setup dialog box.

   c.   Disable the Adobe Gamma utility by removing it from the control panel.

   d.   Deselect the Display Using Monitor Compensation in the RGB setup dialog box.

CHAPTER 19

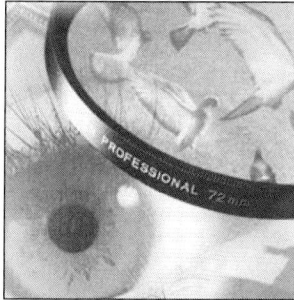

AUTOMATING PHOTOSHOP

An *action* is Photoshop's version of a macro, which is a predefined set of commands that you can save and apply to single or multiple images. Photoshop 5.0 has not only increased the number of actions available, but new features have been added under the File > Automate command. For the exam, it will be important that you understand how to create actions, how to manipulate and categorize them, and how to run actions on a batch of files. In addition, you will need to know the new options available under the Automate command.

Domains & Objectives

Actions/Automation

3.1   Determine the appropriate feature, command or procedure related to the Actions palette, including creating and recording actions, playing actions, editing actions, inserting non-recordable commands, slowing actions during playback, writing descriptors, creating sets of actions, and batch processing.

3.2   Determine the appropriate feature, command, or procedure related to automating tasks with the Automate command, including Conditional Mode Change, Contact Sheet, Execute JavaScript, Fit Image, and convert Multi-page PDF to PSD.

ACTIONS

Photoshop has many prerecorded actions available. There are actions to create a wide variety of textures, buttons, frames, and effects. The power of actions is enhanced by the user's ability to customize existing actions and to create new ones. If you find a series of filters that produce an effect you would like to reproduce, you can record an action as you are performing the steps to have that technique available at a later time. The action can be applied to one image, or to groups of images.

One advantage of actions is that they can be saved and then distributed so that many people can create identical effects. Standards can be established for the management of images within an organizational setting through the use of actions. Many actions are freely available on the World Wide Web, further increasing both their convenience and standardization.

Almost all of Photoshop's commands can be included in actions. In general, you can include any command that affects the entire image or a selection in an action. Commands you can use in actions include most of the filters and color correction tools. Most commands that affect areas of an image such as the paint bucket, gradient, and magic wand also can be included in actions. Furthermore, actions can be nested within other actions.

Many commands and menu items, while they cannot be recorded, can be inserted into actions. You cannot record the creation of a path, for example, but it can be inserted into an action. Tools and commands that generally cannot be recorded are the use of the painting tools, the View commands, and certain menu items. These tools and commands, however, can often be simulated through the clever use of paths and selections.

THE ACTIONS PALETTE

Figure 19.1 shows the Actions palette and the hierarchy of sets, actions, commands, and command settings. A *set* is a grouping of actions. Usually, an action set contains actions that produce similar effects. For example, the Image Effects action set contains a group of actions that change the overall appearance of an image. An *action* is a collection of commands. A command can be a selection, a filter effect, the application of a gradient, or any other command or tool that can be included in an action. The command settings are the position, color, or other specific information required to perform the command. Some commands also enable the user to enter information into dialog boxes to specify certain settings. These commands are referred to as having *modal controls*.

TIP

Be sure that you check the Actions folder on the Photoshop CD for more actions.

Figure 19.1

The Actions palette is
used to record, edit, and
manage actions and
action sets.

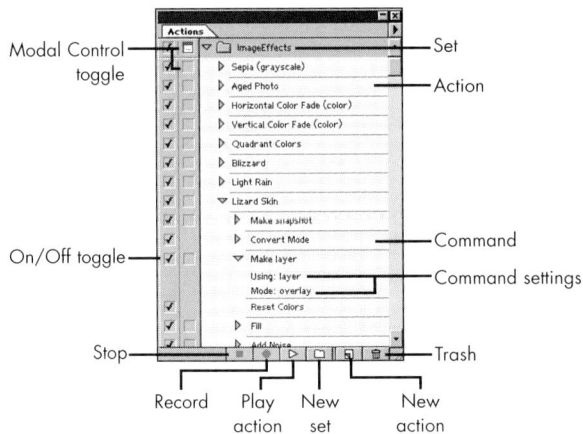

Figure 19.1

The Actions palette is used to record, edit, and manage actions and action sets.

Modal Control toggle — Set — Action — Command — Command settings — On/Off toggle — Stop — Trash — Record — Play action — New set — New action

PLAYING ACTIONS

To apply an action to an image, select the action in the Actions palette, then click the Play button at the bottom of the Actions palette. Be aware that actions may require some conditions to be present in order to execute properly. For example, many filters require the image to be in RGB mode, the action may expect to find a selection or a channel, or the image may need to be a certain size or have a specific foreground color for the action to work.

Now you try it...

Playing Actions

NOTE

If you don't have the Image Effects set loaded, select Load Actions from the Actions palette menu (see Figure 19.3), and load this set.

1   Open the file "Lesson01.psd" from the Chapter 19 lessons folder on the CD (see Figure 19.2).

2   Select the triangle to the left of the Image Effects folder icon in the Actions palette to display the actions available within this set (see Figure 19.4).

3   Select the Lizard Skin action and click the Play button.

4   Select the triangle to the left of the Lizard Skin action to display the commands that produce this effect. Notice the way the action has been built, starting with a snapshot to save the current image in the History palette, and ending with a series of filters to produce the desired effect (see Figure 19.5).

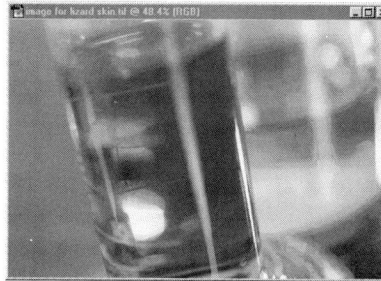

Figure 19.2

The image at the beginning of the exercise.

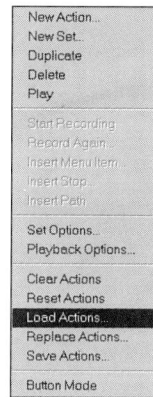

Figure 19.3

Actions can be saved as files, and then loaded into Photoshop.

Click here to display the actions within the set.

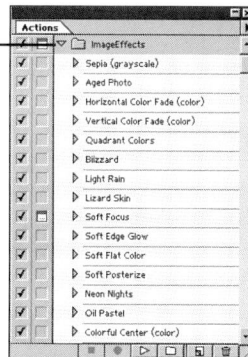

Figure 19.4

Displaying available actions in the Actions palette.

continues

Figure 19.5

Displaying commands
within actions.

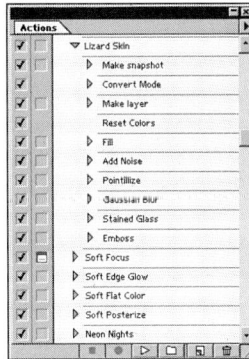

5   Now display the settings for the Fill command by clicking the triangle next to the command. Note the settings for the fill color, the opacity, and the painting mode.

If you would like, try expanding the other actions in this action set and look at their command settings. Notice especially their use of the Snapshot at the beginning of each action. This is useful in case you want to undo the action and return the image to its previous state before the action was executed because Undo reverses only one command.

PLAYBACK SPEED

You can control the speed of an action's playback by selecting Playback Options in the Actions palette menu and then choosing the playback settings (see Figure 19.6). Accelerated is the default playback mode, which plays back commands with minimal user intervention. Step by Step mode completes each step, and then displays the results before going to the next step. Pause mode allows you to interject a delay between each command in an action.

Figure 19.6

Set the speed that actions
play back in the Playback
Options dialog box.

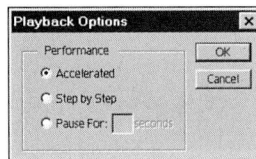

BUTTON MODE

You can display actions as colored buttons without seeing the individual commands by setting the Actions palette to Button Mode (see Figure 19.7). Set the Actions palette to display only the actions and their keyboard shortcuts by selecting the Button Mode toggle from the Actions palette menu. While in Button Mode, an action is played by simply clicking its corresponding button. Because you cannot see the group of commands that make up an action while in Button Mode, you can't edit or insert commands or record new actions. Sets may not be discernible in Button Mode because the same color can be used for any action.

Figure 19.7

The Actions palette in Button Mode shows the action's name and keyboard shortcut.

CREATING AND EDITING ACTIONS

To create a new action, click the New Action button from the Actions palette or select New Action from the Actions palette menu and enter a name for the action, the set into which it should be placed, the keyboard shortcut, and the color of the action's button. The keyboard shortcut must be either a function key (F2-F12) or a combination of the function key and Shift, Ctrl/ Command, or both. You can change any of this information later by double-clicking on the action's name. Figure 19.8 shows the options available when creating a new action. Once the information is entered, click the Record button to begin creating the action.

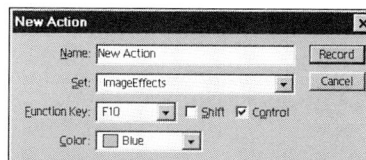

Figure 19.8

Set the name and keyboard shortcut of an action in the New Action dialog box.

TIP

When recording an action, create a snapshot in the first step so that you can easily go back to the state of the image before running the action.

Once recording begins, the Record button in the Actions palette turns red, and each command you perform displays in the Actions palette under the action you are creating. When you have finished recording, click the Stop button in the Actions palette.

Some commands in the action may have *modal controls*, which are commands that require pressing the Enter or Return key or clicking an OK button. Examples of these commands are transformations and filters with dialog boxes. You can choose to accept the values entered when recording the action by turning off the modal control toggle to the left of the action. If turned on, Photoshop prompts you to enter appropriate information during the execution of the action. The modal control toggle may appear black if all the actions within a set or all the commands within an action will prompt for user input, or red if only some do. You can toggle modal control for all the commands in an action, or for all actions within a set (see Figure 19.9).

Figure 19.9

The modal control check boxes determine whether user intervention is required.

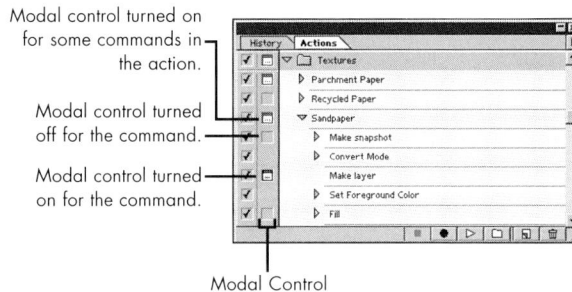

If you need to exclude certain commands within an action, you can accomplish this by turning commands on or off with the on/off toggle next to the action. Similar to the modal control, the color of the toggle next to the action will be either black if all the commands are turned on and red if only some are (see Figure 19.10). It will be blank if the entire action is turned off. You can also turn off an entire action set.

INSERTING COMMANDS

A new command can be added at any time to an existing action by selecting the action, and then clicking the Record button to begin the addition. You can also select a command in an action to begin recording from that point in the action. This technique can be used to add commands that can be recorded in actions. To add path definitions and Menu Items, which can't be recorded, the pop-up menu in the Actions palette must be used.

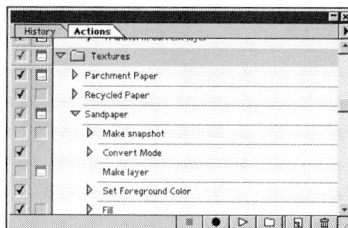

Figure 19.10

Use the on/off toggle to exclude commands from an action.

INSERTING PATHS

To insert a path into an action, the path must already be defined. While recording the action, or after the action has been recorded, select the path you wish to insert from the Paths palette, and then choose Insert Path from the Actions palette menu. If you are inserting a path into an existing action, the path will be inserted immediately following the command you have selected.

The path that is inserted uses the same position and size as it did when it was originally created. The path may be outside the canvas if it were created in a larger image or the current image has been resized, so be sure to keep this in mind when creating actions that involve paths.

INSERTING MENU ITEMS

Menu items are commands selected from the pull-down menus and can include non-recordable commands. Examples of these non-recordable commands are the View commands, the Open As command, and any access to the Preferences. To insert a menu item, choose either Insert Menu Item from the Actions palette menu while recording the action or after selecting the command that should be executed immediately before the menu item. When inserting a menu item, choose the command from the menus. Alternately, you can type either the entire name of the item or just the first letters, and then use the Find button to let Photoshop search for the menu item.

TIP

Use a path with the Stroke Path/Subpath command if you want to incorporate some of the painting tools into your action. Other similar results can be achieved by combining the paths with the Fill Path/Subpath command. Both commands are in the Paths palette menu.

Now you try it...

Inserting Paths and Menu Items

1 Begin by opening the file "Lesson02.psd" from the Chapter 19 folder on the CD. This image already contains a defined path.

continues

2 Make sure the Actions palette is visible.

3 Use the New Set button to create a new set of actions and call it **Legal**.

4 Now that you have created a new action set, start recording an action by clicking the New Action button in the Actions palette. Call this new action **Copyright**. Make sure you place this new action in the set you just created by selecting Legal from the Set pop-up menu in the Actions dialog box (see Figure 19.11).

Figure 19.11

The Copyright action
is placed
in the Legal
action set.

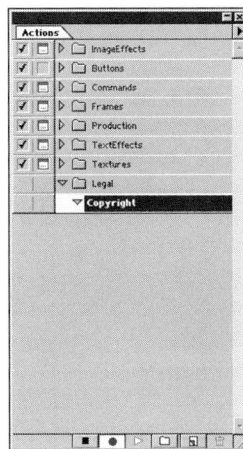

5 Note that the action is now being recorded. Make sure the Paths palette is visible and select the Path "Copyright". From the Actions palette menu, select Insert Path.

6 From the Actions palette menu, choose Insert Menu Item. Type **fit** and click the Fnd button. The Fit Image command is correct, so click OK.

7 Now, fill the current work path by selecting the Fill Path in the Paths palette menu. Set the color to Black, the Opacity to 100%, and the mode to Normal.

8 Finally, insert another menu item by choosing Insert Menu Item from the Actions palette menu. This time choose View > Hide Path (see Figure 19.12).

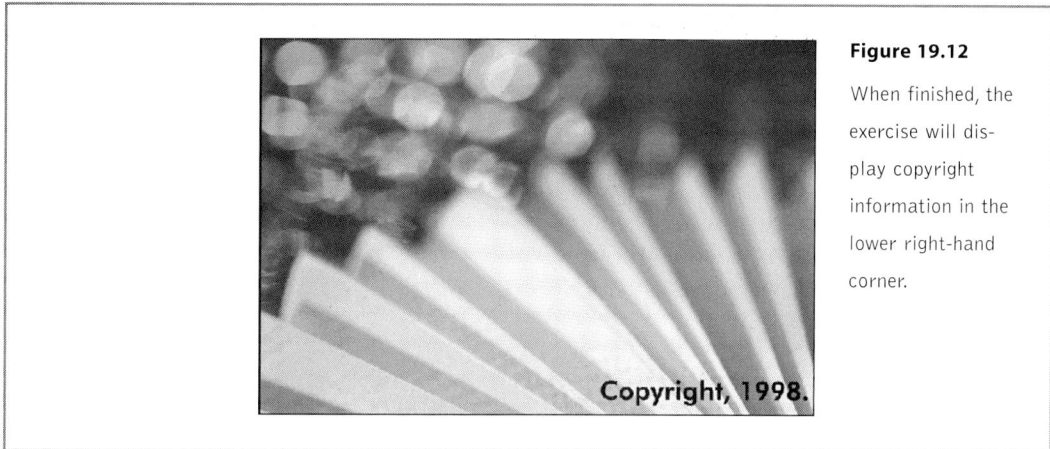

Figure 19.12

When finished, the exercise will display copyright information in the lower right-hand corner.

INSERTING STOPS

It is occasionally necessary to insert a stop into an action. A *stop* is a point at which the action pauses, either to allow the user to enter some information, complete a task, or provide the user with descriptive information. To insert a stop into an action, choose the command within the action after which the stop should occur, and then choose Insert Stop from the Actions palette menu. Figure 19.13 shows the Record Stop dialog box that appears after choosing this option. Enter the text you wish to display in the box provided. If you want the user to be able to continue, make sure that the Allow Continue box is checked.

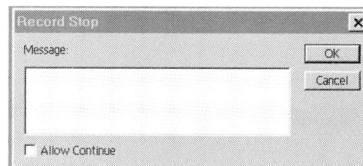

Figure 19.13

The Record Stop dialog box appears when the Insert Stop option is chosen.

Now you try it...

Inserting Stops

1   In the action created in the previous exercise, select the Set Work Path command.

2   Use the Actions palette menu and choose Insert Stop.

3   Type in the following description of this step of the action:

This action fills a path with the foreground color. The path was created by using the Type Mask Tool and then converting the selection to a path.

4   Be sure that you check the Allow Continue box so that the user can move to the next step of the action. If you do not, the action will stop at this point, and you will need to manually restart the action.

ACTION SETS AND ACTION MANAGEMENT

As mentioned previously, Photoshop enables groups of similar actions to be combined into action sets. These sets are folders into which actions are placed. To change the set in which an action resides, drag the action that you want to move into the appropriate set. If you want to change the order that the action sets appear, you can drag the sets to new positions in the palette.

At any level of the action hierarchy, command, action, or set, these items can be duplicated and deleted. Both the Duplicate and Delete commands can be found in the Actions palette menu. If you choose the Clear Actions command, all actions and action sets will be deleted from the Actions palette.

Choose the Reset Actions command from the Actions palette menu to return the actions to the default set. You can load sets of actions by using the Load Actions command. If you want to replace the action sets in the palette with a saved action set, choose Replace Actions.

AUTOMATE COMMAND

Photoshop 5 contains several new built-in automation tools. These tools are used to perform common production tasks such as the construction of contact sheets, batch processing for actions, and the conversion of multi-page PDF files to a format that Photoshop can read. You can use many of the automation tools in conjunction with actions. Some are particularly well suited for use within actions, such as the Conditional Mode Change and the Fit Image.

BATCH PROCESSING

An action can be applied to a group or a batch of files. These files can be acquired from either a folder or through a TWAIN import. In either case, you must choose the action and the set in which the action resides from the Batch dialog box (see Figure 19.14).

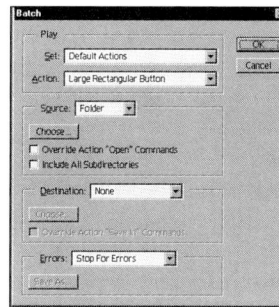

Figure 19.14

Use the Batch dialog box to control which files are processed, how they are processed, and which action is used.

There are three destination options available when saving files: None, Save and Close, and Folder. If None is selected, the files remain open after the action is applied. If Save and Close is chosen, the files are saved, overwriting the originals. If the Folder option is used, the files are saved into a new folder with the same names as the originals. There are also overrides for both opening and saving files. If the action already has an Open or a Save command, these should be overridden to ensure that the files in the specified folder are opened and that the files are saved to the correct folder. If the Override Action "Save In" Command checkbox is not selected, the files will be processed, but each file will be saved with the same name, resulting in only one file created from the last one opened. Photoshop will not warn you that existing files are being overwritten.

CONDITIONAL MODE CHANGE

The Conditional Mode Change allows you to change the image mode if it is already in a specified mode. For example, you may want to convert a series of images to RGB, but only those which are currently in Indexed Color mode. The Conditional Mode Change command can also be used in an action with the Batch option to open all the files in a folder and then convert those which are in Indexed Color to RGB. Figure 19.15 shows the options available for the Conditional Mode Change.

TIP

Use the Conditional Mode Change within an action to change the Image Mode if necessary. For example, if you need to use a filter, such as Lens Flare (which only works with RGB images) as part of an action, convert the image to RGB first. This will eliminate some of the errors regarding filter unavailability.

Figure 19.15

Use the Conditional
Mode Change dialog box
to selectively change the
mode of an image.

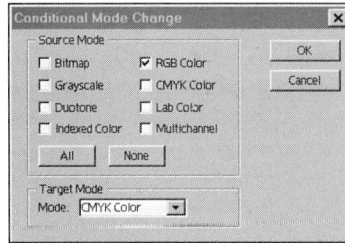

CONTACT SHEET

A contact sheet is a single page that displays a collection of images. In
Photoshop, the Contact Sheet command enables you to construct a contact
sheet by making thumbnail images of all the files in a directory. The contact
sheet can then be printed, which is very useful for managing large quantities of graphic files. Figure 19.16 shows the Contact Sheet options and
Figure 19.17 shows a completed contact sheet.

Figure 19.16

Use these options for
creating the Contact
Sheet.

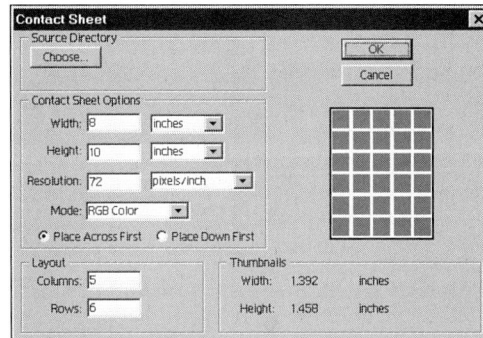

Figure 19.17

A completed contact
sheet can be used to
catalog images.

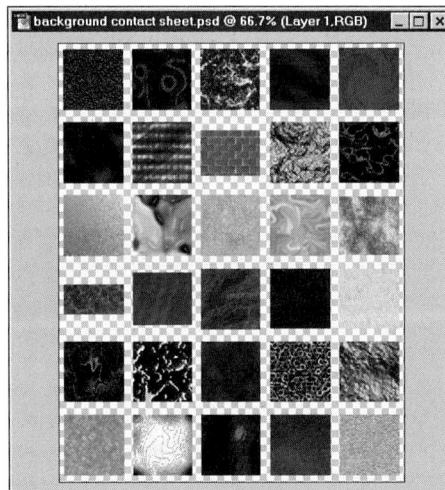

To make a contact sheet from a collection of images, specify from which folder Photoshop will get the images, the size, resolution, and image mode of the file which contains the thumbnails, and the number of thumbnails to appear on each page. The image modes available are RGB, CMYK, Lab, and Grayscale. Take into account the use for the finished contact sheet to determine both the image mode and resolution. See Chapters 16 and 17 for information about choosing appropriate options for prepress and Web production. Before using the Contact Sheet command, close any files that will be thumbnailed.

FIT IMAGE

The Fit Image automation tool can be used to resample an image to a specified size, measured in pixels. The aspect ratio of the original image will be maintained. When combined with the batch option, this can be used to produce thumbnails of a collection of images or to resize an entire folder of images to a particular size.

CONVERT MULTI-PAGE PDF TO PSD

This command creates a Photoshop file for each page of an Adobe Acrobat PDF file. You must specify the original PDF file, the pages to be converted, the print resolution, and image mode of the resulting Photoshop files. In addition, you can choose the destination folder for the converted files by clicking the Choose button. You can also specify a Base Name (see Figure 19.18). By default, the Base Name is the same as the PDF file being converted. When the Photoshop documents are created, they are saved with a file name derived from the Base Name followed by the page number.

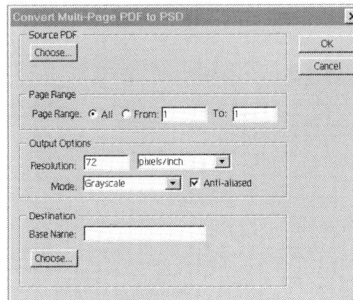

Figure 19.18

The Multi-Page PDF to PSD command is used to create multiple Photoshop documents from a multi-page PDF.

SUMMARY

Actions and Photoshop's automation tools encompass the use of all the commands, tools, and techniques covered in this book. The proper understanding and use of actions will enable you not only to pass the exam, but also to use Photoshop easily and effectively in a production environment. From Web design to prepress, actions and automation provide an invaluable method of not only improving efficiency, but also of ensuring consistency between users on a daily basis.

REVIEW QUESTIONS

1. What is the first step to add a new action while in Button Mode?

    a. Select the Record button from the Actions palette.

    b. Select the New Action button from the Actions palette.

    c. Select the Insert New Action from the Actions palette menu.

    d. Select the Button Mode option from the Actions palette menu to turn off Button Mode.

2. How do you insert a path into an action?

    a. Start recording an action, and then create a path.

    b. Start recording an action, then select Insert Path from the Actions palette menu and create a path.

    c. Start recording an action, then select an existing path and select Insert Path from the Actions palette menu.

    d. Start recording an action, use the selection tool to specify which direction points to include, and then select Insert Path from the Actions palette menu.

3. What do you click on to create a new action set?

    a. The New Set button in the Actions palette

    b. The Record button in the Actions palette

    c. The New Action button in the Actions palette

    d. The New Set and Action button in the Actions palette

4. During playback, which options place a delay of set duration after each command?

    a. Pause

    b. Step by step

    c. Accelerated

    d. Decelerated

5. Which of the following tools can be used in an action?

    a. Eraser

    b. Airbrush

    c. Paintbrush

    d. Paintbucket

6.   Which of the following is an option for the keyboard equivalent for an action?

   a.   Ctrl+C/Command+C

   b.   Alt+F/Option+F

   c.   Ctrl+Shift+F4/Command+Shift+F4

   d.   Alt+Shift+F4/Option+Shift+F4

7.   How do you create an action that turns the ruler's visibility on and off?

   a.   Begin recording, and then select View > Show Rulers.

   b.   Begin recording, select Insert Menu Item, and then select View > Show Rulers.

   c.   Begin recording, and then select Window > Show Rulers.

   d.   Begin recording, select Insert Menu Item, and then select Window > Show Rulers.

8.   What command do you use so that you can open all of the pages of a PDF file in Photoshop?

   a.   Open command

   b.   Open As command

   c.   Contact Sheet command

   d.   Multi-page PDF to PSD command

ANSWERS TO REVIEW QUESTIONS

CHAPTER 1—REVIEW QUESTIONS

1. What is the maximum amount of scratch disk space allowed?

    a. 2GB

    b. 4GB

    c. 8GB

    d. <u>Unlimited</u>

2. What is the default scratch disk arrangement?

    a. No scratch disk is created.

    b. <u>A scratch disk is created on the startup drive.</u>

    c. A scratch disk is created on any secondary drive.

    d. Photoshop creates as many scratch disks as it can.

3. What is the maximum number of scratch disk volumes that can be created?

    a. 1

    b. 2

    c. 3

    d. <u>4</u>

4. You get an error message that Photoshop cannot complete the command because the primary scratch disk is full. What should you do?

   a. Restart Photoshop.

   b. Reinstall Photoshop.

   c. Close any open applications.

   d. <u>Delete unnecessary files from the disk being used as a scratch disk.</u>

5. What is the minimum amount of RAM that Photoshop 5.0 requires?

   a. 8MB

   b. 16MB

   c. <u>32MB</u>

   d. 64MB

6. Photoshop cannot do the following (choose the three that apply):

   a. <u>Play a sound.</u>

   b. <u>Play an animation.</u>

   c. Open a raster image file.

   d. <u>Open a spreadsheet.</u>

7. Which of the following is the fundamental element in a Photoshop image?

   a. Vector

   b. Color Space

   c. <u>Pixel</u>

   d. Path

8. How many colors are supported by an 8-bit image?

   a. 8

   b. 16

   c. <u>256</u>

   d. 65,000

9. You are working on an image and some of the filters are unavailable. What should you do? (Choose 2)

   a. Turn off virtual memory.

   b. <u>Check the plug-in's search path in the preferences.</u>

   c. Delete the Photoshop preferences file to reset them.

   d. <u>Make sure that the plug-ins are in the correct folder.</u>

10. You are working on a 10MB image. What is the minimum recommended amount of RAM you should have available?

   a. 16–32MB

   b. <u>30–50MB</u>

   c. 32–64MB

   d. 50–64MB

CHAPTER 2—REVIEW QUESTIONS

1. When displaying the Document Sizes option in the status bar, what does the number on the left indicate?

   a. Scratch disk size

   b. The size of the document with layers

   c. The size of the document with channels

   d. <u>The size of the document after it is flattened</u>

2.   When displaying the Scratch Sizes option in the status bar, what does the number on the left indicate?

a.   How large your document is

b.   How large your scratch disk is

c.   How much RAM has been allocated to Photoshop

d.   <u>How much memory is required for all open images</u>

3.   How do you display a Context-Sensitive menu?

a.   Double-click on the image.

b.   Command/Alt+click on the image.

c.   <u>Control+click/right+click on the image.</u>

d.   Position the cursor over the tool in the toolbox.

4.   How do you view an image at 100%?

a.   Option-click on the image.

b.   Choose View > Fit in Window.

c.   Double-click the hand tool.

d.   <u>Double-click the zoom tool.</u>

5.   What is the function of the measure tool?

a.   To measure a crop before cropping occurs

b.   <u>To measure the distance between two points</u>

c.   To measure the number of pixels in an image

d.   To measure a transform command before the transformation occurs

6.   How do you recreate your preferences file after you've thrown it away?

a.   Reinstall Photoshop.

b.   Restart your computer.

c.   Copy the default preferences file to the plug-ins folder and restart.

d.   <u>Launch Photoshop.</u>

7.   How do you reposition a guide?

a.   <u>Select the move tool and click and drag.</u>

b.   Option+click and drag while using any tool.

c.   Select any tool in the toolbox and click and drag.

d.   Shift+click and drag key while using any tool.

8.   How do you create a protractor when using a measuring line?

a.   Shift+drag at any angle from either end of the measuring line.

b.   You can't create a protractor when using the measuring line.

c.   Click and drag on one of the endpoints of the measuring line.

d.   <u>Option+drag (Macintosh) or Alt+drag (Windows) at any angle from either end of the measuring line.</u>

CHAPTER 3—REVIEW QUESTIONS

1. If Photoshop warns you that you are running low on memory, which of the following is an acceptable solution?

    a. Delete the Actions.

    b. Purge the Histogram.

    c. Purge the History States.

    d. Purge the preferences file.

2. What is a snapshot?

    a. A saved pattern

    b. A saved histogram

    c. A saved selection

    d. A saved history state

3. When selecting a previous state, which option retains the subsequent states if turned on?

    a. Allow Frame Blending

    b. Allow Linear History

    c. Allow Non-Linear History

    d. Allow Bilinear Interpolation

4. What are the default number of states that Photoshop retains?

    a. 5

    b. 10

    c. 20

    d. 100

5. Which of the following are never saved with the file? (choose 2)

    a. Channels

    b. Snapshots

    c. ICC Profiles

    d. History States

6. To delete all the history states in only the current image, which command should you use?

    a. Clear History

    b. Hold down the Shift key and choose Clear History

    c. Hold down the Alt (Windows)/Option (Macintosh) key and choose Clear History

    d. Hold down the Ctrl (Windows)/ Command (Macintosh) key and choose Clear History

7. To delete all the history states in all open images, which command should you use?

    a. Clear History

    b. Edit > Purge > Histories

    c. Hold down the Ctrl (Windows)/ Command (Macintosh) key and choose Clear History

    d. Hold down the Alt (Windows)/Option (Macintosh) key and choose Clear History

8. If you select a previous history state and all subsequent states are unavailable or dimmed, what does this indicate?

    a. Continuing to change the image from the current state will discard all the unavailable states.

    b. The unavailable states have been discarded and can be recovered by using Undo.

c. The Allow Non-Linear history option has been turned on.

d. You should purge the histories.

9. What will happen if you drag a snapshot to the Create new document from current state button?

a. A new document will be created from the snapshot and duplicate the history states from the original document.

b. <u>A new document will be created from the snapshot and the history will start over in the new document.</u>

c. A new document will be created from the snapshot and the histories will be purged for both the old and new documents.

d. A new document will not be created from the snapshot, because only history states can be used to create new documents this way.

10. What should you do to delete a state and all states that come after it?

a. <u>Make sure that Allow Non-Linear History is turned off, select the state, and then select Delete.</u>

b. Make sure Allow Non-Linear History is turned on, select the state, and then select Delete.

c. Make sure Allow Non-Linear History is turned off, select all the states you want to delete, and then select Delete.

d. Make sure Allow Non-Linear History is turned on, select all the states you want to delete, and then select Delete.

CHAPTER 4—REVIEW QUESTIONS

1. What is the appropriate image resolution for graphics that will appear on Web pages?

a. <u>72 ppi</u>

b. 144 ppi

c. 150 ppi

d. 300 ppi

2. What is the appropriate scan resolution for an image that will be printed at 75 lpi?

a. 75 ppi

b. <u>150 ppi</u>

c. 175 ppi

d. 300 ppi

3. Which types of files can be placed into Photoshop? (Choose 2.)

a. TIFF

b. JPEG

c. <u>PDF</u>

d. <u>EPS</u>

4. For a 3" x 5" image to be printed at 6" x 10" at 150 lpi, what is an appropriate scan resolution?

a. 150 ppi

b. 300 ppi

c. <u>600 ppi</u>

d. 1200 ppi

5. Which interpolation method gives the most accurate results?

   a. Nearest Neighbor

   b. Bilinear

   c. Bicubic

   d. Downsampling

6. If a 100 x 100-pixel image is resampled up to a 200 x 200-pixel image, what will happen to the file size?

   a. It will approximately double.

   b. It will approximately triple.

   c. It will approximately quadruple.

   d. It will remain the same.

7. Which command should you use to include copyright information with an image?

   a. File Info

   b. Export

   c. Preferences

   d. History

8. You are planning to print a black-and-white technical illustration (line art) on a 1200 dpi imagesetter. What scan resolution should you use?

   a. 300 ppi

   b. 600 ppi

   c. 1200 ppi

   d. 2400 ppi

9. You make an elliptical selection in a CMYK image and try to use Image > Crop, but the tool is unavailable (dimmed-out). What might be wrong?

   a. You cannot use cropping in CMYK mode.

   b. You cannot crop an elliptical selection.

   c. You cannot crop a selection in CMYK mode.

   d. You cannot crop a selection with anti-aliasing on.

10. The crop tool is located with what other tool in the toolbox?

    a. The pen tool

    b. The dodge tool

    c. The polygon lasso

    d. The elliptical marquee

CHAPTER 5—REVIEW QUESTIONS

1. In which mode does your image need to be in order to convert it to Bitmap mode?

   a. RGB

   b. Grayscale

   c. Multichannel

   d. Indexed Color

2. When converting from CMYK to Multichannel mode, what are the names of the channels produced?

   a. Cyan, Magenta, and Yellow

   b. Four channels named Alpha

c.   Four channels named Black

d.   Cyan, Magenta, Yellow, and Black

3.   None of the filters are available. Which image mode is your image in (assume 8-Bit/Channel color where applicable)?

a.   CMYK

b.   Grayscale

c.   Multichannel

d.   Indexed Color

4.   You try to add a layer, but the New Layer button in the Layers palette is dimmed. What is a possible reason (assume 8-Bit/Channel color where applicable)?

a.   The image is in CMYK mode.

b.   The image is in Duotone mode.

c.   The image is in Grayscale mode.

d.   The image is in Indexed Color mode.

5.   What does the Halftone Screen option do when converting from Grayscale to Bitmap mode?

a.   It simulates halftone dots.

b.   It creates a custom Dot Gain.

c.   It uses the printer's halftone screen settings.

d.   It sets the halftone screen for the image, but does not display the halftone information.

6.   How many channels does a Quadtone image have?

a.   One

b.   Two

c.   Three

d.   Four

7.   Which color mode is used as an intermediate when converting from RGB to CMYK?

a.   Lab

b.   Grayscale

c.   Multichannel

d.   Indexed Color

8.   What does adjusting the Duotone curves accomplish?

a.   It determines where the spot color should be applied throughout the image.

b.   It determines where trapping should be applied throughout the image.

c.   It determines where the CMYK profile should be applied throughout the image.

d.   It determines where out-of-gamut colors should be corrected throughout the image.

9. While converting from RGB to Indexed Color, the Pattern dither is unavailable. What is a possible reason?

    a. You are trying to use the Web palette.

    b. You are trying to use the Uniform palette.

    c. You are trying to use the Adaptive palette.

    d. You are trying to use the Macintosh System palette.

10. How many colors can an image in Indexed Color mode contain?

    a. 2

    b. 256

    c. 65,000

    d. 16 million

11. When converting an image to Bitmap Mode from Grayscale, the Custom Pattern dither option is unavailable. What is a possible reason?

    a. You have not defined a pattern.

    b. You are trying to use the Uniform palette.

    c. You are trying to use the Adaptive palette.

    d. You cannot convert a Grayscale image to Bitmap Mode.

12. Which color model is device independent?

    a. RGB

    b. CMYK

    c. Lab

    d. Indexed Color

CHAPTER 6—REVIEW QUESTIONS

1. Which tool selects contiguous areas of similar color?

    a. Grow

    b. Similar

    c. Magic wand

    d. Magnetic lasso

2. Which command is used to select areas of similar color throughout an image?

    a. Expand

    b. Similar

    c. Magic wand

    d. Magnetic lasso

3. Which commands or tools, other than the magic wand, rely on the Tolerance setting? (Choose 2)

    a. Similar

    b. Grow

    c. Expand

    d. Contract

4. To adjust the range of colors in the Color Range dialog box, you should adjust which value?

    a. Tolerance

    b. Anti-aliasing

    c. Fuzziness

    d. Feather

5. Which tool does not have an anti-aliasing option?

    a. Magnetic lasso

    b. Elliptical marquee

    c. Rectangular marquee

    d. Polygon lasso

6. Which command creates a smooth transition between selected and unselected pixels?

    a. Grow

    b. Expand

    c. Feather

    d. Transform Selection

7. Which key should you use to copy a selection to the center of another image while dragging and dropping?

    a. Shift

    b. Alt (Windows)/Option (Macintosh)

    c. Ctrl (Windows)/Command (Macintosh)

    d. Alt (Windows)/Command (Macintosh)

8. Which key should you hold down to add to a selection?

    a. Shift

    b. Alt (Windows)/Option (Macintosh)

    c. Ctrl (Windows)/Command (Macintosh)

    d. Alt (Windows)/Command (Macintosh)

9. Which key should you hold down to constrain the elliptical marquee to a circle?

    a. Shift

    b. Alt (Windows)/Option (Macintosh)

    c. Ctrl (Windows)/Command (Macintosh)

    d. Alt (Windows)/Command (Macintosh)

10. To specify the magnetic lasso's sensitivity to edges in the image, which value should be adjusted?

    a. Tolerance

    b. Edge Contrast

    c. Fuzziness

    d. Lasso Width

11. You want to copy a selected area in an image, but when you drag the cursor, only the selection boundary moves. What might you need to do to fix the problem?

    a. Set the tolerance.

    b. Feather the selection.

    c. Select the move tool.

    d. Select the magnetic lasso tool.

12. You click a point with the magic wand tool and only one pixel is selected. What is probably the value of the tolerance?

    a. 0

    b. 100

    c. 255

    d. 256

13. How can you soften the hard edges of a selection? (Choose 2)

    a. Grow

    b. <u>Feather</u>

    c. Smooth

    d. <u>Anti-alias</u>

14. What is the minimum part of an image that can be selected?

    a. 1/2 pixel

    b. <u>1 pixel</u>

    c. 1/10 pixel

    d. 1/256 pixel

15. The crop tool is located with what other tool in the toolbox?

    a. The pen tool

    b. The dodge tool

    c. The polygon lasso

    d. <u>The elliptical marquee</u>

CHAPTER 7—REVIEW QUESTIONS

1. To create a clipping path, you must use which type of object?

    a. A work path

    b. <u>A saved path</u>

    c. A selection

    d. A clipping group

2. When using the magnetic pen tool, which option should you set to change the length of the segments produced?

    a. Tolerance

    b. <u>Curve Fit</u>

    c. Pen Width

    d. Edge Contrast

3. If you increase the length of the segments produced by the magnetic pen tool, what happens to the number of anchor points?

    a. They will increase.

    b. <u>They will decrease.</u>

    c. They will stay the same.

    d. You cannot change the length of the segments produced by the magnetic pen tool.

4. Which of the following cannot be selected with the direct selection tool?

    a. Anchor points

    b. Direction points

    c. <u>Direction lines</u>

    d. Path segments

5. When stroking a path, which key should you use when clicking the Stroke Path button in the Paths palette to select the type of painting tool to use?

    a. Shift

    b. Alt (Windows)/Option (Macintosh)

    c. Ctrl (Windows)/Command (Macintosh)

    d. Shift+Ctrl (Windows)/Command (Macintosh)

6. When converting a selection to a path, what type of path will be created?

    a. Work Path

    b. Open Subpath

    c. Clipping Path

    d. Filled subpath

7. When creating a corner point while using the pen tool, which key should you hold down while dragging the direction line?

    a. Shift

    b. Alt (Windows)/Option (Macintosh)

    c. Ctrl (Windows)/Command (Macintosh)

    d. Alt (Windows)/Command (Macintosh)

CHAPTER 8—REVIEW QUESTIONS

1. What are the steps to paint a straight line?

    a. Press the Shift key while dragging.

    b. Press the Option key while dragging.

    c. Press the Control key while dragging.

    d. You can't draw a straight line with the painting tools.

2. How do you access custom colors?

    a. Choose Import from the File menu.

    b. Choose Open Colors from the File menu.

    c. Click the Custom button in the Color Picker.

    d. Double-click on a swatch in the Swatches palette.

3. What is displayed in the Color Field when the Hue button is selected in the Color Picker?

    a. Saturation on both axes

    b. Brightness on both axes

    c. Saturation on the vertical axis

    d. Saturation on the horizontal axis

4. How do you define a pattern?

    a. Choose Define Pattern from the File menu.

    b. Choose Define Pattern from the Edit menu.

    c. Add the pattern to the pattern list by clicking on the Add button in the Patterns palette.

    d. Control+click/right+click on the pattern, and choose Define Pattern from the context-sensitive menu.

5. How do you apply a stroke to a layer element?

   a. Choose Stroke from the Select menu and enter an amount in the Stroke field.

   b. Choose Stroke from the Layer menu and enter an amount in the Stroke field.

   c. <u>Control+click/right+click on the selection, and choose Stroke from the context-sensitive menu.</u>

   d. Press Command+Shift+Delete (Macintosh) or Control+Shift+Delete (Windows) to stroke with the background color.

6. How do you activate the eyedropper tool while using the painting tools?

   a. Press the Shift key.

   b. <u>Press the Alt/Option key.</u>

   c. Press Command (Macintosh) or Control (Windows).

   d. Press Command+Option (Macintosh) or Control+Alt (Windows).

7. How do you add a color to the Swatches palette?

   a. Choose New Color in the Swatches Options palette.

   b. Drag the foreground color swatch into the Swatches palette.

   c. Choose Add foreground color in the Swatches Options palette.

   d. <u>Click an empty area in the Swatches palette to add the foreground color.</u>

8. What is the function of the Clear?

   a. To delete a layer in an image

   b. <u>To delete any active selection</u>

   c. To remove pixels in an image using the Paintbrush or Airbrush

   d. To make pixels transparent using the paint bucket, line tool, and Fill and Stroke commands

9. What is the function of the Screen mode?

   a. Set the linescreen for the image.

   b. Change the opacity of an image or selection.

   c. Blend the foreground color with the underlying image to produce a darker color.

   d. <u>Blend the foreground color with the underlying image to produce a lighter color.</u>

10. How do you delete a swatch from the Swatches palette?

    a. Alt/Option+click on the swatch.

    b. Press the Delete key.

    c. Command+click (Macintosh) or Control+click (Windows) on the swatch.

    d. <u>Choose Reload Swatches from the Swatches palette menu, and then delete the color.</u>

CHAPTER 9—REVIEW QUESTIONS

1. How do you sample an area of an image using the rubber stamp tool?

    a. Click on the area you want to sample and drag.

    b. Shift+click to select multiple sample pixels.

    c. Option (Macintosh) or Alt (Windows)+click on the area.

    d. Command (Macintosh) or Control (Windows)+click on the area.

2. You use the dodge tool when editing an image to achieve what result?

    a. Darken areas of an image

    b. Delete pixels in an image

    c. Lighten areas of an image

    d. Saturate areas of an image

3. Which filter is commonly applied to channels to reduce banding in a gradient blend?

    a. Noise

    b. Diffuse

    c. Displace

    d. Unsharp Mask

4. How do you rotate a layer or selection?

    a. Choose Rotate from the Select menu.

    b. Click and drag with the rotate tool.

    c. Choose Edit > Transform > Free Transform.

    d. Press Control/Command and drag with the move tool.

5. How do you add perspective to an element using the Free Transform command?

    a. Click on a side handle.

    b. Press Option/Alt+Shift and drag on a side handle.

    c. Shift+click and drag from the center of the bounding box.

    d. Press Command+Option+Shift (Macintosh) or Control+Alt+Shift (Windows) and drag on a side or corner handle.

6. Which is one way you cannot cancel a transformation?

    a. Press the Escape key.

    b. Select a different tool.

    c. Press Control/Command+D.

    d. Press Control/Command+. (period).

7. What happens when you drag the Threshold slider to the right in the Unsharp Mask dialog box?

    a. The amount of sharpening increases.

    b. The amount of sharpening decreases.

    c. The number of pixels surrounding the edge pixels increases.

    d. The number of pixels surrounding the edge pixels decreases.

8. The action of the history brush is the same as using what other tool?

   a. The eraser.

   b. No other tool works like the history brush.

   c. The eraser with the Magic Eraser option checked in the eraser Options palette.

   d. The eraser with the Erase to History option checked in the eraser Options palette.

9. Which tool desaturates areas of an image?

   a. The burn tool

   b. The dodge tool

   c. The sponge tool

   d. Any painting tool that has a Saturation slider in its Options palette

10. How do you change the size of a layer or selection?

    a. Choose Edit > Transform > Scale.

    b. Choose Scale from the Select menu.

    c. Select the scale tool and click and drag the corner points.

    d. Enter the new percentage in the scale tool Options palette.

CHAPTER 10—REVIEW QUESTIONS

1. How do you duplicate a layer?

   a. Choose Edit > Duplicate.

   b. Choose Image > Duplicate.

   c. Choose File > Duplicate Layer.

   d. Drag the layer on top of the New Layer button.

2. How do you change the background into a layer?

   a. Choose Layer > New Layer.

   b. Choose Layer > Transform.

   c. Option-click on the layer thumbnail.

   d. Double-click on the background layer.

3. Which is not a method of changing the stacking order of layers?

   a. Choose Layer > Align Up (or Align Down).

   b. Drag the layer above or below another layer.

   c. Press Control (Windows)/Command (Macintosh)+] (or [).

   d. Choose Layer > Arrange > Bring to Front, Bring Forward, Send to Back, Send Backward.

4. Which blending mode is not available to layers?

   a. Color

   b. Clear

   c. Dissolve

   d. Exclusion

5. When is it appropriate to use a clipping group?

   a. To group layers

   b. To move linked elements

   c. <u>To mask an image inside type or a shape</u>

   d. To create a silhouette for use in a page layout program

6. How do you turn off a layer mask?

   a. <u>Shift+click the layer mask thumbnail.</u>

   b. Option+click the layer mask thumbnail.

   c. Choose Hide Layer Mask from the Layers menu.

   d. Choose Hide Layer Mask from the Layers palette.

7. How do you show a layer mask in the image window?

   a. Shift+click the layer mask thumbnail.

   b. <u>Alt/Option+click the layer mask thumbnail.</u>

   c. Choose Load Layer Mask from the Select menu.

   d. Choose Load Layer Mask from the Layers palette.

8. When an adjustment layer is applied to a clipping group, what happens?

   a. You can't apply an adjustment layer to a clipping group.

   b. <u>Only the layers in the clipping group are affected by the adjustment layer.</u>

   c. An adjustment layer only affects a clipping group when the clipping group is merged.

   d. All layers in an image are affected by the adjustment layer, regardless of the clipping group.

9. Which is not a choice when the Adjustment Layer command options are displayed?

   a. Invert

   b. Threshold

   c. <u>Replace color</u>

   d. Channel Mixer

10. How do you create an adjustment layer?

    a. Choose New Adjustment Layer from the Layer pulldown menu.

    b. <u>Choose New Adjustment Layer from the Layers palette menu.</u>

    c. Shift+click on the Layer thumbnail.

    d. Command+click (Macintosh) or Control+click (Windows) on the Layer thumbnail.

CHAPTER 11—REVIEW QUESTIONS

1. What happens when the anti-aliasing option is turned on in the Type Tool dialog box?

   a. The text is bitmapped.

   b. The text retains the font outline.

   c. <u>The edges of the text are blurred for a smoother appearance.</u>

   d. It has no affect on the text if set in Adobe Illustrator and imported into Photoshop.

2. What does kerning do to text?

   a. It raises or lowers the selected text.

   b. <u>It adjusts the amount of space between two characters.</u>

   c. It equally adjusts spacing between more than two characters.

   d. It adjusts the spacing between two lines of text depending on where the cursor is inserted.

3. What happens when you check the Rotate box in the Type Tool dialog box?

   a. <u>Vertical text is rotated 90°.</u>

   b. Horizontal text is rotated 90°.

   c. Text is rotated in 45° increments.

   d. The Edit > Transform command is enabled.

4. What do you do to increase/decrease type size in 10 point/pixel increments?

   a. Press up and down arrow keys.

   b. <u>Press Shift+up/down arrow keys.</u>

   c. Press Option+Shift+up/down arrow keys.

   d. Press Command+Option+Shift+ up/down arrow keys (Macintosh) or Control+Alt+Shift+up/down arrow keys.

5. When applying a filter to a text layer, what must you do first?

   a. <u>Render the layer.</u>

   b. Choose a filter from the Filter menu.

   c. Make sure the layer isn't linked to another layer.

   d. Make the text an active selection and choose a filter from the Filter menu.

6. How do you reposition text in the image window while still in the Type dialog box?

   a. You must close the Type dialog box in order to move the type in the image window.

   b. Click and drag on the type in the image window.

   c. Select the move tool, and then click and drag the type in the image window.

   d. <u>Move the type with the move tool while in the Type dialog box.</u>

7. What does tracking do to text?

   a. It raises or lowers the selected text.

   b. It adjusts spacing between two characters.

   c. <u>It adjusts the amount of space between characters and words.</u>

   d. It adjusts the spacing between two lines of text depending on where the cursor is inserted.

8. How do you edit a layer effect applied to text?

   a. Choose Text effects from the Edit menu.

   b. Choose Edit > text effects from the Layers palette.

   c. Double-click on the Type icon in the Layers palette.

   d. <u>Double-click on the text effect "f" icon in the Layers palette.</u>

CHAPTER 12—REVIEW QUESTIONS

1. You can add anchor points to which type of wireframe in the 3D Transform dialog box?

   a. Cube

   b. Toroid

   c. Sphere

   d. Cylinder

2. Which filter should be used to remove small dark spots caused by a dirty scanner bed?

   a. Find Edges

   b. Gaussian Blur

   c. Lighting Effects

   d. Dust & Scratches

3. In the 3D Transform filter, what is the Trackball tool used for?

   a. Moving Wireframes and Objects

   b. Rotating Wireframes and Objects

   c. Resizing Wireframes and Objects

   d. Deleting Wireframes and Objects

4. Which of the following filters has configurable options?

   a. Blur

   b. Sharpen

   c. Sharpen More

   d. Unsharp Mask

5. Which of the following is not a wireframe that you can create using the 3D Transform filter?

   a. Cone

   b. Cube

   c. Sphere

   d. Toroid

6. Which file could not be used as a displacement map by the Displace filter?

   a. An image in RGB mode

   b. An image in Lab mode

   c. An image in CMYK mode

   d. An image in bitmap mode

7. You are attempting to apply the Lighting Effects filter, but it is not available (dimmed). What is a possible reason?

   a. The image is in CMYK mode.

   b. The image contains a selection.

   c. The image does not have a background layer.

   d. The image does not contain an alpha channel.

8. You are attempting to apply the Gaussian Blur filter, but it is not available (dimmed). What is a possible reason?

   a. The image is in CMYK mode.

   b. The image contains a selection.

   c. The current layer is not visible.

   d. The image does not contain a background layer.

9. Which filter can load a channel as a texture map?

    a. Sharpen

    b. Displace

    c. 3D Transform

    d. Lighting Effects

10. Which filter should you use to soften the edges of an image?

    a. Blur

    b. Add Noise

    c. Dust & Scratches

    d. Lighting Effects

CHAPTER 13—REVIEW QUESTIONS

1. Which answer is true when using the Apply Image command?

    a. The new image will be in Multichannel mode.

    b. The original channel information in the image is affected.

    c. The individual channels can be specified for both the source and the target.

    d. The original channel information in the image is not affected because you can create a new channel, selection, or document.

2. How do you change the order of color channels?

    a. Color channels cannot be reordered.

    b. Click on the channel name and drag it above or below another channel.

    c. Click on the channel thumbnail and drag it above or below another channel.

    d. Click on the black triangle in the Channels palette and choose Reorder Channels.

3. What does the Solidity value of a spot color represent?

    a. The ink density of the spot color

    b. The opacity of the spot color when printed

    c. An onscreen display of the printed spot color

    d. The tint percentage of the spot color when printed

4. Which answer is true when using the Channel Mixer?

    a. Increasing the values of a specific channel of a RGB image will shift the color toward its complimentary color.

    b. Decreasing the values of a specific channel of a CMYK image will shift the color toward its complimentary color.

    c. Increasing the values of a specific channel of a CMYK image will shift the color toward its complimentary color.

    d. Decreasing the values of a specific channel of an RGB image will shift the color toward its complimentary color.

5. Which answer is incorrect on how to load an alpha channel as a selection?

    a. Choose Select > Load Selection.

    b. Alt/Option+click on the channel thumbnail.

    c. Control/Command+click on the channel name.

    d. Click the load selection button in the Channels palette.

6. What do you need to do first when using Quick Mask mode?

    a. Create a selection.

    b. Select the alpha channel.

    c. Click on the Quick Mask button.

    d. Choose Quick Mask from the Edit menu.

7. Where is a saved selection stored?

    a. In the Select menu

    b. To your hard drive

    c. In the Layers palette

    d. In the Channels palette

8. How do you edit the mask of a saved alpha channel?

    a. Paint on the Layer.

    b. Paint on the layer mask.

    c. Paint on the Quick Mask overlay.

    d. Paint on the alpha channel with black, white, or a shade of gray.

CHAPTER 14—REVIEW QUESTIONS

1. What color should you add to an image that has a blue cast?

    a. Blue

    b. Green

    c. Yellow

    d. Magenta

2. How does the Relative option affect an image when using the Selective Color command?

    a. The Relative option enables selective color correction only on selected channels.

    b. The Relative option enables selective color correction only within an active selection.

    c. The Relative option adjusts only the desired percentage increase or decrease for a particular color.

    d. The Relative option adjusts all four CMYK values to match the desired percentage increase or decrease chosen for a particular color.

3. When using the Color Range command, how do you add colors to the selected range?

    a. Press the Alt/Option key and click on the image.

    b. Press the Shift key and click on the image.

    c. Press Alt/Option+Shift and click on the image.

    d. Select the eyedropper from the toolbox and click on the image.

4. Which color adjustment command is appropriate for an image that has a color cast?

    a. Equalize

    b. Tolerance

    c. Color Balance

    d. Brightness/Contrast

5. How does a high Image Cache Level setting affect the Histogram display?

    a. Accurate pixel information

    b. Inaccurate pixel information

    c. It has no affect on the Histogram information.

    d. It increases the amount of pixel information displayed.

6. Where do you turn off the Image Cache?

    a. Uncheck the Image Cache box in the Histogram dialog box.

    b. Uncheck the Image Cache box in the Levels dialog box.

    c. Toggle the option off by selecting View > Image Cache.

    d. Select File > Preferences > Image Cache.

7. How do you set the white point in an image?

    a. Select the eyedropper tool in the toolbox and click on a highlight in the image.

    b. Select the color sampler tool in the toolbox and click on a highlight in the image.

    c. Select the white eyedropper in the Levels dialog box and click on a highlight in the image.

    d. Select the white eyedropper in the Color Range dialog box and click on a highlight in the image.

8. How do you set the target values for shadows and highlights?

    a. Adjust the settings in the Separations setup dialog box.

    b. Use the eyedropper to select sample pixels in the shadow and highlight areas in an image.

    c. Double-click the eyedroppers in the Curves or Levels dialog box and enter the values in the Color Picker.

    d. Double-click the eyedroppers in the Curves or Levels dialog box to open the Target Value dialog box and enter the values.

CHAPTER 15—REVIEW QUESTIONS

1. Which format does not support lossless compression?

    a. PNG

    b. JPEG

    c. TIFF

    d. Photoshop Native

2. Which format supports spot color channels?

    a. TGA

    b. BMP

    c. DCS 1.0

    d. DCS 2.0

3. Which format only supports 256 colors?

    a. GIF

    b. JPEG

    c. TIFF

    d. PCX

4. Which format is commonly used for the World Wide Web?

    a. EPS

    b. DCS 2.0

    c. TIFF

    d. JPEG

5. Which format supports layers?

    a. Photoshop Native

    b. TIFF

    c. EPS

    d. DCS 2.0

6. Which of the following is a lossy compression?

    a. Run Length Encoding (RLE)

    b. Tagged Image File Format (TIFF)

    c. Lempel-Ziv-Welch (LZW)

    d. Joint Photographic Experts Group (JPEG)

7. Which file format supports images in CMYK mode?

    a. GIF

    b. PCX

    c. PNG

    d. TIFF

8. Which file format can be exported instead of saved?

    a. JPEG

    b. GIF

    c. PNG

    d. TIFF

9. Which format cannot contain an alpha channel?

    a. TIFF

    b. DCS 2.0

    c. JPEG

    d. Photoshop Native

10. Which format is most commonly found on Macintosh systems?

    a. PCX

    b. PICT

    c. PDF

    d. PNG

11. Which format should be used with other Acrobat files?

    a. PDF

    b. PNG

    c. PICT

    d. Photoshop Native

12. Which file format does not support clipping paths?

 a. EPS

 b. GIF

 c. DCS 1.0

 d. DCS 2.0

CHAPTER 16—REVIEW QUESTIONS

1. What happens to an image when GCR is applied?

 a. Cyan, magenta, and yellow are reduced.

 b. Black is added to cyan, magenta, and yellow.

 c. Cyan, magenta, yellow, and black are reduced.

 d. Cyan, magenta, and yellow are replaced with black.

2. Which term is NOT used to describe screen frequency?

 a. Screen angle

 b. Linescreen

 c. Screen ruling

 d. LPI

3. Why would you adjust dot gain?

 a. To create separations

 b. To adjust the color settings

 c. To apply more ink to the paper

 d. To prevent the midtones from printing dark and muddy on press

4. How do you print only one color separation plate?

 a. Convert the plate to a matching spot color.

 b. You can't because the Separation option in the Print dialog box will only print all four plates.

 c. Click on the corresponding cyan, magenta, yellow, or black button in the Print dialog box.

 d. Click off the eye icons of the channels you don't want to print and choose Print.

5. Which is the fastest method for transferring image data to an output device?

 a. PDF

 b. ASCII

 c. Binary

 d. Encoded

CHAPTER 17—REVIEW QUESTIONS

1. Which format should be used to display a photographic image on the World Wide Web?

 a. GIF

 b. EPS

 c. JPEG

 d. TIFF

2. Which format should be used to display a line drawing on the World Wide Web?

   a. GIF

   b. EPS

   c. JPEG

   d. TIFF

3. What is an appropriate print resolution for an image that will be displayed on a monitor?

   a. 72 pixels/inch

   b. 72 lines/inch

   c. 600 pixels/inch

   d. 133 lines/inch

4. Which format should be used to display a photographic image on the World Wide Web without discarding any image information?

   a. EPS

   b. PNG

   c. TIFF

   d. JPEG

5. Which color table should you use to make the colors match as closely as possible to the original image when exporting a GIF file?

   a. Uniform

   b. System

   c. Adaptive

   d. Black Body

6. Which of the following formats uses lossy compression?

   a. GIF

   b. PNG

   c. TIFF

   d. JPEG

7. Which of the following formats does not support transparency?

   a. GIF

   b. PNG

   c. TGA

   d. JPEG

8. In which image mode must an image be in order to run the NTSC Colors filter?

   a. RGB

   b. CMYK

   c. Grayscale

   d. Indexed Color

9. How many colors does the GIF file format support?

   a. 256

   b. 32,000

   c. 65,000

   d. 24 million

CHAPTER 18—REVIEW QUESTIONS

1. What is the default RGB ICC profile used by Photoshop to define the working RGB space?

   a. <u>sRGB</u>

   b. CIE RGB

   c. SMPTE 240M

   d. Colormatch RGB

2. For which device does the Adobe Gamma utility create an ICC profile?

   a. Scanner

   b. Printer

   c. <u>Monitor</u>

   d. Entire system

3. Which of the following RGB color profiles is NOT a standard video format?

   a. NTSC

   b. SMPTE-240M

   c. PAL/SECAM

   d. <u>Colormatch RGB</u>

4. Which file type supports ICC profile embedding?

   a. <u>TIFF</u>

   b. TGA

   c. BMP

   d. PCX

5. Which file type supports ICC profile embedding in Lab mode?

   a. JPEG

   b. PICT

   c. PCX

   d. <u>Photoshop Native</u>

6. Which image mode should never be set for automatic conversion when a profile mismatch is encountered?

   a. Lab

   b. RGB

   c. <u>CMYK</u>

   d. Indexed Color

7. What command should you use to convert the profile of an open image to match the current working profile?

   a. Space to Space

   b. Channel Mixer

   c. Colormatch RGB

   d. <u>Profile to Profile</u>

8. Which of the following is NOT an option to use as a CMYK color space definition?

   a. ICC

   b. <u>CMM</u>

   c. Tables

   d. Built-in

9. What should you do to force Photoshop to display an RGB image directly, with no compensation for the monitor profile?

   a. Select Monitor RGB as the working RGB color space.

   b. Set the primaries to Standard Illuminant A in the RGB setup dialog box.

   c. Disable the Adobe Gamma utility by removing it from the control panel.

   d. Deselect the Display Using Monitor Compensation in the RGB setup dialog box.

CHAPTER 19—REVIEW QUESTIONS

1. What is the first step to add a new action while in Button Mode?

   a. Select the Record button from the Actions palette.

   b. Select the New Action button from the Actions palette.

   c. Select the Insert New Action from the Actions palette menu.

   d. Select the Button Mode option from the Actions palette menu to turn off Button Mode.

2. How do you insert a path into an action?

   a. Start recording an action, and then create a path.

   b. Start recording an action, then select Insert Path from the Actions palette menu and create a path.

   c. Start recording an action, then select an existing path and select Insert Path from the Actions palette menu.

   d. Start recording an action, use the selection tool to specify which direction points to include, and then select Insert Path from the Actions palette menu.

3. What do you click on to create a new action set?

   a. The New Set button in the Actions palette

   b. The Record button in the Actions palette

   c. The New Action button in the Actions palette

   d. The New Set and Action button in the Actions palette

4. During playback, which options place a delay of set duration after each command?

   a. Pause

   b. Step by step

   c. Accelerated

   d. Decelerated

5. Which of the following tools can be used in an action?

   a. Eraser

   b. Airbrush

   c. Paintbrush

   d. Paintbucket

6. Which of the following is an option for the keyboard equivalent for an action?

    a. Ctrl+C/Command+C

    b. Alt+F/Option+F

    c. Ctrl+Shift+F4/Command+Shift+F4

    d. Alt+Shift+F4/Option+Shift+F4

7. How do you create an action that turns the ruler's visibility on and off?

    a. Begin recording, and then select View > Show Rulers.

    b. Begin recording, select Insert Menu Item, and then select View > Show Rulers.

    c. Begin recording, and then select Window > Show Rulers.

    d. Begin recording, select Insert Menu Item, and then select Window > Show Rulers.

8. What command do you use so that you can open all of the pages of a PDF file in Photoshop?

    a. Open command

    b. Open As command

    c. Contact Sheet command

    d. Multi-page PDF to PSD command

Glossary

A

Additive Color A color determined by a model that describes how light is combined, usually RGB. *See* RGB.

Additive Primaries Red, green, and blue light—the fundamental components of the RGB color model. *See* RGB.

Aliasing The stairstep effect at the edge of a line or area of color caused by displaying the line or area of color as pixels. *See* Anti-aliasing.

Amiga IFF Amiga Interchange File Format. A raster image file format prevalent on the Commodore Amiga computer platform (including Video Toaster).

ANPA Color A spot color model developed by the American Newspaper Association and used mainly in newspaper applications.

Alpha Channel 1. In Photoshop, stored mask and selection data in an image.
2. The opacity and transparency data in an image.

Anti-aliasing A technique to reduce the effect of aliasing by interpolating pixels of intermediate color along displayed edges. *See* Aliasing.

ASCII   The American Standard Code for Information Interchange. This system of assigning numbers to characters is recognized by almost all computer platforms. It is commonly used for files containing text.

B

Background Color   In Photoshop, the color used to make gradient fills and fill in the erased areas of an image.

Banding   When producing a gradient, the distinct change of tones that appear as bands of color.

Baseline   An imaginary line on which the majority of the characters in a typeface rest.

Baseline Shift   1. Moving a character or characters vertically from the baseline. 2. The amount of the move from the baseline.

Bézier Curve   A mathematically defined curve, characterized by having two endpoints and two control or direction points.

Bitmap   A raster image containing only black and white tones.

Black Point   The darkest shadow in an image.

Bleed   1. The extension of an image to or beyond the cut line of a page. 2. The amount that the image extends beyond the cut line.

Blur   To smear or make an area less distinct.

BMP   A raster image format common on Windows systems.

Brightness   The attribute of light-source colors by which emitted light is ordered continuously from light to dark in correlation with its intensity.

Browser   An application specially designed to view HTML documents on the World Wide Web.

Bump Map   A raster image, usually grayscale, used to indicate areas of relief and depression.

Bump Plate   On a four-color process job, a fifth plate that carries a spot color to add punch to a particular color.

Burn   The process of selectively darkening an area of an image.

C

Cache   Specialized RAM used as a temporary storage area for information that is transferred between physical RAM and the hard disk.

Calibration   The process of color correcting a device to match other devices (scanners, monitors, printers).

Cast   A color tint throughout an image.

CCITT Group 4   Consultative Committee for International Telephony and Telegraphy. A common compression method used for bitmap images and faxes.

Channel   In Photoshop, stored mask or selection data or spot color information.

CIE Color Model   Also L*a*b or Lab color model. A color model using Lightness and an a* and b* component. The a* component describes the red/green axis, and the b* describes the yellow/blue axis. This is an objective, device-independent color model.

CIELAB Commission Internationale d'Eclairage   The L*a*b color model devised by CIE. *See* CIE color model.

Clipboard   A storage area allocated by the operating system used to store data temporarily.

Clipping Group   In Photoshop, a layer that is used to control the relative transparency and opacity of another layer.

Clipping Path   A path embedded in a raster image, used to designate areas of opacity and transparency in a page layout application.

Color Depth   The number of colors that each pixel in an image is capable of displaying.

Color Lookup Table (CLUT)   A limited number of indexed colors (usually fewer than 256) used to describe each pixel in a raster image.

Color Separations   The individual color plates made from the process and spot colors in an image.

Color Space   1. A coordinate system in which each point represents a color defined by its position in space.
2. In Photoshop, the gamut of colors that a device is capable of reproducing.

Color Wheel   A system of displaying an entire color model's gamut on a 2D disk.

Colorimeter   A machine that measures the way an object either reflects or transmits light across the visible spectrum, and records the values that correlate with the way the human eye sees color.

Color Management Module (CMM)   Software to calibrate the display and printing of color images.

Composite Channel   In Photoshop, the combined results of the individual channels. The individual channels are determined by the image mode.

Compression   Any of a number of processes used to encode image data to reduce file size.

CompuServe GIF   A raster image file format commonly used for images on the World Wide Web; it is limited to 256 colors.

Continuous Tone   An image with intermediate values between highlights and shadows, typified by photographic images.

Contrast   The overall differences in color and tone in an image.

CMYK   Cyan, magenta, yellow, black. The standard color model for printing applications.

Crop   The process of removing unwanted areas from around an image or printed page.

Cursor   The icon that represents the current location of the mouse or insertion point on the monitor.

Curves   In Photoshop, an editable representation of the overall tonal range of an image.

D

DCS Format   Desktop Color Separations. A derivative of the Encapsulated PostScript format, commonly used for spot color separations.

Densitometer   An instrument for determining optical or photographic density.

DIC Color Guide   A spot color system created by Dainippon Ink and Chemicals and used primarily in Japan.

Digimarc   The Digimarc filters embed a digital watermark in a raster image.

Disk Cache   Specialized RAM used as a temporary storage area for information that is transferred between physical RAM and the hard disk.

Displacement Map   A raster image that determines how far pixels in another image should be moved.

Distort   Any change made to an image that alters its original shape or form.

Dithering   A method of simulating unavailable colors by using patterns of available colors.

Dodge   The process of selectively darkening an area of an image.

Dot Gain   Occurs when the specified printer's halftone dots change as the ink spreads and is absorbed by paper.

Double-Byte Fonts   Fonts designed to contain more characters than the Roman fonts, used specifically for Asian languages.

Downsampling   The process of decreasing the pixel dimensions of an image.

Dpi   Dots per inch. Used to measure the maximum number of dots of ink in every inch that a printer can produce. Also used to denote the number of dots in every inch that a scanner is capable of capturing.

Duotone   A printing technique using two colored inks in place of tinted grays.

Dynamic Range   The overall range of tones in an image.

E

EPS, EPSF   Encapsulated PostScript, Encapsulated PostScript Format. A common graphic format, used to describe both raster and vector graphics and found primarily in printing applications.

Exposure   In Photoshop, the amount of change to the image while using the burn or dodge tool.

F

Feathering   In Photoshop, the blending of a selection with its surrounding area.

File Format   Any one of a number of different methods used to store data.

Filmstrip   A file format used mainly by Adobe Premiere but that can also be opened in Adobe Photoshop.

Focoltone Colors   A system of defining process and spot colors devised by Focoltone International.

Foreground Color   In Photoshop, the color used to paint, fill, and stroke selections.

Four-Color Process   A printing process using cyan, magenta, yellow, and black inks.

G

Gamma   The value of the relative brightness of a particular monitor. Adjustments to the gamma are made when calibrating the monitor and color-correcting an image.

Gamut   The range of colors capable of being reproduced by a color model.

GCR   Gray Component Replacement. Substitutes black ink for areas where cyan, magenta, and yellow produce gray.

GIF   Graphic Interchange Format. A raster image file format commonly used for images on the World Wide Web and limited to 256 colors.

GIF89a   A raster image file format commonly used for images on the World Wide Web and limited to 256 colors. The GIF89a format specifically supports interlacing, transparency, and limited animation.

Gradient   A smooth transition from one color into another.

Grayscale   An image consisting only of gray tones, such as a black-and-white photograph.

H

Halftone   Bitmap image in which the illusion of a range of gray tones is created by varying the size or spacing of tiny dots of uniform density. Similar techniques are used for each color in process printing.

Halo   A fringe of pixels caused by anti-aliasing remaining after cutting an image from the background.

High key   An image consisting of mostly highlight tones.

Highlight   The lightest spot or area caused by receiving the greatest amount of illumination.

Histogram   In Photoshop, a graphical representation of the occurrence of the luminosities or different color values in an image.

HSB   Hue, Saturation, and Brightness. A color model using these components to define each color.

HSL   Hue, Saturation, and Lightness. A color model using these components to define each color.

HTML   Hypertext Markup Language. The standardized markup language used to describe text and images on the World Wide Web.

Hue   1. The attribute of colors that permits them to be classed (as red, yellow, green, and so on).
2. A quantifiable measurement of this attribute.

I, J, K

ICC profiles   International Color Consortium profiles. A color space description embedded in an image.

Image Mode   The color model used to describe the pixels in a raster image (for example, RGB, CMYK).

Image Resolution   The number of pixels per inch (ppi) in a raster image.

Indexed Color   A raster image that uses a color lookup table to define a restricted color set (fewer than 256).

Interlaced   The display of every other row of pixels at a time when an image is displayed on screen.

Interpolation   The mathematical process of estimating intermediate values.

JPEG   Joint Photographic Experts Group. 1. The lossy compression scheme used to make the file sizes of continuous tone images smaller.
2. The JPEG File Interchange Format, a common raster image file format that uses the JPEG compression scheme.

Kerning   The adjustment of horizontal space between individual characters in a line of text.

Knock Out   A printing technique that prints overlapping objects without mixing inks. The ink for the underlying elements does not print (knocks out) in the areas where the object overlaps.

KPCMS   Kodak Precision Color Management System. Controls the color mode and display of Photo CD images by specifying profiles for the source film and the destination output device.

L

Lab   Also L*a*b. A device-independent color model designed by the CIE. *See* CIE Color Model.

Layer Mask   In Photoshop, a mask or selection used to determine areas of transparency and opacity on a layer.

Leading   The amount of space added between lines of text. The term originally referred to the thin lead spacers that printers used to physically increase space between lines of metal type.

Levels   In Photoshop, the depiction of tonal information in a histogram that can be edited to adjust shadow, midtone, and highlight areas.

Lightness   The attribute of object colors by which the object appears to reflect or transmit more or less of the incident light; the brightness of a color.

Lossless Compression   Any one of a number of compression methods used to reduce the size of image files without discarding image data, typified by LZW compression.

Lossy Compression   Any one of a number of compression methods used to reduce the size of image files by discarding image data, typified by JPEG compression.

Low Key   An image consisting mainly of shadow tones.

Lpi   Lines per inch. In halftoning, the number of lines of halftone dots per linear inch.

Luminance   1. Brightness of a lighted area as perceived by the eye.
2. The quantified value of this brightness.

Luminosity   Relative brightness of a color.

LZW Compression   Lempel-Ziv-Welch compression. A lossless compression method used widely for reducing the file size of raster images.

M

Mask   A device used to protect areas of an image from change. In Photoshop, this is accomplished through a selection.

Midtone   The tones in an image toward the middle, between the shadows and highlights, typified by a 50% gray value.

Moiré Pattern   An interference pattern produced when two halftone screens are laid on top of one another.

Monitor Resolution   The number of pixels that a monitor is capable of displaying, expressed in width × height.

Monochrome   An image in a single hue.

Monotone   Grayscale images printed with a single, nonblack ink.

Multichannel   In Photoshop, an image mode in which each component channel is separated and there is no composite channel.

N, O

Noise   Random interference in any part of the digital imaging process (for example, dust and dirt on a scanner bed).

Nonlossy Compression   *See* Lossless compression.

NTSC   National Television Standards Committee. The standard composite video signal in the United States. This standard has been largely superceded by the SMPTE-C broadcast standard.

Object Linking and Embedding (OLE)   A way to transfer and share information between applications.

Opacity   The quality of an object that makes it difficult to see through.

Out-of-Gamut   Refers to colors defined in the RGB gamut that do not have equivalents in the CMYK gamut.

P

PAL   Phase Alternation Line. The video encoding/decoding standard used throughout most of Europe.

Palette   A range or group of specialized colors (for example, the Web palette).

PANTONE Colors   A color system devised by PANTONE, Inc., used for print application. PANTONE has palettes for both spot and process colors, and is widely used by graphics professionals in the United States.

Path   A mathematically defined vector-based object.

PCX   A raster image file format.

PDF   Portable Document Format. A page description format used with Adobe Acrobat.

Perspective   Representation in an image of parallel lines as converging in order to give the illusion of depth and distance.

PICT Format   A raster image file format widely used on Macintosh systems

Pict Resource Format   A PICT file contained in a Mac OS file's resource fork.

Pixel   Picture Element. The smallest distinguishable component of a raster image.

Pixel Dimensions   The number of pixels in an image, measured in width x height.

Plate   An individual color separation.

PMS   PANTONE Matching System. *See* PANTONE Colors.

PNG   Portable Network Graphics. A raster image file format developed as a patent-free alternative to the GIF, used mainly on the World Wide Web.

Posterize   To choose the number of tonal levels (or brightness values) for each channel in an image and then map pixels to the closest matching level.

PostScript   A page description language created by Adobe Systems. The industry standard for print applications.

Preserve Transparency   In Photoshop, the option to protect the transparent pixels in a layer.

Primary Colors   The component colors of a color model (for example, red, green, and blue for the RGB color model).

Print Resolution   The number of dots in an inch capable of being produced by a printer.

Process Color   A color constructed using the CMYK color model. *See* CMYK.

Process Printing   Color printing using subtractive primary colorants of cyan, magenta, and yellow, usually with the addition of black.

Proofs   A representation matching the appearance of the final printed piece.

Q

Quadtone   A printing technique using four colored inks in place of tinted grays.

Quartertones   The tones in an image tending toward the highlight areas typified by a 25% gray value.

Quick Mask Mode   In Photoshop, the mode in which selected pixels are displayed as an overlay color (typically red) and selections can be edited using the painting tools. *See* Standard Mode.

R

RAM   Random Access Memory. The physical memory used to store information temporarily in a computer.

Raster   The grid in which pixels reside in an image.

Rasterize   The conversion of vector objects into pixel information.

Raw   An image file format consisting of a stream of bytes describing the color information in the file. Each pixel is described in binary format, with 0 equaling black and 255 equaling white (for images with 16-bit channels, the white value is 65,535).

Resampling   The process of changing the pixel dimensions of an image.

Resampling Up   The process of increasing the pixel dimensions of an image.

Resolution   1. The frequency of pixels in an image, measured in ppi.
2. The pixel dimensions of an image.

Retouching   The process of adding or removing elements to or from an image.

RGB   A color model that uses the additive properties of red, green, and blue light to describe colors. Used exclusively by computer monitors and televisions.

Rubylith   A mask material used to protect areas from accepting paint.

Run Length Encoding (RLE)   A popular lossless compression method that compresses identical sequences of pixels (blocks of color).

S

Saturation   Chromatic purity or degree of difference from the gray having the same lightness.

Scitex CT   Scitex Continuous Tone. An image file format used on Scitex computers.

Scratch Disk   In Photoshop, hard drive space used as virtual memory. *See* Virtual Memory.

Screen Angle   The rotation or the arrays of halftone dots for each process color to avoid moiré patterns.

Screen Frequency   The number of halftone dots per unit area, usually measured in lpi.

SECAM   Sequential Couleur Avec Memoire (Sequential Color with Memory). The video encoding/decoding standard used in France and in the former Soviet Union.

Secondary Color   Colors produced from combinations of primary colors (for example, the additive primaries red and blue combine to produce magenta, a subtractive primary).

Separations   The individual color plates made from the process and spot colors in an image.

Shadow   Partial darkness or obscurity within a part of an image.

Sharpen   To make the details of an area more distinct.

Silhouette   The outline of an object or area viewed as enclosing a mass.

SMPTE-C   Society of Motion Picture and Television Engineers. Broadcast standard for color television in the United States. Largely replaces the NTSC standard.

Specular Highlight   The highlight that appears on an object where the angle of reflection is equal to the angle of incidence.

Spot Color   Printed color other than black and not one of the process colors (cyan, magenta, or yellow).

Standard Mode   In Photoshop, the typical mode used for viewing and editing an image. *See* Quick Mask Mode.

Stroke   In Photoshop, the process of applying a painting tool along a selection boundary or path.

Subtractive Color   A color determined by a model that describes how pigments are combined, usually CMYK. *See* CMYK.

Subtractive Primaries   Cyan, magenta, and yellow pigments, the fundamental components of the CMY color model. *See* CMYK.

SWOP   Specifications for Web Offset Publication. A standard printing model.

T

TGA Format   A raster image file format used primarily for video applications and popularized by the Truevision® Targa video cards.

Three-quarter Tones   The tones in an image tending toward the shadow areas typified by a 75% gray value.

TIFF   Tagged Image File Format. A common raster image file format, used especially in printing and page layout applications.

Tint   An overall color cast in an image.

Tolerance   In Photoshop, the range of colors that will be selected by the magic wand tool.

Toyo Color Finder   A spot color system consisting of colors based on the most common printing inks used in Japan

devised by the Toyo Ink Manufacturing Co.

Tracking   The average space between characters in a block of text. Sometimes also referred to as letter spacing.

Transfer Function   A set of values that enables you to compensate for dot gain between the image and film.

Transparency   The quality of an object that makes it easy to see through.

Trap   The slight intentional overlapping of the edges of printed elements to compensate for minor variations in registration.

Tritone   A printing technique using three colored inks in place of tinted grays.

TWAIN Interface   Toolkit Without an Interesting Name. A standard that enables graphic programs to communicate with image acquisition devices without knowing anything specific about the devices.

U, V, W

UCR   Undercolor Removal. Used to add depth to shadow and midtone areas by reducing the amount of cyan, magenta, and yellow inks and replacing them with an appropriate amount of black.

Unsharp Mask (USM)   In Photoshop, a filter used to sharpen an image by increasing the contrast of detected edges.

Value   The numeric quantities of the component primaries (for example, RGB values).

Vector   A mathematical entity that has both length and direction. Vectors are used to define objects typified by line art and text and can be arbitrarily scaled without losing detail.

Vignette   An image that shades off gradually into the surrounding background.

Virtual Memory   Hard disk space used as RAM.

VLUT   Video Lookup Table. A set of colors controlled by the video card.

Watermark   In Photoshop, a digital signature embedded, usually invisibly, in an image. *See* Digimarc.

White Point   1. The lightest highlight in an image.
2. The whitest white that a monitor can display.

Wizards/Assistants   In Photoshop, subroutines that ask specific questions about a procedure and act accordingly to simplify the task.

X, Y, Z

X-axis   In the Cartesian coordinate system, the horizontal reference line on a grid, chart, or graph.

Y-axis   In the Cartesian coordinate system, the vertical reference line on a grid, chart, or graph.

ZIP Compression   A common compression method used for all types of computer files.

A PPENDIX C

BIBLIOGRAPHY

IN PRINT

Adobe Photoshop 5.0 User Guide (San Jose, CA: Adobe Systems Inc., 1998).

Adobe Photoshop 5 Classroom in a Book (San Jose, CA: Adobe Press, 1997).

Barry Haynes and Wendy Crumpler, *Photoshop 5 Artistry: A Master Class for Photographers, Artists, and Production Artists* (Indianapolis, IN: New Riders Press, 1998).

Frank Cost, *Pocket Guide to Digital Printing* (Albany, NY: Delmar Publishers, 1997).

Linnea Dayton and Jack Davis, *The Photoshop 4 Wow! Book* (Berkeley, CA: Peachpit Press, 1998).

Donnie O'Quinn and Matt LeClair, *Photoshop in a Nutshell: A Desktop Quick Reference* (Sebastopol, CA: O'Reilly, 1997).

Richard Lynch, *Photoshop 5 How-To* (Indianapolis, IN: Sams Publishing, 1998).

Official Adobe Photoshop 5 Book (San Jose, CA: Adobe Press, 1998).

Official Adobe Electronic Publishing Guide (San Jose, CA: Adobe Press, 1998).

Official Adobe Print Publishing Guide (San Jose, CA: Adobe Press, 1998).

Adobe Magazine (San Jose, CA: Adobe Systems).

ELECTRONIC

Adobe Photoshop Online Help at `http://www.adobe.com`

The Graphics File Format Page at `http://www.dcs.ed.ac.uk/~mxr/gfx/`

Graphics File Formats FAQ at `http://www.netmeg.net/faq/computers/graphics/fileformats-faq/`

Graphics viewers, editors, utilities, and information at `http://www2.ncsu.edu/bae/people/faculty/walker/hotlist/graphics.html`

Encapsulated PostScript at `http://infaut.et.uni-magdeburg.de/~arne/helpfile/postscr/eps.html`

INDEX

SYMBOLS

1-bit images, 93
3D Transform filter (Filters menu), 306-307, 311-314
    Anchor Point tool, 309
    camera/trackball controls, 309-310
    Cube tool, 307
    rendering options, 311
    Selection tool, 308
    Sphere tool, 307
8-bit channels, 17, 99
    in saved selections, 115
8-bit images, 106
    in Grayscale mode, 95
16-bit images, 17, 106
    in Grayscale mode, 95
48-bit images, 17
50% Gray option (Fill dialog box), 73, 204
64-bit images, 17

A

.abr files, 195
Absolute mode (Selective Color dialog box), 409
Accelerated mode (Playback Options), 492
Acrobat (Adobe), 87, 430
    see also .PDF files
actions, 489
    copying, 498
    customizing prerecorded, 489
    deleting, 498

duplicating, 498
loading, 498
nesting, 489
new
　Copyright example,
　　495-496
　keyboard shortcuts
　　for, 493
　Legal set example,
　　495-496
　recording, 489
playing
　instructions for, 490
　Lizard Skin example,
　　490-492
　playback speeds, 492
　prerequisites, 490
resetting to defaults, 498
saving batched files, 499
sets, 489
　changing actions in, 498
Snapshots with, 492
structure of, 490
undoing, 492
Actions palette
Button Mode option, 493
commands, 494-495
Image Effects set, 489
modal controls, 494
New Action button, 493
Play button, 490
Playback options, 492
active selections, 342
color adjustments, 405-408
copying, 360
Actual Pixels option
(View menu), 47
Adam7 option, 434
see also .PNG files
adding
arrowheads, 196
channels, 344-345
colors, 180
lighting effects, 322
paths/subpaths, 158
transparency masks, 201
Adjust pull-down menu
(Image menu), 263

adjustment layers, 263
color correction (Rose
　image example), 264-266
merging, 253
Adobe Acrobat, *see* Acrobat
Adobe After Effects, *see* After
Effects
Adobe Certified Experts
(ACEs) requirements, *see*
Photoshop Proficiency
Exam
Adobe Gamma utility,
474-476
monitor calibration, 473
Adobe Illustrator, *see*
Illustrator
Adobe Online, accessing,
43-44
Adobe PageMaker, *see*
PageMaker
Adobe Photoshop Settings
folder, 54-56
Adobe Premiere, *see* Premiere
After Effects (Adobe),
preparing images for, 466
AI (Adobe Illustrator) files,
importing (placing), 86-87
Airbrush tool, 33
Airbrush Options palette,
　190
cursor options, 183
Align Linked option
(Layer menu), 247-248
aligning layer elements,
246-248
alpha channels, 17, 40, 341
channels as masks, 342
converting to spot
　channels, 368
in Duotone mode, 97
duplicating, 346
in Grayscale mode, 95
layer masks as
　channels, 254
reordering, 345
reversing masks using, 410
saving, 359
　file formats for, 349

using with Lighting Effects
　filters, 328
using with Quick Mask, 359
vignette effects, 352
Ambience property
(Lighting Effects filter), 325
Anchor Point tool
(3D Transform filter), 309
anchor points (Bézier curves),
143
adding and subtracting,
　154-155
converting to corner points,
　157
"Andy" example image,
adjusting tonality, 386
angles
of brushes, 194
measuring, 53
animations, 101
ANPA Color
guide to, 179
swatch palettes, 181
Anti-Alias PostScript (General
Preferences dialog box), 22
anti-aliasing, 129-130
in Paint Bucket tool, 199
in Paintbrush tool, 190
in Type tool, 281
Apple Color Picker, 174
Apply Image dialog box
(Image menu), 360-362
applying
layer masks, 259-260
prerecorded actions,
　490-492
areas, selecting
shape-specific, 116-117
Arrange submenu
(Layer menu) options, 243
arrow keys, moving selections
using, 127
Arrowhead option (Line
tools options palette), 196
arrowheads
creating, 198
Line tool for, 196

ASCII encoding
in EPS (Encapsulated
PostScript) files, 427
in printed output, 451
Assistants, *see*
Wizards/Assistants
Assorted Brushes, 195
Auto Erase option
(Pencil tool), 191
Auto Kern option (Type
Tool dialog box), 284
Auto Levels command
(Image/Adjust menu), 388
automated procedures, *see*
actions
automation tools, 498
actions, 499-501
average-key images, 381

B

background colors
changing to
foreground, 173
Color palette, 181
Color Picker for, 174
default, 173
background layers, 239
transforming, 213
Background option
Fill dialog box, 204
Print Setup dialog box, 448
back up, Preferences file, 55
balancing colors, 396-398
Baseline field (Type Tool
dialog box), 284-285
Baseline Shift, 397-300
Batch dialog box (Actions
palette menu), 499
Beep option (General
Preferences dialog box), 22
Behind mode, 271
benchmark testing, 42
Bevel effect (Layer Effects
dialog box), 268
Bézier curves, 281
components, 143-144
see also paths
bicubic interpolation, 213
binary encoding
in .EPS files, 427
in printed output, 451

"Birds" example image
blending using Apply
Image, 362
blending using Calculations,
363-364
Bitmap mode, 93
converting to, 93-95
in electronic publishing,
462
filter support, 305
resolution methods
50% Threshold, 93
Custom Pattern, 94
Diffusion Dither, 94
Halftone Screen, 94
Pattern Dither, 94
bits, in color depth, 17
black, in color separations,
443-444
Black Generation pop-up
menu (CMYK Setup dialog
box), 444
Black option (Fill dialog box),
204
Black Output levels slider, 385
black triangles, meaning of, 34
Blend If option (Layer Options
dialog box), 250
blending
filter effects for, 335-336
in layers/channels
Apply Image for,
360-362
Calculations for, 360
using layer masks for,
256-257, 260
blending modes
Gradient tools, 199-203
Layers palette, 270
Behind, 271
Clear, 271
Color, 273
Color Burn, 272
Color Dodge, 272
Darken, 272
Difference, 272
Dissolve, 271
Exclusion, 273
Hard Light, 272
Lighten, 272

Luminosity, 273
Multiply, 271
Normal, 271
Overlay, 272
Saturation, 273
Screen, 271
Soft Light, 272
using blending modes,
273-274
painting tools, 184
Behind, 185
Clear, 185
Color, 186
Color Burn, 186
Color Dodge, 186
Darken, 186
default, 185
Difference, 186
Exclusion, 186
Hard Light, 186
Hue, 186
Lighten, 186
Luminosity, 187
Multiply, 185
Overlay, 185
Saturation, 186
Screen, 185
Soft Light, 186
using painting tools, 187
Blending option (Stroke
dialog box), 206
blur filters, editing using, 231
Blur submenu (Filter menu),
Gaussian Blur option, 231
Blur tool, 33
editing using, 227
blurring filters
Blur/Blur More filters
(Filters menu), 333
Gaussian Blur filter
(Filters menu), 333-335
Motion/Radial Blur filters
(Filters menu), 335
borders
active color swatches, 182
guides/grids, 52
Navigator palette, 49
in palette groups, 37
"Bottle" example image, using
Equalize command, 411

brightness, adjusting, 409-410
Brightness, in Color
  Picker, 174
Brightness/Contrast dialog
  box (Image/Adjust menu),
  409-410
Brush Size Cursors,
  options, 36
Brush Size option, painting
  tools, 183
brushes
  controls for, 193-194
  creating new, 193
  customizing, 195-196
  default, restoring, 195
  deleting, 194
  history brush, 223-226
  saving, 195
  size
    modifying, 192
    painting tools, 183
    pressure-sensitive
      stylus controls, 189
    size options, 218
  stored brushes, 195
Brushes palette
  brush features, 193-194
  brush sizes, 192-193
  edit tools with, 218
  menu options
    Delete Brush option, 194
    Load Brushes
      option, 195
    New Brush option, 193
    Replace Brushes
      option, 195
    Reset Brushes
      option, 195
    Save Brushes option, 195
  modifying brush sizes, 192
  painting tools with, 184
Built-In CMYK Model (CMYK
  Setup, dialog box), 480
bump (texture) maps, 328
burn tool, 229-230
Button Mode (actions palette),
  493

buttons
  actions for, 489
  Alignment (Type Tool
    dialog box), 285
  Custom (Color Picker), 178
  Delete State
    (History palette), 65
  New Action
    (Action palette), 493
  New Snapshot
    (History palette), 64
  Play (Actions palette),
    490, 493
  shortcut buttons, 44
  Transparency (Gradient
    tool), 203-204
  Zoom (Type Tool dialog
    box), 283

C

Calculations dialog box
  (Image menu), 363-364
calculations, channel, 360
calibrating, 471
  monitors
    Adobe Gamma utility,
      473-476
    chromaticity
      coordinates, 474
    ColorSync-compatible
      utilities, 473
    ICM 2-compatible
      utilities, 473
    phosphor types, 474
    white points, 475
  print/monitor output
    Built-In CMYK
      Model, 480
    CMYK Setup dialog box
      for, 480
    color separation
      tables, 482
    ICC profiles, 481
camera control tools
  (3D Transform filter),
  309-310
"Canoe" example image, Color
  Balance dialog box for color
  correction, 397-398

Canvas Size dialog box (Image
  menu), 82-83
captions
  adding to images, 85
  adding to printed
    images, 449
cascade displays (Windows
  systems), 49
cataloguing image selections,
  contact (sheets for), 500-501
channel calculations, 360
Channel Mixer dialog box
  (Image menu), 365
channels
  8-bit channels, 17
  activating, 343
  adding, 344-345
  alpha channels, 17,
    341, 351
    as masks, 342
    duplicating, 346
    filter effects, 354-355
    gray levels in, 115
    reordering, 345
    reversing masks, 410
    saving, 349, 359
    using with Quick
      Mask, 359
    vignette effects, 352
  in Bitmap mode, 95
  blending, 360-362
  channel calculations, 360
  in CMYK mode, 99
  color channels, 341
    deleting, 348
    duplicating, 346-347
    editing, 345-346
    in Multichannel
      mode, 348
  converting alpha to
    spot, 368
  in Duotone mode, 97
  in Grayscale mode, 95
  in Lab mode, 100
  in Monotone images, 97
  multichannel images,
    creating, 363-364
  in Multichannel mode, 105
  in RGB mode, 99
  splitting/merging, 349

spot channels, 366-369
thumbnails, viewing,
342-343
Channels palette, 342
layer mask alpha
channels, 254
palette menu options,
342-343, 348
Duplicate command, 347
Spot Color dialog box,
367-368
Save Selection as
Channel button, 358
Split Channels command,
349-351
chromaticity coordinates, 474
circular areas, selecting, 117
Clear History command, 65
Clear mode, 271
clipboard, export options, 22
clipping groups, 261-263
Clipping Path dialog box
(Paths palette menu) box, 162
clipping paths, 162, 144
creating, 162, 421
see also paths, 162
Clone Merge option
(Layer menu), 253
cloning, 219-222
see also Rubber Stamp tool
"Clouds" example image,
alpha channel filter effects,
354
CLUTs (Color Lookup Tables),
101
CMMs (Color Management
Modules), sources for, 477
CMYK (cyan, magenta,
yellow, black) mode, 17, 99
color channels, 341
color correcting RGB mode
images, 377
Color Picker features,
177-178
converting from RGB, 100

converting to Multichannel
mode, 105, 348
tips for working with, 375
"CMYK Balloons" example
image, adjusting tonality,
365
CMYK images
color separation options,
441
dot gain percentages, 443
proofs, color correcting, 408
CMYK Preview option
(View menu), 379
CMYK setup dialog box
File/Color Settings menu,
100, 441, 444
File/Color Management
menu, 480
color balance, adjusting
Channel Mixer for, 365
Color Balance dialog box
for, 396-398
Color Bar (Color palette), 182
Color Burn mode, 272
color channels, 341
deleting, 348
duplicating, 346-347
editing, 345-346
in Multichannel mode, 348
color correcting, 383-384
adjustment layers for,
264-266
brightness/contrast,
409-410
CMYK Preview
option, 379
in color channels, 341
converting to black and
white, 411-413
equalizing colors, 411
Input Levels slider
(Levels dialog box), 385
inverting colors, 410
reducing tonality, 414
selective, 408-409
tools for, 376-377
Variations dialog box,
394-396

Color Dodge mode, 272
Color Field (Color Picker),
173-175
"Color Grid" image example,
using blending modes,
273-274
Color Lookup Tables (CLUTs),
101
Color Management Module,
see **CMM**
Color Management submenu
(File menu), 477
CMYK Setup dialog
box, 480
RGB Setup dialog box,
478-479
Color mode, 273
Color palette, 173
changing color mode,
181-182
Color Bar options, 182
sliders, 182
Color Picker
accessing, 174
brightness options, 174
with CMYK Color Model,
177-178
color field options,
173-175
color slider, 174
Custom button, 178
custom colors, CMYK-
equivalent output, 179
default colors, 174
eyedropper. 295-297
with HSB Color Model,
174-175
with Lab Color Model,
176-177
lighting effects, 324
Photoshop vs. Apple and
Windows, 174
print background
options, 448
with RGB Color Model,
175-177
saturation options, 174
when to use, 173

Color Range dialog box (Select menu)
features, 405-406
Fuzziness option, 128-131
instructions for using, 407-408
preview options, 131, 406-407
Color Sampler tool, 377-378
color sampling, 377-378
color separations
black in, 443-444
preparing for layout applications, 453
printing individual separations, 451
setting in CMYK mode, 441
color settings
CMYK Setup dialog box, 480, 482
RGB Setup dialog box, 478-479
Color Settings (Preferences sub-menu), 54
color sliders (Hue/Saturation dialog box), 399-400
color spaces, 18, 477
CMYK Setup dialog box, 480
RGB Setup dialog box, 478-479
Colorize option (Hue/ Saturation dialog box), 400
colors
ANPAcolor, guide to, 179
balancing colors, 396-398
Blending modes, 187
blending tools, 199-203
CMYK Color Model printer output, 177
color channels, 341
color density, in Duotone curves, 97-98
color depth, 17-18
color guides/grids, changing, 52
color palettes, Indexed Color conversions, 463
Color Picker colors, 175

color ranges, 130-132
Color Sampler tool, 377-378
color settings, 54
color sliders, 174, 181-182
color swatches, 180, 182
color values, 175-177
colorizing, 400
correcting colors, tools for, 489
creating custom colors, 178, 180
DIC colors, guide to, 179
fade-out rates, changing, 188
filling using color, 205
flat color, .GIF format for, 457
Focaltone colors, guide to, 179
foreground/background colors, 173, 189
full color, .PNG format for, 458
hue/saturation, 398-400
intermediate colors, anti-aliasing, 129
inverting colors, 132
managing colors, 477-480
matching colors, 22
modes, colors in
  Bitmap, 93
  CMYK, 99
  Color Bar (Color Palette), 182
  Color palette, 181
  Color palette for, 181-182
  Duotone, 96, 179
  Grayscale, 95
  Indexed Color, 101-104
  Monotone, 96
  Multichannel, 105
  Quadtone, 97, 179
  RGB, 99
  Tritone, 97, 179
opacity settings, 187-188
out-of-gamut colors, 99, 132
  in CMYK model, 178
  warnings for, 177, 376

PANTONE colors, guides to, 179
previewing colors, 379
printer output, CMYK colors in, 177, 179
reversing color order, 201
saving color settings, 379
selecting colors
  Color palette for, 181-182
  color pickers for, 173
  Eyedropper tool, 182
  Swatches palette for, 180
spot colors, 366-369
Swatches palette, 180-181
tolerance values, 124
Toyo Color Finder colors, guide to, 179
Trumatch colors, guide to, 179
video-safe colors, 466
see also color channels, 341
Colors palette, 181
in painting tools, 184
ColorSync-compatible utilities, 473
columns, single, selecting, 119
commands
All (Select menu), 135
Auto Levels (Image/Adjust menu), 388
Automate (File menu), 487
collections (actions), 489
Color Range (Select menu), 130-132
Conditional Mode Change (Actions palette menu), 499
Crop (Image menu), 84
Define Pattern (Edit menu), 223
Deselect (Select menu), 134
Duplicate (Channels palette menu), 347
Fade (Filters menu), 335-336
Feather (Select menu), 129, 135
Filter Fade (Filters menu), 335-336
Free Transform, 156

Free Transform (Edit/ Transform menu), 216-217

Grow (Select menu), 133

Insert Menu (Actions palette menu), 495

Insert Paths (Actions palette menu), 495

Inverse (Select menu), 135

Invert (Image/Adjust menu), 410

Layer Via Copy, 245

Layer Via Cut, 246

Load Swatches (Swatches palette menu), 181

Lock Guides (View menu), 51

New View (View menu), 49

non-recordable, inserting in actions, 495

Open (File menu), 49

Preserve Transparency (Layers palette menu)

Purge (Edit menu), 42

Replace Swatches (Swatches palette menu), 181

Reselect (Select menu), 134

Reset Swatches (Swatches palette menu), 181

Save Swatches (Swatches palette menu), 181

selection tool options/settings, 128

Show/Hide Brushes (Window menu), 193

Show/Hide Info (Window menu), 182

Show/Hide Swatches (Window menu), 180

Similar (Select menu), 133

Transform Selection (Select menu), 135-136

Undo (Edit menu), 42

composite images, printing spot colors, 368-369

compositing, 360

compressing

flat color images, LZW-compression, 457

.JPEG files, 433

.PDF files, 430

.PNG files, 435

.PSD files, RLE-encoding, 422-423

.TIFF files, LZW-compression, 424, 457

Compuserve GIF, *see* **GIF**

Conditional Mode Change command (Actions palette menu), 499

Contact Sheet command (Actions palette menu), 500-501

context-sensitive menus, 45

rendering layers using, 289

contrast, adjusting, 409-410

control panel wizard

Adobe Gamma utility, 474-476

controls, lighting, 324

convert point tool, editing paths/subpaths, 157

converting

alpha to spot channels, 368

color images to black and white, 411-413

paths into selections, 161

selections into paths, 161

Copy Merge option (Layer menu), 253

copying

actions, 498

files, 419-420

Layer Effects, 269

layers, 245

paths/subpaths, 158

selections, 113

see also duplicating

"Copyright" example, creating new actions, 495

copyrights, adding to images, 85

corner points (Bézier curves), 143

converting to anchor points, 157

correcting colors

brightness/contrast, 409-410

Input Levels slider (Levels dialog box), 385

processes for, 383-384

selective, 408-409

tools for

Gamut Warning command, 376

Info palette, 377

Create Initial Snapshot option (History palette menu), 67

Create Quick Mask mode, 356

creating

actions, 495

clipping paths, 162

new layers, 242

paths/subpaths

freeform pen tool, 152-154

magnetic pen tool, 150-152

pen tool, 145-149

pattern stamps, 222-223

credits, adding to images, 85

Crop command (Image menu), 84

Crop tool, 84

cropping images

Crop command/Crop tool for, 84

file size issues, 460

Cube tool (3D Transform filter), 307

Current Tool (Status Bar), 43

cursors

brush size, 36

changing into eyedropper, 180

cursor options, 218

default settings, 35

other cursors, 36

painting cursors, 35

painting tool options, 183

setting preferences for, 54

curves

Bézier curves, 143-144, 281

edges, anti-aliasing for, 129

vectors, 16

Curves dialog box (Image/ Adjust menu)
eyedroppers, 387
features, 389-390
keyboard shortcuts, 393
Save/Load buttons, 379
Custom button (Color Picker), 178
Custom Pattern resolution method, 94
customizing, 21
brushes, 196
guides/grid appearance, 52
palette location, groupings, 37, 54
swatch palettes, 180
work area, 36-38, 54
cutting
layers, 246
selections, 113
see also copying; cropping images
cyan, magenta, yellow, black (CMYK) mode, *see* **CMYK mode**

D

Darken mode, 272
.DCS (Desktop Color Separation) files, 429-430, 436
DCS Options dialog box (Save As dialog box), 430
debossing effects, 328-330
Default colors tool, 33
defaults
actions
playback speed, 492
resetting to, 498
blending modes, 271
painting tools, 185
brushes, 195
brushes palette, 192
channels, 344
cursor settings, 35
eyedropper selections, 182
foreground/background colors, 173
halftone screens, 446

history palette, linear option, 66-67
hue (Color Picker), 174
image colors, bits in, 106
initial snapshots, 67
interpolation method, 213
leading values, 284
lighting effects, 325
mask colors, 344
palette, 37
palette location, 37-38
RAM (Windows), 24
resetting defaults, keyboard shortcuts, 132
RGB color space assignments, 478
states, number of, 62
status bar, 40
Swatches palette, 180-181
tools, 38
transparency mask opacity, 203
Define Pattern command (Edit menu), 207, 223
Define Pattern dialog box (Edit menu), 94
Delete Brush option (Brushes palette menu), 194
Delete command
Actions palette menu, 498
Channel palette menu, 348
History menu, 65
Delete State button (History palette), 65
deleting
actions, 498
brushes, 194
channels, 348
lighting effects, 322
paths/subpaths, 158
states (History palette), 62, 65-66
swatches, 180
see also purging, 65
densitometers, calibrating using, 449
Desktop Color Separations files, *see* **.DCS files**

Despeckle filter (Filter/Noise menu), 232
dialog boxes
3D Transform filter (Filters menu), 306
Anchor Point tool, 309
camera/trackball controls, 309-310
Cube tool, 307
rendering options, 311
Selection tool, 308
Sphere tool, 307
using the filter, 307
Add Noise (Filters menu), 318
Apply Image (Image menu), 360-362
Batch (Actions palette menu), 499
Brightness/Contrast (Image/Adjust menu), 409-410
Calculations (Image menu), 363-364
Canvas Size (Image menu), 82-83
Channel Mixer (Image menu), 365
Clipping Path (Paths palette menu) box, 162
CMYK Setup
File-Color Settings menu, 100, 441, 444
File/Color Management menu, 480
Color Balance (Image/ Adjust menu), 396-398
Color Range, 130-132
Color Range (Select menu), 130-132, 405-408
Curves (Image/Adjust menu), 389-390, 393
Define Pattern (Edit menu), 94
Display & Cursors, 35
Display and Cursors (File/ Preferences menu), 218
Dot Gain Curves (Dot Gain pop-up menu), 443

Duotone (Image-Mode menu), 97

Duplicate (Image menu), 360

EPS Options (Save As dialog box), 427

Equalize (Image/Adjust menu), 411

File Info (File menu), 85

Fill (Edit menu), 204-206

General Preferences, 22
  Save Palette Locations, 37

GIF89a Export Options (File/Export menu), 464-465

Gradient Editor, 203-204

Halftone Screens (Page Setup dialog box), 447

Histogram (Image menu), 380-383

Hue/Saturation (Image/Adjust menu), 398-402

Image Size (Image menu), 47, 81-82, 461

Indexed Color (Image-Mode menu)
  conversion options, 101-103
  dithering options, 463-464

JPEG Options (Save As dialog box), 434

Layer Effects (Layer palette), 267-268

Layer Options, 250

Layers Palette Options (Layers palette), 241

Levels (Image/Adjust menu)
  Input Levels slider, 385
  keyboard shortcuts, 388

Lighting Effects filter (Filters menu), 321-322
  controlling lights, 324-325
  embossing/debossing, 329-330
  predefined styles, 325

using filters with, 326-327

Make Work Path (Paths palette menu), 161

Memory, 24

New Adjustment Layer (Layer menu), 263

New Channel (Channels palette menu), 344-345

New Layer (Layer menu), 242

Online for Usage (Export Transparent Image Wizard/Assistant), 39

Page Setup (File menu), 447-449

Posterize (Image/Adjust menu), 414

Print (File menu),
  Print Selected Areas option, 451

Print option (Export Transparent Image Wizard/Assistant), 39

Record Stop (Insert Stop command), 497

Replace Color (Image/Adjust menu), 403-405

RGB Setup (File/Color Management menu), 100, 478-479

Save a Copy (File menu), 419-420

Save As (File menu), 419

Save as EPS (File/Save As menu), 453

Save/Load buttons in, 379

Selective Color (Image/Adjust menu), 408-409

Spot Color dialog box (Channels palette menu), 367-368

Stroke (Edit menu), 206

Threshold (Image/Adjust menu), 411-13

TIFF Options (Save As dialog box), 426

Transfer Functions (Page Setup dialog box), 447

Type Tools, 281-285

Units & Rulers, 50
  font units, 283

Unsharp Mask Preview (Filter/Sharpen menu), 233-234

Variations (Image/Adjust menu), 394-396

Diamond Gradient option (Gradient tool), 200

DIC Color Guide, 179

Difference mode, 272

Diffusion Dither resolution method, 94

direct selection tool, editing paths/subpaths, 155-156

direction lights, 323
  see also lighting effects

direction lines/points (Bézier curves), 143

Director (Macromedia), preparing images for, 466

discarding layer masks, 259-260
  see also deleting

disk space, information about, 40

Displace filter (Filters menu), 315, 317

displacement maps, 315

Display & Cursors options (File/Preferences menu), 35, 183, 218

display options, 54
  layer thumbnails, 241
  layer transparency, 242
  see also monitors

Dissolve blending mode, 185

Dissolve mode, 271

distorting images, 215

Distribute Linked option (Layer menu), 247-248

distributing layer elements, 246-248

dithering
  Custom Pattern option, 94
  Diffusion option, 94

Gradient tool for, 201
Indexed Color dialog
  box options, 463-464
Pattern option, 94
**Document Sizes option
  (Status Bar), 40, 251**
documents, *see* files; images
dodge tool, 229
**Dolly values (3D Transform
  filter), 309-310**
**Dot Gain Curves dialog
  box (Dot Gain pop-up
  menu), 443**
dot gain percentages, 443
downsampling, 74
  see also resampling
drag-and-drop method
  deleting channels, 348
  duplicating channels 347
  duplicating layers, 245
  moving layer elements, 246
  moving selections, 127-128
Drop Shadow brushes, 195
**Drop Shadow effect (Layer
  Effects dialog box), 267**
**drop shadows, creating,
  293-295**
**Duotone color mode,
  93, 96, 179**
  channels, 97
  converting
    to Duotone, 97-98
    *to Multichannel, 105,
      349*
  editing, 349
Duotone curves, 97-98
**Duotone dialog box (Image-
  Mode menu), 97, 379**
**Duplicate command
  (Channels palette menu),
  347**
**Duplicate dialog box
  (Image menu), 360**
duplicating
  channels, 346-347
  layers, 244-245
  see also copying
**Dust and Scratches filter
  (Filters menu), 319**

E

**Edge Contrast option
  (magnetic lasso tool), 123**
**edges, of brushes, controlling,
  193-194**
Edit menu
  Define Pattern command,
    94, 223
  Fill dialog box, 204-206
  Purge command, 42
  Stroke dialog box, 206
  Transform submenu
    Distort command, 215
    *Free Transform
      command, 216-217*
    *Numeric Transform
      dialog box, 215*
    *Perspective
      command, 215*
    Rotate command, 214
    Scale command, 213
    Skew command, 214
editing
  channels, 345-346
  images
    burn tool, 229-230
    cursor options, 218
    dodge tool, 229
    filters for, 231-233
    focus tools, 226-227
    history brush, 223-226
    sponge tool, 230
    stamp tools, 218-223
    toning tools, 229
    *transformation
      commands, 213-217*
    USM for, 234-235
  Layer Effects, 269
  layer masks, 257-259
  layers, 249
    Blend If option, 250
    Opacity percentage, 250
    *Preserve Transparency
      option, 249*
  paths/subpaths
    *add anchor point tool,
      155*
    convert point tool, 157
    direct selection tool, 156
    pen tool, 148-149
    *subtract anchor point
      tool, 155*
  Quick Mask selections
    for, 359
  spot channels, 368
  type layers, 288
  see also retouching;
    special effects
editing tools, palettes for, 218
**effects, special, *see* editing;
  image effects; special effects**
efficiency, improving, 42
**Efficiency indicator (Status
  Bar menu), 42**
electronic publishing
  file formats, 436
    selection criteria, 459
  image modes, 462
    flat color, 457
    full color, 458
    Grayscale, 457
  image resolution, 78-80
**embedded paths, JPEG
  support for, 433**
**Emboss effect (Layer
  Effects dialog box), 268**
embossing effects, 328-330
**Encapsulated PostScript file
  format, *see* .EPS**
encoding printed output, 451
**.EPS (Encapsulated
  PostScript) file format**
  anti-aliasing option, 22
  channels in, 349
  importing (placing), 86
  exporting to
    Illustrator, 421
  saving color
    separations in, 453
  when to use, 436
**EPS Options dialog box
  (Save As dialog box), 427**
**Equalize dialog box
  (Image/Adjust menu), 411**
equalizing colors, 411
Eraser tool, 33, 183, 191-192
errors, misregistration, 452

Exclusion mode, 273
export clipboard option
(General Preferences
dialog box), 22
export paths, 421
Export Transparent Image
Wizard/Assistant (Help
menu), 38-39
exporting
color separations, 453
files, 432
flat color images, 457
full color images, 458
GIF89a files, 464-465
Grayscale mode images, 457
image paths to
Illustrator, 421
to layout programs, 162
Photoshop images to
Illustrator, 421
raster images, 144
transparent images, 38
Eyedropper tools
adding/subtracting
colors using, 131
availability, 131
in Black/White Point
(Levels/Curves dialog
boxes), 391-392
filling/stroking type using,
295-297
in Levels/Curves dialog
box (Image/Adjust
menu), 387
in Options palette, 182
selecting/sampling colors
using, 182
in Swatches palette
cursor, 180

F

50% Threshold resolution
method, 93
Fade command (Filters menu),
335-336
fade-out rates, changing, 188
"Family" example images
retouching instructions,
220-221

Feather command
(Select menu), 129
feathering, 260
Feather command
(Select menu), 129, 135
selection tools for, 128
Transform Selection
command (Select menu),
135-136
values for, 128
Field of View values (3D
Transform filter), 309-310
file formats/filename
extensions, 417, 436
for brush settings, 195
changing, 419
.DCS (Desktop Color
Separation) files,
429-430, 436
in electronic publishing,
459
.EPS (Encapsulated
PostScript), 22, 86, 349,
421, 436, 453
.GIF (Graphic Interchange
Format) files, 432, 436,
457-458, 460
.GIF89a files, 432, 457,
464-465
.JPEG (Joint Photographic
Experts Group) files, 40,
349, 434, 436
in page layout programs,
421
.PCX files, 436
.PDF (Portable Document
Format/Adobe Acrobat)
files, 87, 430, 436
.PGA files, exporting
transparencies using, 465
.PICT files, 432, 436
.PNG (Portable Network
Graphics) files, 434-436,
458
.PSD (Photoshop native)
files, 422-423
saving
Save a Copy command,
419-420
Save As command, 419

.TIFF (Tagged Image File
Format) files, 424, 436
.TGA, transparency export
files, 466
File Info dialog box
(File menu), 85
printing image captions,
449
File menu
Automate command, 487
Color Management
submenu, 477-479
Color Settings submenu,
100, 441
File Info dialog box, 85
General Preferences
submenu, 54, 383
Display & Cursors
options, 35, 183, 218
General Preferences
options, 37
Guides & Grid options,
52
Transparency & Gamut
options, 242
Units & Rulers options,
283
Open command, 49
Page Setup dialog box,
447-449
Print dialog box, 451
Save As submenu, 453
Sharpen submenu, 233-234
files
batched, applying actions
to, 499
compressing, 40
displaying, 49
encoding, 427
image collections, 500-501
locations of, tracking, 40
management preferences,
setting, 54-56
saving
Image Previews
settings, 41
Save a Copy dialog
box, 419-420
Save As dialog box, 419

size concerns
   .GIF files, 458
   preview/thumbnail
      options, 41
   scan-related issues,
      76-79
   status information, 40
   see also compressing; file
      formats; images
Fill commands, 204-205
Fill dialog box (Edit menu),
   204-206
filling areas, keyboard
   commands for, 205
filling type, 295-297
film output, 375
filter effects, instructions
   for creating, 354-355
Filter Fade command
   (Filters menu), 335-336
filters, 303, 305
   3D Transform
      dialog box options,
         306-311
      instructions for using,
         311-314
   Add Noise, 318
      editing images using, 232
   Blur/Blur More, 333
   CMYK mode, 99
   Despeckle, 232
   Displace, 315, 317
   Dust & Scratches, 232, 319
   embossing/debossing,
      329-330
   Fade command, 335
   Gaussian Blur, 231, 333-335
   Glass, 335
   including in actions, 489
   Lab mode, 100
   Lighting Effects, 321-322,
      324-325
   Median, 232
   Motion/Radial Blur, 335
   Multichannel mode, 105
   in RGB mode, 99
   Sharpen/Sharpen More,
      232, 331
   textures, 335

Unsharp Mask, 76, 331
using in layers, 305-306
Filters menu, 305
   3D Transform, 306-314
   Blur submenu options, 231
   Distort submenu
      Displace filter, 315-317
      Glass filter, 335
   dust and scratch removal
      options, 319-320
   Fade command, 335-336
   Gaussian Blur filter,
      333-335
   Motion/Radial Blur
      filters, 335
   Noise submenu options,
      232, 318
   Render submenu,
      lighting effects, 321-327
   sharpening images,
      331-332
   Texturizer filter, 335
   Video submenu
      options, 466
Finger Painting option
   (smudge tool), 227
Fit Image command
   (Actions palette menu), 501
Fit on Screen option
   (View menu), 47
flat colors in electronic
   publishing, 457
Flatten Image (Layer menu/
   Layers palette), 253
flattening images,
   file sizes, 40
flattening layers, 251-253
Focaltone colors
   color guide, 179
   color swatches, loading, 181
focus tools
   cursor options, 218
   editing images using,
      226-227
folders
   action sets, 498
   Adobe Photoshop Settings
      Preferences file, 54-55

Goodies folder, 180-181
   custom brushes in, 195
   Photoshop Extras folder,
      181
Font menu (Type Tool
   dialog box), 283
fonts, choosing, 283
   see also text; type
Foreground color tool, 33
foreground colors, 173
   in Color palette, 181
   filling with, keyboard
      shortcuts, 205
   swatches for, 174
Foreground option (Fill
   dialog box), 204
formats, *see* file formats
frames, actions for, 489
Free Transform command
   (Edit/Transform menu), 156,
   216-217
freeform pen tool, 152-154
full colors in electronic
   publishing, 458
Full Screen mode, 45-46
Full Size option (Image
   Previews), 41
Fuzziness option (Color Range
   command), 128-131
Fuzziness sliders
   Color Range dialog box,
      406
   Replace Color dialog box,
      404

G

gamma, *see* midtones
gamuts
   in CMYK mode, 99
   gamut alerts, 177-178
   see also colors
Gaussian Blur filter
   (Filters/Blur menu),
   333-335
   editing images using, 231
Gaussian noise, 318
GCR (gray component
   replacement) in color
   separations, 444

General Preferences
(Preferences sub-menu)
Anti-Alias PostScript
option, 22
Beep option, 22
export clipboard
option, 22
Pantone names option, 22
Save Palette Locations, 37
Show Tool Tips option, 22
.GIF (Graphic Interchange
Format) files
when to use, 436, 457
file size issues, 458, 460
GIF89a Export Options
dialog box (File/Export
menu), 464-465
GIF89a files, 432
exporting Grayscale mode
images, 457
exporting Indexed Color
files (transparencies), 465
Glass filter (Filters menu), 335
Gloss property (Lighting
Effects filter), 325
Goodies folder, 180-181
brushes in, 195
Gradient command,
including in actions, 489
Gradient Options palette, 201
Gradient Editor, 202-204
Gradient tool, 200-204
gradients
creating new, 202-203
custom, loading, 204
"Grandparents Final"
example image, retouching
instructions, 220-221
Graphic Interchange
Format, *see* GIF
graphics, *see* images
graphs
Curves dialog box
(Images/Adjust menu),
389-390
Histogram dialog box
(Image menu)
interpreting, 381
gray, levels of, 115

Grayscale mode, 17, 93-95
converting to Duotone
mode, 97
converting to
Multichannel mode, 105
in electronic
publishing, 462
.GIF format for, 457
filter support, 305
grayscale bar (Curves
dialog box), 390
grids
appearance of,
customizing, 52
in Curves dialog box
(Images/Adjust menu),
390
rasters, 16
setting preferences for, 54
see also guides/guide lines
guides/guide lines, 51-52
see also grids
Guides & Grid options
(Preferences sub-menu), 52

H

Halftone Screens dialog box
(Page Setup dialog box),
Screen frequency, 447
halftones
transfer functions, 447
screen resolution
method, 94
Hand tool, 33
Hard Light mode, 272
"Heirloom Seed Pack"
example image
creating type effects,
293-295
type setting, 290-293
help
Adobe Online, 43-44
interactive help
*Wizards/Assistants
for, 38*
Help menu
*Export Transparent
Image Wizard/
Assistant, 38*

*Macintosh systems
Help Contents, 43
Resize Image
Wizard/Assistant, 38
Windows systems
Contents sub-menu, 43*
Hide All option (Layer
Mask submenu), 255
Hide Palettes (Window menu),
36
hiding
palettes, 37
layers, 241
high-key images, 381
highlights
adjusting using Input Levels
slider, 384
setting target values, 387
Histogram dialog box
(Image menu), 380
histogram cache levels, 24
interpreting graphs, 381
speed vs. accuracy, 383
statistical information,
382-383
history brush, 223-225
History Brush Source icon
(History palette), 63
History palette, 59
deleting/purging states,
65-66
Eraser tool with, 191
History Brush Source
icon, 63
menu options
*Create Initial
Snapshot option, 67
History Steps option, 67
non-linear history
option, 66-67*
New Snapshot button, 64
snapshots, creating, 63
states
*deleting, 65
discarding, 62
moving among, 62
order of, 61
purging, 65
storing, 62*
using states and snapshots,
63-64

History Steps option
(History palette menu), 67
horizontal mask tool, 289
horizontal type
    setting, 290-295
    tools for, 282
"Hot Pepper" example image,
    type setting, 295-297
HSB (Hue, Saturation, and
    Brightness) Color Model,
    174-175
hue
    adjusting, 398-400
    Color Picker default, 174
Hue/Saturation dialog box
    (Image/Adjust menu),
    398-399
    color bars, 399-400
    Colorize option, 400
    Save/Load buttons, 379
    using hue/saturation
        settings, 401-402

I

ICC (International Color
    Consortium) profiles,
    CMYK Setup dialog box,
    481-482
ICM 2-compatible utilities
    monitor calibration, 473
Icon option (Image Previews
    preference settings), 41
icons
    eye icon (Layers palette),
        241
    History Brush Source
        (History palette), 63
    for linked layers, 244
    Paint Bucket, 180
    protractor icon, Measure
        tool cursor, 53
    Tool icon, 34
illustration programs,
    type/font support, 281
Illustrator (Adobe), 16-17
    AI files, importing
        (placing), 87
    export paths to, 421

support for Photoshop
    formats, 421
type/font support, 281
image effects (special effects)
    3D transformations,
        306-314
    blending/fading filters, 335
    blurring, 333-335
    displacement/distortion,
        315-317, 335
    dust and scratch removal,
        319
    filter effects, 303, 305,
        354-355
    Layer Effects, 266-267
    lighting, 321-326, 329-330
    noise options, 318
    sharpening, 331
    texture, 335
    vignettes, creating, 352-353
    see also Layer effects;
        special effects
Image Effects action set
    (Actions palette), 489
Image menu
    Adjust submenu, 263
        Auto Levels
            command, 388
        Brightness/Contrast
            dialog box, 409-410
        Color Balance dialog box,
            396-398
        Curves dialog box,
            389-390, 393
        editing color channels,
            345
        Equalize dialog box, 411
        Hue/Saturation dialog
            box, 398-402
        Input Levels dialog
            box, 385
        instructions, 346
        Invert command, 410
        Levels dialog box, 388
        Posterize dialog box, 414
        Replace Color dialog box,
            403-405
        Selective Color dialog
            box, 408-409

Threshold dialog box,
    411-413
Variations dialog box,
    394-396
Apply Image dialog box,
    360-362
Calculations dialog box,
    363-364
Canvas Size dialog box,
    82-83
Channel Mixer dialog
    box, 365
Crop command, 84
Duplicate dialog box, 360
Histogram dialog box,
    381-383
Image Size dialog box, 47,
    81-82, 461
    image size management,
        81-84
    sizing image collections,
        500-501
Mode submenu
    Duotone dialog box, 97
    Indexed Color dialog box,
        463-464
Trap option, 452
Image Previews preference
    settings (Preferences
    sub-menu), 41
images
    8-bit, 106
    16-bit, 106
    actions for, 490-492
    adding information to, 85
    blurring tools, 226-227
    brightness/contrast
        adjustments, 409-410
    color adjustments
        Color Balance dialog box,
            396-398
        color selection masks,
            403-405
        converting to black
            and white, 411-413
        equalizing colors, 411
        inverting colors, 410
        Variations dialog box,
            394-396

colorizing images, 400
composite images, spot
  color printing, 268-269
contact sheets, 500-501
cropping images, 84
curves, anti-aliasing for, 129
cutting/copying/pasting
  selections, 113
displaying, monitor
  calibration, 473
Duotone images,
  converting to
  Multichannel, 349
editing images
  adding perspective, 215
  cursor options, 218
  distorting, 215
  filters for, 231-232
  Free Transform
    command, 216-217
  history brush, 223-226
  Numeric Transform
    dialog box, 215
  rotating, 214
  scaling, 213
  skewing, 214
  stamp tools, 218-223
  toning tools, 229
  transformation
    commands, 213
electronic publishing
  formats, 457-459
exporting images
  clipping paths for, 162
  into Illustrator, 421
flattened images, saving, 40
focusing tools, 226-227
highlights/shadows, setting
  using eyedroppers, 387
hue/saturation
  adjustments, 398-400
image modes
  in actions, changing, 499
  Bitmap mode, 93
  CMYK mode, 99
  converting to Bitmaps,
    93-95
  converting to CMYK, 100

converting to
  Duotone, 97-98
Duotone mode, 96-97
in electronic publishing
  files, 457-458, 462
Grayscale mode, 95
Indexed Color mode,
  101-104
Lab mode, 100
Monotone mode, 96
Multichannel mode, 105
Quadtone mode, 97
RGB mode, 99
summary table, 106
Tritone mode, 97
image resolution, 73-76
  50% Threshold, 93
  capturing, resolution
    issues, 75-77
  common problems, 80
  Custom Pattern, 94
  decreating, 461
  Diffusion Dither, 94
  Halftone Screen, 94
  Pattern Dither, 94
image size, reducing, 48
image states, managing,
  61-62, 65
image status information,
  40
image structure, 15
importing/capturing
  images, 86
layer masks, 255-257
  adding, 254
  adjustment layers as,
    263-265
  applying/discarding,
    259-260
  blending, 256-257, 260
  linking/unlinking, 261
  viewing/editing, 257-259
  when to use, 254
layers in
  clipping groups, 261-263
  duplicating layers,
    245-246
  Layer Effects, 266-267

size management issues,
  251-253
magnifying images, 46
  Status Bar for, 48
  Zoom tools, 48
managing appearance using
  Image Effects action set,
  489
moving, drag-and-drop for,
  127-128
multichannel images, 348,
  363-364
multimedia screen
  displays, 467
multiple windows,
  opening, 49
pattern-creation using, 206
previewing CMYK
  colors, 379
printed images (CMYK)
  captions, 449
  color separations, 441
  dot gain percentages,
    442-443
  page setup, 447-448
  printer commands, 451
  using black, 443-444
printed images (pre-press)
  resolution problems, 80
  scan resolution
    formula, 77
  scanning issues, 76-77
raster images, 16
refreshing images, 67
resampling, 74
  Fit Image command, 501
  Image Size dialog box,
    81-82
resizing images, 82-83
RGB/CMYK images, 375
sampling images, keyboard
  shortcuts, 219, 232
saving images, formats for
  .DCS format, 429
  .EPS format, 426.
  .GIF format, 432
  .PDF format, 430
  .PICT format, 432

.PNG format, 434-435
.PSD format, 422-423
.TIFF format, 426
.TGA format, 466
screen-fitting, Zoom tools for, 48
tonal range histograms, 381-383
tonality adjustments, 365, 388-390, 414
toning tools, 229-230
vector images, 16, 86
viewing/previewing images, 45, 48-49
Web displays, preparing images for, 39
resolution issues, 78-80
see also files; image effects
importing vector images, 86
Indexed Color dialog box (Image-Mode menu)
conversion options, 101-103
dithering options, 463-464
Indexed Color mode, 101
CLUTs for, 101
converting to, 101-104, 433
filter support, 305
image files
electronic publishing, 462
exporting, 464-465
type layers in, 285
Info palette
accessing, 182
color corrections, 377
eyedropper information, 182
measurement information, 52-53
protractor feature, 53
transformation information, 213
ink coverage, estimating, 97-98
Inner Glow effect (Layer Effects dialog box), 268
Inner Shadow effect (Layer Effects dialog box), 267
Input Levels slider (Levels dialog box), 385-386

Insert Menu command (Actions palette menu), 495-496
Insert Paths command (Actions palette menu), 495-496
Insert Stop command (Actions palette menu, 498
interpolation, 21, 74, 213
interpolation option (General Preferences dialog box), 22
intersections in selections, 116
Invert command (Image/Adjust menu), 410
Invert option (Color Range command), 132
inverting colors, 410
"Iris" example image (creating pattern stamp), 222-223

J

.JFIF (JPEG File Interchange Format), *see* **JPEG files**
Joint Photographic Experts Group files, *see* **JPEG files**
.JPEG (Joint Photographic Experts Group) files, 40, 434
channels in, 349
when to use, 436
JPEG compression
file size issues, 461
in .JPEG files, 433
in .PDF files, 430
JPEG File Interchange Format (JFIF), *see* **.JPEG files**
JPEG Options dialog box (Save As dialog box), 434

K

kerning, 284, 297-300
see also type
key type, determining, 381
keyboard shortcuts
action-related, 493
blending modes, 187, 274
brush roundness/angle settings, 194
channels, activating/deactivating, 343

Color Bar options, 182
cursor settings, 35-36
Curves options, 393
Deselect command, 134
Eraser tool, 34
Eyedropper options, 182
feathering, 260
filling and stroking, 205
foreground/background settings, 173
Gradient tool, 201-202
hiding palettes, 37
Hue/Saturation dialog box, 402
image sampling, 219, 232
layers
creating clipping groups, 263
duplicating layers, 245
layer masks, 261
Layer Via Copy command, 245
Layer Via Cut command, 246
listing of layers, 274
merging layers, 252-253
moving layer elements, 246
reordering layers, 244
learning keystrokes, importance of, 44
Levels dialog box, 388-389
Line tool, 196
listing of, Help menu for, 43
Lock Guide command, 51
mask activation/deactivation, 356
numeric field toggles, 177
online help access, Windows systems, 43
order of keystrokes, 116
Page Setup options, 447
pattern selection, 206
pulldown menus identification, 44
purging states, Clear History command, 65
Quick Mask mode, editing selections, 359

rendering layers, 289
resetting to defaults, 132
rulers, activating/
  deactivating, 50
selecting/deselecting
  states, 62
selection tool modifiers,
  116-117, 120-121, 127
Show/Hide Guides or
  Grids, 51
swatch management, 180
text field activating/
  deactivating, 286
tool activating/
  deactivating, 34
transformation
  commands, 217
Undo command, 42
Zoom tools, 48
keywords, adding to images, 85

L

**Lab Color Model Color Picker,
  176-177**
Lab mode, 100
  converting to
    Multichannel mode, 105
**"Lake" example image,
  blending images, 362-364**
Lasso tools, 33
  magnetic lasso, 150-151
    keystroke modifiers, 121
  polygon lasso, keystroke
    modifiers, 120
**Lasso Width option (magnetic
  lasso tool, 122**
**Layer Effects dialog box,
  see Layers palette**
Layer Mask, *see* Layer menu
Layer menu
  Align Linked/Distribute
    Linked options, 247-248
  Arrange submenu
    options, 243
  Clone Merge option, 2
  Copy Merge option, 253
  Flatten Image option, 253
  Layer Mask submenu
    options, 254-255
  Merge Down option, 252

Merge Grouped option, 252
Merge Linked option, 252
Merge Visible option, 252
New Adjustment Layer
  dialog box, 263
New Layer dialog box, 242
**Layer Options dialog
  box, Blend If option, 250**
Layer Via Copy command, 245
Layer Via Cut command, 246
layers
  activating, 241
  adjustment, 263
    *color correction using,
      264-266*
  aligning/distributing
    elements, 246-248
  background, 239
    transforming, 213
    type/text as, 285
  Bitmap mode, 95
  blending, Apply Image for,
    360-362
  clipping groups, 261-263
  in CMYK mode, 99
  converting Layer Effects,
    270
  creating new, 242
  in Duotone mode, 97
  duplicating/copying,
    244-246
  editing, 249-250
  filling, 204-205
  flattening
    during mode changes, 93
    saved file size, 40
  Grayscale, 95
  hiding, 405
  keyboard shortcuts for,
    listing of, 274
  Layer Effects, 266
  layer masks, 254-257
    adding, 254
    *adjustment layers as,
      263-265*
    *applying/discarding,
      259-260*
    *blending images,
      256-257, 260*
    *keyboard shortcuts
      for, 261*

    linking/unlinking, 261
    viewing/editing, 257-259
    when to use, 254
  linking/unlinking, 244
  managing layer size
    flattening, 251
    flattening layers, 253
    merging layers, 252-253
  maximum number of, 239
  moving layer elements, 246
  paint bucket tool with, 199
  rendering, keyboard
    shortcuts for, 289
  reordering, 242-243
  repositioning contents, 246
  RGB mode, 99
  showing/hiding, 241
  stroking, 206
  thumbnails, changing
    display, 241
  transparency, display
    preferences, 242
  using filters, 305-306
Layers palette, 241
  blending modes, 184, 270
    Behind, 271
    Clear, 271
    Color, 273
    Color Burn, 272
    Color Dodge, 272
    Darken, 272
    Difference, 272
    Dissolve, 271
    Exclusion, 273
    Hard Light, 272
    Hue, 273
    Lighten, 272
    Luminosity, 273
    Multiply, 271
    Normal, 271
    Overlay, 272
    Saturation, 273
    Screen, 271
    Soft Light, 272
    *using blending modes,
      273-274*
  displaying palette, 241
  Flatten Image option, 253
  Layer Effects dialog box,
    266-267
    bevel effect, 268

drop shadow effect, 267
editing/removing effects,
   269-270
emboss effect, 268
inner glow effect, 268
inner shadow effect, 267
outer glow effect, 268
New Layer option, 242
Opacity percentage, 250
Preserve Transparency
   option, 249
rendering layers, 289
thumbnail size, 241
type layers, 287-288
type mask tools, 288-289
Type option
   Render Layer
      command, 289
   text orientation, 288
leading, in type lines, 284
"Legal" action set
   example, 495-496
"lesson1.psd" example image,
   creating subpaths using pen
   tool, 148-149
"lesson2.psd" example image,
   creating subpaths using
   magnetic pen tool, 151-152
"lesson3.psd" example image,
   creating subpaths using
   freeform pen tool, 154
Levels dialog box (Image/
   Adjust menu)
   Auto Levels command, 388
   eyedroppers, 387
   keyboard shortcuts, 388-389
   Save/Load buttons, 379
libraries, PANTONE
   Coated, 178
   see also colors; PANTONE
Lighten mode, 272
lighting effects
   colors, 324
   Lighting Effects filter for,
      321-322, 324-330
Lighting Effects filter dialog
   box (Filters menu), 321-322
   adding/deleting/moving
      lights, 322
   controlling, 324

embossing/debossing,
   329-330
instructions for using
   filters, 326-327
predefined styles, 325
properties, 324-325
lightness, in Lab mode, 100
line screens, 76-77
Line tool, 196-198
Linear Gradient option
   (Gradient tool), 200
linear histories, 66-67
lines
   text management, 284-285,
      297-300
lines per inch (lpi),
   relation to (ppi), 76-77
linking
   layer masks, 261
   layers, 244, 246-248
Load Actions command
   (Actions palette menu), 498
Load Brushes option (Brushes
   palette menu), 195
Load buttons, 379-380
Load Gradient option
   (Gradient Editor dialog
   box), 204
Load Swatches command
   (Swatches palette menu), 181
loading
   actions, 498
   colors, 181
   custom gradients, 204
Lock Guides command
   (View menu), 51
locking
   guides, 51
   Preferences file, 55-56
lossless compression
   .GIF files, 432
   LZW compression, 424
   .PNG files, 434-435
   RLE encoding, 422
   see also compressing files
low-key images, 380
lpi (lines per inch), relation to
   ppi (pixels per inch), 76-77
Luminosity mode, 273

LZW (Lempel-Ziv-Welch)
   compression
   file size issues, 461
   flat color images, 457
   .TIFF files, 424

M

Macintosh systems
   Assistants, 38
   context-sensitive menus,
      activating, 45
   file size information, 41
   help, accessing, 43
   hidden tools, accessing, 34
   keyboard shortcuts, 289
      adding/subtracting
         pixels, 116
      arrow keys, 127
      color bar options, 182
      Curves dialog box, 393
      deleting swatches, 180
      Deselect command, 134
      Eyedropper options, 182
      Free Transform
         options, 217
      Hue/Saturation
         dialog box, 402
      Lasso tools, 120-121
      Levels dialog box, 388
      Marquee tools, 117
      purging states, 65
      replacing/inserting
         swatch colors, 180
      resetting to defaults, 132
      selecting states, 62
      swatch-activating, 180
   Lock Guide command
      shortcut, 51
   Measure tool, protractor
      feature, 53
   minimizing palettes, 37
   monitor calibrations
      Adobe Gamma utility,
         474-476
      utilities, 473
   Page Setup dialog box, 446
   Preferences file, locking, 55
   preferences storage file
      for, 54

system requirements, 19
View Box, changing
size, 49
Macromedia Director,
see **Director**
Magic Wand command
including in actions, 489
magic wand tool, 125
magnetic lasso tool, 123-124,
150-151
magnetic pen tool,
creating/editing paths/
subpaths, 150-152
magnifying
images
Status Bar for, 48
status bar information, 40
View menu options, 46
Zoom tools, 48
type views, 283
Make Work Path dialog box
(Paths palette menu), 161
managing
colors, 477-480
file size, 81-82
image collections, 500-501
layered images, 251-253
scanned images, 79
see also files; images; layers
maps
bump (texture) maps, 328
displacement maps, 315
Marquee tools, 33, 116
changing View Box
size using, 49
Crop, 84
elliptical marquee,
keystroke modifiers, 117
masks
alpha channels as, 342
clean masks, 405
clipping groups, 261-263
color adjustments using,
403-405
default colors in, 344
keyboard shortcuts, 356
layer masks, 254-257
adding, 254
adjustment layers as,
263-265

applying/discarding,
259-260
blending images,
256-257, 260
linking/unlinking, 261
viewing/editing, 257-259
when to use, 254
Quick Mask Mode, 256-258
reversing masks, 410
selections as, 113
transparency masks
editing, 203
Gradient tool, 201
type masks, 295-297
creating, 289
new layers for, 289
tools for, 282
Unsharp Mask filter,
233-234
see also alpha channels
Material property
(Lighting Effects filter), 325
Measure tool, 33, 52
protractor feature, 53
resizing/repositioning lines,
53
measurement units
font sizes, 283
preference settings, 50, 283
type spacing, 284
Median filter (Filter/Noise
menu), editing images
using, 232
memory, information about,
40, 42
multiple windows and, 49
Memory dialog box
(Preferences sub-menu), 24
menus
Actions palette menu, 495
Color palette menu, 182
context-sensitive menus, 45
when rendering
layers, 289
Edit menu
Fill dialog box, 204-206
Purge command, 42
Stroke dialog box, 206

File menu
Automate command, 487
Open command, 49
Preferences sub-menu,
21, 35, 183, 283
Font menu, 283
Help menu, 38
palette menu options,
activating, 36
pull-down menus,
keyboard shortcuts in, 44
Select menu
All command, 135
Color Range
command, 130-132
Deselect command, 134
Feather command,
129, 135
Grow command, 133
Inverse command, 135
preview area
options, 131
Reselect command, 134
Similar command, 133
Transform Selection
command, 135-136
Swatches palette menu, 181
View menu
Lock Guides
command, 51
Show/Hide Grid
option, 51
Show/Hide Rulers option,
50
Window menu
Show/Hide Brushes
command, 193
Show/Hide Info
command, 182
Show/Hide Palettes, 36
Merge Down option
(Layer menu), 252
Merge Grouped option
(Layer menu), 252
Merge Linked option
(Layer menu), 252
Merge Visible option
(Layer menu), 252

merging
  channels, 349-351
  layers, 252-253
  spot channels, 368
midtones, adjusting, 385
minimizing palette groups, 37
**misregistration, trapping
  for, 452**
modes
  in actions, changing, 499
  blending, 187, 270
    Behind, 271
    Clear, 271
    Color Burn, 272
    Color Dodge, 272
    Darken, 272
    Difference, 272
    Dissolve, 271-273
    Exclusion, 273
    Hard Light, 272
    Lighten, 272
    Luminosity, 273
    Multiply, 271
    Normal, 271
    Overlay, 272
    Saturation, 273
    Screen, 271
    Soft Light, 272
    *using blending
      modes, 273-274*
  changing modes,
    flattening layers during, 93
  CMYK mode, 99, 375
  color filter support, 305
  Duotone mode, 96-98
  Grayscale mode, 95
  Indexed Color mode, 101
    *converting to,
      101-104, 433*
  Lab mode, 100
  Multichannel mode, 105
    converting to, 105, 348
  Quick Mask mode, 356-358
  Relative/Absolute
    modes, 409
  RGB mode, 99, 375
  summary table, 106

monitors
  calibrating
    *Adobe Gamma utility,
      473-476*
    *chromaticity coordinates,
      474*
    *ColorSync-compatible
      utilities, 473*
    *ICM 2-compatible
      utilities, 473*
    phosphor types, 474
    *with printed output,
      480-482*
    white points for, 475
  resolution, 73
  setup preferences, 54
Monotone images, 96
**Motion Blur filter
  (Filters menu), 335**
Move tool, 127-128
moving
  layer elements, 246
  layers, linking, 244
  lighting effects, 322
  pixels, 127-128
  selections, 127-128
**multichannel images,
  creating, 348, 363-364**
Multichannel mode, 105, 348
  converting to, 348
    from CMYK mode, 105
    *from Grayscale/Duotone
      modes, 105*
    from Lab mode, 105
    from RGB mode, 105
  type layers in, 285
Multiply mode, 271
**"Mushrooms" example image,
  using Quick Mask mode,
  356-358**

N

naming files, 419
  see also file formats
**National Television Standards
  Committee color format,
  see NTSC**
**Navigator palette options,
  48-49**

**New Action button
  (Actions palette), 493**
**New Adjustment Layer dialog
  box (Layer menu), 263**
**New Brush option
  (Brushes palette menu),
  creating new brushes, 193**
**New Channel dialog box
  (Channels palette menu),
  344-345**
**New Layer options (Layers
  palette menu), 242**
**New Snapshot button (History
  palette), 64**
noise filters, 318
  editing images using, 232
**Noise submenu (Filter menu),
  Despeckle option, 232**
non-linear histories, using,
  66-67
non-printing elements, 52-53
**Normal (Threshold) blending
  mode, 185**
Normal mode, 271
**NTSC (National Television
  Standards Committee)
  format, converting
  colors to, 466**

O

objects, named, in
  subpath collections, 158
omni lights, 323
  see also lighting effects
**Online for Usage dialog box
  (Export Transparent Image
  Wizard/Assisant), 39**
online help, *see* help
opacity
  filters for, 335-336
  opacity settings, 187-189
  in transparency masks, 203
**Opacity option
  (Stroke dialog box), 206**
**Opacity percentage
  (Layers palette), 250**
Opacity pop-up slider, 250
**Open command (File menu),
  49**

optimizing PSD files,
    RLE-encoding, 422-423
Options palettes
    Airbrush tool, 190
    Aligned option, 218
    Eraser tool, 191
    Eyedropper tool, 182
    Gradient tool, 201-204
    history brush, 224
    Line tool, 196-198
    Paint Bucket tool, 199
    in painting tools, 184, 188
    Pencil tools, 191
    restoring defaults using, 38
    in stamp tools, 218-219
    Use All Layers option, 219
**"Orange Flower" example
    images, using history brush,
    225-226**
**origin information,
    adding to images, 85**
Other Cursors options, 36
out-of-gamut colors, 99
    selecting, 132
    warning for, 376
**Outer Glow effect (Layer
    Effects dialog box), 268**
**Outline type, program
    support for, 281**
output
    calibrating monitors with
        printers, 480-482
    electronic images
        file formats, 459
        *image mode
            requirements, 457-458*
        image modes, 462
    film images
        RGB/CMYK modes, 375
    print images
        CMYK images for, 99
        color density, 97-98
        *color separation,
            441-444*
        custom colors, 179
        *dot gain percentages,
            442-443*
        *Multichannel mode
            for, 105*
        *out-of-gamut colors,
            177-178*

    page setup, 447-449
    printer commands, 451
    screen displays
        *monitor calibration tools,
            473*
        *multimedia applications,
            467*
**Output Levels slider
    (Levels dialog box), 386**
Overlay mode, 272
overlays
    Quick Mask mode, 356-358
    ruby overlays, 356
oversharpening, 235

P

page layout applications
    clipping paths, 144, 162
    file formats for, 421
    preparing separations
        for, 453
    type support for, 281
**Page Setup dialog box
    (File menu)**
    Background options, 448
    captions, 449
    Halftone Screens
        attributes, 446-447
    Transfer Functions, 447
**page setups for printed
    output, 447-449**
PageMaker (Adobe)
    clipping paths, 144
    support for Photoshop files,
        421
paint bucket tool, 33, 199
    anti-aliasing option, 199
    including in actions, 489
    Options palette, 199
    in Swatches palette, 180
    tolerance levels, 199
    Use All Layers option, 199
**paintbrush tools, common
    blending**
    Behind, 185
    Clear, 185
    Color, 186
    Color Burn, 186
    Color Dodge, 186
    Darken, 186

    default, 185
    Difference, 186
    Exclusion, 186
    Hard Light, 186
    Hue, 186
    instructions for using, 187
    Lighten, 186
    Luminosity, 187
    modes, 184
    Multiply, 185
    Overlay, 185
    Saturation, 186
    Screen, 185
    Soft Light, 186
    see also painting tools
**painting, effects on color
    channels, 341**
**Painting Cursors, changing
    size, 35**
painting tools
    Airbrush, 190
    Brush Size option, 183
    Brushes Palette, 192-196
    cursor options for, 183
    Eraser, 191-192
    Fill commands, 204-205
    Gradient, 199-204
    Line, 196-198
    Options palettes, 184
        blending modes, 184-187
        fade-out rates, 188
        opacity settings, 187-188
        *pressure-sensitive stylus,
            188-190*
    paint bucket, 199
    Paintbrush, 190
        cursor options for, 183
    pattern-creating, 206
    Pencil, 190-191
    Stroke commands, 206
    using with paths/subpaths,
        158-160
**Palette Options (Channels
    palette menu), 342-343**
palettes, 36
    Actions palette, 489,
        493-495
    active, managing, 45-46
    Brushes palette, 184,
        192-195, 218

Channels palette, 254, 342-343, 347-351, 358, 367-368

Color palette, 181-182

displaying, 36

editing and retouching tools, 218

Gradient Options palette, 201-204

grouping palettes, 37

hiding palettes, 37

History palette, 59, 61-67, 191

Info palette, 52-53, 182, 213, 377

Layers palette, 184, 241, 249-250, 254, 267, 270-274, 287-289

Line tool palette, 196-198

list of palettes, 36

location of
customizing, 37, 54
restoring default, 23, 38
saving, 23

Marquee options palette, 128-129

Navigator palette, 48-49

Options palette, 182, 190-191, 218-219

Paint Bucket options palette, 199

painting tools palettes, 184

palette options menus
activating, 36
View Box border color, 49

Paths palette, 158-162

Pen Tool option, 146

regrouping, 37

resizing, 37

Swatches palette, 173, 180-181, 184

pan camera tools (3D Transform filter), 310

PANTONE colors, 178-179

channels for, 366-367

libraries, selecting colors from, 173

matching system for, 22

swatch palettes, loading, 181

pasting

Layer Effects, 269

layers, Layer Via Cut command, 246

selections, 113

type/text, 285

see also copying; cutting

paths, 17, 143

clipping paths, 39, 144, 162, 421

converting to selections, 161

creating/editing
add anchor point tool, 154-155
convert point tool, 157
direct selection tool, 155-156
freeform pen tool, 152-154
magnetic pen tool, 150-152
pen tool, 145-149
subtract anchor point tool, 155

export paths, 421

instructions for using, 162-164, 168

managing, 158-160

subpaths, Bézier curves, 143-144

work paths, 160

Paths palette

palette menu
Clipping Path dialog box, 162
Make Selection dialog box, 161
Make Work Path dialog box, 161

managing paths/subpaths, 158-160

Pattern Dither resolution method, 94

Pattern option (Fill dialog box), 205-206

Pattern Stamp tool, 218, 222-223

patterns

creating, 206, 222-223

selecting, keyboard shortcut, 206

swatches for, 207

.PCX files, 436

.PDF (Portable Document Format/Adobe Acrobat) file format, 430

compressing, 430

importing (placing), 87

when to use, 436

pen size options, 218

Pen tool, 33

creating/editing paths/ subpaths, 145-149

Rubber Band mode, 146

Pencil tool

Auto Erase option, 191

cursor options, 183

when to use, 190

"Peppers" example image

applying/discarding layer masks, 259-260

blending images using layer masks, 256-257, 260

using layer masks, 255-257

viewing/editing layer masks, 257-259

perspective, adding to images, 215

.PGA files, exporting transparencies using, 465

phosphors, 474

photographs, retouching instructions, 220-221

Photoshop 5.0

customizing, 21

Extras folder, 181

features, summary of, 18

installing, 20

limitations, 19

new features, 43, 121, 135, 199, 283, 487, 498
3D Transform filter, 306-310
Adobe Gamma utility, 473
Channel Mixer, 365
Color Sampler tool, 377-378
ColorSync-compatible utilities, 473

freeform pen tool,
  152-153
history brush, 223
hue/saturation
  options, 399
ICM 2-compatible
  utilities, 473
Layer Effects, 266
magnetic pen tool, 150
spot color channels,
  366-367
supported fonts, 283
type-handling features, 279
Photoshop Color Picker, *see*
Color Picker
Photoshop native file format
  (PSD files)
  RLE-encoding, 422-423
  see also .PSD (Photoshop
    native) files
Photoshop Proficiency Exam
  requirements, 13-14
  actions, 487
  channels and masks, 339
  color calibration/setup, 472
  color corrections, 374
  electronic publishing, 457
  file formats, 418
  History palette, 60-61
  image modes, 91-92
  image editing/
    retouching, 211
  importing and
    adjusting images, 73
  keyboard shortcuts, 44
  painting tools, 172
  paths, 141
  pre-press production, 439
  selection tools and
    commands, 112
  type handling, 280
  work areas, 32
.PICT files
  features, 432
  when to use, 436
pictures, *see* **images**
pixels
  adding/subtracting,
    interpolation for, 74, 213

blending, 361
color adjustments, 403-405
examining, 125
histograms, 381-383
mixing, 365
moving, 127-128
in Multichannel mode, 348
pixel dimensions, reducing,
  461
relationship to file size, 79
resampling, 74
resolution issues, 73
RLE-encoding, 422-423
sampling, 405
selecting, 113, 124, 129, 135
pixels per inch (ppi), 73
  relation to lpi, 77
placing images, 86
Play button (Actions
  palette), 490
playing actions, 490-493
plug-in filters, finding, 305
Plug-Ins folder,
  Wizards/Assistants in, 38
.PNG (Portable Network
  Graphics) files, 434-436
  with full color images, 458
Point Sample menu
  (Eyedropper tool), 182
point samples, 182
points, 283
polygon lasso tool, 120
Portable Document Format,
  see **.PDF**
Portable Network Graphics,
  see **.PNG**
Posterize dialog box
  (Image/Adjust menu), 414
posterizing, 414
ppi (pixels per inch), 73
  relation to lpi, 76-77
Preferences file, managing,
  54-56
Preferences sub-menu
  (File menu)
  Color Setting options, 54
  Display & Cursors options,
    35, 183, 218

General Preferences
  Anti-Alias PostScript
    option, 22
  Beep option, 22
  export clipboard
    option, 22
  Pantone names
    option, 22
  Save Palette
    Locations options, 37
  Show Tool Tips
    option, 22
  Guides & Grid options, 52
  Image Previews preference
    settings, 41
  Units & Rulers dialog
    box, 50, 283
Premiere (Adobe),
  preparing images for, 466
pre-press images,
  scanning/capture
  resolution, 76-77
Preserve Transparency options
  (Layers palette), 249
  with Fill command, 205
  with type layers, 287
pressure, adjusting in tools,
  188-190
previewing
  colors, CMYK Preview, 379
  .EPS file format options, 427
  images, display options
    for, 131
  see also thumbnails
Print dialog box (File menu),
  451
Print option dialog box
  (Export Transparent Image
  Wizard/Assistant), 39
print publishing, *see* **printing**
Print Selected Areas option
  (Print dialog box), 451
Print Size fields (Image
  Size dialog box), 47
Print Size option
  (View menu), 47

printers
    calibrating monitors using
        CMYK Setup dialog box,
        480-482
    image resolution, 73
    output colors, 177-178
    printer commands, Print
        dialog box, 451
printing
    color density, Duotone
        curves for, 97-98
    color separations, 441
        blacks in, 443-444
    composite images with spot
        colors, 368-369
    contact sheets, 500-501
    dot gain percentages,
        442-443
    file formats, 436
    page setup
        background options, 448
        captions, 449
        halftone screens, 447
        Transfer Functions, 447
    printed output
        CMYK images for, 99
        Multichannel mode
            for, 105
        printing selected
            areas, 451
        scanning/capture
            resolution for, 76-77
    see also electronic
        publishing; output
profiles, *see* ICC profiles
properties, Lighting
    Effects filter, 325
protractor tool, 53
.PSD (Photoshop native) files,
    422-423
publishing, *see* electronic
    publishing; printing
Purge command (Edit
    menu), 42
purging states in History
    palette, 65-66
    see also deleting, 65

Q-R

Quadtone colors, 179
    images using, 97
QuarkXPress
    clipping paths, 144
    support for Photoshop files,
        421
Quick Mask mode, 356-59

Radial Blur filter (Filters
    menu), 335
Radial Gradient option
    (Gradient tool), 200
RAM (random access memory)
    allocated by system,
        information about, 42
    saving, cache levels for, 24
    settings (Windows
        systems), 24
raster images, 16
    exporting, clipping paths
        for, 144
    saving
        EPS format, 426
        PICT file format, 432
rasterizing vector-based
    images, 16
Record Stop dialog box (Insert
    Stop command), 497
recording new actions, 494-496
rectangular areas, selecting,
    116
Rectangular Marquee tool,
    creating patterns, using, 206
"Red bird" example image,
    converting to black and
    white, 412-413
red, green, blue mode, see RGB
    (red, green, blue) mode
reducing images, Zoom tools,
    48
Reflected Gradient option
    (Gradient tool), 200
refreshing images, 67
regrouping palettes, 37
Relative mode (Selective Color
    dialog box), 409
Remove Gradient option
    (Gradient Editor dialog
    box), 204

removing
    custom gradients, 204
    Layer Effects, 270
renaming paths/subpaths, 158
Render Layer command
    (Layers palette), 289
rendering type layers, 289
reordering
    alpha channels, 345
    layers, 242-243
Replace Brushes option
    (Brushes palette menu), 195
Replace Color dialog box
    (Image/Adjust menu),
    403-405
    Save/Load buttons, 379
Replace Swatches command
    (Swatches palette menu), 181
replacing
    brushes, 195
    colors, 180
repositioning
    alpha channels, 345
    guides, 51
    layer elements, 246
    layers, 242-243
    measurement lines, 53
    palette groups, 37
resampling, 74
    blurriness following, 331
    Image Size dialog box,
        81-82
    images, 501
Reset Actions command
    (Actions palette menu), 498
Reset Brushes option (Brushes
    palette menu), 195
Reset Swatches command
    (Swatches palette menu), 181
resetting actions to defaults,
    498-499
    see also defaults
Resize Image Wizard/Assistant
    (Help menu), 38
resizing
    Canvas Size
        command, 82-83
    images, cropping for, 84
    pixels, resampling for, 74
    type area, 283

resolution
common problems/
concerns, 38, 79-80
image resolution, 73-74
relationship to file size,
46, 460-461
monitor resolution, 73
printer resolution, 73
resolution methods
50% Threshold, 93
Custom Pattern, 94
Diffusion Dither, 94
Halftone Screen, 94
Pattern Dither, 94
Web site and video
images, 78-80
restoring, *see* **defaults;**
resetting; resampling
retouching images
filters for, 231
old photographs, 220-221
tools for, 218
see also editing
Return to History option
(Eraser tool), 191
Reveal All option (Layer
Mask submenu), 255
Reveal Selection option
(Layer Mask submenu), 255
RGB (red, green, blue) mode,
17, 99
color correcting for CMYK
output, 377
converting to CMYK mode,
100
converting to
Multichannel mode, 105
filter support, 305
image files
converting to video-safe
colors (NTSC format),
466
electronic publishing, 462
exporting using GIF89a
export command, 464
Lighting Effects filter,
321-330
speed advantages, 375
tips for working with, 375

RGB Color Model Color
Picker, 175-177
RGB Setup dialog box
File/Color Management
menu, 478-479
File/Color Settings
menu, 100
RLE (Run Length Encoding)
compression, 422-423
"Rockies" example image
alpha channels, vignette
effects, 352-353
splitting and merging
channels, 349-351
"Rose" example image
adjusting colors, 264-266,
404-405
adjusting hue/saturation,
401-402
creating selections, 407-408
Rotate box (Type Tool
dialog box), 285
rotating images, 214
roundness brush settings, 194
rows, single, selecting, 119
Rubber Band mode (Pen Tool
Option palette), 146
Rubber Stamp tool, 33,
218-221
rulers, 50
measurement units, 50
setting origin location, 50
setting preferences, 54
Run Length Encoding, *see*
RLE, 422

S

"Sail" example image,
adjusting colors, 395-396
sampling colors, Color
Sampler tool, 377-378
saturation, adjusting, 398-400
Saturation, in Color
Picker, 174
Saturation mode, 273
Save a Copy dialog box
(File menu), 419-420
Save As dialog box (File
menu), 419

.EPS options dialog box,
427, 453
.JPEG Options dialog box,
434
.TIFF Options dialog box,
426
Save Brushes option
(Brushes palette menu), 195
Save buttons, 379-380
Save Palette Locations
(General Preferences dialog
box), 37
Save Selection as Channel
option (Select menu), 358
Save Swatches command
(Swatches palette menu), 181
saving
actions in batched files, 499
alpha channels, 359
brushes, 195
color adjustment settings,
379
color range settings, 132
custom swatch palettes, 181
documents with alpha
channels. 349
files/images, 40-41, 419-420,
422-423, 429-435
palette locations, 23
paths/subpaths, 158
selections, 115
see also files; images
scaling
images, 213
scanned images, 77
type, 281
scan resolution formula
(pre-press images), 77
scanning images, 86
file size considerations,
76-79
images for print
(pre-press), 76-77
interpolation, 74
resampling, 74
resolution, 73-75
common problems, 80
and intended use, 76
scale considerations, 214

scanners
limitations of, 77
TWAIN interfaces, 86
using, 86
Web/video image
resolution, 78-80
scratch filters, 319-320
**Scratch Size (Status Bar
menu), 42**
**Screen angle (Halftone Screens
dialog box), 446**
**Screen frequency (Halftone
Screens dialog box), 446**
screen modes, 45-46, 271
**screen output, Adobe
Gamma utility, 473**
**Screen shape (Halftone
Screens dialog box), 447**
**search categories, adding to
images, 85**
**searching for filter
plug-ins, 305**
**Select Gradient option
(Gradient Editor dialog
box), 204**
Select menu
Color Range dialog box,
405-408
Feather command, 129
Save Selection as Channel
option, 358
**Selection tool (3D Transform
filter), 308**
selections
active, 342
*Color Range dialog box,
407-408*
*context-sensitive menus
for, 45*
*creating using Color
Range dialog box,
405-407*
adjusting colors in, 394-395
channels and, 115
converting to paths, 161
creating patterns from, 206
Equalize command for, 411
filling, 204-205

free-hand, 119-120
intersections, 116
keyboard shortcuts for, 232
managing, 115
*anti-aliasing option,
129-130*
*common modifier keys,
116*
elliptical marquee, 129
feathering option, 128
magic wand, 125
rectangular marquee, 128
masking using, 113
moving, 127-128
pixels in, 113, 135
preview areas. options, 131
Quick Mask, 356
saving as alpha channels,
342, 359
stroking, 206
Threshold command for,
412-413
when to use, 113
selective color correction, 408
**Selective Color dialog box
(Image/Adjust menu),
408-409**
Save/Load buttons, 379
separations, color
black in, 443-444
separation tables, 54
setting, CMYK Setup
dialog box, 441
sets
actions, 489, 498
brushes, 195
gradients, custom, 204
shadows
adjusting, 384
setting target values, 387
**sharpening images, avoiding
over-sharpening, 235**
shortcut buttons, *see* **buttons**
shortcut keys, *see* **keyboard
shortcuts**
**Show Palettes (Window
menu), 36**

**Show/Hide Brushes command
(Window menu), 193**
**Show/Hide Channels option
(Window menu), 342**
**Show/Hide Grid option (View
Menu), 51**
**Show/Hide History option
(Window menu), 64**
**Show/Hide Info command
(Window menu), 182**
**Show/Hide Layers option
(Window menu), 241**
**Show/Hide Swatches
command (Window menu),
180**
showing layers, 241
**Similar command (Select
menu), Tolerance option,
128**
**Size field (Type Tool
dialog box), 281**
size management, 79-80
layered files, 251-253
reducing using RLE-
encoding, 422-423
skewing images, 214
sliders
brush feature controls,
193-194
color, in Color Picker, 174
color bars, in Hue/
Saturation dialog box,
399-400
in Color palette, 181-182
Fuzziness slider, 131
*in Color Range dialog
box, 406*
*in Replace Color dialog
box, 404*
**SMPTE-C (Society of
Motion Picture and
Television Engineers)
color standard, 466**
smudge tool, 227
cursor options, 218
snapshots, 63-64
in actions, 492
default, 67

"Snow" example image, clipping groups, 261-263
Society of Motion Picture and Television Engineers color standard, *see* SMPTE-C
Soft Light mode, 272
Space pop-up menu (Print dialog box), 451
special effects
  3D transformation filters, 306-314
  actions for, 489
  blending/fading filters, 335
  blurring images, 333-335
  displacement/distortion filters, 315-317, 335
  dust and scratch removal, 319
  filter effects, 303-305, 354-355
  Invert command, 410
  Layer Effects, 266
    adding, 267
    bevel, 268
    converting to regular layers, 270
    copying/pasting, 269
    drop shadow, 267
    editing/removing, 269-270
    emboss, 268
    inner glow, 268
    inner shadow, 267
    outer glow, 268
  lighting effects, 321-326
    embossing/debossing, 329-330
  noise options, 318
  sharpening images, 331
  texture effects, 335
  vignettes, 352-353
  see also editing; image effects
speed-related problems
  file transmission speeds, 432
  troubleshooting speed problems, 55
Sphere tool (3D Transform filter), 307

Split Channels command (Channels palette menu), 349-351
sponge tool, 230
spot channels, 366-368
Spot Color dialog box (Channels palette menu), instructions for using, 367-368
spot colors
  channels for, 366-367
  printing composite images, 368-369
spotlights, 323
  see also lighting effects
square areas, selecting, 116
Square brushes, loading, 195
stacking order, layers, changing, 242-243
stamp tools, editing images using, 218-219
  Pattern Stamp, 222
  Rubber Stamp, 219-221
Standard mode tool, 33
Standard Screen mode, 45
standardizing image effects, prerecorded actions for, 489
states
  deleting/purging, 65-66
  discarding, 62
  instructions for using, 63-64
  non-linear histories, 66-67
  order of, 61
  purging, Clear History command, 65
  selecting, 62
  snapshots, 63
  storing, 62
statistical information, histograms
  for, 382-383
Status Bar, 40
  Current Tool, 43
  document size information, 40
  Document Sizes, 251
  Efficiency, 42
  file size information, 40

  magnifying images using, 48
  Timing, 42
Step by Step mode (Playback Options), 492
storing
  brushes, reloading, 195
  color range settings, 132
  Preferences file, 54-55
  states in History palette, 62
  see also saving, 54
Stroke commands, 206
Stroke dialog box (Edit menu), 206
stroking
  keyboard commands for, 205
  type/text, 295-297
stylus, pressure-sensitive, 189
subpaths, 143
  Bézier curves, components, 143-144
  collections, as named objects, 158
  creating/editing
    add anchor point tool, 154-155
    convert point tool, 157
    direct selection tool, 155-156
    freeform pen tool, 152-154
    magnetic pen tool, 150-152
    pen tool, 145-149
    subtract anchor point tool, 155
  managing, 158-160
Swatch box, guide/grid colors, 52
swatches
  PANTONE Coated, 178
  patterns, 207
Swatches palettes, 173
  adding colors, 180
  color selection, 180
  custom, 181
  defaults, resetting, 181

deleting swatches, 180
loading colors, 181
menu
    Load Swatches
        command, 181
    Replace Swatches
        command, 181
    Reset Swatches
        command, 181
    Save Swatches
        command, 181
painting tools, 184
replacing/inserting
    colors, 180
system resources, maximizing
    purging states/
        snapshots, 65
    see also *speed-related*
        problems

T

Tagged Image File Format,
    see **.TIFF**
target values, highlights/
    shadows, 387
"Temple" example image,
    editing channels using
    Curves, 346
testing, benchmark, 42
text
    lines, managing, 285
    masking images in, clipping
        groups, 261-263
    orienting type layers, 288
    shifting lines, 297-300
    see also fonts; type
texture channels (maps), with
    lighting effects, 328
texture filters (Filters
    menu), 335
textures, actions for, 489
Texturizer filter (Filters
    menu), 335
.TGA file format, exporting
    transparencies, 466
Threshold (Normal
    blending mode), 185
Threshold dialog box
    (Image/Adjust menu),
    411-412

thumbnails
    channels, viewing options,
        342-343
    image collections, 501
    image preview option
        settings, 41
    layers, changing size, 241
    Work Path thumbnail, 160
.TIFF (Tagged Image File
    Format) files, 424, 436
TIFF Options dialog box (Save
    As dialog box), 426
tile displays (Windows
    systems), 49
Timing (Status Bar menu), 42
tolerance levels, painting
    tools, 199
Tolerance option (selection
    tools), 124
tonality
    adjusting
        Auto Levels command,
            388
        Curves dialog box for,
            389-390
        Levels sliders for, 386
        using Channel Mixer, 365
    histograms showing, 381-383
    reducing, Posterize
        dialog box for, 414
toning tools for, 229-230
    cursor options, 218
    using with paths/subpaths,
        158-160
Tool Tips option (General
    Preferences dialog box), 22
toolboxes
    color swatches, 173
    hiding, 36
    horizontal mask tool, 289
    repositioning, 36
    selection tools, 115
    type tools, 282
    see also tools
tools
    activating, 34
    active, 43, 45
    add anchor point tool, 155
    Airbrush tool, 33

automation tools, 498
    Conditional Mode
        Change, 499-501
in Bitmap mode, 95
Blur tool, 33
Color Picker tool, 173
Color Sampler tool,
    377-378
color-correction tools
    Gamut Warning
        command, 376
    including in actions, 489
    Info palette, 377
convert point tool, 157
Crop tool, 84
cursor options, 218
Default colors, 33
defaults, restoring, 38
direct selection tool, 156
in Duotone mode, 97
editing and retouching
    tools, palettes for, 218
Eraser tool, 33, 191-192
Eyedropper tool, 182
filter tools, including in
    actions, 489
focus (sharpening/
    blurring) tools, 226-227
Foreground color tool, 33
freeform pen tool, 152-154
Gradient tool, 200-204
in Grayscale mode, 95
Hand tool, 33
hidden tools, accessing, 34
history brush tool, 223-226
identifying, 34
Lasso tool, 33
Line tool, 196-198
magnetic pen tool, 150-152
Marquee tool, 33
Measure tool, 33, 52
    protractor feature, 53
Move tool, 127-128
in Multichannel mode, 105
Paint Bucket tool, 33, 199
Paintbrush tool, 190
painting tools
    blending modes, 187
    Brush Size option, 183

Brushes Palette, 193-196
cursor options, 183
fade-out rates, 188
Fill commands, 204-205
list of, 35
opacity settings, 187-188
Options palettes, 184-189
pattern-creating, 206
pressure-sensitive stylus
    controls, 189
Stroke commands, 206
with pressure-sensitive
    stylus, 188-190
palettes and, 36
Pen tool, 33, 145-149
Pencil tool, 190-191
in RGB mode, 99
Rubber Stamp tool, 33
selection tools, 115
    anti-aliasing option,
        129-130
    common modifier
        keys, 116
    elliptical marquee, 129
    feathering option, 128
    magic wand, 125
    rectangular marquee, 128
stamp tools, 218
    pattern stamp, 222
    rubber stamp, 219-221
in Standard mode, 33
subtract anchor point
    tool, 155
toning tools,
    burn tool, 229-230
    dodge tool, 229
    sponge tool, 230
Type Mask, 288
Type tool, 281-282
Zoom tool, 48
Toyo colors
channels for, 366-367
Color Finder guide, 179
swatch palettes,
    loading, 181
tracking type/text, 284, 297-300
Transfer Functions dialog box
(Page Setup dialog box), 447

Transform submenu
(Edit menu)
    Distort box, 215
    Free Transform dialog box,
        216-217
    Numeric Transform dialog
        box, 215-216
    Perspective command, 215
    Rotate command, 214
    Scale box, 213
    Skew box, 214
transformation commands
    distort command, 215
    Free Transform command,
        216-217
    Numeric Transform dialog
        box, 215
    perspective command, 215
    rotate command, 214
    scale command, 213
    skew command, 214
transforming layers,
    linking, 244
transparencies
    electronic publishing
        format, 462
    exporting
        .GIF89a Export Options,
            464-465
        .PNG format, 465
        .TGA format, 466
    layer transparency, display
        preferences, 242
    support for in .PNG
        files, 434
Transparency & Gamut
    options (File menu), 242
Trumatch colors
    color guide, 179
    libraries, selecting colors
        from, 173
    swatch palettes,
        loading, 181
TWAIN interfaces, 86
    see also scanning
type
    anti-aliasing, 281
    fonts, 283

kerning, 294, 297-300
lines of, leading, 284
masks, 282, 289, 295-297
Outline, 281
resizing, 283
scaling, 281
setting horizontal, 290-292
setting vertical, 295-297
spacing, 284
special effects, 293-295
tracking, 294, 297-300
when to use, 281
see also fonts; text
type layers
    editing, 288
    for masks, 289
    Indexed-color mode, 285
    Layer palette, 287
    Multichannel mode, 285
    rendering, 289
    special effects, 287
    text orientation, 288
    see also layers
Type Mask tools, 288
Type Tool dialog boxes,
    281-282
    Alignment buttons, 285
    anti-aliasing, 281
    Baseline field, 284
    cutting/pasting from
        outside applications, 285
    Fit in Window
        checkbox, 283
    Font menu, 283
    horizontal/vertical, 282
    kerning, 284
    leading, 284
    opening, 282
    Preview option, 283-285
    resizing type, 283
    Rotate box, 285
    Size field, 281
    tracking, 284
    type layers, editing, 288
    type spacing options,
        283-284
    Zoom button, 283

U

Undo command (Edit menu), 42
  states and, 62
undoing actions, 492
Uniform noise, 318
Units & Rulers dialog box (Preferences sub-menu)
  font units, 283
  measurement units, 50
  quick access, 50
unlinking
  layer masks, 261
  layers, 244
Unsharp Mask filter (Filter/Sharpen menu), 76, 234-235, 331-332
Unsharp Mask Preview dialog box (Filter/Sharpen menu), 233-234
Use Accurate Screens option (Halftone Screens dialog box), 447
Use All Layers option (magic wand tool), 125
Use All Layers option (paint bucket tool), 199
Use Cache for Histograms option (File menu), 383

V

values, settings
  arrowhead settings, 196
  brush options, 193-194
  in CMYK Color Model, 177-179
  fade-out rates, changing, 188
  in HSB Color Model, 174-175
  in Lab Color Model, 176-177
  opacity settings, 187-189
  in RGB Color Model, 175-177
  stroke widths, 206
  tolerance levels, 199

transparency mask opacity, 203
type elements, 281, 284
Variations dialog box (Image/Adjust menu)
  adjustment options, 394-395
  color-cast image adjustments, 395-396
  Save/Load buttons, 379
vector images, saving, 426
vectors, 16
vertical type, setting, 295-297
  tools for, 282
video applications
  color standards, NTSC format, 466
  exporting transparencies, TGA format for, 466
  image resolution, 78-80
  screen displays, 467
  video-safe colors, NTSC format, 466
View Box (Navigator palette), 48-49
View menu
  Actual Pixels option, 47
  CMYK Preview option, 379
  Fit on Screen option, 47
  Lock Guides command, 51
  Print Size option, 47
  Show/Hide Grid option, 51
  Show/Hide Rulers option, 50
  Zoom In option, 47
  Zoom Out option, 47
viewing
  images
    at 100%, 48
    changing using Navigator palette, 48
    magnifying options, 46
    Navigator palette for, 49
    screen modes for, 45
    screen-fitting, 48
  layer masks, 257-259
  multiple windows, 49
  type, magnifying, 283
vignette effects, 352-353

W

Web pages
  full color images, .PNG format for, 458
  .GIF files, 432
  image modes for, 462
  image resolution for, 76-80
  Indexed Color images, 101
  color palettes for, 463
  .JPEG files, 433
  preparing images for using Wizards/Assistants, 39
  Web-safe palettes, loading, 181
Web sites, Adobe Online, 43-44
Wet Edges option (Paintbrush tool), 190
White option (Fill dialog box), 204
White Output levels slider, 385
white points, 475
windows, handling multiple, 49
Windows Color Picker, selecting, 174
Window menu
  Show/Hide Brushes command, 193
  Show/Hide Channels option, 342
  Show/Hide History option, 64
  Show/Hide Info command, 182, 213
  Show/Hide Layers option, 241
  Show/Hide Palettes, 36
  Show/Hide Swatches command, 180
Windows systems
  context-sensitive menus, activating, 45
  help, accessing, 43
  hidden tools, accessing, 34
  keyboard shortcuts
    adding/subtracting pixels, 116
    arrow keys, 127

color bar options, 182
Curves dialog box, 393
deleting swatches, 180
Deselect command, 134
Eyedropper options, 182
Free Transform options, 217
Hue/Saturation dialog box, 403
Lasso tools, 120-121
Levels dialog box, 389
Marquee tools, 117
purging states, 65
rendering keyboard shortcuts, 289
replacing/inserting swatch colors, 180
resetting to defaults, 132
selecting states, 62
swatch-activating, 180
Lock Guide command shortcut, 51

Measure tool, protractor feature, 53
minimizing palettes, 37
monitor calibrations in, 473-476
Page Setup dialog box, 446
Preferences file, locking, 55
RAM, default, 24
Status Bar, Show/Hide option, 43
system requirements, 19
View Box, changing size, 49
Wizards in, 38
wireframes, 3D Transform filter tools, 307-310
Wizards/Assistants
accessing, 38
Adobe Gamma utility control panel, 474-476
Export Transparent Image, 38

locating, 38
Resize Image, 38
work area
components, 33-34, 36-37
customizing, 36-38
Status Bar, 40
work paths, 160
see also paths
World Wide Web, *see* **Web pages**

X-Z

ZIP compression, .PDF files, 430
Zoom button (Type Tool dialog box), 283
Zoom In option (View menu), 47
Zoom Out option (View menu), 47
Zoom tools, how to use, 48

Adobe Certified Expert Program

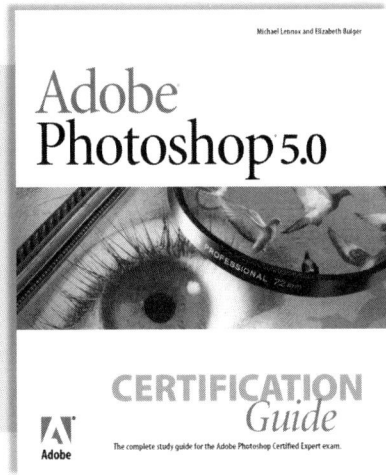

Michael Lennox and Elizabeth Bulger

Adobe
Photoshop 5.0

PROFESSIONAL

CERTIFICATION *Guide*

Adobe

The complete study guide for the Adobe Photoshop Certified Expert exam.

Adobe Certification Guides contain comprehensive study material as well as Practice Proficiency Exams to help better prepare users for Adobe product Proficiency Examinations!

What is an ACE?

An Adobe Certified Expert is an individual who has passed an Adobe Product Proficiency Exam for a specific Adobe software product. Adobe Certified Experts are eligible to promote themselves to clients or employers as highly skilled, expert-level users of Adobe software. ACE certification is a recognized worldwide standard for excellence in Adobe software knowledge.

An Adobe Certified Training Provider (ACTP) is a certified teacher or trainer who has passed an Adobe Product Proficiency Exam. Training organizations that use ACTPs can become certified as well. Adobe promotes ACTPs to customers who need training.

ACE benefits:

When you become an ACE, you enjoy these special benefits:
- Professional recognition
- An ACE program certificate
- Use of the Adobe Certified Expert program logo

Additional benefits for ACTPs:

- Listing on the Adobe Web site
- Access to beta software releases
- *Classroom in a Book* in PDF

For information on the ACE and ACTP programs or on the certification guides, go to www.adobe.com, and look for Training Programs under the Support and Services section.

Adobe Photoshop 5.0
Certified Expert Exam

GOOD FOR 30% OFF
at all Sylvan/Prometric Testing Centers*

You've studied the book. Now register for the exam and be on the way to becoming an Adobe Photoshop ACE.

It's easy. All you need to do is:

- ❏ Study using the book and do the hands-on exercises.

- ❏ Call and register for the exam.

- ❏ Mention the promo code when registering for the exam to receive a 30% discount.

- ❏ Take the exam! You're almost there!

In the U.S. and Canada, please call 800-356-EXAM to make your exam appointment today! To receive your discount, mention the code PS5CPB when you register for the exam.

Adobe

Please call 800-356-EXAM
to make your exam appointment today!

Your code is: PS5CPB

* Applies only to Adobe Photoshop 5.0 Product Proficiency Exam. Limit one per customer.

LICENSING AGREEMENT

By opening this package, you are agreeing to be bound by the following:

This software product is copyrighted, and all rights are reserved by the publisher and author. You are licensed to use this software on a single computer. You may copy and/or modify the software as needed to facilitate your use of it on a single computer. Making copies of the software for any other purpose is a violation of the United States copyright laws.

This software is sold *as is* without warranty of any kind, either expressed or implied, including but not limited to the implied warranties of merchantability and fitness for a particular purpose. Neither the publisher nor its dealers or distributors assumes any liability for any alleged or actual damages arising from the use of this program. (Some states do not allow for the exclusion of implied warranties, so the exclusion may not apply to you.)